LIFE ON THE HIGHEST PLANE

Life on the Highest Plane

By RUTH PAXSON

This is the complete (three volumes in one) edition.

Part 1 THE PERSON AND WORK OF CHRIST

Part 2 THE RELATION BETWEEN CHRIST AND THE CHRISTIAN

Part 3 THE BELIEVER'S RESPONSE TO THE HOLY SPIRIT'S INWORKING

LIFE ON THE HIGHEST PLANE

A Study of the Spiritual Nature and Needs of Man

By

RUTH PAXSON

MOODY PRESS

CHICAGO

© 1928, by
THE MOODY BIBLE INSTITUTE
OF CHICAGO

Paperback edition, 1978

ISBN: 0-8024-4730-9

Scripture quotations are from the King James Version, except those noted R.V., which are from the Revised Version, the British equivalent of the American Standard Version (1901).

Printed in the United States of America

To my friend and co-worker
EDITH DAVIS,
who,
through her faithful intercession, helpful suggestion,
constructive criticism, painstaking correction and
selfless expenditure of time and strength, has
given invaluable assistance, this book is
lovingly and gratefully
dedicated.

Contents

Part 3

THE BELIEVER'S RESPONSE TO THE HOLY SPIRIT'S
INWORKING

DIAGRAMS

Introduction

EVERY CHRISTIAN has inherited untold riches. As a child of the King and a joint heir with Christ he is a spiritual multimillionaire. But comparatively few Christians bear the marks of spiritual affluence. Their conversation, character and conduct give the impression of spiritual impoverishment. Throughout the Church of Christ there is a universal complaint of dearth and deadness.

Many Christians do not seem to be conscious of their lack or their need. They are indifferent and self-satisfied. But, on the other hand, there are many whose lives are characterized by a humiliating consciousness of defeat and failure, by a growing unrest, and by a perpetual striving for something never attained. Their hearts cry out insistently, "Lord, is there nothing better than this for me in the Christian life?"

The purpose of these studies is to teach what are the Christian's possessions in Christ and how they may be appropriated, enjoyed and used.

These Bible studies were first given in embryo to pastors, evangelists, teachers and other Christian leaders in conferences held in China. Later they grew into full-size as they were taught in weekly Bible classes stretching over a period of six months. In response to many requests from both Chinese and missionary friends that this message might be made available for their use, it has been prepared for publication.

God is building a spiritual house for His own glory and use. This house is composed of a foundation, a superstructure and furnishings. These studies attempt to furnish the plan of such a habitation and to show step by step the process of its building. Each chapter is, as it were, a story complete in itself yet connected both with the story underneath it and the one above it. The work is divided into three parts as here indicated:

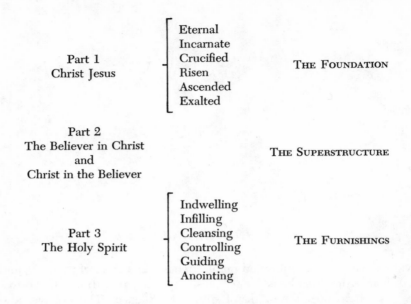

| Part 1
Christ Jesus | Eternal
Incarnate
Crucified
Risen
Ascended
Exalted | THE FOUNDATION |

| Part 2
The Believer in Christ
and
Christ in the Believer | | THE SUPERSTRUCTURE |

| Part 3
The Holy Spirit | Indwelling
Infilling
Cleansing
Controlling
Guiding
Anointing | THE FURNISHINGS |

Every architect has blueprints which visualize the construction to be erected. The fourteen diagrams used in this book furnish blueprints of God's spiritual house which He is in the process of building.

It is the hope of the author that these studies may be used by groups. For such the bibliography will suggest additional material.

The author wishes to acknowledge her indebtedness to Mrs. Mary McDonough for the use of Charts 2, 3 and 4 which are in her book *God's Plan of Redemption;* to the many authors whose books have been consulted for inspiration and confirmation and to the many friends who have had a large share in the sending forth of this message in print through their faithful and believing intercession.

This book is now given back to God with the prayer that He will use it to lift many to *Life on the Highest Plane.*

Part 1

THE PERSON AND WORK OF CHRIST

1

Human Life on Three Planes

THE BIBLE is a mirror in which man may see himself just as he is. Any person who wishes a true picture of himself will find it there. The Bible is God's studio in which will be found the picture of each of His created beings. Your photograph is there. It has been taken by the divine Photographer, therefore it is flawlessly accurate. Do you wish to see *your* photograph?

The Holy Spirit through the apostle Paul has divided the human race into three clearly distinguished groups and every member of the human family, irrespective of racial or natural inheritance, belongs to one of these groups. God's description of each is so accurate and so true that every person may know with certitude in which class he is.

This classification presents a study of human life on three planes, the lowest, the highest, and a middle plane: or the natural man, the spiritual man, and the carnal man.

We will start with the study of life on the lowest plane, that of

THE NATURAL MAN

1 Corinthians 2:14, "But *the natural man* receiveth not the things of the Spirit of God: for they are foolishness unto him: neither can he know them, because they are spiritually discerned."

Romans 8:9, "But ye are not in the flesh, but in the Spirit, if so be that the Spirit of God dwell in you. Now if any man have not the Spirit of Christ, he is none of his."

1 Corinthians, 12:3, R. V., "No man can say, Jesus is Lord, but in the Holy Spirit."

John 14:6, "Jesus saith unto him, I am the way, the truth, and the life: no man cometh unto the Father, but by me."

Is the natural man a Christian? No one can be called a Christian who is not rightly related to God. Is the natural man then rightly related to God? To get our answer let us begin with John 14:6 and work backward to 1 Corinthians 2:14.

Jesus says that no one can get into right relationship with God the Father except through Himself. The Bible shows us with unmistakable clearness that this necessitates receiving Jesus Christ into the life as Saviour and as Lord. Paul tells us that no one can truly call Jesus Lord, except "in the Holy Spirit," and that if the Holy Spirit does not dwell in one he cannot belong to God as one of His own. It is the Holy Spirit alone who knows the things of God which He desires to give us freely in Christ. But 1 Corinthians 2:14 tells us that the natural man refuses to receive the things of the Spirit, they appear mere foolishness unto him. More than that, he cannot know them because it takes a spiritual mind to discern spiritual truth and he is without the Holy Spirit. So it is very clear that the natural man is not in the right relationship to God. Consequently from God's viewpoint, no matter how exemplary a life he may live on the plane of the natural, he is not a Christian.

THE ATTITUDE OF THE NATURAL MAN TO GOD

Let us study what Scripture says of the attitude of the natural man to God:

Galatians 4:8	He does not know God.
Romans 2:21	He has no gratitude to God.
Romans 3:11	He has no desire for God.
1 John 4:10	He has no love for God.
John 3:18	He has no faith in God.
Romans 3:18	He has no fear of God.
Romans 1:21, 25	He does not worship God.
2 Timothy 3:8	He resists the truth.
1 Corinthians 2:14	He receives not the things of God.
2 Thessalonians 2:12	He rejects God's truth.
2 Thessalonians 1:8	He disobeys God's Gospel.
Romans 5:10	He is an enemy of God.

THE RELATIONSHIP OF THE NATURAL MAN TO GOD

The attitude of the natural man to God determines his relationship to God. Romans 5:10 and Colossians 1:21 make it quite clear that the natural man is an open and avowed enemy of God. This attitude on his part determines what God's relationship to him must be.

Ephesians 2:17	He is far from God.
Romans 3:19	He is guilty before God.
John 3:18	He is condemned by God.
John 3:36	He is under God's wrath.
Ephesians 4:18	He is alienated from the life of God.
Ephesians 2:12	He is without God in this life.
2 Thessalonians 1:9	He is without God in the life to come.

The natural man is without the Lord Jesus Christ as his Saviour, therefore he lives wholly and only unto himself. "The old man" is the center of his life and has undivided control over his whole being. Self dominates his thoughts, affections, speech, will and actions. His nature is sinful, therefore his conduct is sinful.

The natural man is dead to God but alive to sin, self and Satan. He is under the dominion of "the prince of the power of the air," and is the bond servant of sin. He is a lost man, helpless and hopeless. The tragic part of it is that "the god of this age" has so blinded his mind that he does not comprehend the seriousness of his condition and consequently he has no power within himself to know God, to love God, to receive God, nor even to seek God. Surely this brief sketch of the natural man reveals life lived on the lowest plane.

Let us next study life on the highest plane, that of

THE SPIRITUAL MAN

1 Corinthians 2:15, "But *he that is spiritual* judgeth all things, yet he himself is judged of no man."

Galatians 6:1, "Brethren, if a man be overtaken in a fault, *ye which are spiritual*, restore such an one in the spirit of meekness; considering thyself, lest thou also be tempted."

The spiritual man is the exact antithesis of the natural man.

THE RELATIONSHIP OF THE SPIRITUAL MAN TO GOD

The spiritual man is rightly related to God through faith in Jesus Christ. This relationship has been brought about by the Holy Spirit who has convicted him of the sin of unbelief in God's way of salvation and of the necessity of a righteousness not his own, if he would ever have fellowship with a holy, righteous God. He has revealed Jesus Christ to him as a Saviour from sin and as the Saviour *he* needs. The Holy Spirit has so wrought upon the mind, heart and will of the natural man that he has been convinced of the truth of the Gospel, convicted of the sin of his own heart, and has been led to put his faith in the crucified One as his Saviour, and so has been "born of the Spirit" into the Kingdom of God.

The spiritual man has the Holy Spirit dwelling in him, filling him, leading him, teaching him, empowering him. Through the new birth God's own life, eternal and uncreated, has been imparted to him and now Jesus Christ is his very life.

The spiritual man has a threefold relationship to the Lord Jesus Christ which is manifested in his character, in his conversation, and in his conduct.

The spiritual man has *accepted* Christ as his *Saviour*.

The spiritual man has *yielded* to Christ as his *Lord*.

The spiritual man has *appropriated* Christ as his *Life*.

Jesus Christ and he are one as the vine and the branch are one. Christ is the supreme need of his life and has the supreme place in his affections. Christ is all and in all to him.

THE CONDITION OF THE SPIRITUAL MAN

The spiritual man having taken the crucified, risen, glorified Christ as Saviour, Lord and Life, lives his life wholly unto God. The Lord Jesus is the center of his life and has undivided control over his whole being. Jesus Christ dominates his thoughts, affections, speech, will and actions. He has become a partaker of the nature of God so that there are two natures in the spiritual man but the divine nature is sovereign.

The spiritual man is habitually alive to God and dead to sin and self. He is a bond servant to God and gladly, joyously, acknowledges and submits to the sovereign lordship of Jesus.

Jesus Christ is intensely real and precious to the spiritual man, and he considers, loves, serves, adores and worships Him. This condition is not due to anything in himself but is true because of his yielding himself unreservedly to the influence and operation of the Holy Spirit, through whom he has been enabled to seek, to receive, to love and to know Christ Jesus as his Saviour and through whom he is filled with His life. Surely this brief sketch of the spiritual man reveals life lived on the highest plane.

Let us lastly study life on the middle plane, that of

THE CARNAL MAN

1 Corinthians 3:1-4, "And I, brethren, could not speak unto you as unto spiritual, but *as unto carnal*, even as unto babes in Christ.

I have fed you with milk, and not with meat: for hitherto ye were not able to bear it, neither yet now are ye able.

For *ye are yet carnal:* for whereas there is among you envying, and strife, and divisions, are ye not carnal, and walk as men?

For while one saith, I am of Paul; and another, I am of Apollos; *are ye not carnal?*"

The carnal man is a hyphenated man, belonging to two spheres.

THE RELATIONSHIP OF THE CARNAL MAN TO GOD

The carnal man is a Christian because he has obtained sonship through faith in Jesus Christ as his Saviour. Therefore he is rightly related to God.

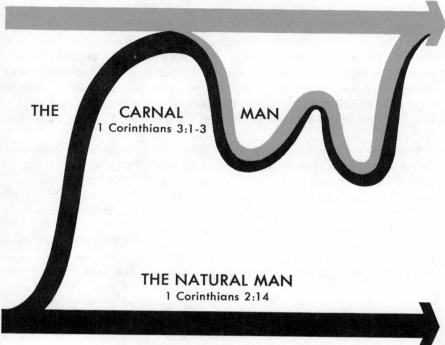

THE SPIRITUAL MAN
1 Corinthians 2:15

THE CARNAL MAN
1 Corinthians 3:1-3

THE NATURAL MAN
1 Corinthians 2:14

Diagram 1: Life on Three Planes

But he has entered into neither the possessions nor the privileges of a son and his practices are not those becoming his position in the family of God.

The carnal man has the Holy Spirit dwelling in him but He is constantly being grieved and quenched so that He has restricted power in and dominion over the life.

The carnal man has been renewed through the new birth but he is still a "babe in Christ." He sits at the table of the Lord to partake of His bounties but he has no appetite nor capacity for "strong meat." He subsists on "milk." He is not a full-grown man. He actually has been united to the Lord Jesus but he is an "adulterer" loving the world and caring far more for its people and pleasures than for Jesus Christ (James 4:4).

The carnal man has accepted Christ as his Saviour but he has little or no apprehension of a life of complete surrender to, and of full appropriation of, Jesus Christ as his Lord and his Life. He feels a need of Christ and desires some relationship with Him but he is not satisfied in Him. Christ has *a* place in his heart but not *the* place of supremacy and preeminence.

THE CONDITION OF THE CARNAL MAN

The carnal man lives his life partly unto God and partly unto himself. The Lord Jesus is really at the center of his life but "the old man" is usually on the throne. There is a divided control over his life. Sometimes Christ dominates his thoughts, affections, speech, will and action but more often they are under the dominion of self. Two natures are side by side in the carnal man, the divine and the fleshly, and he is under the sway of each in turn according as he yields to one or to the other. He is alive to God spasmodically but he is equally alive to sin, self and Satan. He attempts to live in two spheres, the heavenly and the earthly—and he fails in both.

The carnal man is in a miserable condition and his life is always one of defeat and discouragement, often one of despair. This condition is due to ignorance of the deep things of God, unwillingness to yield himself unreservedly to the Lord Jesus Christ, and unbelief in apropriating Christ with all His graces and gifts. Surely this brief sketch of the carnal man reveals life lived on a middle plane. (See Diagram 1.)

We have looked into God's mirror. Have you seen yourself? We have been in God's studio. Have you seen your photograph? We have seen human life on three planes. On which plane are you living?

2

God's First Man—The First Adam

As WE DAILY observe the lives of men and women we see a vast difference in the quality of those lives. We readily admit that people are living on totally different planes with a consequent vast divergence in character and conduct. We must seek the cause of such disparity. What or who is to blame?

If we acknowledge God to be the Creator of all things in His universe, then we are compelled to place the responsibility for such inequality either upon Him or upon man. It must be the result either of God's fiat or of man's choice. To say that it is due to the difference in the heredity, circumstances, environment or opportunities of people, is to beg the question altogether. Countless ones have come up out of the depths of poverty, illiteracy, superstition, affliction and persecution to heights of nobility in character and conduct. Many have fallen from heights of wealth, education, ease, opportunity and privilege to the lowest depths of sin and shame. Upon whom then should the blame rest for such inequality in human life?

Is God responsible for it? The only fair way to answer this question is to turn to His own record of creation and to read what He says of His first man, and to determine upon what plane He intended him to live.

> Genesis 1:26-27, "And God said, *Let us make man in our image, after our likeness:* and *let them have dominion* over the fish of the sea, and over the fowl of the air, and over the cattle, and over all the earth, and over every creeping thing that creepeth upon the earth.
> *So God created man in his own image,* in the image of God created he him; male and female created he them."

> Genesis 1:31, "And God saw every thing that he had made, and, behold, *it was very good.*"

If language has any power whatever to express thought, these words clearly teach us five things regarding God's first man,

1. That he was created by Someone who already existed.
2. That his creation was the result of God's deliberate, direct, creative will.

3. That he was created in the image of God.
4. That he was pronounced "very good."
5. That he was given dominion over all the earth and made the head of the entire terrestrial creation.

God's first man was made just as God wanted all men to be. He was made after a pattern. God's first man came direct from God's own hand and bore a definite resemblance to his Creator. "The root idea of the Hebrew word translated 'image' is that of a shadow." God's first man, then, was God's shadow. He was like God. But in what respect?

To answer this question we are forced to ask another: What was God like? "*God* created *man*." The statement is made without any previous explanation of God Himself; He appears upon the first pages of revelation as a Being acting independently in the creation of a universe and of man with no explanation of Himself and with no reference whatever to His origin.

Who, then, created God? How many mothers have had to answer that query! It is, likewise, the first and greatest issue that confronts the philosopher as he studies into the secrets of the universe. In answering this question correctly one takes his first step in knowing who God is.

Scripture gives to men and women of faith an absolutely satisfying and final answer in the simple but sublime words, "In the beginning *God*." God never *became* for He always *was*. God is the great "I AM." "And God said unto Moses, I AM THAT I AM: and he said, Thus shalt thou say unto the children of Israel, I AM hath sent me unto you." God had no beginning and will have no end. *From* everlasting *to* everlasting He is God. "For with thee is the fountain of life." "For as the Father hath life in himself; so hath he given to the Son to have life in himself." God is the Uncreated: the Always-Existent. He is the eternal, infinite One. He is the Beginning of all beginnings.

This, then, is what God is. But if this is what God is in what respect could God's first man ever be said to resemble Him? Let us press on in our search for an understanding of this great truth. While God never explains Himself in Scripture He does reveal Himself. He wants men to know who and what He is, for if we did not have this knowledge we could never know God's original intention for man who was made in His image.

Let us turn to the first twenty-five verses of the opening chapter of God's Word and see if we find any revelation of Himself that throws light upon the kind of resemblance God's first man bore to God. We read:

"God said. . . ."   "God made. . . ."

"God saw. . . ." "God set. . . ."
"God divided. . . ." "God created. . . ."
"God called. . . ." "God blessed. . . ."

These phrases each record something which God did. Outward action is the expression of inward being. What one does reveals what one is.

"God said," therefore God must have thought.

"God blessed," therefore God must have loved.

"God created," therefore God must have willed.

Genesis 1:1-25 reveals personality. God is a Person. He is a Person who thinks, loves, and wills.

We have now found out two things about God. We have learned that God is the Uncreated, the Eternal, the Infinite, the Fountainhead of all life. And we have learned that He is a Person who thinks, loves and wills. The deduction which we may make from this twofold revelation is that God is a Person who thinks, loves and wills on the plane of uncreated, unlimited, eternal, divine life.

Are we ready now to answer the question, In what respect was God's first man like God? Perhaps we might clarify our thinking on one very fundamental point by first saying in what respect God's first man was not like Him.

> Genesis 2:7, "And *the Lord God formed man of the dust of the ground,* and breathed into his nostrils the breath of life; and man became a living soul."
>
> 1 Corinthians 15:47, "*The first man is of the earth, earthy:* the second man is the Lord from heaven."

God was man's Creator. Man *became* a living soul. Man was *formed* from the dust of the ground. He is of the earth, earthy. It will be clearly seen from these verses that God and God's first man Adam were not in the same order of beings nor did they live on the same plane of life.

God is *uncreated,* man is *created.* God is *infinite,* man is *finite.* God is *heavenly,* man is *earthy.* God is *divine,* man is *human.* Between what God is in His uncreated, essential, divine being and what man is in his created, finite, human being there is an absolutely impassable gulf, an immeasurable distance. God is not superman, man is not inferior God.

In what respect then did God's first man resemble God? Wherein was man God's shadow? It was in the wondrous gift of personality. Man is a person as God is a Person. Let us trace this likeness in the opening chapters of Genesis.

As a Person God thought and expressed His thought in words thus revealing the truth that intelligence is inherent in personality. God made Adam in His image.

Genesis 2:19-20,"And out of the ground the LORD God formed every beast of the field, and every fowl of the air; and *brought them unto Adam to see what he would call them:* and *whatsoever Adam called every living creature,* that was the name thereof. And Adam gave names to all cattle, and to the fowl of the air, and to every beast of the field."

Adam was created with the power to think and to express thought in words. Adam had intelligence.

As a Person God loved and expressed His love in blessing thus revealing the truth that emotion is inherent in personality. God made Adam in His image.

Genesis 2:18, "And the LORD God said, It is not good that the man should be alone; and I will make him an help meet for him."

God gave Eve to Adam to be his wife and God said, "Therefore shall a man leave his father and his mother, and shall cleave unto his wife: and they shall be one flesh" (Genesis 2:24).

Adam was created with the power to love and to express that love in fidelity. Adam had emotion.

As a Person God willed and expressed His will in action thus revealing the truth that will is inherent in personality. God made Adam in His image.

Genesis 3:6, "And when the woman saw that the tree was good for food, and that it was pleasant to the eyes, and a tree to be desired to make one wise, *she took of the fruit thereof,* and did eat, and gave also unto her husband with her; and *he did eat.*"

Adam was created with the power to will and to express that will in choice. Adam had volition.

God's first man was made in God's image in the sense of having a personality patterned after God's in its power to think, to love and to will; but with this difference, that God thought, loved and willed on the plane of uncreated, unlimited, eternal, divine life, while Adam thought, loved and willed on the plane of created, limited, finite, human life. The intellectual, emotional and volitional life of God's first man was perfect within a limited sphere. Above and beyond this was the perfection of God's personality within an unlimited sphere. (See Diagram 2.)

The resemblance which God's first man bore to God through likeness in personality made communion and cooperation between them possible; while the difference of plane on which each lived determined the basis of their relationship. God was the Creator, Adam was the created. God was the Sovereign, Adam was the subject. It also set the boundaries of Adam's intellectual, emotional and volitional life; all must lie within the realm of divine sovereignty. The sovereignty of God expressed in His divine will was to be the circumference of Adam's human life. Unlimited liberty in

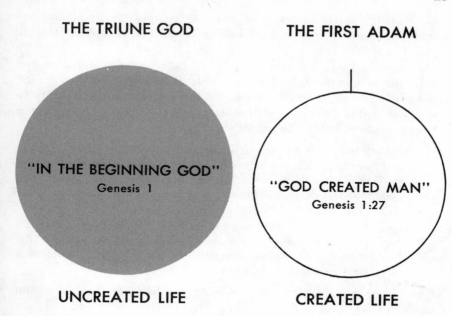

THE TRIUNE GOD   THE FIRST ADAM

"IN THE BEGINNING GOD"
Genesis 1

"GOD CREATED MAN"
Genesis 1:27

UNCREATED LIFE   CREATED LIFE

Diagram 2: Uncreated and Created Life

thinking, loving and willing was given him. But one condition had to be met. He must think, love and will within the circle of God's will.

Such a limitation was not for the purpose of making God a glorified despot: a sovereign who ruled arbitrarily with no thought for the well-being of his subject. On the contrary the limitation was wholly beneficent. It was purely for the purpose of keeping man in the only sphere in which he could remain perfect, in which he could come into the fullest and most complete realization of the possibility of his being, in which, in fact, he could remain in communion and cooperation with God.

That God intended man to become even more than we see him to be in the unfallen first man of Eden the whole trend of the Bible shows. Adam was made in the image of God plus the capacity for sonship. "Man as originally created, was not only in the image of God, he was also made to live in union with God, so that all his limitation might find its complement in the unlimited life of the Eternal. It is a great mistake to think of man as made, and then as put into some position where he might rise or fall, according to the capacity of his own personality. It is rather to be remembered that he was created in the image of God, and then put into a probationary position through which he was to pass unharmed to some larger form of existence, if his life were lived in union with the God who had created him. If however he chose a separate existence, and cut himself off from union, in that act he would fall" (G. Campbell Morgan, *The Crises of the Christ,* p. 28).

What would God's first man do? Would he accept the limitation and live his life in union with God, content to let it be kept wholly within the circle of God's will, or would he exercise his will in a choice contrary to the will of God and so cut himself off from the life of God? There would be but one way to know—the way of a test. God gave the test.

> Genesis 2:8-9, "And the Lord God planted a garden eastward in Eden; and there he put the man whom he had formed. And out of the ground made the Lord God to grow every tree that is pleasant to the sight, and good for food; the tree of life also in the midst of the garden, and the tree of knowledge of good and evil."

> Genesis 2:16-17, "And the Lord God commanded the man, saying, Of every tree of the garden thou mayest freely eat: but of the tree of the knowledge of good and evil, thou shalt not eat of it: for in the day that thou eatest thereof thou shalt surely die."

"Of every tree thou mayest freely eat"—unlimited freedom of choice within the will of God. "But of the tree of the knowledge of good and evil thou shalt not eat of it"—limitation of choice bounded by the will of God.

"The Lord God commanded the man saying, *Thou* shalt not—" Here was the great divide. This was the watershed between the sovereignty of the Creator and the subjection of the created. All on one side was within the circle of God's will: all on the other side was without the circle of God's will. All on one side meant union with God: all on the other side meant separation from God. All on one side spelled life: all on the other side spelled death. God gave the test. Adam was to make the choice. God gave the command. Adam could obey or disobey.

Just here we must pause to penetrate a bit deeper into the study of Adam's personality to see if there was anything within him to hinder or to help him in the making of his choice. Did God make Adam so that he could will to live wholly within the circle of God's will and have every other part of his being in active sympathy with such a decision? In the very constitution of Adam's being did God place anything that would favor and foster such complete and continuous obedience?

Scripture does not say a great deal about the threefold nature of man but what it does say is very illuminating and indubitable. It does tell us how man came to be what man now is.

> Genesis 2:7, "And the Lord God formed man of the dust of the ground, and breathed into his nostrils the breath of life; and man became a living soul."

Scripture names for us the component parts of man as thus created by God.

> 1 Thessalonians 5:23, "And the very God of peace sanctify you wholly; and I pray God your whole *spirit* and *soul* and *body* be preserved blameless unto the coming of our Lord Jesus Christ."

In Genesis 2:7 God gives us the divine order in the creation of the component parts of man.

THE FORMATION OF THE HUMAN BODY

"And the LORD God formed man of the dust of the ground." "The first man is of the earth, earthy." The earth was to be man's dwelling place. In order that it might have communication with the external world in which it dwelt, the body of man was formed of earth, and then equipped with five senses, sight, hearing, taste, touch and smell. Because of its connection with the earthly, the body is the lowest part of man. Yet it has the exalted privilege of being the home of the spirit and of being its only outlet to the world of sense. The body is the port city of the human personality.

THE EMANATION OF THE HUMAN SPIRIT

"And breathed into his nostrils the breath of life." The divine Potter formed the human frame and then breathed into it the breath of life. This life principle which came as a direct emanation from God became the human spirit. Some one has aptly said, "Man is dust inbreathed by Deity."

God Himself defines the human spirit in these words, "The spirit of man is the lamp of Jehovah, searching all the innermost parts." The spirit is the crowning part of man's being. It is God's masterpiece in human creation. It is the part of man which has relationship to the unseen, spiritual world, which has fellowship with God. Through the spirit man apprehends, loves and worships God. Dr. A. T. Pierson says, "The spirit receives impressions of outward and material things through the soul and the body, but it belongs itself to a higher level and realm, and is capable of a direct knowledge of God by relation to its own higher senses and faculties. In an unfallen state it was like a lofty observatory with an outlook upon a celestial firmament" (*The Bible and Spiritual Life*, p. 116). The spirit is the capital city of the human personality.

THE CREATION OF THE HUMAN SOUL

"And man became a living soul." Above the body and beneath the spirit stands the soul, the medium between the two. It has been said that in its relationship to the body and bodily senses it might be likened to the photographer's darkroom. The impressions regarding the external world received through the senses are gathered up and conveyed to this darkroom where they are developed into distinct expressions of thought, emotion or will.

In its relationships to the spirit and the spiritual world the soul might be likened to the judge's bench. The evidence regarding God and spiritual realities which the spirit finds in its research in the spiritual realm is brought to the bar of the soul and there either accepted or rejected.

Man, then, is a trinity; spirit, soul, and body are the integral parts of his triune being. In the constitution of God's first man two independent elements were used; the corporeal and the spiritual; the material and the immaterial. Each was essential because man was to be related to two worlds; the seen and the unseen; the material and the spiritual. He was made primarily for God and in order to have intercourse with God he must have a spirit capable of communion and fellowship with the divine Spirit. But man was to be placed in God's material universe that he might have tangible relationship with the external world of people and things. So he must have a body capable of such contact and communication. Man was to be in close, continuous touch with both heaven and earth; with the external and the temporal; with the spiritual and the material.

When God placed the spirit within the body its home on earth, the union of these two produced a third part and man became a living soul. The soul uniting spirit and body gave man individuality, it was the cause of his existence as a distinct being. The soul, consisting of intellect, emotion and will became the central part, the seat, as it were, of man's being.

The soul acted as the middleman between the spirit and the body; it was the bond which united them and the channel through which they acted upon each other. The soul stood thus midway between two worlds: through the body it was linked to the visible, material and earthly; through the spirit it was linked with the unseen, spiritual and heavenly. To it was given the power to determine which world should dominate man.

The very great importance of this theme in its relationship to succeeding lessons and the intense desire that each reader may have a clear understanding of it leads me to quote at length from Andrew Murray's book, *The Spirit of Christ:*

"The Spirit quickening the body made man a living soul, a living person with the consciousness of himself. The soul was the meeting place, the point of union between body and spirit. Through the body, man, the living soul, stood related to the external world of sense; could influence it, or be influenced by it. Through the spirit he stood related to the spiritual world and the Spirit of God, whence he had his origin; could be the recipient and the minister of its life and power. Standing thus midway between two worlds, belonging to both, the soul had the power of determining itself, of choosing or refusing the objects by which it was surrounded, and to which it stood related.

"In the constitution of these three parts of man's nature the spirit, as linking him with the Divine, was the highest; the body, connecting him with the sensible and the animal, the lowest; intermediate stood the soul, partaker of the nature of the others, the bond that united them, and through which they could act on each other. Its work as the central power was to maintain them in due relation; to keep the body, as the lowest, in subjection to the spirit; itself to receive through the spirit, as the higher, from the Divine Spirit what was waiting for its perfection; and so pass down even to the body, that by which it might be the partaker of the Spirit's perfection, and become a spiritual body.

"The wondrous gifts with which the soul was endowed, specially those of consciousness and self-determination, or mind and will, were but the mould or vessel into which the life of the Spirit, the real substance and truth of the Divine life, was to be received and assimilated. They were a God-given capacity for making the knowledge and will of God its own. In doing this the personal life of the soul would have become filled and possessed with the life of the Spirit, the whole man would have become spiritual.

"To gather up what has been said, the spirit is the seat of our God-consciousness; the soul of our self-consciousness; the body of our world-consciousness. In the spirit God dwells: in the soul self, in the body sense."

It is clear from all this that God's original intention was that the human spirit through which alone man can be related to the Spirit of God and to the spiritual world should be the dominant element in the human personality. The spirit was to be sovereign and as long as it remained so the whole being would be kept spiritual.

But while the human spirit was to be sovereign in the realm of the human personality with both soul and body yielded to its dominance, yet it was to be subject in turn to a higher power. Dr. A. T. Pierson says, "One obvious lesson in this Biblical psychology is that God evidently designed that the human spirit, indwelt and ruled by the Holy Spirit, should keep man in constant touch with Himself, and maintain in everything its proper preëminence, ruling soul and body" (*The Bible and Spiritual Life*, p. 123). (See Diagram 3.)

Thus we see that the human spirit was to be a sovereign under a Sovereign. It was also to be the middleman between the eternal and the temporal; the unseen and the seen; the divine and the human; the heavenly and the earthly. The spirit had its windows opened heavenward and

THE SINLESS ADAM

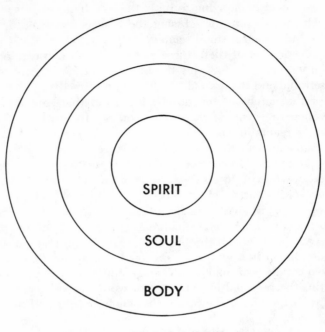

SPIRIT

SOUL

BODY

"VERY GOOD"
Genesis 1:31

Diagram 3: The Sinless Adam

Godward and through spiritual perception, insight and vision it was constantly receiving spiritual impressions which were to be sent outward by way of the soul to the body. The spirit through unbroken fellowship with the Holy Spirit was to be the channel through which the whole being of God's first man would be linked to the life of God and so made and kept spiritual.

This brief study of the threefold nature of God's first man, Adam, shows us that his human personality was so constituted that he could always think, love and will within the circle of God's will. He could choose to live under the authority of his divine Sovereign. There was nothing within himself to hinder perfect obedience to the will of God.

One other question remains to be answered. Was there anything without his life to hinder? Was Adam's environment conducive to complete and continuous obedience to God's will?

God placed His perfect man in a perfect environment. The picture given in Genesis of the Garden of Eden is that of a place in which there was satisfaction and sufficiency for every need of man's spirit, soul and body. The Creator had made Himself responsible for meeting bountifully every need of His creature. Even the brief account given of the life of Adam in Eden reveals perfect adjustment to his environment. Righteousness ruled; therefore, peace resulted. There was nothing within his environment to hinder perfect obedience to the will of God.

God not only placed this perfect man in a perfect environment but His own relationship with Adam was perfect. It was a relationship both of communion and cooperation.

Adam had communion with God. Man was made for God. There is ample scriptural authority for this statement in such verses as Isaiah 43: 7, 21; Colossians 1:16; Revelation 4:11. The fact that man was made in the image of God in his intellectual, moral and volitional life shows that God desired fellowship with him and made him with the capacity for such fellowship which was not given to any other of His creatures. The beautiful words in Genesis 3:8, "And they heard the voice of the LORD God walking in the garden in the cool of the day," reveal God even taking the initiative in seeking communion and comradeship with Adam and Eve. So God's first man walked and talked with God as friend with friend; he was able to know and to enjoy God as a kindred nature; he was in inner, spiritual harmony with God.

God's first man also had cooperation with God in His governmental activities. Adam was God's vice-regent, as it were, over all His works: he was the executive instrument by divine appointment to carry out the divine purpose. God made Adam His representative as the visible monarch of all living things. "He had dominion over the fish of the sea, over the fowl of the air, and over the cattle, and over all the earth, and over every creeping thing that creepeth upon the earth." Within his own sphere he was made a sovereign, subordinate only to God.

One thing more remains to be said concerning God's first man. Adam was not only an individual but he was the federal head of the human race. God made His first man the head and representative of man. Bishop H. C. G. Moule in his *Outlines of Christian Doctrine,* says: "Adam was a true individual, as truly as Abel. But, unlike his son, he was, what only one other Being has ever been, the moral, intelligent Head of a moral, intelligent race; not only the first specimen of a newly created Nature, but in such a sense the Spring of that nature to his after-kind that in him not only the individual but the race could, in some all important respects, be dealt with" (p. 168). Adam by God's appointment was the source of human life of all mankind: the head of the human family. He was God's first representative man. Through him in creation God established a union with the whole human race. Then He commanded Adam to be fruitful and multiply.

God's first man, then, was perfect; he was put in a perfect environment and he had perfect fellowship with God. Harmony reigned within himself, within all his relationships both with the inferior creatures beneath him and with the sovereign Creator above him. There was everything within and without his life to foster complete submission to the sovereignty of God and perfect obedience to His will. Would he be content to remain a sovereign under a Sovereign? Would he choose continuously to live within the circle of God's will? Would his whole personality be kept under the control of the divine Spirit and so maintain its life on the spiritual plane? If so, then through this first man, made in His own image and controlled by His divine Spirit, God would people the earth with beings who would also bear His likeness, yield to His sovereignty, serve Him with fruitfulness, and live together in righteousness and peace.

G. Campbell Morgan in *The Crises of the Christ* states Adam's position before God in the following paragraph, "Finite will is to be tested, and it will stand or fall as it submits to or rebels against the Infinite Will of the Infinite God. Thus unfallen man was a being created in the image of God, living in union with God, cooperating in activity with God, having the points of limitation of his being marked by simple and definite commands laid upon him, gracious promises luring him to that which was highest on the one hand, and a solemn sentence warning him from that which was lowest on the other. He was a sovereign under a Sovereignty, independent, but dependent. He had the right of will, but this could only be exercised in perpetual submission to the higher will of God" (p. 32).

> Genesis 2:16-17, "And the Lord God commanded the man, saying, . . . of the tree of the knowledge of good and evil, *thou shalt not eat of it.*"

Here is God's will expressed in concrete form. Through this command God puts the test to His first man. Adam had the right to will and *he had the power to will Godward.*

3

Life on the Lowest Plane—The Entrance of Sin into Man

IT MUST BE EVIDENT to every thoughtful person that life on the spiritual plane is God's intention for man. In God's first man the divine Spirit had direct relationship with the human spirit and through it as a channel could so control the whole being as to make and keep it spiritual. That which was God's intention for His first man was also His purpose for all mankind.

But candidness compels us to admit that the overwhelming majority of the human race today is living on the lowest plane of life—that of the natural man. In all parts of the world we see man out of adjustment with God, with his fellow men and with himself. Hatred, war, discontent, restlessness, crime, lawlessness, anarchy, prevail.

What then is the reason for such a terrible and tragic fall? Was God's human creation a colossal failure? Did He initiate something which He could not execute? Or must we find a reason for the present condition of humanity in something outside of God? Does the Bible tell us how that which God created without sin and pronounced "very good" became sinful and was denounced by Him as "no good"? A scriptural study of the history of the natural man gives a clear and full explanation.

THE CONDITION OF THE NATURAL MAN

Ephesians 2:12, "That at that time ye were *without Christ*, being aliens from the commonwealth of Israel, and strangers from the covenants of promise, having *no hope*, and *without God* in the world."

The apostle Paul is writing to those in the church at Ephesus who were then living on the spiritual plane but who previously had lived on the plane of the natural. Paul says, "At that time"— when you were living on the lowest plane—"ye were without God, without Christ, and without hope."

31

1 John 5:11-12, "And this is the record, that God hath given to us eternal life, and this life is in his Son. He that hath the Son hath life; and *he that hath not the Son of God hath not life.*"

Eternal life is in Jesus Christ, the Son of God. But Ephesians 2:12 says that the natural man is "without Christ," therefore he must be without eternal life. God offers unto every man the gift of eternal life which he has power to accept or to refuse. To accept it opens the way for him to the highest plane of life, that of the spiritual man; to refuse it leaves him on the lowest plane of life, that of the natural man.

Ephesians 2:1, "And you hath he quickened, *who were dead in trespasses and sins.*"

The natural man refuses the gift of eternal life, therefore he is "dead." Every person who has not accepted from the Father the gift of eternal life bestowed upon him in Christ Jesus, the Son, is described by God as "dead."

Perhaps the reader will think instantly of some unsaved relative or friend who seems to have abounding life and he will challenge, even resent this statement regarding his condition. This person may be a perfect specimen of physical strength and energy. He may be an intellectual giant, perhaps a fine classical scholar, abounding in worldly wisdom and knowledge. He may be a model of morality, living his personal, family and civic life on a high plane. He may even be religious, occasionally attending divine service and contributing toward the maintenance of church or temple. Surely God's description of the natural man does not fit him for he is abounding in life! How can such a man be described as "dead"? There seems to be abounding life in his whole being.

But let a test be made in the realm of his spirit. We have seen that the human spirit is the seat of God-consciousness and that in God's first man there was a direct and vital relationship between the divine Spirit of God and the human spirit of Adam. God's first man responded to God in communion and cooperation. A spiritual man delights to respond to every outreaching of God's grace and love toward him. Does your unsaved friend *respond to God?*

Talk with him about God and spiritual things and your very language is foreign and unintelligible to him, to say nothing of the truth you are attempting to convey. Invite him to go to God's house and he frankly tells you he prefers the club, the cinema or the guild. Give him a Bible to read and it seems insufferably dull and insipid to him and in no measure compares in interest with the newspaper or the latest novel. Invite him to spend an evening in your home in company with God's people and he is fearfully bored and out of place, not knowing how to act or what to say, and longing for the time to depart. Speak to him of his personal spiritual need, explain to him his condition and danger, urge him to accept Christ as his personal Saviour and to ally himself openly with God's people, and he either ridicules the idea or resents it.

Something somewhere seems wrong with the man. Something is wrong with him in the realm of his spirit for there is no response whatsoever to God. There is apparently no God-consciousness. There is no sense of need of God; no desire for God. Something in the man seems *dead*. Something in the man is dead. Death reigns in his spirit.

ADAM, THE CHANNEL OF SIN'S ENTRANCE INTO THE HUMAN RACE

God is the Author of all life and after His creation of living things "God saw every thing that he had made, and behold, it was *very good*." But to-day death reigns everywhere. No living thing is exempt from its touch or its toll. It has wrought ruin everywhere. Surely God is not the author of death. Where then did it come from? God does not leave us in darkness on this question but in language simple enough for a child to understand He tells how death came into the world of living things.

> Romans 5:12, "*By one man sin entered into the world, and death by sin; and so death passed upon all men, for that all have sinned.*"

This clearly teaches that death is a result; that sin is the cause. Death came because of sin.

But how did sin come into the world? *Sin entered by one man.* The blame then for the entrance of sin and death into His beautiful world cannot be placed upon God, for in His own Word He absolutely clears Himself from such a charge.

But who could the man be through whom such terrible havoc, such awful disaster to the whole human race, was wrought? God never leaves an honest, truly seeking soul without an answer that satisfies. In Romans 5:12 God plainly says that all mankind was involved in the disaster caused by one man's sin so he must have been a representative man, one in whom the human race was latent. The context, Romans 5:13-23, sets in sharp contrast sin and death, salvation and life, and traces each to its source in the only two representative men of all history: Adam and Christ. A study of this passage clearly reveals Adam, God's first man, to have been the one through whom sin and death came, and Christ, God's second Man, to have been the One through whom came salvation and life.

But if one has any question in his mind regarding this passage God states the case boldly and unmistakably in

> 1 Corinthians 15:22, "For as *in Adam all die*, even so in Christ shall all be made alive."

Adam is the man through whom sin entered into the human race. The consequence of sin was death. But we have seen in our previous study that Adam was created without sin and that he was put into an environment and enjoyed a fellowship with God both of which were conducive to a continuance in such a state of innocence and fellowship.

So the question forces itself upon one: How could sin enter into such a man with its blighting curse? How was the tragedy of death ever enacted in that beautiful garden? The story is told in the second and third chapters of Genesis. This portion of God's Word spiritually apprehended and humbly accepted gives an answer which satisfies every true and sincere believer.

To answer the question we need to define sin. What could Adam do that could be called sin? The answer is simple. The only sin that Adam could commit was to transgress God's divine law, to will to disobey the clearly revealed will of God. As long as Adam continued to will to live his whole life within the circle of God's revealed will he could not sin. Adam had the right to will but he could remain without sin only as he exercised his will in perpetual submission to the higher will of God. Sin, then, is known disobedience to the clearly revealed will of God. Sin is the willful, deliberate, resistance of a subject to the rightful authority of a Sovereign. "Sin, in the Biblical view, consists in the revolt of the creature will from its rightful allegiance to the sovereign will of God, and the setting up a false independence, the substitution of a life-for-self for life-for-God" (James Orr, *The Christian View of God and the World*, p. 172). Sin as God Himself defines it is "transgression of the law" (1 John 3:4). God called Adam's sin "transgression."

Let us see from God's own record how sin entered into Adam with its curse of death.

> Genesis 2:16-17, "And the Lord God commanded the man, saying, Of every tree of the garden thou mayest freely eat:
>> But of the tree of the knowledge of good and evil, *thou shalt not eat of it*: for *in the day that thou eatest thereof thou shalt surely die.*"

> Genesis 3:6, "And when the woman saw that the tree was good for food, and that it was pleasant to the eyes, and a tree to be desired to make one wise, *she* took of the fruit thereof, and *did eat*, and *gave also unto her husband* with her; and *he did eat.*"

God gave Adam nearly unlimited liberty. Only one commandment was imposed. Only one transgression was possible. Of every other tree he could freely eat. Of only one tree was he forbidden to eat and even for this prohibition God had a beneficent reason. Adam was on trial. He ate of the forbidden fruit. He willed to have something which God for a loving and beneficent reason had willed that he should not have. By that one act he sinned for sin is the transgression of the law. By his own volition Adam deliberately transgressed a divinely marked boundary; he overstepped a clearly revealed divine limitation.

SATAN, THE ORIGINATOR OF SIN IN GOD'S UNIVERSE

But someone may ask, When Adam was a perfect man with a sinless nature, living in a perfect environment and having perfect fellowship with God how could he be tempted to disobey? With all in his own personality and all in his environment favoring his complete and continuous obedience to the will of God, from what source could temptation to disobedience and self-will come? It is a legitimate question and demands an answer which God gives.

> Genesis 3:1, "Now *the serpent was more subtil* than any beast of the field which the LORD God had made. *And he said unto the woman,* Yea, hath God said, Ye shall not eat of every tree of the garden?"

"Now the serpent was more *subtil. . . .* And he *said. . . .*" Here we have words used which can be used only in characteristics, attitudes and acts which belong to personality, either natural or supernatural. But was there any other person in the garden besides the Lord God and His two created beings, Adam and Eve? There evidently was. But it was someone who apparently desired to conceal his identity, so he came under the deceiving cover of impersonation. Who then was this other one?

The conversation between the serpent and Eve recorded in Genesis 3 reveals the twofold fact that this person is an enemy of God and that he is there in the garden for an evil purpose. Does Scripture give us any clue by which this cunning, wicked impersonator may be identified? It does. His name identifies him.

> Revelation 12:9, "And the great dragon was cast out, *that old serpent, called the Devil, and Satan,* which deceiveth the whole world: he was cast out into the earth, and his angels were cast out with him."

Holy Scripture is a unity and Scripture interprets Scripture. "The serpent" of Genesis 3:1 is none other than "that old serpent, called the Devil, and Satan" of Revelation 12:9 and 20:2.

In Revelation 12:9 he is revealed as a deceiver. His nature identifies him. The Bible tells us clearly that that is the part he was playing in the Garden of Eden in his first dealings with humanity. The fingerprints of the archdeceiver are clearly discerned in Genesis 3.

> 1 Timothy 2:14, "And Adam was not deceived, but *the woman being deceived* was in the transgression."

2 Corinthians 11:3, "But I fear, lest by any means, as *the serpent beguiled Eve through his subtilty,* so your minds should be corrupted from the simplicity that is in Christ."

There is evidence then that before the creation of Adam and Eve there was in God's universe a being who was both a sinner and a traitor. Does God's Word give us any light upon who he is and how he came into such a condition?

Ezekiel 28:11-19 and Isaiah 14:12-20 seem to give this clue. A careful study and comparison of these two passages with other Scriptures seem to indicate very clearly that the one referred to is none other than Satan.

The passage in Ezekiel reveals the truth regarding the person and position of Satan originally. It states that Satan was a created being and that he was created perfect. He was "full of wisdom," "perfect in beauty," "perfect in thy ways," "the sum of perfection was found in him."

Not only was he perfect as regards his person but he held a very exalted position in the service of God. He was "the anointed cherub that covereth" and served "in the holy mountain of God." Perhaps no other created being held so exalted a position or was so intimately connected with God.

That he also had some relationship to and power over God's created universe given to him by God Himself is seen in the two titles, "the prince of this world" (John 14:30) and "the prince of the power of the air" (Ephesians 2:2).

That he had been given a high position of trust to which he had been a traitor is very certain. He was a prince over a kingdom for three times the Lord Jesus called him "the prince of this world," and when he took the Lord into a high mountain and offered Him all the kingdoms of the world with their glory Jesus did not dispute his claim to their disposal.

But with all Satan's perfection and power, he was still a created being and, as such, he must be subservient to his Creator and remain dependent and obedient. Scripture, however, from beginning to end reveals Satan as God's archenemy. He is an open and avowed rebel. He is not a subject of the kingdom of light but is a sovereign over the kingdom of darkness.

When and how did this rebellion toward God take place? "The anointed cherub" who was "in the holy mountain" sinned.

Ezekiel 28:15-16, "Thou wast perfect in thy ways from the day that thou wast created, till iniquity was found in thee . . . *thou hast sinned:* therefore I will cast thee as profane out of the mountain of God."

The sin that led to Satan's downfall is intimated in the words, "Thine heart was lifted up because of thy beauty, thou hast corrupted thy wisdom by reason of thy brightness" (Ezekiel 28:17). Pride led to self-exaltation which expressed itself in self-will.

Let us now examine Isaiah 14:12-20 and see to what lengths self-exalta-tion carried Satan in rebellion against his Creator and Sovereign.

> Isaiah 14:12-14, "How art thou fallen from heaven, O Lucifer, son of the morning! how art thou cut down to the ground, which didst weaken the nations!
>
> For thou hast said in thine heart,
> I will ascend into heaven,
> I will exalt my throne above the stars of God:
> I will sit also upon the mount of the congregation , . . .
> I will ascend above the heights of the clouds;
> I will be like the most High."

Self-exaltation led to self-will, self-will led to rebellion against God, and Lucifer, son of the morning, became Satan, father of the night. The mo-ment "the anointed cherub" said in his heart "I will" as opposed to God's will sin began. The moment the subject sought to dethrone the Sovereign by saying "I will be like the most High" sin's work in the universe com-menced. But it did not end there. The sin that began in the holy mountain of God was carried into the Garden of Eden.

SATAN, THE DECEIVER AND THE TEMPTER, IN EDEN

Satan, God's avowed enemy, is there. This apostate spirit is the fourth person in the Garden of Eden. And what is his mission? He is there with the definite, deliberate, diabolical purpose of tempting Adam and Eve to do just what he himself had done—through an act of self-will to step out-side the circle of God's will, to dethrone God by enthroning self. He is there to gain recruits for his rebel ranks; to win subjects for his kingdom of darkness and death.

It is instructive to follow the cunning machinations of this diabolical strategist as he succeeds in tempting Adam and Eve into doubt, dis-obedience and disloyalty. God grant that it may throw needed illumina-tion upon the path of temptation some reader may be treading.

Let us ask and answer three questions:

What was Satan's aim in tempting Adam and Eve?
What was Satan's method of approach to them?
How did he achieve his success?

Satan's aim, let us remember, was to exalt himself to God's place of sovereignty and authority and to secure for himself the worship from God's created beings which belonged to God alone. So he was in Eden to draw Adam and Eve away from God, to persuade them into disobedience and disloyalty, which would automatically cast them out of God's kingdom into his own. To accomplish this he did not need to incite them to gross sin or vice; one act of disobedience would carry out his purpose. He needed only to destroy confidence in God and to lead them to disbelieve and disobey Him.

Satan's method of approach was very cunning and subtle. It was not the method of open warfare against God but that of undermining faith in God by malicious propaganda. Satan did not come out into the open and contest God's sovereignty over His created beings but he sought to discredit God in their sight by creating within them discontent with their circumstances and by holding before them a false utopia, thus hoping to instigate a revolt against God.

His method has not changed from that day to this. He is attempting the same thing and using the same method now that he did four thousand years ago. The seed germ of discontent and disorder sown in the Garden of Eden has borne fruit and is reaping a terrible harvest in all parts of the world today. Churches and chapels are being demolished; Bibles are being torn to pieces; anti-Christian demonstrations are being staged; threats are being made of dethroning God in His own universe. Back of all this subtle, efficient, destructive propaganda is the master mind of the first spiritual Bolshevik who began his world revolution in the Garden of Eden.

To accomplish his purpose there he put before Eve the lure of a far better condition of life than they enjoyed under God's beneficent, loving rule, and urged securing it by illegitimate, revolutionary means. Satan must reach the spirit of Adam and Eve and in some way break the connection between the divine and the human. He did this by the proffer of a knowledge even such as "the gods" possessed. Through the human spirit illumined by the divine Spirit they did know God, which knowledge was the summum bonum of benefit and blessing. But Satan intimated that there was more to be known which God was willfully and wrongfully withholding from them. They were not having their due.

To reach the spirit, to which Satan had no means of access, he must get at the soul. The emotions must be stimulated to desire this tree of the knowledge of good and evil which could make one wise. Their eyes must be opened to see how pleasant was this tree that they might covet its fruit.

So an indirect appeal was made to the soul through the senses. Satan gained his entrance to the innermost being of Eve through the body. The tree was good for food so he tempted Eve to eat of the forbidden fruit.

Every part of the human personality had been undermined by this satanic propaganda. Satan had appealed to the whole man, spirit, soul and body but his method of approach had been from circumference to center; from body through soul to spirit.

Let us examine God's Word to see how Satan achieved his success.

> Genesis 3:1, "And he said unto the woman, *Yea, hath God said,* Ye shall not eat of every tree of the garden?"

A subtle insinuation is couched in these words which was intended by the tempter to arouse suspicion of God's goodness. "Did God really tell you that you couldn't eat of every tree in this garden? Wasn't the garden made for you? Are you not laboring to dress it? Then haven't you a right to its fruit?" The devil did not come to Eve at once with a glaring accusation of God's unkindness but merely with a subtle insinuation. He knew that harmony reigned in the Garden of Eden and that Adam and Eve were perfectly adjusted to each other, to their environment and to God. Satan laid hold upon the only thing he could in their external environment and used it to cause disruption in their relationship with God. Satan's aim was to create doubt first and thus gain a foothold by disturbing the inner harmony of Eve's moral being.

The reply of Eve showed that the devil's insinuating question had had the desired effect. She acknowledged God's goodness in granting them the liberty to eat of the fruit of the trees in the garden and admitted the one and only restriction. But in so doing she omitted from God's gracious promise the words "every" and "freely" and added to the prohibition the words "neither shall ye touch it," thus revealing a secret acquiescence in the serpent's insinuation against God's goodness. Doubt of God's goodness was at work in her heart so the devil grew bolder.

Eve not only stated the restriction made upon their liberty but also God's explicit warning of the penalty of death in case of disobedience, varying it however by changing God's Word "thou shalt surely die" to "lest ye die." Then Satan made a bold, shocking assertion, an out-and-out denial of God's Word, "Ye shall not surely die." This was immediately followed by his final and fatal appeal.

> Genesis 3:5, "For God doth know that in the day ye eat thereof, then your eyes shall be opened, and ye shall be as gods, knowing good and evil."

The bold blasphemy, the cunning deception, the seductive allurement of his sugarcoated lie, were worthy of the source from which they came. Satan implied in this diabolical statement that God was maliciously robbing man of knowledge which he not only had a right to possess but which would raise him to an exalted position hitherto undreamed.

"Your eyes shall be opened and *ye shall know.*" Was not the desire to know a lawful one? Was not the ambition for self-improvement through the pursuit and acquisition of knowledge a legitimate one? Eve had been daily coming into a larger and fuller knowledge of God and His universe no doubt and now, if by merely eating of the fruit of the tree of the knowledge of good and evil she could at once obtain a knowledge as limitless as God's own and be assured God's penalty of death would not be enacted why should she not eat of it?

Satan had reached the acme of evil when he had said, "I will be like the most High," and now in some modified form suited to the innocence of the sinless pair he tempted them to a similar aspiration, "Ye shall be as gods." He held out to them the luring possibility of advancement in knowledge even to the plane of the divine and unseen.

In the appeal of Genesis 3:5 the tempter assailed the whole personality of the woman; intellect, emotion, and will. "Do not be such fools as to believe God's word when it is so evidently against all right and reason; do not be such dupes as to be cheated out of something you rightfully should have; do not be such cowards that you fear to assert your own will in this matter."

"Thus it is seen that at the back of the method of the devil is an aspersion cast upon the character of God. Man was made to question the goodness of law. Appealing to the intelligence of man, the enemy created an aspersion, which was calculated to change the attitude of his emotion, and so capture the final citadel, that namely of his will. He declared that man's intellectual nature was prevented from development by this limitation. By this declaration he created in the mind of man a question as to the goodness of the God who had made the law, and thus imperiled the relation of the will to God, as he called it into a place of activity outside, and contrary to the will of God" (G. Campbell Morgan, *The Crises of the Christ*, p. 33).

The Sin of Adam and Eve and Its Effect upon Themselves

Some response had to be made to such an appeal. The will must function in acceptance or rejection of such an accusation against God. There was no neutral ground. Eve must take sides either with or against God. "*God said*" and "*the serpent said*," and they said totally contradictory things. Eve listened to Satan's voice rather than to God's. She believed the devil's lie rather than God's truth. "The serpent beguiled Eve through his subtilty" (2 Corinthians 11:3), and she ate of the forbidden fruit. Adam listened to Eve's voice rather than to God's. Eve enticed her husband through his affections and he ate of the forbidden fruit. He was the one to whom God had given the command. To eat of the fruit was a deliberate transgression of the divine law.

Genesis 3:6, "And when the woman saw that the tree was good for food, and that it was pleasant to the eyes, and a tree to be desired to make one wise, she took of the fruit thereof, and did eat, and gave also unto her husband with her; and he did eat."

Genesis 3:17, "And unto Adam he said, Because thou hast hearkened unto the voice of thy wife, and hast eaten of the tree, of which I commanded thee, saying, Thou shalt not eat of it: cursed is the ground for thy sake; in sorrow shalt thou eat of it all the days of thy life."

Adam and Eve had the God-given right to will and the power to will Godward. They exercised the right to will and *they chose to will Satanward.* The moment they so chose they stepped outside the circle of God's will and into the realm of self-will. They dethroned God and enthroned self. That one act, that one choice, that one decision, was sin. Satan triumphed, sin entered, ruin ensued.

Sin penetrated to the innermost part of Adam's being, the spirit, the meeting place of God and man. And with what result? The very result which God had predicted—*death.* To apprehend the magnitude of sin, one must know the meaning of death.

And what is death? Mrs. McDonough in *God's Plan of Redemption* gives a clear and helpful answer. "The scientific definition of death helps us to perceive His meaning. It is as follows, 'Death is the falling out of correspondence with environment.' The following illustration will help to better understand the subject. Here is an eye of a human being, apparently able to see any object placed before it; the objects of nature, bathed in the bright sunshine surround it, but there is no response from the eye. It does not see; for the optic nerve is severed. It is dead to the beauty before it.

"Here is a person whose ears are completely deafened. Birds are singing, bells are ringing, voices speaking, but those ears do not respond to the sound waves that are carrying melody to other ears which are open to receive the same. They are dead to sounds.

"Upon the very day of Adam and Eve's disobedience *sin severed the delicate intuitive knowledge of God in the spirit of Adam and Eve.* They failed to respond to Him who was their Environing Presence. They were dead to God. . . . The death process established in the spirit of our first parents was quickly manifested throughout the whole of the inner man and after a time the possibility of dissolution of the body, which had been held in abeyance while man remained obedient and dependent before the Fall, became an actuality" (p. 33).

Death in its twofold aspect, spiritual, the separation of the human spirit of man from the divine Spirit of God, and physical, the separation of the spirit and the body of man, came by sin. A grain of truth was mixed with the lie of the serpent.

> Genesis 3:7, "And the eyes of them both were opened, and *they knew that they were naked;* and they sewed fig leaves together, and made themselves aprons."

> Genesis 3:8, "And they heard the voice of the Lord God walking in the garden in the cool of the day: and *Adam and his wife hid themselves from the presence of the Lord God* amongst the trees of the garden."

Their eyes had indeed been opened but to behold what? Their own nakedness. They both acquired knowledge but of what? Their own sin and shame. They had come into a new self-consciousness but in that one act of sin they had lost God-consciousness. Their newly acquired knowledge served only to produce such a sense of shame that they counted themselves unfit for God's presence and were afraid to meet Him. The twilight hour of communion with God was robbed of all its sweetness and satisfaction by the sense of shame and sin. Eager response to God was changed into seeking refuge from God. Sin separated man from God and separation from God, who is Life, is death.

Physical death was the certain, even though more remote, result of sin. The judgment upon Adam included the curse of physical death.

> Genesis 3:19, "In the sweat of thy face shalt thou eat bread, till thou return unto the ground; for out of it wast thou taken: *for dust thou art, and unto dust shalt thou return."*

From the day Adam sinned, the seed of physical death was in his body and finally reaped its harvest in full.

> Genesis 5:5, "And all the days that Adam lived were nine hundred and thirty years: and *he died."*

Thus we see God's sentence of death, both spiritual and physical, meted out as a result of sin.

The Effect of Adam's Sin upon the Human Race

We have seen the disastrous effect of Adam and Eve's sin upon themselves. The question naturally arises, Did it affect any one else? Can we trace the sin in the human family back to the first sin in the first man, its federal head? Let us reason backward.

Sin is a Fact

Man is a sinner. One needs only to be closeted with himself for a single day to have sufficient proof of this statement. But if he should be loath to admit the evidence given in his own thoughts, feelings, desires, words and acts, let him listen to the gossip of a small town, or read in the daily paper of doings in town or city. Man is a sinner. To deny the reality of sin is not only to disbelieve God's Word and to make Him a liar but it is to discredit one's own experience and observation.

> 1 John 1:8, 10, "If we say that we have no sin, *we deceive ourselves,* and the truth is not in us.
>
> If we say that we have not sinned, *we make him a liar, and his word is not in us.*"

SIN IS A UNIVERSAL FACT

Every man is a sinner. There are no exceptions to this rule except the Man, Christ Jesus. God's Word says, "There is no man that sinneth not."

> Romans 3:10, "As it is written, There is *none righteous,* no, *not one.*"
> Romans 3:12, "They are all gone out of the way, they are together become unprofitable; there is *none that doeth good,* no, *not one.*"

Every truly honest man knows and admits that he is a sinner. At one time self-righteous scribes and Pharisees brought to the Lord Jesus a woman taken in the act of adultery. To tempt Him that they might accuse Him, they asked if they should fulfill the Law of Moses by stoning her. In reply the Lord Jesus said, "He that is without sin among you, let him first cast a stone at her." And "being convicted by their own conscience, they went out one by one." Who among the readers of this book is "without sin"? Men differ in the degree of sin in the life but not in the fact of sin. Many men are naturally kind, generous, genial and loving but "there is none righteous."

EVERY MAN IS A SINNER BEFORE HE SINS

Sin is far more than an act; it is a state, a nature, a disposition, a tendency. Sin is an inner reality before it is an outer manifestation. Sin is a desire before it is a deed.

> James 1:15, R. V., "Then *the lust, when it hath conceived, beareth sin:* and the sin, when it is fullgrown, bringeth forth death."

Who has not seen a baby give vent to temper, self-will, stubbornness and anger before it could talk or walk! Men were born in sin. We are all of us "by nature the children of wrath." Humanity inherited a sinful nature.

By God's appointment Adam was the federal head of the human family. He was the seed of the race, and all the coming generations were in him. Adam was not only man but he was the womb of mankind. As forerunner of the human race, he was also its representative.

Therefore Adam's sin was not his sin alone. All mankind was vitally affected by it. Adam's sin put the poison of sin in the human germ; the result was the moral and spiritual ruin of the race, collectively and individually. Adam was created without sin. By an act of his own will he became a sinner. "What man thus became, men are."

"Who can bring a clean thing out of an unclean?" (Job 14:4). "That which is born of the flesh is flesh" (John 3:6). Adam fell and by that fall received a corrupt nature. Then he begat sons in his own likeness (Genesis 5:3). They inherited his sinful nature and so the poison of sin went on down through the human race until all men are involved.

> Romans 5:12, "Wherefore, as by one man sin entered into the world, and death by sin; and so *death passed upon all men, for that all have sinned.*"

> Romans 5:19, "For as *by one man's disobedience many were made sinners,* so by the obedience of one shall many be made righteous."

By Adam's disobedience all men were made sinners and the death sentence rested upon all.

Spiritual deterioration and death began immediately upon Adam's Fall and the depths into which the human race soon sank are revealed in the following words.

> Genesis 6:3, R. V., "And the LORD said, My Spirit shall not strive with man for ever, for in their going astray *they are flesh.*"

> Genesis 6:5-6, "And God saw that the wickedness of man was great in the earth, and that every imagination of the thoughts of his heart was only evil continually.
> And it repented the LORD that he had made man on the earth, and it grieved him at his heart."

Physical deterioration began immediately upon Adam's fall, and death and decay were the final outcome. Adam lived *and died.* The sad record of Genesis 5 shows that the seed of death implanted in Adam was transmitted to his posterity until each human being has to pay the death toll.

THE EFFECT OF ADAM'S SIN UPON THE SOCIAL ORDER

In the Garden of Eden before the tempter entered it we see the social order as God intended it to be. Adam and Eve were perfect and were living in perfect adjustment with God; therefore there was perfect adjustment between themselves. Godliness and holiness were followed by righteousness and peace.

But sin entered the human spirit and severed its relationship with the divine Spirit. Immediately man was thrown out of adjustment with God and *ungodliness* was the result.

Sin entered the human personality and reigned over every part of it. Man's whole being was thrown into confusion and conflict. Man was thrown out of adjustment with himself and *unholiness* was the result.

Sin entered the human relationship God had established between his first man and woman and produced friction. They were thrown out of adjustment with each other and *unrighteousness* was the result. Each had sinned in eating of the forbidden fruit but each was unwilling to bear the blame for it. Eve had tempted Adam but Adam had of his own free will hearkened unto the voice of his wife and disobeyed God's command. When brought face to face with his sin Adam played the part of a churlish coward blaming both God and Eve for his own misdoing.

> Genesis 3:12, "And the man said, *The woman whom thou gavest to be with me, she gave me of the tree,* and I did eat."

The sin that had introduced disorder into man's relations with God and into his own personality now introduced it into the relationship of fellow beings. Friction between man and man began in God's social order. "The break upward brought the break crosswise. That is the tragic Eden crisis. It touches us all most intimately today. The gloom and blight of the Eden crisis has cast its inky shadow over all the race, and over all life, ever since" (S. D. Gordon, *Quiet Talks on the Crisis and After,* p. 56).

Its inky shadow cast gloom over that first home. The sin of the first parents was visited upon the first children. The eldest son Cain killed his brother Abel. Friction between parents bore fruit in murder between brothers. The maladjustment in God's social order begun in Eden has continued and grown apace into personal, family, civic, national and international frictions until the whole world today is one seething, struggling mass of discontent, envy, greed, suspicion, jealousy, hatred and revenge.

THE EFFECT OF ADAM'S SIN UPON THE MATERIAL UNIVERSE

The blighting, withering effect of sin was felt in the material universe for even the earth was cursed because of the sin of Adam.

> Genesis 3:17-19, "And unto Adam he said, Because thou hast hearkened unto the voice of thy wife, and hast eaten of the tree, of which I commanded thee, saying, Thou shalt not eat of it: *cursed is the ground for thy sake;* in sorrow shalt thou eat of it all the days of thy life;
> Thorns also and thistles shall it bring forth to thee; and thou shalt eat the herb of the field; *in the sweat of thy face shalt thou eat bread.*"

The soil should henceforth be comparatively barren, man would no longer be blessed by its spontaneous, prodigal abundance but would have to coax from it by the sweat of his face and much suffering the necessities of life.

The Effect of Adam's Sin upon God

While the sin of Adam brought incalculable suffering and sorrow to himself and to his posterity yet the One most wounded and wronged by sin was God. The defeat of His purpose in the human race and the dethronement of Himself in His own universe was the twofold aim of Satan in Eden's tragedy. Behind the temptation was the tempter. "The fall began in heaven. Sin entered into God's house before it invaded man's. Christ felt its sting before man felt its stab" (Patterson, *The Greater Life and Work of Christ*, p. 82). The sin enacted in Eden immediately created two very vital issues and brought God into a new relationship both to the tempted and the tempter, to the sinner and to Satan.

The issue at stake between God and God's first man was God's union with the human race. Through Adam in creation God had become united with humanity. But now through sin that union had of necessity been broken. God, who is absolute Holiness, could never countenance nor condone sin, much less dwell in its presence. Sin must be punished and the sinner banished. Adam and Eve, through yielding to temptation, had become sinners. God who had been their beneficent Creator, their bountiful Provider, their intimate Companion, in the light of their transgression of His holy law must assume a different relationship to them and the race latent in them from that which He had before.

God could never remain holy and just unless sin were punished according to its deserts and in such a way as to satisfy fully His holiness. When He gave His command regarding the eating of the fruit of the tree of the knowledge of good and evil He had clearly stated the penalty if the command were disobeyed. To be true to Himself He must now exact that penalty for their sin. He must become their Judge and pronounce upon them the curse which sin merited.

But He had made the human race for Himself and His own glory. He could not willingly stand by and condemn it either to destruction or to eternal separation from Himself for He loved it with an everlasting love. God's holiness compelled Him to become a Judge but His love compelled Him to become a Redeemer. If His union with the human race had been broken through the first man's disobedience, He would send another Man to reestablish it through His obedience. If the race had been ruined through the first man's sin it should be redeemed through the second Man's Saviourhood. Thus God assumes a twofold relationship to Adam and Eve in their sin: that of a Judge and that of a Redeemer. The promise of a Saviour and the pronouncement of a doom were made. Both promise and pronouncement must be fulfilled.

So we see God in Eden seeking the sinner who, because of his sense of guilt and shame with its resultant fear, was hiding from Him.

> Genesis 3:9, "And *the Lord God called unto Adam,* and said unto him, Where art thou?"

What a marvelous unveiling of the infinite, abounding grace of God! A wounded, wronged God seeking a guilty, ungodly sinner! The Lord God taking the initiative to bring Adam and Eve back home to Himself! And this is but the opening scene in the continuous unfolding of God's infinitely gracious dealings with fallen humanity from that hour to this.

God then brought Adam and Eve face to face with the fact and guilt of their sin and gave them a fair, full opportunity to confess it. But instead of a contrite, brokenhearted confession there came a cowardly, halfhearted one mixed with much of palliation and shifting of responsibility.

Again the exceeding riches of God's grace shone forth in His giving the promise of a Saviour. "It shall bruise thy head, and thou shalt bruise his heel" foretold to those guilty sinners who were soon to be banished from God's presence that He would open for them and for the race a way of access to Himself through the suffering of another.

Having now given vent to His infinite mercy and love in the gracious promise of a Saviour, God does full justice to His holy nature and His holy law in pronouncing a curse upon their sin. The God of all grace becomes the sinner's Judge. Sweat, suffering and sorrow are the awful consequences of sin. Then comes the sentence of death, for "the wages of sin is death," and the banishment from God's presence.

> Genesis 3:19, "In the sweat of thy face shalt thou eat bread, till thou return unto the ground; for out of it wast thou taken: *for dust thou art, and unto dust shalt thou return.*"
>
> Genesis 3:23-24, "*Therefore the Lord God sent him forth from the garden of Eden,* to till the ground from whence he was taken. So he drove out the man."

Having dealt with the sinner in grace God now deals with Satan in wrath. There could be no mercy manifested here. The issue between God and Satan was a far more serious one. In the Eden temptation Satan had contested God's right to the ownership of and the dominion over His own creation. Through their yielding to sin God had lost the sovereignty over the world and the race. Such insult and treachery must be dealt with according to their deserts.

THE PROPHECY OF A CONFLICT AND THE PRONOUNCEMENT OF A DOOM

God Himself declares a war against this arch-rebel that He will fight to the finish and in which He will show no mercy. God prophesies an age-long conflict and pronounces an eternal doom.

Genesis 3:15, "*And I will put enmity between thee and the woman, and between thy seed and her seed; it shall bruise thy head,* and thou shalt bruise his heel."

From this sentence of eternal enmity there could be no reprieve.

4

Life on the Lowest Plane—The Rule of
Sin over Man

SIN IS A DESPOT and the Bible shows very clearly that man came under the despotic rule of sin. Sin not only "entered" and "abounded," but it also "reigned" in man (Romans 5:12, 20-21). He lives under a threefold bondage, from which it is impossible for him to extricate himself.

He is in bondage to sin.

> John 8:34, R. V., "Jesus answered them, Verily, verily, I say unto you, Every one that committeth sin is *the bondservant* of sin."

He is in bondage to self.

> 2 Corinthians 5:15, "And that he died for all, that they which live should not henceforth *live unto themselves*, but unto him which died for them, and rose again."

He is in bondage to Satan.

> 2 Timothy 2:26, "And that they may recover themselves out of the snare of the devil, *who are taken captive by him at his will.*"

The natural man is in helpless captivity to sin, self and Satan.

THE RUIN WROUGHT BY SIN IN THE HUMAN PERSONALITY

Not only were *all men* drawn into the whirlpool of sin but *all of man* was ruined by its pollution. Man's personality was corrupted at the very center and the dry rot of sin contaminated his whole being from center to circumference. Death breathed upon spirit, soul and body its destructive fumes. Sin stalked over the human being, that beautiful thing created in the image of God, and left its deadly trail everywhere, marring it until scarcely a trace of godlikeness could be found. Sin caused civil war within the human personality.

SIN MADE THE HUMAN SPIRIT A DEATH CHAMBER

The blasting breath of death first touched the human spirit. Sin closed the windows of the spirit Godward and made it a death chamber. Sin severed the human spirit's relationship with the divine Spirit.

> Ephesians 4:18, "Having the understanding darkened, *being alienated from the life of God* through the ignorance that is in them, because of the blindness of their heart."

Sin also dethroned the human spirit as sovereign over the human personality and made it a captive, a slave. Both soul and body were permeated with sin and were brought under sin's control. Each claimed and sought an equal right to the rule of man. The immediate effect of sin was the complete inversion of the relationship between the spiritual and the physical in human nature. The fall of man from the plane of the spiritual to the plane of the natural took place.

"In the fall the soul refused the rule of the spirit and became the slave of the body with its appetites. Man became flesh; the spirit lost its destined place of rule, and became little more than a dormant power; it was no longer the ruling principle but a struggling captive. And the spirit now stands in opposition to the flesh, the name for the life of soul and body together in their subjection to sin" (Andrew Murray, *The Spirit of Christ*, p. 34).

So the natural man "who is born of the flesh" is flesh. He is of the earth, earthy, and dominated by the flesh rather than by the spirit. The human spirit is darkened, deadened and dethroned.

SIN MADE THE HUMAN SOUL A RUIN

Sin invaded the realm of the soul and laid hold upon the intellectual, emotional, and volitional life.

1. The mind of man was blinded.

> 2 Corinthians 4:3-4, "But if our gospel be hid, it is hid to them that are lost:
> In whom *the god of this world hath blinded the minds of them which believe not*, lest the light of the glorious gospel of Christ, who is the image of God, should shine unto them."

> Titus 1:15, "Unto the pure all things are pure: but unto them that are defiled and unbelieving is nothing pure; but *even their mind and conscience is defiled*."

> Colossians 1:21, "And you, that were sometime *alienated and enemies in your mind* by wicked works, yet now hath he reconciled."

God's first man was made with the capacity for knowing God and one cannot help but believe that had Adam continued to live his life entirely within the circle of God's will that capacity would have been enlarged and enriched. But he sought knowledge God had willed he should not have. By that one act of self-will he placed his intellect outside the circle of God's will. He had the knowledge of evil but he had neither the wisdom nor the power to resist it. As a result sin wrought such ruin in the mind of man that God was compelled to say "that every imagination of the thoughts of his heart was only evil continually" (Genesis 6:5). He even calls evil, good, and good, evil.

Separated from God man's mind became so darkened that his thinking is materialistic. "God is a Spirit: and they that worship him must worship him in spirit and in truth." God is eternal and spiritual and can never be apprehended by what is merely temporal and natural. Apart from living union and communion with God the operation of the human intellect is entirely within the realm of material things.

Separated from God man's mind became so darkened that his thinking is sensual. The soul, unaided by the spirit, in its struggle with sin is open to continuous and terrible temptation through the body.

Separated from God man's mind became so darkened that his thinking is rationalistic. Being outside of God's will his thinking is inevitably outside of God's thought. His wisdom is not God's wisdom: in fact God draws a clean-cut line between His wisdom and that of the natural man.

> 1 Corinthians 1:20-21, "Where is the wise? where is the scribe? where is the disputer of this world? *hath not God made foolish the wisdom of this world?*
>
> For after that in the wisdom of God *the world by wisdom knew not God,* it pleased God by the foolishness of preaching to save them that believe."

The wisdom of the natural man has its source in himself. He rejects anything and everything which cannot be apprehended and explained by his own unaided reason.

> 1 Corinthians 2:14, "But *the natural man receiveth not the things of the Spirit of God:* for they are foolishness unto him: *neither can he know them,* because they are spiritually discerned."

Sin has so twisted and perverted the intellect of the natural man and Satan has so blinded his mind that he often thinks he knows more than God. Pride leads him to exalt his own mentality to such an extent that, if God says anything which his tiny intellect and puny reason cannot comprehend, then he declares God's saying "foolishness." He boldly proclaims God's sacred truth to be fable; God's eternal Word to be an earth-born myth. His endeavor to fathom God's ocean of truth with his little teacup of a mind is pathetic, and his arrogant method of casting aside God's supernatural revelation when it goes contrary to his sin-saturated reason is pitiful indeed.

2. The heart of man was defiled.

> Jeremiah 17:9, *"The heart is deceitful* above all things, *and desperately wicked."*

> Mark 7:21-23, "For from within, *out of the heart of men,* proceed evil thoughts, adulteries, fornications, murders, thefts, covetousness, wickedness, deceit, lasciviousness, an evil eye, blasphemy, pride, foolishness: *all these evil things come from within,* and defile the man."

What a picture of the human heart! Yet it is a true one because it was taken by the divine Photographer "who knows what was in man." Who can look upon this awful picture and others given on the same divine authority, such as Romans 1:29-32, Galatians 5:17-21, Psalm 14:1-3, and not call man's case absolutely hopeless except somehow a miracle be wrought?

Man was made to love God with all his mind, heart, strength and soul. His heart was created with the capacity to respond to the love of God with love. Man was made to love his fellow men. God wishes man to love his neighbor as himself.

But what is the condition in the world today both as regards man's relationship to God and to his neighbor? It is an awful but a tragically true prediction which God made in His Word of the present world condition.

> 2 Timothy 3:1-4, "This know also, that in the last days perilous times shall come.
> For men shall be lovers of their own selves, covetous, boasters, proud, blasphemers, disobedient to parents, unthankful, unholy,
> Without natural affection, trucebreakers, false accusers, incontinent, fierce, despisers of those that are good,
> Traitors, heady, highminded, lovers of *pleasure more than lovers of God."*

When did man fall into such an evil state as is here described? The moment God's first man stepped outside of God's will by his own voluntary choice and carried the human race with him, that moment he dethroned God and enthroned self in his own affections. From that moment man left to himself has been inherently and incurably selfish.

3. The will of man was perverted.

To will to do God's will is man's highest privilege, his most godlike prerogative. To live wholly within the will of God is to have righteousness, peace and harmony reign everywhere. This was God's intention in His universe. All angelic beings, as well as man, were made to be obedient subjects of God the Creator. But in Satan pride led to self-will; self-will to rebellion; rebellion to refusal of authority; and the refusal of authority to lawlessness. Satan, having stepped outside the will of God and become a rebel, tempted Adam and Eve to do the same. They yielded to his temptation and ever since the will of mankind has been off the main track.

But if man has not been willing to submit to the will of God which is always kind, beneficent and loving, surely he will not submit to the will of his fellow man which is often selfish, tyrannical and despotic. So the world of politics, commerce, industry, education and even religion, is intersected with sidelines built by the ingenuity of masterful minds who wish to satisfy their unquenchable thirst for power over other men's lives or their insatiable thirst for other men's possessions. A heaven-inspired description of the perversion sin made in man's will and of the lengths of lawlessness into which it led him, is given in these verses:

> Judges 17:6, "In those days there was no king in Israel, *but every man did that which was right in his own eyes.*"

> Romans 8:7, "Because the carnal mind is enmity against God: for it is *not subject to the law of God, neither indeed can be.*"

G. Campbell Morgan, *The Crises of the Christ*, sums up the ruin wrought in the human soul by Adam's fall as follows: "Thus in the spiritual part of his nature, man by the fall has become unlike God, in that his intelligence operates wholly within the material realm, whereas the divine wisdom is spiritual, and therefore explanatory of all material facts; his emotion acts from wrong principles of self-love, whereas the divine love ever operates upon the principle of love for others; and his will asserts itself upon the basis of passion for mastery, whereas the divine will insists upon obedience, through determination to serve the highest interests of others."

SIN MADE THE HUMAN BODY A BATTLEFIELD

Sin not only invaded the realm of the spirit and the soul but also that of the body and made that which was intended to be the spirit's congenial home its prison house. That which should have been spiritual tends to become sensual. That which God purposed to be the channel through which the spirit within man could touch the external world and bring blessing to it was turned into the instrument through which Satan reached the spirit with his defilement. The body became Satan's broadcasting station.

> Romans 7:23, "But I see another law in my members, warring against the law of my mind, and *bringing me into captivity to the law of sin which is in my members.*"

In Paul's exhortation to those who had accepted Christ as Saviour, "Let not sin therefore reign in your mortal body, that ye should obey it in the lusts thereof," he implied that the body of the natural man had been sin's territory. The members of the body became Satan's tools and instruments of sin.

> Romans 6:13, "Neither yield ye *your members as instruments of unrighteousness unto sin:* but yield yourselves unto God, as those that are alive from the dead, and your members as instruments of righteousness unto God."

> Romans 7:5, R. V., "For when we were in the flesh, the sinful passions, which were through the law, *wrought in our members* to bring forth fruit unto death."

The human body defiled by sin is corrupt, dishonored and weak and it awaits deliverance from a bondage under which it groans (Romans 8:23).

> 2 Corinthians 5:4, "*We that are in this tabernacle do groan, being burdened:* not for that we would be unclothed, but clothed upon, that mortality might be swallowed up of life."

The Manifestation of Sin in the Natural Man

Sin began to do its deadly work at the core of Adam's being. This core, his human nature, became sinful. Sin became its native atmosphere. Sin became its governing, impelling principle. The fountainhead of his thoughts, emotions, attitudes, instincts and purposes, was vitiated by sin.

The word we commonly use today to express this sinful root is *self*. The core of the natural man is self. Scripture gives us another name. That corrupt human nature, that inborn tendency to evil in all men received by inheritance from our first parents, is called "the old man."

> Colossians 3:9, "Lie not one to another, seeing that ye have put off *the old man* with his deeds." (Cf. Romans 6:6, Ephesians 4:22.)

But man is not a silent, inactive creature. His thoughts are expressed in words; his instincts are translated into actions; so if the fountain is corrupt, then that which flows out from it will be correspondingly corrupt. This inner nature manifests itself in outward acts. The hidden desires of "the old man" come to the surface in deeds. Covetousness grows into theft; deceit becomes falsehood; impurity of thought and desire manifests itself in sins of the flesh; unforgiveness and hatred crystallize into revenge and murder; fear becomes fretting; unbelief shades off into worry; dislike degenerates into backbiting; impatience becomes nagging; dissatisfaction and discontent clothe themselves with murmuring and complaining; self-righteousness slips into censoriousness; pride takes on the color of boastfulness; envy becomes slander; ambition arms itself for war; selfishness grows into oppression; and jealousy attempts to end its torment in suicide or homicide.

This truth is made very plain in the Bible in the clear-cut distinction between *sin* and *sins*.

1 John 1:8-9, "If we say that we have *no sin*, we deceive ourselves, and the truth is not in us.

If we confess *our sins*, he is faithful and just to forgive us *our sins*, and to cleanse us from all unrighteousness."

Leon Tucker in his *Studies in Romans* states the difference as follows:

"Sin is the character; sins are conduct.
Sin is the center; sins are the circumference.
Sin is the root; sins are the fruit.
Sin is the producer; sins are the product.
Sin is the sire; sins are his offspring.
Sin is the fountain; sins are its flow.
Sin is what we are; sins are what we do."

Sin then is the old nature itself; sins are the manifestations of the old nature.

This picture of the ravages of sin in the life of the natural man is an exceedingly dark one but a thorough, prayerful study of God's Word on this subject together with an honest observation of human life as it is must convince an open-minded, humble man that it is a true picture. It does not mean that each person has committed every one of these sins. There is a difference in the degree of sin manifested in the natural man but not in the fact of inherent sin. God who knows what is in man says, "There is none righteous; no, not one." It does mean that every man is a sinner in the sight of God and that the whole world is guilty before Him (Romans 3:19). It does mean that man who was made in the image of God has become flesh.

The Destiny of the Natural Man

God and sin cannot dwell together; they cannot stay in the same place at the same time for they are mutually exclusive. They are exact opposites. Perhaps you are now sitting in a room full of light; a few hours will pass by and it will be filled with darkness. Where has the light gone? It has been displaced by darkness. Again a few hours pass by and the room is filled with light. Where has the darkness gone? It has been displaced by light. Light and darkness cannot dwell together; they are exact opposites; they are mutually exclusive.

> 1 John 1:5-6, "*God is light,* and in him is *no darkness at all.* If we say that
> we have fellowship with him, and walk in darkness, we lie, and do not
> the truth."

> Ephesians 5:8, "For *ye were* sometimes *darkness,* but *now are ye light in
> the Lord:* walk as children of light."

God is light, sin is darkness; therefore God must displace sin or sin displaces God. God and sin cannot stay in the same place at the same time for they are mutually exclusive.

Sin separated Adam from God; it made him want to hide from God's presence. Sin separated God from Adam and compelled Him to pronounce the sentence of death and to send him forth from the garden of Eden.

If God cannot dwell with sin in the sinner on earth neither could He dwell with sin in the sinner in heaven. So if the natural man persists in his sin and rejects the way of salvation which God provides in Christ Jesus, by that very choice he debars himself from the presence of God throughout eternity. His own unrighteousness will then shut him out of the Kingdom of God.

> 1 Corinthians 6:9, "Know ye not that *the unrighteous shall not inherit the
> kingdom of God?*"

> Revelation 21:27, "And *there shall in no wise enter into it any thing that
> defileth,* neither whatsoever worketh abomination, or maketh a lie: but
> they which are written in the Lamb's book of life."

Let us now sum up the truth we have studied thus far. God's first man, Adam, was without sin; he was created in God's image on the plane of human life. He was made with the capacity for life on the highest plane, the spiritual, and with the power to choose such a life. God made man with his face turning Godward. God's will was both the center and the circumference of his life: consequently he lived in righteousness and peace because in perfect adjustment with God, with himself, and with all created beings.

But Adam chose to disobey God's command. He used his power to choose Satanward, and placed his life voluntarily under Satan's sovereignty. He stepped outside of God's sphere of righteousness, light and life into Satan's sphere of sin, darkness and death. He dethroned God and enthroned self. He ceased to be spiritual and became flesh. Sin made him a sinner with his face turning Satanward and his course tending downward. Self-will became both the center and the circumference of his life; consequently he lives in ungodliness, unrighteousness and discord because there was maladjustment with God, with himself, and with all created beings.

Adam himself was the father of children. He was not merely an individual creation of God but he was the appointed federal head of the human race. All the evil consequences of sin in him were transmitted to all men so that by nature all men are guilty and defiled. The most awful consequence of sin, however, was not the moral and spiritual ruin of the human race but the denial of the Godhood of God in His own universe.

This view of the origin and the consequences of sin, even though it is so clearly taught in God's Word, is not accepted by all. Sin even in many pulpits today is treated very lightly if not passed over altogether. Nevertheless everyone knows that humanity is saturated with sin and that sin is really at the bottom of all the world's trouble. But many people are unwilling to admit the real nature of sin. They treat it like a superficial skin disease rather than like a malignant cancer.

Men are unwilling to acknowledge the truth of God's estimate of the natural man, that left to himself he is hopelessly, incurably bad. They place the blame of his misconduct onto his environment or limited cir-

THE SINFUL ADAM

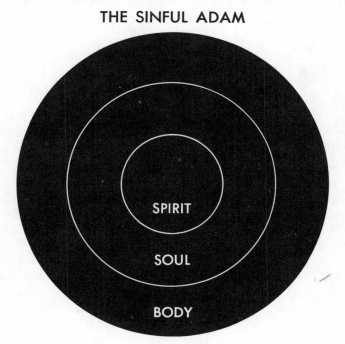

SPIRIT

SOUL

BODY

"NO GOOD"

Romans 7:18

Diagram 4: The Sinful Adam

cumstances and by seeking to improve these external conditions and to afford him larger opportunities through education and civilization they believe he can be evolved into what God intended him to be.

Such thinking is due to a fundamental misconception of what sin is. The essence of the first sin in Eden is clearly defined in God's Word and it is the essence of all sin from that day to this.

> 1 John 3:4, R. V., "Every one that doeth sin doeth also lawlessness; and *sin is lawlessness.*"

The exceeding sinfulness of Adam's sin lay in the fact that it was high treason of the created against the Creator; of the subject against the Sovereign. Such at heart is all sin. The natural man is a spiritual Bolshevist.

Man is not only guilty and defiled but he is rebellious and lawless. He is not only separated from God by sin but he is unreconciled by enmity. In God's sight he is a sinner, an enemy, an outlaw. (See Diagram 4.)

5

God and Satan in Conflict

THAT EVIL EXISTS in this world no one could deny. Evil forces are at work in countless ways and through manifold channels. An evil power operates everywhere working intelligently for the degeneration of mankind and for the defeat of God. There is in the world an aggressive opposition to God and to God's purpose.

Power is the product of personality, therefore the acknowledgment of the presence of power necessitates the recognition of the presence of a personality originating and directing it.

Nowhere in the Bible is evil treated as a mere abstraction. A lie is the spoken language of a liar.

> Acts 5:3, "But Peter said, *Ananias, why hath Satan filled thine heart to lie to the Holy Ghost,* and to keep back part of the price of the land?"

A murder is the actualized desire of a murderer.

> 1 John 3:12, "Not as *Cain, who was of that wicked one,* and *slew his brother.*"

Ananias was the mouthpiece and Cain was the tool of another. Behind the human personality was a supernatural personality. Their evil was the revealed power of a concealed person.

The Bible tells us that such an evil one exists. Christ is the authority for the statement that there is an evil one and that he is the devil.

> Matthew 13:19, R. V., "When any one heareth the word of the kingdom, and understandeth it not, *then cometh the evil one,* and snatcheth away that which hath been sown in his heart."

> Matthew 13:39, "*The enemy that sowed them is the devil;* the harvest is the end of the world; and the reapers are the angels."

Good forces are at work also. A good power operates everywhere intelligently for the regeneration of mankind and for the exaltation of God. There is in the world an aggressive opposition to Satan and to Satan's purpose.

Nowhere in the Bible is good spoken of as a mere abstraction. It is invariably the product of personality. Christ is the authority for the statement that there is a good one and that He is God.

> Matthew 13:24, "Another parable put he forth unto them, saying, The kingdom of heaven is likened unto *a man which sowed good seed in his field.*"

> Matthew 13:37, "He answered and said unto them, *He that soweth the good seed is the Son of man.*"

> Luke 18:19, "Jesus said unto him, Why callest thou me good? *none is good, save one, that is, God.*"

The evil one is the antithesis of the Good One. Scripture sets Satan forth as the greatest enemy of both God and man. This is clearly seen in the names and titles given him.

He is called *"Satan,"* which means "opponent," or "adversary." This title is used of him fifty-six times and invariably reveals him as the opponent of God and the adversary of man.

> Matthew 4:10, "Then saith Jesus unto him, *Get thee hence, Satan:* for it is written, Thou shalt worship the Lord thy God, and him only shalt thou serve."

> 1 Peter 5:8, "Be sober, be vigilant; because *your adversary* the devil, as a roaring lion, walketh about, seeking whom he may devour."

He is called *"the devil,"* which means "slanderer," or "accuser." This title occurs thirty-five times in the Bible and shows him to be the slanderer of God and the accuser of man.

> Matthew 13:39, *"The enemy that sowed them is the devil;* the harvest is the end of the world; and the reapers are the angels."

> Revelation 12:10, "And I heard a loud voice saying in heaven, Now is come salvation, and strength, and the kingdom of our God, and the power of his Christ: *for the accuser* of our brethren is cast down *which accused them before our God* day and night."

The devil slanders God to man (Genesis 3:1-7) and man to God (Job 1:9-12; 2:1-7).

He is called *"the wicked one."*

> Matthew 13:19, "When any one heareth the word of the kingdom, and understandeth it not, then cometh *the wicked one,* and catcheth away that which was sown in his heart."

He is not only the personification of evil, "the wicked one," but he is the source of evil in others.

> 1 John 3:8, *"He that committeth sin is of the devil; for the devil sinneth from the beginning.* For this purpose the Son of God was manifested, that he might destroy the works of the devil."

The devil is a liar and cannot speak the truth. He is a murderer and bent on the ruin and destruction of men. He was the first sinner; therefore he is the forefather of sinners.

> John 8:44, *"Ye are of your father the devil,* and *the lusts of your father ye will do.* He was a murderer from the beginning, and abode not in the truth, because there is no truth in him. When he speaketh a lie, he speaketh of his own: for he is a liar, and *the father of it."*

He is called *"the tempter."* He tempted the Son of man and he tempts all men.

> Matthew 4:3, "And when *the tempter* came to him, he said, If thou be the Son of God, command that these stones be made bread."

> 1 Thessalonians 3:5, "For this cause, when I could no longer forbear, I sent to know your faith, lest by some means *the tempter have tempted you,* and our labour be in vain."

He is called *"the deceiver."* He deceives both individuals and nations. He began his wicked work in Eden by deceiving Eve.

> Revelation 12:9, "And the great dragon was cast out, that old serpent, called the Devil, and Satan, *which deceiveth the whole world:* he was cast out into the earth, and his angels were cast out with him."

> 1 Timothy 2:14, "And Adam was not deceived, but *the woman being deceived* was in the transgression."

On the threshold of divine revelation we read the prophecy of a conflict between Satan and God and every page from that on is but an unfolding of its progress toward its divinely appointed end, the ultimate and absolute defeat of Satan, the eternal and perfect victory of God.

The Commencement of the Conflict

That a good God created everything good is a logical supposition, for the character of God must be expressed in His works. But when God says that every creation of His was "very good," then the statement is lifted out of the realm of supposition into that of fact.

God, then, did not create evil nor did He create the evil one as the evil one. Where then did evil come from? How did "the anointed cherub" become the "devil," "the wicked one," "the tempter," "the deceiver"? How did the beautiful archangel who held the highest rank in heaven become the diabolical traitor who will be cast into the depths of hell? How did

he who "abode in the truth" become an apostate and "the father of lies"?
We have seen already that it was because he said,

> "I will ascend *into heaven.*
> I will exalt *my throne* above the stars of God.
> I will *sit* also upon the mount of the congregation.
> I will *ascend above the clouds.*
> I WILL BE LIKE THE MOST HIGH."

Every word of this defiant, presumptuous declaration is the very breath
of treason and anarchy. Lucifer is unwilling longer to be a subject in and
a prince over the world; he is determined not to be a subordinate but a
sovereign.

God could brook no such independence of action; He could countenance no such effrontery to His sovereignty over the universe or His
moral government of created beings. Such treason brought Satan and
God into deadly conflict.

THE CONSEQUENCES OF THE CONFLICT

The die had been cast. Satan was henceforth to contest with God the
possession of the earth and all therein; to set himself up as a rival claimant
to the world's sovereignty and to man's worship. He would establish a
kingdom of his own. God, for a purpose which we shall understand as we
proceed with the unfolding of His wondrous plan of redemption, permitted Satan to go forward with his evil designs.

TWO SOVEREIGNS

There are now in the universe two separate distinct kingdoms, the Kingdom of God and the kingdom of Satan. Two sovereigns claim authority
over heaven and earth.

By His creatorship God is the rightful Lord, for all things were created
by Him and for Him. God has never given away to any created being,
angelic or human, any part of His universe. He holds the possession of
the whole universe in perpetuity.

> Deuteronomy 10:14, "Behold, *the heaven and the heaven of heavens is
> the Lord's thy God, the earth also, with all that therein is.*"

> Psalm 24:1, "*The earth is the Lord's, and the fulness thereof; the world,
> and they that dwell therein.*"

The Kingdom of God is the central government, the only government
recognized by God and the spiritual hosts of heaven and earth. It is composed of all moral intelligences, angelic or human, celestial or earthly,
of all centuries and all climes, who willingly place themselves within the

circle of the divine will and who of their own free choice acknowledge and accept God as their Sovereign. The Kingdom of God embraces the entire universe over which God is enthroned as the absolute Sovereign.

The Lord Jesus teaches that there is such a Kingdom of God and who are eligible to citizenship in it.

> Luke 13:28-29, "There shall be weeping and gnashing of teeth, when ye shall see Abraham and Isaac, and Jacob, and all the prophets, *in the kingdom of God, and you yourselves thrust out.* And they shall come from the east, and from the west, and from the north, and from the south, and shall sit down *in the kingdom of God.*"

> John 3:5, "Jesus answered, Verily, verily, I say unto thee, *Except a man be born of water and of the Spirit,* he cannot enter into the kingdom of God."

God states with clearness the essential credentials for entrance into His kingdom.

> James 2:5, "Hath not God chosen the poor of this world *rich in faith,* and heirs of the kingdom which he hath promised to *them that love him?*"

However unthinkable it may seem there is also in God's universe a kingdom of Satan. The Lord Jesus teaches that there is such a kingdom. On one occasion when casting out a demon He was charged by some of the people with casting out demons through Beelzebub the chief of demons. Jesus made the following reply in which He brought the kingdom of Satan and the Kingdom of God into sharpest contrast.

> Luke 11:17-20, "But he, knowing their thoughts, said unto them, Every kingdom divided against itself is brought to desolation; and a house divided against a house falleth.
>
> If Satan also be divided against himself, *how shall his kingdom stand?* because ye say that I cast out devils through Beelzebub.
>
> And if I by Beelzebub cast out devils, by whom do your sons cast them out? therefore shall they be your judges. But if I with the finger of God cast out devils, no doubt *the kingdom of God is come upon you.*"

God acknowledges that Satan did set up a kingdom and that he sits on a throne of his own making.

> Revelation 2:13, R. V., "I know where thou dwellest, *even where Satan's throne is;* and thou holdest fast my name, and didst not deny my faith, even in the days of Antipas my witness, my faithful one, who was killed among you, *where Satan dwelleth.*"

Christ never acknowledged Satan to be king but three times He did call him "the prince of this world."

John 12:31, "Now is the judgment of this world: *now shall the prince of this world be cast out.*"

God also acknowledges the worship Satan has succeeded in obtaining, for He calls him "the god of this world."

2 Corinthians 4:4, "In whom *the god of this world hath blinded the minds of them which believe not.*"

There is still another title given him in Scripture which shows that Satan not only obtained and exercises great power on earth among men but that he carried his rebellion against God even into heaven and secured a following among the angelic host.

Ephesians 2:2, "Wherein in time past ye walked according to the course of this world, *according to the prince of the power of the air,* the spirit that now worketh in the children of disobedience."

Ephesians 6:12, R. V., "For our wrestling is not against flesh and blood, *but against the principalities, against the powers,* against the world-rulers of this darkness, against the spiritual hosts of wickedness in the heavenly places."

It is evident, then, that through Satan's treason and Adam's disobedience Satan gained a temporary conquest of the earth, which became a revolted province in God's universe. Satan is a sovereign over a rebel government; it is a government against government. It is composed of all moral intelligences, angelic or human, celestial or earthly, of all centuries and of all climes, who are without the circle of the divine will and who continue to be subjects of Satan. The kingdom of Satan embraces the whole world of mankind that is without the Lord Jesus Christ.

TWO SPHERES

In a recent issue of the *National Geographic Magazine* there is a remarkable picture. It was a view taken from a hydroplane at an elevation of five thousand feet of two rivers, the Negro and the Amazon, meeting and mingling. The picture reveals two distinct streams, each identified by its color. The waters of the Negro are black, those of the Amazon yellow, and even at the place where they meet the sharp color line of distinction can be seen.

One looking down upon humanity from the viewpoint of the heavenlies can see in this world two distinct streams of life, the natural and the spiritual, each easily identified by its color. The waters of the natural are black, those of the spiritual yellow, and even at the place where they meet and mingle whether in business, in society or in the home, the sharp color line of distinction may be seen.

The Negro and the Amazon have different sources and each partakes all through its course of the color of the water at the fountainhead. The natural and the spiritual in human life come from two distinct sources and each partakes all through its course of the quality of life at its fountainhead.

There are two spheres into which all humanity is divided; the one is the sphere of sin and the other is the sphere of righteousness. These two spheres are identified by three outstanding characteristics: the sphere of sin by darkness, death and disorder; the sphere of righteousness by light, life and liberty. Satan is the sovereign in the sphere of sin and Christ is the Sovereign in the sphere of righteousness.

That there are these two spheres of life and that Christ Jesus died and rose again to bring men out of the one into the other is declared in many passages of Scripture. We shall study only three passages. In Paul's defense before Agrippa he states his God-given commission as a minister and a missionary to the Gentiles. God told Paul exactly what He expected him to do.

> Acts 26:17-18, "Delivering thee from the people, and from the Gentiles, unto whom I now send thee, to open their eyes, and *to turn them from darkness to light,* and *from the power of Satan unto God,* that they may receive forgiveness of sins, and inheritance among them which are sanctified by faith that is in me."

Those to whom Paul preached were blinded, befogged, bound men and he was sent that they might be enlightened and emancipated. They were to be turned from something to Something, they were to be turned from some one to Some One.

> Colossians 1:13, R. V., "Who *delivered us* out of *the power of darkness,* and *translated us* into *the kingdom of the Son of his love."*

The believer has been *rescued from* Satan's dominion and *removed into* God's Kingdom.

> Ephesians 5:8, R. V., "For ye were *once darkness,* but are *now light* in the Lord: walk as children of light."

There are these two sharply contrasted and distinctly marked spheres in which men live and each reader this moment is in one or the other of these spheres.

Two seeds

With the defection of Adam, Satan thought he had won the first step in God's defeat and dethronement. A terrible conflict began. God did not minimize its sinister seriousness but on the very threshold of the conflict He triumphantly claimed victory over his enemy.

> Genesis 3:15, "And *I will put enmity* between thee and the woman, and *between thy seed and her seed; it shall bruise thy head,* and thou shalt bruise his heel."

This prophecy-promise contains God's declaration of war. A battle is to be fought to a finish between two seeds. The issue at stake is the sovereignty of God. The immediate object in the conflict is the redemption and reconciliation of the human race ruined through sin. The ultimate object is the restoration to God of undivided sovereignty over all His universe; in other words the rule of the Kingdom of God.

Enmity is to exist between two seeds—the seed of the serpent and the seed of the woman. Satan's seed traced through Scripture is the Antichrist; the woman's seed is the Christ. Toward these two persons pitted against each other in a final conflict all Scripture prophecy converges.

Satan knows that Jesus Christ is "the seed of the woman." It is He whom the devil hates. Ever since this first Messianic prophecy was uttered in Eden Satan's virulent attacks have been against the Person and work of the Lord Jesus. From the moment God said "I will put enmity between thy seed and her seed; it shall bruise thy head and thou shalt bruise his heel" until Christ, the Saviour, fulfilling that prophecy on Calvary cried, "It is finished," Satan waged incessant warfare against the *Person* of the Lord Jesus.

Old Testament history unfolds to view repeated attempts to destroy the line through which "the woman's seed" would come, thus preventing the incarnation. These being brought to naught by God's protecting intervention, he then sought to kill the Christ Child at birth. Failing in this he tried to thwart the fulfillment of God's eternal purpose in His Son by tempting the Lord Jesus in the wilderness to declare His independence of God. Defeated in his direct appeal he used indirect means to keep Him from the cross of Calvary. He used both Christ's enemies and His friends as his tools. He instigated His enemies to kill Him and repeated attempts were made upon His life. He used His friends to dissuade Him from the voluntary sacrifice of Himself as the world's Saviour. His defeat in all these varied attempts maddened him into an attack upon the spirit, soul and body of the Son of Man in Gethsemane, his last futile effort to blockade the way to Calvary. Jesus Christ went to the cross, He died and rose from the tomb: the seed of the woman bruised the serpent's head.

Failing to hurt the Person of the Lord Jesus Satan has been occupied through the past nineteen centuries with attempts to nullify His *work*. He has done this by deceiving men and blinding their minds thus leading them to disbelieve and deny the truth of the Gospel. By so doing he hopes to delay the final fulfillment of the prophecy regarding his own utter defeat.

From the moment of the pronouncement of this prophecy-promise God has made steady progress in its fulfillment. In the Garden of Eden it was *announced;* in the manger cradle at Bethlehem it was *actualized;* on the cross of Calvary it was *accomplished;* and on Mount Olivet it will be *attested.*

The Kingdom belongs to God. Satan maintains his claim only as a traitor and an usurper. Christ came, lived, died, rose, ascended into heaven and will come again that He may sit upon His throne and reign (Acts 2:30) until every foe is conquered (Acts 2:35) and all is put again under the divine sovereignty of the triune God (1 Corinthians 15:22-28).

In Eden the final fate of Satan is clearly announced. "It shall bruise thy *head.*" It is to be a fatal stroke which effects his ultimate defeat, dethronement and destruction. The doom pronounced upon the devil in Genesis 3:14-15 is an eternal doom: the end for him is eternal torment in the lake of fire prepared for him and his angels (Matthew 25:41).

In the manger cradle of Bethlehem the final fate of Satan is actualized. The incarnation of the Lord of heaven means the beginning of the end for Satan, and he knows it. That is why he fought the birth of the Christ Child and why he now denies the God-breathed truth of the virgin birth. His destruction was actualized when God-manifest-in-Christ entered openly and aggressively into the field of operation to lead His forces on to victory.

On the cross of Calvary the final fate of Satan was accomplished. There his doom was sealed. God's eternal purpose in Christ's Saviourhood was realized. Henceforth heaven looks upon the devil as a defeated foe. Christ in anticipating His death upon the cross regarded it as the time and place of the devil's defeat for He said, "Now shall the prince of this world be cast out" (John 12:31).

But not until on the Mount of Olivet the Lord Jesus Christ comes from heaven in all His majesty and glory will the final fate of Satan be attested. The sentence pronounced upon him in Eden will then be executed. Through God's permission the traitor-prince still rules the kingdom of Satan, but when God's eternal purpose in Christ Jesus is carried out fully then God's judgment upon Satan will be executed finally.

SUBJECTS IN THE TWO KINGDOMS

From the moment Satan set up a kingdom of his own he has been busy recruiting subjects and mobilizing his forces for warfare. Today he has a multitudinous satanic host in the aerial heavens, on earth and in the underworld.

Scripture speaks of "the devil and his angels." It tells us there are angels that sinned.

> Matthew 25:41, "Then shall he say also unto them on the left hand, Depart from me, ye cursed, into everlasting fire, *prepared for the devil and his angels.*"

> Jude 6, "And *the angels which kept not their first estate, but left their own habitation,* he hath reserved in everlasting chains, under darkness, unto the judgment of the great day."

As "prince of the power of the air" and "prince of demons" Satan rules a vast host of spirit beings in the aerial heavens. The "demons" or "evil spirits" who are employed in Satan's service are probably those who were under his rule when he was "the anointed cherub" and who followed him in his rebellion against God. The heavenlies swarm with these spiritual hosts of wickedness which are united in a most complete organization consisting of principalities and powers over which are intelligent world-rulers. The headquarters of this vast organization, Satan's seat (Revelation 2:13), is above the earth and the sphere of activity of this satanic host is on the earth and in the atmosphere that envelops it.

> Matthew 8:16, R. V., "And when even was come, they brought unto him many *possessed with demons:* and he cast out the *spirits* with a word, and healed all that were sick."

> Ephesians 6:12, R. V., "For our wrestling is not against flesh and blood, but *against the principalities,* against *the powers,* against *the world-rulers of this darkness,* against *the spiritual hosts of wickedness in the heavenly places.*"

Satan is also ruler over a satanic order on earth. He is called "the prince of this world." The posterity of Satan's seed is found not only among angels and demons but among men. The seed of the serpent can be traced from Genesis to Revelation. They are men and women who choose to live in self-will rather than in God's will, who refuse God's sovereignty over their lives, who in pride and self-righteousness reject Jesus Christ as their Saviour. Cain is the first one mentioned as the seed of the serpent.

> 1 John 3:12, "Not as Cain, *who was of that wicked one,* and slew his brother. And wherefore slew he him? Because his own works were evil, and his brother's righteous."

The Lord Jesus recognized the serpent's brood in the self-loving, self-willed, Christ-hating, Christ-rejecting Pharisees of His day and did not hesitate to call them by their rightful names.

Matthew 23:33, *"Ye serpents, ye generation of vipers,* how can ye escape the damnation of hell?"

On another occasion in speaking to those who rejected Him, He disclosed their spiritual ancestry, the devil, and said they were subjects in his service. *"Ye are of your father the devil,* and *the lusts of your father ye will do."*

At still another time Jesus called the unsaved among men "the children of the wicked one." He had told them the parable of the tares and the wheat and they asked for an explanation.

Matthew 13:38, "The field is the world; the good seed are the children of the kingdom; but *the tares are the children of the wicked one."*

God has a multitudinous host in heaven, in paradise and on earth who are His subjects. The seed of God can be traced from Genesis to Revelation and includes all those who from the beginning of human history have been rescued from Satan's kingdom and removed into God's through faith in the atoning sacrifice of the Son. Abel was the first of the heroes of the faith.

Hebrews 11:4, *By faith Abel offered unto God a more excellent sacrifice than Cain, by which he obtained witness that he was righteous,* God testifying of his gifts: and by it he being dead yet speaketh."

All down through the centuries men continued to offer those "more excellent sacrifices" which required the shedding of blood, thus expressing their need of and faith in the Saviour who was to come.

Then the Saviour came and made one sacrifice for sins through the shedding of His own blood. Since then through the preaching of the Gospel multitudes from out of all nations and peoples of the earth have renounced their citizenship in the kingdom of Satan and have become subjects in the Kingdom of God.

Colossians 1:13, "Who hath *delivered us from the power of darkness,* and hath *translated us into the kingdom of his dear Son."*

Added to these vast multitudes of God's subjects on earth are the innumerable hosts of angels in heaven whose delight is in unceasing worship of the Lamb that was slain.

Revelation 5:11-12, "And I beheld, and I heard *the voice of many angels round about the throne* and the beasts and the elders: and the number of them was ten thousand times ten thousand, and thousands of thousands;

Saying with a loud voice, Worthy is the Lamb that was slain to receive power, and riches, and wisdom, and strength, and honour, and glory, and blessing."

Two SYSTEMS

Satan has a purpose, a project and a program. His purpose is to "be like the most High," his project is to set up a kingdom in opposition to the Kingdom of God, his program is to better the condition of the world and the circumstances of humanity so that men will be satisfied to remain his subjects and will have no desire for the Kingdom of God.

Satan has been represented in much of the literature of the world as the fiend of hell. He has been caricatured as a heinous creature with horns and hoofs, reveling in all that was cruel, vicious and unclean. But he is the exact opposite of all this. He never wanted to be the god of hell but the God of Heaven. It was God's judgment upon his sin that made him king of the bottomless pit. He is the inspirer and instigator of the very highest standards of the God-less, self-made world of mankind. His purpose was and still is to be and to do without God what God is and does. Let us ever keep in mind that Satan's purpose was to dethrone God in His universe and in the hearts of men and then to take His place. To succeed in his attempt Satan must try not to be unlike God but like God. To incline the hearts of men to himself as a ruler and to draw out their hearts to him in worship he must imitate God. To annul the work of Christ Satan must counterfeit it as far as possible.

His project was in line with his purpose. He would leave his position as a subordinate in God's kingdom and set up a kingdom of his own. The foundation of it would be self. Self-will, self-love, self-interest, self-sufficiency would constitute its cornerstone. Lawlessness, a revolt against the rule of God, and irreverence, a refusal to worship God, would be its superstructure.

Satan knew that such a project would have to be safeguarded by a cleverly planned program. Not even the natural man would submit knowingly to the sovereignty of Satan or fall down and worship him. So Satan's program from the beginning has been one of deception. Satan has sought to keep the natural man satisfied with himself and with the world in which he lives. This is not as easy a task as it might seem. The spirit of man can never be satisfied save in God from whom it emanated and for whom it was created. Something in even the worst of men at certain times and under some circumstances cries out for God. Man lives and toils in sweat, suffering and sorrow. His spirit, soul and body cry out for release from the intolerable burden.

In the light of this knowledge Satan framed a very clever program. It was to unite all his subjects into a huge world federation for the reformation and betterment of the world. This would be accomplished through carefully worked out plans for the promotion of education, culture, morality and peace upon the earth. Human relationships, international, civic, social, family and personal, are undeniably in a terrible tangle but through peace conferences, leagues of nations and world courts, international mal-adjustments would be righted: through mass education movements and social-service programs, civic and social conditions would be bettered: through new thought processes which foster self-culture and self-con-straint, the civil war within man's own personality would be ended and so more amicable relations with those to whom he was bound by ties of blood and of friendship would be established. Thus Satan would succeed in deceiving men into thinking the Kingdom of God had come on earth.

Satan knows there is but one true God and that Jesus Christ is His Son whom He sent to be the Saviour (James 2:19; Matthew 8:29). But this truth he would keep men from knowing. He must even keep them from feeling any need for God. So his program must provide for the per-fect satisfaction of man's soul and body that his spirit may be kept dark-ened and deadened. So Satan's program includes every conceivable thing that could minister to self-enjoyment, self-ease, self-gain and self-satisfac-tion in the realm of the physical, intellectual, affectional, aesthetic, moral, even religious nature of man.

Moreover his program must provide for man an outward environment that matches this inward need. The earth is cursed but Satan must do what he can to remove the effects of that curse. Man will never be satis-fied unless the earth is a more comfortable, pleasant place in which to live. So Satan's plan is to make this world very attractive and then or-ganize human society that it may be so engrossed with its pursuits and pleasures men will have no thought for God.

Earnest, serious-minded men will see through this flimsy veil and will be concerned over the world's maladjustments. But Satan will engage such men in the task of repairing the ruin he himself has wrought. They will give millions upon millions of dollars, some will even lay down their lives in the accomplishment of the task thinking they are engaged in God's service. Satan will drug men with the tangible and transient and so detach them from the heavenly and eternal.

This huge federation of evil spirits and evil men is organized into a cunning system over which Satan is the presiding genius. He determines its principles, directs its policies, decides upon its program and devises its propaganda. This satanic system is "the world." The Lord Jesus re-vealed both its name and its nature in His farewell message to His disciples and told them clearly what its attitude to Him would be. The attitude of this system to Jesus Christ, which is one of unmitigated hatred, brands it as satanic.

John 15:18-19, "If *the world* hate you, ye know that *it hated me before it hated you.*

If ye were of the world, the world would love its own: but because ye are not of the world, but I have chosen you out of the world, therefore *the world hateth you.*"

John 17:14, 16, "I have given them thy word; and *the world hath hated them,* because *they are not of the world, even as I am not of the world.*"

God says that this satanic system is inherently "evil"; hopelessly "corrupt"; thoroughly "polluted"; irreconcilably hateful.

Galatians 1:4, "Who gave himself for our sins, that he might deliver us from *this present evil world,* according to the will of God and our Father."

2 Peter 1:4, "Whereby are given unto us exceeding great and precious promises: that by these ye might be partakers of the divine nature, having escaped *the corruption that is in the world* through lust.

2 Peter 2:20, "For if after they have escaped *the pollutions of the world* through the knowledge of the Lord and Saviour Jesus Christ, they are again entangled therein, and overcome, the latter end is worse with them than the beginning."

John 15:18, "If the world hate you, ye know that *it hated me* before *it hated you.*"

Thus God states His estimate of "the world." He speaks with equal clearness regarding its works.

John 7:7, "The world cannot hate you; but me it hateth, because I testify of it, *that the works thereof are evil.*"

This satanic system, "the world," is like a colossal octopus that has sent forth myriads of tentacles to lay hold upon every phase of human life and draw it unto itself. It has its grip upon the corporate life of mankind in its homes, marts, schools, politics, even its churches. It has penetrated into every relationship of the individual's life, personal, family, social, national and international.

"The world," which is human society with God left out, is Satan's snare for capturing men and holding them in bondage. "What the web is to the spider: what the bait is to the angler: what the lure is to the fowler: so is the world to Satan a means of capturing men." "The world" is the devil's paw with which he strikes men: it is his lair into which he entraps men: it is the devil's ally in fighting God for the sovereign control of men.

But is there anything within men that responds to Satan and to his system? In the Bible we read they have an accomplice who name is "the flesh."

Romans 7:5, "For when *we were in the flesh,* the motions of sins, which were by the law, did work in our members to bring forth fruit unto death."

Romans 8:12-13, "Therefore, brethren, we are debtors, *not to the flesh, to live after the flesh.*

For *if ye live after the flesh,* ye shall die: but if ye through the Spirit do mortify the deeds of the body, ye shall live."

In Scripture the word "flesh" has several meanings but in the verses quoted it is used in the ethical sense and means the whole natural man, spirit, soul and body, living in self-will and alienated from the life of God. The flesh is what man became through the Fall. It is man "without God" (Ephesians 2:12).

The "flesh" manifests nothing but antagonism to God and defiance of authority. It is irrevocably opposed to God and to His Law.

Romans 8:7, "Because *the carnal mind is enmity against God:* for it is *not subject to the law of God, neither indeed can be.*"

The "flesh" then is the material in mankind upon which Satan works to keep man a part of his system. This trinity of evil, the world, the flesh and the devil, is organized into a diabolical combine against God and His saints.

Satan has a cleverly thought out plan but God has a divinely wrought out purpose. God's purpose antedated Satan's plan: God's purpose anticipated Satan's plan: God's purpose annulled Satan's plan: God's purpose was formed in the eternity of the past and reaches into the eternity of the future. "God was in Christ reconciling the world unto himself."

Christ Jesus was the One through whom God's purpose was to be fulfilled. He constantly spoke of Himself as One who had been sent from heaven by the Father to do the Father's will, not His own. He did not belong to earth but to heaven and was here only to fulfill a special mission.

John 6:38, 40, "For *I came down from heaven, not to do mine own will, but the will of him that sent me.*

And this is the will of him that sent me, that every one which seeth the Son, and believeth on him, may have everlasting life: and I will raise him up at the last day."

Jesus disclaimed any part in or relationship to the satanic system called "the world."

John 17:16, "They are not of the world, *even as I am not of the world.*"
John 14:30, "For *the prince of this world cometh,* and *hath nothing in me.*"

In fact He declared that this satanic system had an unchangeable attitude toward Him—that of unrelenting hate which would spend itself ultimately in crucifying Him.

John 15:18, "If the world hate you, ye know that *it hated me before it hated you.*"

John 15:20, "Remember the word that I said unto you, The servant is not greater than his lord. *If they have persecuted me,* they will also persecute you; if they have kept my saying, they will keep yours also."

There is nothing in Scripture to indicate that God makes any attempt to change or to convert "the world." The Lord Jesus frankly acknowledges that "the whole world lieth in the evil one" (1 John 5:19, R.V.) and is under Satan's control.

God's purpose in Christ is to call men out of the world: to emancipate them from love for it, even to crucify them unto the world and it unto them.

John 15:19, "If ye were of the world, the world would love his own: but because . . . *I have chosen you out of the world,* therefore the world hateth you."

1 John 2:15, "*Love not the world, neither the things that are in the world.* If any man love the world, the love of the Father is not in him."

Galatians 6:14, "But God forbid that I should glory, save in the cross of our Lord Jesus Christ, *by whom the world is crucified unto me, and I unto the world.*"

God's purpose in this age Scripture makes unmistakably clear to the spiritual mind. It is to call out individuals, here and there, from all nations, kindreds, peoples and tongues, who through faith in the atoning sacrifice of Jesus Christ on the cross become a very part of Him and He of them. This living organism He calls His Body, the Church.

Colossians 1:18, "And *he is the head of the body,* the church: who is the beginning, the firstborn from the dead; that in all things he might have the preeminence."

Christ's purpose in this age is to call out of the world and into union with Himself those "chosen in him before the foundation of the world," who become a holy, heavenly people fit to be members of the Body of which the holy Christ in heaven is the Head.

Ephesians 1:4, "According *as he hath chosen us in him before the foundation of the world,* that we should be holy and without blame before him in love."

Ephesians 1:22-23, "And hath put all things under his feet, and *gave him to be the head over all things to the church,*
Which is his body, the fulness of him that filleth all in all."

1 Corinthians 12:27, "*Ye are the body of Christ,* and members in particular."

From God's viewpoint "the world" and "the Church" are exact opposites. "The world" is a vast organization of the whole mass of unbelieving mankind under Satan's leadership. "The Church" is an invisible organism of all true believers under Christ's headship. These two are in conflict on the earth and are pitted against each other as the instruments of Satan and of Christ in their attempt to get and keep possession and control of men.

How does God win response to His appeal to men to come out of the world and into fellowship with Christ? Does He have an associate in this task? We shall see in succeeding lessons that this is the work of the Holy Spirit who kindles life anew in the human spirit and then comes Himself to dwell in it.

> Ezekiel 36:26-27, "A new heart also will I give you, and *a new spirit will I put within you:* . . .
> And *I will put my spirit within you.*"

> Romans 8:9, "But ye are not in the flesh, but *in the Spirit,* if so be that *the Spirit of God dwell in you.* Now if any man have not the Spirit of Christ, he is none of his."

The Consummation of the Conflict

God's eternal purpose in man's redemption has been in gradual process of fulfillment ever since it was formed and each succeeding century has brought it nearer to its consummation. The heart of God's plan of redemption was a Saviour. This Saviour was to come through the seed of a woman. God was to become man. So God chose a people and set them apart that through them the Saviour might come "according to the flesh." In the fullness of time Christ came, lived, died and rose again. Man redemption was accomplished.

> Romans 9:4-5, "Who are Israelites; . . . whose are the fathers, and *of whom as concerning the flesh Christ came.*"

Following thereon a written Word was needed to proclaim this wondrous Gospel to sinners everywhere. So God chose and set apart a people through whom the written Word might come.

> 1 Corinthians 15:3-4, "I delivered unto you first of all that which I also received, how that Christ died for our sins *according to the scriptures;* And that he was buried, and that he rose again the third day *according to the scriptures.*"

> Romans 3:1-2, "What advantage then hath the Jew? . . . Much every way: *chiefly, because that unto them were committed the oracles of God.*"

Through the Israelites, God's chosen people, He gave both the incarnate Word and the written Word to the world.

God's next move was to preach this Gospel through His own ministers and missionaries throughout the whole world that all men everywhere might have the opportunity to behold the Son and to believe on Him.

> Mark 16:15, "And he said unto them, *Go ye into all the world, and preach the gospel to every creature.*"

When this work has been completed to God's satisfaction and the Bride is made ready for the Bridegroom, the Lord Jesus Christ will come again to take His own unto Himself and to set up His Kingdom upon earth.

This is the beginning of the end for Satan. He will be bound, cast into the bottomless pit for one thousand years. Then he will be loosed for a little season. He will go forth to deceive the nations and to gather them together for battle against the Lord, thus proving his unchanging and unchangeable attitude of self-will and of opposition to God (Revelation 20:1-3, 7-9).

Then comes God's final and full judgment upon him. He is cast into the lake of fire and brimstone to be tormented day and night forever and ever (Revelation 20:10).

Christ Jesus having consummated to the full God's plan to redeem men and reconcile all things unto Himself now restores the absolute, undivided sovereignty of God over His entire universe.

> 1 Corinthians 15:24-25, 28, "Then cometh the end, *when he shall have delivered* up the kingdom to God, even the Father; when he shall have put down all rule and all authority and power. *For he must reign, till he hath put all enemies under his feet.*
>
> And when all things shall be subdued unto him, then shall the Son also himself be subject unto him that put all things under him, *that God may be all in all.*"

6

False and Futile Attempts for Salvation

In His Word God has taught one truth which is beyond all contradiction. It is that sin has created an awful chasm between Himself and man. Man may ignore or condone sin, he may treat it very lightly, he may even be so foolish as to deny its reality, but that does not alter the unalterable fact that sin exists and that it separates from God. God does not treat sin lightly. God hates it; God condemns it. "Sin unatoned for must be an insuperable barrier between the sinner and God."

If the natural man is to be brought into favor and fellowship with God, it is evident that something must be done with sin. Man's first step in returning to God must be a consciousness that deepens into a conviction of sin. So the question which comes to every person who awakens to his condition through sin and its consequences, is the same as that which came to the Philippian jailor, "What must I do to be saved?" (Acts 16:30).

The Nature of Salvation

Let us analyze the jailor's question. First, "What must *I* do to be saved?" Who is the "I"? A lost man enslaved by sin, self and Satan; a blind man, whose mind has been darkened by the god of this world and whose eyes are closed to the beauty and glory of God; a dead man alienated from the life of God.

Second, "What must I do to be *saved?*" He does not ask what he must do to be reformed or repaired or repolished, but to be saved. The question he asks is, "How can I, an enslaved man, have deliverance; a blind man have sight; a dead man have life?"

Third, "What must I *do* to be saved?" What can a bondslave do to free himself? Or what can a blind man do to gain sight? Or what can a dead man do to make himself alive?

Let us answer the jailor's question by defining the kind of salvation which will fully meet the sinner's need. *It must be a salvation God can accept as wholly sufficient and satisfactory.* God is the One who has been offended and most wounded by sin. By his sin Adam forfeited all right to relationship with God and it is God alone who can say by what means and in what manner the relationship with sinful men can be restored. Man has no ground upon which he can approach God. If God ever receives the natural man it must be upon some ground where he confesses himself a helpless, hopeless sinner. "Between him and God is the impassable gulf of moral inability. Between him and God is the barrier of penal judgment." God alone can determine how this chasm shall be bridged and this barrier removed.

It must be a salvation that deals effectually with sin and all its consequences. This salvation must put away sin and give man a new nature, without which there would be no basis for establishing a relationship with God. This salvation must blot out man's sins and their attendant guilt. Sins committed cannot be undone merely by an expression of sorrow or by a promise of amendment through a New Year resolution or by the turning over of a new leaf.

It must be a salvation that carries out the sentence of death upon the sinner. God's law is holy and it cannot be trifled with. God's judgments are righteous and they must be fulfilled. God has said, "The soul that sinneth it shall die." The penalty must be paid; the judgment must be executed. Any salvation that saves must take into acount the payment of this penalty and the execution of this judgment.

It must be a salvation that accomplishes the defeat, dethronement and destruction of Satan. God's judgment upon Satan who brought sin into the universe must be executed as truly as God's judgment upon the sinner. God has said that the seed of the woman shall bruise the head of the serpent. This is one half of the original promise of salvation. Christ's final victory necessitates Satan's full defeat. Such must be the nature of any salvation that fully saves.

MAN'S FALSE AND FUTILE ATTEMPTS FOR SALVATION

But there are those who, refusing to accept God's estimate of the natural man, deny the necessity of any such radical and revolutionary change in him. They delight in the exaltation of the flesh, and they deny the self-evident fact that human nature is in utter ruin though they are compelled to admit that it is greatly in need of repair. They believe and teach that human nature is imperfect because it is in the process of formation. But given proper environment, liberal education and the chance to make the best of what he already possesses, man by his own natural development ultimately will achieve godlikeness and attain a place in the Kingdom of God. In other words salvation is not by grace but by growth; it depends upon an evolution of life from within rather than upon an impartation of life from without.

There are those even in the pulpit and in the theological seminary who teach that the natural man is not dead but diseased; not wicked but weak; not fallen but fainting; and they attempt resuscitation through ethical culture, social reform and mass education while ridiculing the necessity of redemption through the atoning work of the crucified Saviour and regeneration through the power of the indwelling Spirit.

Their kind of preaching is well summed up in the word of a prominent preacher who said, "Do your part and God will surely do His. To deny that a man is forgiven when he turns away from wrong and asks forgiveness would be to deny the moral character of God." In such teaching man is made his own savior, and salvation is nothing more than a feeble sense of regret resulting in slight changes in conduct to which God is asked to affix His seal of forgiveness.

This kind of thinking and teaching leads men to seek out ways of salvation which are futile and to rest upon hopes which are false. If the meaning of salvation is what we have indicated in these pages then the means of its accomplishment must be supernatural. But man is ever prone to put his trust in the purely natural, in himself.

When the eyes of Adam and Eve were opened to evil and they came into a realization of their sin and shame, instead of seeking God, confessing their sin, and acknowledging their undone condition, they made themselves aprons of fig leaves to cover their nakedness (Genesis 3:7). From that day to this the natural man has been at the same foolish, futile task of trying to cover his sin and guilt with some garment of his own making which he trusts will be acceptable to God.

But no dress which the natural man provides for the flesh will ever please God. No matter of what material it is made or how beautiful, fitting and durable it may seem to be to the world, it will wither into nothingness, even as Adam's and Eve's aprons of fig leaves, before the righteousness and holiness of God.

No garment of salvation except the one He Himself provides will be acceptable to God.

> Genesis 3:21, "Unto Adam also and to his wife *did the Lord God make coats of skins, and clothed them.*"

By this act God acknowledged that the shame of Adam and Eve was not groundless, and that they did need a covering; but He also showed the utter inadequacy of the one they had provided for themselves, their lack of apprehension of the enormity and heinousness of their sin against Him, and of the nature of the salvation required to restore them to His fellowship.

God had said, "In the day that thou eatest thereof thou shalt surely die." They had eaten. "The wages of sin is death." If they did not die someone acceptable to God must die in their stead. This is the meaning of salvation. But God had already given the promise of a Saviour-Substitute. The seed of the serpent would *bruise* the heel of the woman's seed. The garments of skin with which the Lord God clothed Adam and Eve were procured through the slaying of animals, through the shedding of blood. By this gracious act of God the means of salvation was symbolized; the death of His own well-beloved Son was shadowed forth. God Himself furnished the skins, God made the coats, God clothed them in acceptable garments.

Now let us look at some of the aprons of fig leaves with which the natural man is trying to make himself acceptable to God and fit for heaven.

SALVATION THROUGH CHARACTER

"Character—homebrew" is the sign over the door of the self-righteous man's life. He has to admit weakness and failure but he does not call sin *sin* nor does he grant that he has any great need. There is nothing in him so wrong that he cannot remedy it himself if given time, a proper environment and enlarged opportunities. The self-righteous man thinks that he starts with something already very good, something even with the very essence of the divine in it. His business is to make this good thing gradually better.

In this process of self-cultivation the self-righteous man measures himself with himself and he is very pleased; he measures himself also with other men and, like the self-righteous Pharisee of Luke 18:9-14, he is more than pleased. He congratulates himself on himself and even commends his virtues to God. But there is one measurement that he has forgotten to take. He has never placed his self-righteous life alongside the spotless, stainless, sinless, life of the Son of Man to see how infinitely far short he falls of a righteousness which God accepts. He ignores the fact that the absolute righteousness of God demands nothing less than absolute righteousness in all who are acceptable to Him, which is a demand no human being in himself ever can meet.

Someday when this man stands before the Lord Jesus Christ, once a proffered but a rejected Saviour, now his Judge, he will expect Him to approve this man-made production of righteousness, to pronounce it as good as anything the Lord could have done, and to let him pass into heaven to abide forever in the presence of an absolutely righteous God.

I was talking once with a friend concerning his need of a Saviour. He was a man of splendid ideals, high standards and excellent principles. He was cultured, kind, moral, and from a human standpoint, lived what the world would commend as a highly respectable life. When I pressed the necessity of accepting Jesus Christ as his Saviour, he said, "Why do I need anyone to die for me? I do not want any one's blood shed for me!" The root of that reply was self-righteousness. That young man was trusting to be saved through character. God looks down upon all such "which trusted in themselves that they were righteous" and says,

> Romans 3:10, 12, "There is *none righteous*, no, not one.
> They are all gone out of the way, they are together become unprofitable; there is *none that doeth good, no not one.*"

And of the righteousness which has been so carefully cultivated He gives His estimate through the mouth of His prophet,

> Isaiah 64:6, "But we are all as an unclean thing, and *all our righteousnesses are as filthy rags;* and we all do fade as a leaf; and our iniquities like the wind, have taken us away."

To rely upon self-righteousness as the ground of salvation is utterly futile. God declares plainly that His wrath against it will be revealed.

> Romans 10:3, "For they being ignorant of God's righteousness, and going about to establish their own righteousness, have not submitted themselves unto the righteousness of God."

> Romans 1:18, "For *the wrath of God is revealed from heaven against all ungodliness and unrighteousness of men*, who hold the truth in unrighteousness."

How very different is the self-righteous, self-made man from the one who has had a glimpse of the Holy One and His righteousness!

> Isaiah 6:5, "Then said I, Woe is me! for *I am undone;* because I am *a man of unclean lips;* and I dwell in the midst of a people of unclean lips: for mine eyes have seen the King, the LORD of hosts."

> Job 42:5-6, "I have heard of thee by the hearing of the ear: but now mine eye seeth thee.
> Wherefore *I abhor myself*, and repent in dust and ashes."

> 1 Timothy 1:15, "This is a faithful saying, and worthy of all acceptation, that Christ Jesus came into the world to save sinners; *of whom I am chief.*"

The last quotation is from the lips of a man who, if anyone, could have rested upon his own righteousness as a sufficient ground of acceptance with God. With perfect sincerity he said of himself that "touching the righteousness which is in the law" he was "blameless." Yet after seeing the Lord of glory he was convinced of the foolishness and futility of such confidence in the flesh. From that time he had but one consuming desire, "that I may win Christ, and be found in him, not having mine own righteousness, which is of the law, but that which is through the faith of Christ, the righteousness which is of God by faith" (Philippians 3:6, 8-9). The only righteousness that makes any man acceptable with God is the righteousness of God by faith in Jesus Christ.

> Romans 3:22-23, "Even *the righteousness of God which is by faith of Jesus Christ unto all and upon all them that believe:* for there is no difference: for all have sinned, and come short of the glory of God."

No one whose eyes have seen the King, the Lord of hosts, and who has contrasted his own sinfulness with His holiness will have a shred of hope of acceptance with God through his own character. The man who relies upon any righteousness in himself as his ground of salvation and who refuses Christ's imputed righteousness as God's free gift only proves the Word of God that the god of this world has blinded his mind so that the light of the glorious Gospel of Christ, who is the image of God, should not shine into his heart.

SALVATION THROUGH EDUCATION

Another bridge which men attempt to erect over the yawning sin-made chasm between God and man is that of education. Ignorance due to lack of opportunity is deemed the cause of much of the sorrow, suffering and strife in the world. The cry is, "Give everyone an education and so elevate standards, raise ideals and change environment. By thus creating a desire for better conditions of life a better life itself will eventuate." There are intelligent men and women today who are proclaiming that the one thing needed for the salvation of individuals and of nations is mass education. Knowledge is made the cure for sin.

Such argument is absolute fallacy. For *to know* is but a fragment of man's responsibility in the matter of living and is by far the easier part of the task. Life challenges us *to do,* above all *to be.* Knowledge is of no value whatsoever until it has been transmuted into character and conduct. In fact the Bible tells us in one of its most solemn words that unless it is so transmuted knowledge becomes positive sin. "To him that knoweth to do good, and doeth it not, to him it is sin" (James 4:17).

Education has sometimes even led to a deterioration of character and conduct. It has opened new avenues into sin and taught men greater cleverness in the ways of evil. It has not only made men more selfish, more proud, more grasping, but has placed them in positions where their selfishness, ambition and greed could have full right-of-way against others less favored.

We hear much in certain circles today about religious education and many people believe this to be the sufficient remedy for the need of the world. If religious education means teaching the Word of God itself under the direction and operation of the divine Teacher, the Holy Spirit, with the purpose of securing man's regeneration and renewal, then it is indeed one of the world's greatest and deepest needs. But, if it means urging the natural man to study Christ's teachings and to learn His principles of life for men as individuals and as members of society in order that through obedience to His teaching, through application of His principles, and through imitation of His example there may be a reconstruction of human society and an amelioration of social wrongs, then it is an absolutely foolish and futile thing. The natural man could know the content of the teachings of God from Genesis to Revelation and still have no power, and more, no desire to obey them. He might be thoroughly conversant with every Christian principle for the government of man in his personal, social and civic relationships and yet fail to apply them in his own life.

I heard of a group of students who talked loud and long about the selfishness and greed of officials in high places in the government of their country. They took part in patriotic movements to remove these men from office. Yet they themselves were found guilty of taking a "squeeze" from their fellow students who had entrusted to them the task of buying food under a self-government scheme in operation in the college. In their smaller sphere of activity they had done exactly what the officials had done in their larger sphere. Any system of religious education which merely unfolds to the natural man the teachings and principles of Jesus Christ and tells how to apply them in the life of the other fellow is utterly inadequate.

The Bible is the only textbook given man on salvation from sin and from cover to cover there is not a ray of hope held out of salvation through education or through anything that aims merely at the improvement of the natural man. In fact God plainly tells us in the first and second chapters of 1 Corinthians that it is "the wisdom" of the natural man that keeps him from accepting the only way of salvation, Christ crucified. Education, if it be truly Christian, may be one of the agents used by God to create the desire for salvation but it can never furnish the dynamic which makes salvation possible.

SALVATION THROUGH WORKS

One man looks for salvation through character or what he *is;* another trusts in education or what he *knows;* while a third seeks it in service or what he *does.* He believes he can be saved through good works. He comes to God with self-confidence and says, "What shall I do that I might work the works of God?"

God answers his question by asking one which teaches that the natural man can do no good work that will accomplish his salvation.

> Jeremiah 13:23, "Can the Ethiopian change his skin, or the leopard his spots? *then may ye also do good, that are accustomed to do evil.*"

Please note God does not say, "Can the Ethiopian powder or rouge his skin?" That has been done. The question is "Can the Ethiopian *change* his skin?" The natural inference is that it would be changed from its natural color to another. Can that be done?

Suppose a girl from Ethiopia comes for the first time into the presence of a group of fair-skinned girls. Never before has she seen any color of skin but black. She wishes her skin to be fair and determines to do something to make it so. Procuring water and soap she proceeds to lather her face and rubs it vigorously. The process ended she goes triumphantly to the mirror expecting to see a great change. Instead she confronts the same black skin only a bit more highly polished. She decides that she did not do enough, that she failed to use sufficient water or soap or muscle, so she repeats the process increasing the use of soap, water and strength. But the second attempt ends in the same bitter disappointment. To *change* her skin is beyond her power.

"*Can* the Ethiopian change his skin?" We are compelled to answer God's question for His answer to ours depends upon it. *If* the Ethiopian *can* change his skin then the natural man will be able to *do* something to change his sinful heart, he will be able to do good who has always been accustomed to do evil. But if the Ethiopian cannot change his skin, then what must we infer regarding the power of the natural man to change his evil heart? God's Word gives a conclusive answer.

> Jeremiah 2:22, "For though thou wash thee with nitre, and take thee much soap, *yet thine iniquity is marked before me*, saith the Lord God."

Through self-cultivation, self-discipline and self-effort many men and women have been able to accomplish certain reforms within themselves which have made them more acceptable to themselves and to the world but no living person has ever been able to make himself righteous, and without righteousness no man is acceptable to God.

Another way in which the natural man attempts his own salvation is to do something *for* God which will be acceptable.

This was Cain's mistake, moreover, it was Cain's sin. Why was Abel's offering accepted and Cain's accepted not? (Genesis 4:4-5). Abel realized that he was a sinner and that the offering he brought to God must confess that fact and be an acknowledgment of his need of another to cleanse him. Cain, on the contrary, brought an offering which revealed no sense of sin but rather of complete self-sufficiency. He offered *his* best, the work of *his* hands, the fruitage of *his* toil. He needed not the help of anyone. And he expected God to accept his gift, the offering of a sinner still in his sins, and to call the account against him squared. Cain did not come to God "by faith" (Hebrews 11:4) but "by works."

There is no phase of modern teaching more ancient or pagan than the doctrine proclaimed so generally throughout the world today that we can be made acceptable to God by good works, that we are saved through service. It is indeed true that, if we are saved, we will serve; but it is altogether untrue that we are saved because we serve.

Jews in our Lord's time who were unwilling to acknowledge Him as their Messiah and to accept Him as their Saviour, came to Him with the question, "What shall we do that we might work the works of God?" The reply of the Lord Jesus is very significant. "This is the work of God, that ye believe on him whom he hath sent." But this "good work" they stubbornly refused "to do."

What God required was not that they should do something for Him but that they should accept what He had done for them. The foundation stone of salvation is not what man gives to God but what God gives to man; it is not what man offers to God but what he receives from God.

> Romans 4:4-5, "Now to him that worketh is the reward not reckoned of grace, but of debt.
>> But *to him that worketh not, but believeth on him* that justifieth the ungodly, *his faith is counted for rightoeusness.*"
>
> 2 Timothy 1:9, "Who hath saved us, and called us with an holy calling, *not according to our works*, but according to his own purpose and grace, which was given us in Christ Jesus before the world began."

The Pharisees considered themselves the prophets of religion. They fasted and prayed; they paid tithes and "built the tombs of the prophets and garnished the sepulchers of the righteous." They did countless good works yet Jesus called them "hypocrites" and the apostle Paul prayed that they might be "saved." So in this twentieth century many are deceived into thinking they are saved because they serve tables at a church supper; make garments for the poor or bandages for the sick; act as chairman of the finance committee to put over a big drive; or contrive schemes for the physical and social betterment of mankind.

Salvation through good works either for God or man is pure paganism. I have a friend in China whose dear old grandmother was an ardent Buddhist. At seventy-six years of age she rose every morning at four o'clock and spent the hours until noon without food in performing the rites of her heathen worship. She walked long distances to the temple, she burned her bundles of incense and lighted her candles, she gave of her money. Her days were largely spent in religious works, but at seventy-six she was still an ignorant, superstitious, idolatrous, unsaved woman. But not one whit more unsaved than the man or woman, even though dressed in cap and gown, who offers to the Saviour who died upon the cross to redeem him "the stone" of philanthropy, good works and social service, for "the bread" of faith, adoration and worship.

SALVATION THROUGH RELIGION

Someone has said, "Man is incurably religious." Another has beautifully written, "God created in man a deep and everlasting void. The soul in its highest sense is a vast capacity for God but emptiness without God." It is most assuredly true that man was made for God and his heart never can be fully satisfied until it is satisfied in Him. It is equally true that God made man not only in His likeness but also with the capacity for fellowship with Him, yes, even for sonship. Therefore God's heart can never be fully satisfied except as this relationship with man is realized and enjoyed.

The natural man can neither satisfy nor please God (Romans 8:7). Therefore God could never enjoy his presence, even were it possible for him to stay in the presence of a holy God. Something must be done by God to make man acceptable to Him.

From the day sin entered into the human race, God has been working to win men and women, one by one, back to Himself. He has sent His messengers, prophets and apostles to open the eyes of sinners and "to turn them from darkness to light and from the power of Satan unto God." At the same time the devil has been equally busy blinding the minds of men "lest the light of the glorious Gospel of Christ who is the image of God, should shine unto them" (2 Corinthians 4:4).

Satan's path is not altogether smooth. Two forces are working against him. One is the religious instinct in man. He cries out for something he knows he needs. He senses his insufficiency in seasons of trial, suffering and sorrow; often his heart reaches out for the help and comfort of one stronger than himself. He cannot let loved ones pass out of sight and touch without an insistent longing to know where they have gone and if all is well. That unsatisfied something in man's soul that cries out to an unknown God is very much against Satan.

The second hindrance to the devil is the Holy Spirit. It is His business to convict of sin, to reveal the love of God in Christ, and to draw the heart of the sinner out in faith and love to God.

Just here the devil reveals himself at his worst. He will lay siege to that unquenchable thing in man's nature which craves an object of worship and hold it for himself. He will delude men into thinking they can be saved by systems of religion which he inspires them to make.

Contrary to the salvation of which Jesus Christ is the source, Satan's system is not one and the same for all men alike irrespective of family, race, education, privilege or environment. These man-made, Satan-inspired religions have various names and manifold methods each suited to the type and temperament of the man who believes them. There is one kind for the ignorant and illiterate; another for the educated and erudite; one for the simple and superstitious; another for the wise and cultured; one for the poor; another for the prosperous.

There is a system of religion for the idolater. Satan is an arch-deceiver and his practice of deception is seen in its most cruel and malicious form in idol-worship. Even in this twentieth century Satan still holds in his power millions upon millions of men who are worshipers of gods of their own making. They have been led to believe a lie and so have been plunged into dense darkness.

There is a system of religion for the ritualist. In carrying out His eternal purpose in Christ, God called forth a people from among the nations through whom the seed of the woman would come. The Jews were set apart as the people of God by the rite of circumcision. To this God added the covenants and the law so that the worship and service of the Jew was based on a God-appointed, God-honoring ritualism. Through the manifold ordinances and sacrifices of the Jewish ritualism God made the Jew familiar with the idea of redemption. Then God raised up prophets who foretold the coming of a Messiah who would be their Redeemer. In the fullness of time the Saviour was born. The need of sacrifices was past, for the one Sacrifice had offered Himself.

But the expounders of the law, the most ardent religionists of Jesus' day, instead of receiving Him rejected Him. And why? Because they permitted religious ordinances to take a larger place in their lives than God's redemptive order. They exalted ritualism above righteousness and substituted prayer for penitence, tithing for trust and fasting for faith.

There are other great religious systems in the world today in which the real Christ of the Bible, the Redeemer of the Gospels, is veiled through ordinances and ceremonies in which there is no saving power, yet through which countless are deceived into thinking they are made acceptable to God.

There is a system of religion for the rationalist. The pronouncement of the curse upon Satan and the promise of salvation through Christ following the Fall precipitated a conflict as we have seen. The conflict begun then has never ceased; it is being waged more fiercely today than ever before.

To prevent the exception of the curse and the fulfillment of the promise Satan tried in every conceivable way to destroy the seed of the woman. At the cross of Calvary he thought himself triumphant. But the very place of his supposed victory was the place of his judgment and the forerunner of his final doom. Christ arose, the Victim became the Victor. Christ Jesus returned to the glory from whence He came. He went beyond the devil's reach. There is no way in which Satan again can touch or tempt the person of the adorable Lord. How then would he continue the conflict? Now that he could not focus the venom of his hate upon the incarnate Word upon what would he focus it?

The revelation of this conflict is unfolded in a Book. The incarnate Word has gone home to His Father but the written Word is still on earth. In it the defeat of the devil and the victory of the Christ is recorded in large type. The way of salvation through the atoning death and the triumphant resurrection of the Lord of glory is written in red letters from Genesis to Revelation. *This is the Gospel.* This Gospel the devil hates with all the hatred of which the father of hate is capable. So against it he will now direct his attack. Around the Gospel of Christ the conflict will revolve henceforth.

The Gospel is in the Bible and the Bible is in the world. It has been printed in hundreds of languages and has gone to the far corners of the earth. More millions of copies of it are being sold annually than of any other book. Men everywhere are reading the Bible and are believing the Gospel. Being saved through it they are taken from Satan's dominion and removed out of his kingdom.

What can he do to stop its progress and its power? Destroy it? He has tried that and failed. The Bible is not printed on paper only but it has been graven on human hearts by the Spirit of God, so that if every copy of the printed Bible in the world today were destroyed a new copy could be made from its truth stored in human hearts.

Perhaps, then, Satan could ridicule the Bible and hinder its progress and power through scoffing. He has tried that also and failed. He has used some of the world's most brilliant men as his preachers of infidelity and atheism. Today they are in their graves and their words are forgotten while the Bible lives on more powerful than ever.

But is there not a more effectual way of denying the Gospel and of keeping sinners from the benefit and blessing of the salvation it offers? There is and Satan is making use of it in these days in ever increasing measure. God tells us that the devil's most subtle maneuver in the conflict is to turn preacher and with the Bible as his textbook to concoct out of it a gospel of his own. When Satan found that attacking the written Word from without failed then he began attacking it from within. As Christ uses men to preach His Gospel so Satan would find men who would consent to become "his ministers."

> 2 Corinthians 11:13-15, R. V., "For such men are false apostles, deceitful workers, fashioning themselves into apostles of Christ. And no marvel; *for even Satan fashioneth himself into an angel of light.*
>
> It is no great thing therefore if *his ministers also fashion themselves as ministers of righteousness;* whose end shall be according to their work."

What would Satan's gospel be and where would it begin? God's Gospel is a Gospel of grace and begins with Genesis, chapters 1-3. But how could Satan accept these three chapters as they stand fresh from the heart and hand of God containing as they do the revelation of God's perfect work in the creation of the universe and man; the invasion of an enemy, he being that enemy; the injection of sin into God's perfect work; the awful consequence in the Fall of Adam and Eve; the terrible curse of God upon himself, upon man and upon the earth; the precious promise of a Saviour and the glorious prophecy of his own defeat through the death upon the cross? Of course he could not accept these chapters for in them is the germ of the whole Gospel of man's salvation.

He would defeat his own purpose if he did so bold and blatant a thing as deliberately to cut these chapters out of the Bible. But the arch-deceiver is quite equal to the emergency. He will preach a gospel that reserves the right of interpretation of the Word of God according to the dictates of reason. He will insist upon a faith that is rational.

It is always difficult for reason to accept anything beyond its own range. God thinks and works on the plane of uncreated, divine, unlimited, supernatural life. Man thinks and works on the plane of created, human, limited, natural life. The rationalist refuses to recognize any such dividing line between himself and his Creator. Consequently he refuses to accept anything, even from God, that goes beyond his reason. So whatever the rationalist believes, his religion must be on his own plane of life—the natural.

So a system of religion is framed to suit him. A gospel is manufactured "which is another gospel" (Galatians 1:6), a clever, malicious counterfeit. Satan knows that he must inspire man to make a religion which does away altogether with God's revelation of the creation and the fall of man, otherwise how can he dispose of the promise of a Saviour and the prophecy of his own ultimate defeat through Christ's glorious victory on Calvary and His triumphant return as King?

Consequently the basic tenet of the rationalist's system of religion is evolution. Man did not come direct from God's hands—a perfect work which God Himself pronounced "very good." God's first man was not created in the image of One infinitely higher than himself, but was evolved from something infinitely lower than himself. This something had evolved through various stages by natural processes until man was produced. So God's part in the production of man was not so much that of a Creator as of a semidivine supervisor or foreman "of resident natural forces." In other words *the supernatural* in man's creation was eliminated through evolution. So much for man's creation in this man-made, Satan-inspired gospel.

How does this gospel of the rationalist deal with sin? Sin is in the world.

Sin is in man. How does the rationalist account for its origin and what does he say of its end? He evades the issue altogether by calmly denying the necessity of anyone having such knowledge.

I read recently a chapter on "Sin and its Forgiveness" from the pen of a noted preacher in which he said, "Whence did sin come? What was its origin? How did it get into God's universe? That is a question to which no satisfactory answer has ever yet been given. . . . Jesus is disappointing in His treatment of human sin. The origin of evil He never touched. He left that problem as opaque as it was before He came. He seemed to take it for granted that the origin of evil is a problem to be thought about and worked out in some other world than this. . . . It is not necessary for us to know either the beginning of evil or the end of it; it is enough to know that sin is a burden to the heart of God, and that God has provided a way for our deliverance." Such deliberate evasion is equivalent to out-and-out denial. For any honest man, whose mind has not been blinded by the god of this world, could not but believe from the reading of Genesis 3 and Romans 5 that sin came into this world through Adam who yielded to the will of Satan. Therefore sin must have had its origin in the devil. Jesus, far from leaving this opaque, threw a flood of light upon it when He said that the devil was "a murderer *from the beginning* . . . he is a liar, and the *father* of it" (John 8:44).

But not only is sin in the world but Christ is also in the world. And He is in the world primarily as a Saviour. He became a Saviour by going to the cross. His work in this world as Saviour is to draw sinners unto Him for salvation. "And I, if I be lifted up from the earth, will draw all men unto me." His power of attraction is mighty and permeates the world of humanity today. When once the Lord Jesus Christ is accepted by one as Saviour, yielded to as Lord, and appropriated as Life, then the devil's power over that life is broken. The devil knows this full well. So what will he do with Christ in the system of religion he inspires men to make, and in the gospel he inspires them to preach?

Satan cannot do away with Christ altogether for even the most simple would see that any system of religion which claims to be based on the Bible and calls itself Christianity must give Christ some place. It is a galling thing to do but the devil is compelled for policy's sake to preach Christ in his "gospel, which is another gospel." But will he allow "his ministers of righteousness" to preach Jesus Christ as the Saviour from the guilt, penalty and power of sin through His substitutionary death upon the cross and His bodily resurrection and His ascension into heaven as the God-man, the interceding High Priest? Never! To do so would be allowing his own funeral sermon to be preached, fulfilling Genesis 3:15. But he will preach Jesus as the world's greatest teacher, its purest example, its most ethical leader, its most powerful reformer. He will appeal to the natural man still in his sin and hostility, still under condemnation and the sentence of death, to obey Christ's teaching, emulate His example, follow His leadership and submit to His reforms. Such a caricature of the real Christ as this is found in the rationalist's system of religion.

True Christianity is grounded upon the supernatural. Two *supernatural facts* are its foundation. The first is the supernatural creation of man by the divine Creator whose perfect work was ruined by an enemy through the injection of sin. The second is the supernatural regeneration of man accomplished by God's grace through the supernatural birth, life, death, resurrection, ascension and exaltation of His Son.

Rationalism, liberalism, modernism or whatever one wishes to call it, is grounded upon the natural. Two *fallacies* are its foundation. The first is the fashioning of man through evolution by which natural process he will continue to grow from the imperfect to the perfect. The second is the natural reformation of man accomplished through self-development by the help of a human Jesus, whose earthly life furnishes an example to be imitated, whose teachings provide a rule for right living, and whose principles constitute a guide for the overcoming of evil and the gradual betterment of individual and corporate life.

There is, then, a system of religion made by man but inspired by Satan. It is a religion which eliminates the supernatural. I am speaking now of the system not of the man who accepts it: of modernism not of the modernist. There are varying degrees and grades of faith and of unbelief in those who subscribe to this false system of religion. Some who call themselves modernists were brought up and nourished on the fundamental truths of evangelical Christianity and there is now in their belief a strange mixture of the false and the true. Our purpose in writing this is not to judge any man but to warn any who may be putting confidence for salvation in this man-made, Satan-inspired system of religion.

There is a gospel of Satan and a Gospel of Christ; the one is the exact antithesis of the other. Satan's gospel has no place for the grace of God. Satan's gospel reverses God's estimate of the natural man. It does not admit that in himself he is hopelessly incurable and incorrigible, even though it does have to say that he is still imperfect. The basic tenet of his gospel is man's natural worthiness which can be increased and for which man will take to himself the glory. Satan's gospel admits the natural man's need for spiritual garments, but it teaches men that these garments can be made by themselves and urges them to borrow the pattern from the earthly life of Jesus and then make the garments to fit themselves. In Satan's gospel the sinner does not penitently beseech God to save him, but he politely requests God to help him save himself and then endorse what he has done.

The Gospel of Christ has place for nothing but the grace of God by which a salvation is provided that the sinner accepts by faith as a gift. God's Gospel declares that the natural man is a sinner, a rebel and an outlaw and that he is separated from God and condemned by God. In God's Gospel the sinner admits that this is his standing and his state before God and that he is absolutely helpless to change it and therefore hopeless. He comes to God in true penitence and cries to God for salvation. The basic tenet of God's Gospel is the infinite worth of His Son and the efficacious worthiness of His finished work of redemption. God's Gospel declares the spiritual nakedness of the natural man and his inability to stand in the presence of God unless clothed in the garment of His Son's righteousness which He will graciously bestow upon all who will accept Him by faith.

Which Gospel are *you* believing? There is but one Gospel that is the power of God unto salvation. Anything which departs an iota from the truth of that Gospel is "another gospel," even the gospel of Satan.

> Romans 1:16, "For I am not ashamed of *the gospel of Christ:* for it is the power of God unto salvation to every one that believeth."
>
> Galatians 1:6-9, "I marvel that ye are so soon removed from him that called you into the grace of Christ *unto another gospel:*
> Which is not another; but there be some that trouble you, and *would pervert the gospel of Christ.*
> But though we, or an angel from heaven, preach *any other gospel* unto you than that which we have preached unto you, *let him be accursed.* As we said before, so say I now again, *If any man preach any other gospel unto you than ye have received, let him be accursed."*

We have been facing the question, "What must I do to be saved?" and endeavoring to answer it. I trust it has been made clear that salvation does not consist in anything that man makes of himself or that education and environment make of him. Nor does it consist in anything that he does either for God or for man. Neither is salvation a mere matter of a changed manner of living. It does not mean the elevation of the life of the natural man to a better state of living still on the natural plane. As long as he remains on the plane of the natural he is unsaved, no matter how cultured, educated, moral or even religious he is.

Salvation is not man's work for God but God's work for man. Salvation calls us to put our faith not in what man is or does but in what Christ is and has done. Salvation's first concern is not what kind of a life a man lives but what is his relationship to God. So its first dealing is not with the good in man but with the bad. Salvation does not try to improve the standing and state of the natural man through reformation, but it transfers him into a totally new sphere of life through regeneration.

Every attempt to save the natural man through character, education, good works or religion, will prove utterly futile because it has failed to deal effectually with that trinity of evil, sin, self and Satan. Anything that leaves a man "in Adam," "in the flesh," and under "the power of Satan" is not salvation and is not acceptable to God.

Dear reader, which way are you going to take?

Will you proudly and arrogantly try to save yourself or will you humbly and penitently accept the salvation provided for you in Another?

Will you go the way of Cain, who presented to God as a sacrifice the finest fruit of his garden and the best product of his toil, or will you go the way of Abel who acknowledged his need of a Saviour, and accepted by faith God's sacrifice?

Will you attempt to secure access to and acceptability with God on the ground of good works or will you rest on the finished work of God's Son?

Will you try to improve the old sinful nature which is your inheritance in Adam or will you partake by faith of that new divine nature which God bestows in Christ?

Will you try to conform your character and conduct to the standards of Satan's worldly system or will you yield yourself to Christ to be transformed into His image through the infilling of the Holy Spirit?

Will you follow Satan's way or God's? Upon your answer to this question your present happiness and your eternal destiny depend.

NO MIDDLE GROUND—ONLY A CHASM

"The Faith which was once for all delivered unto the saints."

Modernist Theology

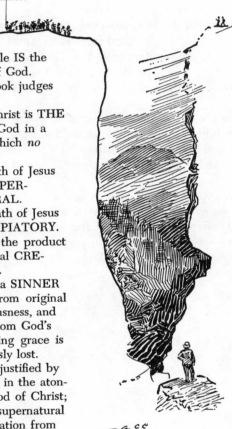

1. The Bible IS the Word of God. "The Book judges man"
2. Jesus Christ is THE Son of God in a sense which *no* other is.
3. The birth of Jesus was SUPER-NATURAL.
4. The death of Jesus was EXPIATORY.
5. Man is the product of special CRE-ATION.
6. Man is a SINNER fallen from original righteousness, and apart from God's redeeming grace is hopelessly lost.
7. Man is justified by FAITH in the aton-ing blood of Christ; result—supernatural regeneration from ABOVE.

1. The Bible CON-TAINS the Word of God. "Man judges the book"
2. Jesus Christ is A Son of God in the sense which *all* men are.
3. The birth of Jesus was NATURAL.
4. The death of Jesus was EXEMPLARY.
5. Man is the product of EVOLUTION.
6. Man is the unfortu-nate VICTIM of environment but through self-culture can "make good."
7. Man is justified by WORKS in follow-ing Christ's exam-ple; result—natural development from WITHIN.

7

The Chasm Bridged

GOD AND GOD'S FIRST MAN enjoyed sweet and intimate communion until they were separated by sin. How could this great, impassable chasm which sin had made between God and man be bridged? From the very nature of the case man could do nothing, even had he wanted to, for sin had closed all possible access to God. Clearly, if anything was to be done, God would have to do it.

But what would God do? Adam's sin presented a terrific problem: one which not only affected God's personal relationship to man but His governmental relationship to the whole universe; it even affected His own personal character.

Adam's sin was spiritual anarchy; it was resistance to God's authority; disobedience to God's command; rebellion against God's law. How would God treat sin? Would He punish it and pass judgment upon it? Or would He condone it and pass over it? If God failed to deal righteously with such a flagrant case of disobedience and disloyalty, how could He maintain order through obedience to law in any other part of His universe? God's governmental administration of the universe was involved in this stupendous difficulty.

But Adam's rebellion created an even greater problem than this. By it God's holiness had been outraged; His righteousness denied; His veracity questioned; His goodness doubted; His Word disbelieved; His command disobeyed; His love spurned. Surely such treatment deserved drastic action. Why did He not then and there abandon Adam and Eve utterly and leave them and their posterity to the consequences of their sin?

He did not because He could not. "God is love," and "love never faileth." God's love is an everlasting love which nothing can quench, not even sin. Awful, terrible as sin is, it is not powerful enough to defeat God's purpose in the creation of man. Man was created not only *by* God but *for* God. Man was made for fellowship with God, much more, for ultimate sonship.

95

Apart from a living, loving relationship with man God could never be satisfied. God, who is love, could not cast away the sinner in his sin and still be love. The claims of God's love must be met.

But "God is light" and "in him is no darkness at all." As light cannot fellowship with darkness, so holiness cannot commune with sin. A holy God cannot have intimate relationship with a sinful man. God and sin cannot dwell together. The claims of God's holiness must be satisfied as truly as the claims of His love.

"We speak of law and love, of truth and grace, of justice and mercy, and so long as sin does not exist, there is no controversy between any of these. If there be no sin, law and love are never out of harmony with each other; truth and grace go ever hand in hand; justice and mercy sing a common anthem. If the law be broken, what is love to do? If truth be violated, how can grace operate? In the presence of crime, how can justice and mercy meet? This is the problem of problems. It is not a problem as between God and man. It is not a problem as between God and angels. It is a problem as between God and Himself" (G. Campbell Morgan, *The Bible and the Cross*, p. 125).

Let us think deeply into this greatest of problems created by Adam's sin. How would he satisfy the claims of both His love and His holiness? His holiness must condemn sin and command the sinner to depart. His love must open its arms to the sinner and bid him come. A holy God could not tolerate sin, a loving God could not turn away from the sinner. God could not desert the sinner but what should He do with the sin? God's attitude toward sin would reveal His true character quite as much as His attitude toward the sinner.

Would Adam's sin not only separate God and man but would it even bring division into God's own being? "Sin, whether as anticipated by the Creator, or as become actual in our world, created an antinomy in the very being of God, created a new ethical exigency for God and for the universe, so that the legitimate expression of either or both of these polarities (holiness and love) in question a new reconciliation was necessary: that is, a reconciliation of opposite moral relationships within God's being itself. On the one hand, as we must believe, the self-affirmatory character of the divine purity must compel displeasure against sin: and on the other hand, the divine clemency which on God's part yearns to impart its own holy nature to His creatures would constrain Him to forgive and cleanse from that sin" (H. C. Mabie, *The Divine Reason of the Cross*, p. 54).

What, then, would God do that both would be consistent with His holiness and conciliatory to His love; which would mercifully and yet righteously bridge that awful chasm between Himself and man?

THE CHASM BRIDGED

A perfect reconciliation was brought about within God's being by a synthesis of His holiness and His love by which the claims of each were satisfied. God's holiness and righteousness compelled Him to pronounce the curse upon the serpent, the man, the woman and even upon the earth. God had said, "For in the day that thou eatest thereof thou shalt surely die." God's word is true and is from everlasting to everlasting; God's righteousness compelled Him to carry out His judgment upon sin.

"But God's love put an exquisite, fragrant, fadeless rose in the midst of the thorns." Right in the very heart of the pronouncement of that awful curse recorded in Genesis 3:14-19 is that gracious, wondrous promise of salvation through a Saviour.

> Genesis 3:15, "And I will put enmity between thee and the woman, and between thy seed and her seed; it shall bruise thy head, and thou shalt bruise his heel."

God's holiness and love are melted together in this precious promise and out of this golden crucible emerges *the cross of the Lord Jesus Christ,* and stretches itself across the impassable chasm sin has made between God and man. "The reconciliation was effected through the self-provided, suffering reconciliation of God in Christ. 'Mercy and truth are met together: righteousness and peace have kissed each other.' Thus the antinomy in the divine Being itself was dissolved."

Before Adam and Eve left the Garden of Eden the promise was made of a way of salvation for the whole human race which had been plunged into moral and spiritual ruin through sin. It was not man's way but God's— salvation through a Saviour.

THE CROSS IN GOD'S ETERNAL PURPOSE

But just here we may ask—and reverently so—Did Adam's and Eve's sin take God by surprise and did He have to think out a way of escape for man after his fall? Here we come to the very acme of the infinite grace of God. May the Holy Spirit grant each reader spiritual understanding to apprehend "the breadth and length and depth and height of the love of God which passeth knowledge."

No, Adam's sin did not take God by surprise, nor was God's way of redemption an afterthought. God knew even before the foundation of the world and the creation of man the sad and tragic devastation sin would work in the human race. God had anticipated the Fall and was ready for it.

The cross which was to bridge the chasm made by sin was set up in love in the dateless eternity of the past before it was set up in promise in Eden or in history on Calvary. "The divine redemptive movement, *in purpose anterior to creation,* once determined upon, never paused until it victoriously expressed itself in the language of Calvary. . . . The atonement in principle and in God is dateless, but as taking effect on man it is historical, though dateless. . . . Redemption then, in the large, is anything but an afterthought, a mere appendix to make good an unexpected disaster which had overtaken God's universe. Both sin and redemption were foreseen from the beginning" (H. C. Mabie, *The Divine Reason of the Cross,* chap. 2).

There was a cross set up in heaven before it was ever set up on earth. The atonement for man's sin made visible, effectual and historical on Calvary, was wrought out in purpose and in principle in the heart of the triune God: Father, Son and Holy Spirit in the dateless past.

> Revelation 13:8, "And all that dwell upon the earth shall worship him, whose names are not written in the book of life of *the Lamb slain from the foundation of the world.*"
>
> Ephesians 1:4, "According as *he hath chosen us in him before the foundation of the world,* that we should be holy and without blame before him in love."
>
> Acts 2:23, "Him, *being delivered by the determinate counsel and foreknowledge of God,* ye have taken, and by wicked hands have crucified and slain."
>
> 2 Timothy 1:9, "Who hath saved us, and called us with an holy calling, not according to our works, but according to his own purpose and grace, *which was given us in Christ Jesus before the world began.*"

What can these words mean but that in the counsels of the triune God in the eternity of the past the awful tragedy in Eden was foreknown and that, then and there, the wondrous plan of salvation through the Son's redemptive work was formed by which God-in-Christ should reconcile a lost, sinning race to Himself?

REVELATION OF REDEMPTION

The Bible is the book of redemption, its one theme from the beginning to the end is *salvation through a Saviour.*

> Luke 24:27, "And beginning at Moses and all the prophets, *he expounded unto them in all the scriptures the things concerning himself.*"
>
> Luke 24:44, "And he said unto them, These are the words which I spake unto you, while I was yet with you, that all things must be fulfilled, *which were written in the law of Moses, and in the prophets, and in the psalms, concerning me.*"

All through the Law, the Psalms and the Prophets, God is unfolding to man His plan of salvation through a Saviour. By the sacrifices of the Old

Testament He foreshadows the one supreme sacrifice. By pen pictures and prophetic promises He foretells Him who is "The Lamb of God that taketh away the sin of the world."

The story of His life with the record of its words and works; His death, resurrection and ascension as recorded in the Gospels; His doings as continued in the history of the Acts; the deeper revelation of Himself as the living, victorious, glorified Lord in the epistles, and the promise and prophecy of a coming King in the Revelation; all have but one underlying purpose: namely, to reveal Him, not as the founder of a new religious order, nor as the propagator of a new ethical code, nor as the teacher of moral principles, nor as the reformer of man's external environment, but to reveal Him as the Saviour of mankind. The Father announced the coming of His Son as the coming of a Saviour.

> Matthew 1:21, "And she shall bring forth a son, and thou shalt call his name JESUS: for *he shall save his people from their sins.*"

> Luke 2:11, "For unto you is born this day in the city of David *a Saviour,* which is Christ the Lord."

Jesus Christ did not come only to teach or to preach or to heal: He came to *save.* Jesus Christ came for but one purpose which He Himself states in these words,

> Luke 19:10, "For the Son of man is come *to seek* and *to save* that which was lost."

He came to bridge the chasm which sin had made between God and man. No one else and nothing else could do this.

8

God's Second Man—The Last Adam

THREE THINGS ARE CLEAR: man cannot save himself, God has undertaken to save him, Jesus Christ is the means. The question follows:

What method would God use in salvaging the wreckage wrought in humanity? Would He try to repair the ruin in the old creation or would He replace it by a totally new creation? Would He reestablish the old order of humanity or would He inaugurate a radically new order?

The race had been ruined through a man, therefore it must be redeemed through a man. The first man had failed to fulfill God's original intention in creation so a second Man must come forth who would succeed in fulfilling it. The old order of which the first Adam was the head had gone down in ruin so a new order of redeemed men under the headship of the last Adam must be started. The sentence of death had fallen upon all mankind through the first Adam's disobedience; it must be lifted through the obedience of another Adam, whose work would be so perfect that He could be rightly called "the last Adam" for none other would ever be needed. The redemption wrought through the last Adam is set in sharp contrast to the ruin accomplished through the first Adam in Romans 5:12-21.

THE FIRST MAN			THE SECOND MAN
THE FIRST ADAM			THE LAST ADAM
	"BY ONE MAN"		
Disobedience			Obedience
Sin			Grace
Death	*Ruined*	*Redeemed*	Life
Judgment			Justification

THE NECESSITY OF A MEDIATOR

God, then, will redeem man through a Man. What then would be required in a Redeemer? Remember that sin has caused a terrible breach between God and man. God is morally unable to have fellowship with the sinner and the sinner is morally unable to have access to God. If any real reconciliation is to be effected between them there is need of a Mediator, one who would stand between God and man. Such a Mediator must needs be one accepted and trusted by both parties, one who partakes both of God's nature and of man's nature, one who in the work of reconciliation would represent both God and man equally, one who would satisfy every claim of God upon man and of man upon God. In other words a true Mediator must be a God-man. The Saviour of men must be a God-man. Christ Jesus, the Mediator, is the *God*-man. He is not the man-*God*. He is not a man who became God but God who became man. He is not a man who for a special purpose and at a special time was invested with Deity but He is God who for a special purpose and at a special time was invested with humanity. He always was God: He became man.

> Hebrews 1:1-3, "God, who at sundry times and in divers manners spake in time past unto the fathers by the prophets, hath in these last days spoken unto us by *his Son, whom he hath appointed heir of all things, by whom also he made the worlds;*
> *Who being the brightness of his glory, and the express image of his person, and upholding all things by the word of his power,* when he had himself purged our sins, sat down on the right hand of the Majesty on high."

No words could teach more clearly that Christ Jesus, the Saviour, the God-appointed Mediator, is God. He is the eternal Son, the Heir, the Creator, the Upholder of the universe and all therein. He is the Son who is the commencement, the continuance, and the consummation of all things. He is the Son, the effulgence of the Father's glory and the very essence of His person. He is the eternal Son who said of Himself, "Before Abraham was, I am" (John 8:58); who declared, "I came forth from the Father, and am come into the world: again, I leave the world, and go to the Father" (John 16:28); and on the eve of returning to His Father, prayed, "And now, O Father, glorify thou me with thine own self with the glory which I had with thee before the world was" (John 17:5).

Only God could represent God in this mediatorship. As in creation so in redemption the Father works in and through the Son. "God in Christ was reconciling the world unto himself." Christ Jesus, the Mediator between God and man is God, the eternal Son, "the Lord from heaven."

But where could God find one who would qualify as the God-*man?* Most surely not among the sons of men on earth, nor among the angelic hosts of heaven for they are neither God nor man. One and only One even in heaven itself could ever be thought of for such an exalted task—the eternal Son of God.

But how could even He be a Mediator for man? It is easy to see how the Lord from heaven could represent a holy God but could He be a just, righteous, impartial representative for sinful man? If such a reconciliation demanded a divine-human Mediator how could He qualify who had been throughout all the eternity of the past the holy Son of God?

Just here we come to the place where the human mind has to acknowledge its finiteness, where human reasoning is silenced, where human comprehension confesses defeat, for we are lifted above all that is human, earthly and natural, up—up—up—into the realm of that which is divine, heavenly and supernatural, to the wondrous grace of God. Nothing but the grace of God could have provided such a divine-human Mediator, could have conceived the thought of a God-man.

Again we are driven back in thought to that which took place in the eternal councils of the Godhead as the Omniscient Father, Son and Holy Spirit looked out upon the universe they were to make, upon the man they were to create, and foresaw the tragedy in Eden with all its terrible consequences. Then and there the triune God looked from eternity to eternity and compassed fully in thought and plan all that would take place between, "In the beginning God created the heaven and the earth" (Genesis 1:1) and "I saw a new heaven and a new earth: for the first heaven and the first earth were passed away" (Revelation 21:1). It was then and there determined that the eternal Son of God, the Alpha and the Omega, "the beginning and the end, the first and the last" (Revelation 22:13), should lay aside for a brief space of time His essential glory, and be "made in the likeness of men . . . [to become] obedient unto death, even the death of the cross" (Philippians 2:7-8) that He in returning to glory might bring "many sons unto glory" (Hebrews 2:10), to be forever with the Lord. There in the glory of eternity the grace of God fashioned the wondrous plan of redemption by which the eternal Son of God would become the incarnate Son of Man; the divine-human Mediator; the God-*man* whom both God and man would need when sin entered into the human race and separated man from God. Christ Jesus is the divinely provided Mediator.

> 1 Timothy 2:5, R. V., "For there is one God, *one mediator also between God and men,* himself man, *Christ Jesus.*"

In no book of the Bible is the person of Christ Jesus, the God-man and His work as the divine-human Mediator more clearly set forth than in the epistle to the Hebrews. In it we can trace back to glory the unfolding of truth regarding His glorious person and follow from heaven to earth and from earth to heaven again His gracious work as Redeemer.

We shall consider His work in the following chapters. May we concentrate our thought now upon His person. Who is He?

The divine-human Mediator—the eternal Son of God—"The Lord from heaven."

> 1 Corinthians 15:47, "The first man is of the earth, earthy: the second man is *the Lord from heaven.*"

> John 1:1-2, "In the beginning was the Word, and the Word was with God, and *the Word was God.*
> The same was in the beginning with God."

The divine-human Mediator—the incarnate Son of Man—"The Word made flesh."

> John 1:1, "In the beginning was the Word, and the Word was with God, and *the Word was God.*"

> John 1:14, R. V., "And the Word became flesh, and dwelt among us (and we beheld his glory, glory as of the only begotten from the Father), full of grace and truth."

"The Word became flesh." "The statement is appalling, overwhelming. Out of the infinite distances into the finite nearness; from the unknowable, to the knowable; from the method of self-expression appreciable by Deity alone, to a method of self-expression understandable of the human" (G. Campbell Morgan, *The Crises of the Christ,* p. 73). Christ Jesus, the Mediator, is the God-*man.* The eternal Son of God became the incarnate Son of Man. Heaven came to earth.

In Hebrews, chapter 1, the Mediator is divine. He is called "Lord," "God," "the Son." In Hebrews, chapter 2, He is human. He is called "Jesus," "brother," "high priest." In chapter 1 He is as far above us as the heavens are above the earth; He is absolutely separate from us; He is in a class by Himself; He is the unapproachable; the incomprehensible; the incomparable One. In chapter 2 He is on the level of our humanity, He has stooped to come to our human plane of life.

> Hebrews 2:9, "But we see *Jesus, who was made a little lower than the angels for the suffering of death,* crowned with glory and honour; that he by the grace of God should taste death for every man."

In chapter 2 He is one with us, He has entered into our humanity, He has actually become part of our flesh and blood.

> Hebrews 2:11, "For *both he that sanctifieth and they who are sanctified are all of one:* for which cause he is not ashamed to call them brethren."

> Hebrews 2:14, "Forasmuch then as the children are partakers of flesh and blood, *he also himself likewise took part of the same;* that through death he might destroy him that had the power of death, that is, the devil."

In chapter 2 He is the tender, sympathetic, understanding Son of Man: the gracious, gentle One.

> Hebrews 2:17-18, "Wherefore *in all things it behoved him to be made like unto his brethren,* that he might be a merciful and faithful high priest in things pertaining to God, to make reconciliation for the sins of the people.
> For in that *he himself hath suffered being tempted,* he is able to succour them that are tempted."

Only Man could represent man in this mediatorship. Christ Jesus, the Mediator between God and man is Man: the incarnate Son: "the Word made flesh."

From the beginning to the end of Scripture this story is told: Christ Jesus, the Mediator between God and man is *God;* the eternal Son; the Lord from heaven; the Alpha and the Omega. Christ Jesus, the Mediator between man and God is *Man;* the incarnate Son; the Man of Galilee; the Babe of Bethlehem.

How the Eternal Son Became the Incarnate Son

That Christ Jesus was a divine-human Mediator is not only a fact of revelation but of history as well. Not only the words of Scripture but the A.D. on our desk calendar tells us that at some one point of time "The Word was made flesh, and dwelt among us."

> Luke 2:11-12, "For unto you is *born this day in the city of David a Saviour,* which is Christ the Lord.
> And this shall be a sign unto you; Ye shall find *the babe* wrapped in swaddling clothes, lying in a manger."

"Christ the Lord"—"a babe"! *"A Saviour"*—"wrapped in swaddling clothes"! *The Creator* of the universe—"lying in a manger"! *The Author* and *Sustainer of life*—"born"! *The Father of eternity*—beginning to count His life by days and weeks and years! A *God-man!* It is a fact of revelation and of history staggering: stupendous: sublime. In this fact we are face to face with the miracle of miracles, the mystery of mysteries.

Many have asked the question, How can such a thing be? How did the eternal Son of God become the incarnate Son of Man? How was the uncreated Lord of glory born a babe in Bethlehem? The answer is plainly given in the annunciations of the angels to Joseph and to Mary.

> Matthew 1:20, "But while he thought on these things, behold, the angel of the Lord appeared unto him in a dream, saying, Joseph, thou son of David, fear not to take unto thee Mary thy wife: *for that which is conceived in her is of the Holy Ghost.*"

Luke 1:30-31, 34-35, "And the angel said unto her, Fear not, Mary: for thou hast found favour with God.

And, behold, thou shalt conceive in thy womb, and bring forth a son, and shalt call his name JESUS. Then said Mary unto the angel, How shall this be, seeing I know not a man?

And the angel answered and said unto her, *The Holy Ghost shall come upon thee, and the power of the Highest shall overshadow thee: therefore also that holy thing which shall be born of thee shall be called the Son of God."*

Perhaps nothing in God's holy Word challenges man to greater reverence, deeper humility, sublimer faith, than this divine record of God's supernatural entrance into human life. Yet to the truly humble, reverent, worshipful man of faith there is no difficulty in accepting the statement of revelation that through the supernatural operation of God, the Holy Spirit, the virgin Mary gave birth "to that holy thing which was called the Son of God." He reads and accepts these two annunciations without making any attempt to explain the heart of the mystery therein because he humbly acknowledges that it transcends all human understanding.

He sees in Christ Jesus, the God-man, essential Deity and real humanity, very God and very Man. He gladly acknowledges the supernatural in the Person of the Lord Jesus Christ. He finds no way to account for such a result except in an adequate cause. A supernatural life demands a supernatural birth. So he joyfully accepts as true God's divine revelation that in the origin of the God-man there was to be found the coöperation of Deity and humanity. He believes that Christ Jesus, the God-man, was "conceived by the Holy Ghost, born of the Virgin Mary," as the evangelical church has believed through the centuries.

Thus the supernatural birth of the Lord Jesus is the connecting link between eternity and time: between heaven and earth: between Deity and humanity: between God and man. Through the doorway of that supernatural conception there came into this world such a Person as had never lived in it before or ever has since. In Him there is essential Deity and essential humanity each in its wholeness and completeness. He is "the Son of God, the Word of the Father, begotten from everlasting of the Father, very and eternal God, of one substance with the Father. Being such, He took man's nature in the womb of the blessed Virgin, of her substance, so that two whole and perfect Natures, that is to say, the Godhead and the Manhood, were joined together in one Person, never to be divided, whereof is one Christ, very God and very Man" (H. C. G. Moule, *Outlines of Christian Doctrine,* p. 57).

All that God is, Christ Jesus is. All that unfallen man was, He is. Nothing that belonged to Deity or to sinless humanity was lacking in Him.

The divine and the human nature are each fully manifested in His unique personality. Both God and man are equally represented in the constituent elements of the personality of the God-man. He is veritable God and veritable man in one person.

Even though the God-man is a unit in whom God and man meet in a harmonious union of natures yet the root of His wonderful personality is God. Through all eternity He was God. At one moment of time He became Man. "The Son of God came from the eternities. The Son of Man began His Being." *"In the beginning* was the Word, and the Word was God." The deity of Christ Jesus is basic and primary. *"The Word was made flesh"* and there was "born this day in the city of David a Saviour— a Babe wrapped in swaddling clothes." The humanity of Christ Jesus is assumed and therefore secondary though essential. In the union of God and man, God is the dominant factor. "The incarnation is the humanizing of deity and not the deification of humanity." The God-man is "God . . . manifest in the flesh" (1 Timothy 3:16).

In the following scriptural classic we have a very clear and beautiful revelation of the person of the God-man and the process by which He became such and the purpose.

> Philippians 2:5-8, R. V., "Have this mind in you, which was also in Christ Jesus: *who, existing in the form of God,* counted not the being on an equality with God a thing to be grasped, but *emptied himself,* taking the form of a servant, being made in the likeness of men; and *being found in fashion as a man, he humbled himself,* becoming obedient even unto death, yea, the death of the cross."

He was the Eternal Son, "existing in the form of God" and "on an equality with God." But in the presence of Eden's tragedy and man's need of redemption He counted not the being on an equality with God a thing to be grasped but by a sublime act of self-emptying He qualified to be the world's Saviour. While not divesting Himself of His essential nature as God, He became the incarnate Son, "taking the form of a servant, being made in the likeness of men," and submitted to the temporary nonmanifestation of His divine prerogatives.

"He emptied Himself." He did this by permitting the essential glory and majesty of His divine person to be covered and hidden for a while by the flesh, by voluntarily putting His several attributes, omnipotence, omniscience, and omnipresence, under temporary limitations; and by placing Himself under the sovereign will of the heavenly Father and under the control of the Holy Spirit.

"The emptying indicates the setting aside of one form of manifestation, in which all the facts of equality with God were evidently revealed, for another form of manifestation, in which the fact of equality with God must for a time be hidden, by the necessary submissiveness of the human to the divine. . . . The Word passed from government to obedience, from independent cooperation in the equality of Deity to dependent submission to the will of God" (G. Campbell Morgan, *The Crises of the Christ*, pp. 76-77).

"He humbled Himself." God took man's form, the Lord of glory stooped to an actual union with human nature. In His humiliation He endured every conceivable suffering, the culmination of which was His cruel death on the cross as a condemned criminal.

His voluntary self-humbling and self-emptying were for a purpose. "He became obedient unto death, yea, the death of the cross" that through His divine-human mediatorship He might become mankind's all-sufficient Saviour. (See Diagram 5.)

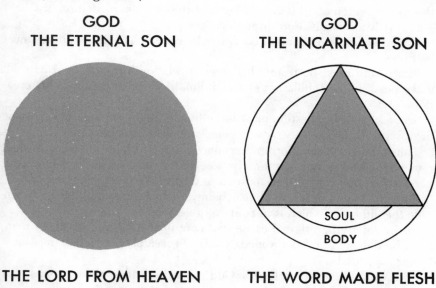

GOD
THE ETERNAL SON

GOD
THE INCARNATE SON

SOUL

BODY

THE LORD FROM HEAVEN
1 Corinthians 15:47

THE WORD MADE FLESH
John 1:14

Diagram 5: God—Manifest in the Flesh

9

Four Spans in the Bridge of Salvation— Incarnation

GOD IN HIS INFINITE LOVE has undertaken the restoration of mankind and the reconciliation of all things to Himself through the mediation of Christ Jesus. It is to be salvation through a Saviour.

If man's complete salvation is effectually accomplished, five things must be done.

First: Man must be restored to such a relationship with God as shall make possible the fulfillment of the original, divine intention in his creation.

Second: The sin question must be fully and finally settled. Sin must be dealt with in respect to its guilt, penalty, power and presence.

Third: Such propitiation and reconciliation must be effected as shall remove the barrier of separation between God and man and give to every person the opportunity of restoration to God's favor and fellowship.

Fourth: A new order of human beings must be inaugurated to supersede the old order which is in ruin and rejection.

Fifth: Satan, the original cause and continual instigator of sin in man, must be defeated and dethroned. God's sovereignty over all things must be fully restored.

To accomplish such a salvation God erected a bridge of four spans over the chasm made by sin. Each span is an integral part of the whole. Without any one span the bridge would be incomplete and inadequate. The four spans are incarnation, crucifixion, resurrection and ascension. Incarnation is the first span in the bridge of salvation.

That there would be an incarnation God's prophet had plainly foretold.

Isaiah 7:14, "Therefore the LORD himself shall give you a sign; Behold, *a virgin shall conceive, and bear a son,* and shall call his name Immanuel."

Isaiah 9:6, "*For unto us a child is born,* unto us a son is given: and the government shall be upon his shoulder: and his name shall be called

Wonderful, Counsellor, The mighty God, The everlasting Father, The Prince of Peace."

The moment sin stained the heart of humanity God gave the promise of a Saviour. All down through the centuries those who, like Simeon and Anna were eagerly anticipating the coming One, could hear the advancing steps of the Lord of glory on His way from heaven to earth.

In the fullness of time He came. "Jesus was born in Bethlehem of Judea in the days of Herod the king." "God manifest in the flesh" was God's first step in the fulfillment of His prophecy-promise in Eden.

God's original intention in the creation of man was a being made in His own image. Through sin man lost all true knowledge both of God and of himself as God meant him to be.

Living in a world of sinful men the sinner had no one better than himself with whom to compare himself. So he measured himself with himself and with others like himself and the result has been self-complacency and self-sufficiency. Left to himself alone there is no desire for anything better for there is no sense of need. In his moral and spiritual darkness and degradation man is incapable of knowing aright either God or himself. Hence it is clearly evident that if man is to be restored to favor with God he needs a twofold revelation, a revelation of God as He is, and of himself as he is and as God means him to be.

Revelation—The Preliminary Purpose in Incarnation

God gave that twofold revelation in Christ Jesus, the God-man. Only the Son could reveal accurately and authoritatively the Father because He alone had seen the Father.

John 1:18, "No man hath seen God at any time; *the only begotten Son, which is in the bosom of the Father, he hath declared him.*"

Matthew 11:27, "No man knoweth the Son, but the Father; *neither knoweth any man the Father, save the Son.*"

But how could the Son make known to sinners on earth the ineffable beauty, the infinite love, the immeasurable worth of the Father in heaven if He remained in the Father's bosom? There was but one way that the age-long cry of "orphaned humanity," "Shew us the father," could be answered and that was by way of the incarnation. This is the way the Lord Jesus took and He told those who saw Him on earth that when they had seen Him they had seen the Father.

John 14:9, "Jesus saith unto him, Have I been so long time with you, and yet hast thou not known me, Philip? *he that hath seen me hath seen the Father;* and how sayest thou then, Shew us the Father?"

In the incarnate Son the everlasting Father stooped to the level of man's power to comprehend Him. "Jesus is God spelling Himself out in a language that men can understand."

In the glorious Person and the gracious work of the Son, God was manifest. What the Son was God is. His character and conduct on earth are a mirrored reflection of His Father in heaven. Blessing the little children and bidding them come unto Him; entering into the joys of the wedding feast and the dinner party; weeping with the bereaved sisters at the brother's tomb; seeking the companionship of kindred spirits in the Bethany home; talking with an outcast woman at Jacob's well; feeding the hungry multitudes who have followed Him into the desert; giving sight to the eyes of the man born blind; cleansing the Temple of the avaricious moneychangers; denouncing the hypocrisy and self-righteousness of the unbelieving Pharisees; suffering in Gethsemane; dying upon Calvary; in all these ministries the invisible God is made intelligible to men.

But Jesus Christ came not alone to reveal God to man but to reveal man to himself. Through sin man was blinded both to the worth of God and the worthlessness of self. But in the man Christ Jesus, God revealed to humanity His perfect Man, the divine ideal. In Him man not only found all that he could ever want in God but all that God could ever want in man. What the God-man was on earth God desires every human being to be. "In him we see in perfect form what man in the divine idea of him is." By comparison of his life with that of the man Christ Jesus each one may see the depth of sin into which he has fallen and the height of holiness to which he may rise.

The twofold revelation in the God-man of God as He is and of man as he may be is surely the preliminary purpose in the incarnation but it is not the primary one. If the natural man had nothing beyond this revelation it would do him very little good. In the first place, how could his blinded mind apprehend it? His darkened heart accept it? His biased will act upon it? And if he could apprehend, accept, and act upon this revelation of God and of himself given in Jesus, where would it bring him? Such a revelation does not touch the sin question except to reveal to what depths man has fallen. In no sense can it settle it. It would only leave the awakened sinner with a greater consciousness of condemnation and a deeper experience of despair.

Redemption—The Primary Purpose in Incarnation

Revelation in itself is not a sufficient reason for the incarnation. God was not manifest in the flesh to mock sinners by giving them an example of a perfect life which they had absolutely no power within themselves to imitate. The God-man is an example for the saint to follow but not for the sinner.

Again Jesus Christ did not come to impart teachings which the natural man could obey. Nor did He come to earth to make it a more comfortable and habitable place for the sinner through the social reforms He would effect. Nor did He come as the founder of a new religion, the spiritual head of another sect, which would go a step beyond other religions in resuscitating the old creation and in lifting the human race through gradual development to a higher moral and spiritual attainment.

Jesus Christ clearly conceived His mission to this sinful world to be that of a Saviour. Scripture always speaks of the incarnation in relationship to sin and to God's purpose in redemption. Redemption is the primary purpose in the incarnation. Christ came to save sinners like you and me.

> Luke 19:10, "For *the Son of man is come to seek and to save that which was lost.*"

> Galatians 4:4-5, R. V., "But when the fulness of the time came, God sent forth his Son, born of a woman, born under the law, *that he might redeem them that were under the law,* that we might receive the adoption of sons."

> 1 John 3:5, R. V., "And ye know that *he was manifested to take away sins:* and in him is no sin."

The incarnation is undoubtedly the first span in God's bridge of salvation. But in what way is the fulfillment of God's redemptive purpose begun in the incarnation? What part does it have in man's restoration to the favor and fellowship of God?

We have already stated two consequences of the fall; first, the utter failure of God's first man to fulfill God's original intention in His creation; secondly, the total ruin of the old order of humanity of which Adam was the head. The first Adam failed both as a man and as a representative man. Through his sin God's union established in creation with himself and through him with the whole human race was broken. This must be restored. Sin had injected into man an evil nature which made man hostile to God. He must be reconciled. Salvation demands reconciliation and reconciliation must be followed by conformity. Salvation from God's viewpoint does not mean merely the recovery of men from the guilt, penalty and power of sin but it means restoration to the likeness of God, even conformity to the image of His Son. It is not only a negative deliverance from a state of estrangement from and hostility to God but it is a positive entrance into a state of righteousness and holiness in God.

To accomplish such a salvation an altogether new union with the race must be made and it must be a union based on kinship of nature so that

both God and man could find their fullest satisfaction and greatest blessedness in such fellowship. It was impossible for God to permit, or for man to
enjoy, such a union as long as man had only an evil nature. For man to
enjoy fellowship with God he must have a nature like God's. But how
could he become a partaker of the divine nature? Here we discover the
measure of God's grace. Here God's grace at its highest height stoops to
man's need at its deepest depth. In order that man might become a partaker of the divine nature, God would Himself become a partaker of human nature. In order to condemn sin in the flesh, God would send His own
Son in the likeness of sinful flesh.

> Hebrews 2:14, 16-17, "*Forasmuch then as the children are partakers of
> flesh and blood, he also himself likewise took part of the same;* that
> through death he might destroy him that had the power of death, that
> is, the devil.
>
> For verily he took not on him the nature of angels; *but he took on
> him the seed of Abraham.*
>
> Wherefore *in all things it behoved him to be made like unto his
> brethren,* that he might be a merciful and faithful high priest in things
> pertaining to God, to make reconciliation for the sins of the people."

> Romans 8:3, "For what the law could not do, in that it was weak through
> the flesh, *God sending his own Son in the likeness of sinful flesh,* and
> for sin, condemned sin in the flesh."

The act of the Son of God in becoming a partaker of our nature is the
incarnation. This is followed very shortly by His death, resurrection and
ascension by which we may become partakers of His nature. Thus in the
incarnation we find the cornerstone of the new union between God and
man. But let us go further into its meaning.

God was faced with two necessities in any effectual plan of salvation:
first, the sending forth of a second Man who would fulfill His original intention in man's creation; second, the providing of another Adam who
would act representatively for the human race as the Head of a new order.
The Man Christ Jesus meets both these necessities. He is God's second
Man.

> 1 Corinthians 15:47, "The first man is of the earth, earthy: *the second
> man is the Lord from heaven.*"

He is God's last Adam.

> 1 Corinthians 15:45, "And so it is written, The first man Adam was made
> a living soul; *the last Adam was made a quickening spirit.*"

In the God-man, God made a new union with the human race; the ultimate issue of this union is a new race of redeemed men of whom Christ
Jesus is the Head.

To fully qualify, however, as the last Adam in this mediatorial redemptive work, God's second Man must succeed where His first man failed, and He must succeed under the same circumstances and limitations. The first man failed on earth: the second Man must succeed on earth. The first man had a tripartite human nature subject to human limitations. The second Man must have a tripartite human nature subject to human limitations. The first man was tempted from without by Satan to doubt, disobedience and disloyalty. The second Man must be tempted in the same way, by the same person, to do the same thing. If God's second Man succeeded where God's first man failed then He would qualify as the last Adam to become the Redeemer of the human race and the Head of a new order of beings.

Let us see how God's second Man in the incarnation met every one of these requirements.

The eternal Word was made flesh and dwelt among us. The only begotten Son left the Father's bosom in glory to be born of a virgin in a manger in Bethlehem. A Saviour was born in the city of David. The Lord from heaven came to earth.

God's second Man was human, subject to human limitations. Christ's humanity began where ours did and went through all the stages of human life from infancy to manhood. Christ had a human ancestry.

> Romans 1:3, "Concerning his Son Jesus Christ our Lord, *which was made of the seed of David according to the flesh.*"

> Acts 13:23, *"Of this man's [David] seed* hath God according to his promise raised unto Israel a Saviour, Jesus."

The Son of God became the Son of Man by a human birth. He was "a babe wrapped in swaddling clothes." Mary was His mother.

> Luke 1:30-31, "And the angel said unto her, Fear not, Mary: for thou hast found favour with God.
> And, behold, *thou shalt conceive in thy womb, and bring forth a son,* and shalt call his name JESUS."

He was a "child" subject to the law of regular development, living in a home with brothers and sisters and growing under the training and discipline of His home life as other boys grow.

> Luke 2:40, "And *the child grew,* and waxed strong in spirit, filled with wisdom: and the grace of God was upon him."

He was "a man" and as a son and brother in the home, as a neighbor and tradesman in the community, as a citizen of the nation, He performed every duty and met every obligation that these human relationships demanded. Christ Jesus was not only "made in the likeness of men" but He was in His earthly life "found in fashion as a man" (Philippians 2:7-8). "In all things it behoved him to be made like unto his brethren" (Hebrews 2: 17). In everything the Son of Man was not only humanly perfect but He was perfectly human.

God's second Man had a tripartite human nature.

> Luke 23:46, "And when Jesus had cried with a loud voice, he said, Father, into thy hands I commend *my spirit:* and having said thus, he gave up the ghost."

> Matthew 26:38, "Then saith he unto them, *My soul* is exceeding sorrowful, even unto death: tarry ye here, and watch with me."

> Matthew 26:12, "For in that she hath poured this ointment on *my body,* she did it for my burial."

God's second Man had a spirit. It was ever open Godward and heavenward. He loved His Father and delighted in His Father's world, word and will. Communion with His Father was His supreme delight and He ever lived in the consciousness of the Father's presence (John 8:29) and in the joy of the Father's smile (Matthew 17:5). In Jesus the human spirit was always in perfect adjustment with the Spirit of God and was dominant over both His soul and body.

God's second Man had a soul. The last Adam thought, loved and willed as the first Adam had done. His familiarity with the Holy Scripture shows how He must have read and pondered the sacred writings. His parables taken largely from nature or the events of human life reveal the mold that shaped His thought life. He loved people and enjoyed fellowship with them. He was capable of intense sympathy and sorrow, of great indignation and anger, of deep joy and gladness, of exquisite appreciation and gratitude. Jesus had a soul in which was manifested a mighty capacity to think, love and will.

God's second Man had a body. He was made "in the likeness of sinful flesh." The Samaritan woman knew Him to be a Jew. Mary Magdalene thought Him to be a gardener. Those who saw and heard Him in the synagogue at Nazareth while wondering at His gracious words still took Him to be only Joseph's son. He ate, slept, walked, worked and lived as other men did. While in His countenance, conversation and carriage there must have been that which His sinlessness and holiness produced which made Him different from all other men, yet in His physical form there was nothing which differentiated Him.

God's second Man was not only human but He was subject to all sinless infirmities and limitations of humanity. Jesus hungered, thirsted, slept, wept, wearied, mourned, suffered and died. "There is not a note in the great organ of our humanity which, when touched, does not find a sympathetic vibration in the might, range and scope of our Lord's being, saving, of course, the jarring discord of sin."

> Hebrews 2:10-11, "For it became him for whom are all things, and by whom are all things, in bringing many sons unto glory, *to make the captain of their salvation perfect through sufferings.*
> For both he that sanctifieth and they who are sanctified are all of one: for which cause he is not ashamed to call them brethren."

Lastly God's second Man was tempted from without by Satan to doubt, disobedience and disloyalty.

When Satan said "I will" to God, setting his creaturely will in opposition to that of his Creator, he broke the unwritten law that in God's universe there can be but one will and that the will of the Maker of all things. Lawlessness then became a fact in the celestial realm. It entered the world and began coursing through the veins of human life when God's first man broke God's law and disobeyed God's command.

From that day on down through the centuries until the angels sang the first Christmas carols over the manger cradle in Bethlehem there had never lived a man who had been perfectly obedient to God, who had fully kept God's law. Men had turned to their own way and done that which was right in their own sight. Even among those who through faith followed the Lord there was not one who lived only and wholly in the will of God.

But through the incarnation there entered into human life a second Man in whom mankind was again to be put to the test; a last Adam in whom the human race had its only and final hope of restoration to God.

The first man, Adam, and the whole race latent in him had gone down into ruin and rejection through disobedience. Now God had sent forth a second Man, a last Adam, who might lift the race into restoration and reconciliation upon the one condition of obedience. It must, however, be obedience from the beginning to the end of life; obedience at all times, in all things, under all circumstances, to all limits, in spite of all consequences; obedience, too, not merely in the letter but in the spirit; obedience to the whole will of God as the unalterable rule of life; such obedience as made the will of God the center of His life, the circumference, and all in between. The ruling passion of His whole being must be "God's will—Nothing more, nothing less, nothing else."

> Romans 5:19, "For as by one man's disobedience many were made sinners, so *by the obedience of one shall many be made righteous.*"

Would the Son of Man be able to qualify for Saviourhood under such a condition? Would He choose in all things to will Godward?

In coming into the world Christ Jesus had declared that the purpose of the incarnation was to do His Father's will.

> John 6:38, "For I came down from heaven, *not to do mine own will, but the will of him that sent me.*"

Part of His humbling in becoming the Son of Man was His willingness to leave the place of equality in sovereignty as God to take the place of subordination in subserviency as man. The Father's will was the Son's delight; it was the very sustenance of His life.

> John 4:34, "Jesus saith unto them, *My meat is to do the will of him that sent me,* and to finish his work."

He came, He lived, He worked, all with one purpose and one passion—to do His Father's will. And what was the Father's will in relation to the human race and to the incarnation of His Son?

> John 6:40, "And *this is the will of him that sent me,* that every one which seeth the Son, and believeth on him, may have everlasting life: and I will raise him up at the last day."

God's will was that every sinner should see in His Son a Saviour and believe on Him as such so that the Father might lift from him the sentence of death and raise him up into eternal life in Him.

That this was the Father's will Satan knew; that Jesus Christ had yielded Himself unreservedly to the Father to carry out that will Satan also knew. His satanic desire, his devilish determination, was to keep the Son of Man from doing the Father's will if possible. The slightest shadow of questioning regarding His Father's goodness would be doubt: failure to keep the holy law of God even in one point would be disobedience: the merest deflection of desire toward self-will would be disloyalty, and God's second Man, His last Adam, would have been disqualified for becoming the world's Saviour and the Head of a race of holy, heavenly men. That He would be tempted by Satan from the center to the circumference of His life, that His Father must even permit such temptation would be easily understood even if Scripture did not state it so plainly.

> Hebrews 4:15, "For we have not an high priest which cannot be touched with the feeling of our infirmities; but *was in all points tempted like as we are, yet without sin.*"
>
> Hebrews 2:18, "For in that *he himself hath suffered being tempted,* he is able to succour them that are tempted."
>
> Hebrews 2:10, "For it became him, for whom are all things, and by whom are all things, in bringing many sons unto glory, *to make the captain of their salvation perfect through sufferings.*"

To qualify as the Saviour of men and the Head of a race of redeemed men, the Man Christ Jesus must be a victor over humanity's temptations one by one.

Throughout the thirty years of private life as a child, a boy and a young man, He had no doubt been tempted over and over again to doubt the Father's goodness, to disobey the Father's Law and to be disloyal to the Father's will. In the home, at the carpenter's bench, in the manifold contacts of community life He met a daily assault in the common temptations of man. That He came through these years of obscurity with His manhood unsullied and unstained is amply attested by the Father's voice speaking those words of unqualified approval at His baptism. "This is my beloved Son, in whom I am well pleased." As a Man, Jesus had lived in private a life not only of absolute sinlessness but one that was wholly obedient to the will of God.

He emerged from private into public life and engaged upon His three years of public ministry. He publicly proclaimed Himself as the Messiah. But before He did this an event of tremendous significance occurred. At the Jordan Jesus was baptized by John. This was His first act of identification with humanity's sin, it was the preliminary step in becoming the sinner's Substitute.

Crowds of people were thronging to John to be baptized, confessing their sins. Jesus came to be baptized. He had no sin to confess and He had no disobedience to God's law to repent of. But there on the banks of the Jordan God's second Man publicly acknowledged and accepted His responsibility as the world's Saviour by thus identifying Himself with the world's sin. The last Adam through His baptism committed Himself to bear all the consequences of a broken law on the part of sinners. At His baptism the Man Christ Jesus began to be numbered with the transgressors and the work of personal substitution, which ended at Calvary, was commenced.

Immediately after His baptism His public ministry began and we read, "Then was Jesus led up of the Spirit into the wilderness *to be tempted of the devil.*" As a man, Jesus had met the manifold testings through the daily temptations incidental to private life and in them all had come forth Victor. But now as the Son of Man He is to have the decisive test of His whole life in a personal conflict with the devil himself. Man's salvation does not consist in deliverance from temptation but in deliverance from the possession and power of the tempter. The utter defeat and destruction of the devil himself was part of Christ's work as Saviour. Jesus Christ was committed to the salvation of mankind from sin in toto; this necessitated His going back to the very origin of sin in man and confronting and conquering its instigator. To such a task and to such a test "Then was Jesus led up of the Spirit into the wilderness."

In this wilderness conflict the God-man is there not alone as a man but as the Son of Man, not only as an individual but as the Representative of mankind. Satan is there not only as a personal enemy of "the seed of the woman" but as the avowed foe of God and of the human race. The enmity prophesied in Eden is having there a concrete fulfillment; the conflict foretold, which has gone on in secret for centuries and which has its manifest fulfillment on Calvary, is brought out into the open and crystallized into actual combat here in the wilderness. The devil is no longer allowed to cover his identity through impersonation but is exposed as the devil and his purposes are openly revealed. There in the wilderness the spoiler of the human race faces the Saviour of the human race in a decisive and terrible conflict. It will be proven here for all ages to come who is the vanquished and who the Victor.

Satan had tempted Adam with one purpose of gaining sovereignty over him and securing his worship. He had tempted God's first man in the Garden of Eden at the one point where he could be disobedient and had met marked success. He had come forth victor. Adam had made a personal choice against the choice of God. He had acted independently of God and by so doing had stepped outside of God's will into self-will.

In the wilderness Satan, impelled by the same purpose, tempted God's second Man, employing the same methods and working toward the same end. A careful study of the great temptation (Matthew 4:1-11) will show that Satan made three separate attacks along three distinct avenues but with one purpose: to draw the God-man in desire and in deed outside the will of God; to induce Him to make a personal choice against the choice of God; to persuade Him to act independently. The supreme effort in each attack was to dislodge the God-man from the center of God's will and to lead Him into disloyalty to His Father.

The temptation in the wilderness was the decisive test not only for Christ but for Satan as well. If Satan could only triumph over the last Adam as he had over the first then he would be victor for all time to come. So he offered to Him in the wilderness all that he had gained in the garden, even the kingdoms of this world if He would only fall down and worship him. Then he would indeed have dethroned God, and the satanic passion to be "like the most High" would have been realized. The only hope of man's salvation would have gone, for Christ is the last Adam.

God's first man exercised his right to will and willed Satanward. God's second Man had also been given the same right to will and the power to will Godward. He exercised the right to will and chose to will Godward. The first Adam became the *victim* of sin and of Satan; the last Adam became the *Victor* over sin and Satan.

The question is bound to force itself upon us, "Was it as God or as man that the God-man triumphed over Satan?" Unconsciously perhaps, we may comfort ourselves in defeat by thinking that He made use of the prerogatives and powers of Deity and that His victory was gained through means beyond the reach of man. If this be true the whole benefit to mankind of that wilderness experience is lost, and it was only a personal and not a racial victory which the God-man gained. He alone would have profited by it but there would have been no meaning in it for you and for me. For if He had recourse to Deity and to divine power not at our disposal, then His triumph over sin and Satan does not avail for us.

This, however, was the very thing the devil was tempting Him to do and the very thing He resolutely refused to do. Satan tempted Him to use His power as the Son of God. "He declined to use the prerogatives and powers of Deity in any other way than was possible to every other man. He did not face temptation or overcome it in the realm of His Deity but in the Magnificence of His pure, strong Manhood: tested for thirty years in ordinary private life and for forty days in the loneliness of the wilderness. Jesus was in the wilderness as Man's representative" (G. Campbell Morgan, *The Crises of the Christ*, p. 170).

The last Adam gained His victory precisely where the first Adam failed. Scripture reveals two constituent elements in the God-man's triumph in the wilderness. The first is the sovereign control of the Holy Spirit over His whole being, spirit, soul and body. The second is His implicit obedience to God's Word.

> Matthew 4:1, "Then *was Jesus lĕd up of the Spirit into the wilderness* to be tempted of the devil."

God, the Holy Spirit, led Him into the wilderness to gain this racial victory. The temptation in the wilderness was no accident; it was not even the devil's doings; it was part of the plan. The temptation from without did not take Jesus unawares; He was prepared for this crisis. In His earthly life He was begotten, ruled, led, filled and empowered by the Holy Spirit. While still having all the attributes of Deity, yet as God's second Man, He voluntarily submitted to a life of human limitations so that He might be tempted in all points like as we are and gain the victory over temptation in the only way in which we can gain the victory. So He voluntarily put Himself under the control of the Holy Spirit, and lived His life and did His work only in the Spirit's power.

The temptation of the last Adam in the wilderness was an assault upon His entire personality. Satan approached Jesus through "the lust of the flesh," "the lust of the eye," and "the pride of life," but He found no vulnerable spot in Him. The human spirit in Jesus was dominant over both soul and body because it in turn was yielded wholly to the Spirit of God. The constituent parts of Jesus' wondrous personality were in perfect adjustment to each other because the whole life was lived in right relationship to God. Hence when Satan came he "found nothing in Him." It was victory gained through submission to the dominant control of the Holy Spirit. Such a victory may daily be yours and mine.

The second factor in the triumph of the God-man was His obedience to and use of God's Word. In Eden God's first man was defeated because he had listened to the devil's voice instead of to God's; he had believed the devil's lie instead of God's truth. In the wilderness God's second Man was victorious because He had listened to God's voice instead of to Satan's; He had believed God's Word instead of the devil's lie. More than that, He had used that Word as a weapon against the devil and with it alone repulsed the threefold attack.

> Matthew 4:4, "But he answered and said, *It is written.*"
>
> Matthew 4:7, "Jesus said unto him, *It is written.*"
>
> Matthew 4:10, "Then saith Jesus unto him, Get thee hence, Satan: *for it is written.*"

"Then the devil leaveth him" for the victory was won. It was the victory of perfect obedience to the will of God revealed in the Word of God. Such a victory may daily be yours and mine.

The victory won in the wilderness over the tempter was both perfect and permanent. For both Satan and Christ it had been a decisive test. From that time the devil never again approached Christ in the same way and Christ ever treated Satan and his emissaries as a Victor treats the vanquished.

But the temptation in the wilderness was humanity's test as well as Christ's. God was giving man another chance, a last chance. Therefore the victory was humanity's victory. The Lord Jesus was there as God's second Man qualifying to become man's Saviour and as the last Adam preparing to become the Head of a new race of men. "The Lamb of God, which taketh away the sin of the world" must be without spot. Satan had used every avenue of approach and every method of attack to make Him sin and to win His allegiance but he had failed utterly. The Son of Man came forth from this fierce conflict unscathed, unsullied, unstained. At every point where the first man had failed, the second Man had succeeded; at every place where the first Adam met defeat, the last Adam won victory. The fight against sin, self and Satan had been completely won. His sinlessness qualified Him for Saviourhood. The victory in the wilderness was more than personal, it was racial; it was your victory and mine, if we will.

Sinlessness, however, is a negative condition of life and God requires

more than that. For the fullest fellowship with Himself He demands
something positive, even the perfection of holiness. So Christ went forth
from the wilderness to live a perfect life—perfect in its words, walk, ways
and work. Perfection marked everything in His character and conduct.
He Himself testified both negatively and positively to the perfection of His
life when He said 'The prince of this world cometh, and *hath nothing in
me*" (John 14:30) and "The Father hath not left me alone; for I do always
those things that please him" (John 8:29). He was not only the sinless One
but the perfect One.

The perfection of His life was the perfection of obedience, of unwavering, unvarying submission to His Father's will. When He emptied Himself
of His equality with the Father and yielded the place of sovereignty for
one of subserviency He surrendered completely His right to speak, to act,
to will independently of His Father.

> John 12:49-50, "For *I have not spoken of myself;* but the Father which
> sent me, he gave me a commandment, what I should say, and what I
> should speak.
> And I know that his commandment is life everlasting: *whatsoever I
> speak therefore, even as the Father said unto me, so I speak.*"

> John 5:19, "Then answered Jesus and said unto them, Verily, verily, I
> say unto you, *The Son can do nothing of himself,* but what he seeth
> the Father do: for what things soever he doeth, these also doeth the
> Son likewise."

> Matthew 26:39, "And he went a little further, and fell on his face, and
> prayed, saying, O my Father, if it be possible, let this cup pass from me:
> *nevertheless not as I will, but as thou wilt.*"

His obedience was the obedience of the God-*man:* of the divine-*human*
Mediator, of God's second *representative* Man. It was therefore not due to
any divine attributes of the Son of God but was an obedience the Son of
Man learned through sufferings and sorrow, through trial and tribulation
as He trod the pathway of all humanity.

> Hebrews 5:8-9, "Though he were a Son, *yet learned he obedience* by the
> things which he suffered;
> And *being made perfect,* he became the author of eternal salvation
> unto all them that obey him."

> Hebrews 2:10, "For it became him, for whom are all things, and by
> whom are all things, in bringing many sons unto glory, *to make the
> captain of their salvation perfect through sufferings.*"

It was an obedience that did not end simply in the perfection of moral
beauty and spiritual grace in daily life but one which led Him to drink

the cup of suffering to its very dregs. It constrained Him, even compelled Him to be obedient unto death, even the death of the cross, because this was the Father's will. He measured up to the full stature of the perfection of holiness in God the Father through His perfect obedience as the incarnate Son.

In the person of the God-man the broken unity between God and man has been reestablished. For what purpose? For none other than that of restoring in man the image of God, disfigured and marred by sin. In the holiness of the perfect Man, sinful humanity has not only a revelation of what God meant man to be but also a pledge of what man may become. God was in Christ reconciling the world unto Himself that He might lift man out of what he is into what God is.

> Romans 5:10, "For if, when we were enemies, we were reconciled to God by the death of his Son, much more, being reconciled, *we shall be saved by his life.*"

God proposes the inauguration of a new order of beings who are to be as heavenly and holy, as pure and perfect as He is; a race of redeemed men who shall be "conformed to the image of his Son." Undiscouraged by sin's tragic work God purposes to carry out His original intention that man shall be like Himself. The new union God made with humanity in the incarnation is His pledge of the fulfillment of such a purpose. He stooped to an actual identification with human nature and by that stoop He lifted human nature into an actual identification with the divine nature.

Reconciliation—The Plenary Purpose in the Incarnation

The revelation of God in Christ to man and the redemption by God in Christ of man were undoubtedly the preliminary and the primary purpose in the incarnation. But they do not exhaust the exceeding riches of God's grace in salvation nor complete His purpose in sending His only begotten Son into the world.

Sin despoiled both the human race and the natural universe. Sin produced chaos in the place of cosmos. Both heaven and earth suffered through sin.

Christ the Son is the Alpha and He is the Omega. He is the goal of all things in God's universe as He is the beginning. Christ Jesus is the Firstborn of all creation; by Him all things consist and in Him shall all things be gathered together. God's eternal purpose in Christ His Son will be consummated in the reconciliation of all things in heaven and in earth unto Himself.

> Colossians 1:20, "And, having made peace through the blood of his cross,

by him to reconcile all things unto himself; by him, I say, whether they be things in earth, or things in heaven."

Ephesians 1:10, "That in the dispensation of the fulness of times *he might gather together in one all things in Christ,* both which are in heaven, and which are on earth; *even in him.*"

Incarnation then is the first span in the bridge of salvation, the first great movement toward the restoration of man to God and toward the reconciliation of all things in God's universe. It is no wonder the angels of heaven sang on that first Christmas morning. The birth of the Lord Jesus was the beginning of the fulfillment of the prophecy-promise of Genesis 3:15. It was the first step in the overthrow of God's archenemy; the first victory in the agelong conflict; the beginning of the end of sin. It was to the angels as to us, "the central point from which all events were to be hereafter measured. To heaven as to earth it was to be the reckoning point of all time, and more, for B.C. and A.D. are to be the extensions of eternity" (A. Patterson, *The Greater Life and Work of Christ,* p. 136). (See Diagram 5.)

10

Four Spans in the Bridge of Salvation—
Crucifixion

INCARNATION brought God to man but it could not bring man to God. The first span in the bridge of salvation demands a second.

In the incarnation God had not yet dealt with the sin question. He could go no further through the revelation of His own sinless, perfect life than to show men what they ought to be. Sin, the insuperable barrier between God and man, remained, and Satan, the archenemy of God, the tempter and deceiver of men, still held the human race in his control. Men did not even know how sinful they were; their darkened minds had no conception of God's real attitude toward sin, nor did they apprehend the awful certainty of its inexorable consequences.

The life and teaching of Christ Jesus had stirred the heart of a very few to desire something better and to seek Him as the Giver but the majority of those who saw and heard Him were indifferent to Him, and not a few even hated Him. Had He only lived His pure, holy life and died a natural death He would have been enshrined in the memory of but few of the choice, rare souls who appreciated His worth.

That something more than the life even of the holy Lord Jesus was needed to save men's souls is patent, something that would deal adequately with sin and all its consequences, something with power in it to defeat and to destroy the devil, something with the germinating seed of a holy, heavenly life. The world is full of leaders and reformers. Its fundamental need is a God-sent Saviour, One who can deal with sin in such a way as to bring satisfaction to God and salvation to man.

DEATH THE GOAL OF INCARNATION

The incarnation was not an end but a means to an end. In itself it had no redemptive value but it paved the way for His death which alone has redemptive value. It could never make an end of sin but it did give to the world a Saviour. Our Lord Himself and every New Testament writer set forth the death of Christ as the goal of the incarnation. He was born not merely a Man but a Saviour. He came not alone to live but to save, and to save He must die.

> Matthew 1:21, "And she shall bring forth a son, and thou shalt call his name JESUS: *for he shall save his people from their sins.*"
>
> Luke 2:11, "*For unto you is born* this day in the city of David *a Saviour, which is Christ the Lord.*"

The eternal Son became the incarnate Son that He might lay down His life as the crucified Son. He became the Son of Man that He might die for the race of men.

> Matthew 20:28, "Even as *the Son of man came* not to be ministered unto, but to minister, and *to give his life a ransom for many.*"

He took a body in incarnation that He might lay it down in crucifixion. He entered into a body supernaturally prepared for Him, which no sin had tainted and upon which death had no claim that He might offer it as a voluntary sacrifice unto God, that through death He might destroy him that had the power of death, that is the devil. "The body was prepared not so much for the birth as for the bruising" (Genesis 3:15).

> Hebrews 10:5, "Wherefore when he cometh into the world, he saith, Sacrifice and offering thou wouldest not, *but a body hast thou prepared me.*"
>
> Hebrews 10:10, "By the which will *we are sanctified through the offering of the body of Jesus Christ once for all.*"
>
> Hebrews 2:14, "Forasmuch then as the children are partakers of flesh and blood, *he also himself likewise took part of the same; that through death he might destroy him that had the power of death, that is, the devil.*"

Christ Jesus not only came into the world to die but He knew that He came for that purpose. From the very beginning of His public ministry the Son of Man had a brooding anticipation of "an hour" that was to come— an hour which in some eventful way would be the culmination of His ministry. "The sense of something tragic in His destiny was present in the mind of Jesus."

Let us trace His anticipation of this hour through John's gospel.
> John 2:4, "Jesus saith unto her, Woman, what have I to do with thee? *mine hour is not yet come.*"

This word was spoken on a joyous occasion at the beginning of His public ministry when He was popular, when the people were receiving and following Him.

John 7:6, "*My time is not yet come:* but your time is alway ready."

A large multitude of those who had been fed with the loaves and fishes had followed Him as He went from Capernaum across the sea. He used the occasion to give the wonderful discourse recorded in John 6 where He claims to be the Bread of Life sent by the Father to give His life for the life of the world. Life out of death was possible for all but only actual in the life of the one who "ate his flesh and drank his blood." The message of the cross was foreshadowed in these words. It was a hard saying even for His own disciples and many of them went back and walked no more with Him. The claim of Messiahship and Saviourhood angered the Jews beyond measure and instilled such bitter hatred into their hearts that they sought to kill Him. But Jesus was unperturbed, simply saying, "My time is *not yet come.*" He knew full well the time would come when their hate would expend itself on Him in cruel malignity.

Three times in John 7 this expression is used. The Jews' Feast of Tabernacles was at hand and the Lord Jesus was conscious of the plot on the part of the Jews to kill Him, so He says to the disciples,

> John 7:8, "Go ye up to the feast: I go not up yet unto this feast; *for my time is not yet full come.*"

How significant are those words "full come." The shadow of the cross had already fallen over His life. From that time on He would walk in its ever deepening darkness.

At this feast the Lord Jesus was brought into open conflict with the Jews over the question of the authoritative origin of His doctrine. Again He made claims for Himself which so incensed them that we read,

> John 7:30, "Then they sought to take him: but no man laid hands on him, *because his hour was not yet come.*"

The same thing was repeated as the Lord Jesus taught in the Temple (John 8:20). Jesus grew in popularity with the people. He makes even more daring claims to Deity and Messiahship and proved the truth of His words by the wonder of His works. The man born blind is given sight. Lazarus is raised from the dead. The religious leaders of the day are compelled to acknowledge the uniqueness of His power and they fear its influence upon the people. They frankly confess that "the world is gone after him" and openly declare that the thing must be stopped immediately. The hour draws nearer.

Just at this time when the Jews are most fiercely censuring and opposing Him a very significant thing happens. A deputation of Greeks (Gentiles) came to worship Him. Everything converges to show Christ that "the hour" He has so long anticipated is now near at hand. So when Andrew and Philip bring the message of the Greeks to Him, with majestic calmness and kingly control He replies, "The hour *is* come."

Up to this time He has not explained what He means by the often repeated words "my hour." Several times He has foretold His death and resurrection but the disciples did not grasp His meaning. On this occasion, however, He speaks more explicitly.

> John 12:23-24, "And Jesus answered them, saying, *The hour is come, that the Son of man should be glorified.*
>
> Verily, verily, I say unto you, *Except a corn of wheat fall into the ground and die*, it abideth alone: *but if it die*, it bringeth forth much fruit."

> John 12:27, 31-33, "Now is my soul troubled; and what shall I say? Father, *save me from this hour:* but *for this cause came I unto this hour.*
>
> Now is the judgment of this world: now shall the prince of this world be cast out.
>
> And I, *if I be lifted up from the earth*, will draw all men unto me. This he said, *signifying what death he should die.*"

The interval now was very short. Not a single event of that last week takes the Lord Jesus by surprise. He knows that His hour has come. In His last conversation and prayer with His disciples He anticipates His exodus from this world and His return to His Father in heaven.

> John 16:28, "I came forth from the Father, and am come into the world: *again, I leave the world, and go to the Father.*"

> John 17:1, "These words spake Jesus, and lifted up his eyes to heaven, and said, Father, *the hour is come;* glorify thy Son, that thy Son also may glorify thee."

When the Lord had spoken these words He went forth with His disciples unto a place called Gethsemane. There His soul began to be very sorrowful and oppressed, so much so that He left the companionship of the disciples and went alone with His Father to pray. Falling upon His face He cried,

> Matthew 26:39, "O my Father, if it be possible, *let this cup pass* from me: nevertheless not as I will, but as thou wilt."

Returning unto His disciples and finding them asleep, He, still overborne with sorrow, went away a second time and prayed,

> Matthew 26:42, "O my Father, *if this cup may not pass away from me, except I drink it*, thy will be done."

Again He came to the disciples and found them sleeping and again He left them to pray. Then He returned to them for the last time and said,

Matthew 26:45, "Sleep on now, and take your rest: behold, the hour *is at hand,* and the Son of man is betrayed into the hands of sinners."

Never in the history of man was such anguish of spirit and agony of soul endured as that of the Son of Man as He went to Calvary by way of the Garden of Gethsemane. Heaven mercifully veiled the Sufferer from the gaze of men and left us only the thrice repeated pleadings of His prayer to indicate the nature and the depth of the suffering.

Two utterances in His prayer take us to the very heart of His anguish. "Let this cup pass from me" and, "Behold the hour is at hand." Surely the two bear some intimate relationship to each other. But what is the dreaded "cup" that must be drunk? What is the inevitable "hour" so long anticipated and now at hand? Did He not interpret the meaning of this often used expression when He said "The Son of Man is betrayed into the hands of sinners"? From this and the events that follow in quick succession "the hour" could be none other than the hour of His death.

But why should He dread that or shrink from its approach? But an hour or two before He had said "Now I go my way to him that sent me." Would not death be to Him an hour of glorious release from a life environed by sin, suffering and sorrow? Would it not be the hour of reinvestment with all His kingly majesty and glory? Above all would it not be a return to the blessedness of immediate, intimate fellowship with His Father? Had He died a death such as other men die then it would indeed have been just such a glorious release. Had death for Him been merely the culminating event in a life of unsullied perfection then it would have been such a gracious coronation. Some adequate explanation must be found for His dread of the approach of that "hour" that meant the drinking of a bitter "cup."

But another question must surely press in upon one who has beheld the Son as He is mirrored in the pages of the four gospels and who has entered into a study of His matchless, pure life with any degree of spiritual appreciation and apprehension. The question is "Why need Jesus Christ die?" Scripture is very clear in its statement of what death is and who dies.

Romans 6:23, "For *the wages of sin is death.*"

Romans 5:12, "Wherefore, as by one man sin entered into the world, and *death by sin; and so death passed upon all men.*

Ezekiel 18:20, *"The soul that sinneth, it shall die."*

Death is the consequence of sin: it is the sinner who dies. And Jesus Christ died! The irresistible logic of these facts places before one two alternatives. Either Jesus was a sinner as all other men are and His death like theirs was the wages of His own sin, or else He died a death different from the death of all other men and for a reason entirely outside of His own life.

Was Jesus Christ a sinner? Did death come to Him as the penalty of His own sin? Even His bitterest enemies in the time in which He lived and in all succeeding ages have never accused Him of sin. He said once to a group who were opposing and denying Him, "Which of you convinceth me of sin?" But not one word of accusation did they bring against Him. Even Pilate said he could find no fault in Him. God testified to the absolute sinlessness and holiness of His life even before His birth in saying through the angel to Mary, "that *holy thing* which shall be born of thee shall be called the Son of God." After Jesus had lived in a world where He was continuously environed by sin and defilement God again testified through those who knew His character and conduct under all circumstances that He "*did* no sin" (1 Peter 2:22); "*In* him is no sin" (1 John 3:5); He "*knew* no sin" (2 Corinthians 5:21). In His character, conversation and conduct He was the holy One of God "without blemish and without spot." If then death is the wages of sin, it had no claim upon Jesus Christ.

Why then did Jesus Christ die? How foolish and futile to look anywhere else for an answer to such a question but to God's divine revelation. There an absolutely sufficient and altogether satisfying answer is given.

> 1 Corinthians 15:3, "For I delivered unto you first of all that which I also received, how that *Christ died for our sins* according to the scriptures."

> Isaiah 53:6, "All we like sheep have gone astray; we have turned every one to his own way; and *the Lord hath laid on him the iniquity of us all.*"

> Isaiah 53:4-5, "Surely *he hath borne our griefs,* and *carried our sorrows:* yet we did esteem him stricken, smitten of God, and afflicted. But *he was wounded for our transgressions, he was bruised for our iniquities: the chastisement of our peace was upon him; and with his stripes we are healed.*"

> 1 Peter 2:24, "*Who his own self bare our sins* in his own body on the tree, that *we,* being dead to sins, should live unto righteousness: by whose stripes ye were healed."

In every one of these passages "death" and "sin" are shown to have an inextricable relationship to each other but it is invariably the death of Christ and the sin of men.

Words could not make it clear that Jesus Christ died not because of anything in Himself but because of something in us; that it was not the wages of His sin but of ours that He paid on the cross. It was *our* sin He put away; *our* sins that He bore; *our* iniquities which were laid upon Him. Death had no claim on Him; then the death He died was for the sake of others and to accomplish something for them which they were unable to accomplish for themselves. The death of Christ was obviously for the purpose of taking up the sin question and dealing with it in such a way as to bring salvation to man.

But would it also deal with it in such a way as to bring satisfaction to God? God has an unalterable, irrevocable attitude toward sin which is most clearly revealed in His judgment upon it. "The wages of sin is death." Death is the expression of God's implacable condemnation of sin. "Death is the man's liability in relation to sin." Did the death of Christ deal with this divine judgment upon sin in a way that was satisfactory to God? God says it did.

> 2 Corinthians 5:14-15, R. V., "For the love of Christ constraineth us; because we thus judge, that *one died for all, therefore all died;*
> And *he died for all,* that they that live should no longer live unto themselves, but unto him *who for their sakes died and rose again.*"

The sinner's twofold relationship to God, the divine Judge and God, the gracious Saviour, may be stated as follows,

"The wages of sin is death,"
"All have sinned,"
"So death passed upon all men."
BUT
"One died for all,"
"Therefore all died."

Death is the racial doom. In Adam all die because in Adam all sinned. Death is God's judgment upon sin and it rests equally upon all men. From the execution of this divine judgment there is no escape because it is the decree of a holy God and is therefore unalterable. Sin and death are inextricably interwoven: the sinner must die.

But the holy God is also a loving God. While He cannot change His attitude toward sin and His judgment upon it without denying His own nature yet His love with perfect consistency can make some escape for the sinner, providing whatever He does maintains unity in His own divine being. This necessitates meeting in full the requirement of His holy Law.

What, then, would that requirement be? That an adequate Substitute able to meet the full penalty of the Law should voluntarily offer to take the sinner's place and die the sinner's death.

But where could such an adequate substitute be found? Only "a lamb without spot and blemish" could be accepted as an offering for sin. Only an absolutely sinless one could be the sinner's Substitute. It would require one who himself had fulfilled every demand of God's holy Law to pay the sinner's penalty for a broken Law. There was but one who had ever lived such a life on earth and He was the incarnate Son of God.

Would He voluntarily offer Himself as the sinner's Substitute and thereby assume all responsibility for the removal of the penalty, the power and the presence of sin in man, knowing as He did that the penalty of sin was death, that the power of sin meant anguish of suffering consummating in crucifixion, and that the presence of sin involved even separation from God? Would He who never knew sin willingly be made sin on the sinner's behalf knowing full well that all the wrath of a holy God against sin would be spent on Him? (A very helpful treatment of this to which I am indebted is found in Armour, *Atonement and Law*).

Yes, He would do it. For the very purpose of becoming the sinner's Substitute the eternal Son had become the incarnate Son. But have we not discovered in this truth the secret of His dread of that "hour," His shrinking from the "cup"? It was not death He dreaded but the death of the cross which was "the wages of sin." What else could the thrice repeated pleading to the Father to remove "the cup" mean but that, in the death He was about to die as the sinner's Substitute, all the sin of the whole race of sinners with all its stain and stench would be upon Him? It is no wonder that the soul of the sinless Son of God cried out in an agony of suffering at the thought!

But the weight and wickedness of the world's sin was not all the "cup." Sin separates from God. God cannot stay in the presence of sin even when that sin is upon His own beloved Son. The Son of Man in the garden faces this awful consequence of Saviourhood. Could He assume *this* consequence of sin for the sinner's sake? Could He, who through all eternity in glory had rested in the intimate fellowship of the Father's bosom and who in His life on earth had enjoyed the vivid consciousness of His Father's abiding presence, consent to the inevitable even though momentary separation from His Father which the presence of the world's sin on Him would cause? Death is separation from God and separation from God is hell (2 Thessalonians 1:7-9).

This, then, is "the cup" He could not drink were there any other possible way for the Father's will in man's salvation to be accomplished. This is "the cup" that caused the agony of soul in Gethsemane—an agony so terrible that His sweat was as it were great drops of blood falling to the ground; an agony so awful it took Him back three times to the Father to cry out for release; an agony so intense that a heaven-sent angel appeared to strengthen Him. This is "the cup" that caused the intolerable anguish of spirit, which wrung from the Sufferer upon Calvary that heartbreaking cry, "My God, my God, why hast thou forsaken me?" Could He drink *that* "cup"? Yes, even that if it were the Father's will and there were no other way in which sin could be dealt with to God's satisfaction and man's salvation. He who had been obedient to the will of His Father every moment of His earthly life would be "obedient unto death, even the death of the cross."

There evidently was no other way for "while he yet spake, lo, Judas, one of the twelve, came, and with him a great multitude with sword and staves." In quick succession follow the betrayal, arrest and trial of the Lord Jesus and then—the crucifixion of the Lord of glory.

The "hour" *had come.* The event foretold and foreshadowed for centuries had taken place; "the most stupendous event in the history of man, the only event in the history of God." The noon hour not only of time but of eternity had come; indeed it was the pivotal hour in the life both of heaven and of earth. "The Son of God has died by the hands of men. This astounding fact is the moral center of all things. A bygone eternity knew no other future; an eternity to come shall know no other past. That death was this world's crisis" (Sir Robert Anderson, *The Gospel and Its Ministry,* p. 12).

The death of Jesus Christ is the pivotal fact in Christianity. It is its very heartbeat; its life's blood. Without it Christianity would not be. His worth lay not in the life He lived but in the death He died. His death was not so much the culmination of the victorious, obedient, holy life as its coronation. His incarnation was but paving the way for death; His death was the goal of incarnation.

It is not merely the fact that Christ died that is vital but that He died *the death of the cross.* The prophecy of Genesis 3:15 foretold a bruising and it was in the bruising of the heel of the woman's seed that the promise of the sinner's salvation was to be found. The Old Testament sacrifices made for the sake of sins year by year required the blood of goats and calves. These sacrifices and this blood-shedding were the foreshadowing of the one perfect sacrifice of the Son of God as He poured out His life's blood on Calvary for the salvation of sinners. While the prophets of old did tell us something of the circumstances that would attend the birth of Jesus Christ yet the burden of their message was of One who would be "wounded," "bruised," "scourged," "oppressed," "afflicted." By the mouth of all the prophets God foretold that Christ should suffer. Over and over again the Lord Jesus told the disciples that He "must go unto Jerusalem, and suffer many things of the elders and the chief priests and scribes, and be killed, and be raised again." On the way to Emmaus as He walked and talked with the two disciples who were recounting to Him the tragedy of His crucifixion He said unto them,

> Luke 24:26, "Ought not Christ *to have suffered these things,* and to enter into his glory?"

The theme of the entire Bible is *the Lamb slain* from the foundation of the world. "Cut the Bible anywhere and it bleeds; it is red with redemption truth." A suffering, crucified Christ was the Christ preached by the apostles and to them His sufferings were a vital factor in the sinner's salvation because of their expiatory nature. Paul testifying before King Agrippa preached a suffering Christ.

Acts 26:22-23, "Having therefore obtained help of God, I continue unto this day, witnessing both to small and great, saying none other things than those which the prophets and Moses did say should come:
That Christ should suffer, and that he should be the first that should rise from the dead."

Peter told us that it was through the victorious atoning sufferings of Christ that men were brought back to God.

1 Peter 3:18, *"For Christ also hath once suffered for sins, the just for the unjust*, that he might bring us to God, *being put to death in the flesh*, but quickened by the Spirit."

John taught that there was no cleansing power except in the blood of Christ shed on Calvary.

1 John 1:7, *"The blood of Jesus Christ his Son cleanseth us from all sin."*

Respectable sinners will flock to the church today to hear ministers preach on the life of Jesus; many are even not averse to listening to an occasional sermon of the death of Christ, providing that death is preached only as the greatest example of sacrificial love, or as the culminating event in a life of obedience, or as an act of martyrdom in a good cause. But in this age there is a widespread refusal on the part of the man in the pew, and on the part of the man in the pulpit a conspicuous rejection of the biblical, evangelical teaching regarding the death *of the cross.* The reason for this will grow more apparent as we proceed with our studies.

THE CROSS OF CHRIST—THE GREAT DIVIDE

The cross of Christ makes a clean-cut cleavage between the two spheres, the sphere of death, darkness and disorder, and the sphere of life, light and liberty, and it challenges sinners to decide in which they purpose to live. The cross of Christ is the battlefield on which the conflict between Satan and God over the sovereignty of human lives is being waged and it compels men to take sides either for or against God. The cross of Christ marks the boundary line between the kingdom of Satan and the Kingdom of God and it calls subjects in the one to come out and to become subjects in the other. The cross of Christ finds men living on the plane of the natural and it opens a way for them to live on the plane of the spiritual and then appeals to them to enter the open door. The cross of Christ is the great divide: it separates men into two classes, the unsaved and the saved.

> 1 Corinthians 1:18, "For the preaching of the cross is to them that perish foolishness; *but unto us which are saved* it is the power of God."

THE CROSS OF CHRIST—A DOUBLE EXPOSURE

The cross of Christ is the place of exposure. There as nowhere else is revealed the hatred of man for God and the love of God for man. Sin is seen at its worst and love is seen at its best in the cross. Man's sin and God's love both reach a climax on Calvary. There the hideousness of the one and the glory of the other are brought out into the sharpest relief.

> Acts 2:23, "*Him,* being delivered by the determinate counsel and fore-knowledge of God, *ye have taken, and by wicked hands have crucified and slain.*"

The desperate, despicable wickedness of the human heart is uncovered at Calvary. All the rebellion, self-will and enmity of the natural man found vent in this one act. In the crucifixion of the Holy One sin came out into the open and disclosed its inwardness.

"Him—ye have taken and by wicked hands have crucified and slain." *Sin* nailed the *Saviour* to a cross and by doing so exposed to the world its ugly hideousness. Sinners stained their hands with the blood of their Saviour and thereby revealed the length and breadth, the height and depth of the infamy of sin.

However, the sin of man could not outstrip the love of God. Nor could sin defeat God by taking Him unawares. Before that hydra-headed monster had raised its head in rebellion against God He had accomplished its defeat. "Him, being delivered by the determinate counsel and foreknowledge of God." In the eternal counsels of the Godhead the cross of Christ was set up *in love* before man was made or the world created. In the atoning death of the well-beloved Son on the cross of Calvary, God was fully prepared to assume responsibility for sin and all its consequences. God, the Father, spelled out in capital letters on the cross His unquenchable love for sinners.

The cross of Christ reveals not only the love of the Father but the love of the Son as well. In the lament over Jerusalem, in the parable of the father's love for the prodigal, in the tender look at the denying Peter, and in the pathetic question to Judas the betrayer, Jesus Christ showed His sorrow for sin and the outreaching of His loving heart to the sinner. But only in the laying down of His sinless life in death as the sinner's Substitute do we see the perfect outshining of His infinite, limitless love. With the most perfect apprehension of what the sin of man was on the one hand, and of what the mind of God toward sin was on the other and of sin's due from God, there went up from the depths of Christ's sinless humanity a perfect amen to the righteous judgment of God against sin, and a willingness to bear that judgment.

The cross of Christ is the heart of God broken by sin. It tells you and me that God who must judge and punish sin will save and forgive the sinner. It discovers to us unfathomable depths of God's love.

> Romans 5:8, "But *God commendeth his love toward us,* in that, while we were yet sinners, Christ died for us."

> John 3:16, "*For God so loved the world,* that he gave his only begotten Son."

> Galatians 1:3-4, "Our Lord Jesus Christ, *who gave himself for our sins,* that he might deliver us from this present evil world, according to the will of God and our Father."

THE CROSS OF CHRIST—THE PLACE OF VICTORY

God has but one problem in His universe—it is sin. All other problems of whatever nature emanate from this one. The sweat of grinding toil, the suffering of broken hearts, the sorrow of the world's crushing maladjustments, all have their beginning in sin. God has but one enemy in the universe—it is Satan. All other enmities, whether among angels or men, have their ultimate source in him. To regain His rightful sovereignty over the world and in the human race God had a double victory to win. This twofold victory was won through the Saviourhood of Jesus Christ. Salvation from sin and all its consequences, deliverance from Satan and his allies, were gained for the sinner at the cross.

The Old Testament classic which reveals Jesus Christ as the Sin-bearer is Isaiah 53.

> Isaiah 53:4, 6, 10-12, "Surely *he hath borne our griefs,* and *carried our sorrows.*
> And *the Lord hath laid on him the iniquity of us all.*
> When thou shalt make *his soul an offering for sin.*
> For he shall *bear their iniquities.*
> *He bare the sin of many.*"

The New Testament is full of the same truth.

> John 1:29, "The next day John seeth Jesus coming unto him, and saith, Behold, *the Lamb of God, which taketh away the sin of the world.*"

> Hebrews 9:28, "*So Christ was once offered to bear the sin of many;* and unto them which look for him shall he appear the second time without sin unto salvation."

Jesus Christ faced the problem which sin had created and solved it by taking upon Himself the whole responsibility for it. When He entered into human life and as the Son of Man became the connecting link between God and the ruined race, He pledged Himself to become responsible for sin and its effects.

Sin had brought upon man four terrible consequences for which Christ as Sin-bearer assumed responsibility. The first is guilt. The whole world is guilty before God (Romans 3:19). The whole of man is defiled and depraved. That this guilt might be removed God made Christ sin and then treated Him as sin.

> 2 Corinthians 5:21, R. V., *"Him who knew no sin he made to be sin on our behalf;* that we might become the righteousness of God in him."

The second is death. "The wages of sin is death." The sentence of death rested upon the whole human race. As the last Adam, Jesus Christ assumed all responsibility for the first Adam's sin and its consequences. Therefore He executed the death sentence upon sinners by Himself dying.

> Romans 5:6, "For when we were yet without strength, in due time *Christ died for the ungodly."*

The third consequence of sin is the curse. Sin is lawlessness and the penalty for broken law is the curse. Jesus Christ acknowledged the justice in God's judgment upon sin and voluntarily offered to assume even this responsibility on the sinner's behalf.

> Galatians 3:13, *"Christ hath redeemed us from the curse of the law, being made a curse for us:* for it is written, Cursed is every one that hangeth on a tree."

The fourth consequence of sin is the wrath of God. God hates sin. God's holiness demanded that He take some action against it. So God was compelled to decree that sin would bar sinners from His presence through time and eternity. Here again Jesus Christ assumed responsibility for the presence of sin in men and on the cross of Calvary bore the full force of God's wrath against it even to the point of conscious separation from His Father's presence.

> Romans 5:9, "Much more then, being now justified by his blood, *we shall be saved from wrath through him."*

In becoming the Sin-bearer Jesus Christ fully met and solved the problem of sin. "In His death everything was made His that sin had made ours . . . everything in sin except it sinfulness" (James Denney, *The Death of Christ*).

The cross of Christ is God's starting point of victory over Satan and all his allies. God is the One who has been hurt most by sin. "Satan was putting the knife into God's heart through Adam's hand." So any effectual dealing with sin must go back to its first cause and any permanent victory for God must be a crushing defeat for Satan.

The first curse pronounced after the Fall was upon the serpent. The serpent's curse and the Saviour's cross are inextricably interwoven. The prophecy containing the curse foretells a double bruising. "It shall bruise thy head, and thou shalt bruise his heel."

Men and women are being taught that the record of the Fall in Genesis 3 is just a myth and that no scholarly person believes it today. This is indeed the devil's lie and he has a very good reason for telling it. By the death of Christ his head was bruised, his doom was sealed. The cross of Christ robbed that satanic usurper of every vestige of rightful claim to the world and of all dominion over any man or woman who fully trusts in the atoning blood of the Saviour and who yields to the Lordship of Jesus. Christ's cry of victory from Calvary's cross "It is finished" was Satan's death knell. The victory over the devil commenced in the wilderness, continued in Gethsemane, culminated on Calvary. The hour of Christ's death was the hour of Satan's defeat.

> John 12:31, "*Now* is the judgment of this world: *now shall the prince of this world be cast out.*"

The death of the cross deprived him of his power and rendered him inoperative.

> Hebrews 2:14, R. V., "Since then the children are sharers in flesh and blood, he also himself in like manner partook of the same; *that through death he might bring to nought him that had the power of death, that is, the devil.*"

The death of Jesus Christ meant an open and decisive victory for God over all the principalities and powers in rebellion against Him. It severs the believer from the powers of darkness.

> Colossians 2:14-15, "*Blotting out the handwriting of ordinances that was against us,* which was contrary to us, and took it out of the way, nailing it to his cross;
> And *having spoiled principalities and powers, he made a shew of them openly, triumphing over them in it.*"

The devil has two active, aggressive allies in his diabolical work of keeping sinners living in self-will and rebellion toward God. They are the "world" and the "flesh." For the defeat of both of these God has made ample provision in the cross of Christ.

> Galatians 6:14, "But God forbid that I should glory, save *in the cross of our*

Lord Jesus Christ, by whom the world is crucified unto me, and I *unto the world."*

Galatians 5:24, "And they that are Christ's have *crucified the flesh* with the affections and lusts."

In the cross of Christ the sinner who truly desires it may find complete deliverance from the evil one and all his entanglements. Satan's reign over him may end there if he seeks release through the cross.

The Cross of Christ—A Divinely Provided Meeting Place

Sin made every man unrighteous in God's sight, (Romans 3:10-12) and by so doing it created an impassable chasm between a righteous God and an unrighteous sinner. It did more than that, it totally disqualified man for doing anything to bridge this chasm thus placing upon God the whole responsibility of making a way of access into His presence and of providing a meeting place between Himself and the sinner.

But how could a righteous God be just and the justifier of sinners (Romans 3:26)? How could God maintain His holiness in His dealing with sin and at the same time manifest His graciousness in mercy toward the sinner? How could God provide such a meeting place and not deny Himself through compromise?

Before God was a Law which was holy and right. It was the expression of His own character; the essence of His own nature. To ignore or condone man's rebellion and disobedience as evidenced in that Law broken would be to deny Himself. God could not do that; He must be true to Himself so He must treat sin as sin and deal with it as such. It must be condemned and its merited punishment meted out. "Even God cannot change the character of righteousness by altering, or lessening to the slightest degree, its holy demands. What is done for the satisfaction of His love in saving any one whom His righteousness condemns must be done in full view of all that His righteousness could ever require" (L. S. Chafer, *Salvation,* p. 27).

Before God was not only a broken Law but a broken relationship, a broken bond of love which had united Him to the human race. Before Him, too, was the desperate need of those whom He loved with an everlasting love, the undone condition of those who were precious in His sight. Before Him was His own broken heart made desolate by the prodigal's departure into the far country.

Viewing the sinner in his relationship to God his fundamental need is a way of access and acceptance with God despite his guilt. Viewing God in His relationship to the sinner His fundamental necessity is a way of granting favor and fellowship to the sinner despite His holiness. A meeting place between a righteous God and an unrighteous sinner is the demand made upon the righteousness of God. But it is equal to even this necessity for in His death upon Calvary's cross Jesus Christ became the propitiation for the sins of the world.

> 1 John 2:2, R. V., "And *he is the propitiation for our sins;* and not for ours only, *but also for the whole world."*

> Romans 3:25-26, R. V., "Whom God set forth to be a propitiation, through faith, in his blood, to show his righteousness because of the passing over of the sins done aforetime, in the forbearance of God; for the showing, I say, of his righteousness at this present season: *that he might himself be just,* and *the justifier of him that hath faith in Jesus."*

To the spiritually minded Christian who has a realization of the awful chasm sin had made between him and his God the truth that centers on the word "propitiation" is inexpressibly precious. But to the natural man living still in pride, rebellion and self-satisfaction, it is insufferably offensive.

"Propitiation" means a mercy seat or covering, a divinely provided meeting place. In Old Testament times on the Day of Atonement the great high priest took the blood of the sacrificial lamb into the Holy of Holies and with it sprinkled the Mercy Seat. Within the ark under the cover of the blood was the broken Law. The blood-sprinkled Mercy Seat provided a meeting place between God and the sinner where the guilty one could come to God without remembrance of his past offenses and without fear of judgment and where the Holy One could receive the sinner without compromise and yet without condemnation. "A holy God could righteously meet a sinful man and a sinful man could fearlessly meet a holy God."

God set forth His well-beloved Son to be such a propitiation for all the guilty sinners in all the world. Through the shedding of the precious blood of the Lamb of God on the cross of Calvary such a covering for sin and for broken Law was provided. In His death Jesus Christ honors God's holy Law by bearing in full the punishment meted out to the sinner for breaking it. Thus in the crucified Lord the sinner has found a meeting place with God and a way of access into His favor and fellowship.

THE CROSS OF CHRIST—A DIVINELY PREPARED TURNING POINT

A double barrier separates God and the sinner. Sin has caused man to be offended toward God as truly as it has caused God to be offended toward man. The cross of Christ shall have failed to deal adequately with sin if it only removes the cause of offense in its Godward aspect and does not equally remove it in its manward aspect.

And this is exactly what the cross of Christ does. "We love him because he first loved us" (1 John 4:19). "By grace are ye saved through faith." The grace of God built the bridge of salvation before ever a single sinner made a start toward crossing it. Grace took God into the garden in the cool of the day to seek the first two sinners and to offer them the gracious promise of salvation through a Saviour even before He dealt righteously with their sin in pronouncing upon them the judgment of the curse. Even in the prophecy-promise given in Eden, God was in Christ reconciling the world unto Himself. God took the initiative in effecting reconciliation by giving His Son to die.

> Romans 5:10, "For if, when we were enemies, *we were reconciled to God by the death of his Son*, much more, being reconciled, we shall be saved by his life."

> Colossians 1:21-22, "And you, that were sometime alienated and enemies in your mind by wicked works, *yet now hath he reconciled In the body of his flesh through death*, to present you holy and unblameable and unreprovable in his sight."

> 2 Corinthians 5:18, "And all things are of God, *who hath reconciled us to himself by Jesus Christ.*"

The Son of God endured the suffering and the shame of the cross that thereby He might tell a world of sinners who have turned their backs on God that God loves them with an everlasting love. When the sinner sees the Saviour suffering, the just for the unjust, when he sees Christ crucified by *his* sin, dying *his* death, enduring *his* punishment, then his heart is melted, his rebellion is removed, his whole attitude toward God is changed from enmity to love, from estrangement to fellowship, from indifference to devotion, from fear to faith, from shame to peace.

In Christ crucified, God has provided such propitiation and reconciliation as has made possible the removal of the barrier of separation between God and man, and has opened a merciful yet righteous way of access and acceptance; thus giving to every man who will avail himself of God's grace the opportunity for full restoration to God's favor and fellowship.

THE CROSS OF CHRIST—THE END OF THE OLD CREATION AND THE BEGINNING OF THE NEW

Through propitiation and reconciliation, accomplished in the death of Christ, adequate provision has been made for a change of relationship between the sinner and God which effects a radical change in the sinner's position before God. But is there provision for a change in his condition also? The natural man is a slave, "sold under sin" (Romans 7:14).

Where sin abounded grace did much more abound. God's boundless grace was undaunted by the sinner's helpless, hopeless condition. God's right to proprietorship through creation still remained but it had been lost to Him through man's surrender of himself to the sovereignty of another. But God would Himself go down to the slave market of sin and buy back that which was His own. He would then take the sinner out of the sphere of Satan, out of the slave market of sin, and set him free in the glorious liberty of a new life in Christ.

Such redemption demanded a ransom. It required a life for a life. "The life is in the blood." To redeem the race from the bondage of sin involved the paying of a price which was nothing less than the precious blood of the spotless Lamb of God. To buy back His own for a possession God paid the costly price of His own blood.

> Acts 20:28, "Take heed therefore unto yourselves, and to all the flock, over the which the Holy Ghost hath made you overseers, to feed the church of God, *which he hath purchased with his own blood.*"

> 1 Peter 1:18-19, "Forasmuch as ye know that ye were not redeemed with corruptible things, as silver and gold, from your vain conversation received by tradition from your fathers; *but with the precious blood of Christ,* as of a lamb without blemish and without spot."

> Revelation 5:9, "And they sung a new song, saying, Thou art worthy to take the book, and to open the seals thereof: for thou wast slain, and *hast redeemed us to God by thy blood* out of every kindred, and tongue, and people, and nation."

But God did not go into the slave market of sin only to buy the captive sinner but also to bring him out from that old sphere of bondage and set him free in a new sphere of liberty. Not alone would He lead him out of Egypt but He would bring him into Canaan. Christ Jesus would become not only the sinner's Saviour but He would be the believer's Lord and Life. In the cross of Christ, God rejected the old order of fallen, sinful humanity "sold under sin" through the first Adam's disobedience that He might raise up a new order of holy, heavenly beings redeemed from sin through the last Adam's obedience.

The death of Christ upon the cross not only redeems but it re-creates; it not only provides complete emancipation from the old life but abundant entrance into the new.

> Exodus 13:3, "And Moses said unto the people, Remember this day, *in which ye came out of Egypt, out of the house of bondage;* for by strength of hand *the Lord brought you out from this place.*"

> Exodus 13:11, "And it shall be *when the Lord shall bring thee into the land of the Canaanites,* as he sware unto thee and to thy fathers, and shall give it thee."

Titus 2:14, "Who gave himself for us, *that he might redeem us from all iniquity,* and *purify unto himself* a peculiar people, zealous of good works."

THE CROSS OF CHRIST—THE PLACE OF DECISION THAT DETERMINES DESTINY

"The Cross of Christ has measured out the moral distance between God and man and has left them as far asunder as the throne of heaven and the gates of hell" (Sir Robert Anderson, *The Gospel and Its Ministry,* p. 25). Scripture bears ample testimony to the solemn truthfulness of these words.

But praise God it is equally true that the cross of Christ has measured out the length and breadth and height and depth of the love of God in the gift of a Redeemer who closed the gates of hell and opened the gates of heaven for all who will believe.

As sin through Adam had been universal, so salvation through Christ must be made potential to all. Where sin abounded grace did much more abound and opened a way back to God for every sinner. The bridge of salvation provided a way out of the old sphere into the new for all who will acknowledge themselves sinners needing a Saviour.

Titus 2:11, "For the grace of God that bringeth salvation *hath appeared to all men.*"

1 Timothy 2:5-6, "One mediator between God and men, the man Christ Jesus; *who gave himself a ransom for all.*"

Isaiah 53:6, "*All we* like sheep have gone astray; we have turned *every one* to his own way; and the LORD hath laid on him the iniquity of *us all.*"

Hebrews 2:9, "But we see Jesus, who was made a little lower than the angels for the suffering of death, crowned with glory and honour; *that he by the grace of God should taste death for every man.*"

In tenderest compassion God broods over every sinner and bleeds for his sin. His great yearning heart of love reaches to the uttermost corner of His universe and seeks to draw each heart unto Himself through His Son.

1 Timothy 2:3-4, R. V., "This is good and acceptable in the sight of God our Saviour; *who would have all men to be saved,* and come to the knowledge of the truth."

1 Timothy 4:10, "For therefore we both labour and suffer reproach, because we trust in the living God, *who is the Saviour of all men,* specially of those that believe."

2 Peter 3:9, R. V. "The Lord is not slack concerning his promise, as some count slackness; but is longsuffering to you-ward, *not wishing that any should perish,* but *that all should come to repentance.*"

BUT THIS MAN
after he had offered one sacrifice
for sins forever sat down
on the right hand of God
Hebrews 10:12

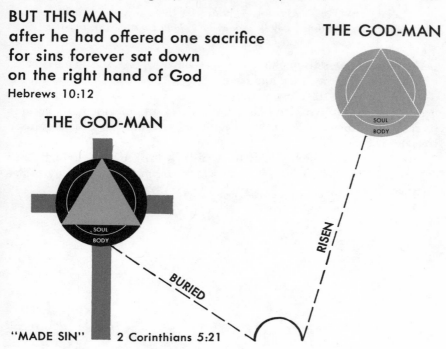

THE GOD-MAN

THE GOD-MAN

SOUL
BODY

RISEN

BURIED

SOUL
BODY

"MADE SIN" 2 Corinthians 5:21

Diagram 6: The God-man—Crucified, Risen, Ascended

That all men might have an adequate opportunity to know God's way of salvation He commanded the disciples to carry the Gospel to the ends of the earth preaching it to every creature.

> Acts 1:8, "But ye shall receive power, after that the Holy Ghost is come upon you: and ye shall be witnesses unto me both in Jerusalem, and in all Judea, and in Samaria, and *unto the uttermost part of the earth.*"

> Mark 16:15, "And he said unto them, Go ye into all the world, and *preach the gospel to every creature.*"

God commands every sinner who hears the Gospel to repent and turn to Him.

> Acts 17:30, "And the times of this ignorance God winked at; but *now commandeth all men every where to repent.*"

God invites all sinners to come to Him and promises eternal life to all who truly believe and receive His Son.

> John 6:37, "All that the Father giveth me shall come to me; and him that cometh to me I will in no wise cast out."

John 3:16, "For God so loved the world, that he gave his only begotten Son, *that whosoever believeth in him should not perish, but have everlasting life.*"

Countless sinners throughout the ages have refused the grace of God manifested in His salvation and have rejected Christ, the Saviour, but the death of Christ on the cross of Calvary opened a way back to God for all men everywhere. "No man is lost for want of an atonement, or because there is any other barrier in the way of his salvation than his own most free and wicked will."

Dear reader, on which side of the cross of Christ are you living? Your relationship to the crucified Christ will determine your destiny. (See Diagram 6.)

11

Four Spans in the Bridge of Salvation— Resurrection

HAVING GRANTED that incarnation and crucifixion are necessary spans in the bridge of salvation, one is driven to the acceptance of resurrection as the third span or all that has been gained through the other two will be lost.

The intimate relationship between these three fundamental truths, their unbreakable connection in fact, is brought out very wonderfully in Peter's sermon on the day of Pentecost recorded in Acts 2:22-36. The resurrection of the Lord Jesus Christ is shown to be the essential vindication of His incarnation and crucifixion. Without the resurrection the other two spans in the bridge of salvation would be futile; through the resurrection every claim God had made regarding the Person and work of His Son both had been vindicated and realized.

Let us get the setting of these words. A tremendous event had taken place. It was a postresurrection event. The risen, ascended, exalted Christ had poured forth the Holy Spirit who had filled every believer and had caused each one to speak in another tongue the wonderful works of God so that people from every nation under heaven gathered in Jerusalem at that time had heard them speak in their own language. The multitude was confounded and amazed and asked for an explanation.

This the apostle Peter gave in a sermon the theme of which was the resurrection of Christ. He deals with it both in retrospect and in its relationships. The outpouring of the Holy Spirit which they had seen and heard had been promised, but it was conditioned upon the realization of God's eternal purpose which He had purposed in Christ, His Son (Ephesians 3:11) and upon the fulfillment of His divine plan. According to that purpose and plan it was the risen, exalted Christ who was to shed forth the Holy Spirit.

> Acts 2:32-33, "This Jesus hath God raised up, whereof we all are witnesses.
>
> Therefore *being by the right hand of God exalted,* and *having received of the Father the promise of the Holy Ghost, he hath shed forth this,* which ye now see and hear."

145

The outpouring of the Holy Spirit was an accomplished fact attested to not only by the little company of believers but by devout Jews from every nation. The shedding forth of the Holy Spirit was proof that Christ had risen from the dead. Now that we have the setting of the words under consideration let us study their significance.

The Resurrection—An Essential Vindication

Acts 2:22, "Ye men of Israel, hear these words; *Jesus of Nazareth, a man approved of God among you* by miracles and wonders and signs, which God did by him *in the midst of you,* as ye yourselves also know."

In these words the apostle Peter records God's satisfaction in the Person and work of the incarnate Son. He had sent His Son into the world to live such a life as none other had ever lived and to do such a work as none other had ever done. He had lived the life and done the work and had received the Father's unqualified approval.

Let us get clearly before us in review what the task was to which the Father had set His Son. In the equality of Deity, Father and Son had worked together to create a universe and the race which was to inhabit it. Into this perfect creation sin had entered first through a celestial being and then through a human being. Death, darkness and disorder followed in the trail of sin and threw everything in God's world out of harmony with Him. God Himself was even dethroned both in His world and in the hearts of men.

As Father and Son had worked together in the creation of the race so would they work together for its regeneration. God in Christ would reconcile the world unto Himself. As sin had entered the world through God's first man, salvation would enter through God's second Man.

To this end the eternal Son would become the incarnate Son. The second Man would start exactly where the first man started, with a perfect life, a human nature, a direct fellowship with God through the Holy Spirit, the right to will and the power to will Godward, but He would start in a world where everything would work to drag Him down into defeat and destruction. In such a world He must live a life such as none other had ever lived—a life of unspotted holiness, unceasing victory and unwavering obedience. It must be a life literally "without spot or wrinkle, or any such thing," unsullied by either the slightest desire to sin born from within or by the yielding to any temptation to sin brought from without. It must be a life from center to circumference lived wholly within the will of God.

Through such a holy Man, God would establish a new union with the human race and through such a sinless Mediator, God would open a way of reconciliation and redemption to rebellious sinners.

The apostle Peter in the sermon at Pentecost witnessed to the fact that the incarnate Son had lived such a life on earth. Three times God had even opened heaven and spoken to all who would hear the words of divine satisfaction in the perfection of His Son. But the world did not reckon to it such worth or give to it such honor. Many had rejected Him; some had even dared call Him an impostor and a blasphemer. A further public witness and open vindication of the Father's satisfaction in the perfection of the Son was essential. This God gave in the resurrection.

The Resurrection—A Consummated Victory

Acts 2:23, *"Him,* being *delivered by the determinate counsel and fore-knowledge of God, ye* have taken, and by wicked hands *have crucified and slain."*

In undertaking the reconciliation and redemption of the world God obligated Himself to deal fully and finally with sin and all its consequences. Every man was a sinner and the sinner's greatest need is a Saviour.

In the incarnation God provided a potential Saviour in the Holy One who was always everywhere Victor. But to make this potential Saviourhood effectual for man's salvation it must be actualized. Christ's personal victory must become a racial victory if it avails for the sinner. But the only way in which the benefit of Christ's victory over sin could be bestowed upon the sinner was by having the guilt, penalty and judgment of sin borne by the Saviour. If the sinner were to take Christ's place of holiness, victory and obedience Christ must take the sinner's place of sin, death and judgment. If any sinner were ever saved Christ must take upon Himself the sin of all sinners and bear its full responsibility. To pay the wages of sin the Author of life died. In the deep and unfathomable mystery of the cross His Spirit was separated from God and went into hades, and from His body which went into the grave (Acts 2:27).

The eternal Son becoming the incarnate Son had given the world a perfect Man; the incarnate Son becoming the crucified Son had given to the human race a perfect Saviour. He had been victorious in the wilderness temptation, in the Gethsemane struggle and finally in the Calvary conflict. But now what? He lies buried in a tomb and a stone seals His grave. Has He been conquered at last? Was His victory but a seeming victory? Has the world had bequeathed to it nothing but the example of a sinless, perfect life it is impossible to follow and the memory of a well-meaning but futile sacrifice for sin? Will the Author, Preserver and Upholder of all life Himself succumb to death, and will the palm of victory after all belong to him "who has the power of death, that is the devil"? Such will surely be the case if the God-man remains in the grave.

But this is unthinkable. Christ had said that He would not only lay down His life but that He would take it again (John 10:17-18). And He did rise from the dead. Death could never hold Him who had said, "I am *the resurrection,* and *the life:* he that believeth in me, though he were dead, yet shall he live" (John 11:25).

> "Death could not keep his prey—
> Jesus, my Saviour,
> He tore the bars away—
> Jesus, my Lord!
> Up from the grave He arose,
> With a mighty triumph o'er His foes;
> He arose a Victor from the dark domain,
> And He lives forever with His saints to reign.
> He arose! He arose! Hallelujah, Christ arose!"

The victory over death was complete.

> 1 Corinthians 15:55-57, "O death, where is thy sting? O grave, where is thy victory? The sting of death is sin; and the strength of sin is the law. *But thanks be to God, which giveth us the victory through our Lord Jesus Christ.*"

The victory of the resurrection gathered up into its embrace all the other victories in His life and death and gave to them meaning and power. The victories of incarnation and crucifixion were merged into THE VICTORY; perfect, powerful, permanent victory over the triumvirate of hell: sin, death and Satan.

THE RESURRECTION—THE DIVINE SEAL

> Acts 2:24, "*Whom God hath raised up,* having loosed the pains of death: because it was not possible that he should be holden of it."

Upon the life of the perfect Man and the work of the perfect Redeemer, God, the Father, set His divine seal of approval and appraisal by raising the God-man from the dead. Christ Jesus had cried from the cross, "It is finished," and it was the cry not of a victim of Satan, but of a Victor over Satan; not of one vanquished by death, but the cry of the Vanquisher of death. In that cry of victory Christ showed that He anticipated His resurrection; He expected the Father to raise Him from the dead. Had He a right to expect His Father so to act? Most assuredly.

To His perfection of life as God's second Man the Father had set His seal of approval both at His baptism and at His transfiguration by opening the heavens and saying, "This is my beloved Son, in whom I am well pleased." Would the Father remain silent now? Would there be no witness to the Father's satisfaction in the all-sufficiency of the Son's sacrifice of Himself upon Calvary's cross to save men? To Christ's death on the cross as the perfect Saviour, God would set His seal by opening the tomb and raising His Son from the dead, thus expressing in language more eloquent than words His satisfaction with the Saviour's redemptive work and its sufficiency for the sinner's salvation. "Upon all the virtue of His life and the value of His death and the victory of His conflict, God set the seal in the sight of heaven and earth and hell, when raising Him from the dead" (G. Campbell Morgan, *The Crises of the Christ*, p. 364). "The resurrection is the Father's 'Amen' to the Son's exclamation 'It is finished.'"

THE RESURRECTION—A SURE PLEDGE

The body that had been specially prepared for Him in incarnation (Hebrews 10:5), that had been laid down in death upon the cross (Hebrews 10:10) was now raised and came forth from the tomb.

> Matthew 28:5-6, "And the angel answered and said unto the women, Fear not ye: for I know that ye seek Jesus, which was crucified.
> He is not here: *for he is risen*, as he said. *Come, see the place where the Lord lay.*"

> John 20:27, "Then saith he to Thomas, Reach hither thy finger, and *behold my hands;* and reach hither thy hand, and *thrust it into my side:* and be not faithless, but believing."

In resurrection as in incarnation He was still the God-man. He arose from the grave on that first Easter morning with the body which He had taken in incarnation, which had been nailed to the cross in death, which had been placed in Joseph's tomb, which had been preserved from corruption and which after three days had been raised from the dead. In that body He appeared to the disciples, proving to them His identity by the nail prints in His hands and feet and the spear print in His side. In that body He ascended to heaven and sits today at the right hand of the Father, receiving the worship of countless multitudes out of every kindred, and tongue, and people and nation who are redeemed to God by the blood of the Lamb slain on Calvary. In that glorified yet scarred body He will live through the ages of the ages, the visible reminder to redeemed sinners "of the exceeding riches of his grace in his kindness toward us through Christ Jesus."

While the body of the risen God-man was the same body yet it was a changed body. From the truth revealed in Philippians 3:20-21 and 1 Corinthians 15:42-50 it is clear that the body Christ Jesus had in resurrection was a glorified, incorruptible, mighty, spiritual, heavenly body. The limitations of His earthly life were those of His human nature; the limitations incident to the humiliation to which He had voluntarily submitted. But in the resurrection He threw off all these fetters of the flesh. "His birth marked the voluntary self-limitation of His Godhood in His descent into our race in His incarnation. His resurrection marked His ascent out of these limitations and His return to His former glory. It was the passageway through which He went to the resumption of the unlimited powers of His Godhood" (A. E. Wood, *The Person and Work of Jesus Christ*, p. 56)..

The resurrection of Jesus Christ is the sure pledge of the resurrection of the believer. When comforting Martha about her brother Lazarus who had been dead four days Jesus said, "I am the resurrection and the life; he that believeth in me, *though he were dead, yet shall he live.*" Just as truly as Christ's prophecy concerning His own resurrection was literally fulfilled will this promise to Martha concerning the resurrection of every believer also be fulfilled. The resurrection of Him who is the Head of the Body makes the resurrection of every member of the Body not only certain but essential.

> 1 Corinthians 15:20-23, "But now is Christ risen from the dead, and become the firstfruits of them that slept.
>
> For since by man came death, by man came also the resurrection of the dead.
>
> For as in Adam all die, *even so in Christ shall all be made alive.*
>
> But every man in his own order: Christ the firstfruits; *afterward they that are Christ's at his coming.*"

And as He rose with a glorified, incorruptible, mighty, spiritual, heavenly body, so shall we. "As we have borne the image of the earthy, we shall also bear the image of the heavenly" (1 Corinthians 15:49).

> Philippians 3:20-21, R. V., "For our citizenship is in heaven; whence also we wait for a Saviour, the Lord Jesus Christ: *who shall fashion anew the body of our humiliation, that it may be conformed to the body of his glory,* according to the working whereby he is able even to subject all things unto himself."

THE RESURRECTION—A NEW BEGINNING

> Colossians 1:18, "And he is the head of the body, the church: *who is the beginning, the firstborn from the dead;* that in all things he might have the preeminence."

Through the last Adam, God has provided another way of union with the human race and in Him He has made a new beginning. Through the perfection of His incarnate manhood, God's second Man has qualified to become the Head of a new creation, through the victory of His crucifixion He has put an end to the old creation, and now through the power of His resurrection a new order of beings is formed of which He is appointed the executive Head. As firstborn from the dead He becomes the Progenitor of a new race of redeemed men, the Head of a new company of people whose life on earth is to be transformed daily into His image from glory to glory and who are ultimately to share the perfection of His glorification.

Through the death and resurrection of Jesus Christ, as twin events, certain definite issues in the conflict between God and Satan were met and eternally settled. The victory over Satan was fully and finally won which robbed him of the last vestige of claim to sovereignty over the earth or the race. He is henceforth a usurper and a thief. Jesus Christ gained back all that had been lost and now the earth and all that is therein are His not only by right of creation but by right of conquest.

To the believer in Jesus Christ it means that the sovereignty of Satan over his life is ended and the sovereignty of God begins; that he leaves the sphere of sin, death, darkness and disorder, and enters the sphere of righteousness, life, light and liberty; that he ceases to be a subject in the kingdom of Satan and becomes a subject in the Kingdom of God; that he severs his alliance with Satan's system, the world, and avows his allegiance as a member of Christ's Body the Church, to Christ Himself who is its Head. It means, in other words, that the old creation with all that pertains to it ends at the cross and is buried in the tomb and that a new creation comes forth in the resurrection. It means that the old relationship with sin, self and Satan is altogether annulled and a new union with God in Christ Jesus is made, and that in this new relationship Christ becomes not only the believer's Saviour but his Lord and his Life.

Through His death on the cross Christ Jesus willed to every man who will take it perfect salvation from the pollution, penalty and power of sin; perfect victory over death, both spiritual and physical; perfect release from the bondage of Satan. Through the resurrection from the dead He is appointed by the Father to be Executor of this will; to be the Mediator of the new covenant; to be the Dispenser of all the blessings and benefactions which were given through grace to all those who have become sons and heirs of God through faith in Him. The resurrection of Christ Jesus is the third span in the bridge of salvation. (See Diagram 6.)

12

Four Spans in the Bridge of Salvation—
Ascension and Exaltation

THERE REMAINS but one double span to complete God's wondrous bridge of salvation. The God-man, crucified, buried and risen, must go back to His Father in glory and be exalted to the place of honor and power at His right hand. Only then would His work be completed. At the resurrection Christ Jesus was constituted the last Adam and became the Progenitor of a new order of beings but not until His ascension and exaltation could He actually be inducted into His work as Head of the Church. He must first enter into heaven to present the blood of Calvary's Sacrifice to His Father and then be enthroned by God as "the King of kings and the Lord of lords."

THE HOMECOMING OF THE SON

In His glorified body the God-man left the earth and passing through the heavens, entered into heaven itself.

> Acts 1:10-11, "And while they looked stedfastly toward heaven *as he went up*, behold, two men stood by them in white apparel;
>   Which also said, Ye men of Galilee, why stand ye gazing up into heaven? *this same Jesus, which is taken up from you into heaven*, shall so come in like manner *as ye have seen him go into heaven*."

> Hebrews 9:24, "For Christ is not entered into the holy places made with hands, which are the figures of the true; *but into heaven itself*, now to appear in the presence of God for us."

Oh! What a homecoming that must have been! Thirty-three years before the well-beloved Son, who through all eternity had been in the bosom of the Father, had left His home in glory to be born in the womb of a virgin. Earth had never held such a One as He and the world, not knowing the worth of the precious gift, received Him not. But, having glorified His Father on earth and having finished the work which He gave Him to do, the Son now goes home. He is marred and scarred by His treatment on

152

earth. Hands and feet and brow all tell the story of the crucifixion on Calvary's tree. The precious body of flesh and bones (Luke 24:39) is a silent witness to the blood shed on the cruel cross. Surely heaven had never homed such a One as He. But heaven knew the worth of the treasure it held on that wonderful ascension day and the angelic host, the number of whom was ten thousand times ten thousand, and thousands of thousands, praised Him with a loud voice and heaven reverberated with the anthem of welcome that greeted the triumphant Redeemer as He entered its portals.

Psalm 24:7-10, "Lift up your heads, O ye gates; and be ye lift up, ye everlasting doors; and *the King of glory shall come in.*
Who is this King of glory? The LORD strong and mighty, the LORD mighty in battle.
Lift up your heads, O ye gates; even lift them up, ye everlasting doors; *and the King of glory shall come in.*
Who is this King of glory? The Lord of hosts, he is the King of glory."

THE EXALTATION OF THE SON

The Father awaited the return to glory of His well-beloved Son that He might bestow upon Him the place of highest honor; that He might exalt Him to the place of greatest power; that He might give Him a name which is above every name; that He might crown Him Lord of all.

Ephesians 1:20-22, "Which he wrought in Christ, when he raised him from the dead, *and set him at his own right hand in the heavenly places,*
Far above all principality, and power, and might, and dominion, and every name that is named, not only in this world, but also in that which is to come:
And hath put all things under his feet, and gave him to be the head over all things to the church."

Philippians 2:9-11, "*Wherefore God also hath highly exalted him,* and *given him a name which is above every name:*
That at the name of Jesus every knee should bow, of things in heaven, and things under the earth;
And that *every tongue should confess that Jesus Christ is Lord,* to the glory of God the Father."

The exaltation of Jesus Christ meant His enthronement. The eternal Son who once voluntarily had emptied and humbled Himself was now exalted to the throne of God and all power in heaven and upon earth was granted unto Him. The crucified Saviour is now the preeminent Lord.

Matthew 28:18, "And Jesus came and spake unto them, saying, *All power is given unto me in heaven and in earth."*

Acts 2:36, "Therefore let all the house of Israel know assuredly, that *God hath made that same Jesus,* whom ye have crucified, *both Lord and Christ."*

The Present Work of the Living Christ

There are three tenses in salvation, past, present and future. Three statements may be made regarding the sinner which are apparently contradictory, yet absolutely true; the believer has been saved, the believer is being saved, the believer will be saved. There is a salvation that is to be appropriated in a moment of time by the sinner, that day by day is to be actualized in the believer's life, that some future day will be fully accomplished. The work which the God-man began on the cross for the sinner He continues on the throne for the saint.

The divine-human mediator

There is but one way of approach to God whether for sinner or for saint and that is by way of Christ Jesus, the divine-human Mediator. The sinner has no way of access to God for salvation except through Christ.

John 14:6, "Jesus saith unto him, I am the way, the truth, and the life: *no man cometh unto the Father, but by me."*

The saint has no way of approach to God for sanctification except through Christ.

Hebrews 7:25, "Wherefore *he is able also to save them to the uttermost that come unto God by him,* seeing he ever liveth to make intercession for them."

Whether we wish to be delivered out of the bondage of sin, or whether we desire to enter into the fullness of our glorious liberty as sons and heirs of God, we must do it through Christ. Through the mediation of Christ Jesus we obtain life; through the same mediation we obtain life more abundant. Our eternal inheritance is in Him. All blessings promised under the new covenant are hid away in the God-man. The glorified Lord is the depository of all the spiritual treasures kept for God's people. He holds them in trust to be bestowed by Him as Mediator when claimed by faith. The representative Man who was on the cross as the sinner's Substitute is on the throne as his Surety.

Hebrews 9:15, R. V., "And for this cause *he is the mediator of a new covenant,* that a death having taken place for the redemption of the transgressions that were under the first covenant, *they that have been called may receive the promise of the eternal inheritance."*

THE GREAT HIGH PRIEST

Just before Jesus gave up the ghost He cried "It is finished." What was finished? The completion of His work as the Sacrifice for man's sin. He Himself was that Sacrifice.

> Hebrews 9:26, "For then must he often have suffered since the foundation of the world: but now once in the end of the world hath he appeared to put away sin *by the sacrifice of himself.*"

But in olden times the sacrifice made for sins had to be ministered by a priest. On the great Day of Atonement the great high priest alone went into the Holy of Holies to offer the sacrifice for the sins of the people. The sacrifice would have been of no avail had it not been offered by a God-appointed, God-anointed, priest. Christ is the Lamb of God offered as a Sacrifice to put away sin for us. But have we a great High Priest who can act as minister of the sanctuary and make the sacrifice for sin avail for our forgiveness, cleansing and renewal? Praise God we have just such a great High Priest.

> Hebrews 8:1, "Now of the things which we have spoken this is the sum: *We have such an high priest,* who is set on the right hand of the throne of the Majesty in the heavens."
>
> Hebrews 10:12, "But *this man,* after he had offered one sacrifice for sins for ever, *sat down on the right hand of God.*"
>
> Hebrews 4:14, "Seeing then that *we have a great high priest,* that is passed into the heavens, *Jesus the Son of God,* let us hold fast our profession."

The Man who was the Sacrifice also offered the sacrifice.
"It is finished"—"He sat down."
The priest in olden times always stood; he never sat because his work was never finished, "for it is not possible that the blood of bulls and of goats should take away sins" (Hebrews 10:4). So in those sacrifices there was a remembrance year by year of sins (Hebrews 10:3). But when "this man had offered one sacrifice for sins forever," then *"He sat down."* A perfect Sacrifice for sin had been made; the Saviour's work was done.

> Hebrews 7:26-27, "For such an high priest became us, who is holy, harmless, undefiled, separate from sinners, and made higher than the heavens; Who needeth not daily, as those high priests, to offer up sacrifice, first for his own sins, and then for the people's: for this he did once, when he offered up himself."

But in order that the precious blood of the Lamb might avail for the forgiveness, cleansing and renewal of the believer a God-appointed, God-anointed high priest is needed. Such a great High Priest Jesus Christ became. In virtue of His perfect life on earth, in virtue of His perfect sacrifice upon the cross, in virtue of His finished work for man's redemption, the God-man sits at the right hand of God as our great High Priest. He is there as our Forerunner, having made a blood-sprinkled path from earth to heaven—even into the Holy of Holies—for sinful men (Hebrews 6:20; 10:19). He is there as our Representative before God, "a merciful and a faithful high priest in things pertaining to God." While down here on earth He was tempted in all points like as we are so He is a High Priest who is touched with the feeling of our infirmities (Hebrews 4:14-15). He knows our trials, afflictions, disappointments, difficulties, sufferings and sorrows, for He has met and passed through them on earth. Therefore He is able now to succor them that are tempted (Hebrews 2:18).

THE SYMPATHETIC ADVOCATE

God cannot condone sin nor company with it whether that sin is in the sinner or in the saint. Sin always, everywhere, separates from God. When the believer sins, his fellowship with God is broken, but he cannot restore himself any more than the sinner could save himself. As the sinner needed a Saviour to open a way to God through redemption so the saint needs an Advocate to keep that way open through restoration.

Such an Advocate must be one who sympathetically understands the awful power of sin and himself has felt its tremendous pressure upon spirit, soul and body, and yet one who has been uncompromising in his refusal to yield to it in thought, word or deed.

Such an Advocate must be one who is able to have access moment by moment to God and one who has a remedy to offer God for the things he attempts to make right.

Such a righteous and effectual Advocate the believer has in Christ Jesus. Such an efficacious remedy for cleansing and restoration Christ has in His shed blood.

> 1 John 2:1, "My little children, these things write I unto you, that ye sin not. *And if any man sin, we have an advocate with the Father, Jesus Christ the righteous.*"

> 1 John 1:6-7, "*If we say that we have fellowship with him, and walk in darkness, we lie,* and do not the truth:
> But if we walk in the light, as he is in the light, we have fellowship one with another, *and the blood of Jesus Christ his Son cleanseth us from all sin.*"

As the sinner is cleansed once for all from the guilt of sin through the precious blood of Christ, so the saint in the same way is cleansed daily from the defilement of sin.

THE FAITHFUL INTERCESSOR

God was not satisfied with delivering the sinner from the old sphere of death, darkness and disorder but He wished him to claim and use to the full his possessions and privileges in the new sphere of life, light and liberty. He is not content merely to have a man saved but He purposes to have him saved to the uttermost. God is able not only to lift the sinner from the lowest depths of life on the plane of the natural but also to exalt the saint to the highest heights of life on the plane of the spiritual. For this He has made ample provision in the faithful intercession of the exalted Lord.

> Romans 8:34, "Who is he that condemneth? It is Christ that died, yea rather, that is risen again, who is even at the right hand of God, *who also maketh intercession for us.*"
>
> Hebrews 7:25, *"Wherefore he is able to save them to the uttermost* that come unto God by him, *seeing he ever liveth to make intercession for them.*"

The intercession of the exalted Son is the capstone of His finished work. What He made potential through His crucifixion on the cross He makes actual through His intercession on the throne. "The intercession of the exalted Christ for the saint is the projection into experience of the saving act of the crucified Saviour for the sinner. It is by His work from heaven that we appreciate His work upon earth."

In His last prayer with the disciples on earth, recorded for us in John 17, He unveils the nature and the content of His high-priestly intercession for all believers. He prays for their safety and their sanctification; He anticipates the oneness of life which He as Head will have with them, as members of His Body; and prays for His perpetual presence in them that it may mean the perfection of His life in theirs. "Christ ever liveth to make intercession for us," praying that God's eternal purpose which He wrought out in the incarnation, crucifixion, resurrection, ascension and exaltation of His Son may be perfectly realized in the life of the believer in his complete deliverance from bondage and in his full acceptance of Christ.

In the ascension and exaltation of Jesus Christ, God completes the fourth span in the bridge of salvation.

13

The Crowning Work of Jesus Christ in Salvation

THERE REMAINS yet one thing to be done to perfect God's gracious plan of salvation. A connecting link between the Saviour in heaven and the sinner on earth is needed. The finished work of Christ by some means must be made applicable to and operative in the souls of men. A way must be provided whereby the life of the crucified Saviour, now enthroned as Lord in heaven, may be communicated to, and maintained in, the believer on earth.

TWO WONDROUS GIFTS

Upon the sinner God has bestowed a wondrous gift, that of His Son as Saviour; upon the believer God has bestowed a second wondrous gift, that of His Spirit as Sanctifier.

> Galatians 4:4-6, "But when the fulness of the time was come, *God sent forth his Son,* made of a woman, made under the law,
>
> To redeem them that were under the law, *that we might receive the adoption of sons.*
>
> And because ye are sons, *God hath sent forth the Spirit of his Son* into your hearts, crying, Abba, Father.
>
> Wherefore thou art no more a servant, but a son; and *if a son, then an heir of God through Christ."*

God sent forth His Son that the sinner might enter the family of God as a child. God sent forth His Spirit that the child might enter into the fullness of his inheritance as an heir. God gave His Son to make salvation *possible for us;* God gave the Spirit to make salvation *real in us.* God gave His Son that we might have life; God gave the Spirit that we might have life abiding and abounding.

GOD'S CROWNING WORK

Without the Holy Spirit's work all that was accomplished through Christ's death, resurrection and exaltation would be of no avail. One cannot study thoughtfully the Lord's last conversation with His disciples on earth recorded in John 13-16 without seeing that He teaches most clearly that the sending of the Holy Spirit from the Father upon His return to glory was to be the crowning work in His salvation of men. Let us turn then to these chapters for a study of this truth.

There were many things that He longed to say to His disciples that last night but they were unable to bear them (John 16:12). A few things, however, He must make clear. One was the kind of life He expected them to live. It was to be both an abiding and an abounding life. His life was to be to their life what that of the vine is to the branch. In Him dwelt all the fullness of the Godhead bodily and that fullness was to be made theirs until they were "filled with all the fulness of God" (Colossians 2:9-10; Ephesians 3:19).

As He talked along about this wonderful abiding and abounding life, He said, "But because I have said these things unto you, sorrow hath filled your heart" (John 16:6). No doubt He was watching their faces and saw a confused, troubled look as He spoke of going away from them and yet of expecting them to live any such life as this. He had told them that it was to be a life characterized by peace, joy, power, fruitfulness, friendship and love, yet it was to be interwoven with suffering, tribulation, persecution, even possible death by violence. How could they ever hope to live such a life if He went from them when in those three years in which they had enjoyed the blessing and helpfulness of His personal presence there had been so much of envy, criticism, discouragement, cowardice, fear, and unbelief in their lives? His quick sympathy understood what they feared to express and He hastened to comfort them by saying: "I will not leave you comfortless: *I will come to you.*"

What a strange thing to say—to tell them in the same breath that He was going away from them and yet coming to them. But He explains further: "Yet a little while, and *the world seeth me no more; but ye see me.*" He was to be with them and seen of them but in a way unknown and invisible to others. It must be, then, in a spiritual rather than in a physical presence. Still they were perplexed and could see no real benefit in His leaving them. Then He said, "Nevertheless I tell you the truth; It is expedient for you that I go away: for if I go not away, *the Comforter will not come* unto you; but if I depart, *I will send him* unto you." But what would be gained by the going of Jesus Christ and the sending of someone else in His place? Had it not been very wonderful to have the Lord with them on earth, talking and praying with them, teaching and leading them, letting them work with Him, showing them by the life He lived and the work He did how they ought to live and work? Yes, it had been very wonderful but not altogether successful. While there had been much of joy in fellowship with Him yet there had been also much of discouragement. He said so much the meaning of which they could not grasp and even what they did understand they so often failed to obey. He had been much with them but they had not grown like Him in the three years. What gain then could it be to have Him go away so that even His bodily presence was denied them? He does not leave them without answering every questioning of their sad, perplexed hearts.

> John 14:16-17, "And I will pray the Father, and he shall give you another Comforter, that he may *abide with you for ever;* even the Spirit of truth . . . for *he dwelleth with you, and SHALL BE IN YOU.*"

Oh! here is something entirely new: wholly different from any of God's dealings with men before. God the Spirit had been with men and He had come upon men but never had He been in men as a perpetual presence. Now it would seem that through Jesus Christ's going back to the Father by way of the cross and the tomb and the clouds an entirely different relationship was to be established between God and men, a relationship more close and intimate than anything man had experienced through all the centuries. "We will come unto him and make our abode with him" (John 14:23). God, the righteous, holy One, was to live in men in actual presence. How could such a thing be? The Lord Jesus tells us.

> John 14:20, "At that day ye shall know that *I am in my Father,* and *ye in me,* and I in you."

> John 17:21, "As thou, Father, art in me, and I in thee, that they also may be one in us."

How would the Son who was leaving to go back to the Father in heaven and to live at His right hand be able to live also in Peter, and in James, and in John on earth? "O the depth of the riches both of the wisdom and knowledge of God! how unsearchable are his judgments, and his ways past finding out!" Here indeed is the crowning work of the Lord Jesus.

> John 16:7, "Nevertheless I tell you the truth; It is expedient for you that I go away: for if I go not away, the Comforter will not come unto you; but if I depart, *I will send him unto you.*"

> John 16:13-14, "Howbeit when he, the Spirit of truth, is come, he will guide you into all truth: *for he shall not speak of himself;* but whatsoever he shall hear, that shall he speak: and he will shew you things to come.
>
> *He shall glorify me:* for *he shall receive of mine, and shall shew it unto you.*"

> John 15:26, "*He shall testify of me.*"

Jesus taught clearly in these words that the chief mission of the Holy Spirit in being sent forth from the Father to dwell in the believer was that He might make the presence of the risen, glorified, living Lord an actual spiritual reality. He also taught them that the Holy Spirit was to be both the sole and the sufficient Messenger of spiritual truth and the Medium of spiritual revelation. In other words all that they would ever know of, or receive from, their risen Lord was to be communicated by and through the Holy Spirit. Without Him there would be no means for the presence and power of the risen Christ to be manifested in their lives, and no way for them to realize in their spiritual experience the blessing and benefit gained for them by Jesus Christ through His death and resurrection. The Holy Spirit was to be the Middleman between heaven and earth. The salvation that had come from the Father through the Son would be applied by the Spirit. By the power invested in the Holy Spirit the believer would be lifted to the plane of the spiritual man and his life maintained there.

THE PROMISE OF CHRIST FULFILLED

Christ had promised that, if He went away, the Holy Spirit would come and His promise was fulfilled literally. He died and rose again. He met the disciples individually and collectively several times, revealing Himself to them as their risen Lord. He gave them a last commission; then He repeated His promise and commanded them to wait for its fulfillment.

> Luke 24:49, "And, behold, *I send the promise of my Father upon you: but tarry ye in the city of Jerusalem, until ye be endued with power from on high.*"

> Acts 1:4-5, "And, being assembled together with them, *commanded them that they should not depart from Jerusalem, but wait for the promise of the Father,* which, saith he, ye have heard of me.
> For John truly baptized with water; but *ye shall be baptized with the Holy Ghost not many days hence.*"

Jesus Christ then ascended into heaven (Acts 1:10-11). They waited according to His command (Acts 1:12-14). God's time was fulfilled. The day of Pentecost came (Acts 2:1-4). The promise of the Father was actualized in the descent of the Holy Spirit in baptism upon the waiting group of believers.

THE TWOFOLD ASPECT OF THE HOLY SPIRIT'S BAPTISM

The descent of the Holy Spirit upon the disciples had a double import: it accomplished two definite, distinct things.

First, the Holy Spirit came upon each believer, filling him with Himself. Through this baptism the exalted Christ took up His abode in the individual believer where He was enthroned as Lord and appropriated as Life.

Through the baptism in the Holy Spirit the abundant life of the living Lord was manifested in power in each believer.

Acts 2:4, *"And they were all filled with the Holy Ghost."*

Second, the Holy Spirit came upon the whole group of believers and baptized them into one Body, the Church. Through this baptism they were united to Christ, its Head, and to one another as fellow members of the Body of Christ. Through the Holy Spirit's descent on the day of Pentecost the exalted Christ was installed as Lord over, and instilled as Life into, the Church.

> 1 Corinthians 12:12-14, "For as the body is one, and hath many members, and all the members of that one body, being many, are one body: *so also is Christ.*
>
> For *by one Spirit are we all baptized into one body,* whether we be Jews or Gentiles, whether we be bond or free; *and have been all made to drink into one Spirit.* For the body is not one member, but many."

THE RESULT OF THE HOLY SPIRIT'S BAPTISM

Through His death, resurrection and exaltation, the Lord Jesus not only removed the penalty of sin but He broke its power. Through union with Him by faith He had made potential for the believer on earth the same life of victory, power and holiness, which He lived in heaven. This life was to be communicated to and maintained in each believer through the incoming, indwelling and infilling of the Holy Spirit.

On the day of Pentecost, Peter, James, John and all the other believers who tarried in the upper room were baptized with the Holy Spirit. The question is bound to rise in our hearts, "Did that baptism make any difference in their lives? If so, what difference?" Even a casual comparison of the record of the life of the disciples before and after Pentecost will con-. vince any one that a marvelous change had been wrought. These men had been in almost daily companionship with Jesus during the years of His public ministry. They had been taught deep truths by Him, they had shared His wonderful prayer life. They had lived under the spell of that matchless personality day by day. He had been both their Teacher and their Example for three years.

But witness the failure, defeat, and sin of their lives as they are laid open to our gaze in the gospels! See the jealousy, ambition, selfishness, pride, self-seeking, self-assertion, self-love, weakness, and fruitlessness. In spite of their fellowship with the Holy One who tried in all possible ways to help them they remained very largely what they were before they followed Him.

And why was this true? Because He was only living with them, one without, working upon them by His word and personal influence. But what a change was wrought when on the day of Pentecost, through the baptism in the Holy Spirit, Christ came down into those men to take the perfect possession, the complete control, and the unhindered use of their whole being. Self was dethroned and Christ was enthroned as Lord. Christ became the Life of their life.

A fourfold fruitage was manifested in their lives immediately. They became men of *purity*. "God, which knoweth the hearts, giving them the Holy Spirit, purified their hearts by faith." A mighty inward change first was wrought. The Spirit of God is a holy Spirit and He can only dwell in a holy place. So His primary work is always the cleansing of the innermost recesses of the life. "Be ye holy for I am holy" is God's mandate to the saved soul. When the disciples were baptized with the Holy Spirit He first purified them, displacing pride with humility; selfishness with love; cowardice with courage; carnal with spiritual; worldly with heavenly; human with divine; temporal with eternal.

They became men of *power*. "Ye shall receive power after that the Holy Ghost is come upon you." This promise abundantly was fulfilled in them. Inward purity begat outward power. The book of the Acts is one unbroken record of the mighty power of God the Holy Spirit coursing through purified channels. "Rivers of living water" flowed through those first apostles and believers into Jerusalem, Judea, Samaria, and even to the uttermost parts of the earth.

They became men of *passion*. One and all they gave themselves to the winning of souls. Their own hearts, all aglow with fervent gratitude and adoring praise to Him who loved them enough to give Himself for them, were kindled into a flame of passionate desire to bring others into the joy and peace and security of a personal, saving relationship to the Lord Jesus Christ. They became men of one passion—"This one thing I do" animated their lives.

> "Oh! for a passionate passion for souls!
>   Oh! for a pity that yearns!
> Oh! for a love that loves unto death!
>   Oh! for a fire that burns!
> Oh! for a prayer power that prevails!
>   That pours itself out for the lost;
> Victorious prayer in the Conqueror's name,
>   Oh! for a Pentecost!

They became men of *prayer*. Communion with God through prayer, and cooperation with God through intercession in making the finished work of Christ operative in other men's lives, became their chief delight and constant occupation. The book of the Acts is one continuous record of answered prayer. All their wonderful works were begun, continued, and ended in prevailing prayer.

The repeated impression made upon the student of the book of the Acts is that through the baptism in the Holy Spirit at Pentecost those first believers were changed from carnal into spiritual Christians and that from that time on they purposed to live their lives on the highest plane. What life on the highest plane was to them is defined aptly and adequately in a description used repeatedly in connection with them, "They were filled with the Holy Spirit."

Through our studies thus far we have seen that in the finished work of Jesus Christ, the eternal, incarnate, crucified, risen, ascended, exalted Son crowned by the sending forth of the Holy Spirit, God has made all-sufficient provision for lifting any and every person from the deepest depths of life on the natural plane to the highest heights of life on the spiritual plane. (See Diagram 7.)

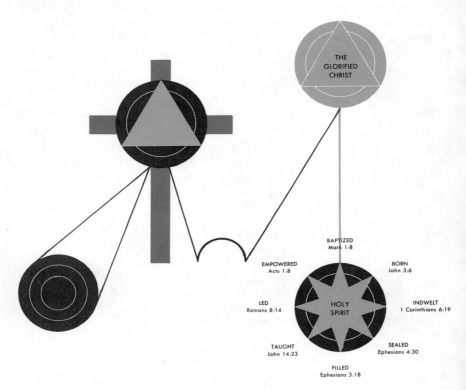

Diagram 7: The Holy Spirit

Part 2

THE RELATION BETWEEN CHRIST AND THE CHRISTIAN

14

Grace Triumphant over Sin

THE MOST TRIUMPHANT WORDS ever spoken were those which fell from the lips of the Lord Jesus Christ when on the cross He said, "It is finished." It was the divine proclamation that grace had triumphed over sin. It was God's pronouncement to the world that all that had been lost both to Him and to man through the first Adam had been regained through the last Adam.

> Romans 5:20, "But where *sin abounded, grace did much more abound.*"
>
> Romans 5:12, 15, "*By one man sin entered* into the world."
> "Much more the grace of God, and *the gift by grace, which is by one man,* Jesus Christ, hath abounded unto many."

THE CHALLENGE OF GRACE—IN ADAM OR IN CHRIST

So far in our studies we have considered God's dealings with the human race *representatively* through two men, the first and the last Adam. Through the federal headship of the first Adam, God established a union with the whole human race in creation. All that Adam was in creation God intended all mankind latent in him to be.

But Adam sinned and thereby received a sinful nature, becoming a sinner both in desire and in deed. He came into bondage to sin, self and Satan. He became a subject in the kingdom of Satan and entered into the sphere of death, darkness and disorder. He became "flesh" and descended to life on the plane of the natural. There was upon him a sinner's guilt, over him a sinner's condemnation, and before him a sinner's doom.

Through his federal headship Adam bequeathed to the human race latent in him all that became his in the Fall. He became the progenitor of a race "begat . . . in his own likeness after his image" (Genesis 5:3). His posterity inherited his sinful nature and shared in the consequences of his sin. Every man by physical birth is "In Adam."

In Adam's creation God had established a union with the human race on the basis of personal communion and governmental cooperation. In Adam's

167

Fall that union was broken and mankind was alienated from God. Sin put an impassable chasm between a righteous, holy God and guilty, sinful men.

But as God dealt representatively with the human race in the first Adam so did He also in the last Adam. What was ruined in the Fall of the first man God redeemed in the victory of the second Man. The loss that both God and the race sustained by the sinful act of the first Adam was recovered by the righteous act of the last Adam. The union that was broken through His first man God reestablished through His second Man. The impassable chasm made by the first Adam's sin was bridged by the last Adam's sacrifice.

On the cross of Calvary Christ Jesus, the divine-human Mediator, took the sinner's place and became the sinner's Substitute. The sinner's guilt was borne, the sinner's condemnation was removed, and the sinner's doom was met, by the Sin-bearer. Adam's sin was put away and all of its consequences were borne by God's Son.

Through His federal headship Christ made *potential* for all sinners all that became His through the victory of His death and resurrection. As all men have been united to the first Adam in creation and in the Fall, so all men may be united to the last Adam in grace through faith. As all men are "In Adam" so all men may be "In Christ."

Through the death, resurrection, ascension and exaltation of the Lord Jesus Christ mankind was *potentially* redeemed and God reestablished a relationship with the race "by grace through faith" so that all men may come out of bondage to sin, self and Satan into the glorious liberty of the children of God and into the bounteous inheritance of the heirs of God. "In Christ" all men may now find a way of escape from the sphere of death, darkness and disorder and an abundant entrance into the sphere of life, light and liberty and they may be delivered from the kingdom of Satan and translated into the Kingdom of God's dear Son. "In Christ" all men may now leave the plane of the natural and rise to the plane of the spiritual. Every man by spiritual birth may be "In Christ."

God deals representatively with the whole human race in these two federal headships. It may be said, that judicially God has relation to but two men in all the universe, Adam, the first and Adam, the last.

> Romans 5:18-19, R. V., "So then as *through one trespass the judgment came unto all men to condemnation;* even so *through one act of righteousness the free gift came unto all men to justification of life.*
>
> For as *through the one man's disobedience the many were made sinners,* even so *through the obedience of the one shall the many be made righteous.*"

But through these two men God has a personal relationship with every individual on earth because every person is now either "In Adam" or "In Christ," either still is alienated from God through sin or is accepted by God through His Son.

Sin entered, abounded, and reigned (Romans 5:12, 20-21); on Calvary's cross grace entered and did much more abound and now reigns wherever God's gift is accepted by faith.

> Romans 5:21, "That as sin hath reigned unto death, *even so might grace reign* through righteousness unto eternal life *by Jesus Christ our Lord.*"

And now every living person is challenged by grace to come out of the life of sin, to leave the life "In Adam" for the life "In Christ."

15

Christ Our Saviour—The Bridge Crossed

IN THIS BOOK we are writing, as it were, the spiritual biography of man. Our story encompasses his life in creation, in the Fall, in grace, and in glory. We have seen what God meant him to be in creation, what he became in the Fall, and what God has done for him through grace. We have now come to the most crucial point in his whole history. A choice must be made that will give direction to all that lies beyond both for time and for eternity. It is a decision that determines destiny. Will the natural man remain on the plane of the natural or will he choose to live on the plane of the spiritual? Will he receive or refuse God's gift through grace? Will he cling to his sin or lay hold upon God's Son?

THE INEVITABLE CHOICE—YOUR SIN OR GOD'S SON

God's first gift to man is that of a Saviour because this is man's primary need. It was God's love for *sinners* that led Him to give His Son to die for us (Romans 5:8). Christ was born into this world a Saviour.

> Luke 2:11, "For *unto you is born* this day in the city of David a *Saviour,* which is Christ the Lord."

It was Christ's love for *sinners* that brought Him from heaven to earth. By His own testimony He came to seek and to save the lost.

> 1 Timothy 1:15, "This is a faithful saying, and worthy of all acceptation, that *Christ Jesus came into the world to save sinners;* of whom I am chief."

> Luke 19:10, "For *the Son of man is come to seek and to save that which was lost.*"
>
> > " 'Man of Sorrows,' what a name,
> > For the Son of God, who came
> > *Ruined sinners to reclaim,*
> > Hallelujah! What a Saviour!"

Christ crucified is the sinner's only way back to God. He is the sinner's only door of access into the presence of God and God's only door of access into the heart of the sinner.

170

John 14:6, "Jesus saith unto him, *I am the way*, the truth, and the life: *no man cometh unto the Father, but by me.*"

John 10:9, "*I am the door: by me if any man enter in, he shall be saved,* and shall go in and out, and find pasture."

The initial relationship of the natural man to God must be that of a sinner penitently acknowledging his sin and accepting God's gracious gift of a Saviour. The sinner must come to God through *the crucified* Christ, or he cannot come to God at all.

This is an exceedingly humiliating position for the natural man to take, it knocks the underpinning from beneath his entire life for it strikes at the very root of his self-will, self-love, self-trust and self-exaltation. By it he is compelled to acknowledge that he has made an utter failure, that he is wholly incapable of living his own life in his own strength, but more than that, that he is absolutely unfit to live in the presence of One who is righteous and holy. It brings him altogether to the end of himself, to the foot of the cross to acknowledge his sinful, helpless, hopeless condition, and to look up in simple faith to the crucified Saviour, who alone can lift him to a higher plane of life.

Many sinners in the world today will not go thus far. They will acknowledge their lack of light and their need of a teacher; they will confess they do not know the right way of life and need a leader; they will admit the low level of their standards and their need of an example; but they will not acknowledge that they are out-and-out sinners needing a Saviour. They simply place themselves outside the class for which Christ died. But the Lord of glory did not leave the bosom of His Father and the joy of heaven for the suffering and sorrow of earth and the shame and scourging of Calvary's cross merely to receive the patronizing admiration of men and to help them to live a somewhat more intelligent, respectable, useful life as sinners on the plane of the natural man. He came only because men were lost and must be found: because they were sinners and must be saved. He came not to call the righteous but sinners to repentance.

Through Christ, *as Saviour,* God has provided the only way back to Himself that He deems effectual: He has opened the only door from earth into heaven. Through His Son, as Saviour, God had made salvation from sin a potential gift to all sinners so that since Christ died and rose again all men everywhere are shut in to an inevitable choice—the choice between their sin and His Son. *"Neither is there salvation in any other: for there is none other name under heaven given among men, whereby we must be saved."*

Since the shedding of the precious blood of His only begotten Son on the cross of Calvary, God the Father sees every person on earth either with or without a Saviour.

The Gracious Invitation

God not only provided a Saviour for every sinner but He has through the Gospel sent forth an invitation to those "of every tongue, and people, and nation" to accept His gift, to partake of His feast, to inherit His riches, to share the blessings of His heavenly home.

His infinite grace, His tender love, His compassionate mercy, have made room for all. He declares that none is too good to come, for if he is, the salvation provided for him in Christ is useless, and that none is too bad for salvation would thereby be proved ineffectual. Not one who has put his trust in the shed blood of the Saviour, however long he has lived in sin or however deep into it he has sunk or however crimson is its stain upon his life, will be turned away from the Father's heart or home. To the weary and heavy laden; to the hungry, thirsty and poor; to the wandering and the wayward; the loving Father says, "Come unto me."

> Matthew 11:28, "*Come unto me*, all ye that labour and are heavy laden, and I will give you rest."
>
> Isaiah 55:1, "Ho, every one that thirsteth, *come ye to the waters*, and he that hath no money;*come ye*, buy, and eat; yea, *come*, buy wine and milk without money and without price."
>
> John 7:37, "In the last day, that great day of the feast, Jesus stood and cried, saying, If any man thirst, *let him come unto me*, and drink."
>
> John 6:37, "All that the Father giveth me shall come to me; *and him that cometh to me I will in no wise cast out.*"

Dear reader, are you still among the number who have not accepted God's gracious invitation to come unto Him? Are you troubled, perplexed, anxious, restless? Christ says, "Come unto me, for in me ye may have peace."

Are you unhappy, discontented, and dissatisfied, and is your heart devoid of joy? Christ says, "Come unto me, my joy shall remain in you that your joy may be full."

Does life seem intolerable to you because of its burdens, its sufferings, its tribulations? Christ says, "Come unto me, in the world ye shall have tribulation but I have overcome the world."

Are you discouraged by the repeated temptation at the same vulnerable spot which you are utterly powerless to resist? Christ says, "Come unto me, and in me ye shall be more than conquerors."

Is your heart filled with an insatiable hunger which no one and no thing has ever been able to satisfy? Christ says, "I am the bread of life, he that cometh to me shall never hunger."

Is your soul parched with a thirst that you have tried to quench in a thousand ways and have failed? Christ says, "If any man thirst, let him come unto me and drink."

Is your path strewn with disappointments, afflictions, trials, and does the road ahead seem to be dense darkness? Christ says, "I am the light of the world: he that followeth me shall not walk in darkness, but shall have the light of life."

Are you terrified at the sin stains on your soul and doubt if ever they can be removed? Then the Saviour says, "Only come unto me, though your sins be as scarlet, they shall be as white as snow; though they be red like crimson, they shall be as wool."

Do you really wish to be free from sin, to end the despotic rule of self, and to sever your partnership with Satan? You may come out of this three-fold bondage into the glorious liberty and the bounteous inheritance of a son and heir of God if you will avail yourself of God's gracious invitation. Christ Jesus is able to save you to the uttermost of your sin and to satisfy you to the uttermost of your need. The first step out of the natural into the spiritual is such a very simple one that even a little child may take it for it is just the choice of God's Son instead of your sin; it is the personal acceptance of God's wondrous gift of a Saviour.

> "Out of my bondage, sorrow and night,
> Jesus, I come, Jesus, I come;
> Into Thy freedom, gladness, and light
> Jesus, I come to Thee.
> Out of my sickness into Thy health,
> Out of my want and into Thy wealth,
> *Out of my sin and into Thyself,*
> *Jesus, I come to Thee."*

THE RESPONSE OF FAITH—THE BRIDGE CROSSED

Man has had nothing whatever to do with the building of the bridge of salvation. That was God's work and His alone. God furnished both the material and the workmanship by which this wondrous bridge was builded. *"By grace* are ye saved."

> Titus 2:11, *"For the grace of God that bringeth salvation* hath appeared to all men."

> 2 Timothy 1:9, *"Who hath saved us,* and called us with an holy calling, not according to our works, but *according to his own purpose and grace,* which was given us in Christ before the world began."

But God leaves it to the sinner to decide whether he will cross this bridge or not. What God's grace has provided man's faith must possess. The salvation made potential by grace God expects to be made experiential by faith. Salvation is not something to be purchased or earned or gained through merit of any kind, for salvation is a gift and a gift is received. Salvation is for all men but only those who believe and receive are saved. "By grace are ye saved *through faith.*"

> 1 Timothy 4:10, "For therefore we both labour and suffer reproach, because we trust in the living God, *who is the Saviour of all men, specially of those that believe.*"
>
> Ephesians 2:8-9, "For *by grace are ye saved through faith;* and that not of yourselves: *it is the gift of God:* not of works, lest any man should boast."

While man has had nothing to do with the building of the bridge yet he has everything to do with regard to the use of it for he decides whether or not he will cross it. Have you crossed this bridge? Has God's gracious invitation met with a glad response on your part? I must press the question home for it is one that will have to be answered either here and now, or yonder at the great white throne. No decision you will ever be called upon to make can begin to compare with this one in importance because upon it hangs your happiness and usefulness in this life and your destiny in the life to come.

Perhaps among the readers of this book are some earnest inquirers who are saying in their hearts, But what does crossing the bridge involve? and What must I do to be saved? Let us together now consider these questions in turn.

Crossing the bridge means a decisive break with all that pertains to the old creation in the old sphere. If, then, one decides to become a Christian, his first step will be to turn his back on sin, and turn his face toward Christ his Saviour. In that first step he will renounce his sin and receive God's Son. The first step out of the life on the plane of the natural into life on the plane of the spiritual involves a twofold reversal in the sinner's relationship to God which the Bible calls repentance and faith.

> Acts 20:21, "Testifying both to the Jews, and also to the Greeks, *repentance toward God,* and *faith toward our Lord Jesus Christ.*"
>
> Acts 26:18, "To open their eyes, and to *turn them from darkness to light, and from the power of Satan unto God,* that they may receive forgiveness of sins, and inheritance among them which are *sanctified by faith that is in me.*"
>
> 1 Thessalonians 1:9, "For they themselves shew of us what manner of entering in we had unto you, and *how ye turned to God from idols* to serve the living and true God."

The cross of the Lord Jesus Christ is the place at which this decisive break with the old life is made. It is the birthplace of real repentance and true faith.

In the parables of the Kingdom (Matthew 13:1-52), Christ likened the Kingdom of heaven to a field in which there were both wheat and tares, and to a net in which were both good and bad fish. He states that no attempt will be made to separate them until the harvest time at the end of the age. False professors and true possessors are in the visible church today and will continue to be until Christ comes again.

The false professor has never genuinely repented, for let us remind ourselves that repentance means *a change of mind,* a complete reversal of attitude toward God and consequently a change of mind toward all that is opposed to God. There is much in Christian experience today that is called repentance which is sheer camouflage. It is not genuine abhorrence and loathing of sin as something hateful and heinous in the sight of God, but is selfish and sinful regret in having sin exposed or in having to suffer its punishment. It is not a real turn about-face but it is a pretence at looking Godward while walking sinward. A repentance that makes one a possessor of God's gift through grace is born of a consciousness of sin that deepens into conviction and compels one to cry out in honesty of heart, "What must I do to be saved?"

Such a repentance has its birth at the cross of Christ. Gazing upon the spotless, sinless, Son of God crucified upon a criminal's cross, bearing the sin of the world with all its stain; drinking the cup of suffering even to its bitter dregs; enduring the penalty and punishment of sin even unto death; the sinner comes to a realization of the sinfulness of sin. With the light of God's holiness and the warmth of God's love streaming into his own soul the sinner has his first real revulsion toward sin. Repentance which is "not only a heart broken *for* sin but *from* sin" follows. To see sin as God sees it in the light of the cross is to have the taste for it and the delight in it taken away.

Neither has the false professor ever truly believed for let us remember that to *believe* is to *receive* a Person into the life to possess and to control it as His own. There is much in Christian experience today that is called faith which is not faith at all. Sometimes one is deceived into thinking emotional feeling is faith. The emotions are played upon by sentimental appeals and a superficial response is made. But the seed sown has not taken root so a change of feeling results in a casting away of faith. That is sometimes called faith which is merely the assent of the mind to the great historical facts regarding Jesus Christ but is wholly divorced from any intention of accepting Him as Saviour, yielding to Him as Lord, and appropriating Him as Life. But, a faith that makes one a possessor of God's gift through grace is born of a consciousness of helplessness and hopelessness that compels the sinner to cry out in sincere longing of heart, "God, be merciful to me a sinner."

Such a faith has its birth at the cross of Christ. The Holy Spirit having brought the sinner to acknowledge his own helpless and hopeless condition then fixes his gaze upon the all-sufficient Saviour. He points him to the One who bore his sins in His own body on the tree; to the Lamb of God who taketh away the sin of the world which included *his* sin. He reveals Christ Jesus as the One who tasted death for him and enables him to say, "He loved *me* and gave Himself for *me*." He assures the sinner now burdened by the guilt and pollution of his sins that there is forgiveness and cleansing for him in the blood of the slain Lamb. Then He leads him to put his trust in Jesus Christ as his own personal Saviour and by an act of his will to receive Him into his life as such.

Having considered what is involved in a genuine crossing of God's bridge of salvation let us now turn to the other question, "What must I do to be saved?" God's Word gives an abundant answer to this question.

> John 20:31, "But these are written, that ye might believe that Jesus is the Christ, the Son of God; and that believing ye might have life through his name."

> Acts 16:30-31, "And brought them out, and said, Sirs, what must I do to be saved?
> And they said, *Believe on the Lord Jesus Christ, and thou shalt be saved,* and thy house."

> John 1:12, "But *as many as received him,* to them gave he power to become the sons of God, *even to them that believe on his name.*"

God wishes the poor, the unfortunate, the illiterate, the young and the untalented to come to Him and to have the blessings of salvation, as well as the rich, the favored, the learned, the aged, and the gifted. He has made the way of salvation so simple that all may walk in it and nobody need be excluded because of any lack in himself. Salvation is all wrapped up in a Saviour who is a gift of God to be received upon the one condition of faith. "Whosoever believeth on him shall not be ashamed."

Faith is very simple yet it is a very comprehensive thing and involves in its operation the mind, the heart, and the will. Faith includes belief which is the assent of the mind to the things written in God's Word concerning the Saviour. We believe that He is the Christ, the Son of God, who died for our sins. Faith includes trust, which is the consent of the heart to the gracious work of Christ. We not only believe the things which the Word teaches about Christ, the Saviour, but we believe *on* Him. We put our trust and our dependence upon Him alone for our salvation. But faith also includes appropriation which is the decision of the will to receive Christ Jesus. Faith enables me first to *perceive* Christ as the Saviour of all men and then to *receive* Him as my own personal Saviour. Faith leads me to believe that "God so loved the world that whosoever believeth in him should not perish" and then leads me to receive "Him who loved me and gave himself for me."

We see, then, that salvation is far more than mere assent to the doctrinal truth of the Bible, for one could believe every word in the Book and still not be saved. It is also far more than mere church membership for one could perform every ordinance and ceremony the church requires and still not be saved. Salvation centers not in a doctrine nor in an ordinance but in a Person and he only is saved who has put his trust in Christ as Saviour to the point of receiving Him into his whole being as *the Saviour from his sins.*

Such salvation is typified for us in the redemption of the children of Israel from their awful bondage to Pharaoh and their deliverance from the terrible judgment of death in Egypt. Because of Pharaoh's rebellion toward God, the firstborn in all the land were to be smitten with death. God gave definite instructions to the children of Israel through Moses as to what they were to do to avert this terrible sentence of death upon their households. They were told to take a lamb without blemish, slay it, and put the blood upon the two side posts and on the upper doorpost of the house. As God passed through the land of Egypt at midnight He would pass over every house upon which He saw the blood and into that home the plague of death would not come. "When I see the blood I will pass over you." The only thing that saved the firstborn in any household on that memorable night was the blood of the lamb on the doorpost.

Since God's dear Son laid down His life in death on Calvary's cross the sinner's only shelter from the wrath of God is under the cover of His precious blood. God has told us that we are "redeemed with the precious blood of Christ, as of a lamb without blemish and without spot" and asks us to take by faith the blood of Christ to cover all our sins. As He looks upon each of us today He sees us either with or without that covering.

> Matthew 26:28, "For this is *my blood of the new testament, which is shed for many for the remission of sins.*"
>
> 1 Peter 1:18-19, "Forasmuch as ye know that *ye were* not *redeemed* with corruptible things, as silver and gold, from your vain conversation received by tradition from your fathers;
>   But *with the precious blood of Christ,* as of a lamb without blemish and without spot."

The cross of Christ is the only place where God and the sinner can meet and the Lamb of God is the bond of union. The sinner looks up and trusts in the shed blood of the Saviour. God looks down and says "I see the blood and will pass over you." Faith has responded to grace and the Saviour and the sinner are made one at the cross.

My friend, whoever and wherever you are, have you crossed God's bridge of salvation? Have you responded to the unsearchable riches of God's grace as manifested in Christ, through faith? Have you believed on Him and received Him into your life as your own personal Saviour? Are you resting safe and secure today under the sheltering cover of the blood of the Lamb of God? If not, will you not lay this book down and right now look up in faith to Him?

> "I take, O Cross, thy shadow,
>   For my abiding place;
> I ask no other sunshine
>   Than the sunshine of His face,
> Content to let the world go by,
>   To know no gain or loss,
> My sinful self my only shame,
>   My glory all the Cross." (See Diagram 8.)

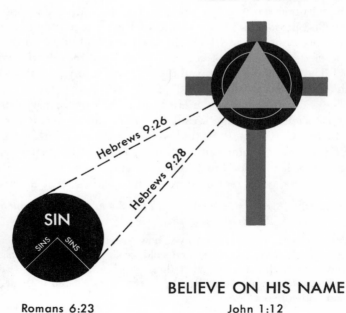

Diagram 8: Receiving Christ the Saviour

THE FIRSTFRUITS OF FAITH

The inheritance into which the believer enters as a son and heir of God is a very rich and beautiful one and includes every spiritual blessing in Christ. But the blessing primarily coveted is relief from the burden of sins, the sense of forgiveness, the assurance of pardon. The circumstances of conversion vary greatly and people come to God in vastly diverse ways. Some are born of Christian parents and are nurtured in an atmosphere surcharged with the love and worship of God. The name of Jesus is on the lips almost as soon as the name of "Father" or "Mother." Sometimes one cannot tell when that personal choice of Jesus Christ as Saviour was made, for love to Him seems always to have been in the heart. With others the new birth has meant a decided and definite break in the life. Not all have the keen realization of the awful sinfulness of sin nor does the guilt and condemnation of it rest on them as a terrible burden as it did upon Pilgrim in Bunyan's classic story, but to almost everyone there is the bondage to some besetting sin from which he seeks release. So the first blessing of which the sinner is conscious and the one in which he primarily rejoices is the forgiveness of sins.

Ephesians 1:7, "In whom we have redemption through his blood, *the forgiveness of sins,* according to the riches of his grace."

The moment the sinner acknowledges his sin and turns in real faith to Christ as Saviour, that very moment God grants perfect and permanent pardon for all his sins: his past is blotted out and he will not be judged for sin that his Saviour has borne to the cross. But lack of assurance regarding forgiveness is a very common thing even in the lives of some who have been Christians for years. Because of ignorance of God's Word when perchance one falls again into some besetting sin, doubt comes into the heart and robs it of the joy of salvation. In order that the believer may rest in the conscious assurance of full acquittal, God unfolds in His Word the completeness of forgiveness. Are you resting today in the assurance of sins forgiven? If not, may God speak to you in these precious statements of His Word and enable you to claim each for yourself.

Isaiah 38:17, "Behold, for peace I had great bitterness: but thou hast in love to my soul delivered it from the pit of corruption: *for thou hast cast all my sins behind thy back.*"

All my sins behind God's back! Out of God's sight! Never to be seen again! O! the comfort of knowing that the sins God has forgiven *He* will never see again!

Psalm 103:12, "As far as the east is from the west, *so far hath he removed our transgressions from us.*"

All of my sins put the distance of the world's circumference from me! Out of my sight as well as out of the sight of God! While in China I received a cable telling of the death of a dearly loved sister in America. During the weeks that followed in which I waited for a letter giving further particulars of her death, I realized how far the east is from the west and there came a new, sweet experience of the assurance of my salvation in these precious words, *"As far—So far."* O! the comfort of knowing that the sins which God has forgiven *I* shall never see again!

> Micah 7:19, "He will turn again, he will have compassion upon us; he will subdue our iniquities; and *thou wilt cast all their sins into the depths of the sea."*

All my sins cast into the depths of the sea! Not only out of sight but out of reach! A few years ago the steamship *Titanic* built at a cost of millions of dollars and carrying a cargo valued at many millions more went to the bottom of the Atlantic Ocean. So far as I know no attempt has ever been made to bring either the *Titanic* or her cargo from the depths of the sea. O! the comfort of knowing that the sins forgiven by God are out of reach, pardoned for time and for eternity!

> Isaiah 44:22, *"I have blotted out, as a thick cloud, thy transgressions, and, as a cloud, thy sins."*

> Hebrews 8:12, "For I will be merciful to their unrighteousness, and *their sins and their iniquities will I remember no more."*

All my sins blotted out and forgotten! Not only out of God's sight and out of God's reach, but out of God's memory! But in the unsearchable riches of His grace God has blotted out my sins so completely that there is not a trace of them left to remind Him that once they were. O! the comfort of knowing that the sins which God has forgiven He has also forgotten!

But the forgiveness of sins is but half, and that the negative half, of the firstfruits of faith. Merely removing the penalty for and the punishment of sins does not undo all the work of sin. For the natural man is not only a sinner: he is a rebel and an outlaw as well. He needs not only to be redeemed but to be reinstated to favor with God. A criminal may be pardoned and released from prison but he returns to the community in which he lives as a pardoned criminal. No human judge has the power to reinstate him into society as one who never sinned. What man cannot do God can. Justification is the positive half of the firstfruits of faith.

> Acts 13:38-39, "Be it known unto you therefore, men and brethren, that *through this man* is preached unto you the forgiveness of sins.
> And *by him all that believe are justified from all things,* from which ye could not be justified by the law of Moses."

2 Corinthians 5:21, R. V., "Him who knew no sin *he made to be sin on our behalf;* that *we might become the righteousness of God in him.*"

Christ, our Saviour, not only pardoned our sin but He gave us the *standing* before the Father of one who had never sinned. The only way in which He could do this was to exchange places with us. He took our place upon the cross becoming sin for us that we might take His place before the Father becoming righteousness in Him. His death was one act with a double blessing. The negative side was forgiveness which took something from us, the penalty of our sins; the positive side was justification which gave something to us, the righteousness of God. The death of Jesus Christ accomplished a twofold work in the believer: it unclothed him by removing the filthy rags of sin and it clothed him by bestowing the pure garments of His perfect righteousness. "For he hath made him to be sin for us, who knew no sin," here Christ Jesus is saying to His Father, "Put their sins to my account." "That we might be made the righteousness of God in him," here Christ Jesus is saying to His Father, "Put my righteousness to their account." Through His death upon the cross Jesus Christ not only took us out of the old standing in Adam, but He brought us into a new standing in Christ. The grace of God provides for justification, the blood of Jesus Christ procures it, and the faith of the believer possesses it.

> Romans 3:24, "*Being justified freely by his grace* through the redemption that is in Christ Jesus."
>
> Romans 5:9, "Much more then, *being now justified by his blood,* we shall be saved from wrath through him."
>
> Romans 5:1, "Therefore *being justified by faith,* we have peace with God through our Lord Jesus Christ."

Through justification certain definite and glorious blessings are secured to the believer. Chief among these is peace with God. Resistance and rebellion through self-will have ceased and the heart rests in the assurance of God's favor.

> Romans 5:1, "Therefore being justified by faith, *we have peace with God through our Lord Jesus Christ.*"

All distance between God and the sinner is obliterated. All barriers are torn down. The believer is made near to God's heart through the blood of Christ.

> Ephesians 2:13, "But now *in Christ Jesus ye* who sometimes were far off *are made nigh by the blood of Christ.*"

"O the love that sought me,
O the blood that bought me,
O the grace that brought me to the fold!"

THE GREAT REFUSAL

Jesus Christ spoke some very sad and solemn words during His earthly ministry but among the saddest and the most solemn are these:

John 5:40, "And *ye will not come to me*, that ye might have life."

These words were spoken to men who professed to believe and to love the Scriptures and who even searched them in the hope of securing eternal life. The very Scriptures that they searched pointed everywhere to Jesus Christ as the Author and Giver of life, yet *Him* they stubbornly and persistently refused and rejected. To Him they would not come acknowledging themselves sinners needing Him as their Saviour. These men were guilty of the great refusal. They rejected God's Son as their Saviour. The cause of their refusal was self-will. Please note Christ said "ye *will* not come to me." Their rejection of Jesus Christ was not due to inability but to unwillingness. They *could* come but they *would not*. Note too that all Christ asked them to do was *to come to Him* that He might give them that which they needed more than they needed anything else.

Their decision determined their destiny. God left it with them to make the choice between their sin and His Son but having made it He determined what the result of that choice should be.

John 8:24, "I said therefore unto you, that ye shall die in your sins: for *if ye believe not that I am he, ye shall die in your sins.*"

John 8:21, "Then said Jesus again unto them, I go my way, and ye shall seek me, and shall die in your sins: *whither I go, ye cannot come.*"

To refuse grace is to invite judgment. To retain a sinner's guilt is to receive a sinner's doom. If the natural man chooses to live and to die on the natural man's plane then he must expect the natural man's destiny.

The Gospel of the Lord Jesus Christ has been preached all over the world yet millions upon millions of those who have heard it are living as though Christ had not died, as though God had not taken up the sin question and settled it in such a way as to provide salvation for all men. Throughout the world today are multitudes who are guilty of the great refusal, who are choosing to remain in their sins rather than accept God's Son as their Saviour.

Out of this number are some who apparently have no concern whatever over their souls. Their minds and hearts are set upon the pursuits and pleasures of this life as though there were no God to reckon with and no life beyond this to prepare for. There are others who through self-righteousness and self-exaltation refuse God's way of the cross. It is an offense unto them. They indulge in very shallow and superficial sentiments about the love of God which they think too great to ever condemn anyone to separation from Him forgetting altogether that the love of God spent itself on that very cross. Up to the cross God has infinite love for the sinner but if in self-exaltation he passes it by and rejects the Saviour, then on the other side that very love is wrath. There are others who say they want to believe but cannot. Unbelief is never due to inability. It may be due to unwillingness. Thomas was an honest doubter and said, "I *will* not believe *except* I shall see." God gave him to see and he believed. It may be due to ignorance of what faith is and requires. The all-important thing in faith is not its measure but its object. Christ Himself stated this when He said "Come unto me." Anyone *can* come.

There are countless sins of which every sinner is guilty but there is one above all others for which God is today condemning him and holding him accountable and that is the sin of refusing Jesus Christ as his Saviour. Wrapped up in that sin are all the others. That is the sin of sins. It is upon that sin the Holy Spirit puts all the pressure of conviction to bring a soul to God. This is His initial work in the sinner.

> John 3:18, "He that believeth on him is not condemned: but he that believeth not *is condemned already, because he hath not believed in the name of the only begotten Son of God.*"

> John 16:8-9, "And when he [the Comforter] is come, *he will reprove the world of sin,* and of righteousness, and of judgment; *of sin, because they believe not on me.*"

God gives clear and unmistakable warnings to those who are facing the inevitable choice between their sin and His Son. The great refusal means death.

> Romans 6:23, "*For the wages of sin is death;* but the gift of God is eternal life through Jesus Christ our Lord."

The great refusal means the wrath of God abiding upon the unbeliever.

> John 3:36, "He that believeth on the Son hath everlasting life: and *he that believeth not the Son* shall not see life; but *the wrath of God abideth on him.*"

The great refusal means the judgment of the great white throne.

> Revelation 20:12, "And *I saw the dead,* small and great, *stand before God;* and the books were opened: and another book was opened, which is the book of life: and *the dead were judged out of those things which were written in the books, according to their works.*"

The great refusal leads to eternal separation from the presence of God.

2 Thessalonians 1:8-9, "In flaming fire taking vengeance on them that know not God, and that obey not the gospel of our Lord Jesus Christ: *Who shall be punished with everlasting destruction from the presence of the Lord, and from the glory of his power.*"

God invites you to receive Christ into your life as Saviour *today.* To drift is to refuse; to ignore is to refuse; to postpone is to refuse; to face the claim of Christ and to turn silently away is to refuse. The rich young ruler refused and is never mentioned again. A young official in China faced the claim and call of Christ one night but he said, "Tomorrow, wait until tomorrow." He refused; that night he was assassinated.

2 Corinthians 6:2, "Behold, *now* is the accepted time; behold, *now* is the day of salvation."

Hebrews 3:15, "While it is said, *To-day* if ye will hear his voice, harden not your hearts, as in the provocation."

Proverbs 27:1, *"Boast not thyself of to morrow;* for thou knowest not what a day may bring forth."

Isaiah 55:6, "Seek ye the LORD *while he may be found,* call ye upon him *while he is near.*"

"AND YE WILL NOT COME TO ME THAT YE MIGHT HAVE LIFE."
John 5:40

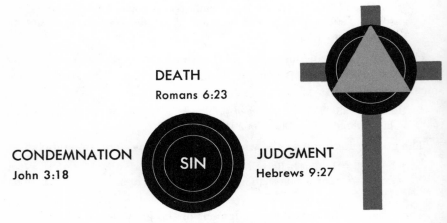

Diagram 9: Rejecting Christ the Saviour

"Choose ye *this day* whom ye will serve."

The cross of the Lord Jesus Christ is the great divide. On which side of it are *you* today? The choice is inevitable—your sin or God's Son. (See Diagram 9.)

16

Christ Our Head—A New Creation Formed

CROSSING GOD'S BRIDGE of salvation begins with the believer's justification but it does not end there for justification in its twofold aspect deals largely with our past and carries us only over the borderline into the new sphere. It gives us a new standing before God, but it does not equip us to live in a state becoming our standing. It paves the way for us into the presence of a holy God but it cannot make us holy. It opens the door for the establishment of the new order in Christ but it needs regeneration to furnish the certificate for membership in that order. Justification and regeneration are simultaneous in experience.

THE RISEN CHRIST—HEAD OF A NEW ORDER

In Christ crucified God made an end of the old creation and all that pertained to it; in Christ risen, He made the beginning of a new creation. Through His resurrection Christ Jesus became the Head of a new order of beings, who are to be as heavenly and holy, as pure and as perfect as He is; the Progenitor of a new race of redeemed men whose ultimate glory through grace is to be complete conformity to His image.

> Romans 8:29, "For whom he did foreknow, he also did predestinate *to be conformed to the image of his Son,* that he might be the first born among many brethren."

But life in the new order requires a wholly new equipment which Scripture clearly describes.

THE IMPLANTATION OF A NEW LIFE

The first necessity for fellowship with the living God is life; the first requirement for union with the divine Head is divine life; to live in the sphere of the Spirit one must have spiritual life. To belong to the new order one must have the same kind of life as the Head of the order.

But the natural man is "without Christ" therefore he is without "life." By nature every sinner in Adam whether rich or poor, literate or illiterate, moral or immoral, religious or irreligious, is spiritually dead. Every child born into this world, whatever his parentage or position in society, enters it entirely destitute of the divine life of God.

The primary need, then, for membership in the new order, for citizenship in the new Kingdom, for sonship in the new family, is life that fits one for his new relationships and environment. To be related to God either as a son in His family or as a subject in His Kingdom necessitates the possession of His eternal, divine, spiritual life. But how would a dead man become possessed of this life? The answer to this all-important question our Lord Himself gives in His conversation with Nicodemus recorded in the third chapter of John's gospel.

Nicodemus was a man of the Pharisees. So great was his fear of his co-religionists, yet so insistent was his desire for something the Lord Jesus possessed, that he came to Him under cover of the night. As a ruler of the Jews also he occupied an influential position yet despite his religious privileges his heart was unsatisfied and craved something which Phariseeism was unable to give him. Without question Nicodemus came to the Lord Jesus driven by a deep sense of need. What then did he come for? The answer to this question is important in the light of what Christ Jesus gave him; it may also help some reader to interpret his own greatest need and to understand the right method of approach to the One who alone is able to meet it. We are not told directly why he came but John 3:2 suggests a clue.

Nicodemus was himself a teacher but perhaps he recognized in Jesus' teaching an authority and attractiveness which were lacking in his own. He was a great religious leader yet he had no such miracle-working power as had Jesus. He was a ruler of the Jews and Jesus was only a humble itinerant preacher yet God was not with him as He was with Jesus. Did Nicodemus come seeking light upon the secret of such wisdom and power which possibly even for unselfish reasons he craved to possess? Did he come as a teacher to a greater teacher merely to be taught? As a leader to a greater leader simply to be led? Was the deepest need he felt in his life the need of *light*? Had he who professed to be the physician of others' soul-sickness failed to diagnose correctly his own? If so, there are many in similar positions today who have made the same mistake.

The conversation that follows shows that the Great Physician instantly went to the seat of Nicodemus's trouble. He who "knew what was in man" diagnosed his case aright and saw a much deeper and more imperative need than that of which Nicodemus himself was yet conscious. Nicodemus came for *light* but he needed *life:* and the light he wanted could only come out of the life he needed.

John 1:4, "In him was life; and *the life was the light of men.*"

Nicodemus wanted divine wisdom and spiritual power, these are the fruit of divine, spiritual life. Nicodemus came to Him who said, "I am the light of the world" to receive light but he had not come to Him who said, "I am the life" to receive life. Nicodemus came only as a teacher to be taught. The Lord Jesus saw that he needed to come as a sinner to a Saviour to be saved. So in His reply He met not the desire but the need of Nicodemus. He went to the core, He touched the quick of his need.

> John 3:3, "Jesus answered and said unto him, Verily, verily, I say unto thee, *Except a man be born again, he cannot see the kingdom of God.*"

The proof that the Lord was right in His diagnosis and that Nicodemus was devoid of the life of God is plainly seen in his utter lack of spiritual apprehension of the Master's words. He had not the faintest idea of the meaning of the words "born again," as his perplexed question to Jesus revealed.

> John 3:4, "Nicodemus saith unto him, How can a man be born when he is old? *can he enter the second time into his mother's womb, and be born?*"

What could Nicodemus have thought a man could gain through a second physical birth that he had not received through the first? What additional inheritance could be given him through the same parents in a second birth? The very question he asked revealed his need of light, but of spiritual light that is the product of spiritual life. Nicodemus was blind because he was dead. The thing which Nicodemus did not know, but which Christ did know, was that he was still in the sphere of death, outside the Kingdom and family of God, and living on the plane of the natural man.

Consequently Nicodemus did not know that nothing which he had through the flesh could be put to his account in the realm of the spirit; that the position, possessions and privileges, upon which he prided himself in the sphere of the natural, were like counterfeit coins in the sphere of the spiritual. Nicodemus did not apprehend that nothing which he could have received through a thousand physical births could make him eligible to citizenship in the Kingdom of God or to sonship in the family of God.

The whole purpose of Jesus' conversation was to show Nicodemus that he was an alien and that citizenship in the Kingdom of God required naturalization through regeneration. Is it any wonder that the perplexed cry came from his heart, "How can these things be?" For was he not a Jew *by birth*, therefore was he not born into the Kingdom of God? Had he not scrupulously and punctiliously observed every ordinance and ceremony and fulfilled every religious duty, therefore had he not earned his way into the Kingdom of God *by good works?* Was he not a man of the Pharisees, even a ruler of the Jews, therefore was he not eligible to citizenship in the Kingdom of God *by his religion?* Nicodemus was all that he claimed to be by birth, by good works, and by religion, yet Jesus told him that none of these things in itself or all of them put together would serve as naturalization papers in the Kingdom of God. One thing was absolutely essential in a Kingdom that was built upon the supernatural, and that one thing was supernatural life. Without this no one, whatever his parentage, privileges or position, could qualify for entrance.

Seeing the perplexity of Nicodemus's mind, yet understanding the hunger of his heart, Jesus repeated and amplified His words on the absolute necessity of the new birth.

> John 3:5, 7, "Jesus answered, Verily, verily, I say unto thee, *Except a man be born of water and of the Spirit, he cannot enter into the kingdom of God.*
> Marvel not that I said unto thee, *Ye must be born again.*"

Is it possible that some reader of these pages is, like Nicodemus, trusting to his godly parentage, his good works, his exemplary morality, his inherited religion, for entrance into the Kingdom of God? If so, will you not heed the words which Jesus spoke to Nicodemus for He is speaking them to you as well?

The absolute necessity of the new birth as a requirement for entrance into the Kingdom of God could not have been expressed in more emphatic words, than the Lord uses here. If you will trace His conversations in the gospels you will notice that He never employs the use of the words "Verily, verily," except when teaching something of paramount importance. In John 3:5, 7, He uses three very emphatic words, "except," "cannot," and "must." The Lord of the Kingdom is declaring the first and fundamental requirement of life in the Kingdom when He says "Ye"—no matter who you are—"*must* be born again." There are absolutely no exceptions to this law of the spiritual realm.

If anyone could have hoped for exemption from this requirement Nicodemus would have been that man. Yet his high moral character, his clean, upright life, his orthodox religious creed, his influential social position, his membership in the Sanhedrin, his faithful performance of religious duties, and his acknowledgment of Jesus as a great teacher and a good man, were insufficient to gain an entrance for him into the Kingdom of God. Jesus Christ, who looks at men from the viewpoint of heavenly standards, told Nicodemus that even he could not see, much less enter, the heavenly Kingdom except this divine miracle of the new birth was wrought in his spirit.

THE IMPARTATION OF A NEW NATURE

Jesus has expressed to Nicodemus the imperativeness and the inflexibility of the necessity of a new birth for the implantation of the new life. But has Jesus made an arbitrary, perhaps even an unreasonable demand, or has He only stated a law of the spiritual Kingdom, which admittedly is as reasonable as the law which governs the physical kingdom?

In the physical realm we recognize two laws which operate everywhere and always; physical life is the result of physical birth, and the thing that is born partakes of the nature of that which gave it birth. Like begets like. Natural begets natural. Jesus told Nicodemus that the same kind of a law prevails in the spiritual realm; the spiritual life is the result of spiritual birth and that which is born of God partakes of the nature of God. Like begets like. Divine begets divine.

> John 3:6-7, "That which is born of the flesh is flesh; and *that which is born of the Spirit is spirit.*
> *Ye must be born again."*

In these verses Jesus has stated with intentional conciseness and clarity four profound truths:

1. There are two distinct spheres in which men live.
2. Entrance to each sphere is by birth.
3. Flesh begets flesh and Spirit begets spirit.
4. Anyone who wishes to pass out of the sphere of the flesh into the sphere of the Spirit can do so only by a second birth.

Nicodemus coveted for himself something which Jesus possessed. That which Nicodemus coveted was a spiritual thing. It belonged only to those living in the spiritual sphere; it could be bestowed only upon those who possessed a spiritual nature. But Nicodemus was living in the sphere of the flesh. He was no doubt living up to the best that he knew *in that sphere;* in fact he came to Jesus for *more light* on how to live a still better and more useful life in that same sphere. Was it not a reasonable and even laudable desire and should it not be granted?

Again Jesus goes to the very heart of the difficulty and shows the utter impossibility of making the flesh spiritual. "That which is born of the flesh *is flesh"* and it can never be anything else. It may be educated flesh, cultured flesh, traveled flesh, moral flesh, yes, even religious flesh, but it is still flesh.

Even God makes no attempt to make the flesh anything but flesh. He tells us why in His Word.

> Romans 8:7-8, R. V., *"Because the mind of the flesh is enmity against God;*

> for *it is not subject to the law of God,* neither indeed can it be.
> And *they that are in the flesh cannot please God."*

The flesh is God-hating and God-defying. It is irreconcilably hostile to God. Because the flesh is what it is, it is unchangeable and unimprovable. So God makes no attempt either to repair the ruin or to reconcile the enmity of the old, corrupt, defiled, rebellious, lawless nature. Even when outwardly clothed in the beautiful garments of geniality, amiability, kindliness, generosity, courtesy and gentleness, it is still at heart God-hating and God-defying. "They that are in the flesh cannot please God."

How then could God permit one to enter His family as a son, or His Kingdom as a citizen, who had *only* the old nature of the flesh? How could one obey the laws of a spiritual Kingdom with only a fleshly nature? How could a corrupt, defiled nature that loved sin and hated holiness ever make a man holy? Upon what would God have to build to conform the natural man into the image of His Son? Or what enjoyment would heaven offer to an unregenerate soul? If on earth those living in the flesh find no pleasure in the companionship and converse of those living in the Spirit surely this would be even more true in heaven. The pursuits and pleasures, the desires and the deeds of the natural man, are the exact antitheses of those of the spiritual man. If Nicodemus were to possess and enjoy the spiritual thing for which his heart hungered he must have a spiritual nature.

"That which is born of the flesh *is* flesh." The old, fleshly nature equips one to live in the sphere of the flesh but nowhere else. So Jesus held out to Nicodemus no hope of his heart's desire and need being met and satisfied through any change either sudden or gradual in his old nature. Jesus makes no proposal to reinvigorate or reinforce the old nature by the addition of spiritual gifts and graces or by the subtraction of evil tendencies and practices. Jesus will not put a new piece on an old garment. Jesus shows unmistakably that "there is no process, even of divine alchemy, by which the base metal of the flesh can be transformed into the fine gold of the Spirit." The flesh cannot be improved, changed or utilized by God. There is nothing in it which God can accept.

What then does God purpose to do to equip a repentant, believing sinner for membership in the new order of heavenly holy men? He purposes to endow him with a new nature that fits him for citizenship in His Kingdom and for sonship in His family. He purposes to bestow upon him His own divine nature which will fructify in a supernatural life. To live the life of God one must have the nature of God, therefore through the new birth God plants His own seed in the spirit of man to abide there.

2 Peter 1:4, "Whereby are given unto us exceeding great and precious

promises: that *by these ye might become partakers of the divine nature,* having escaped the corruption that is in the world through lust."

1 John 3:9, R. V., "Whosoever is begotten of God doeth no sin, *because his seed abideth in him:* and he cannot sin, because he is begotten of God."

The believer in Christ Jesus becomes the possessor of something which he never possessed before—the nature of God Himself. The eternal life of the uncreated God is implanted in the innermost part of his human personality and his whole being throbs with the divine energy of a new life. The new birth is the impartation of a new intellectual, emotional, volitional nature which produces in man a totally new life and fits him to live in a totally new sphere.

In the light of the Lord Jesus' conversation with Nicodemus it is a self-evident fact that God cannot accept any substitute for the new birth. *Reformation cannot be substituted for regeneration.* If God makes no attempt to reform "the old man" surely He cannot accept any fragmentary improvement man might effect. Reformation is purely man's work; it leaves the flesh flesh, for it is the human trying to better itself. Reformation may improve the character of the flesh by the lopping off of certain evil habits but it cannot change flesh into spirit. Reformation may make a man somewhat more kind, generous, courteous, but it cannot make him holy, and "without holiness no man shall see the Lord." Reformation may help a man to better the condition of his living on the plane of the natural but this does not meet God's requirement for a totally new life on the plane of the spiritual.

Respectability cannot be substituted for regeneration. Many people are deluding themselves into thinking that if their character and conduct conform to the moral standards of the best society, that is a sufficient passport into the companionship of an altogether holy God. But God's standards are as far above man's as the heavens are above the earth.

Religion cannot be substituted for regeneration. Nicodemus was an ardent, active religionist but he was not a son of God or a citizen in the Kingdom of God. Over the doorway to the Kingdom of God no one will ever see written, "Admittance granted to those who have been baptized, who have been punctilious in church attendance, who have partaken of the Holy Communion, who have read the Scriptures and prayed, who have given their tithe." In His holy Word God has already written these solemn and irrevocable words over that doorway, *"Except a man be born again, he cannot see the kingdom of God."* Jesus Himself, the righteous Judge, bars the gate of heaven to the unregenerate. "And there shall in no wise enter into it any thing that defileth, neither whatsoever worketh abomination, or

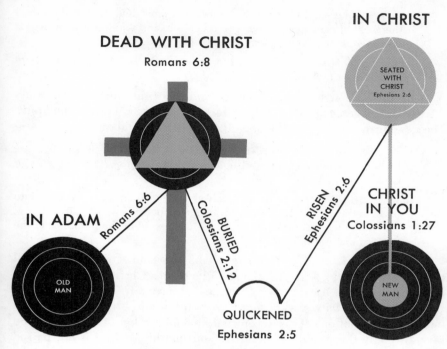

Diagram 10: A New Creation

maketh a lie; but they which are written in the Lamb's book of life" (Revelation 21:27). "Marvel not that I said unto thee, Ye must be born again." (See Diagram 10.)

THE HOLY SPIRIT—THE AUTHOR OF THE NEW LIFE

But Nicodemus did marvel at what our Lord was saying and could only reply "How can these things be?" Nicodemus like many others today had preconceived ideas and prejudices which made it difficult for him either to understand or to accept the divine simplicity of God's plan of salvation. "He had to dsecend from the lofty heights of Rabbinical learning and traditionary religion and learn the alphabet of the Gospel in the school of Christ." Then, too, it would be a most humiliating thing for this prominent leader in religious circles who was supposed to teach others concerning the Kingdom to admit that he himself could not enter the Kingdom except he came as a sinner to a Saviour, confessing his need of a new nature.

But the Lord Jesus takes infinite pains to throw light into the darkened mind of Nicodemus because He knows that He is dealing with a hungry soul. So He tells him the "how" of the new birth.

> John 3:8, "The wind bloweth where it listeth, and thou hearest the sound thereof, but canst not tell whence it cometh, and whither it goeth: *so is every one that is born of the Spirit.*"

> John 3:6, "That which is born of the flesh is flesh; and *that which is born of the Spirit is spirit.*"

As in justification so in regeneration God takes the initiative and does the work. *"By grace* are ye saved." The spiritual man is born of the Spirit. The new birth is God's work alone. It is a birth from above.

> 1 John 3:9, R. V., "*Whosoever is begotten of God* doeth no sin, because his seed abideth in him: and he cannot sin, *because he is begotten of God.*"

> John 1:12-13, "But as many as received him, to them gave he power to become the sons of God, even to them that believe on his name:
> *Which were born,* not of blood, nor of the will of the flesh, nor of the will of man, *but of God.*"

"Born"—"not of blood." Regeneration has no connection with natural descent. Recently I asked a gentleman if he were a Christian. Instantly he replied, "Certainly, I was born a Christian." I have a friend who felt quite sure that her *first* baby was born a Christian but now she has come to be more sure that not one of her seven could have been born Christians. God says distinctly that the divine, eternal, spiritual life of God is not passed from father to son but is implanted by God, the Holy Spirit, directly in the spirit of man. "Salvation does not run in the blood." Eternal life is not an inheritance from godly parents but it is the gift of God in Christ His Son.

"Born"—"not of the will of the flesh." Regeneration has no connection with natural volition. The will of the flesh is hostile to God and left to itself it would never move Godward. Did not Christ say to those who opposed Him, "Ye *will not* come to me that ye might have life"? Self-will would never abdicate in favor of God. But even if it would choose to do so it is altogether "without strength" (Romans 5:6). Good resolutions made when the heart is touched by an emotional appeal, or the turning over a new leaf on one's birthday, or at the beginning of the new year, or the fixed determination to cut one's self loose from an evil practice, do not constitute regeneration. Except grace takes the initiative and the Holy Ghost operates on the will of man he would never desire a new nature or be able to obtain one. "*So then it is not of him that willeth,* nor of him that runneth; but of God that sheweth mercy" (Romans 9:16).

"Born"—"not of the will of man." Regeneration has no connection with natural relationships. God uses the faithful preaching and teaching of the Word by pastor and Sunday school teacher, the believing prayer of parents and friends, the earnest exhortation, warning and pleading of the personal worker to show another his need of a Saviour and to teach him the way of salvation, but no effort of theirs can beget in another the divine, supernatural life of God. No ordinance or rite, however sacred and holy, administered by priest or preacher has life-begetting power.

"Born"—"but of God." Regeneration is solely the work of God. It is patent that no one can give the life of God to another but God Himself. To become a son of God one must receive the life of God from God. God, the Holy Spirit, is the sole author of this new life which He implants by a creative act in the sinner.

Sin's first devastation was wrought in the human spirit. So here is where the Holy Spirit begins His work in regeneration. In the human spirit of the believer is implanted the life of God.

> Ephesians 2:1, "And *you hath he quickened,* who were dead in trespasses and sins."
>
> Ephesians 2:5, "Even when we were dead in sins, *hath quickened us together with Christ,* (by grace ye are saved:)."

Into this renewed human spirit the Holy Spirit comes to dwell. Here He will operate to make the implanted life a living reality. So the believer will be transformed into the image of Christ from glory to glory.

> Ezekiel 36:26-27, "A new heart also will I give you, and *a new spirit will I put within you:* and I will take away the stony heart out of your flesh, and I will give you an heart of flesh.
>
> *And I will put my spirit within you,* and cause you to walk in my statutes, and ye shall keep my judgments, and do them."
>
> 1 Corinthians 3:16, "Know ye not that ye are the temple of God, and that *the Spirit of God dwelleth in you?*"

In regeneration the Holy Spirit uses both a divine and a human instrument. The divine instrument is the Word of God.

> 1 Peter 1:23, "*Being born again,* not of corruptible seed, but of incorruptible, *by the word of God,* which liveth and abideth for ever."
>
> James 1:18, "*Of his own will begat he us with the word of truth,* that we should be a kind of firstfruits of his creatures."

To place the Word of God in the hands of those not yet born again or to unfold its truth to them God uses human instruments.

> 1 Corinthians 4:15, "For though ye have ten thousand instructors in Christ, yet have ye not many fathers: *for in Christ Jesus I have begotten you through the gospel.*"
>
> Galatians 4:19, "My little children, *of whom I travail in birth again* until Christ be formed in you."

The Cross—The Place of Spiritual Birth

The Lord Jesus has told Nicodemus of the necessity, the nature, and the Author of the new birth, but he still said, "How can these things be?" Was it a *personal* question? Did Nicodemus want to know how such a miracle as regeneration could be wrought in himself even though he might still be unwilling to admit the need of it? Whether this be true or not Jesus now used the Scriptures with which this master in Israel was very familiar to tell him how he could be born again.

> John 3:14-15, "And as Moses lifted up the serpent in the wilderness, *even so must the Son of man be lifted up:*
> *That whosoever believeth in him should not perish,* but have eternal life."

The Old Testament incident was well known to every Jew. The Israelites were murmuring against God and Moses. The Lord sent fiery serpents among the people, they were bitten by them and large numbers were dying. Moses prayed for their deliverance and the Lord told him to make a serpent of brass and to put it upon a pole that every one who was bitten, when he looked upon it, should live.

The serpent of sin has put its deadly poison into every descendant of Adam. But God lifted up His Son, "made in the likeness of sinful flesh" to the cross where He put away sin and all its deadly effects by the sacrifice of Himself. One believing look at the serpent meant life to the death-smitten Israelite. One believing look at the crucified One means life to the one "dead in trespasses and sins."

> "There is life for a look at the Crucified One;
> There is life at this moment for thee;
> Then, look, sinner, look unto Him, and be saved,
> Unto Him who was nailed to the tree."

The cross of Christ reveals to us the Son of God dying as our Saviour. We look to Him in faith and the Holy Spirit implants in us the life of God and imparts to us the nature of God and we are born again. The cross of Jesus Christ is the believer's spiritual birthplace.

At the cross of Christ through the new birth the sinner leaves the family of Satan and becomes a son and an heir in the family of God. The new birth causes a radical reversal in his filial relationship. . .

> Galatians 3:26, "For *ye are all the children of God by faith in Christ Jesus.*"

> 1 John 3:8-10, "*He that committeth sin is of the devil;* for the devil sinneth from the beginning. For this purpose the Son of God was manifested, that he might destroy the works of the devil.

Whosoever is born of God doth not commit sin; for his seed remaineth in him: and he cannot sin, because he is born of God.

In this the children of God are manifest, and the children of the devil: whosoever doeth not righteousness is not of God, neither he that loveth not his brother."

Romans 8:16-17, R. V., "The Spirit himself beareth witness with our spirit, *that we are the children of God:*

And *if children, then heirs; heirs of God, and joint-heirs with Christ;* if so be that we suffer with him, that we may be also glorified with him."

At the cross of Christ through the new birth the rebel, the alien, the outlaw, becomes a citizen in the Kingdom of God.

Philippians 3:20, R. V., "*For our citizenship is in heaven;* whence also we wait for a Saviour, the Lord Jesus Christ."

A NEW CREATION FORMED

The new birth entitles the believer to membership in the new order of beings of which the risen Christ is the Head. Through the implantation of the divine life and the impartation of the divine nature in the believer a completely new entity is formed. The man in Christ is a new creation.

2 Corinthians 5:17, R. V., margin, "Wherefore *if any man is in Christ, he is a new creation;* the old things are passed away; behold they are become new."

Galatians 6:15, R. V., margin, "For neither is circumcision anything, nor uncircumcision, *but a new creation.*"

In this new creation everything must partake of the character of the new nature which is its fountainhead; therefore the old things must pass away. Members of the new order have a new ambition which is to be altogether well pleasing unto the Lord, its Head (2 Corinthians 5:9). To be like Christ is their supreme ambition. To attain this they are willing to count all things belonging to the old life but loss.

Philippians 3:7-8, "*But what things were gain to me, those I counted loss for Christ. Yea* doubtless, and *I count all things but loss* for the excellency of the knowledge of Christ Jesus my Lord: for whom I have suffered the loss of all things, and do count them but dung, *that I may win Christ.*"

Members of the new order have new affections. The object of their affections has changed from self to Christ. The Holy Spirit has made the Lord Jesus so attractive and so satisfying that they can say from the heart:

"Thou, O Christ, art all I want,
More than all in Thee I find."

The love of Christ constrains them to live unto God instead of unto themselves and to love God with all the mind, heart, strength and soul.

> 2 Corinthians 5:14-15, R. V., *"For the love of Christ constraineth us:* because we thus judge, that one died for all, therefore all died:
> And he died for all, that *they that live should no longer live unto themselves,* but unto him who for their sakes died and rose again."

> Matthew 22:37, "Jesus said unto him, *Thou shalt love the Lord thy God* with all thy heart, and with all thy soul, and with all thy mind."

Loving God in this way with every faculty of the whole being means loving the things He loves and hating the things He hates. The expulsive power of this new affection removes the old things that grieve and displease Him; the things which are not to His honor and glory. The creative power of the new affection produces within us love for the things He cares for most, His Word, His house, His people, His day, His Kingdom.

Love for the Father includes love for all His children. The love of the Head of the new order constrains every member to love all the other members. Love for our brothers and sisters in Christ is one proof of our own rebirth.

> 1 John 3:14, "We know that we have passed from death unto life *because we love the brethren.* He that loveth not his brother abideth in death."

The new order demands a new standard of life. Self-exaltation was the norm of the old life. Sin was less sinful than it really is and holiness was less holy than it really is.

In this new creation there is a new conception of sin. Things that before seemed altogether right now seem altogether wrong. Habits, haunts, practices, pursuits, pleasures, companionships, conversations, clothes, that were harmonious and suitable in the old sphere seem wholly out of place in the new. Their presence in the new sphere spoils its harmony and vitiates its atmosphere. After breathing the fresh, pure air of the higher altitude, the truly born-again one finds the atmosphere of the natural plane reeking with worldliness, selfishness and sin, stifling and sickening. The one born of God cannot go on sinning as he once did: he cannot continue in the practices which he knows to be contrary to God's will and Word. He has now a conception of sin which makes him loathe them.

> 1 John 3:9, *"Whosoever is born of God doth not commit sin;* for his seed remaineth in him: *and he cannot sin, because he is born of God."*

In the new creation there is also a new standard of measurement. In the old life the sinner measured himself by himself or by others like himself. But in the new order the victorious, obedient, holy life of the incarnate Son becomes the believer's pattern for his own life on earth and all his living is measured by that perfect standard.

Christ's unchanging and unchangeable teachings and principles are now the rule by which he lives and he rejoices in being free from the despotism of the constantly shifting customs and styles of worldly society. The new creation in Christ has a new standard of values. Time becomes an extremely precious thing, the use of which is to be sacredly guarded and prayerfully made. Money becomes invested with new meaning and power, for consecrated to the Lord and used in His service it may be the means of saving souls infinitely precious in God's sight. Men and women, boys and girls, become vastly more than flesh and blood; they are seen as God sees them, human souls lost in sin, redeemed by the precious blood of the Son of God, and waiting to be saved through faith in Him. In all things Christ the Son becomes the believer's Example.

> John 13:14-15, "If I then, your Lord and Master, have washed your feet; ye also ought to wash one another's feet.
> *For I have given you an example,* that ye should do as I have done to you."

> 1 Peter 2:21, "For even hereunto were ye called: because Christ also suffered for us, *leaving us an example that we should follow his steps.*"

But need we continue to enumerate the things made new through the new birth when God says so plainly that *"all things* are become new?" Indeed, they must become so because we have a new spring from which all things in our life come. "All things are of God" (2 Corinthians 5:18). The source of all our thoughts, feelings, motives, ambitions, aspirations, actions, affections, purposes and plans, is God Himself. The new birth is just the beginning of a new life. "It is a crisis with view to a process; a rebirth with the prospect of a constant renewal."

Have you, my friend, been born again? Are you a member of the new order? Are you a new creation? If not, will you not begin that new life just now by one believing look at the crucified One?

But perchance, you have professed to come into the family of God through faith in Jesus Christ and yet you are discouraged today because of the countless old things that still persist in the new life. Is yours the case of new pieces on an old garment?

One day on the streets of Peking I saw an old countryman. He had on an old, faded, worn-out garment. It had been blue once but it was blue no longer. Right across the front and across the back of his faded garment were big, bright blue, new patches. On seeing the innocent old countryman's garment I laughed aloud. I could not help it for it looked so funny. But why did I laugh? The patches were all right. They were big and new and bright and blue and covered the whole of his garment, front and back. There was nothing the matter with the patches! Then why did I laugh? I will tell you why. Because the garment and the patches were out of harmony with each other. The garment was old and faded and worn out; the patches were new and bright and blue. The garment and the patches did not belong to each other.

I wonder if as God looks down upon us today He sees some patched Christians! Some professors of Christianity rather than possessors of Christ! Perhaps you go to church, read your Bible, have daily prayer, partake of the Holy Communion, all of which are part of every genuine Christian life. But in your life are these things like new patches on an old garment? Are they simply good habits added on to the old life of sin and self? Are you a patched Christian? A professor instead of a possessor? Or have the old things passed away and all things become new because you are in deed and truth a new creation in Christ?

17

Christ Our Lord—A New Sovereign in a New Sphere

CROSSING GOD'S BRIDGE of salvation the believer enters into a totally new sphere which requires the enthronement of a new Sovereign over his life. The Head of the new creation must become its Lord if all things are to become new.

When the risen Christ ascended to heaven His Father exalted Him to the place of Lordship over the universe and He included within that sovereignty the enthronement of Christ as Lord over the individual believer. To understand better the absolute necessity for such a change of sovereigns let us study these two spheres more in detail.

THE CHARACTERISTIC MARK OF EACH SPHERE

These two spheres are the exact antitheses of each other so that life in the one precludes life in the other. They may be readily distinguished because each has a characteristic mark.

> Romans 8:5, "For they that are *after the flesh* do mind *the things of the flesh;* but they that are *after the Spirit the things of the Spirit.*"
>
> Romans 8:9, "But ye are not *in the flesh,* but *in the Spirit,* if so be that the Spirit of God dwell in you. Now if any man have not the Spirit of Christ, he is none of his."

The characteristic mark of the old sphere is the "flesh" and of the new the "Spirit." The unbeliever is "in the flesh" and the believer is "in the Spirit."

The Bible teaches very plainly that "the flesh" and "the Spirit" are mutually irreconcilable enemies in totally diverse camps.

> Romans 8:6, "For to be *carnally minded* is death; but to be *spiritually minded* is life and peace."
>
> Galatians 5:17, "For *the flesh lusteth against the Spirit,* and *the Spirit against the flesh:* and *these are contrary the one to the other:* so that ye cannot do the things that ye would."

Man became "flesh" through Adam's sin.

> Genesis 6:3, R. V., "And Jehovah said, My spirit shall not strive with man
> for ever, *for that he also is flesh.*"

The flesh is the whole natural man, the life of nature, whether good or
bad, received through the first birth. It is the earthward, sinful life received through human generation. It is *all* that I am as a son of Adam.

> John 3:6, *"That which is born of the flesh is flesh;* and that which is born of
> the Spirit is spirit."

God invariably describes "the flesh" as the cause of sin's power, of the
Law's weakness, and as enmity toward Himself. God declares "the flesh"
to be irreconcilably lawless.

> Romans 7:25, "I thank God through Jesus Christ our Lord. So then with
> the mind I myself serve the law of God; but *with the flesh the law of sin.*"

> Romans 8:3, "For what the law could not do, in that *it was weak through
> the flesh,* God sending his own Son in the likeness of *sinful flesh,* and for
> sin, condemned sin in the flesh."

> Romans 8:7, *"Because the carnal mind is enmity against God:* for it is not
> subject to the law of God, neither indeed can be."

God sees nothing good in "the flesh." Even the very best product which
physical generation can produce He casts away as altogether useless.

> Romans 7:18, "For I know that *in me (that is, in my flesh,) dwelleth* NO
> GOOD THING: for to will is present with me; but how to perform that
> which is good I find not."

Paul's estimate of the flesh as given in this verse is God-inspired as anyone must readily admit who knows his former high regard for himself
(Philippians 3:4-6). Through human generation Paul was indeed richly
endowed. Yet inspired by the Holy Spirit he wrote "I know that in *my*
flesh dwelleth *no* good thing." When he entered into the sphere of the
Spirit he saw that the finest and best thing in him, his righteousness, was
as "filthy rags" because it, too, was permeated and defiled by sin—it was
self-righteousness. No, God sees no redeeming feature in any son of Adam.
The flesh offers nothing which is acceptable to God. Indeed the flesh is
the soil in which Satan works to keep the sinner alienated from God.

So there is but one possible attitude which God can have toward the
flesh. It is the attitude of condemnation and rejection. God refuses to deal
with the flesh on any terms for it is irretrievably displeasing to Him. "They
that are in the flesh CANNOT please God" (Romans 8:8).

Regeneration opens the way for man to become spiritual. At the new birth, as we have already seen, it is the Holy Spirit who quickens our human spirit and then comes to dwell therein to make our entire life spiritual and supernatural, heavenly and holy. It is the Holy Spirit in us who causes sin's power to be broken, God's law to be kept, and love of God to be supreme.

Romans 8:2, 4, "For *the law of the Spirit* of life in Christ Jesus *hath made me free from the law of sin* and death.
That the righteousness of the law might be fulfilled in us, who walk* not after the flesh, but *after the Spirit."*

Romans 5:5, "And hope maketh not ashamed; because *the love of God is shed abroad in our hearts by the Holy Ghost* which is given unto us."

The Reign of the Old Man

In each of these spheres is a sovereign who purposes to rule with undivided authority.

Colossians 3:9-10, "Lie not one to another, seeing that ye have put off *the old man* with his deeds; and have put on the new man, which is renewed in knowledge after the image of him that created him."

The sovereign in the old sphere is "the old man." The very essence of the flesh is self-will in the form of this God-resisting, God-rejecting nature. The heart of the flesh is this deep-dyed traitor which hates everything that God loves and loves everything that God hates.

The expression "the old man" is used but three times in the Bible, in Ephesians 4:22, Colossians 3:9, and Romans 6:6. It has an equivalent in the "I" of Galatians 2:20 and in the word "sin" as used in Romans 6. The term commonly used is "self." Through the first Adam's fall, "self" usurped the throne of man's personality and has held it in its control and use ever since. Every child is born into the world with king "self" on the throne, a fact which is made evident before he can even walk or talk.

"The old man" on the throne determines what the whole life from center to circumference shall be. His evil desires become evil deeds; his unholy aspirations are transmitted into unholy acts; his unrighteous character manifests itself in unrighteous conduct; his ungodly will is expressed in ungodly works.

Ephesians 2:3, "Among whom also we all had our conversation in times past in the lusts of the flesh, *fulfilling the desires of the flesh* and of the mind."

Colossians 3:9, "*Lie not* one to another, seeing that ye have put off *the old man with his deeds."*

Galatians 5:19-21, "*The works of the flesh are manifest, which are these;*

Adultery, fornication, uncleanness, lasciviousness, idolatry, witchcraft, hatred, variance, emulations, wrath, strife, seditions, heresies, envyings, murders, drunkenness, revellings, and such like; of the which I tell you before, as I have told you in time past, that they which do such things shall not inherit the kingdom of God."

"The old man" demands an environment that is in full accord with his tastes and inclinations, all of which are earthborn. He feeds on the things that are seen, he walks by sight, he revels in "the lust of the flesh," "the lust of the eyes," and "the pride of life." So the only atmosphere in which he could live and breathe is that of the world. "The world" is "the old man's" native heath.

> 1 John 2:16, "For all that is in the world, the lust of the flesh, and the lust of the eyes, and the pride of life, *is not of the Father, but is of the world.*"

DETHRONEMENT OF THE OLD MAN—COCRUCIFIXION WITH CHRIST

The vast majority of Christians stop short in their experience of the blessings of salvation with the joy of forgiveness of past sins and with the hope of heaven in the future. But the present is a forty-year wilderness experience full of futile wanderings, never enjoying peace and rest, never arriving in the promised land.

The history of God's dealing with the children of Israel is full of helpfulness and instruction for us at this point. Indeed it is typical of every phase of our deliverance from the old sphere and our entrance into the new. Egypt is the type of the world; the oppression of Pharaoh typifies the bondage to Satan in which the sinner is held; Canaan, the promised land flowing with milk and honey, typifies the heavenlies in which the believer has every spiritual blessing.

God purposed not only to bring the children of Israel out of Egypt but into Canaan, not only out of bondage but into rest. There are three distinct stages recorded of this deliverance; while still in Egypt they were delivered from the judgment of death through the sprinkling of the blood of the Paschal lamb upon the doorposts; then they were delivered out of Egypt and from the enemies who pursued them by the miraculous passage of the Red Sea. Due to their rebellion and unbelief the forty long, weary years of futile wandering in the wilderness followed, during which all of the people, except Caleb and Joshua, died, never having "possessed their possessions." Then came the last stage in their deliverance when the two, who had wholly followed the Lord, led the new generation of Israelites into the promised land through the miraculous passage of the river Jordan. There they had victory over their enemies, entered into the possession of their inheritance and had rest.

God purposes not only to bring the sinner out of the world but into the heavenlies: not only out of sinnerhood but into sainthood. There are three distinct stages in this deliverance which represent three different aspects of the death and resurrection of the Lord Jesus Christ. They are not stages in the sense of being marked off in point of time for they all belong to the believer through his relationship to the crucified, risen, exalted Lord and are his in experience the moment he apprehends and claims them by faith.

While still in bondage God speaks to the sinner telling him the way of deliverance from death, through faith in the shed blood of the Lamb of God. This results in the joy and peace of forgiveness, this covers the past. But the sinner needs much more than this for he needs to be taken out of the old sphere and to be freed from the grip of his old enemies, the world, the flesh and the devil. This is the passage of the Red Sea—the death and resurrection of the Lord Jesus Christ which makes a way clean out of the old sphere for the believer and at the same time swallows up the pursuing enemies in utter defeat and destruction. This is the believer's justification which gives him the standing before God of a freed and justified man and places the cross and the open tomb between him and his enemies.

Just here many believers stop; satisfied with release from the servitude of Pharaoh's land but not seeking the delights and rest of God's land of promise. They stop short of the last stage of the journey; hence the years of wilderness wandering, constantly going but never getting anywhere. They have been taken out of Egypt but Egypt is still in them. They hanker for the things of the world and of the flesh. Their lives are characterized by selfishness, murmuring, defeat, dissatisfaction, rebellion and fruitlessness. The Jordan crossing is still ahead for them. I wonder if this book has found such a wilderness wanderer in you? If so, may it come as God's Joshua to lead you over the Jordan into the land of your perfect inheritance in Christ Jesus. Through justification and regeneration the believer is separated from the old sphere of the natural man and all that pertains to it; through identification with Christ in His death, resurrection and ascension, he is brought out of the wilderness wanderings of the carnal life and into the victory, peace and rest of the spiritual life. Let us study together now what the crossing of the Jordan typifies for the believer.

Few people are willing to admit that "the old man" sits upon the throne and rules the whole being with despotic power. Even among Christians there are gross ignorance of and indifference to the subtle, insidious workings of the old "I." If the grosser "works of the flesh" are absent from the life, the individual rests in a complacent sense of goodness failing altogether to apprehend how obnoxious to God are the more refined and less openly manifest sins of the spirit and how they separate one leagues upon leagues from His pure holiness. No man living, except the one who through the enabling Spirit has seen Christ in His righteousness and holiness, will ever willingly say, "I know that in me (that is, in *my* flesh,) dwelleth *no* good thing."

Let us, then, pause for a moment to take a full-length portrait of this hideous, heinous self; let us face honestly his manifold operations and see if we are not forced to accept God's estimate of him and to acquiesce in the method of deliverance from his sovereignty. The foundation of life in the natural man is foursquare; self-will, self-love, self-trust, and self-exaltation, and upon this foundation is reared a superstructure that is one huge capital "I." Self-will is the cornerstone and self-exaltation is the capstone.

Self-will—"We have turned every one to his own way." The flesh wants its own way and is determined to have it even if it defies and disobeys God and overrides others. "I will" is the alphabet out of which self fashions its language of life.

Self-centeredness—"the old man" feeds upon himself. He is the beginning and the end. Life presents little that interests or affects him except as it relates to himself. He is the center of the world in which he lives and moves and he always looks out for number one.

Self-assertion—"the old man" believes that everyone is as interested in him and as fascinated by him as he himself is, so he protrudes and projects himself into the sight, hearing and notice of others continually. He monopolizes conversation and the theme is always "I," "my" and "mine." He walks with a swagger and expects the world to stop work and look at him. And he never dreams how offensive his self-importance is to others.

Self-depreciation—"the old man" is very versatile and sometimes it suits his purpose better to clothe his pride in a false humility. He curls up in his self-depreciation and shirks a lot of hard work which other people have to do. He magnifies his littleness and feebleness to his own advantage, yet with strange inconsistency he resents others' taking his professed estimate of himself and treating him accordingly.

Self-conceit—"the old man" lives so much in himself that he does not know how big the world is in which he lives and how many other really intelligent people there are in it, so he has little regard for the opinions of others, especially if contrary to his own. He looks with proud and supercilious pity upon those less favored and gifted than himself.

Self-love—"the old man" loves himself supremely, one might say almost exclusively. He loves God not at all and his human love for others is tainted more or less with selfishness, jealousy, envy or impurity. Indeed "the old man" makes an idol of himself which he not only loves but worships.

Self-indulgence—"the old man" eats, drinks, and is merry. For him to want anything is equivalent to having it. He pampers and coddles himself; he can even indulge his extravagant, fleshly appetites while others starve to death before his eyes.

Self-pleasing—"the old man" chafes under discomfort and deprivation and is grumpy and peevish unless everything in the life of his day ministers to his real or imagined needs. He lives unto only one person whose name is *self*.

Self-seeking—"the old man" is on a quest: he is after whatever will advance the cause of self. He seeks with feverish ambition and activity praise, position, power, prominence, and anything that checks his gaining them is attributed to others.

Self-pity—his love for himself often creates within "the old man" rebellion against his circumstances or relationships; he exaggerates his own possible suffering, discomfort or sorrow and makes himself and others miserable by his habitual murmuring.

Self-sensitiveness—"the old man" is extremely hard to live with because he is covered with wounds and is continually being hurt afresh. He is not very companionable because usually he is dissolved in tears, shrouded in silence, or enjoying a pout.

Self-defense—"the old man" is very jealous of his rights and busy avenging his wrongs. He indulges freely in lawsuits. In his pursuit of his own vindication and justification in cases of disagreement and estrangement with others he is blinded by his own sin.

Self-trust—"the old man" is very self-confident and feels no need of one wiser and stronger than himself. Trusting in his own powers and resources he is prone to say "Though all men shall deny Thee, yet will not I."

Self-sufficiency—the self-confidence of "the old man" fosters an egotistical, smug self-satisfaction which leaves him stagnant. He has neither desire nor sense of need for anything beyond what he already possesses.

Self-consciousness—"the old man" never forgets himself: wherever he goes he casts a shadow of himself before. He is constantly occupied with photographing himself and developing the plates. He is chained to himself and as he walks one hears the clank of the chains. He is often morbidly self-introspective.

Self-exaltation—"the old man" is absorbed in his own excellencies: he overestimates himself and his abilities: he thirsts for admiration and praise and he thrives on flattery. He secretly worships at the shrine "self" and he wishes others to do so publicly.

Self-righteousness—"the old man" loves to dress himself in the garments of morality, benevolence and public-spiritedness. He even patronizes the church and often assists in drives for raising money for philanthropic and religious purposes, heading the list of donors with a handsome gift. He keeps a double entry account book—both with the church and with the world and expects a reward both on earth and in heaven.

Self-glorying—perhaps "the old man" resents this plain delineation of himself as he really is and thinks the condemnation too sweeping. Immediately he begins to enumerate his good qualities, his amiableness, geniality, tolerance, self-control, sacrificial spirit and other virtues. In doing so he takes all the credit to himself for what he is, exhibiting ill-concealed pride and vanity.

All that we have desired to say of this hideous ugly self is said most tellingly by Gerhard Tersteegen in the following lines:

> "Apart from Thee
> I am not only naught but worse than naught,
> A wretched monster, horrible of mien!
> And when I work my works in self's vain strength,
> However good and holy they may seem,
> These works are hateful—nay, in Thy pure sight
> Are criminal and fiendish, since thereby
> I seek, and please, and magnify myself
> In subtle pride of goodness, and ascribe
> To *Self* the glory that is Thine alone.
> So dark, corrupt, so vile a thing is self.
> Seen in the presence of Thy purity
> It turns my soul to loathing and disgust;
> Yea, all the virtues that it boasts to own,
> Are foul and worthless when I look on Thee.
> Oh that there might be no more *I* or *mine!*
> That in myself I might no longer own
> As mine, my life, my thinking, or my choice,
> Or any other motion, but in me
> That Thou, my God, my Jesus might be all,
> And work the all in all! Let that, O Lord,
> Be dumb, forever die, and cease to be,
> Which Thou doest not Thyself in me inspire,
> And speak and work."

Is this delineation of self true or untrue? You have three ways by which you may judge and decide; what God's Word says of him, what you have seen of his manifestation in other lives, and what you know to be true of yourself. In the light of our own experience is there one of us who would not have to confess to every one of these hateful manifestations of self at some moment in a greater or less degree? We each of us know what a hydra-headed monster that old "I" is. Luther knew it and said "I am more afraid of my own heart than of the Pope and all his cardinals. I have within me that great Pope Self."

What, then, shall be done with this most stubborn foe? this most tyrannical sovereign? this bold usurper of God's place? God has declared very
plainly in His Word what He has already done with him. He has but one
place for "the old man" and that is the cross, and but one plan for the
termination of his despotic rule and that is by his crucifixion with Christ.

> Romans 6:6, R. V., "Knowing this, that *our old man was crucified with
> him*, that the body of sin might be done away, that so we should no
> longer be in bondage to sin."
>
> Galatians 2:20, R. V., "*I have been crucified with Christ;* and it is no longer
> I that live, but Christ liveth in me: and that life which I now live in the
> flesh I live in faith, the faith which is in the Son of God, who loved me,
> and gave himself up for me."
>
> 2 Corinthians 5:14-15, R. V., "For the love of Christ constraineth us: be-
> cause we thus judge, that *one died for all, therefore all died:*
> And he died for all, that *they that live should no longer live unto
> themselves, but unto him* who for their sakes died and rose again."

Two things explicitly stated in these verses should be noted; first, that
the crucifixion of "the old man" is an already accomplished fact, and second, that it is a cocrucifixion.

Notice the tenses: "was crucified"—past, and "have been crucified"—
past perfect. The judicial crucifixion of "the old man" took place centuries
ago. Whether or not a single soul ever accepted this glorious fact that the
entire old creation in Adam was carried to the cross and there crucified
with Christ, it is as gloriously true as the fact that Christ Himself was
crucified.

"One died for all."

Substitution—the Saviour on the cross *for* the sinner.

"Therefore all died."

Identification—the sinner on the cross *with* the Saviour.

It is part of the flawless provision of God's grace for the believer that
everything that pertains to the old nature should terminate its sinful course
at the cross. Whether from "sins" or from "self" the cross is God's only
place of deliverance. But as surely as Christ Jesus "bore my sins in His
own body on the tree" just so surely was my "old man crucified with Him"
there. If I accept and act upon the one fact by faith, consistently I must
accept and act upon the other fact by faith.

Deliverance from the old sphere "in the flesh" and entrance into the
new sphere "in the spirit" demands the dethronement of self. It is very
evident that a house divided against itself cannot stand. No house can
entertain two masters without unceasing conflict. If the Lord Jesus is to
take the throne and rule over the human personality then "the old man"
must abdicate. That he will never do. So God must deal drastically with

him. He is a usurper whom God has condemned, and sentenced to death. In His infinite grace God carried out that sentence on Calvary's cross. And now God declares to every person who cries out for deliverance from the tyranny of self, "the old man was crucified with Christ." Do you believe it and find it increasingly true?

I was once leading a series of meetings in a school in China and was showing the way of deliverance from both the penalty and the power of sin through the death and resurrection of the Lord Jesus Christ. One message was particularly on the theme we are now considering. The most attentive listener in the audience was a man who had been the classical teacher in that school for eleven years. Although he had daily heard the Gospel in chapel and had attended church he had never become a Christian. But during those days the Spirit of God worked mightily in his heart convicting and convincing him and finally leading him to an open confession of Christ. In conversation with a missionary afterward this teacher said that, although he had believed the Gospel truth that Christ died for his sins, he had never accepted Him as Saviour because this did not seem to fully meet his need. He said that he was under the dominion of sin, and was governed by that old sinful nature and that not until he learned that God in Christ's cross had dealt with that root, *sin,* out of which came the fruit, *sins,* did he believe it was a salvation sufficient to deliver him. But he found in this glorious truth of the crucifixion of "the old man" that God is able to save to the uttermost those that come to Him in Christ and accept the full work of His cross.

The second fact which these verses make clear is that this is a *co*crucifixion. "Our old man" was crucified *with Christ.* This declares both the method and the time of this crucifixion. There is often confusion at this point.

Paul says, "I have been crucified *with Christ.*" He did not try to crucify himself nor did his crucifixion take place at some special point in his spiritual experience through some act on his part. With that death Paul had no more to do than he had with the death of Christ Himself. The crucifixion of that old "I" was not *self*-crucifixion neither did it take place in Damascus, Arabia, or when Paul was "caught up to the third heaven." But the death of the "I," which was Saul, took place on the cross when Christ died there.

The truth becomes easy of apprehension if we but remember that God sees every person either in Adam or in Christ. He deals with the human race through these two representative men. When Adam died the human race died in him. You died in Adam. So did I. Through that spiritual death "the old man" found birth and usurped God's place on the throne of man's life. Christ came as the last Adam to recover for God and for the race all that had been lost to them through the first Adam. God's method of defeating death is through death, so Christ died and the race of sinners died in Him. "One died for all: *therefore all died*." When the last Adam died "the old man" died with Him. The old "I" in you and in me was judicially crucified with Christ. "*Ye died*" and your death dates from the death of Christ. "The old man," the old "self" in God's reckoning was taken to the cross with Christ and crucified and taken into the tomb with Christ and buried.

> Romans 6:3-4, R. V., "Or are ye ignorant that all we who were baptized into Christ Jesus were baptized into his death? *We were buried therefore with him through baptism into death:* that like as Christ was raised from the dead through the glory of the Father, so we also might walk in newness of life."

The perfection of God's grace is marvelously manifested in this glorious fact of cocrucifixion—the sinner with the Saviour on the cross. It needs only the perfection of man's faith to make it a glorious reality in his spiritual experience. Assurance of deliverance from the sphere of the "flesh" and of the dethronement of "the old man" rests upon the apprehension and acceptance of this fact of cocrucifixion.

THE CREATION OF THE NEW MAN. CORESURRECTION WITH CHRIST

Cocrucifixion opens the door into coresurrection. Death is the gate to life. Identification with Christ in His death and burial is but the beginning of the believer's union with Him in endless life. Death is both an ending and a beginning, an exit and an entrance.

> Romans 6:5, R. V., "For if we have become *united with him in the likeness of his death*, we shall be *also in the likeness of his resurrection*."

> Romans 6:8, R. V., "But if *we died with Christ,* we believe that *we shall also live with him*."

Identification with Christ in His quickening, resurrection and ascension, takes the believer into the new sphere of the "Spirit" and begins the life of "the new man."

> Ephesians 2:4-6, "But God, who is rich in mercy, for his great love wherewith he loved us, even when we were dead in sins, *hath quickened us together with Christ* (by grace ye are saved;) and *hath raised us up together,* and *made us sit together in heavenly places in Christ Jesus*."

> Ephesians 4:24, "And that *ye put on the new man,* which after God is created in righteousness and true holiness."

"Together with Christ" on the cross, in the tomb, in the heavenlies!

Thus would the exalted Lord of glory, Head of the new creation, share with every believer the glorious victory of His death, the mighty power of His resurrection, and the regal bounty of His throne.

> "If Christ would live and reign in me,
>   I must die;
> With Him I crucified must be;
>   I must die;
> Lord, drive the nails, nor heed the groans,
> My flesh may writhe and make its moans,
> But in this way, and this alone,
>   I must die.
>
> When I am dead, then Lord to Thee
>   I shall live;
> My time, my strength, my all to Thee
>   I shall give.
> O may the Son now make me free!
> Here, Lord, I give my all to Thee;
> For time and for eternity
>   I will live."

THE NEW SPHERE—THE BELIEVER IN CHRIST

The moment a penitent sinner puts his faith in the atoning blood of the crucified Christ that moment he steps out of life "in Adam" and enters into life "in Christ." Forever after he is ensphered and environed by the Lord of glory. He is *"in Christ Jesus"* and will be through the ages upon the ages to come. All that he is and has he is and has "in Christ." In God's reckoning the believer has no life apart from His Son. Christ is the ground in which he is rooted and planted. Through the new birth the believer became a new creation with a new nature which demanded a new environment, a new atmosphere, as it were, where the new life could mature into an ever deepening conformity to the image of Jesus Christ. This new environment is "in Christ."

Let us read a few passages out of scores in the Bible in which this expression "in Christ" is used to show that from the eternity of the past through our present life on into the eternity of the future God thinks of who have accepted Christ as Saviour only in this relationship to His Son.

> Ephesians 1:4, "According as he hath *chosen us in him* before the foundation of the world, that we should be holy and without blame before him in love."
>
> Ephesians 1:6, "To the praise of the glory of his grace, wherein he hath made us *accepted in the beloved.*"
>
> Ephesians 2:13, "But now *in Christ Jesus* ye who sometimes were far off *are made nigh* by the blood of Christ."

1 John 2:6, "He that saith he *abideth in him* ought himself also so to walk, even as he walked."

Philippians 3:9, "And be *found in him,* not having mine own righteousness, which is of the law, but that which is through the faith of Christ, the righteousness which is of God by faith."

Romans 16:10, "Salute Apelles *approved in Christ.*"

Colossians 2:7, "*Rooted and built up in him,* and stablished in the faith, as ye have been taught, abounding therein with thanksgiving."

2 Corinthians 5:17, "Therefore if any man be *in Christ,* he is *a new creature:* old things are passed away; behold, all things are become new."

2 Corinthians 2:14, "Now thanks be unto God, which always causeth us to *triumph in Christ,* and maketh manifest the savour of his knowledge by us in every place."

1 Corinthians 1:2, "Unto the church of God which is at Corinth, to them that are *sanctified in Christ Jesus,* called to be saints, with all that in every place call upon the name of Jesus Christ our Lord, both theirs and ours."

Colossians 2:9-10, "For in him dwelleth all the fulness of the Godhead bodily. And ye are *complete in him,* which is the head of all principality and power."

Colossians 1:28, "Whom we preach, warning every man, and teaching every man in all wisdom; that we may present every man *perfect in Christ Jesus.*"

That every reader of this book might be led into a clearer apprehension of this marvelous truth I would commend the reading of the late Dr. A. T. Pierson's book *In Christ.* To whet the appetite for it I would quote the following from the introduction:

"A very small key may open a very complex lock and a very large door and that door may itself lead into a vast building with priceless stores of wealth and beauty. This brief phrase 'In Christ,' a preposition followed by a proper name, is the key to the whole New Testament. Those three short words, 'In Christ Jesus' are without doubt the most important ever written, even by an inspired pen, to express the mutual relation of the believer and Christ. They occur with their equivalents over one hundred and thirty times. Such repetition and variety must have some intense meaning. When, in the Word of God a phrase like this occurs so often and with such manifold applications, it cannot be a matter of accident; there is a deep design. These two words unlock and interpret every separate book in the New Testament. Here is God's own key whereby we may open all the various doors and enter all the glorious rooms in this Palace Beautiful and explore all the apartments in the house of the heavenly Interpreter from Matthew to the Apocalypse, when the door is opened into Heaven."

This relationship of the believer to the Lord Jesus determines his position, his privileges and his possessions. To be in Christ is to be where He is, to be what He is and to share what He has.

The believer in Christ is where Christ is. Christ is in His Father's immediate presence, He is at the Father's right hand, He is in the Father's sight; so is the believer in Christ.

> Ephesians 2:6, "And hath raised us up together, and made us *sit together in heavenly places in Christ.*"
>
> Colossians 3:3, "For ye are dead, and *your life is hid with Christ in God.*"

Christ has left the earth as His place of abode and now dwells in the heavenlies. The believer is in Christ, therefore even now while still on earth his real citizenship is in heaven and he is a pilgrim upon earth for his real life is in Christ.

> Philippians 3:20, R. V., "For *our citizenship is in heaven;* whence also we wait for a Saviour, the Lord Jesus Christ."
>
> Hebrews 13:14, "For *here have we no continuing city,* but we seek one to come."

Therefore the believer's heart is set upon heavenly things; he values and seeks heavenly things more than earthly.

> Colossians 3:1-2, "If ye then be risen with Christ, *seek those things which are above,* where Christ sitteth on the right hand of God. *Set your affection on things above,* not on things on the earth."

Do I hear someone say, This is too high a standard for me; it is not only impossible but unattractive. I am on the earth and in this world, therefore why should I not live as though I were and enjoy what this earth and this world have to give me and leave the enjoyment of heaven until I reach there? Such is the reasoning of vast numbers of Christians and their lives are in full harmony with their reasoning. As someone has aptly said they have become Christians much as a man takes out a life insurance policy—something that does not in any way alter one's manner of living but will be of use after death and is maintained with the payment of a yearly premium. With many a person becoming a Christian has made little if any difference in either his character or conduct. He is still of the earth—earthy.

Is it not conceivable that God would have us become acclimated to our eternal home in heaven with Christ during our transient stay on earth? If the atmosphere of heaven is stifling to me here what will it be to me there? If the heavenly pleasures and pursuits are unattractive to me now, what will they be to me then? There is music in heaven but it is not jazz; there are pleasures there but they are not the pleasures of the ballroom, the card table, or the cinema; there are pursuits in the glory land but not that of making money or a name or a place in society. Death is both an exit and an entrance all in one. For the believer it closes the door on earth to open one into heaven. There is not one instant for preparation for that higher altitude. If my heart cannot stand it here how will it stand it there?

Or is it unthinkable that God would wish to open a window into that blessed realm of light and life to some wayward, worn traveler on the road of darkness and death through the Spirit-filled lives of believers on earth? In fact is that not one of His most effectual ways today of making known the beauties and excellencies of that other world? Does He not want to bring heaven to earth that He may woo earth to heaven? And how else can He do it but through heaven-born, heaven-filled men and women?

Again is there one so selfish, so grasping, as to wish to get all from God and give nothing to God? Is there one who would accept a pass from earth to heaven provided only through God's matchless grace and marvelous love, who still will spend all his time and substance in pleasure-seeking?

No, God means that life down here shall be in harmony with life up there; that even while sojourning on earth we shall live a life partaking of the nature of heaven, a life holy and heavenly in character and conduct.

In Christ Jesus the believer is what Christ is in the reckoning of God. Christ, the Head, and the believer, a member of His Body, are one. Through this wonderful identification God looks upon us as joint-heirs with Christ, entering into and occupying the same position and enjoying the same privileges as His Son.

> Romans 8:17, "And, if children, then heirs; heirs of God, and *joint-heirs with* Christ; if so be that we suffer with him, that we may be also glorified together."

We are so enfolded and environed by the Lord Jesus that God cannot see Christ today without seeing us. This moment as God looks upon His Son at His right hand He sees you and me if we are in Christ Jesus.

> "Near, so very near to God
>   Nearer I could not be;
> For in the person of His Son,
>   I'm just as near as He.
> Dear, so very dear to God,
>   Dearer I could not be;
> For in the person of His Son,
>   I'm just as dear as He."

In Christ Jesus the believer shares with Christ all His possessions. Every spiritual blessing is ours in Christ. Dare we believe it? All things are ours in Christ. Dare we act as though we believed it?

> Ephesians 1:3, R. V., "Blessed be the God and Father of our Lord Jesus Christ, who hath blessed us *with every spiritual blessing* in the heavenly places in Christ."
>
> Romans 8:32, "He that spared not his own Son, but delivered him up for us all, *how shall he not with him also freely give us all things?*"
>
> 1 Corinthians 3:21, "Therefore let no man glory in men. *For all things are yours.*"

God says in these and many other passages that the possessions of the exalted Christ are the possessions of the one united to Him by faith. Identification with Him in His death, burial, resurrection and ascension includes identification with Him in all the gain and the glory, all the privileges and possessions gained by Him through His passion. Christ's victory over Satan and all the forces of evil is ours and His present life of rest, peace and joy is ours.

What, then, should be the Christian's chief business in life? To possess his possessions in Christ Jesus that in daily life and service he may realize and utilize to the full his spiritual inheritance. How may this be done?

1. Through *spiritual apprehension* of our riches in Christ.

> 1 Corinthians 2:12, "Now we have received, not the spirit of the world, but the spirit which is of God; *that we might know the things that are freely given to us of God.*"

We could never know of ourselves but the Spirit knows and indwells us that He may illumine us regarding our riches in Christ.

2. Through *spiritual aspiration* for our riches in Christ.

> Colossians 3:1-2, "*Seek* those things which are above. . . . *Set* your affection on things above."

Not only through the Holy Spirit's illumination but also through His impelling shall we possess our riches in Christ. The indwelling Spirit creates within us the desire for all our spiritual inheritance.

3. Through *spiritual appropriation* of our riches in Christ.

> 2 Corinthians 3:18, R. V., "But we all, with unveiled face beholding as in a mirror the glory of the Lord, are transformed into the same image from glory to glory, *even as from the Lord the Spirit.*"

Faith lays hold on our inheritance in Christ and appropriates that which God has so prodigally provided. We are energized by the Holy Spirit to take these things by faith.

THE NEW SOVEREIGN—CHRIST IN THE BELIEVER

Through the new birth the believer enters into the Kingdom of God where God's will is supreme. The life of every loyal subject is lived wholly in the will of God. The government of God has spiritual laws which operate beneficently for the well-being both of the individual and of society in every department of life. Wherever these laws are implicitly obeyed, there the will of God is done on earth as in heaven, and peace, rest and unity prevail. Through the new birth the believer enters into the family of God where the Father's will is supreme. The life of every filial child is lived wholly in the will of the Father.

Self-will is the cornerstone upon which Satan's kingdom is built and he constantly tempts the Christian to disobey. No man in his own strength is able to resist. Only one Man ever has wholly resisted it and refused the control of Satan over his will. Now as Head of the new creation He is absolute Lord in the new sphere.

By virtue of entering into that sphere every believer acknowledges Christ Jesus to be the Lord of his life and accepts the will of God as his rule of life. When Christ is thus crowned as Lord, then the responsibility is His to keep the believer from falling and to enable him to resist every temptation of Satan.

John 13:13, *"Ye call me Master and Lord:* and ye say well; *for so I am."*

Romans 14:8-9, R. V., "For whether we live, we live unto the Lord; or whether we die, we die unto the Lord: whether we live therefore, or die, *we are the Lord's.* For to this end Christ died and lived again, *that he might be Lord of both the dead and the living."*

To many Christians the most difficult thing they have to do is to consent willingly to the Lordship of Jesus Christ over their whole being. They are loath to admit the necessity of the absolute dethronement of "the old man" and the perfect enthronement of the Lord Jesus. As someone has very aptly said, "I was quite willing that Jesus Christ should be King, so long as He allowed me to be Prime Minister." But Christ shares His Lordship with no one and unless "He is Lord of all, He is not Lord at all."

But the perfection of God's grace meets even this weakness and inability in us in His gift of the indwelling Holy Spirit who enables us by His inward working to crown Christ Lord.

Thus Christ Jesus establishes His throne at the very center of the new creation and from there rules to the circumference of the believer's being. He becomes Lord of all.

18

Christ Our Life—A Perfect Oneness Effected

CHRIST JESUS was made like us that we might be made like Him. In the incarnation there was the union of Deity with humanity that in regeneration there might be the union of humanity with Deity. When the Holy Spirit begat in the believer a new nature He opened the door to a living, organic union between Christ and the Christian which will exist through the ages upon ages to come. Christ and the Christian are eternally one. The exalted Christ lives now to bestow upon us in all of its fullness His own triumphant, joyous, holy life.

To be a Christian is nothing less than to have the glorified Christ living in us in actual presence, possession and power. It is to have Him as *the Life of our life* in such a way and to such a degree that we can say even as Paul said, "To me to live is Christ." To be a Christian is to *grow up into Christ in all things:* it is to have that divine seed which was planted in our innermost spirit blossom out into a growing conformity to His perfect life. To be a Christian is to have Christ the life of our minds, our hearts, our wills, so that it is Christ thinking through us, loving through us, willing through us. It is increasingly to have no life but the life of Christ within us filling us with ever increasing measure.

But I can hear some modern Nicodemus say, "How can these things be?" How can I live such a life in my home where I receive no sympathy nor help but rather ridicule and scoffing, and where I have for so long lived a sinful and a defeated life? How can I live a truly consistent Christ-life in my social circle where there is scarcely a person who ever gives Him a thought and where His name is never mentioned? How can I live "in the Spirit" in a place of business where I am surrounded by those living altogether "in the flesh" and where the very atmosphere seems surcharged with evil? How can I even learn to live the life more abundant when my membership is in a thoroughly worldly church where little is given to feed and strengthen my spiritual life?

As we are in Christ in the heavenlies so is He in us on earth. Christ in us can live this life anywhere, and that is what He longs to do. This truth our

Lord gave in germ in His last conversation with His disciples on earth. He had told them that He was going away from them and they were wondering how they could ever be true disciples apart from Him. The burden of this last conversation was to assure them He would be with them in a spiritual Presence far more real and vital than the relationship they had with Him up to that time. The same life that was in Him as the Vine would flow through them as branches.

> John 15:5, "I am the vine, ye are the branches: He that abideth in me, and *I in him*, the same bringeth forth much fruit: for without me ye can do nothing."

It was likewise the burden of our Lord's high priestly prayer on that last night.

> John 17:23, 26, "*I in them*, and thou in me, that they may be made perfect in one; that the world may know that thou hast sent me, and hast loved them, as thou hast loved me. And I have declared unto them thy name and will declare it: that the love wherewith thou has loved me may be in them, and *I in them*."

"*I in them*"—these three simple but significant words close the prayer with that little inner circle in which He breathed forth the passionate desire of His heart for His own on down through the centuries. Now as well as then, it is the consuming desire of Jesus Christ to reincarnate Himself in the Christian.

The apostle Paul in the revelation given him laid hold upon this precious, glorious truth and it is woven into the warp and woof of his experience, his preaching, and his missionary service. "Christ liveth in me" was the very acme of his personal spiritual life.

> Galatians 2:20, R. V., "I have been crucified with Christ; and *it is no longer I that live, but Christ liveth in me:* and the life which I now live in the flesh I live in faith, the faith which is in the Son of God, who loved me, and gave himself up for me."
>
> Philippians 1:21, "For *to me to live is Christ*."

"Christ liveth in me" so that "To me to live is Christ"—there was nothing beyond this for Paul. Having the glorified Christ as his very life was all-inclusive in Paul's spiritual experience. This to him was *life on the highest plane*.

"*Christ in you*" was the heart of his message to the churches. It rang out with clarion clearness in all Paul's teaching and preaching. A cross section from any of Paul's epistles would reveal this truth written in capital letters.

> Colossians 1:27, "To whom God would make known what is the riches of

the glory of this mystery among the Gentiles; *which is Christ in you*, the hope of glory."

"*Christ in you*" was the very passion of his missionary service. Paul might employ different methods in his service for God, he might be all things to all men, but the end, the aim, the goal of it all was just one thing with him—that Christ Jesus Himself might be formed in each one who heard the Gospel message.

> Galatians 4:19, "My little children, of whom I travail in birth again *until Christ be formed in you.*"

To be a Christian is to accept Christ as Saviour and to crown Him as Lord. But there is one step more: it is to appropriate Him as Life. As the works within the watch are the real life of the watch so the Lord Jesus within the believer is the real life of the believer. "The Christian life is not merely a converted life nor even a consecrated life but it is a Christ-life." Christ is the Christian's center; Christ is the Christian's circumference; Christ is all in between. As Paul has put it "Christ *is* all and *in* all."

> Colossians 3:4, "When Christ, *who is our life*, shall appear, then shall ye also appear with him in glory."

A Perfect Oneness Effected

The spiritual history of a believer could be written in two phrases, "Ye in me" and "I in you." In God's reckoning Christ and the believer have become one in such a way that Christ is both in the heavenlies and upon earth and the believer is both on earth and in the heavenlies. The Church without Christ is a Body without a Head; Christ without the Church is a Head without a Body. The fullness of the Head is for the Body and the Body is "the fulness of him that filleth all in all."

> Colossians 2:9-10, R. V., "For *in him dwelleth all the fulness of the God-head bodily, and in him ye are made full*, who is the head of all principality and power."
>
> Ephesians 1:22-23, R. V., "And he put all things in subjection under his feet, and gave him to be head over all things to *the church, which is his body, the fulness of him that filleth all in all.*"

Could God tell us more clearly that in His divine purpose He means for the fullness of Christ to be the fullness of the Christian? It is a staggering thought! Its plain import is that you and I and all other Christians are to bring Christ down from heaven to earth and to let men see even in us who He is and what He has done and what He can do in a human life. It is to have Christ's life in such a perfection of likeness that men see Him in us and are drawn to Him in faith and love. It is to be such a oneness of life that one's human personality is but a vessel in which the beauty, holiness and glory of the Lord Jesus shine forth in undimmed transparency.

But here I hear the murmur of a doubting Thomas, "Except I see this Christ-life more perfectly in my fellow Christian or experience it more fully in my own life I will not believe it is possible!" All I can say in answer to this is "I believe because I have seen." For six weeks I lived in a heaven upon earth in a Chicago boardinghouse, incredible as that may seem. It was run by a little woman who weighed about eighty-five pounds and who was kept from falling into a heap upon the floor by a brace which was worn night and day. She had lived on the third floor for two years with no outlook but the blue sky above and a patch of green grass a few feet square below. But her eyes shone like stars, upon her face was a smile that intense bodily suffering, straitened financial circumstances, few social contacts, limited opportunities for enjoyment of God's great and wonderful world, had not been able to remove, and mirrored in that face was a light that one never sees on sea or land except where the Light of the world dwells in undimmed brightness. Christ was the Life of her life.

A young Chinese man who had been a Christian less than two years came one day for a bit of Christian fellowship. From a godless life he had been very marvelously converted and transformed. Christ had in deed and truth become all and in all to him. After he left the house that day a gentleman who saw him for only a brief moment said, "Who was that young man? I never met anyone who so instantly compelled me to think of Christ as did he."

A Christian businessman lay dying of cancer in a hospital. Friends called to comfort him and they left feeling that they had not only been taken to the very door of heaven but even that they had seen the King in His beauty. Christ had been the Life of his life in health and continued to be so in sickness.

A young woman of nobility and wealth was on the road that led into worldliness and ease, when she met her Lord. Captivated by His mighty love and power, even as was the apostle of old, she too said, "Lord, what wilt thou have me to do?" The answer was, "I would go through you to carry the Gospel to China." For nearly thirty years she has been there without a furlough, working and praying through the cold of winter and the heat of summer, with only an occasional vacation of a week or two. In more than twenty places are groups of worshipers of the true God and many hundreds have been eternally blessed through that life crucified, buried, and risen with Jesus Christ. You say, "She must be old, worn and haggard." Far, far from it. In her beautiful face is all the joyous gladness of youth and yet all the wondrous peace of the twilight years of a life lived in the constant and conscious presence of the living God. Even a stranger immediately recognizes in that life something more than human; something that belongs to another world than this. Christ is the Life of her life.

A little girl of eleven years of age lay dying. She deeply and dearly loved her Lord and as He came to take her home she seemed fairly transfigured. She called father, mother, brothers and sisters to her and with the very love of Christ filling and flooding her little heart she pleaded with them to meet her in heaven. An elder sister who loved that child as she loved no one else went from that room crushed but with her heart steeled against her sister's Christ. Out into a life of reckless worldliness she went but ever haunted by the face of Christ and the voice of Christ as she had seen and heard it in her little sister. Two years passed by but the vision of His face and the sound of His voice were not dimmed and finally that cold, resisting heart was melted into such love of the Lord Jesus that she joyously accepted Him as her Saviour, and her life was marvelously transformed. Christ was the Life of that eleven-year-old child.

Is He the Life of your life? Could this be said of you?

> "Not I, but Christ be honoured, loved, exalted,
> Not I, but Christ be seen, be known, be heard;
> Not I, but Christ in every thought and action,
> Not I, but Christ in every look and word."

The thought of living such a Christ-life could well make us tremble and fear did God not make it so clear that He does not expect us to live it in our own strength and power but that in the gift of the Holy Spirit He has made ample provision for our growing conformity into the image of His Son and for a continuous renewal of Christ's life within us. It is the Holy Spirit who brings the fullness of Christ's life in the heavenlies into our life on earth.

> 2 Corinthians 3:18, R. V., "But we all, with unveiled face beholding as in a mirror the glory of the Lord, are transformed into the same image from glory to glory, *even as from the Lord the Spirit.*"

> Ephesians 3:16-17, 19, "That he would grant you, according to the riches of his glory, *to be strengthened with might by his Spirit in the inner man; that Christ may dwell in your hearts by faith. That ye might be filled with all the fulness of God.*"

> "There's a Man in the Glory
> Whose Life is for me,
> He's pure and He's holy,
> Triumphant and free.
> He's wise and He's loving,
> Tender is He;

And His Life in the Glory,
My life must be.

"There's a Man in the Glory
Whose Life is for me,
He overcame Satan;
From bondage He's free.
In life He is reigning,
Kingly is He;
And His Life in the Glory,
My life must be.

"There's a Man in the Glory
Whose Life is for me,
In Him is no sickness:
No weakness has He.
He's strong and in vigour,
Buoyant is He;
And His Life in the Glory,
My life may be.

"There's a Man in the Glory
Whose Life is for me.
His peace is abiding;
Patient is He.
He's joyful and radiant,
Expecting to see
His Life in the Glory
Lived out in me."

19

Christ Our Sanctification—A People for His Possession and Use

THE CHRISTIAN is a new creation, in a new sphere with a new Sovereign, living a new life, all of which speaks of differentiation and distinctiveness. The Christian is a marked man. There is a distinct line of cleavage between the man "in the flesh" and the man "in the Spirit." There is a definite boundary between "the world" and "the heavenlies" and the man who through redemption has stepped over that border line is thereby a sanctified man. Christ, the Saviour, has become his sanctification.

The necessity for sanctification will be clearly seen when we remember that man was created for God's possession and use but through sin he fell into the possession and use of Satan. In sanctification God recovers His own and fits him for communion and cooperation with Himself.

Sanctification, as Scripture reveals, has a very vital relationship to the believer's calling, position and condition. This is typified in God's redemptive dealings with the children of Israel. Through His call to Abraham God chose and set apart a nation for Himself. With them He made a covenant by which they were to be separated from all other peoples upon the earth and were to become a holy people who would show forth the praise and glory of His name among the heathen nations. The children of Israel were set apart as God's peculiar possession, under His sovereign control and for His exclusive use.

> Deuteronomy 14:2, "For thou art an holy people unto the LORD thy God, and *the Lord hath chosen thee to be a peculiar people unto himself, above all the nations that are upon the earth.*"

But the children of Israel were sold into the bondage of Egypt and became the subject—slaves of Pharaoh. That He might repossess His own, God redeemed them and brought them out of Egypt and into Canaan. In position as well as by calling they became a separated people; God's own possession.

Leviticus 20:24, 26, "But I have said unto you, Ye shall inherit their land, and I will give it unto you to possess it, a land that floweth with milk and honey; *I am the Lord your God, which have separated you from other people.* And ye shall be holy unto me: for I the LORD am holy, and *have severed you from other people, that ye should be mine.*"

Numbers 3:13, *"Because all the firstborn are mine;* for on the day that I smote all the firstborn in the land of Egypt *I hallowed unto me all the firstborn in Israel,* both man and beast: *mine shall they be:* I am the LORD."

Then God commanded them to live as a people who belonged wholly unto Him. The separateness which He had wrought through their changed position was to be manifested through a changed condition. As a people in covenant with a holy God they were to live a holy life in the midst of altogether unholy nations and were to be God's instrument in the conquest of the promised land.

Leviticus 20:7-8, *"Sanctify yourselves therefore, and be ye holy:* for I am the LORD your God. And *ye shall keep my statutes, and do them:* I am the LORD which sanctify you."

THE BELIEVER A SAINT BY CALLING

In the New Testament God says that believers are a chosen, called, and separated people. In Christ the believer was set apart as God's own peculiar possession even before the foundation of the world. Every believer is chosen in Christ to be holy; he is called to be a saint; he is set apart to show forth the beauty, glory and holiness of His God.

Ephesians 1:4, *"According as he hath chosen us in him* before the foundation of the world, *that we should be holy* and without blame before him in love."

Romans 1:6-7, "Among whom are ye also *the called of Jesus Christ:*
To all that be in Rome, beloved of God, *called to be saints:* Grace to you and peace from God our Father, and the Lord Jesus Christ."

1 Peter 2:9, "But *ye are a chosen generation, a royal priesthood,* an *holy nation, a peculiar people; that ye should shew forth the praises of him* who hath called you out of darkness into his marvellous light."

Thus we see that every believer was chosen and called to be a saint and that a saint is one set apart as belonging to God and as separated unto Him for His use. Throughout Scripture this is invariably the meaning of the words "to sanctify" or "sanctification" whether used in connection with things or persons. That which is sanctified is something wholly set apart for God's possession and use and when God lays claim to anything and separates it unto His use it is by that act "sanctified." God's undivided proprietorship of the believer lies enfolded in the very heart of the truth of sanctification. In the eternity of the past God called us to be His own possession. He said, "Thou art mine."

THE BELIEVER A SAINT BY POSITION

When, where, and how is the believer sanctified? At what point of time, at what stage in spiritual experience, and through what means is the believer wholly separated unto God and set apart as the special possession of the Lord? There has been much confusion on these points that has led to bewilderment on the part of many and even delusion on the part of some.

But God's Word is crystal clear on this theme as on all others connected with salvation if we keep to the scriptural meaning and method of the spiritual experiences God intends we should enjoy. Let us never forget that God is infinitely more concerned about our entrance into the fullness of our inheritance in Christ than we can possibly be. How hurt and harmed is the separate, holy Christ by the mixedness and unholiness in the lives of Christians. Then surely He would take great care that this wondrous truth of sanctification should be made very plain.

So the Word of God answers the above questions by showing us that sanctification is primarily a change in position and secondarily but of necessity a change in condition.

God tells us very plainly when, where and how the children of Israel were sanctified.

> Numbers 8:17, "For all the firstborn of the children of Israel are mine, both man and beast: *on the day that I smote every firstborn in the land of Egypt I sanctified them for myself.*"

> Leviticus 11:45, "*For I am the Lord that bringeth you up out of the land of Egypt, to be your God:* ye shall therefore be holy, for I am holy."

By the blood of the Paschal lamb they were redeemed *in* Egypt and set apart as a people for God's own possession. By the crossing of the Red Sea they were redeemed *from* Egypt and separated from other people for the Lord's use. Even during the wilderness wanderings in which there was much of murmuring and rebellion they were, as far as their position before God was concerned, a sanctified people.

Just so the cross of the Lord Jesus Christ marks the place of the believer's sanctification; the blood of the Lamb of God is the means; and the moment in which the sinner puts his faith in that atoning blood for salvation marks the time.

> Hebrews 10:10, "By the which will *we are sanctified through the offering of the body of Jesus Christ once for all.*"

Hebrews 13:12, "Wherefore Jesus also, *that he might sanctify the people with his own blood,* suffered without the gate."

Acts 26:18, "To open their eyes, and to turn them from darkness to light, and from the power of Satan unto God, that they may receive forgiveness of sins, and inheritance among *them which are sanctified by faith that is in me.*"

God never acts apart from Christ. Everything that God does whether in creation or salvation He does through His Son. And everything that God does in Christ for man's salvation He begins at the cross. So our sanctification begins there. At the cross the sinner becomes a saint. Every believer has been set apart for God's own possession and use by the sacrifice of His Son. The believer is a saint by position. As in justification the guilty sinner is accounted righteous through the blood of the cross so in sanctification the defiled sinner is accounted holy. By the sacrifice of the Lord Jesus Christ he "hath been perfected once for all." In this objective aspect sanctification is absolute and complete. Christ Himself and Christ alone is our sanctification.

Hebrews 10:14, "For by one offering *he hath perfected for ever* them that are sanctified."

1 Corinthians 1:30, "But of him are *ye in Christ Jesus, who of God is made unto us* wisdom, and righteousness, and *sanctification,* and redemption."

Thus we see that sanctification in this aspect is not "a second work of grace" at some time subsequent to conversion; nor a result of any act of consecration or faith on part of the believer; but that it takes place through God's first and initial work of grace—the death of His Son—and is simultaneous with justification and regeneration. "The primary and fundamental idea of sanctification is neither an achievement nor a process, but a gift, *a divine bestowal of a position in Christ.*"

In this *positional* aspect of sanctification all believers share equally: the youngest, weakest and most immature is as truly and as much sanctified as the oldest, strongest and most spiritual Christian.

This fact we see in the spiritual history of the Corinthian Christians as given in Paul's epistles. These letters were written to rebuke and correct gross sins, outstanding evils, even fearful immoralities in the Corinthian church yet the apostle writes to them as those that have been sanctified, those who are "holy in Christ." While he tells them that he cannot write unto them as unto spiritual but rather as unto carnal Christians yet he calls them saints. Even though they are still in the wilderness as regards spiritual experience yet he considers them a people separated unto God for His possession and use. It is because they have been so set apart and given such an exalted position that he reproves them for their unholy condition.

> 1 Corinthians 1:2, "Unto the church of God which is at Corinth, *to them that are sanctified in Christ Jesus, called to be saints,* with all that in every place call upon the name of Jesus Christ our Lord, both theirs and ours."

Their position as sanctified ones is the basis of his appeal for a corresponding condition of life. He reminds them that fornicators, idolaters, adulterers, drunkards, and revilers, shall not inherit the Kingdom of God (1 Corinthians 6:9-11), and then frankly says, "and such were some of you" in the old sphere when you were wholly separated unto sin and wholly separated from God. But it is all different now for "you are sanctified" and are thereby set apart unto God. Therefore your condition should correspond with your position. You were once in the devil's possession and use but now you are set apart unto God for His possession and use. You *are* saints; therefore live like saints.

> 1 Corinthians 6:11, "And such were some of you: but ye are washed, *but ye are sanctified,* but ye are justified in the name of the Lord Jesus, and by the Spirit of our God."

Are you a true believer in the Lord Jesus Christ? Then you are a saint. Have you put your trust for salvation in Christ's shed blood? Then you are sanctified and set apart as one belonging wholly and only unto God. Are you "a new creation in Christ Jesus"? Then you are also "a saint in Christ."

THE BELIEVER A SAINT BY CONDITION

A holy God must have a holy people. That which God has taken to be His own, which He has separated unto Himself must be holy even as He is holy. God took Israel out of Egypt into Canaan that they might be made a separate people shut in to Himself that through His presence in their midst as their Lord and Leader they might learn to do His will and obey His laws. He had called them to be a holy people. He had separated them that they might become a holy people. Their changed position from Egypt to Canaan presupposes a corresponding changed condition in all their manner of living. His very proprietorship of them demanded holiness. That which belongs to God must be holy, for God cannot presence Himself with unholiness neither can He use in His service that which is unclean. If He did so, He would deny His own nature, dishonor His own name. What God is, that which belongs to Him must be, or else God would lay Himself open to the charge of being a partaker of the sin of His people. Because they were a separated people God commanded them to be a holy people and to put all uncleanness of every kind away from them. He told them that the real purpose of their redemption had been their sanctification.

> Leviticus 20:24, 26, "I am the LORD your God, which have separated you from other people.
>
> And *ye shall be holy unto me; for I the Lord am holy,* and *have severed you from other people, that ye should be mine."*

> 2 Chronicles 29:5, 15-16, "And said unto them, Hear me, ye Levites, *sanctify now yourselves,* and *sanctify the house of the Lord God* of your fathers, and *carry forth the filthiness out of the holy place.*
>
> And they gathered their brethren, and *sanctified themselves,* and came, according to the commandment of the king, by the words of the LORD, *to cleanse the house of the Lord.*
>
> And the priests *went into the inner part of the house of the Lord, to cleanse it,* and *brought out all the uncleanness that they found in the* temple of the LORD into the court of the house of the LORD."

God has taken the believer to be His own and His proprietorship of the life is in itself a call and a challenge to holiness. God has redeemed us that He might possess us and He possesses us that He may conform us to the image of His Son. Christ saved us that He might sanctify us.

> 1 Thessalonians 4:7, "For God hath not *called us unto* uncleanness, but unto *holiness."*

> Ephesians 5:25-27, "Husbands, love your wives, *even as Christ also loved the church, and gave himself for it; that he might sanctify and cleanse it* with the washing of water by the word, that he might present it to himself a glorious church, not having spot, or wrinkle, or any such thing, *but that it should be holy and without blemish."*

The position of the believer in Christ is a call and a challenge to holiness. It also reveals God's provision for the life of holiness which He expects of the believer. God requires Christians to live "as becometh saints" but the power for such a life is not in ourselves but in Christ Himself. Through identification with Him in His death and resurrection we have been planted into Christ and He environs us with His own holiness. We are "holy—in Christ."

> Ephesians 5:3, "But fornication, and all uncleanness, or covetousness, let it not be *once* named among you, *as becometh saints."*

> Philippians 4:21, "Salute every *saint in Christ Jesus."*

The presence of Christ in the believer is a call and a challenge to holiness. "I am holy—be ye holy." Perfection of life is God's only standard. In Christ incarnate we find divine holiness in a human life and nature.

Through Christ crucified, that holy, divine nature was imparted to us. In the risen, ascended Christ indwelling we have the very presence of the Holy One in power. In virtue of what Christ did *for* us we are made holy and in virtue of what He does *in* us we are kept holy. Christ Himself is our sanctification.

> 1 Peter 1:15-16, R. V., "But like *as he who called you is holy, be ye your-selves also holy in all manner of living;* because it is written, Ye shall be holy; for I am holy."
>
> 1 Thessalonians 5:23-24, "And the very God of peace *sanctify you wholly;* and I pray God your whole spirit and soul and body be preserved blameless unto the coming of our Lord Jesus Christ. Faithful is he that calleth you, *who also will do it.*"

In this conditional aspect of sanctification there is a vast difference in believers. Some who have been Christians for a quarter of a century may show few evidences of a holy life while one who has known Christ but a short time may have much "fruit unto holiness." The progressive realization of holiness in life depends upon the believer's response to God's provision for it in Christ. With some this progress is a steady inflow, while with others it comes through a special experience which seems to them as marked as that of conversion. Let us now consider what that provision is.

SANCTIFICATION IS A RADICAL REVERSAL IN RELATIONSHIPS

Entrance into the new sphere involves a decisive, clean-cut reversal of every relationship obtaining in the old sphere. What the sinner was alive to the saint becomes dead to, and what the sinner was dead to the believer becomes alive to. The radical change wrought in the believer's position demands a complete reversal in every relationship if a corresponding change is to be wrought in his condition. Sanctification is one act with a double significance: negatively it means separation; positively it means holiness. Christ, our sanctification, separates us from all that is opposed to the will of God and He separates us unto all that is consistent with that will.

Let us consider first the things to which the believer becomes dead.

THE BELIEVER BECOMES DEAD TO SIN

Three phases of three words each which the apostle Paul uses throw marvelous light upon this reversal in the believer's relationship to sin. Please note that it is a study in prepositions.

> Ephesians 2:5, "Even when we were *dead in sins,* hath quickened us to-gether with Christ."

Romans 6:8, "Now if we be *dead with Christ,* we believe that we shall also live with him."

Romans 6:2, "God forbid. How shall we, that are *dead to sin,* live any longer therein?"

"Dead *in* sins"—such is the sinner's relationship to sin in the old sphere. He is so permeated and saturated with sin that God can only describe his relationship to sin as one of immersion in it. Sin in his environment.

"Dead *with* Christ"—such is the sinner's identification with the Sin-bearer. Salvation had to put both the Saviour and the sinner on the cross to reverse the relationship to sin.

"Dead *to* sin"—such is the believer's relationship to sin in the new sphere. He is so insulated and enveloped by Christ that God can only describe his relationship to sin as one of death to it. Christ is his environment. (See Diagram 11.)

Death defeats death and annuls its power over the sinner. The believer is so united with Christ in His death that he enters into precisely the same relationship to sin that Christ enjoys—Christ Jesus was never "dead in sins," the Lamb of God was "without spot and blemish" for there was no sin in Him. But as the last Adam, the representative Man, the sinner's Substitute, He was in a very real sense *"made sin* for us." The sin of the whole

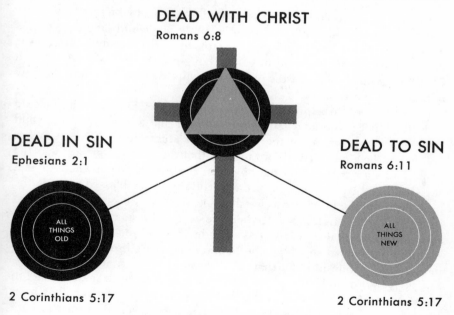

DEAD WITH CHRIST
Romans 6:8

DEAD IN SIN
Ephesians 2:1

ALL THINGS OLD

DEAD TO SIN
Romans 6:11

ALL THINGS NEW

2 Corinthians 5:17

2 Corinthians 5:17

Diagram 11: Changed Relationships

world of sinners was upon Him so that on the cross of Calvary in a very real and awful sense He was so separated unto sin for our sakes that He was separated from God. But, praise God, His death once and for all changed not only His relationship to sin but that of the believing sinner in Him.

> Romans 6:10, R. V., "For the death that he died, *he died unto sin once* [Gr., once and for all]: but the life that he liveth, he liveth unto God."

> Romans 6:11, R. V., "*Even so reckon ye also yourselves to be dead unto sin*, but alive unto God in Christ Jesus."

Let us not through unbelief or fear of the consequences minimize the force of the words in Romans 6:11. To make this truth stand out before us in all its daring ruggedness let this verse fall into its constituent parts before our eyes.

Dead unto sin
Alive unto God } The believer's changed relationships.

In Christ Jesus —The divine Medium.
Reckon   —The Human Means
Even so   —The defined Measure.

Simpler words could not have been used to convey to the mind and heart one of the most profound truths in the Bible nor could language tell us more plainly the severing power of the cross of Christ: nor make more clear the meaning of sanctification in God's thought. The believer "dead with Christ" is dynamited out of the old relationship "dead in sins" into the new relationship "dead to sin."

But what does the expression "dead to sin" mean? Does it mean that sin is dead or that it is eradicated? Does it mean that the believer is beyond the reach of temptation or the possibility or ability to sin? No, it means nothing of the kind. God's Word teaches that the believer on earth has the penalty of sin removed and the power of sin broken but nowhere does it say that he is freed from the presence of sin. That blessed state is the believer's future inheritance as we shall see in a later study. Nor is he freed from temptation. In fact temptations are even more severe and more constant as one maintains in faith the attitude of "dead to sin." But "dead to sin" does mean that in Christ the believer has been brought *positionally* into such a relationship to it that he is beyond the reach of sin's dominion, that he is environed by Christ Jesus in such a measure as to share to the full His victory over sin. It means also that through the new birth he has been given a nature which hates sin and loves holiness. Where formerly there was response to sin, and apathy toward God, now the attitude is completely reversed. Sin meets with a cold reception and a quick rebuff while the whole being is aglow with an ever deepening love and devotion to its Lord. "The new man which after God is created in righteousness and true holiness" refuses sin and chooses holiness; says no to sin and yes to God.

This positional victory over sin through grace is perfect. In Christ, God has taken the believer beyond the necessity of sin's lordship. In Christ sin's power is broken and its claim is canceled. Several times in Romans 6 God declares the believer's perfect freedom from the power of sin.

> Romans 6:18, 22, R. V., "And *being made free from sin,* ye became servants of righteousness.
> *Now being made free from sin* and become servants to God, *ye have your fruit unto sanctification,* and the end eternal life."
> Romans 6:14, "*For sin shall not have dominion over you:* for ye are not under law, but under grace."

These words if they teach anything clearly tell us that the believer in Christ need not sin, that sin has no rightful claim upon him. Let us get this thing straight and have no confusion in our minds about it. God nowhere says *that we are not able to sin* but He clearly says *that we are able not to sin.* In other verses in Romans 6 God states explicitly that sin still has power over the believer because the believer permits it. In other words, the believer sins because he wants to, because he yields to the allurements, the charms, the call of sin or he sins because he does not claim his privileges in Christ.

Just here I can almost hear the murmur of doubt in the heart of some reader as he says, "Is such victory possible?" Most of us have an inadequate conception of the meaning of the cross and of the power of Christ. We imagine Him able only to carry us safely over the borderline of the new sphere of life and unlock for us the door into heaven, but utterly impotent to keep us victorious and Christlike in the midst of the temptations of a sinful world. We are so ready to believe in the strength of the devil and so loath to believe that we are indeed spiritual multimillionaires, "heirs of God, and joint-heirs with Christ." But such you and I are, even while living as spiritual paupers. But "He is able to do exceedingly abundantly above all that we ask or think," and will prove that He is so able if we but give Him the chance.

Perhaps some reader, if we were talking together personally, would put to me the questions that have been asked scores of times. Can this truth of complete and continuous victory over sin be brought from heaven to earth, can it be brought out of the realm of the doctrinal into the realm of the experiential? Will it really *work* if applied to *my* temper, jealousy, worry, pride, resentment and hatred? Can I in *my* daily walk in a world reeking in sin and placing temptation before me at every step really be kept unspotted and unsullied? Can the relationship "dead to sin" be actualized in *my* spiritual experience here and now on earth?

My answer to you would be, "Test the power of Jesus Christ's victory over sin on your besetting sin and give Him a fair chance to prove to you that He can save to the uttermost, even to make you dead to that sin. Take the sin that is dragging you down into the very depths of despair and let Him who is your sanctification make you dead to it."

A missionary came once for a talk. Her face was the picture of despair. By her own confession hers was a joyless, peaceless, powerless life. She found no joy in Bible study; no reality in prayer; and she had no love for souls. She had dreaded having me come to that school to lead a series of evangelistic meetings because she thought she would be expected to do personal work among the girls and she was utterly devoid both of desire and of power for such a task. Her body as well as her spirit was ill and she had already told her Chinese co-workers and her fellow missionaries that because of ill health she did not intend to return to China after her furlough. We talked together of the life of victory in Christ but she repeated over and over again that while she believed it was for others she knew it was not for her. She knew intellectually the Bible truth about victory over sin and was altogether familiar with every Bible verse that I quoted. She had read many books on victory in Christ and could have told any person who came to her seeking help the way to victory. But she herself was living in utter defeat and abject discouragement. Deep down in her heart was *a hurt*. There it had been for four years eating away at her spiritual vitals like a cancer. To that hurt she was wholly "alive." We talked for hours but she left me as she came—in despair. However, a deep, quiet assurance of complete victory for her came into my heart. I knew that victory in Christ was God's will for her for He had said so in His Word so I confidently claimed His promise in 1 John 5:14-15 and thanked God for the answer to the prayer as I fell asleep.

Before breakfast there was a tap on the door. What a gloriously radiant face greeted my eyes as I opened it and she exclaimed: "Oh! it's gone and I know it will never come back again!" What gone? The hurt. How? The Lord Jesus Christ, her Victor, had presenced Himself in the spot where the hurt was and had made her dead to it. Since that time, fully seven years ago, God has used that missionary to help many another defeated one into the joy and peace of victory over sin.

Sanctification is separation from sin and Christ is the Separator and He sanctifies by indwelling, possessing and controlling. Victory is not a mere blessing, doctrine, or experience, but it is a Person. To have Him acknowledged as sole Proprietor of the whole being and allowed to act as such is to be assured of victory over sin. To have Him crowned as Lord and in control *is to have victory already*. This throws light on what real victory is and what it is not. Some of us may not have victory because we are altogether too superficial in our thinking. We trifle with this very important thing. We think we shall obtain victory by reading literature on the subject or by hearing messages at a conference, or by an interview with some Christian leader while all the time we are unwilling to face God alone that He may show us both what sin is and what victory is.

God does not speak of being dead to "sins" but to "sin." He does not talk of "victories" but of "victory." He does not command us to be troubled over our sin but to be "dead" to it. He makes it very clear that He does not mean mere control over *outward* expressions of sin but a definite dealing with *inner* disposition. Real victory is a glorious and marvelous change in the innermost recesses of the spirit which transforms the inner disposition and attitude as well as the outward deed and act. "Real victory never obliges you to conceal what is inside." No, more than that, if one has real victory over sin he longs with intensity to let others know what his treasure is.

If we are to look to the Lord Jesus to make our freedom from sin actual and if "dead to sin" is to be lifted out of its doctrinal setting in Romans 6 and made an experiential fact in your life and mine, then we must know both what sin is and what victory is. Satan blinds the minds, dulls the consciences, deadens the spiritual sensibilities so that countless Christians never think of calling some sinful things sin. Of course we are forced to call some glaring, outstanding offense against God and man that becomes more or less public, sin. But what about that black, defiling, evil thing, hidden away in the spirit, heart or thought which has not yet found its way out into a word or a deed, but which is open to the all-seeing, all-searching eye of our holy God? Is that sin? God would lead us to think it is.

Psalm 19:12, 14, "Who can understand his errors? Cleanse thou me from *secret faults*. Let the word of my mouth, and *the meditation of my heart*, be acceptable *in thy sight*, O LORD, my strength, and my redeemer."

Psalm 51:6, 10, "Behold, thou desirest truth *in the inward parts*: and *in the hidden part* thou shalt make me to know wisdom.

Create in me a clean heart, O God; and renew *a right spirit* within me."

2 Corinthians 7:1, "Having therefore these promises, dearly beloved, *let us cleanse ourselves from all filthiness of the* flesh and *spirit*, perfecting holiness in the fear of God."

Let us face a few simple tests and see if we have been cleansed "from all filthiness of the spirit" and if there is freedom from sin "in the inward parts."

You used to lose your temper and give way to violent outbursts; now there is a large measure of outward control but a very great residue of inward irritation and secret resentment. Is that real victory?

Someone says something unkind or unjust to you; you do not answer back and outwardly you appear polite but inwardly you are angry and are saying to yourself, "I'd like to give her a piece of my mind!" Is that freedom from sin?

Someone has wronged you; you do not openly retaliate or seek to revenge the wrong but in your innermost heart you wish the person misfortune and rejoice when it comes. Is that having "a right spirit"?

You are a favored one through family, position or wealth. You do not openly boast but your heart is filled with secret pride, vanity and a sense of superiority. Is that counted as being "dead to sin"?

At a summer conference in China a woman came seeking help. She was unhappy and others around her were made unhappy. There was unlove in her heart; in fact, there was someone she hated. She was a Christian worker and recognizing the havoc this feeling was working in her own life and in that of others she tried to gain gradual victories over it. She had hated even the sight of the other person but she acknowledged finally the sinfulness of that. So she invited the person to dinner in her home *but hoped she wouldn't come!* When she came to me she had reached the point where she was *"ready to forgive"* but *"would never forget!"* Then she compelled herself to say that she *"wouldn't hate"* but she *"couldn't love."* Not until God, who is love, really possessed her heart did she become "dead" to that sin.

In Christ Jesus full provision has been made for you and me to be "dead to sin." But Romans 6:11 tells us that the believer must respond to God's act of grace by an act of faith. Man's faith is the cooperative complement of God's grace. Through faith God makes real in experience what through grace He has made real in fact. Through grace God has reversed the believer's relationship to sin and now God calls upon him to "reckon" upon this reversal as a fact and so to act, walk and live.

Furthermore, Romans 6:12-13 tells us that the believer must respond to God's act of grace by an act of the will.

> Romans 6:12, *"Let not sin therefore reign in your mortal body, that ye should obey it in the lusts thereof."*

This is a call, a challenge and a command all in one. It is a call to higher ground, to life on the highest plane. It is a challenge to take God at His Word and prove His power as Victor. It is a command to assert the rights of one whose real life is in the heavenlies in Christ.

Through the finished work of Jesus Christ, God has done all He can do toward the believer's sanctification. If he enjoys in experience real separation from sin he must now act. His will must coalesce with God's will and work as a unit if he is to live as one "dead to sin." And God does not let this step be shrouded in misty vagueness but in Romans 6:13 tells in simplest and plainest language just what the believer must do to keep sin from reigning in his body.

> Romans 6:13, "Neither yield ye your members as instruments of unrighteousness unto sin: but *yield yourselves unto God,* as those that are alive from the dead, and *your members as instruments of righteousness* unto God."

"Yield," "*yield,*" "YIELD"—by a definite, intelligent, voluntary act of the will the believer must choose Christ as his new Master and yield himself to Him as Lord. Christ and sin cannot both "reign" over your life at the same time. There is no possibility in God's plan for such a compromising alliance. Jesus Christ not only desires to enter every life as Saviour but to rule as Lord and to reign as King. He not only designs to take possession but to assume control. He is not content to be recognized only as the owner of the house but purposes as well to be manager of the household. He is not satisfied to become something only to us but wishes to be everything.

Romans 6:14-22 reveals two incontrovertible facts:

1. We are able not to sin.

2. If we sin, we sin because we want to sin; because we will to sin; because we choose to yield to our old master instead of to our new Master.

But it also clearly implies that by "reckoning" ourselves dead unto sin and by "yielding" ourselves unconditionally to Christ we may come to have a totally changed attitude to sin. Love for it and indulgence in it will become hatred for it and resistance to it. Sin is not dead and it will continue to entice but it will meet with no response from us. Our former master still lives and works hard at his task but Christ, our new Master, makes us deaf to sin's appeals by making us dead to sin itself.

THE BELIEVER BECOMES DEAD TO THE LAW

If one is to come into real liberty in the Lord and be released from the futile striving to attain by his own effort what by faith he may obtain as God's gift, he must apprehend this second reversal in his relationships. Paul in the light of his own experience expounds this truth quite fully in Romans 7. Paul as a sinner had tried to become righteous by keeping the Law of God. He had failed utterly and had come to Christ as his Saviour that he might be made righteous in Him. But in Romans 7 as a saint, he was trying to become holy by attempting to keep God's Law in his own strength. He had learned that he could not be saved by his own efforts but he had still to learn that he could not be sanctified in that way.

The Law is holy and demands of man both perfect righteousness and perfect holiness, but it cannot give to anyone the power to be righteous or holy. So when one comes into a realization of the holy nature of God's Law and of its rightful demand for holiness of life the attempt is made to live such a life in one's own strength. It is this that Paul is telling us in Romans 6 and 7, we neither can do nor need try to do. He tells us this in three different statements each of which unfolds a distinct phase of this truth.

First, the saint in the new sphere is under a distinctly different regime from the sinner in the old sphere. He is no longer under Law but under grace.

Romans 6:14, "For sin shall not have dominion over you: for *ye are not under the law, but under grace.*"

Second, the believer has come under the regime of grace through his union with the Lord Jesus Christ in His death and resurrection. So now under grace he fully shares Christ's relationship to the Law. In His incarnate life Christ Jesus as the representative Man met every demand of the Law both for righteousness and holiness. In His death, as the sinner's Saviour, He met every claim of the Law for righteousness against the sinner and in His resurrection, as the Head of the new creation, He met every claim of the Law for holiness against the saint. The Law has no further claim against the believer either for righteousness or for holiness for every claim has been fully satisfied.

Third, the believer is, therefore, dead to the Law.

Romans 7:4, "Wherefore, my brethren, *ye also are become dead to the law by the body of Christ; that ye should be married to another, even to him who is raised from the dead,* that we should bring forth fruit unto God."

Galatians 2:19, "For *I through the law am dead to the law,* that I might live unto God."

It is the function of grace to do for us what we cannot do for ourselves. It is the work of grace to undo the work of sin. Sin made us unholy: grace makes us holy. Grace always operates through Jesus Christ who dwells within us in the very perfection of His own holiness through the power of the Holy Spirit.

Does this not show us how needless and futile are our efforts to compel ourselves to live well pleasing unto God, to achieve victory over sin through good resolutions or through willpower, and to live a holy life through legal bondage to certain principles or practices? The way of sanctification is as simple as the way of salvation. As truly as Christ is our

Saviour just so truly He is our sanctification. Our part is to believe and to receive.

Holiness is a gift and a gift is not "attained" but "obtained." Christ Himself is our holiness. Holiness does not come as a result of "works" but is a "fruit." Becoming "servants to God, ye have your *fruit unto holiness*" (Romans 6:22).

Becoming "dead to the law" does not give to any Christian the license to sin. Far from it. His death to the Law is accomplished only through his marriage union with the Holy One Himself and that for one definite, distinct purpose, that he may "bring forth fruit unto God" and live wholly unto Him. It is for the one purpose of enabling him to do the will of God in every department of his life.

THE BELIEVER BECOMES DEAD TO SELF

The exact words are not in Scripture but the thought is clearly there in the following passages which show the believer's radical reversal in his relationship to self.

> 2 Corinthians 5:15, R. V., "And he died for all, that *they that live should no longer live unto themselves*, but unto him who for their sakes died and rose again."

> Galatians 5:24, "And *they that are Christ's have crucified the flesh* with the affections and lusts."

"The old man" never acknowledges himself as dead. Self-will is married to self-love and they and their entire offspring will work night and day to retake the throne of the believer's life permanently, if possible, but if not, temporarily. But Christ enables us to say a continuous and firm no to every appeal of self and to refuse it even a foothold in any of the territory which He has conquered. The divine Proprietor is amply able to guard and keep His property for Himself. Our part is to maintain a persistent and consistent attitude of death to self.

THE BELIEVER BECOMES DEAD TO THE WORLD

Christ, as our sanctification, brings out a very radical reversal in the believer's relationship to the world and in its relationship to the believer. The apostle Paul uses a very strong expression in stating it.

> Galatians 6:14, "But God forbid that I should glory, save in the cross of our Lord Jesus Christ, *by whom the world is crucified unto me, and I unto the world.*"

He says it is a twofold crucifixion. A double death takes place at the cross of Christ when the sinner becomes a saint. The absolute necessity for this is clearly seen when we remember that the sinner is part of the system, called the world, which is Satan's channel of manifestation and his instrument for service. The world and the Church are wholly antagonistic in their whole manner of living and working: their pleasures, pursuits, plans and programs are as different from each other as Christ is different from Satan. So when Christ sanctifies the believer as His own possession and for His own use, He takes him so altogether out of this world-system and separates him so wholly unto Himself that he is thereafter "dead to the world."

As soon as the believer really takes this attitude toward the world and maintains his position in Christ as a consistent member of His Body then the world hates him and disclaims any relationship or affiliation with him. As long as the believer compromises and maintains a friendly attitude toward the world the latter will be friendly with the hope of winning the Christian back into its fold. But the world only loves its own and hates all that is not of it so that when the believer comes out into an open, decisive separateness the world thereafter is crucified unto him.

> John 15:19, *"If ye were of the world, the world would love his own:* but because ye are not of the world, but I have chosen you out of the world, *therefore the world hateth you."*

> 1 John 3:1, "Behold, what manner of love the Father has bestowed upon us, that we should be called the sons of God: *therefore the world knoweth us not, because it knew him not."*

The real secret governing our abandonment of the world is our love for the Lord Jesus Himself. He loved us so much that He gave Himself for us. We are captivated by that love and we open our hearts to receive Him, then He gives Himself to us. He in His loveliness becomes much more attractive than anything the world can offer; He in His tender sympathy, loving understanding and exquisite love bestows upon us much more than the world can give; He in His own wondrous divine-human Person satisfies our hearts as all that the world has to give could never satisfy.

It was so in the life of a university student who was enamored of the world. She fed on worldliness, she walked and lived in it. Her clothes, her companionships, her pleasures, her conversations, her tastes, her choices, in fact everything about her bore the mark of the world. She had been indulging in the gaieties of the university life to an excess that troubled even her worldly minded friends. But one night in the beginning of the spring term of her senior year she found Christ as her Saviour and her Master. Only a few days later she was to have attended the biggest dance of the season. She did not go but spent the entire evening in communion with her newfound Lord over His Word and in prayer. Throughout the remaining weeks of her senior year she refused scores of invitations to similar parties.

A something had come into her life that made some who had known and prayed for her very happy and that made others who had companioned with her in the past very contemptuous. She would have told you that that something was a Someone, it was the Lord Jesus. Love for Him had made her dead to the world, which, when she no longer belonged to it had become dead to her.

This radical reversal of our relationship to sin, to the Law, to self and to the world is brought about through our identification with Christ in His death and resurrection. In Christ crucified and risen we are made a *separate* people for His possession and use.

Christ our sanctification not only made a clean-cut reversal in our relationship to Satan and to everything pertaining to his sphere but He made an equally revolutionary change in our relationship to God and to everything that belongs to His Kingdom.

THE BELIEVER BECOMES "ALIVE UNTO GOD"

Having been born into God's family as a child and into His Kingdom as a citizen his whole life is now centered in the family and Kingdom interests. Having been accepted as Saviour, united with as Head, and crowned Lord, Christ has become both the center and the circumference of his life and all in between. In Christ Himself the believer finds his deepest joy, his greatest delight and his completest satisfaction.

As being "dead to sin" detracts from sin's charms and breaks its power to lure and entice so being "alive unto God" enhances Christ's charms and heightens the Holy Spirit's power to woo and to win us to love our Lord and to delight in Him. To be "alive unto God" is to love the Lord Jesus as we love no other person or thing in heaven or upon earth. It is to adore Him as the Beloved, to give Him the place of preeminence in our lives. *It is for Christ Jesus Himself to be all and in all to us.*

> Colossians 1:18, "And he is the head of the body, the church: who is the beginning, the firstborn from the dead; *that in all things he might have the preeminence.*"
>
> Song of Solomon 5:10, "*My beloved* is white and ruddy, *the chiefest among ten thousand.*"
>
> Colossians 3:11, "*But Christ is all, and in all.*"

But is there in the lives of very many Christians whom you know such a personal passion for the Lord Jesus? Does the average church member impress the world as being "alive unto God"? Is the Christian businessman more eager for God's projects to succeed than his own? Upon which does the Christian mother put most thought and time—her daughter's health, her place in society, or growth in her spiritual life? Which does the ordinary church member attend most regularly, the cinema or the prayer meeting? Is there not a sluggishness and stagnancy in the lives of thousands upon thousands of professed Christians today that amounts almost to deadness toward God and His interests? Many of God's children in all parts of the world believe that the Church of Christ is in just such a dead condition and that there is great need of revival.

Perhaps this book will fall into the hands of some persons who are altogether unconscious of the need of such a quickening. They are conventional, respectable Christians. They always attend church, go to prayer meeting and fulfill faithfully what they consider to be their financial obligation to the church. They never do anyone any harm; neither do they do anyone any good. They would not consciously put a stumbling block in the way of somebody's becoming a Christian; neither would it ever dawn upon them to put forth an effort to win one. They are colorless Christians. They would be disgusted with the frivolous person who found pleasure for a morning in reading a trashy book but just so they would be bewildered at the joy some earnest soul found in several hours' study of the Word. To them the pleasure places of the world have no attraction but neither does the trysting place of prayer. They are the lineal descendants of the elder brother in the parable of the prodigal, who did not bring disgrace to his father's name but neither did he bring joy to his father's heart.

What I am trying to say is that you and I may be separate and yet not be holy; we may be orthodox and yet not be spiritual; we may be "dead to sin" and yet not be "alive to God." We may have cut ourselves loose from every form of worldliness but in so doing have become critical and self-righteous. We may be loyal defenders of the faith, ready even to lay down our lives for it and in so doing become bitter and unloving. We may be faithful in the fulfilling of every obligation to God and have given ourselves in self-sacrificing devotion to His cause and yet have no warm glow of love in our hearts, no spring of joy in our souls, no fervency of spirit in our communion with the Lord Jesus Himself.

But the divine-human God-man can never be satisfied with negation. If He died and rose again to separate us from sin, He ascended into heaven and was exalted to the throne that He might separate us unto the Lord. The work of the cross is to be perfected through the work of the throne. What the Saviour began the Sanctifier is to continue. The ascended Lord lives to keep us holy through His Spirit.

This He does as our great High Priest, our Advocate and our Intercessor. He has lived on earth and He knows how unceasingly we are in contact with that which defiles. He knows the insidiousness of Satan's temptations and how he takes advantage of our times of trial, affliction, weariness, loneliness, sickness, disappointment, stress and sorrow to press upon some vulnerable spot in our character to tempt us into sin. So there He is as our Representative before the Father's throne pleading our case and as we turn to Him in frank open confession of our sin He applies the precious blood that cleanses and enables us to walk again in the light of His holy presence. Christ has come not only to save us but to save us to the uttermost. A life as pure and perfect as His own is His only standard for us. For this He intercedes constantly at His Father's throne.

> 1 John 2:1, "My little children, these things write I unto you, that ye sin not. And *if any man sin, we have an advocate with the Father,* Jesus Christ the righteous."

> Hebrews 7:25-26, "Wherefore *he is able also to save them to the uttermost that come unto God by him, seeing he ever liveth to make intercession for them.*
> For *such an high priest became us,* who is holy, harmless, undefiled, separate from sinners, and made higher than the heavens."

But how could the believer's conscience ever become enlightened to discern the presence of sin and how would his heart be made to recoil from its defilement and his spirit to resent its intrusion? Here again we see the perfection of God's grace in the gift of the Holy Spirit by whom the initial work of sanctification in us is begun and through whom its progressive work is carried on. It is He who makes us feel the need of cleansing and leads us to Him who alone can cleanse.

> 1 Peter 1:2, "Elect according to the foreknowledge of God the Father, *through the sanctification of the Spirit,* unto obedience and sprinkling of the blood of Jesus Christ."

> 2 Thessalonians 2:13, "God hath from the beginning chosen you to salvation *through sanctification of the Spirit* and belief of the truth."

A holy God has opened the way into His presence and has taken unto Himself a people to live there in abiding communion with Himself. Blessed the man or the woman who has found his way into that holy sanctuary and delights himself in the Holy One! Upon such God sets His seal signifying that they are His own possession forever and that He has begun to work within them conformity to the image of His Son. This seal is none other than the Holy Spirit.

> Ephesians 1:13, "In whom ye also trusted, after that ye heard the word of truth, the gospel of your salvation: *in whom also after that ye believed, ye were sealed with that holy Spirit of promise.*"

> 2 Corinthians 1:21-22, "Now he which stablisheth us with you in Christ, and hath anointed us, is God; *who hath also sealed us, and given the earnest of the Spirit in our hearts.*"

20

Christ Our Captain and Conqueror—Conflict and Conquest

WHEN JESUS CHRIST ascended into heaven He went as Conqueror over the evil one and all his hosts. When God exalted Him to Lordship over the universe He set Him at His own right hand far above all the principalities and powers that belonged to the kingdom of Satan and put them all under His feet. Through His death upon the cross Jesus Christ wrested from Satan every vestige of his claim upon the world and upon men. Through His resurrection and ascension He passed as Conqueror through the enemy's territory. At His exaltation God and all the heavenly host united in crowning Him King of kings and Lord of lords, the one and only Potentate. Through His Saviourhood He has now a claim upon every man's life, and through His installation as Head of the new creation He gained the right to the worship of all that believe. He has regained for God His sovereignty over millions upon millions of lives which are now in the possession and use of their rightful Owner. Jesus Christ has entered into the enemy's territory and inch by inch has won it back for God.

> Ephesians 1:20-22, "Which he wrought in Christ, when he raised him from the dead, *and set him at his own right hand in the heavenly places,*
> *Far above all principality, and power, and might, and dominion, and every name that is named,* not only in this world, but also in that which is to come:
> *And hath put all things under his feet,* and gave him to be the head over all things to the church."

> 1 Timothy 6:14-15, "*Our Lord Jesus Christ:* which in his times he shall shew, *who is the blessed and only Potentate, the King of kings, and Lord of lords.*"

Satan was judged, sentenced and doomed at the cross of Christ but, until that sentence is executed, he is contesting fiercely the Lord's victory and with all the might of his supernatural power is fighting to hold his ground and to regain what he has lost.

This conflict is typified in the conquest of the children of Israel over the wicked nations dwelling in Canaan as recorded in the book of Joshua. The land of Canaan was the land that God promised to the seed of Abraham. It was theirs by the right of God's gift. But it was occupied by the Canaanites who were an accursed race (Genesis 9:25), and other kindred nations who also were steeped in iniquity and wickedness.

These wicked nations in the land of promise were under the leadership and control of Satan to defeat God in carrying out of His divine purpose for, in, and through, His chosen people. Satan, through his emissaries, would keep God's people from the possession, enjoyment and use of their promised inheritance. These wicked nations were very powerful and, although each was under its own ruler, were easily welded together as one in aggressive alliance against God's people.

God commanded the children of Israel first to enter the promised land and then to possess and to hold it.

> Joshua 1:11, "Pass through the host, and command the people, saying, Prepare you victuals; for within three days *ye shall pass over this Jordan, to go in to possess the land,* which the LORD your God giveth you to possess it."

God equipped them for the conquest of the land with a promise and a Presence; the promise was of victory, the Presence was that of the Victor.

> Joshua 1:5, "*There shall not any man be able to stand before thee all the days of thy life:* as I was with Moses, so *I will be with thee:* I will not fail thee, nor forsake thee."

As they moved toward Jericho to begin the conquest of these strong, powerful enemies, there appeared unto Joshua a man with a sword drawn in his hand. It was Jehovah, the Lord, who then and there became the Captain of the hosts of the Israelites as they went forth into battle against the Lord's enemies and theirs.

> Joshua 5:13-14, "And it came to pass, when Joshua was by Jericho, that he lifted up his eyes and looked, and, behold, there stood a man over against him with his sword drawn in his hand: and Joshua went unto him, and said unto him, Art thou for us, or for our adversaries?
>
> And he said, Nay; *but as captain of the host of the Lord am I now come.* And Joshua fell on his face to the earth, and did worship, and said unto him, What saith my lord unto his servant?"

Under the command of the Lord of hosts Israel went forth to take Jericho, Ai, Gibeon and to win victory over thirty-one kings. "The Lord delivered them into the hand of Israel." The victory of God's children was accomplished through the presence of the Victor.

Joshua 10:42, "And all these kings and their land did Joshua take at one time, *because the Lord God of Israel fought for Israel."*

The book of Joshua in the Old Testament has its counterpart in the New in the epistle to the Ephesians. The conflict and conquest of the children of Israel under Jehovah, the Captain of the host, foreshadows the conflict and conquest of the new creation, the Body of Christ, under the Lord Jesus Christ, its Head and Conqueror.

THE CONFLICT IN THE HEAVENLIES

"In Christ" in the heavenlies is the believer's promised land. This is his God-given inheritance promised even before the foundation of the world (Ephesians 1:4, 11). "In Christ" in the heavenlies every spiritual blessing is his possession by right (Ephesians 1:3). Through his identification with Christ the believer has already entered into the heavenlies (Ephesians 2:5-6).

Christ, his *Saviour*, has won him from the kingdom and family of Satan to the Kingdom and family of God; Christ, his *Head*, has given him His own divine nature; Christ, his *Lord*, has dethroned self and has assumed the undivided control of his life; Christ, his *Life*, has shared with him His risen, glorified, supernatural life in all its fullness; Christ, his *Sanctification*, has put His blood, His cross and His throne between the believer and the world, the flesh and the devil; and Christ, his *Conqueror*, gives Himself in His high-priestly and intercessory ministry for the believer's continuous and complete victory.

All this maddens the devil and spurs him into warfare against the saints of God. It is the twofold triumph of Christ in the believer and the believer in Christ that causes the conflict in the heavenlies. It is Satan contesting with Christ His inheritance in the saints and their inheritance in Him.

It is a spiritual conflict. It is a battle between supernatural forces. It is he who is the very personification of evil and wickedness and all his evil subordinates warring against Him who is the very personification of righteousness and holiness and all of His holy warriors. It is the hierarchy of hell against the theocracy of heaven.

Ephesians 6:12, R. V., "For *our wrestling is* not against flesh and blood, but *against the principalities, against the powers, against the world-rulers of this darkness, against the spiritual hosts of wickedness in the heavenly places."*

If in this conflict Christ is to be manifested as the Victor there must be on the believer's part a realization of the power of the enemy. It is a very foolish thing to underestimate the power of the devil for we do it not only to our hurt but to the detriment of the Body of Christ of which we are a member. The devil is mighty and powerful; he is cunning and crafty; he is intelligent and industrious.

His forces of evil are invisible—"not flesh and blood."

They are well organized—"principalities."

They are well governed—"powers."

They work in secret—"the darkness of this world."

They are entrenched in innumerable hosts in the very territory where the believer dwells—"hosts of wickedness in heavenly places."

It behooves the believer to know that he is surrounded by the unseen, cunning, malicious, powerful hosts of the evil one who plots his downfall.

> 1 Peter 5:8, R. V., "Be sober, be watchful: *your adversary the devil*, as a roaring lion, walketh about, *seeking whom he may devour*."

The believer is the channel through which Christ manifests Himself *to* a world in Satan's embrace, and through which Christ witnesses and works *in* that world to win it back to Himself. So if the devil can defeat the believer and cause his testimony, his prayer and his service, to be powerless, he has to that extent defeated Christ for he has held his ground in the world and regained ground in the believer. The only way in which he can hold his kingdom is by keeping his dominion over human lives. The most holy and spiritual Christian is Satan's greatest hindrance so against him will be launched his fiercest onslaughts.

This being true, not only is it necessary to realize the power of our foe but also to recognize his methods of attack. He is a deceiver and seldom fights in the open. He lays snares to entrap the ignorant and innocent and comes as an angel of light to deceive even the elect. He works most successfully through the subtlety of seduction.

> 2 Corinthians 2:11, "Lest Satan should get an advantage of us: for *we are not ignorant of his devices*."
>
> 2 Timothy 2:26, "And that they may recover themselves out of *the snare of the devil, who are taken captive by him at his will*."
>
> 2 Corinthians 11:14, "And no marvel; for *Satan himself is transformed into an angel of light*."
>
> 2 Timothy 3:13, "But evil men and *seducers shall wax worse and worse*, deceiving, and being deceived."

In the Garden of Gethsemane we see the devil making his final attack upon the God-man by trying to drive a wedge between the Father and the Son. To accomplish this he aimed his fiery darts at our Lord's spirit, soul and body. All the hosts of hell were united in that spiritual battle to keep Him from the cross. And now he works in every conceivable way to keep the Body of Christ from appropriating and abiding in the victory He gained for it at the cross and shares with it from the throne. Against both the corporate Body of Christ and its individual members the devil is massing his hosts, for he knows the time is now near when the sentence against him will be executed.

To understand his present method of attack we shall need to remind ourselves that he has two accomplices: the world and the flesh. The flesh is the material in human life upon which he works and the world is flesh in the aggregate. We shall need to understand also just what the devil is doing in this world which is wholly under his leadership and control.

His aim, as we have seen in chapter 5, is the dethronement of God. To accomplish this there must be the undermining of the authority of God in every relationship He bears to man, and the democracy of self-will must be established in its place. To achieve this success Satan planned a world-wide revolution in government, in society, and in religion. His plan is to destroy government through anarchy; society through debauchery; religion through apostasy.

The daily papers chronicle his successes in his worldwide revolution in government. Under the deceiving guise of a fair-looking but falsely working nationalism he is seducing countless numbers of men and women in various countries, some of whom are truly honest patriots at heart, into action that must inevitably end in the overthrow of stable government.

His successes in the worldwide revolutions in society are no less apparent. The immodesty and indecency in women's dress, the surrender of the outward marks of gracious womanliness for an aping mannishness; the laxness in the marriage vow as evidenced in the frequency of divorce; the insubordination of children and lack of parental discipline; the fading of the fair bloom of purity from the heart life of countless boys and girls; the growing unfaithfulness in the sacred relationship of husband and wife which reaches its height in the hell-born doctrine of free love; the feverish pursuit of pleasure on the part of both old and young: all are but a few of the manifestations of the social debauchery into which the devil is leading the world.

His successes in the worldwide revolution in religion is a topic of daily conversation in almost every country of the world today. The devil would have no religion but devil worship; he would do away with all authority but that of self-will. The authority of the sovereign God, delegated to the incarnate Word and revealed in the written Word, is set aside as something obsolete in the modern world. The right of every man to be a law unto himself in all matters of religion is the basic principle in the present appalling apostasy.

This terrible condition which God so plainly predicted would be seen in the last days is clearly outlined in one pasasge of Scripture. In the following verses we see the full-blown flower of anarchy, debauchery and apostasy.

> 2 Timothy 3:1-8, R. V., "But know this, that in the last days grievous times shall come. *For men shall be lovers of self, lovers of money,* boastful, haughty, railers, disobedient to parents, unthankful, unholy, without natural affection, implacable, slanderers, without self-control, fierce, *no lovers of good,* traitors, headstrong, puffed up, *lovers of pleasure rather than lovers of God;* holding a form of godliness, but having denied the power thereof: from these also turn away. For of these are they that creep into houses, and take captive silly women laden with sins, led away by divers lusts, ever learning, and never able to come to the knowledge of the truth. And even as Jannes and Jambres withstood Moses, so do these also withstand the truth; men corrupted in mind, *reprobate concerning the faith.*"

Against the corporate Body of Christ, Satan is working in two very distinct and definite ways at the present time, through degeneration and through division.

First of all, he is sowing tares among the wheat. He is placing his emissaries both in the pulpit and in the pews for the sole purpose of leavening the whole. He is mixing his own progeny among the people of God so as to lower the standard of the entire Body of Christ. Thus Chirst will be so caricatured before those in Satan's kingdom that they will see no advantage in leaving it for the Kingdom of God.

Satan is working through his paid and his lay agents in the professing church to destroy the sovereignty of God; to undermine the authority of His Word; to strip Christ of His deity, and to unseat Him from the place and preeminence of Lordship; and to lead His people away from full conformity to the image of Christ by partial conformity to the standards and fashions of the world. Thus through this degeneration within the visible church, the Body of Christ is being made impotent in the midst of the world's appalling need.

The world has its standard of what the Christian should be, and inconsistent as it may seem, it holds the Church of Christ up to that standard. A worldly minded woman was asked by a minister's wife to become a Christian. Her response was as revealing as it was cutting, "If I should become a Christian, I could never wear the immodest clothes that you wear." The emptiness of the pews speaks of the contempt the world has for a church that degenerates into a lecture hall and a place of entertainment. A friend, who was eagerly praying for a husband's conversion, who out of regard for her went regularly to church, said, "Oh! why doesn't the minister *preach Christ?*" "Anything but Christ crucified, risen, ascended, exalted" is the devil's motto and he is doing his best to get ministers of the Gospel to make it theirs.

But the devil has another mode of attack upon the corporate Body of Christ. He is doing a very deadly work even among the saints of God through division. When he sees that he cannot touch the spiritual man through deceiving him regarding the fundamental truths of God, or undermine his love for God, or deflect him from doing the will of God, then he works to make him so zealous in his defense of the truth, so ardent in his love for it, so set in his own particular interpretation of it, that he will not fellowship with those who, as sound and true and devoted as he, do not see and act as he does. He cannot see that "adorning the doctrine" may be as great a manifestation of real love for Christ and as potent a weapon against the appalling apostasy as "defending" it. Or perhaps in his desire for vital spirituality within the Church he has placed such emphasis upon some segment of truth that he unspiritualizes other brethren who do not give that truth the same emphasis. Thus the devil succeeds in injecting into the very vitals of Christ's Body the poison of acrimonius criticism, unwarranted suspicion, unloving intolerance and bitter feeling. By weakening and dividing the spiritual forces of Christ and by turning their eyes in upon themselves rather than out upon the world lying in sin, Satan gains a tremendous victory in the conflict.

But the devil goes still further and presses on in an attack upon the individual members of Christ's Body who have entered into real oneness with their Lord. He sends forth his fiery darts to carry depression of spirit, delusion of mind, distraction of heart, deflection of will and distress of body.

The human spirit is the headquarters of the Holy Spirit in the believer's life and the vantage ground from which He works to carry the life of Christ out to the uttermost part of the human personality. So it is very necessary to have it untrammelled, joyous, assured. But the evil one works to inject the poison of doubt concerning one's spiritual condition, and discouragement over one's work. Especially are Christian workers being attacked in this manner by Satan.

The world today is flooded with cults. Tons of literature are sent broadcast filled with satanic propaganda. Reading rooms and lecture bureaus are established and everything possible is done to delude people and to seduce them from the simplicity of the faith of Christ. Earnest children of God are often caught unawares in some time of sorrow or affliction when they seek for light and comfort. These cults hold forth spurious hope through specious lies and people are ensnared. Or some through neglect of God's Word and failure to appropriate their inheritance in Christ by faith are unsatisfied in their Christian lives and turn to one of these novelties in religion, hoping by some shortcut to obtain what they have hitherto not had in experience. Others who desire the deepest spiritual life are led to take some truth of God's Word and then go beyond what the Word teaches regarding it into disastrous error. Or sometimes Satan seduces a Christian worker into a study of the books of these various cults under the guise of ability to save others from deception, and he thereby becomes entrapped. Satan has a thousand methods suited to the temperament and circumstances of the one he is trying to ensnare. Satan hates the Word of God and works against it by blinding men's eyes (2 Corinthians 4:4), by substituting his own doctrines (1 Timothy 4:1-2), by contradicting it (Genesis 3:5), by wresting it (Matthew 4:6), by leading men to disbelieve it (2 Timothy 4:3-4), by taking it out of men's hearts (Mark 4:15). Above all he would keep God's children ignorant of the truth concerning himself which the Bible reveals, and of the victory which Christ Jesus has already gained over him at the cross.

Satan works to cause distraction of heart. Many of God's consecrated children are being tortured by cruel and crushing suffering and sorrow which have their source in Satan. He is sending his poisoned shaft into the home, alienating husband and wife through unfaithfulness. He is causing estrangements in family circles based on falsehood, misunderstanding and false interpretation of motives, words and acts. Through the shirking of the burden on the part of one member of the family he is placing an intolerable load upon another. Others who have made their business a real partnership with God he attempts to overwhelm with business perplexities and financial losses through the unscrupulousness of others. The evil one works to rob God's child of the peace of God.

Satan schemes to cause deflection from God's plan and purpose in work. He will do anything to keep God's child from the direct work of saving souls. He directs the attention to secondary matters; he divides the energy over unnecessary tasks, and he darkens the mind over questions of guidance.

Satan works to cause distress of body through weakening it by disease or crippling it by disaster (Job 2:7). Through his continued onslaughts upon every part of the believer's being the devil is trying to move him out of the will of God by getting him experientially out of his position in Christ Jesus.

THE CAPTAIN OF THE HOST

Some believers are ensnared by Satan because they fail to realize his power and to recognize his tactics. But others make the equally fatal mistake of overestimating his power and of overemphasis upon his activities. He is mighty, but there is One infinitely mightier. He is powerful, but there is One who is all-powerful. He can and does attack us from without, but there is an omnipotent, triumphant One who can and does strengthen, sustain and energize us from within. He is the One to whom all power has been given in heaven and upon earth. He is the Captain of our salvation; the Leader of God's hosts.

> 1 John 4:4, "Ye are of God, little children, and have overcome them: *because greater is he that is in you, than he that is in the world.*"
>
> Matthew 28:18, "And Jesus came and spake unto them, saying, *All power is given unto me in heaven and in earth.*"
>
> Romans 8:37, "Nay, *in all these things we are more than conquerors through him* that loved us."
>
> Hebrews 2:10, "For it became him, for whom are all things, and by whom are all things, in bringing many sons unto glory, *to make the captain of their salvation* perfect through sufferings."

The believer should always look upon Satan as a defeated foe. He has already been overcome by the Captain of our host. Any power which he exercises today is only a permitted power that God may get greater glory to Himself through the victory gained by His child before a doubting world, and also that the Christian's life in Christ may be deepened and strengthened. Satan was permitted through his human tools to stone Stephen to death but through Stephen's gloriously triumphant martyrdom God won the crown jewel from Satan's diadem, Saul of Tarsus. He was allowed through human instruments to put to death the Lord of glory but in doing it he sent himself to the bottomless pit.

That wicked one has no claim whatever upon one who is born of God and he has no power to harm or hurt him. The believer who is hid with Christ in God and who is one with his ascended Lord has the right to claim the perfect protection which that position provides and to reckon himself as a conqueror in Christ Jesus.

> 1 John 5:18, "We know that whosoever is born of God sinneth not; but he that is begotten of God keepeth himself, and *that wicked one toucheth him not.*"
>
> Romans 16:20, "And *the God of peace shall bruise Satan under your feet* shortly."

The Captain of the host never commanded the children of Israel to fight *for* a position of victory but to fight *from* a position of victory. In His reckoning the battle was won before it was begun. Even before entrance into a battle He invariably spoke in the *past* tense of the deliverance of the enemy into their hands.

Joshua 6:2-3, "And the LORD said unto Joshua, See, I *have* given into thine hand Jericho, and the king thereof, and the mighty men of valour. And ye *shall* compass the city, all ye men of war, and go round about the city once. Thus shalt thou do six days."

Then why did they have to fight the battle at all? That through faith in their Captain and His Word they might come to share His assurance of complete conquest over the enemy. While the walls of Jericho were still standing and the children of Israel were shut outside the gates Joshua proclaimed to the people that their conquest of the city was an accomplished fact.

Joshua 6:16, "And it came to pass at the seventh time, when the priests blew with the trumpets, Joshua said unto the people, Shout; for the LORD *hath* given you the city."

The battle of the believer is that of faith from his position of accomplished victory over the evil one through his oneness with His ascended Lord.

THE CONQUEST OF THE ENEMY

In Ephesians 6:10-18 our Captain tells us that power to stand against the enemy depends upon our position and upon our protection.

Ephesians 6:10-11, "Finally, my brethren, *be strong in the Lord,* and in the power of his might.

Put on the whole armour of God, that ye may be able to stand against the wiles of the devil."

In ourselves we have no power and we would have to succumb instantly to the attacks of the evil one. But "in Christ" oh! how different! Our Victor over Satan envelops us for we are hid with Christ in God. As someone has truly said, "Before the devil can reach your life to touch it, he must get through God and through Christ." Our part then in the conquest is, calmly and confidently, to meet every onslaught of the enemy from our hidden position in Christ Jesus and to sing as we fight "The Lord *hath* given me the victory." Then it will be ours in the conquering power of His might.

In ourselves we have no power to withstand the continuous attacks of the enemy against every part of our lives. But God has provided an armor that will protect at every point.

Ephesians 6:14-18, R. V., "Stand therefore, *having girded your loins with truth,* and *having put on the breastplate of righteousness,* and *having shod your feet with the preparation of the gospel of peace;* withal *taking up the shield of faith,* wherewith ye shall be able to quench all the fiery darts of the evil one. And *take the helmet of salvation,* and *the sword of the Spirit, which is the word of God: with all prayer and supplication* praying at all seasons in the Spirit, and watching thereunto in all perseverance and supplication for all the saints."

"Stand—girded with truth." The power of the deceiver lies in his ability to persuade people to believe him instead of God and thus to lead them into doubt, disbelief and error. The antidote to this deception is to abide in Him who is the truth. We should saturate our lives in the truth of His love, His faithfulness, His power, His holiness, His purposes—in the truth of Christ Himself so that such truth like a girdle will bind us to Him in unswerving love and loyalty. But we need also to have Him, who is the truth, abide in us so that there may be nothing hypocritical, dishonest or shady upon which the prince of darkness can lay hold and use against us.

"Stand—having put on the breastplate of righteousness." Rooted in Him who is our righteousness and growing up into His own uprightness of life more perfectly day by day through the indwelling and working of the Holy Spirit, the believer can stand before every accusation of the devil with "a conscience void of offense toward God and men," as the tall pine tree whose roots have hid themselves in the bowels of the earth resists the blasts of the winter storm.

"Stand—having shod your feet with the preparation of the Gospel of peace." Our walk is through a world of disorder. Thousands of things happen to us to cut, to bruise, to wound, to grieve, to rob us of the peace of God that passeth all understanding and to hinder our testimony regarding a Gospel of peace and joy and rest. Countless things occur, many of them very trivial, which the devil rejoices to use to cause estrangement and misunderstanding. But the believer has the love of God in his heart so he is enabled to live at peace with all men. Over the mountain roads of Switzerland travelers wear heavy boots with thick soles, often with spikes, so that as they walk over the rough, stony paths they are unbruised, and over the ice and snow they are kept from stumbling and falling. They are rightly shod.

"Stand—taking the shield of faith." Conybeare's translation adds to the understanding of this direction from our Captain by saying "take up *to cover you* the shield of faith." How does the believer know from which direction the enemy under the cover of darkness will send forth a fiery dart, or at what point in his life it may be aimed? Paul speaks of "all" the fiery darts, intimating that possibly the devil sends many of them at the same time. There is great need that faith should be a covering. So the believer needs to walk in faith, to pray in faith, to speak in faith, to praise in faith, to live continuously believing in the faithfulness of God to keep that which has been committed unto Him.

"Stand—taking the helmet of salvation." The helmet is for the head. One

of the most vulnerable places in the believer is his thoughts. Perhaps the devil finds entrance here more quickly than elsewhere. Is this not the reason why the apostle Paul exhorts Christians to think of things that are "true, honest, just, pure, lovely, and of good report?" *Every thought* needs to be brought into captivity to the obedience of Christ if the believer is to know how to refuse the thoughts that come from the evil one. Satan also finds an undisciplined, undiscerning mind an easy prey to his delusions and ofttimes an unconscious instrument in his service. Even earnest Christians are often gullible and commend a sermon that is saturated with the most insidious denial of the Person and work of Jesus Christ because it is couched in eloquent, fervent language and even flattering admiration of the Lord it betrays. If ever there was a time when Christians needed to put on the helmet of salvation it is now. And putting it on will mean such a thorough and intelligent knowledge of salvation in Christ as shall make the believer impervious to every satanic attack even in these days of growing apostasy.

"*Stand—taking the sword of the Spirit.*" Jesus Christ puts into the Christian's heart and hand the only weapon which He Himself used when He won that perfect victory in the wilderness. The sword of the Word of God, when used in the power of the Holy Spirit, is the mightiest weapon in this spiritual conflict. Satan cannot stand before "It is written" spoken out of the assurance of the believer's own experience of its absolute trustworthiness and power. It is the spiritual man who has been taught by the Holy Spirit the very deep things of God who is best able to put the enemy to rout by the use of this powerful weapon.

"*Stand—praying in the Spirit and watching.*" The Christian warrior clad in his protective armor is now ready for the hardest fight of the battle. It is "prayer and supplication in the Spirit and watching thereunto" until the enemy is routed. It takes a truly spiritual man to be a potent prayer warrior. True "praying in the Holy Spirit" leads him out of himself into intercession for the lifting of the whole Body of Christ to life on the highest plane for the victory of the ascended Head to be manifested in the whole life of each member of His Body on earth.

Thus the believer, who is deeply rooted in his position in Christ and who has put on the whole of his protective armor, is able to stand and to withstand every onslaught and attack of Satan. The ground gained for him by Christ is held by him for Christ and a steady and successful advance is made into the territory still held in the dominion of the evil one. The spiritual man becomes an overcomer and, one with his ascended Lord, rejoices in daily and hourly conquest in this spiritual conflict in the heavenlies.

21

Life on the Highest Plane

IN THE QUIET of a village in Switzerland God has been teaching me many precious lessons about this ascent to life on the highest plane. Grindelwald is thirty-six hundred feet above the sea and from my window I can see four majestic, snowcapped mountains rise to immense heights out of this little valley. For days after coming here I was absolutely satisfied with what I could see from my window. What more of beauty, of majesty, of glory could one want or take in! But as I got a glimpse here and there of higher peaks hidden from view by these nearer mountains the desire came to climb to some place where I could look out over them all.

One day a party of us started on such a climb. The way was unknown to us but green paint on rock, tree and fence told us the path. We carried that day only what was necessary for the trip; everything but what we actually needed was left behind. The path led steadily up with almost no stretches on the level, in places quite steep. As the sun shone upon us we grew warm, the rough, stony places made our feet burn and ache, unused muscles were stretched and strained, and we had to stop often to rest; every part of the body felt the tug of the climb. To endure the difficulties of the mountain climb and to enjoy all the beautiful things God has placed along the way to see and hear and smell, every faculty of our being and every member of our body was brought into play.

Very often on the upward climb we stopped to rest and refresh ourselves by looking back over the road already traversed and at the new beauties that greeted us the higher up we went. At one point in the way we caught sight of just the summit of a pyramid-shaped, snow-covered peak different from all others we had seen. It arrested our attention and provoked inquiry because of its distinctiveness in shape and its purity of covering. How thrilled we were to learn that it was the Jungfrau, that queen of the Alps.

But oh! what joy when we reached the Waldspitz and how amply repaid we felt in just one moment's time as we gazed at that indescribably beautiful panorama of several of the highest snowcapped Alpine mountains, which is thought one of three of the most beautiful views in Switzerland. Below us the valley and everything in it seemed dwarfed; the glaciers that in the valley towered so high were now so far below; and the nearer mountains that from the valley seemed so high as to live in the clouds were overtowered by the majestic Schreckhorn and the peerless Jungfrau.

We were very, very far yet from reaching the highest height of the Alps but we had gone far enough on such a mountain climb to know that it was worth all it cost, and to get a vision of what majestic glory must be in store for one who dared to go to the top where he could look up to God's heaven and out over God's world from the highest plane.

Dare I hope that the studies in this book have meant just such a spiritual ascent to some readers? Did the book find you living in the heat and stress and strife of life below sea level, on the plane of the natural but with a true desire to seek relief in a higher spiritual altitude? Or had you already left the old sphere of the natural and were enjoying life a few hundred feet above sea level, on the plane of the carnal? Had you settled down in complacent self-satisfaction with what you could see from the little window of your valley experience and had you become content to live at the half-way house of spiritual achievement? Did you aspire for nothing higher than the pleasant walks you could take on the level road where you would not need spiked shoes, a traveler's kit and a climber's stick but could still wear your best clothes and high heeled shoes and only get comfortably tired? But when the book found you was there a stirring of discontent in your soul because at times when walking in communion with Him alone, or in the companionship with some saint of God who had reached the highest plane and told you of its glories, you had seen glimpses of a life in Christ immeasurably beyond anything you had ever seen or dreamed of, and your whole soul cried within you for an experience of such victory, glory, peace and holiness as you knew were possible?

Dare I hope that you essayed to make the climb and that the studies, chapter by chapter, have pointed the way for you out of the natural into the spiritual life in Christ Jesus? I know from experience that it has not been an easy climb. Besetting sins and hindering weights have had to be left behind and only those things taken with you which would strengthen and assist you on the upward climb toward God; the sunshine of God's chastening has heated you to the highest pitch of endurance at times; your feet have been cut and torn by the temptations and afflictions along the way; unused muscles of faith, love, long-suffering, patience and devotion have been stretched to the point of strain; perhaps you have been easily winded by the buffeting and blows of the world, the flesh and the devil. I am sure that before you had gone very far from the valley experience of life on the carnal plane you found that every part of your being was feeling the pull of the climb; and that spirit, soul and body needed to be wholly sanctified and surrendered to the Lord Jesus Christ and put under the control and guidance of the Holy Spirit, that you might not be overcome by the difficulties and might not miss the blessings God had strewn along the way.

But now you have reached the place where you may look out upon God's spiritual Alpine range of salvation and get one glorious panoramic view of peak upon peak which altogether reveal the infinite grace and boundless love of the triune God. Off yonder in the range of vision are the twin peaks of Forgiveness and Justification; next in sharp, clear outline is the lovely peak of Regeneration; further to the back is a majestic peak which one does not see at all from the valley viewpoint of the carnal life because it is hidden by the nearer mountain of Regeneration, the peak of Identification with Christ in His death, resurrection, ascension and present life in glory. But off in the distance is one peak different from all the rest, distinctive in its snow white purity and holiness, the crown of all the others. It is Sanctification, the Jungfrau of spiritual experience. As you have gazed upon the flawless perfection, the indescribable grandeur, the overpowering majesty of the wonders of God's infinite grace and perfect love has not everything in the valley of your carnal life seemed to sink into utter insignificance? Have not things which seemed high above you and that overpowered you by their weight taken their proper place beneath your feet? Have you not realized how shut in you were down there by narrow interests, selfish enjoyments, petty pleasures, puny aspirations? Do you not feel that life for you can never again be the same now that you have felt the thrill of the climb on the ascent and have viewed God's gracious, glorious plan of salvation from the mountaintop?

If this be true of you, dear fellow traveler, may we not just rest a while with this glorious vision before us and sit in quiet meditation upon what we have seen life on the highest plane to be.

It Is a Life Saved Through God's Gracious Provision

The salvation which God has provided for the sinner is a perfect salvation. It is without flaw. It provides for his past, present and future. It covers every need of every part of his being under every circumstance. It relates him rightly to heaven and to earth; to the divine and to the human; to God and to man for time and for eternity. It is a salvation to the uttermost.

Such a salvation is the gracious provision of God in Christ. Apart from Jesus Christ no man can be saved; in Christ any man may be saved to the uttermost because in Christ incarnate, crucified, risen, ascended and exalted, God found everything needful to restore a believing sinner to fellowship with Himself.

> Acts 4:12, *"Neither is there salvation in any other: for there is none other name under heaven given among men, whereby we must be saved."*
>
> 2 Timothy 2:10, "Therefore I endure all things for the elect's sakes, that they may also obtain the *salvation which is in Christ Jesus* with eternal glory."

The provision that God made in Christ for every believer is threefold. He sent Him to die on the cross as our Saviour; He raised Him from the dead to make Him the Head and the Lord of the Church, His Body; and He exalted Him to His right hand and gave Him all power in heaven and upon earth that He might share Himself and His possession in the heavenlies with His joint heirs on earth. The one who has reached the goal of life on the highest plane has accepted Christ as his Saviour, yielded to Him as his Lord, and appropriated Him as his Life.

It Is a Life Conformed to God's Perfect Pattern

Complete conformity of the penitent, believing sinner to the image of his perfect Saviour was the purpose of the wondrous plan of salvation wrought out in the eternal counsels of the triune God before ever the world or man was made.

God laid the foundation for such an achievement in the creation of the first man in His own image. In His second Man, God gave mankind the perfect pattern to which He would conform every believer in Christ Jesus. May we see, then, what were the constituent elements in the life of this perfect pattern that we may fully understand and quickly respond to the operation of the Holy Spirit as He works to fashion us according to it.

We have seen in our study on the incarnation that the life of the God-man was a truly human life in every sense in which our life is human, except in its sinfulness. He lived in the same kind of a world and was involved in the same kind of relationships. So the constituent elements in His moral and spiritual character that enables Him to be a perfect pattern to all mankind must be in us if we are fully conformed to His image.

The God-man's surpassing perfection is seen most clearly in His relationship to His Father which was one of unimpaired obedience and of unintermittent dependence. The will of God was the center and the circumference of His life, and all that took place from His birth in the manger to His death on the cross was the execution of His Father's will. He came, He lived, He died, that His Father's will might be done on earth as it is done in heaven. Obedience was the invariable, unalterable rule in the life of

Christ on earth. He always said yes to God. Self-will had no place in His life.

> Hebrews 10:9, "*Then said he, Lo, I come to do thy will, O God.* He taketh away the first, that he may establish the second."
>
> John 6:38, "For I came down from heaven, *not to do mine own will, but the will of him that sent me.*"
>
> John 4:34, "Jesus saith unto them, *My meat is to do the will of him that sent me,* and to finish his work."

Christ, the perfect pattern, was also absolutely dependent. Self-trust had no place in the life of the God-man. The last Adam lived the life of dependence which the first Adam refused to live. Never was a life lived on earth so dependent upon God as was His. His thoughts, His words, His works, were those of His Father. He was a Sent One and He did only what He had been sent to do. He never initiated or executed anything which had its spring in Himself for His was a life "insulated in God's will." In His utter dependence upon God the last Adam was the perfect pattern.

> John 5:30, "*I can of mine own self do nothing:* as I hear, I judge: and my judgment is just; because I seek not mine own will, but the will of the Father which hath sent me."
>
> John 14:10, "Believest thou not that I am in the Father, and the Father in me? *the words that I speak unto you I speak not of myself: but the Father that dwelleth in me, he doeth the works.*"

The God-man's surpassing perfection is seen again most transparently in His glorious victory and in His spotless holiness. Tempted in all points as we are, having no companionship but that of sinful men and women in a world of sin, tested by His Father and tempted by the devil, yet He came forth so victorious that both friend and foe alike acknowledged no fault in Him.

> Luke 23:22, "And he said unto them the third time, *Why, what evil hath he done? I have found no cause of death in him:* I will therefore chastise him, and let him go."
>
> 1 Peter 2:22, "*Who did no sin,* neither was guile found in his mouth."

But the perfection of His character did not consist so much in the negative quality of sinlessness as in the positive one of holiness—a holiness so rare, so wondrous, so unearthly that it compelled His Father to break the silence of heaven three times that He might speak forth His divine appreciation and evaluation of it.

> Luke 1:35, "And the angel answered and said unto her, The Holy Ghost

shall come upon thee, and the power of the Highest shall overshadow thee: therefore also *that holy thing which shall be born of thee* shall be called the Son of God."

Matthew 17:5, "While he yet spake, behold, a bright cloud overshadowed them: and behold a voice out of the cloud, which said, *This is my beloved Son, in whom I am well pleased; hear ye him.*"

The God-man's surpassing perfection is seen again most wondrously in His regal righteousness and in His sacrificial love. "He came unto his own, and his own received him not." He was despised, persecuted, rejected and finally crucified by the very ones He came to save yet there was never a trace of bitterness, malice or revenge in His heart. Even from the cross He prayed for His murderers. He was reviled, yet He showed no trace of retaliation; He suffered unjustly, yet He made no threats of redress. When He drove the money changers from the Temple and when He spoke the scorching, scathing denunciations of the hypocritical Pharisees it was but the outward expression of His own regal righteousness. Whether dealing with friend or foe, in mercy or in judgment, Christ Jesus was always the perfect pattern.

1 Peter 2:21-23, "For even hereunto were ye called: because *Christ also suffered for us, leaving us an example, that ye should follow his steps: Who did no sin, neither was guile found in his mouth: Who, when he was reviled, reviled not again; when he suffered, he threatened not;* but committed himself to him that judgeth righteously."

But it was in His sacrificial love for men that the perfection of Christ's character shone forth even more than in His righteous treatment of them. Christ Jesus never pampered or pleased Himself. Though weary and hungry the soul need of a prostitute in Samaria would detain Him by Jacob's well while the others went on into town to buy food; His night's sleep was gladly forfeited that He might talk with the man who feared to come to Him by day; He did not stop short with self-emptying and self-humbling, costly as they were, but kept on giving Himself even unto death, the death of the cross. The God-man pouring out His soul unto death in sacrificial love is the perfect pattern.

John 15:12, "This is my commandment, *That ye love one another, as I have loved you.*"

The spiritual man is the man who lives his daily life according to the perfect pattern. In Him are to be found the same constituent moral and spiritual elements which were regnant in the character and conduct of the God-man. He has made the will of Jesus Christ the center and the circumference of his life, and so he is obedient. He acknowledges that he has no life apart from Christ and takes the Lord Jesus for everything in his inner life, his environment and his service, and so he is dependent. The spiritual man has crowned Christ Lord and placed his life completely under the control of his Master, therefore he is gloriously victorious. He has appropriated Christ as the Life of his life therefore he becomes the partaker of His holiness. The spiritual man has accepted Christ's commission as one sent into the world to save sinners even as Christ accepted this commission from His Father, so his attitude to all men whether friend or foe is based on Christ's principles of righteousness and love.

The spiritual man is one who is being conformed to the image of Christ, the perfect pattern. When this has been said, everything has been said. In God's reckoning there is nothing for man beyond conformity to the image of His Son. Christ is God's perfection and to be fully conformed to His image is to be perfect before Him.

The process of conformity is going on day by day in the spiritual man's life. It is a transformation from obedience to obedience, from dependence to dependence, from victory to victory, from holiness to holiness, from righteousness to righteousness and from love to love. As the spiritual man gets a larger vision of this perfect pattern through daily study of God's Word, he takes higher ground along the line of the God-given revelation, so that his life is a continuous growing up into Christ in all things.

> 2 Corinthians 3:18, R. V., "But we all, with unveiled face beholding as in a mirror the glory of the Lord, *are transformed into the same image from glory to glory,* even as from the Lord the Spirit."
>
> Ephesians 4:15, "But speaking the truth in love, *may grow up into him in all things,* which is the head, even Christ."

The consummation of this conformity will not be experienced until the Lord Jesus returns to take His own to be forever beyond the presence of sin into the presence of the Saviour (1 John 3:2).

It Is a Life Perfected by God's Holy Presence

I hasten to this point because I would not have anyone think even for an instant that conformity to the image of Christ is effected by imitation of a pattern, no matter how perfect. Such conformity as the Bible speaks of is not wrought in the believer through the imitation of a pattern without but through the presence of a Person within. It is only through the union whereby the Vine lives in the branch and the branch in the Vine that such conformity is found. It is only the man who apprehends his position in Christ and Christ's possession in him who grows up into likeness to his Lord. It is only the man who consistently can say, "Christ liveth in me" who can say honestly, "To me to live is Christ." It is not the imitation of the incarnate Son but it is the indwelling of the crucified, risen, ascended, exalted Son that perfects conformity to His image. What He was I am to be because of what He did on the cross and now does from the throne. It is the Father's answer to the last three words of His Son's high-priestly prayer that produces conformity to Christ in the believer. Oneness with the Lord makes likeness to the Lord.

> John 15:5, "I am the vine, ye are the branches: He that abideth in me and *I in him,* the same bringeth forth much fruit: *for without me* ye can do nothing."

> John 17:26, "And I have declared unto them thy name, and will declare it: that the love wherewith thou hast loved me may be in them, and *I in them.*"

It Is a Life Energized by God's Mighty Power

One has only to begin to live his life on the highest plane to know that life can never be maintained on that level in one's own power. Living steadfastly and habitually in the altitude of the heavenlies is the spiritual man's greatest difficulty. Even after taking Christ Jesus as his perfect pattern and realizing His holy presence within, the believer often has periods of dismal failure and terrible defeat.

But the spiritually minded man has learned God's way of maintaining his life in the heavenlies and his life is energized by the mighty power of the Holy Spirit whom God bestows upon every child of His. The Holy Spirit is given when the new nature is imparted to the believer for the very purpose of effecting this growing conformity to the image of Christ.

> Ephesians 3:16-17, 19-20, "That he would grant you, according to the riches of his glory, *to be strengthened with might by his Spirit in the inner man;*
> *That Christ may dwell in your hearts by faith;*
> *That ye might be filled unto all the fulness of God.* . . .
> Now unto him that is able to do exceeding abundantly above all that we ask or think, *according to the power that worketh in us.*"

Life on the highest plane is consistently and continuously maintained by the energizing power of the indwelling power of the indwelling Spirit of God.

It Is a Life Fulfilling God's Eternal Purpose

Before ever the world was created or man was made to inhabit it God had a purpose which He intended to carry out through His Son.

> Ephesians 3:11, "According to *the eternal purpose* which he purposed in Christ Jesus our Lord."

2 Timothy 1:9, "Who hath saved us, and called us with an holy calling, not according to our works, *but according to his own purpose and grace,* which was given us in Christ Jesus *before the world began.*"

This purpose God kept hid in His heart, yet throughout all the centuries preceding the incarnation of His eternal Son He was working toward its fulfillment. Then Christ came, lived, died, rose again and ascended into heaven. Now the time had come both for the revelation and the realization of this purpose. Through the apostle Paul, God's chosen vessel, the revelation of this eternal purpose of God in Christ Jesus was made and its clearest unfolding is given to us in the epistle to the Ephesians.

Through the finished work of Christ upon the cross and from the throne God would call out a people unto Himself who during this present period of His Son's absence from earth would witness and work for Him here as His Body and upon His return to earth to reign would come with Him as His Bride.

Ephesians 1:22-23, "And hath put all things under his feet, and gave him to be the head over all things to the church, *which is his body,* the fulness of him that filleth all in all."

Revelation 21:9, "And there came unto me one of the seven angels which had seven vials full of the seven last plagues, and talked with me, saying, *Come hither, I will shew thee the bride, the Lamb's wife.*"

The Holy Spirit as a purifying and energizing power works within the Church to prepare it to live on earth as Christ's Body and to present it in heaven to Christ as His Bride.

2 Timothy 2:20-21, "But in a great house there are not only vessels of gold and of silver, but also of wood and of earth; and some to honour, and some to dishonour.

If a man therefore purge himself from these, *he shall be a vessel unto honour, sanctified, meet for the master's use, and prepared unto every good work.*"

Ephesians 5:25-27, "Husbands, love your wives, even as Christ also loved the church, and gave himself for it; that he might sanctify and cleanse it with the washing of water by the word, *that he might present it to himself a glorious church, not having spot, or wrinkle, or any such thing; but that it should be holy and without blemish.*"

But there are two things which are absolutely essential in the relationship between Christ and the believer if God's eternal purpose is to be fulfilled; one is communion and the other is cooperation. God is love and love is a reciprocal thing. Love must both give and receive. There is no such thing as love between God and man or man and man unless there exists in the relationship both communion and cooperation, and the greater the love the fuller is the communion and the cooperation.

In the eternity of the past the eternal Son rested in the bosom of the eternal Father—that was communion. And when the triune God initiated the wondrous plan of redemption the eternal Son offered Himself as the Lamb to be slain—that was cooperation. In the Garden of Eden the Lover-Creator and His first man must have walked often in the garden in the cool of the day—that was communion. And the sovereign Lord God gave to His subject the dominion over everything on earth—that was cooperation. The night before His crucifixion the God-man sat at supper with the twelve—that was communion. And before He ascended into heaven He said, "All power is given unto me in heaven and in earth. Go ye therefore, and teach all nations, baptizing them in the name of the Father, and of the Son, and of the Holy Ghost: teaching them to observe all things whatsoever I have commanded you"—that is cooperation.

The spiritual man apprehends this truth and appreciates the significance of it. He sees that it means such a yielding of himself to Jesus Christ as Lord, as will make possible the perfect possession, the complete control and the unhindered use of his entire being. He clearly perceives that salvation includes sanctification and that life on the highest plane demands not only a separation from sin but a separation unto God, and he rejoices in being thus wholly set apart unto communion and cooperation with the Lord of glory.

It Is a Life Fashioned on God's Original Plan

In God's original plan the human personality was a unity. The human spirit, dominated and directed by the Holy Spirit, was supreme in authority over the soul and the body so that the Holy Spirit through the channel of the human spirit made and kept the whole being spiritual.

As we have seen in chapter 17 sin began its deadly work in Adam's spirit by severing it from the divine Spirit thus alienating it from the life of God and making it a death chamber. Sin also dethroned it as sovereign over the human personality and made it a slave to the soul and body. Thus sin left the human spirit darkened and dethroned. Salvation must begin where sin began; the human spirit must be quickened. The sovereignty of the Holy Spirit over it must be restored, and its supremacy over soul and body must be revived.

The human spirit was made the receptacle of the eternal life of God. Salvation always outruns sin for "where sin abounded grace did much more abound." In the quickening of the human spirit God not only made it cease being a death chamber but He made it the receptacle of the eternal life of the triune God. Through the new birth He implanted within it something which had never been there before, the divine, spiritual, eternal life of the triune God in the Person of Christ the Son in whom "dwelleth all the fulness of the Godhead bodily" (Colossians 2:9).

> 1 John 5:11-12, "And this is the record, *that God hath given to us eternal life,* and *this life is in his Son.*
>   *He that hath the Son hath life;* and he that hath not the Son of God hath not life."

Into this quickened spirit the Holy Spirit comes to dwell, feeding and fostering this new life within that it may grow up "into a perfect man, unto the measure of the stature of the fulness of Christ" (Ephesians 4:13). A renewal of this divine life within is made daily by the Holy Spirit.

> Ezekiel 36:26-27, "A new heart also will I give you, *and a new spirit will I put within you:* and I will take away the stony heart out of your flesh, and I will give you an heart of flesh.
>   *And I will put my spirit within you,* and cause you to walk in my statutes, and ye shall keep my judgments, and do them."

> 2 Corinthians 4:16, "For which cause we faint not; but though our outward man perish, *yet the inward man is renewed day by day.*"

The spiritual man is one in whom the human spirit is supernaturally recreated through the implantation of the uncreated life of God at the new birth. Into this quickened spirit the Holy Spirit has come to abide, to control, to renew and to energize. Between them "a perpetual partnership" is established. Through this supernatural reunion of the divine Spirit and the human spirit Christ and the believer are joined into one spirit.

> 1 Corinthians 6:17, "But he that is joined unto the Lord is *one spirit.*"

Through this act of God in regeneration the maladjustment within the believer's human personality is remedied. True balance between the constituent parts is restored; the sovereignty of the spirit over soul and body is revived, and the human spirit is again the premier in the governmental affairs of the human being, and the soul and body are its loyal and faithful underlings.

The human soul becomes the illumined vessel of the divine Spirit.

1. The mind is renewed. The spiritual man is spiritually minded. He thinks the thoughts of God. He craves divine wisdom (1 Corinthians 2:7); he sits at the feet of a divine Teacher (John 16:13); he loves God with all his mind (Matthew 22:37); he minds the things of the Spirit (Romans 8:5); he thinks on the things that are true, honest, just, pure, lovely, and of good report (Philippians 4:8); he is of one mind with his brethren (Philippians 2:2); he has the mind of Christ (1 Corinthians 2:16) so he is of sound mind (2 Timothy 1:7), and every thought is brought into cap-

tivity to the obedience of Christ (2 Corinthians 10:5). Intellect, reason and every faculty of his mind are renewed and illumined by Him who knows the mind of God.

Ephesians 4:23, "And *be renewed in the spirit of your mind.*"

Romans 8:6, "For to be carnally minded is death; but *to be spiritually minded* is life and peace."

Philippians 2:5, "*Let this mind be in you, which was also in Christ Jesus.*"

2. The heart is purified. The spiritual man is pure-hearted. He wants to possess his inheritance in Christ so he sets his affection on things above (Colossians 3:2); he craves the vision of God granted only to the pure in heart (Matthew 5:8); he desires to see his Lord which is only the prerogative of the holy (Hebrews 12:14); he seeks the conformity to Christ promised upon His return to those who purify themselves even as He is pure (1 John 3:2), and so he allows the Holy Spirit to do within him all needed work of pruning and purifying.

Acts 15:8-9, "And God, which knoweth the hearts, bare them witness, *giving them the Holy Ghost,* even as he did unto us;
And put no difference between us and them, *purifying their hearts by faith.*"

1 Thessalonians 3:13, "*To the end that he may stablish your hearts unblameable in holiness before God,* even our Father, at the coming of our Lord Jesus Christ with all his saints."

3. The will is energized. The spiritual man knows that at the center of Satan's being is self-will and that everyone in whose life self-will is supreme is the seed and the subject of Satan. He knows that at the center of Christ's being is God's will and that everyone in whose life God's will is supreme is the seed and the subject of Christ. He has compared and contrasted the "I will" of Satan, Isaiah 14:12-15 and its result in Revelation 20:7-15 with the "I will" of Christ in Hebrews 10:5-13 and its result in Philippians 2:5-11 and has decided to cast in his lot for time and for eternity with Jesus Christ the obedient, dependent One. The spiritual man looks to the Holy Spirit to work *in* and then work *out* God's perfect will within him.

Hebrews 13:21, "*Make you perfect in every good work to do his will, working in you* that which is wellpleasing in his sight, through Jesus Christ; to whom be glory for ever and ever."

Philippians 2:13, "*For it is God which worketh in you both to will and to do of his good pleasure.*"

The human body becomes the habitation of the triune God on earth. The spiritual man apprehends the spiritual significance and sacredness of his body. Under the Holy Spirit's illumination he learns what it becomes through the new birth.

1. The body is the temple of the living God.

> 2 Corinthians 6:16, "And what agreement hath the temple of God with idols? *for ye are the temple of the living God;* as God hath said, *I will dwell in them,* and walk in them; I will be their God, and they shall be my people."

2. The body is the temple of the Holy Spirit.

> 1 Corinthians 6:19-20, "What? know ye not that *your body is the temple of the Holy Ghost which is in you,* which ye have of God, and ye are not your own? For ye are bought with a price: *therefore glorify God in your body,* and in your spirit, which are God's."

3. The body is a member of the Lord Jesus Christ.

> 1 Corinthians 6:15, *"Know ye not that your bodies are the members of Christ.* Shall I then take the members of Christ, and make them the members of an harlot? God forbid."

4. The body is the container of the heavenly treasure.

> 2 Corinthians 4:7, *"But we have this treasure in earthen vessels,* that the excellency of the power may be of God, and not of us."

5. The body is the channel for good works.

> 2 Corinthians 5:10, "For we must all appear before the judgment seat of Christ; *that every one may receive the things done in his body,* according to that he hath done, whether it be good or bad."

6. The body is Christ's broadcasting station.

> 2 Corinthians 4:10-11, "Always bearing about in the body the dying of the Lord Jesus, *that the life also of Jesus might be made manifest in our body.*
> For we which live are alway delivered unto death for Jesus' sake, *that the life also of Jesus might be made manifest in our mortal flesh.*"

The spiritual man perceives through this truth that God wishes to become incarnate and to dwell on earth and that the way in which He has chosen to do this is by having the perfect possession, the complete control and the unhindered use of the human body of the believer. Acting upon this knowledge the spiritual man has presented God with his body here and now as a living sacrifice.

> Romans 12:1, "I beseech you therefore, brethren, by the mercies of God, *that ye present your bodies a living sacrifice,* holy, acceptable unto God, which is your reasonable service."

Not wishing to run any risk of defrauding God or of deceiving himself in regard to the completeness of this transaction he makes a special gift to God of each individual member of his body to be used hereafter as God's instrument.

> Romans 6:13, "Neither yield ye your members as instruments of unrighteousness unto sin: but yield yourselves unto God, as those that are alive from the dead, and *your members as instruments of righteousness unto God.*"

But the spiritual man knows also that the redemption of the body is not yet completed and will not be until the Lord comes again when this body of humiliation will be exchanged for one glorified even as Christ's is glorified now (Romans 8:23, Philippians 3:20–21, R. V.). He knows further that the flesh is still entrenched within him even though he is not now in the sphere of the flesh and that he is still environed by a hostile, hateful world.

> Romans 8:10, "And if Christ be in you, *the body is dead because of sin;* but the Spirit is life because of righteousness."
>
> John 17:15, 18, R. V., "*I pray not that thou shouldest take them from the world,* but that thou shouldest keep them from the evil one.
>   As thou didst send me into the world, *even so sent I them into the world.*"

So he understands the need of constant vigilance over the body that it may be kept under the dominating control of the Holy Spirit lest he yield to any of the appetites, passions and lusts of the flesh or be conformed to the fashions and foibles of the world. The spiritual man is willing for any work of the Holy Spirit within him in the way of discipline that will keep the body under and enable him to possess it in honor and sanctification.

> 1 Corinthians 9:27, "*But I keep under my body, and bring it into subjection:* lest by any means, when I have preached to others, I myself should be a castaway."
>
> 1 Thessalonians 4:4, "That *every one of you shall know how to possess his vessel in sanctification and honour.*"

Thus we see that in grace the human personality was sacredly preserved as an entity as it was made in creation and remained in the Fall. All that was ruined was redeemed and restored, *plus.* For through the new nature imparted and the new life implanted that which in creation was earthly and human only, in re-creation became heavenly and divine. With this perfect adjustment to God, the life becomes righteous and holy; and then of necessity follows adjustment within and without. Through the spiritual man's perfect harmony with God, with himself and with others the Kingdom of God begins on earth and the will of God is done on earth as it is in heaven.

It Is a Life Lived on God's Appointed Plane

As God has never had but one plan for the life of man and that a spiritual one, so He has never had but one plane on which He means man to live and that the plane of the spiritual. Life lived on the highest plane is a life of deep, vital, growing spirituality. When God speaks of the man who is capable of examining and understanding the things of God and of the one whom He can trust to help weak and sinful believers He calls him "he that is spiritual."

> 1 Corinthians 2:15, "But *he that is spiritual* judgeth all things, yet he himself is judged of no man."

> Galatians 6:1, "Brethren, if a man be overtaken in a fault, *ye which are spiritual restore such an one* in the spirit of meekness; considering thyself, lest thou also be tempted."

There are three outstanding marks of the life lived on the highest plane, the first is—*it is an abounding life.* The spiritual man draws all his resources directly from God consequently he never need lack for anything. God's granaries are always full and the doors are opened earthward. In Christ, the believer's life, "dwelleth all the fulness of the Godhead bodily," and in Him the believer may be made as "full" as he wishes to be (Colossians 2:9-10). The spiritual man desires with a deepening intensity to "be filled with all the fulness of God" (Ephesians 3:19) consequently he draws bountifully from Christ.

> 2 Corinthians 8:7, "Therefore, *as ye abound in every thing,* in faith, and utterance, and knowledge, and in all diligence, and in your love to us, see that ye abound in this grace also."

> 2 Corinthians 9:11, *"Being enriched in every thing to all bountifulness,* which causeth through us thanksgiving to God."

1. The spiritual man abounds in grace.

> 2 Corinthians 9:8, "And God is able to make *all grace abound toward you;* that ye, always having all sufficiency in all things, may abound to every good work."

2. The spiritual man abounds in hope.

> Romans 15:13, "Now the God of hope fill you with all joy and peace in believing, *that ye may abound in hope,* through the power of the Holy Ghost."

3. The spiritual man abounds in joy.

> John 15:11, "These things have I spoken unto you, that my joy might remain in you, and *that your joy might be full."*

4. The spiritual man abounds in peace.

> Colossians 3:15, "And *let the peace of God rule in your hearts,* to the which also ye are called in one body; and be ye thankful."

5. The spiritual man abounds in thankfulness.

> Ephesians 5:20, *"Giving thanks always for all things unto God* and the Father in the name of our Lord Jesus Christ."

6. The spiritual man abounds in knowledge.

> 1 Corinthians 1:5, "That *in every thing ye are enriched by him,* in all utterance, and *in all knowledge."*

7. The spiritual man abounds in love.

> Philippians 1:9, "And this I pray, that *your love may abound yet more and more* in knowledge and in all judgment."

The more the spiritual man abounds in the riches of God's grace the more unsearchable and exhaustless he finds them to be so that there exists in his life a strange but joyous paradox—that of always being satisfied in Christ and yet always unsatisfied. The spiritual man never stops growing because he is always reaching upward to that still higher height that is just beyond. It was this passionate upreaching toward Christ in the heart of the apostle Paul that inspired those words to the Christians at Philippi.

> Philippians 3:12-14, "Not as though I had already attained, either were already perfect: but I follow after, *if that I may apprehend that for which also I am apprehended of Christ Jesus.*
>
> Brethren, I count not myself to have apprehended: but *this one thing I do,* forgetting those things which are behind, and *reaching forth unto those things which are before,*
>
> I *press toward the mark for the prize of the high calling of God in Christ Jesus."*

The second mark of life lived on the highest plane is—*it is an overcoming life.* Having taken his position by faith in the heavenlies in Christ the spiritual man lives in the atmosphere of triumph which prevails there. The spiritual man is on top of his difficulties; he is the conqueror not the conquered; the victor not the vanquished. His identification with Jesus Christ in the victory over sin and Satan is a reality to him and he looks upon

Satan as an already defeated foe and treats him accordingly and reckons upon his own death to sin, to self and to the world.

> Romans 8:37, "Nay, *in all these things we are more than conquerors* through him that loved us."

> 1 John 5:4, "For *whatsoever is born of God overcometh the world:* and this is the victory that overcometh the world, even our faith."

The spiritual man aspires to such an overcoming life on earth as will win for him a share in the reigning life of heaven.

> Revelation 3:21, *"To him that overcometh* will I grant to sit with me in my throne, even as I also overcame, and am set down with my Father in his throne."

The third mark of life lived on the highest plane is—*it is an overflowing life.* The spiritual man has enough and to spare. He does not have to hoard his spiritual riches for he is the child of a King and knows that his Father is a royal Giver and has taught His child "that it is more blessed to give than to receive." He is assured that the more he gives the more he will receive. Out of his innermost being flow the rivers of living water to bring life more abundant to every life he touches.

> John 7:38, R. V., "He that believeth on me, as the scripture hath said, *from within him shall flow rivers of living water."*

A life lived on the highest plane is a continuous miracle of God's grace.

22

Carnal or Spiritual

THAT GOD HAS MADE ample provision in Christ for each person to live his life on the highest plane is evident from our previous studies. But that every believer does not exercise this privilege needs no argument. We feel how far short of it we ourselves fall and we observe the low spiritual level upon which other lives are lived. A casual perusal of Paul's letters to the churches will reveal the fact that there is more than one kind of Christian. In the sixth through the eighth chapters of Romans this truth is clearly taught.

Romans 6 is the hub of life on the highest plane. Deep spirituality emanates from a spiritual apprehension, appropriation and assimilation of the truth of this chapter. In this divine revelation God gives us the spiritual seed from which the full-blown flower—a life in growing conformity to the image of Christ—springs. Here man is delivered from the sphere of darkness, death and bondage; here he leaves behind the old servitude to sin and becomes the servant of righteousness; here he comes out from under the yoke of the Law to live under the reign of grace; here he witnesses the crucifixion of the old man to make way for the control of the new nature; here God tells the believer that he not only need not sin but that he may be holy. Romans 6 tells us plainly that God has made full provision in Christ for lifting the sinner from the lowest depths of life on the plane of the natural to the highest heights of life on the plane of the spiritual.

Romans 7 and 8 each picture the life of a Christian but the difference in likeness to the pattern set in Romans 6 is so great as to lead one to think that there are surely two kinds of Christians.

Romans 7 pictures a life of storm, stress and struggle; a life of defeat and discouragement crowned with despair. Romans 7 is the divine photograph of an eager Alpine climber. He starts at the base (Romans 6) of the majestic snowcapped Jungfrau and aspires to scale its highest height (Romans 8). He has studied a guidebook about Alpine climbing and confident of his own strength and ability he presumes to ascend without a guide. After hours upon hours of toilsome climbing, ignorant of the way, floundering in masses of ice and snow, worn out with his effort to ascend the steep and dangerous path, he sinks down exhausted and filled with despair and in the darkness of the night that has overtaken him cries out for deliverance (Romans 7:24).

In Romans 7 we find the believer acknowledging that the Law of God is holy, just and good, and admitting that it should be obeyed. A part of him longs to keep it, even strives to do so in his own strength, while another part of him resists. How to conquer in this conflict he does not know. He knows that he need not sin and resolves that he will not but he goes on sinning. His will functions but he is baffled in knowing how to fulfill its decree to be holy and to do good. He wills and he works to reach the plane of the spiritual but is unsuccessful and inevitably must fail, for a man cannot sanctify himself any more than he can save himself.

Romans 8 pictures discernment after delusion; conquest after conflict, sunshine after storm. The despairing cry of the Alpine climber has been heard by an unseen Guide who has climbed all the way with him. Unwilling to intrude where not wanted, He has remained silent, but the moment He hears the cry for help He flashes light upon the midnight darkness of the traveler's path. He points out the way, He even lifts the weary traveler up and enables him to overcome every difficulty of the way and to reach the goal of his aspiration. The "I" used more than thirty times in Romans 7 is displaced by the "Holy Spirit" who in that chapter is not mentioned once. The mountain is the same, the path is no less difficult or dangerous. But the difference between Romans 7 and 8 is the difference of a *Guide* who knows the way and can enable the traveler to reach the top.

Romans 8 reveals as clearly as does Romans 7 that there is a conflict on within every believer which never ends as long as one dwells on earth, but it reveals *the way of victory*. It removes the delusion that the believer can fight the enemy in his own strength and gives spiritual discernment of God's gracious provision of *the means of victory*. Romans 8 lifts the believer above the clouds of discouragement into the clear sunlight of abiding peace and rest because it assures him at the beginning that "in Christ" there is no condemnation by God as regards his past, and at the end that "in Christ" there is no separation from God as regards his future, and all the verses in between proclaim the perfect provision made "in Christ" for victory over every enemy within and without as regards the present (Romans 8:2-34). The Father has given unto every believer the Spirit of His Son to guide him on life's pathway.

> Romans 8:1, "There is therefore now no condemnation to them which are in Christ Jesus, who walk not after the flesh, but after the Spirit."

Romans 8:35-39, "Who shall separate us from the love of Christ? shall tribulation, or distress, or persecution, or famine, or nakedness, or peril, or sword?

As it is written, For thy sake we are killed all the day long; we are accounted as sheep for the slaughter.

Nay, in all these things we are more than conquerors through him that loved us.

For I am persuaded, that neither death, nor life, nor angels, nor principalities, nor powers, nor things present, nor things to come, nor height, nor depth, nor any other creature, shall be able to separate us from the love of God, which is in Christ Jesus our Lord."

There are, then, two kinds of Christians clearly named and described in Scripture. It is of the utmost importance that every believer should know which kind of Christian he *is* and that, after knowing, he should determine which kind he wishes *to be*. Let us read these verses from Paul's letter to the Corinthian church, and note the names he gives to these two classes. One he addresses as carnal, the other as spiritual Christians.

1 Corinthians 3:1-4, "And I, brethren, could not speak unto you as unto *spiritual*, but as unto *carnal*, even as unto babes in Christ.

I have fed you with milk, and not with meat: for hitherto ye were not able to bear it, neither yet now are ye able.

For ye are yet *carnal*: for whereas there is among you envying, and strife, and divisions, are ye not *carnal*, and walk as men?

For while one saith, I am of Paul; and another, I am of Apollos; are ye not *carnal?*"

THE MARKS OF THE CARNAL CHRISTIAN

The up and down line in the first diagram is photographic. It is almost cruelly self-revealing. It visualizes the average church member. It is like a costly picture cheaply framed or an exquisite garment illy fitted. One look tells you that something is wrong and no matter how often you look it never seems right. We know instinctively that the true Christian life could never be symbolized by a wavering line. Christianity, which is Christ-possessing, controlling and using, must spell straightness and steadiness. It must be life on the spiritual plane. The life of the carnal Christian is not so.

IT IS A LIFE OF UNCEASING CONFLICT

Romans 7:22-23, "For I delight in the law of God after the inward man:

But I see *another law in my members, warring against the law of my mind,* and bringing me into captivity to the law of sin which is in my members."

> Galatians 5:17, "For *the flesh lusteth against the Spirit,* and *the Spirit against the flesh:* and these are contrary the one to the other: so that ye cannot do the things that ye would."

One law "warring against" another law in the same personality; part of a man "serving" one law and part of him serving another—this is indeed the language of conflict. Two forces absolutely contrary to each other are each working to gain and to keep control over the entire personality. Two natures, the divine and the fleshly, are engaged in deadly warfare. The spiritual is sometimes in the ascendancy and the believer enjoys a momentary joy, peace and rest. The divine nature imparted to him at his rebirth is in control and Christ in him is victorious. But the fleshly nature which is always defiant to the authority and rule of God rebels. Conflict ensues. The fleshly nature is again the master, and joy and peace are gone. Such is the miserable existence of the carnal Christian.

A friend told me a story of her six-year-old nephew which tellingly illustrates this manner of living. Her nephew was often tempted to run away and his mother was much distressed by it. One day she told him that if he ran away again she would have to punish him. Soon afterwards the temptation came through a neighbor boy and he yielded to it. Upon returning home his mother said, "James, didn't you remember that I said if you ran away again I would punish you?" "Yes," said James, "I remembered." "Then why did you do it?" asked his mother. Little James replied, "It was this way, Mother. As I stood there in the road thinking about it Jesus pulled on one leg and the devil pulled on the other and the devil pulled the harder!" The Lord Jesus pulling on one leg and Satan pulling on the other is the constant experience of the Christian, but yielding to the devil and giving to him the victory over Christ is the wretched condition of the carnal Christian.

IT IS A LIFE OF REPEATED DEFEAT

> Romans 7:15, R. V., "For that which I do I know not: *for not what I would, that do I practise; but what I hate, that I do.*"

> Romans 7:19, R. V., "For *the good which I would I do not:* but *the evil which I would not, that I practise.*"

As one reads Romans 7 he feels that the apostle Paul is writing someone's spiritual biography. It was no doubt his own. But could it not have been yours and mine as well? It is the revelation of a true desire and an honest attempt to live a right and a holy life but it is surcharged with the atmosphere of deadly defeat; a defeat so overpowering as to burst forth in that despairing cry for deliverance.

Romans 7:24, *"O wretched man that I am!* who shall deliver me from the body of this death?"

Who of us has not uttered it? We have made countless resolutions at the dawn of a new day or of a new year regarding the things we would or would not do. But long before the twilight hour our hearts have been heavy with a humiliating sense of failure. The things we steadfastly determined to do were left undone and the things we solemnly resolved not to do were repeatedly done. Sins both of commission and of omission, like evil spirits, haunt our bedchamber and rob us even of the balm of sleep. Temper, anger, fretting, worry, murmuring, pride, selfishness, malice, worldliness, unfaithfulness, evil speaking, bitterness, jealousy, envy, quarreling, hatred, in fact "the old man's" entire family of evil passions and desires may have worked havoc in one's own personal life, and spoiled the day not only for one's self, but for one's family and friends and, most of all, have grieved God.

The trouble was not with the will for it was very sincere in the decisions made at dawn and fully purposed to carry them out.

Romans 7:18, "For I know that in me (that is, in my flesh,) dwelleth no good thing: *for to will is present with me; but how to perform* that which is good I find not."

But in the carnal Christian Christ is compelled to share the control of the life with another and the result is both inner and outer maladjustment. Self-will, self-love, self-trust and self-exaltation always spell envying, quarreling, bitterness and division.

1 Corinthians 3:3, "For *ye are yet carnal:* for whereas *there is among you envying,* and *strife,* and *divisions, are ye not carnal,* and walk as men?"

The state of the carnal Christian is one of failure and defeat and it *never* can be anything else. If he wishes deliverance he may have it but it will be a deliverance out of Romans 7 into Romans 8.

IT IS A LIFE OF PROTRACTED INFANCY

The carnal Christian never grows up. He remains, stunted and dwarfed, a mere "babe in Christ."

1 Corinthians 3:1-2, "And I, brethren, could not speak unto you as unto spiritual, *but as unto carnal, even as unto babes in Christ.*
I have fed you with milk, and not with meat: for *hitherto* ye were not able to bear it, *neither yet now are ye able."*

The Corinthian Christians should have been full grown; they had been Christians long enough to have become spiritual adults but they were mere "babes in Christ." They should have been strong, healthy, meat-eating grown-ups; instead they were weak, milk-drinking infants. They did not measure up either in stature or strength to what they should have.

Nothing on earth could be sweeter or more perfect to loving parents than *a baby in babyhood* but oh! the indescribable heartache endured by the parents if that precious child remains a baby in body or in mind. Nothing on earth sets the joybells of heaven ringing as the birth of one into the family of God but oh! what pain it must cause the heavenly Father to see that spiritual babe remain in a state of protracted infancy!

Which are you today, dear reader, a spiritual babe or an adult? Are you still in infancy in spiritual things or are you full grown? To answer the question it may help to ask and answer another. What are the marks of a babe? A baby cannot serve himself but is helplessly dependent upon others. He may give enjoyment to others but he cannot help them. A baby absorbs attention, he expects to be the center of his little world. A baby lives in the realm of his feelings, being entirely governed by them. If all goes well, he is pleased and smiling but he is exceedingly touchy, and if his desire is crossed at any point he quickly lets it be known in lusty remonstrance. God's Word shows that the carnal Christian bears these selfsame marks.

> Hebrews 5:12-14, R. V., "For *when by reason of the time ye ought to be teachers, ye have need again that some one teach you* the rudiments of the first principles of the oracles of God; and *are become such as have need of milk*, and *not of solid food*.
>
> For every one that partaketh of milk is without experience of the word of righteousness; *for he is a babe.*
>
> But solid food is for fullgrown men, even those who by reason of use have their senses exercised to discern good and evil."

The Christians to whom this epistle to the Hebrews was written were evidently carnal Christians also. They ought to have been teaching others yet they themselves still needed to be taught even the elementary truths of spiritual experience. They, as well as the Corinthians, should have been able to eat meat but they were still content to feed on milk. They were able neither to help themselves nor others. They were incapacitated through their protracted infancy either to receive the deep things of God or to impart them to others.

Perhaps Paul puts his finger upon the reason for the stunted condition of the Corinthian Christians in the first two chapters of 1 Corinthians. He teaches us that the spiritual man knows the deep things of God through the discernment made possible by the Holy Spirit's illumination. The spiritual man is one who, delighting in God's Word, devours and digests it. By feeding upon it he grows in stature and strength.

But the Corinthian Christians were very evidently not of this type. They were following human leaders, esteeming lightly the wisdom of God and exalting highly the wisdom of men. They were substituting fodder for food and attempting to satisfy hunger on husks. Consequently they were still "babes in Christ"—weak, emaciated Christians.

Much the same condition prevails today in the churches of Christendom. The average professing Christian is not going firsthand to the Bible for food, expecting the Holy Spirit to give him the strong meat of the Word. He is looking to human teachers for his nourishment and gulps down whatever is given him. He is a spiritual parasite living on predigested food, consequently he is underfed and anemic. In this weakened state he is open to all forms of spiritual disease. He is an easy prey for temper, impurity, pride, bitterness and selfishness and because of his close relationship to other members of the Body of Christ, the result is often just such an epidemic of sin as existed in the Corinthian church.

IT IS A LIFE OF BARREN FRUITLESSNESS

Luke 13:6-7, "He spake also this parable; A certain man had a fig tree planted in his vineyard; and *he came and sought fruit thereon, and found none.*

Then said he unto the dresser of his vineyard, Behold, these three years *I came seeking fruit on this fig tree, and find none: cut it down; why cumbereth it the ground?*"

John 15:2, "*Every branch in me that beareth not fruit he taketh away:* and every branch that beareth fruit, he purgeth it, that it may bring forth more fruit."

The influence of the carnal Christian is always negative. The carnal Christian occupies a pew in church on the Lord's Day indicating some love in his heart for the Lord and devotion to Him but he is unable to bring with him any member of his family or associate in business or friend because of the inconsistency of his life before them during the week. He is a branch of the vine but a fruitless, hence a useless, branch.

IT IS A LIFE OF ADULTEROUS INFIDELITY

James 4:4, "*Ye adulterers and adulteresses,* know ye not that the friendship of the world is enmity with God? Whosoever therefore will be *a friend of the world is the enemy of God.*"

1 John 2:15-16, "*Love not the world, neither the things that are in the world.* If any man love the world, the love of the Father is not in him. *For all that is in the world,* the lust of the flesh, and the lust of the eyes, and the pride of life, *is not of the Father, but is of the world.*"

The language of James 4:4 is drastic and austere, there is an irrevocable finality about it. Men may hold two opinions about "the world" but not so with God. In James 4:4 He at least leaves no Christian any room whatever for argument regarding his attitude toward and relationship to "the world" but declares in words of transparent clearness that any Christian who maintains friendship with the world is guilty of adulterous infidelity in his relationship to Christ.

To realize the truth of God's pungent statement the reader need only remind himself of what the world is and of its attitude to Christ. "The world" is Satan's eyes, ears, hands and feet combined to fashion his most cunning weapon for defeating God by capturing the souls of men. "The world" is Satan's *lair* for the unsaved and his *lure* to the saved to keep them from God. "The world" is human life and human society *with God left out*.

What, then, should be the Christian's relationship to the world? The answer is found in the Christian's relationship to Christ. Christ and the Christian are one. They are joined together, as we have seen, in such an intimate union and identification of life that God, the Holy Spirit, does not hesitate to say that the love relationship they bear to each other is one analogous to that of marriage.

Is it any wonder, then, that God says that friendship with the world on the part of a Christian is tantamount to spiritual adultery and that He brands "the friend of the world" "an enemy of God"? Hobnobbing with the world in its pleasures, entering into partnership with it in its pursuits, fashioning one's life by its principles, working to carry out its program, all make one an accomplice of the evil one against one's own Beloved, against the Saviour, Lord and King of one's life. Such adulterous unfaithfulness in love marks one as a carnal Christian.

But perhaps some reader is still in the dark as to what is worldly. He is not clear as to what he may have, do or enjoy. The acid test of worldliness is given in 1 John 2:16. Under the Holy Spirit's illumination test your life by it and you will quickly discern the mark of the worldly.

Worldliness is "all that is not of the Father." Whatever would not be as appropriate and fitting to Christ's life in the heavenlies as to the Christian's life on earth is worldly. Whatever does not come out from God and cannot go back to Him with His blessing is worldliness. Such is the negative aspect of worldliness.

It has a positive aspect as well. Worldliness is "the lust of the flesh," "the lust of the eyes," and "the pride of life." Worldliness may be manifested in one's conversation, in one's style of hairdress, in the clothes one wears, in the company one keeps, in the pleasures one enjoys, in the books one reads, in the appetites one indulges, in the things one buys, in the ambitions by which one is ruled, and in the activities in which one engages.

Anything which feeds or pampers the flesh, the animal part of man, whether it results in gross sensuality, or in taking the bloom from heart purity, or merely in soft self-indulgence and self-ease, is worldliness. Anything that stains the heart, soils the hands, stings the conscience and separates one from the joy and sweetness of communion with Christ, is worldliness. It is "the lust of the flesh."

Anything that caters merely to the fashions of this world, that stimulates desire for possession and property, that aims merely to please men and gain their approval, that keeps the eyes fixed on the lowlands instead of on the heights, on the seen rather than on the unseen, anything that puts a cloud between Christ and the Christian and shuts Him out from one's vision is "the lust of the eyes."

Anything that exalts self, that fosters pomp and pride, that clips the wings of the soul so that it grovels in the dust of earth instead of soaring heavenward, that sets the affections upon the wealth, the fame, the honors of earth rather than upon the treasures of heaven, that robs the Christian of his possessions and privileges in Christ, is "the pride of life."

There can be no confluence between these streams. Their admixture in a human life produces the carnal Christian.

IT IS A LIFE OF DISHONORING HYPOCRISY

> Ephesians 5:8, "For ye were sometimes darkness, but *now are ye light in the Lord: walk as children of light."*
>
> 1 John 1:5-6, "God is light, and *in him is no darkness at all. If we say that we have fellowship with him, and walk in darkness,* we lie, and do not the truth."
>
> 1 Corinthians 3:3, "Are ye not carnal, and *walk as men?"*

The carnal man says one thing and does another; his walk does not correspond with his witness; he professes what he does not possess. The carnal man walks as those who make no profession of being Christians and presents them with such a caricature of Christ that he has no power to win them to his Saviour.

Does anything more need to be said to prove that the carnal Christian falls far short of God's best and is not well pleasing unto Him? But there is abundant hope for the believer who, wearied with the conflict, humiliated by the defeat, chagrined by the immaturity, distressed by the fruitlessness, convicted of the infidelity, and pained by the hypocrisy, turns to God and cries out for deliverance from the wretched captivity of carnality into the glorious liberty of spirituality.

THE MARKS OF A SPIRITUAL CHRISTIAN

IT IS A LIFE OF ABIDING PEACE

John 14:27, *"Peace I leave with you, my peace I give unto you:* not as the world giveth, give I unto you. Let not your heart be troubled, neither let it be afraid."

John 16:33, "These things have I spoken unto you, that *in me ye might have peace.* In the world ye shall have tribulation: but be of good cheer; I have overcome the world."

The peace of the spiritual Christian is that of Christ's presence. "My peace I give unto you." It does not mean that there is no conflict in the life of the spiritual Christian for it is through conquest in conflict that he grows, but it does mean the peace of conscious victory in Christ. The spiritual Christian does not continue in the practice of known, willful sin so he lives in the unclouded sunshine of the Father's presence and in the unshadowed light of the Father's countenance. His communion with the Father is unmarred by the gnawing consciousness of soiled hands, by the pricking of a wounded conscience, or by the condemnation of an accusing heart. There is abiding peace, deepening joy and satisfying rest.

IT IS A LIFE OF HABITUAL VICTORY

1 Corinthians 15:57, "But thanks be to *God,* which *giveth us the victory through our Lord Jesus Christ."*

Romans 8:37, "Nay, in all these things *we are more than conquerors through him* that loved us."

2 Corinthians 2:14, "Now thanks be unto *God, which always causeth us to triumph in Christ,* and maketh manifest the savour of his knowledge by us in every place."

The believer has changed masters and has entered into a new servitude which is perfect freedom. God tells him he has been made "free from sin"; that he is "more than conqueror" through Christ; that "the victory" of the cross was all-inclusive; and that "in Christ" he may walk through life's battlefield "in triumph." The spiritual Christian takes God's word at face value, he dares to believe it and to act accordingly.

The believer's identification with Christ did not secure for him "victories" only but "victory." His victory over sin is all-inclusive, the greater has wrapped within it the lesser. He who has given victory over one sin can give victory over all sin; He who has kept from sin for a moment, can with equal ease keep for an hour or a day. Victory over sin is a gift through Christ.

Victory need not be intermittent but may be habitual. God can cause us *always* in all places, under all circumstances, at all times, in all things, "to triumph in Christ" for "He is able *to save to the uttermost* them that come unto God through him, seeing he ever liveth to make intercession for them."

Perhaps some reader will say, I have experienced occasionally this glorious freedom from some besetting sin but it has been only a transient liberty. Is there really such a thing here on earth as habitual victory over all known sin?

Let us think of the difference between such a transient liberty and a permanent freedom. It was made very clear to me once through an experience in speaking on two Sundays to the women in Cook County Jail in Chicago. At the first meeting one hard-faced, rough-looking woman made considerable trouble, nearly breaking up the meeting. She came at the close imploring me to secure her release from jail, making all sorts of lavish promises of good behavior, even to becoming a Christian if I would do her this favor. Twenty-six times she had been behind those bars for the some offense, she said. This confession told me why she was in jail. Liberty she had had twenty-five times: freedom she had never known. She had no desire to break with sin but only to break from jail.

The following Lord's Day I spoke on the difference between liberty and freedom. Knowing that the woman's attention must be held for the sake of others as well as for herself I had taken some thread and scissors to illustrate the message. During the talk I asked her for the loan of her fingers. I wound the thread lightly around them and then asked her to free herself. With her strong, brawny hands it was an easy matter just to loosen the thread and she did it exultingly. Then I wound it around again and again some fifty times until her fingers were truly "bond servants" to that thread, praying that God would drive home the truth of her terrible bondage to sin. All the time her face grew longer and more perplexed. Finally I stopped and asked her again to loosen her fingers and free herself. With real seriousness she looked into my face and said bluntly, "You know I can't!" I said, "Yes, I know you can't and are you not glad that I have brought these scissors along which can cut this thread and set your fingers free?" Then I told her of the Saviour who came from heaven to die on Calvary's cross that through the outpouring of His precious blood she might be cut loose from sin and set free forever and ever. "If the Son shall make you free, ye shall be free indeed" (John 8:36).

To make that perfect victory permanent He has sent the Holy Spirit to indwell and control. The carnal man is under the power of the law of sin. It operates in his life, bringing him much of the time under its dominion. But there is another and a higher law at work in the believer and as he yields himself to its mighty power the spiritual man is delivered from the law of sin and death. Herein lies his habitual victory over all known sin.

Romans 8:2, "For *the law of the Spirit of life in Christ Jesus hath made me free* from the law of sin and death."

2 Corinthians 3:18, R. V., "But we all, with unveiled face beholding as in a mirror the glory of the Lord, *are transformed into the same image from glory to glory,* even as from the Lord the Spirit."

There is nothing static in true spiritual experience. The upward look and the unveiled face must catch something of the glory of the Lord and reflect it. With a growing knowledge of Him and a deepening communion with Him, there must inevitably be a growing likeness to Him. It is a transformation into His image *from* glory *to* glory. The spiritual nature is ever reaching out after and laying hold of that which is spiritual in order that it may become more spiritual. "As the bursting acorns lay hungry hold only on what will produce oaks" so the spiritual man lays hungry hold only on what will produce likeness to Christ Jesus.

John 15:2, 5, "Every branch in me that beareth *not fruit* he taketh away: and every branch that beareth *fruit,* he purgeth it, that it may bring forth *more fruit.*

I am the vine, ye are the branches: He that abideth in me, and I in him, the same bringeth forth *much fruit:* for without me ye can do nothing."

Surely there is progression in Christlikeness—"*not* fruit," "*fruit,*" "*more* fruit," "*much* fruit." Do these phrases not unveil before us the possibilities and potentialities for Christlikeness open to every branch in the vine? Do they not also show us the positive progression "*from* glory *to* glory" God expects to see in us? These expressions are descriptive. Which one describes you? There is but one branch that fully satisfies the heart of the divine Husbandman.

John 15:8, "*Herein is my Father glorified, that ye bear much fruit;* so shall ye be my disciples."

God makes very clear what is the fruit which He expects to find on the branch.

Galatians 5:22-23, R. V., "But the *fruit of the Spirit* is love, joy, peace, long-suffering, kindness, goodness, faithfulness, meekness, self-control; against such there is no law."

The "fruit of the Spirit" is the full-orbed, symmetrical character of the Lord Jesus Christ in which there is no lack and no excess. The apostle Paul did not speak of "*the fruits* of the Spirit" as he is so often misquoted. It is just one cluster, and all nine graces are essential to reveal the beauty and glory of true Christlikeness. But how often we see a great heart of love spoiled by a very quick temper—there is "love" but not "self-control." Or we see long-suffering marred by boastfulness—the person being so afraid the long-suffering will not be noted and appreciated that there is a repeated reminder of it. There is "long-suffering" but not "meekness." Occasionally one sees a Christian long on faith but very short on gentleness. He has in his makeup the thunder of Mount Sinai more than the love of Calvary. He believes the doctrine and defends it with better success than he adorns it. He has "faith" but not "kindness." Or often we see one whose life is the embodiment of goodness but the goodness is overshadowed by anxiety, worry, and fretting. The presence of "goodness" is limited in its beneficent working by the absence of "peace." Oh! how the lack or the excess of one of these graces mars the beauty, the completeness, the symmetry of the cluster! In the spiritual Christian all nine of these graces blend in such beautiful and winsome attractiveness and harmony that the world sees Christ living within.

I was traveling upon the Yangtsze River in central China. A heavy rainstorm had just cleared away and the sun had come out brightly from behind the banked-up clouds. I felt an inward impelling to go out upon the deck and the Lord had a precious message awaiting me. The water of the Yangtsze River is very muddy. But as I stepped to the railing and looked over I did not see the dirty, yellow water that day but instead the heavenly blue and fleecy white of the heavens above and all so perfectly reflected that I actually could not believe that I was looking down instead of up. Instantly the Holy Spirit flashed 2 Corinthians 3:18 into my mind and said, "In yourself you are as unattractive as the water of the Yangtsze River but when your whole being is turned Godward and your life lies all open to Him so that His glory shines upon it and into it then you will be so transformed into His image that others looking at you will see not you but Christ in you." Oh! friends, are you and I "reflecting as in a mirror the glory of the Lord"?

IT IS A LIFE OF SUPERNATURAL POWER

> John 14:12, "Verily, verily, I say unto you, He that believeth on me, *the works that I do shall he do also; and greater works than these shall he do;* because I go unto my Father."

These words were spoken by Jesus Christ to a little group of unlettered men. One of them was a sunburned, weather-beaten, rough old fisherman. He would be ill at ease in a modern college crowd and very probably would fail to pass entrance examinations into a present-day theological seminary. But he belonged to the company of believers to whom this promise was given and one day it was marvelously fulfilled in his life when through one sermon he won six times as many souls to true discipleship as Jesus did in the three years of His public ministry.

In what did Peter's power consist and does it avail for you and me? Was it the power of personal charm? of gracious manner? of giant intellect? of eloquent speech? of massive scholarship? of dominant will? While there were many lovable qualities in the impulsive, eager, loving old fisherman yet none of them could begin to account for such an overwhelming fulfillment of our Lord's promise in him. God clearly reveals the secret of Peter's power.

> Acts 1:8, "But *ye shall receive power after that the Holy Ghost is come upon you:* and ye shall be witnesses unto me both in Jerusalem, and in all Judea, and in Samaria, and unto the uttermost part of the earth."

The power to do "the same works and even greater" is not the power which resides in anything human. On the contrary it is the power of God the Holy Spirit which is fully at our disposal when we are fully yielded to Him. Is His supernatural power manifested in your life and works today?

IT IS A LIFE OF DEVOTED SEPARATENESS

> 1 Thessalonians 4:3, "*For this is the will of God, even your sanctification.*"

> Hebrews 7:26, "For such an high priest became us, *who is holy, harmless, undefiled, separate from sinners,* and made higher than the heavens."

> John 14:17, "Even the Spirit of truth; *whom the world cannot receive, because it seeth him not, neither knoweth him:* but ye know him; for he dwelleth with you, and shall be in you."

The spiritual man apprehends the will of the Father, the walk of the Son, and the work of the Spirit, in relation to his sanctification. The Father willed that he should be set apart and separated wholly unto Himself and the spiritual man acquiesces in the Father's purpose and wills to separate himself from everything that he knows would keep him from becoming a vessel fit for the Master's use.

The spiritual man takes Christ as his Example and determines to walk as He walked. Christ lived a life that was "holy, undefiled, separate from sinners." He was in the world but not of it. He had the closest contact with the world but without conformity to it or contagion from it. He lived in a world evil, corrupt, polluted, yet He remained unspotted, unstained and unsullied. The spiritual man aspires to a similar separateness of walk in this evil world.

The spiritual man lives habitually under the dominating control of the Holy Spirit who indwells him. The Holy Spirit and the world have nothing in common. The world cannot see or know the Holy Spirit for He is unseen and invisible and the world comprehends only the seen and the tangible. The Holy Spirit working within the believer enables the risen Lord to continue from the throne the work of sanctification begun in the believer at the cross. The spiritual man yields unconditionally to the Spirit's power as He works out God's full purpose in him.

God, the Father, works through His Son, by the Holy Spirit, to carry out His will of complete sanctification.

> 1 Peter 1:2, "Elect according to the foreknowledge of God the Father, through sanctification of the Spirit, unto obedience and sprinkling of the blood of Jesus Christ."
>
> 1 Thessalonians 5:23, "And *the very God of peace sanctify you wholly; and I pray God your whole spirit and soul and body be preserved blameless* unto the coming of our Lord Jesus Christ."

The Holy Trinity are at work within the believer to separate him wholly unto the Lord and to set him apart as a vessel fit for the Master's use. God is ever working to bring the believer into full conformity to the image of His Son.

When there is complete separateness the Christian will bear the same relationship to the world as Christ bore to it and the world will bear the same relationship to him as it bore to Christ. The Christian will regard the pleasures, the pursuits, the principles and the plans of the world exactly as Jesus Christ did. He is not of the world, therefore the world hated, persecuted and crucified Him. Such an experience the spiritual Christian will likewise have.

> John 17:16, "*They are not of the world,* even as I am not of the world."
>
> John 15:19-20, "If ye were of the world, the world would love his own: but *because ye are not of the world, but I have chosen you out of the world,* therefore *the world hateth you.*
>
> Remember the word that I said unto you, The servant is not greater than his lord. If they have persecuted me, *they will also persecute you;* if they have kept my saying, they will keep yours also."

There can be no successful attempt at a compromising admixture of the world and the heavenlies, of the flesh and the Spirit in the life of the one who truly aspires to life on the highest plane. God has separated these two unmixables by the cross of Christ. Any believer who submits to the perfect work of that cross both *for* and *in* him must choose to leave the world and the flesh behind and be wholly separated unto the pleasures and pursuits of life in Christ in the heavenlies.

God calls the believer to a life of spiritual "isolation" and "insulation" in order that he may be conformed to the image of His Son and filled by His

Spirit. The spiritual Christian responds to the call and obeys God's command to come out and live a life of devoted separateness.

> 2 Corinthians 6:14-18, *"Be ye not unequally yoked together with unbelievers:* for what fellowship hath righteousness with unrighteousness? and what communion hath light with darkness?
>
> And what concord hath Christ with Belial? or what part hath he that believeth with an infidel?
>
> And what agreement hath the temple of God with idols? for ye are the temple of the living God; as God hath said, I will dwell in them, and walk in them; and I will be their God, and they shall be my people.
>
> *Wherefore come out from among them, and be ye separate,* saith the Lord, and *touch not the unclean thing;* and I will receive you,
>
> And will be a Father unto you, and ye shall be my sons and daughters, saith the Lord Almighty."

But it is not merely the apprehension of and acquiescence in the will of God that loosen the grip of the world and the flesh upon the believer. It is the deeper appreciation of the gracious love of the Father and the sacrificial love of the Son that woos and wins him into a life of devoted separateness. We consent to be truly separated when once we spiritually discern how for our sakes He sanctified Himself that we might be sanctified. It is the one, who beholding the Lamb of God taking away the sin of the world, says, "He loved *me* and gave Himself for *me*" who gladly consents to be crucified unto the world and to have the world crucified unto him.

May the writer bear testimony that it was so in her experience. Life in the flesh and in the world kept her for some years after her conversion and entrance into church fellowship from victory and peace in her inner life and from power in service. Hour upon hour had been spent in argument with a dear friend and a separated Christian upon the harmlessness and rightfulness of her worldly walk. But one day face to face with God the decision of the will was made and the front door of her life was opened and the King of kings and Lord of lords was invited to enter and to take real control. Thereupon the vagabonds and hirelings that had robbed her of her possessions and privileges in Christ sneaked out the back door and desire for and delight in their companionship were gone forever. It was with her in deed and truth "the expulsive power of a new affection" that kept her so occupied with her adorable Lord and so happy in His service that there was no sense of loss but rather of incalculable gain.

IT IS A LIFE OF WINSOME HOLINESS

> Exodus 15:11, "Who is like unto thee, O LORD, among the gods? who is like thee, *glorious in holiness,* fearful in praises, doing wonders?"

1 Peter 1:15-16, R. V., "But *like as he who called you is holy, be ye your-selves also holy in all manner of living;*
    Because it is written, *Ye shall be holy; for I am holy.*"

God's holiness is His crown of glory. It is His holiness that measures the awful distance between Himself and the sinner. Yet He calls His own to be holy *because* He is holy and there is no other way by which he may come to have fellowship with Him for "without [holiness] . . . no man shall see the Lord" (Hebrews 12:14).

Every Christian is called by his new position in Christ to a life of holi-ness. But there are many Christians who frankly do not want to be holy. There are others however who truly desire to be spiritual but are neverthe-less afraid to be "holy." This may be due to their misunderstanding of what holiness is, either through their own neglect of the study of God's Word or through the false teaching on this subject which makes them shy of it through fear.

If one aspires to life on the highest plane he must be holy according to scriptural holiness. What, then, is it? First, may we say what it is not. Holiness is not sinless perfection, it does not place one beyond the pos-sibility of sinning nor remove from him the presence of sin. Scriptural holiness is not "faultlessness." That is a condition he will reach only upon the return of the Lord Jesus who takes him beyond all contact with a world of sin. Scriptural holiness is not "faultlessness" but it is "blamelessness" in the sight of God. We are to be "preserved blameless" *unto* His coming and we shall be "presented faultless" *at* His coming.

1 Thessalonians 5:23, "And the very God of peace sanctify you wholly; and I pray God your whole spirit and soul and body be *preserved blameless unto the coming* of our Lord Jesus Christ."

Jude 24, "Now unto him that is able to keep you from falling, and *to pre-sent you faultless before the presence of his glory* with exceeding joy."

This truth was unfolded to me with fresh meaning four years ago when I was called upon to dispose of the personal belongings of a dearly loved sister whom God had called home. Among the things she especially treas-ured was found a letter written to her when I was seven years of age. She had gone on a visit; I loved her and missed her and that letter was the love of my heart expressed in words. The letter was by no means "faultless" for the penmanship was poor, the grammar was incorrect and the spelling was imperfect, but it was "blameless" in the sight of my sister for it came out of a heart of love and was the best letter I could write. For me, a grown woman, to write the same letter today would not be "blameless" for my experience in penmanship and my knowledge of grammar and of spelling are far greater.

Holiness is a heart of pure love for God expressed in character, conversation and conduct. Holiness is Christ, our sanctification, enthroned as Life of our life. It is Christ in us, living, speaking, walking. The character of even the greatest saint will have in it some lack, his conversation will often fail in magnifying his Lord and his conduct in some respect will fall short of his calling in Christ Jesus. He will not be sinless but his heart will be pure love for God and he will give Christ the place of supreme pre-eminence in his mind, heart, strength and soul. There will be nothing static in his holiness, but daily by the Holy Spirit's faithful sanctifying work in his inmost life Christ Jesus will be formed more perfectly within him. The result will be a "transformation into His image from glory to glory."

> 1 Thessalonians 3:13, "To the end he may stablish *your hearts unblameable in holiness* before God, even our Father, at the coming of our Lord Jesus Christ with all his saints."

Such holiness is winsome for it spells the holy calm of God mirrored in the face, the holy quietness of God manifested in the voice, the holy graciousness of God expressed in the manner, and the holy fragrance of God emanating from the whole life. It is God so inhabiting His holy temple, which temple you are, that He reveals Himself through human personality.

A sermon I heard when a student at the Moody Bible Institute thirty years ago brought me the meaning of true holiness. The sermon was not a long one, neither was it preached by a famous preacher. It was a sermon of just six words preached to an audience of one by Amelia, the maid who waited upon the door. Amelia's sermon was occasioned by the call upon me of a very poor woman needing help on a very hot day when I was packing a very big trunk in a very small room. Several times I had gladly gone to this woman's home to help her but on this particular day I did not want to see her. Of course, I did not want Amelia to know that, so smiling sweetly I said, "I will be down soon." Amelia turned and went a few steps, then came back and with a pained expression in her face said, "Why, Miss Paxson, you *looked* cross!" Amelia taught me that day that holiness is an inward possession and not an outward profession and a possession that implies a Presence—that penetrates to the inmost spirit, that permeates the whole being and that purifies it in every part.

The life of the spiritual Christian which has been unfolded is that which every true believer desires but which very few expect to live on earth. To many such a life seems to be the prerogative of only a few rare souls chosen by God for especially high and holy tasks and to be utterly impossible for others. On that contrary, it is not the prerogative of a few but the privilege of all. To some it is a life which they have admired in others but have feared for themselves because of the demand it made for complete surrender. To others there has been utter ignorance either of the possibility of such a life or how to live it. But I believe there are a very large number of Christians today who are not satisfied with the lives they are living and who desire to know what are the cause and the cure of carnality. Diagnosis precedes cure. We have attempted in this chapter to make a diagnosis. Let us now seek to find a cure.

23

The Christian's Choice—Self or Christ?

THERE ARE TWO KINDS of Christians, easily identified and clearly distinguished from each other. How can there be such a paradox? is the question that must present itself to every thoughtful mind. The fountainhead of the Christian life is the same for all. Then how can there be two streams from it which flow so widely apart? When every Christian, as we have seen, has been brought through God's grace into the same position and put under the same control how does one become carnal and another spiritual? How can two persons, each of whom is born again, live such differing lives? An answer to this question is essential if one is to choose intelligently to be a spiritual Christian and to carry out that choice steadfastly.

THE COEXISTENCE OF TWO NATURES IN EVERY BELIEVER

Every Christian is conscious of inward conflict, of a duality within himself which he experiences but perhaps does not understand. Part of him aspires to be well pleasing unto God, another part of him wants to satisfy every demand of self. Part of him longs for the peace and rest of the promised land, another part of him lusts for the leeks, onions and garlic of Egypt; part of him grasps Christ and part of him grips the world. He has to admit that there seems to be a law of gravitation which tends ever to pull him sinward while at the same time a counteracting law lifts him Christward.

The scriptural explanation of this duality in Christian experience is found in the coexistence of two natures within the believer: the old, sinful Adamic nature and the new, spiritual Christ nature. Let us turn to the first epistle of John for its clear unfolding of this very important truth. The apostle John is a mature Christian and he is writing to those who are at least capable of receiving very deep spiritual truth. In the simplest of language he teaches the coexistence of the two natures in every believer.

> 1 John 1:8, "*If we say that we have no sin, we deceive ourselves, and the truth is not in us.*"

If any Christian, no matter how full grown he is or how many special experiences he has had, says that he is entirely freed from the old sinful nature, he deceives himself. But such a person does not deceive his family, or his neighbors, or his fellow Christians, nor does he deceive God. In the next verse God makes provision for the very sins which will come out of the root of sin still existing in this self-deceived Christian (1 John 1:9). These "sins" which are forgiven and the "unrighteousness" which is cleansed, are the sins and the unrighteousness of saints.

But the apostle John goes further. "If we say we have *no sin*" the inevitableness of logic compels us to say that we do *not sin* for if the root of sin is eradicated, then from what source could sins come? Every stream no matter how tiny must have a source. A few days ago looking out upon the Alps in a heavy rainstorm I saw ten streams of water flowing down the mountainside. In today's sunshine I look out again and not one of those streams can be seen. If there is "no sin," then the believer "*cannot sin.*" The old apostle uses very drastic language here—it may be that he knew he was writing to some who in the very earnestness and intensity of desire were in danger of believing this unscriptural doctrine.

1 John 1:10, "If we say that we have not sinned, *we make him* [God] *a liar, and his word is not in us.*"

The gross, vulgar, more open sins may have gone from us but what of the hidden sins of the heart; the pride even in our spiritual attainment, the attitude of self-righteousness toward others who are still on a lower plane, the harshness of judgment of those who do not believe as we do, the secret irritability, sometimes even toward those we love best, the unloving thought toward relative, friend or servant, the intolerance toward the weak or willful, or the countless sins of omission that must be charged against the Christian by the One who said, "To him that knoweth to do good and doeth it not, to him it is sin." Sin is not merely an act; it is also an attitude and an absence. It is not alone what we do but what we do not do. It is what we are and what we are not in the innermost part of our being as God sees us. Who that has a scriptural apprehension of sin as it is in man and of holiness as it is in God could ever say he is without sin?

There is in every believer that old nature which can do nothing but sin. John traces this sinful nature back to its original source in Satan. Inherent within the old nature is a threefold inability: it cannot know God, it cannot obey God, it cannot please God. By physical birth every person becomes the possessor of this God-ignorant, God-defying and God-displeasing nature and it remains in him as long as he lives on earth.

But there is in every believer that new nature which cannot sin. The old apostle leads us along the trail to its source in God. Inherent within the new nature is a threefold capacity: it can and does know God, obey God and please God. By spiritual birth every person becomes the possessor of this God-knowing, God-obeying, God-pleasing nature.

> 1 John 3:6-9, "Whosoever abideth in him sinneth not: whosoever sinneth hath not seen him, neither known him. Little children, let no man deceive you: he that doeth righteousness is righteous, even as he is righteous.
>
> *He that committeth sin is of the devil;* for the devil sinneth from the beginning. For this purpose the Son of God was manifested, that he might destroy the works of the devil.
>
> *Whosoever is born of God doth not commit sin;* for his seed remaineth in him: and *he cannot sin, because he is born of God."*

These two natures coinhabit every believer. This truth is repeatedly brought out in 1 John. John wrote to those believers as though he did not expect them to sin because they had within them this God-inspired, God-begotten nature.

> 1 John 2:1, "My little children, these things write I unto you, *that ye sin not."*

Yet he made full provision for their sinning because they had within them this Satan-inspired, devil-begotten nature.

> 1 John 2:1, "And *if any man sin,* we have an advocate with the Father, Jesus Christ the righteous."

God makes no attempt to change or to improve the old nature because it is unchangeable and unimproveable. Cultivation through education and travel do not change it one iota but simply clothe it in a more refined and respectable costume. God makes no attempt to subject it for it is incorrigible and irreconcilable. Government and laws may keep it partially suppressed but it is planning and secretly executing a world revolution against God and His government, and stands ready to break out in vehement action at every favorable opportunity. God makes no attempt to eradicate it, because He has a far more wonderful way of conquest over this sinful nature which we shall soon consider.

THE CONFLICT OF THESE TWO NATURES IN EVERY BELIEVER

To admit the coexistence of these two diametrically opposed and mutually exclusive natures is to admit the necessity of fiercest conflict. It is indeed the agelong conflict between Satan and Christ with the believer's inner life as the battlefield. It is self contesting Christ's right to His purchased possession.

This conflict is personalized in the spiritual experience of the apostle

Paul. He has been reborn, he was justified and sanctified in Christ Jesus. The Lord Jesus had come in to possess His possession and to take control. But there was one who contested His right. A conflict ensued between the old Saul and the new Paul. Two antagonists were fighting a deadly battle for a coveted prize. Romans 7 pictures a Christian torn to pieces by this awful conflict and baffled and discouraged beyond words by it all. He wonders if there is any possible way into victory and rest.

It is this conflict which staggers many a young Christian, and often causes a total eclipse of faith or a gradual backsliding into the world. He took the first step into the Christian life because his conscience was awakened to the evil of his doings. His chief concern was for his *sins*. He had been convicted of the sinfulness of acts and habits, and felt a sense of guilt because of them. He came to Christ and accepted Him as Saviour that he might be rid of certain *sins*. In the realization of forgiveness and the assurance of pardon he experiences great joy and gladly witnesses for Christ.

But he soon finds himself doing the old things again; the evil habits persist; the sinful disposition manifests itself in hydra-headed fashion; wicked practices return; worse than all, the joy in fellowship with Christ lessens; the heart grows cold; the spirit is dulled; he grows utterly discouraged. But his love for God has not been altogether quenched and flames up into intense desire under the inspiration of some message from God's Word or by the glimpse into a life which reflects peace and joy. Something in him cries out for God while another something contests every inch of God's claim upon the life. He is wholly nonplussed by this duality within himself.

Something within him will not let him release his hold upon God. Consequently he strives against these sins, agonizes over them, prays for release, makes every effort possible within his own power to get victory. But in spite of all he does his life is a kingdom divided against itself. Then something tells him it is no use trying to live a victorious life and he may as well give up. Over and over again he asks himself the question, Is it all worthwhile? He tries even to persuade himself that the man who makes no profession of Christ is much happier than he. But one day when on the very verge of absolute despair he cries out of deep heart desire for deliverance, "O wretched man that I am! who shall deliver me from the body of this death?"

What seems like his utter downfall is really his hour of deliverance for it is the time of abject self-despair to which he had to come before God could step in and open before him the way of deliverance.

Dear friend, are you living in Romans 7 today? Are you worn out with the conflict? Do you wish to know the way out? Then just close this book for a moment and tell Him so; then open it and ask Him to show you the way out into conquest and victory.

The Conquest of the Old Nature

God gives to us very clear and definite instruction regarding our part in the dethronement of this usurper self and the enthronement of Christ as sole Possessor and only Ruler over His inheritance in us.

We must condemn the flesh

God condemns the flesh as altogether sinful (Romans 8:3); He sees in it "no good thing" (Romans 7:18) and no Christian will ever have conquest over it until he accepts God's estimate of it and acts accordingly. This may seem like an easy thing to do but on the contrary it is exceedingly difficult. God's standard is very exacting. He says there is "no good thing" in the flesh. God says that "the flesh" both at its center and circumference is sinful; He condemns both its innermost desires and its outermost deeds (Ephesians 2:3, Colossians 3:9), and declares that it is unworthy of any confidence on our part. The first step which the apostle Paul took to the life on the highest plane was this—to condemn as unsafe, unclean and untrustworthy, the flesh which formerly he had so highly regarded.

> Philippians 3:3-4, "For we are the circumcision, which worship God in the spirit, and rejoice in Christ Jesus, *and have no confidence in the flesh.*
> Though I might also have confidence in the flesh. *If any other man thinketh that he hath whereof he might trust in the flesh, I more.*"

But we do have a great deal of confidence in the flesh. We divide it into the good and the bad. Certain things in the flesh we are compelled to distrust because they have got us into trouble. Certain other things we have gone so far as to acknowledge as weaknesses, faults, possible danger points. But there is another good-sized portion of the flesh that we rate rather high and in which we trust without reserve. It may be our refined and cultured tastes; the opinions and judgments which are the product of our educated minds; our generous, noble, philanthropic feelings; our high standard of morality; or, like Paul, our ancestral heritage. So that when we make a cross section of *our* "flesh," taking good and bad together, it seems in our sight to measure up fairly well; at least we can see no reason for such a wholesale condemnation of it as God makes.

But let us put this best product of the flesh to the test. Let us take it from a home in which love reigned and sweet companionship was its daily portion, where books lined the library shelves, beautiful pictures adorned the walls, snow white linen covered the table, and from a community life which offered everything needful to satisfy the intellectual, social, aesthetic and spiritual desires and needs. Transplant this life to an interior village on the mission field to live within a house with several people of varying temperaments and tastes, with limited household appointments, with untaught, untrained servants, with nothing without upon which to rest the eye but mud walls and dirty narrow streets, surrounded by jarring voices and unpleasant odors, and a furlough seven years off—would this best product of the flesh stand the test and come off more than conqueror? More than one missionary has left the mission field even before furlough was due and for no other reason than that "the flesh" broke down under the test.

Or let us put it to a different kind of a test. Perhaps "the flesh" boasts of that godlike quality of character called love. So choose the deepest, purest human love we can find and place it alongside of the love of 1 Corinthians 13. Is it a love that in nothing or at no time seeketh its own, that is absolutely free from the slightest taint of jealousy? Does it suffer long and is it always kind or is there sometimes not a feeling of secret irritability toward the one most deeply loved? Has it unfailingly been so charitable that it has never taken account of evil? Would it not have to blush with shame at its jealousy, envy, snobbishness, intolerance, selfishness, impatience and irritability? Has our "flesh" never broken down under this divine test?

May we make one more analytical test of "the flesh." This time let it be a chemical analysis in God's laboratory. Here is a man who boasts of his generosity and is considered one of the best givers in the city. He lavishes expensive gifts upon his family and gives costly dinners to his friends and subscribes largely to campaigns when the newspapers print the list of donors. But he grinds the most possible labor out of his employees for the least possible pay, he quarrels with his tailor over his bill, and he robs God of even the tithe which is His by right. Here is a woman who rides triumphantly upon the social wave as one of the most gracious and charming women in the community. But she nags her husband, is impatient with her children and scolds her servants. "The flesh" always has its blind side.

But I can almost hear someone rise up in defense of "the flesh" and say, But is it not natural to resent wrong? to dislike some people? to crave certain things? to stand up for your own rights? Yes, it is *natural* and that is just why it is sinful. That is just what "the flesh" is, it is our natural life; including all we call highest and best as well as all we deem worst and weakest. What God asks us to do is to take the cross section of "the flesh" we have made and condemn it all, to believe in its utter impotence to do good and in its mighty power to do evil.

WE MUST CONSENT TO THE CRUCIFIXION OF THE OLD MAN

Having condemned "the old man" as a hideous, hateful, heinous thing we are prepared for the next step God asks us to take. He has declared "the old man" worthy of crucifixion, in fact, He has already accomplished his crucifixion with Christ. Now God asks the believer to give his hearty consent to this transaction and to consider it an accomplished fact in his experience. Again this would seem like an extremely easy thing to do. In theory it is, in practice it is not, for "the old man" will fight like a tiger for his life.

"Self will make any concession if allowed to live. Self will permit the believer to do anything, give anything, sacrifice anything, go anywhere, take any liberties, bear any crosses, afflict soul or body to any degree—anything, if it can only live. It will consent to live in a hovel, in a garret, in the slums, in faraway heathendom, if only its life can be spared. It will endure any garb, any fare, any menial service rather than die."

But God says nothing short of the crucifixion of self will do. This was the second step which the apostle Paul took to life on the highest plane—he gave his whole-souled consent to his cocrucifixion with Christ Jesus and considered it something now past.

> Galatians 2:20, R. V., "*I have been crucified with Christ; and it is no longer I that live,* but Christ liveth in me: and that life which I now live in the flesh I live in faith, the faith which is in the Son of God, who loved me, and gave himself up for me."

"The Cross only severs what you consent to part from. The severing of the Cross is not an actual experience, unless the will of the believer desires and consents to the actual separation in fact and practice."

Have you consented to your crucifixion with Christ? There can be no reservations, no holding back part of the price. The whole "I" must be counted dead. God asks you to put your signature to this statement, "I have been crucified with Christ." If you have never done so, will you do it today?

WE MUST COOPERATE WITH THE HOLY SPIRIT IN KEEPING THE
OLD MAN CRUCIFIED

What Christ has made possible for us the Holy Spirit makes real within us, but only with our intelligent cooperation. God states very clearly in His Word what our part is and it is the duty of every believer to know and to do his part.

1. Reckon yourself dead unto sin.

> Romans 6:11, "Likewise *reckon ye yourselves to be dead indeed unto sin,* but alive unto God through Jesus Christ our Lord."

Through the crucifixion of "the old man" with Christ, the believer has been made dead unto sin, he has been completely freed from sin's power, he has been taken beyond sin's grip, every claim of sin upon him has been nullified. This is the flawless provision of God's grace but this accomplished fact can only become an actual reality in the believer's experience as faith lays hold upon it and enables him moment by moment, day by day, though temptation assail him, "to reckon" it true. As he *reckons* the Holy Spirit makes *real;* as he continues to reckon, the Holy Spirit continues to make real. Sin need have no more power over the believer than he grants it through unbelief. If he is alive unto sin it will be due largely to the fact that he has failed "to reckon himself dead unto sin in Christ." We cannot expect God to do His part and our part too. His part has been done perfectly, He waits now for us to cooperate with Him through faith in making this perfect salvation a reality in experience. Through grace "the old man" was nailed to the cross and buried in the tomb: through faith "the old man" will be kept there. Continuously reckon yourself to be totally severed from all that belonged to the old life and all that pertained to the old sphere, and faith will eventuate into experience.

Because I know in personal experience the defeat and discouragement that ensues from failure to reckon one's self dead unto sin and because I believe it is the common experience of scores of Christian workers I am quoting at length from a letter received from a missionary. God will use this testimony to help many, I confidently believe, to see the place of failure.

"Last night I had a long conference with my Father. It was like other nights in my life, when after long periods of perplexity and prayer for light, the Lord has settled matters for me. I asked Him to show me why I was failing, why my life was not more even and assured. He knew I was keeping back nothing, and that I believed Jesus had met the whole sin question, branches and root, on the Cross. Why was my experience so fluctuating?

"It was not long before the answer came, and I saw, what I had never realized before, that while I had taken the work of Christ on the Cross as the perfect and complete satisfaction for the *guilt* of my sin, so that the devil in all his assaults had not been able to move me from my confidence that all my sins, past, present and future are under the blood, and powerless to bring me again under the condemnation of God; I had never appreciated to the full the value of His dealing with the *root* of sin in me. I believed He *had* dealt with it. I believed He *had* identified me with Himself on the Cross, and that in Him I was crucified, 'dead unto sin and alive unto God.' I believed it as a *fact* in the Lord's glorious work, but I had been appropriating the value of it only piecemeal, so to speak. It had been the way of victory to me for years. Many of the temptations resisted, the victories won, were through a definite reckoning of myself as dead to sin and alive to God. Such victories have lasted months sometimes, blessed seasons! But I saw that just as I would have fallen into distressing condemnation under Satan's assaults, if I had not taken Christ's atoning work in its entirety, once for all; so my failure to appropriate the work of the Cross for my sinful *self*, in its entirety, had left me an occasional prey to its power. I had been reckoning just parts of myself dead, instead of my whole self. As a result I was afraid of self, often uneasy and not sure of victory. And he that feareth is not made perfect in love.

"Your words Sunday helped me, 'Who giveth us the victory, not victories.' Well, dear friend, I have taken Christ in death and resurrection as the full and perfect solution for the whole of the sin problem. He has done it and it is done. I have asked for the same immovable assurance about *sin* as I have enjoyed for years about my *sins*, and I believe He has given it and will maintain it. He has given me deep calm about it all.

"I see how my failure to trust *fully* the work of the Cross has hindered the inflow and outflow of the Holy Spirit. The failure to give Christ the *full glory* due Him has meant that my carnal self was able to keep me, much of the time, without the Holy of Holies of the presence of Father and Son, where in the Spirit it is my privilege to *dwell*.

"Glory be to God, the triune God! You will give Him glory with me, for this unfolding of His truth to His unworthy child. I believe this was the one thing needed to enable me to be used *to work all the good pleasure of His will*."

2. Make no provision for the flesh.

Romans 13:14, "But put ye on the Lord Jesus Christ, and *make not provision for the flesh, to fulfil the lusts thereof*."

Galatians 6:8, "For *he that soweth to the flesh shall of the flesh reap corruption; but he that soweth to the Spirit shall of the Spirit reap life* everlasting."

Romans 8:5, "For they that are after the flesh *do mind the things of the flesh;* but they that are after the Spirit the things of the Spirit."

Romans 8:4, "That the righteousness of the law might be fulfilled in us, *who walk not after the flesh, but after the Spirit*."

Here before us is very definite and practical instruction on the way of conquest of "the old man" which is constantly ignored and often willfully disobeyed by Christians. How can the Holy Spirit make real within us our complete severance from "the old man" and all that pertains to the old creation when we daily make ample provision for the renewal of that life within us by feeding him upon the food that makes fat? What is food to "the flesh" is fodder to the Spirit and *vice versa*. Search your own life under the Spirit's guidance to discover what stores you have on hand that are making "the flesh" fat in you and then throw the entire supply away and stock your shelves with those things upon which the Spirit can feed.

God's law of sowing and reaping in the spiritual realm is as inexorable as it is in the material realm. If we sow to "the flesh" we shall reap of "the flesh." What folly for a Christian woman to think she can sow to "the flesh" in mannish hair dress, indecent clothes, trashy books and worldly pleasures and then reap in return an unspotted husband, Christian children and spiritual fellowship in the home! And what inconceivable absurdity for a church to sow to its young people the dance and the movie and expect to reap a prayer meeting or a revival! To which are you sowing your time, your strength, your money—to "the flesh" or to the Spirit?

What things do you "mind"? It is a strong word. Upon what things are your mind, heart, will set? In what kind of things are you so immersed as to be oblivious to other things? With the desire for what kind of things are you saturated? With a consuming, compelling passion for what kind of things are you filled? You are responsible for the direction your desires take because in cooperation with the Holy Spirit He will direct you away from the things of "the flesh" toward the things of the Spirit. Are you making provision for "the flesh" in the things that you "mind"?

The world judges a Christian very largely by his "walk." To a world deaf to every other kind of a message the Christian may witness by his "walk." But what kind of a witness is the Christian if the worldly man finds him walking just where and just as he walks? What power will a Christian walking "in the flesh" have to deliver a sinner from the sphere of the flesh? Here is largely the secret of the shameful fruitlessness of the Church of Christ in the world today. Are you walking "in the flesh" or in the Spirit?

God commands every believer to take a definite, decisive attitude toward "the flesh" and to maintain it by the Holy Spirit's power under all circumstances.

> 1 Peter 2:11, "Dearly beloved, I beseech you as strangers and pilgrims, *abstain from fleshly lusts, which war against the soul.*"

> Galatians 5:24, "And *they that are Christ's have crucified the flesh with the affections and the lusts.*"

It resolves itself into a total abstinence of all that feeds or fosters the life of "the flesh" and a full appreciation of all that starves and stifles it.

3. Ignore the claims of the flesh.

Romans 8:12, "Therefore, brethren, *we are debtors, not to the flesh*, to live after the flesh."

'The flesh" is a fighter and will never abdicate the throne of its own will nor will it ever renounce its claim upon the believer's life. We owe "the flesh" nothing: we owe the Saviour, who severed us from its deadly, deathly poison, everything. Our invariable, unswerving attitude to every claim of "the flesh" upon us should be one of insistent refusal. It is the believer's privilege in the face of any claim it may advance to quietly, persistently say, "I am dead to that thing." Take sides instantly with the Holy Spirit whenever "the flesh" puts forth a claim to any part of your life and victory in Christ will be yours.

4. Mortify the members of the body.

Colossians 3:5, "*Mortify therefore your members which are upon the earth;* fornication, uncleanness, inordinate affection, evil concupiscence, and covetousness, which is idolatry."

Romans 8:13, "For if ye live after the flesh, ye shall die: but *if ye through the Spirit do mortify the deeds of the body*, ye shall live."

The body is the playground of "the flesh." Through it as a channel the believer is continuously open to temptation; its members have long been the tools of sin. But by yielding every member of the body as an instrument of righteousness to Jesus Christ we may cooperate with the Holy Spirit in routing "the flesh" from its long fortified stronghold.

WE MUST CAST OFF THE OLD MAN

Ephesians 4:22, R. V., "*That ye put away as concerning your former manner of life, the old man,* that waxeth corrupt after the lusts of deceit."

Colossians 3:9, "Lie not one to another, *seeing that ye have put off the old man with his deeds.*"

The old nature is cast aside as a filthy, worthless garment. It is as though a beggar had become betrothed to the King of all the earth and cast aside her filthy rags that she might don her bridal robe.

THE LORD JESUS IN CONTROL

But the conquest of the old nature is but the negative side of a life that is spiritual. The positive aspect of it is the supernatural control of every department of the believer's being by the Lord Jesus. It was not enough that the children of Israel should cross the Jordan, they were commanded to possess the land and by dispossessing every enemy live in victory and peace.

WE MUST CROWN JESUS CHRIST AS LORD

> 2 Corinthians 5:15, "And that he died for all, that *they which live should not henceforth live unto themselves, but unto him* which died for them, and rose again."
>
> Galatians 2:20, R. V., "I have been crucified with Christ; and it is *no longer I that live, but Christ liveth in me.*"
>
> Philippians 1:21, "For *to me to live is Christ,* and to die is gain."

The very purpose of Jesus Christ's death and resurrection is to dispossess, to displace and to dethrone that old "I," and to give the throne of the human personality to Him to whom it belongs by the right of creation and of purchase, that He might reign there as its sole Lord and King. "To me to live is Christ" is the life God expects every believer to live. The apostle's cry of despair, "O wretched man that I am! who shall deliver me from the body of this death?" and his shout of victory, "I thank God through Jesus Christ our Lord," were spoken almost in the same breath. By one supreme act of the will he seemed to step out of the grip of the old nature into the control of the new.

Dear friend, has Christ's coronation day as King been celebrated yet in your life? Who sits today on the throne of your being, self or Christ? Unless by a definite act of your will you have chosen Him as Lord it is futile for you to expect Him to control your life.

WE MUST COVET THE THINGS OF CHRIST

> Colossians 3:1-3, "If ye then be risen with Christ, *seek those things which are above,* where Christ sitteth on the right hand of God.
> *Set your affections on things above,* not on things on the earth.
> For ye are dead, and *your life is hid with Christ in God.*"

It will never do merely to crown Christ as a puppet King by an act of the will and then live under the democracy of self-*desire.* Of self, for self and by self, seems to be the threefold principle governing countless Christian lives. If self-will dethrones God in human lives today, it is self-love that votes to keep Him dethroned. It is not enough to have the will fixed in its purpose to crown Him as Lord and then have the affections lusting for the things of the world, the flesh and the devil. The desires of the heart must keep step with the decision of the will; the believer must "seek those things which are above" and joyfully, eagerly, "set his affections" upon them. How incongruous for him to be "in Christ" seated in the heavenlies at the right hand of God and hid away with Christ in the Father's innermost sanctuary and yet be hankering for the things of earth and of time and of sense!

If one truly covets Christ, he will be willing to count all things loss. He will not only cut loose from every besetting sin and entangling alliance but he will stand ready to lay aside every hindering weight. He will make himself ready to be a victor in the race of life here on earth (1 Corinthians 9:24-27), and he will have his bridal robe ready for the coming marriage to the Lamb (Revelation 19:7-8).

> Philippians 3:7-8, R. V., "Howbeit what things were gain to me, *these have I counted loss for Christ.*
>   Yea verily, and *I count all things to be loss for the excellency of the knowledge of Christ Jesus my Lord: for whom I suffered the loss of all things,* and do count them but refuse, *that I may gain Christ.*"

> Hebrews 12:1, "Wherefore seeing we also are compassed about with so great a cloud of witnesses, *let us lay aside every weight,* and *the sin which doth so easily beset us,* and let us run with patience the race that is set before us."

The apostle Paul put before him a prize to be gained—Christ Jesus Himself—and this prize he coveted above all else in life. His passionate desire for the Lord Jesus made him willing, even eager, not only to renounce all known sin but even to cast aside anything and everything that tended to make his spiritual experience stagnant and sluggish.

The Alpine climber prepares to ascend the Jungfrau—at last a long-cherished ambition is to be realized. Into his pack go necessities as he thinks them to be. A heavy load it becomes. Early in the climb he is overcome. His body is wearied through its excessive burden. Finally the guide tells him a choice must be made because not only is he hindering his own progress but that of the other climbers to whom he is roped. He must either give up his hope of reaching the summit or he must cast aside the weights. Does he covet his prize enough to count all these things but loss that he may gain the summit of the Jungfrau?

My friend, have you been living in the valley, self-satisfied and self-complacent? As you have gone with me through these studies has your eye traveled up, up, up to the very summit of spiritual experience—Christ Jesus, crucified, risen, ascended, exalted, living in all the fullness of His beauty, power, glory, and holiness in human life, conforming it to His image, and then using it to bring other lives into the same conformity? Have you aspired to reach the top—to live your life on that highest plane? The ascent is steep and difficult but it is possible and a thousand times repaying. But, if you attempt it, you will have to follow the explicit direction of the Guide not only for your own sake but for the sake of others. The divine Spirit will command you to renounce all known sin; He will even ask you to cast away some things which *He* sees are weighing you down and wearying you so that you cannot keep pace with your spiritual companions, which, if carried, will keep you from reaching the top. Perhaps He will require you to make that choice today. God grant that you may count all things but loss that you may win Christ.

WE MUST COOPERATE WITH THE HOLY SPIRIT IN KEEPING CHRIST ENTHRONED

It is not crowning Christ as Lord that troubles many an earnest soul but the keeping Him enthroned. It is not reaching the high altitude in the spiritual realm but it is the maintaining of life on that highest plane. But for this specific purpose God's second gift, the Holy Spirit, was bestowed upon every believer. Through His indwelling the Christian He enables him to glorify Christ in character, conversation and conduct. But His omnipotent working depends upon the believer's constant and consistent cooperation. And He tells him just what he must do to cooperate.

1. "Reckon yourself alive unto God."

> Romans 6:11, "Likewise reckon ye yourselves to be dead indeed unto sin, but *alive unto God* through Jesus Christ our Lord."

Through identification with Jesus Christ in His resurrection the believer has been made "alive unto God." Through the burial of "the old man" with Christ in the tomb he was completely separated *from* all that belonged to the old creation. Through the emergence of "the new man" with Christ from the tomb he was completely separated *unto* all that belongs to the new creation. This is the faultless provision of God's grace for every believer. Every believer is already in the heavenlies in Christ; Christ is now the source and sustenance of every Christian's life. All that the Man in the glory is and has is the rightful possession of every believer here and now. But what God provides through grace He expects the believer to possess through faith. Emissaries from the realm of darkness and death will come to lure him away from his hidden life in Christ but as he "reckons himself to be alive unto God" he will be able to resist the evil one and to maintain his position in Christ. As he "reckons" upon this accomplished fact based on his Saviour's resurrection the Holy Spirit works within to make it real. As he continues to "reckon" moment by moment that he has no life but life in Christ, the Holy Spirit keeps him abiding.

2. Make every provision for the Spirit.

> Romans 8:9, "But ye are not in the flesh, *but in the Spirit, if so be that the Spirit of God dwell in you.*"

The moment the believer becomes the possessor of the new nature he leaves the sphere of the flesh to abide in the sphere of the Spirit, and the Spirit comes to abide in him. In other words, he is in the Spirit and the Spirit is in him. The maintenance of such a life in such a world as this requires the most careful and constant provision.

Only the Holy Spirit knows what will sustain and strengthen life in His sphere. He alone can provide that food. This He has done for every believer and all He asks is for the acceptance of the food He offers. He knows both the age and the capacity of each believer and will suit his food to his need.

> 1 Peter 2:2, "As newborn babes, *desire the sincere milk of the word*, that ye may grow thereby."
>
> Hebrews 5:14, *"But strong meat belongeth to them that are of full age, even those who by reason of use have their senses exercised to discern both good and evil."*

3. Follow the leading of the Spirit.

> Romans 8:14, *"For as many as are led by the Spirit of God,"* they are the sons of God."

The only way to combat successfully the claims of the flesh is to obey implicitly every prompting or motion of the Spirit, be it ever so slight. Whether it be a warning, a check, a leading, or a teaching, all are given by Him as He sees necessary, and should be followed instantly.

4. Yield to Christ the control of every member of the body.

> Romans 6:13, "Neither yield ye your members as instruments of unrighteousness unto sin: but yield yourselves unto God, as those alive from the dead, and *your members as instruments of righteousness unto God."*

It is utter folly to talk about Christ's control over and use of our lives if we have blinded our eyes to His vision and deafened our ears to His voice and tied our tongues as His witnesses and fettered our hands as His tools and lamed our feet as His messengers, through yielding them to the devil as instruments of unrighteousness unto sin. But it is just such a stultified life that countless Christians expect Christ to use. If Christ's control is to count for anything in our lives and through us in the lives of others, every member of our bodies must be at His absolute disposal.

WE MUST CLOTHE OURSELVES WITH CHRIST

> Galatians 3:27, "For as many of you as have been baptized into Christ *have put on Christ."*
>
> Romans 13:14, "But *put ye on the Lord Jesus Christ,* and make not provision for the flesh, to fulfil the lusts thereof."

Did you discern in reading these two verses that in the first one God declares that the believer has already put on the Lord Jesus Christ and in the last one He exhorts—may we put it stronger yet—He commands him to do so? Through the grace, mercy and love of God the believer has been unclothed and clothed upon in the new position in Christ to which he has been brought. The snow white linen of Christ's righteousness and holiness are his. But God requires the cooperative response of the believer's love, devotion and faith in keeping these garments clean and rightly fitted to the believer's daily walk and warfare.

Dear fellow Christian, perhaps we have come to the second crucial milestone in your spiritual experience. Already you have accepted Christ as Saviour. You faced the choice of your sin or God's Son and you chose Christ as your Saviour. But have you wandered forty years in the wilderness of defeat, of discouragement and oftentimes of despair? Are you weary and footsore? Does your heart cry out for the peace, joy, victory and power you see others enjoying? If so, are you ready just now to take the second step into the life on the highest plane by crowning Jesus Christ as Lord over your spirit, soul and body and by placing your whole being unconditionally under His control? Before you is this choice, self or Christ?

> "Oh! the bitter shame and sorrow,
>   That a time could ever be,
> When I let the Saviour's pity
>   Plead in vain, and proudly answered—
>   '*All of Self and none of Thee.*'
>
> "Yet He found me: I beheld Him
>   Bleeding on the cursed tree;
> Heard Him pray, 'Forgive them, Father,'
>   And my wistful heart said faintly—
>   '*Some of Self and some of Thee.*'
>
> "Day by day His tender mercy,
>   Healing, helping, full and free,
> Sweet and strong, and oh! so patient,
>   Brought me lower while I whispered—
>   '*Less of Self and more of Thee.*'
>
> "Higher than the highest heavens,
>   Deeper than the deepest sea;
> Lord, thy love at last has conquered:
>   Grant me now my soul's petition—
>   '*None of Self and all of Thee.*'"

Part 3

THE BELIEVER'S RESPONSE TO THE HOLY SPIRIT'S INWORKING

24

The Spirit-filled Life

IN OUR STUDIES so far we have considered God's wondrous plan of salvation as wrought out in the Lord Jesus Christ. We have seen what Christ came to do for us, to be in us, and to work through us. We have faced what life in Christ may be and, therefore, ought to be in every Christian. Let us now honestly face its real worth to us individually.

Is God's salvation in Christ *perfect?* Can anything be added to it? Can anything be taken from it? Surely the answer will quickly come from any life in vital relationship with the Lord Jesus: Yes, God's salvation is perfect; it provides for every need; it satisfies every desire; it furnishes an all-sufficient Saviour. As I look into my life's deepest need I can think of nothing to add to it nor of anything that could be taken from it. God's salvation wrought out in Christ for me is of infinite worth through its perfection.

But is it *practical?* Is it possible for an ordinary person to live a life in Christ such as God seems to expect? I can imagine the answer of some to be: The truth regarding a life lived on the highest plane is biblical and logical but it does not match my experience nor the experience of many Christians of my acquaintance. Is not God's plan of salvation too perfect to be practical for such a world as this? Is not life on the highest plane possible only to those who are called into special Christian service?

Everything in God's Word contradicts this suggestion. God's plan of salvation is not only perfect but it is practical and possible for every individual believer. The Good Shepherd spoke concerning every sheep within His fold when He said, "I am come that they might have life and that they might have it *more abundantly.*" Whoever has Christ's life in any measure may have it in its fullness.

> Colossians 2:9-10, R. V., "For in him dwelleth all the fulness of the Godhead bodily, and *in him ye are made full,* who is the head of all principality and power."

John the Baptist in two wonderful proclamations declared the entire scope of Christ's work in salvation when he said, "Behold the Lamb of

God, which taketh away the sin of the world" and "He that sent me to baptize with water, . . . the same is that which baptizeth with the Holy Ghost" (John 1:29, 33). Christ would do a twofold work for those who trust Him as Saviour; He would take away their sin and He would baptize them in the Spirit. Thus John the Baptist states that part of Christ's work is to bring the believer into as definite a relationship to the Holy Spirit as he bears to Christ, although it is to be a different relationship.

What John the Baptist had said Christ corroborated in two remarkable invitations which He gave to sinners to come to Him and drink of the water of life.

> John 4:14, R. V., "But whosoever drinketh of the water that I shall give him shall never thirst: but the water that I shall give him shall *become in him* a well of water springing up unto eternal life."

> John 7:37-38, R. V., "Now on the last day, the great day of the feast, Jesus stood and cried, saying, If any man thirst, let him come unto me and drink. He that believeth on me, as the scripture hath said, *from within him* shall flow rivers of living water."

Jesus Christ promised to bestow a gift upon the one who believed in Him as Sin-bearer which would bring perfect satisfaction and sufficiency within the believer's inmost life and which would then overflow in rich and abounding blessing into the lives of others. Christ's offer to the Samaritan woman was a gift which would change her source of supplies from a water pot to a well and then convert her life into a channel through which rivers of this living water would flow.

The Holy Spirit—Christ's Gift to the Believer

We are left in no doubt as to what this gift was, for the Lord Jesus states most explicitly that it was the gift of the Holy Spirit.

> John 7:39, R. V., *"But this spake he of the Spirit, which they that believed on him were to receive: for the Spirit was not yet given; because Jesus was not yet glorified."*

Please note that in this verse the Lord Jesus tells us three things:

1. What the gift was—"This spoke he of the Spirit."
2. To whom it was to be given—"Which they that believe on him were to receive."
3. When the gift was to be bestowed—"Jesus was not yet glorified."

It is evident from these words that His finished work as Sin-bearer must first be accomplished and then as the glorified Lord in heaven He would bestow this wondrous gift upon every believer which would make *real within him* that abiding and abounding life which Christ had made *possible for him.*

Still further light was thrown upon the nature of this gift in Christ's last conversation with the disciples on the eve of His exodus. He told them He was to live in them as an abiding spiritual Presence; that there would be a divine inflow of life supernatural in quality, and a divine outflow of life supernatural in power. They were to live as He lived and to work as He worked. To provide power for such a life He promised that "another Comforter" would come to take up His permanent abode in them.

> John 14:16-18, "And I will pray the Father, and *he shall give you another Comforter, that he may abide with you for ever.* Even the Spirit of truth; whom the world cannot receive, because it seeth him not, neither knoweth him: but ye know him; for *he dwelleth with you, and shall be in you.* I will not leave you comfortless: *I will come to you.*"

"Another Comforter"—these words are descriptive and defining and very significant. The "Comforter" (Paraclete) means "one who is called alongside of another to help." "Another" means one just like Himself. Someone was to come to dwell in each of them in perpetual presence and through His indwelling Christ Himself would be brought back to live within them. The One who was to abide in them was the Spirit who had indwelt, infilled and empowered the God-man when He was upon earth. Christ promised that upon His return to glory He would send back this same Spirit to indwell, to infill and to empower them. This He did on the day of Pentecost when the Holy Spirit came down to form the Church, the mystic Body of Christ, and to dwell in it on earth. On that day the disciples who tarried in the upper room were baptized in the Spirit.

From that day, as the divine record shows, everyone who through faith in Christ as Saviour, has been organically and vitally united with the living Lord as a member of His Body, has received the gift of the Holy Spirit.

> Acts 2:38, "Then Peter said unto them, Repent, and be baptized every one of you in the name of Jesus Christ for the remission of sins, and *ye shall receive the gift of the Holy Ghost.*"

> Acts 11:15, 17, "And as I began to speak, the Holy Ghost fell on them, as on us at the beginning.
> Forasmuch then as *God gave them the like gift as he did unto us, who believed on the Lord Jesus Christ;* what was I, that I could withstand God?"

The moment one receives the Sin-bearer as his Saviour he is "in the Spirit" and the Spirit is in him. Whatever his spiritual condition every Christian is indwelt by the Holy Spirit as an abiding, perpetual Presence. It is impossible to accept the Son and to refuse the Spirit.

> Romans 8:9, "But ye are not in the flesh, but *in the Spirit,* if so be that the

Spirit of God dwell in you. *Now if any man have not the Spirit of Christ, he is none of his."*

1 Corinthians 3:16, *"Know ye not* that ye are the temple of God, and *that the Spirit of God dwelleth in you?"*

In the divine plan there is as definite a purpose in the gift of the Spirit as in the gift of the Son. Through the Son the sinner has life; through the Spirit the believer has life more abundant. Through the Son the sinner leaves the sphere of the natural and enters the sphere of the spiritual. Through the Spirit the believer is lifted to the highest heights of life on the spiritual plane. God has a purpose for every Christian—a life of true, deep, vital, growing spirituality—and the Holy Spirit lives within every believer as God's gracious provision for the accomplishment of this very purpose.

But do not let us think for a moment that the Spirit works apart from the Son. Life more abundant is by the Spirit. He shares with Christ the Head of the Body, His intense desire that the fullness of life in the Head in heaven shall be manifested in the Body on earth. But the believer must know that the fullness is for him, he must desire to have it, and there must be a means of communicating it to him. All this is the work of the Holy Spirit. It is His task to reveal Christ in all the perfection of His heavenly, holy life to the believer; to unfold to him the unsearchable riches which are his as an heir of God in Christ; to create within him a desire to possess his possessions; and then, to act as the channel through which the abundant life of the glorified Lord in heaven is communicated to him.

John 16:14-15, *"He shall glorify me: for he shall receive of mine, and shall shew it unto you.* All things that the Father hath are mine: therefore said I, that he shall take of mine, and shall shew it unto you."

Romans 8:16-17, R. V., *"The Spirit himself beareth witness with our spirit, that we are children of God:* and if children, then heirs; heirs of God, and joint-heirs with Christ; if so be that we suffer with him, that we may be also glorified with him."

It is the Holy Spirit who works within the believer to bring him to make the choice between self and Christ. But as He works He is opposed, thwarted, challenged and resisted every step of the way by that bitter opponent. "The flesh" works as diligently to keep the believer fleshly as the Spirit works to make him spiritual.

Galatians 5:17, "For *the flesh lusteth against the Spirit, and the Spirit against the flesh: for these are contrary the one to the other."*

Romans 7 records the victory of "the flesh" and we see the Holy Spirit ignored, silenced, thwarted and quenched. Romans 8 records the victory of the Holy Spirit and we see Him victorious, active, regnant and supreme.

We are compelled to believe that some advance in relationship to the Holy Spirit has taken place which has given Him this wonderful victory and we are constrained to ask God to show us what it is.

THE SPIRIT-FILLED LIFE

In one terse, concise command God shows us the highest point the believer can reach in his relationship to the Holy Spirit.

> Ephesians 5:18, "And be not drunk with wine, wherein is excess; *but be filled with the Spirit.*"

You, who have the Holy Spirit in you, give Him full right-of-way in your life; let Him dominate your whole being; let Him who dwells within you fill you from the center to the circumference of your life. You are in the sphere of the Spirit, therefore let the Spirit live out His life in you. Through regeneration God has endowed you with Himself and in the Person of the Spirit He dwells within you. Allow Him now to work out His perfect will unhindered through the undivided control of your whole being. Permit Him to energize you with His almighty power through filling you with Himself.

"Be filled with the Spirit" is a command given to every believer. No Christian is refused the blessing of such a precious experience and none is exempt from its responsibilities. As the refusal of life in Christ is the greatest sin of the unbeliever so the refusal of life more abundant in the Holy Spirit's fullness is the greatest sin of the believer. To be filled with the Holy Spirit is not the privilege of a few but it is the prerogative of all believers. Since it is a command, it is not optional, but it is incumbent upon *every* Christian to be so filled.

> Acts 4:31, "And when they had prayed, the place was shaken where they were assembled together; and they were *all* filled with the Holy Ghost, and they spake the word of God with boldness.

"Be filled with the Spirit"—"Filled."
"Full of the Holy Ghost"—"Full."
"That ye may be filled unto all the fulness of God"—"Fulness."

These words suggest that there is an infinite, exhaustless fullness which the believer may receive according to his receptive capacity. He may be "filled" today yet tomorrow he shall need to be "filled" again so that his life may be habitually "full"; and the process of continuous infillings will need to continue as long as he lives since the source of supply is "all the fulness of God." A life "full of the Holy Ghost" should be and may be the normal life of every believer. "We may be always full, yet ever filling, the first reception of the fulness being a crisis that leads to a process."

> Acts 6:3, "Wherefore, brethren, look ye out among you seven men of honest report, *full of the Holy Ghost* and wisdom, whom we may appoint over this business."

> Acts 11:24, "For he [Barnabas] was a good man, and *full of the Holy Ghost* and of faith: and much people was added unto the Lord."

To be spiritual, then, one must be filled and be kept filled with the Holy Spirit. The habitual fullness of the Holy Spirit is the divine provision for a life lived on the highest plane. The Holy Spirit is the divinely appointed means of communication of "the abundant life" of the ascended, glorified Lord in heaven to the believer on earth. There is a threefold manifestation of the Holy Spirit's infilling.

THE REALIZATION OF CHRIST'S ABIDING PRESENCE

Is not the realization of Christ's abiding presence the greatest need as, I dare say, it is the deepest desire of some of us? He said, "I will come unto you" and with our intellect we believe He has come but our hearts cry out for a deeper realization of His blessed presence within. The lives of the early Christians seemed fairly surcharged with such a joyous, vivid consciousness of the presence within them of their living, glorified Lord. He was so real to them that He seemed to be the home of all their thoughts and the horizon of all their affections. Is the spiritual presence of the living Lord such an intense reality to you? Are you occupied with Christ? Are you satisfied in Christ? Can you say from your heart,

> "Thou, O Christ, art all I want;
> More than all in Thee I find"?

To have Christ abiding in us in all His fullness is to have every need supplied, every desire fulfilled, every hunger satisfied, every thirst quenched. It is to have our whole life perpetually refreshed and replete in Him. Such a realization of His abiding presence in its fullness is one of the rich rewards of a Spirit-filled life.

> Ephesians 3:16-17, 19, R. V., "That he would grant you, according to the riches of his glory, that ye may be *strengthened with power through his Spirit in the inward man; that Christ may dwell in your hearts through faith. That ye may be filled unto all the fulness of God.*"

THE REPRODUCTION OF CHRIST'S HOLY LIFE

The reproduction of Christ's holy life within the believer is another unspeakably precious benefit of the Spirit-filled life. Who of us has ever had a real vision of the Lord Jesus who has not abhorred his own sinfulness and longed passionately for Christ's holiness? Who has ever really seen the King in His beauty and not longed intensely to be like Him? But His is a life that defies imitation. No counterfeit is ever so quickly detected and so heartily detested as a counterfeit of the Christ. There is no possibility of likeness to the character seen in Jesus Christ except through the reproduction of His life in us.

To communicate the life of the living Head in heaven to the Body on earth, making the visible part of Christ of the same character as the invisible part, is the work of the Holy Spirit. To reproduce the life of the Lord Jesus in us in a growing perfection is the mission of the Holy Spirit and His ability to perform this task is in proportion to the freedom given Him to do it. The Spirit-filled Christian is the one who is most like his Lord.

> 2 Corinthians 3:18, R. V., "But we all with unveiled face beholding as in a mirror the glory of the Lord, *are transformed into the same image from glory to glory, even as from the Lord the Spirit.*"

> Galatians 5:22-23, R. V., "But *the fruit of the Spirit* is love, joy, peace, longsuffering, kindness, goodness, faithfulness, meekness, self-control: against such there is no law."

Compressed into these nine exquisite graces is a marvelous word-picture of the character of Jesus Christ in its essential beauty, symmetry and perfection. Such character can never be produced through human effort for it is not the product of human nature but the fruit of the divine nature. Only the divine can produce the divine. "As without the sun the photographic image cannot be printed upon the sensitized film, so apart from the Holy Spirit, the moral glories of the Lord Jesus can never become ours in any sense save that of desire." But, when the Holy Spirit is permitted to fill us, He brings forth His own fruit in a character of growing likeness to that of our Lord.

THE REENACTMENT OF CHRIST'S SUPERNATURAL POWER THROUGH US

The reenactment of Christ's supernatural power through us is the third outstanding mark of a Spirit-filled life. All power belongs unto God and He has delegated this power to His Son and the Son in turn transmits that power to the one whose life is united with His. When He gave that last commission to the disciples He said, "All power hath been given unto me in heaven and upon earth, *go ye therefore* and make disciples of all the nations." The "therefore" fully implies that, as He sent them forth to accomplish such a superhuman task, He promised to endue them with supernatural power. Just before His ascension He told them to wait until they were "endued with power from on high" and in giving this command He reiterated His promise to send forth to them the Holy Spirit upon His return to glory (Luke 24:49). So their enduement with power and their reception of the Holy Spirit evidently had a vital connection. The last words He spoke, as He was lifted up out of their sight, declared this.

> Acts 1:8, "But *ye shall receive power, after that the Holy Ghost is come upon you:* and ye shall be witnesses unto me both in Jerusalem, and in all Judea, and in Samaria, and unto the uttermost part of the earth."

A study of the book of Acts shows us that those who were filled with the Holy Spirit were full of power. They had power to suffer and to sacrifice; to teach and to preach; to witness and to work. Thousands of souls were born into the Kingdom of God and blessed through their ministry. But this work of grace was not wrought through human energy, zeal, wisdom or eloquence, but through the power of the ascended Lord poured forth through Spirit-filled lives.

Have you the power of the Holy Spirit? Through you is He working mightily to convict men of sin, to constrain them to believe in Christ, and to conform them to the image of the Lord Jesus? If not, is it because you are not *filled* with the Holy Spirit? Wherever He is in fullness He manifests Himself in power. "In order to have the Holy Spirit's competency we must have His control."

One day while rowing I noticed a break in the bank and a veritable river was flowing out of the lake through the adjoining fields, making everything round about rich in foliage and fruitage. Inquiring of one of my companions why with such a continuous outflow of water the lake did not go dry, he replied, "Oh! there are innumerable springs in the bottom and as much water as flows out through the river flows in through the unseen springs." Such inflow and outflow symbolizes a Spirit-filled life.

"In him a well." The Holy Spirit in His fullness is Christ's gift to every believer. He dwells within, a well of living water, a continuously upspringing fountain. With Him within there is no need for dearth. The promise is he *"shall never thirst."* The supply will be commensurate to the need. Satisfaction and sufficiency characterize the Spirit-filled life.

"Out of him rivers." The inflow demands and provides an outflow. Satisfaction in Christ means the overflow of Christ. The Holy Spirit in complete, continuous control is a well of living water within us, constantly springing up in ever increasing fullness until there are rivers of living water flowing into other lives. Thus the Spirit-filled life is one of perennial freshness, fragrance, fullness and fruitfulness.

Is such a life yours? If not, do you desire it? It is available; it is obtainable; it is for you if you thirst. *"If any man thirst."* Do you know there is more of the Holy Spirit for you than you have yet claimed? Have you enough of Him to make you want more? Then listen to the invitation freely extended to you. "If any man thirst let him come unto me and *drink.*" Drink until you are satisfied, until you are full, yes, until you are overflowing. The fullness of the Holy Spirit is for everyone who thirsts for it and who will meet God's simple and clearly stated conditions.

> "Our blest Redeemer, ere He breathed
>   His tender, last farewell,
> A Guide, a Comforter, bequeathed
>   With us to dwell.
> And every virtue we possess,
>   And every victory won,
> And every thought of holiness,
>   Are His alone."

25

The Prerequisite to Fullness—Cleansing

"GOD HATH NOT CALLED US unto uncleanness but unto holiness," and if we measure up to our calling as saints, all uncleanness must go. The infilling of the Holy Spirit demands the cleansing of the life. Two commands given to Christians in regard to their relationship to the Holy Spirit reveal this fact very strikingly.

> Ephesians 4:30, "And *grieve not the holy Spirit of God,* whereby ye are sealed unto the day of redemption."

Grieve is a love word. You cannot grieve one who does not love you. You can hurt him or anger him but you cannot grieve him. To grieve the Holy Spirit means that we are causing pain to Someone who loves us. What, then, in us causes this divine One grief?

He is the Spirit of *truth* (John 14:17) so anything false, deceitful, hypocritical, grieves Him.

He is the Spirit of *faith* (2 Corinthians 4:13) so doubt, unbelief, distrust, worry, anxiety, grieve Him.

He is the Spirit of *grace* (Hebrews 10:29) so that which is hard, bitter, ungracious, unthankul, malicious, unforgiving or unloving, grieves Him.

He is the Spirit of *holiness* (Romans 1:4) so anything unclean, defiling or degrading, grieves Him.

He is the Spirit of *wisdom and revelation* (Ephesians 1:17) so ignorance, conceit, arrogance and folly, grieve Him.

He is the Spirit of *power, love and discipline* (2 Timothy 1:7) so that which is barren, fruitless, disorderly, confused and uncontrolled, grieves Him.

He is the Spirit of *life* (Romans 8:2) so anything that savors of indifference, lukewarmness, spiritual dullness, and deadness, grieves Him.

He is the Spirit of *glory* (1 Peter 4:14) so anything worldly, earthly or fleshly, grieves Him.

He dwells within us to enable us "to grow up into him in all things" (Ephesians 4:15); to bring us daily into conformity to Christ's image (2

320

Corinthians 3:18); until we have reached "unto the measure of the stature of the fulness of Christ" (Ephesians 4:13); so anything in us which hinders Him in carrying out this purpose grieves Him. Knowingly, willfully, to permit anything which is contrary to what the Holy Spirit Himself is to remain in your life, now His domain, must mean that you love sin more than you love Him. Such unfaithfulness grieves Him. Refusing obedience to God's revealed will constitutes a rejection of Him in favor of His enemy.

Spirituality depends upon a harmonious and happy relationship with our divine Helper and Advocate. Sin, then, which impairs such relationship must inevitably hinder any true spirituality. As long as we are indulging known sin we are living in the same abode with a grieved Spirit who is thereby hindered from manifesting Himself fully in and through us. It is clear, then, that if one is to be filled with the Holy Spirit all conscious, willful sin must be put away. "God does not require golden vessels, neither does He seek for silver ones, but He must have clean ones." To be filled one must be cleansed.

1 Thessalonians 5:19, *"Quench not the Spirit."*

We "grieve" the Spirit when we say yes to Satan when he lures us into sin. We "quench" the Spirit when we say no to God when He woos us into sanctification and service. To bring the believer to will to let God's will have absolute sway over the entire being is part of the Spirit's work, perhaps it is His hardest task. Self-will is a latent thing in every one of us which is prone to manifest itself in secret if not in open rebellion against God.

The only cure for self-will is a deliberate, determined choice to do God's will in all things, at all times, at all costs. It is to have one's heart firmly fixed upon the doing of God's will as the rule for daily life and to permit no exception to this rule. "So a yieldedness to the will of God is not demonstrated by some one particular issue; it is rather a matter of having taken the will of God as the rule of one's life. To be in the will of God is simply to be willing to do His will without reference to any particular thing He may choose. It is electing His will to be final, even before we know what He may wish us to do. It is, therefore, not a question of being willing to do some one thing; it is a question of being willing to do *anything*, when, where and how it may seem best in His heart of love" (L. S. Chafer, *He That Is Spiritual*, p. 113).

God's first man had the right to will and the power to will Godward. But he chose to will Satanward. God's second Man had the right to will and the power to will Godward which He invariably did in every choice. If you are a Christian, you are God's new man in Christ. You have the right to will and the Holy Spirit dwells within you to enable you always to will Godward. But if you say no to God at any point you have allied yourself with the evil forces which are in rebellion against God. Such resistance and rebellion are sin and the Holy Spirit cannot occupy fully His abode in your life until you are cleansed.

The indwelling Spirit longs to fill the life of each one whom He indwells. So He is constantly working toward the purifying of the life. Indeed He is there for that very purpose. In a darkened room there would be much of dust which would pass unnoticed but, when the sun shines in, it is all brought out into the light. The more fully the light fills the room the more perfectly the dust is revealed. The Holy Spirit dwelling in the believer brings out into the light the sin in the life and the more fully He indwells the more perfect will be the revelation and recognition of sin. The nearer God comes to us the more sensitive to sin are we made. Some things which five years ago or a year ago or a month ago you would not have called sin you now acknowledge to be sin. The Holy Spirit who dwells in us is there to purify our hearts and to sanctify our lives. "Giving them the Holy Ghost, purifying their hearts by faith."

The Means of Cleansing

1 John 1:7, *"The blood of Jesus Christ his Son cleanseth us from all sin."*

For sinner and saint alike nothing but the blood of Jesus suffices to cleanse from sin. For the unsaved sinner it removes the guilt of sin. For the sinning saint it removes the defilement of sin. The Christian is in constant contact with sin and the very tense of the verb used in this verse "cleanseth" shows that he never gets beyond the need of the cleansing blood of Christ.

The Method of Cleansing

The grieved Spirit will let us know that He is grieved and what it is that grieves Him. He will convict us of the sin that thwarts and throttles Him and He will point us to the cleansing blood of Christ. He will open the Word to 1 John 1:9 and show us what our part is. Then our responsibility begins. God requires but one thing of us—a frank, full confession prompted by a true heart-repentance.

1 John 1:9, *"If we confess our sins,* he is faithful and just to forgive us our sins, and *to cleanse us from all unrighteousness."*

But, while He requires only this simple, honest confession, He will accept no substitute for it. Regret and remorse because of suffering from sin's punishment are not confession; a forced acknowledgment when caught in some offense which is in reality merely the admission of transgression rather than of *the sin* of the transgression, is not confession;

prayer in which a short, vague, half-concealed acknowledgment of sin is overshadowed by a long accompaniment of justification and vindication of self, will not pass with God for a bona fide confession from the heart. Confession of sin is made primarily to God and often only to Him. But, if one has wronged another and sin has placed a barrier between them, confession of that sin before the other may be required to remove the barrier. God's cleansing of us may await our confession to a brother. But this precious promise does hold out to us the blessed assurance that, when honest confession of known sin is frankly made to God, He instantly forgives and cleanses. We are thereby brought into perfect adjustment to an ungrieved, unquenched Spirit and every hindrance to His infilling is removed.

THE MEASURE OF CLEANSING

The measure of cleansing is from all defilement of both flesh and spirit. Separation from every defiling thing is a prerequisite to the infilling of the Holy Spirit.

> 2 Corinthians 7:1, "Having therefore these promises, dearly beloved, *let us cleanse ourselves from all filthiness of the flesh and spirit,* perfecting holiness in the fear of God."

God demands a cleansing that reaches from the innermost desire to the outermost deed; that goes from the core to the circumference. He asks us to take His conception of sin which regards a lustful look as truly sin as a lustful act; which calls hate in the heart sin as much as murder by the hand; which sees in irritability of spirit the seed of the outburst of temper. God asks for the cleansing of both the inner and outer part of the temple which He indwells. Even after we have "cleansed ourselves" by deliberately putting out of our lives everything which we know to be sinful there will be much when once He fills the life which the Holy Spirit will convict us of as unclean and unholy.

God's withholding of His presence in power from His own children until sin is put away is very strikingly revealed in His dealings with the children of Israel over Achan's sin. They had gained a marvelous victory at Jericho. The city and all that was in it had been delivered to them by the Lord. God had told them beforehand that everything in the city was accursed and that no one of them was to take anything of the spoils for himself or he, too, would be accursed. Achan, coveting gold, silver, and a Babylonish garment, took them and hid them under his tent. No eye but that of the all-seeing God saw him do it. The children of Israel, rejoicing in the signal victory over Jericho, marched against the smaller city of Ai with absolute assurance of a similar victory, only to meet with an overwhelming defeat.

Joshua fell on his face before God and offered a prayer in which he charged God with blame for such humiliation before their enemies. But God commanded him to stop praying and told him that He would continue to withhold His presence from the children of Israel until the accursed thing was taken away from among them. Not until the man who had coveted, stolen and deceived was found and confession of sin was made did God again dwell in victory and in power among the children of Israel.

Perhaps you have been praying fervently for the fullness of the Holy Spirit while all the time there has been the continued indulgence of some known sin, the willful disobedience of some known command, or the deliberate resistance to God's clearly revealed will. If so, God is saying to you just now, "Get thee up, wherefore liest thou upon thy face? Thou hast sinned, neither will I be with you any more except ye destroy the accursed from among you. Up, sanctify yourselves, thou canst not stand before thine enemies until ye take away the accursed thing from among you" (cf. Joshua 7:10-13). So long as you are living with a grieved or a quenched Spirit you cannot be filled. To be filled one must be cleansed.

I looked the other day upon the snow-clad summit of the Silberhorn as it glistened in the sun. It was a marvelous symbol of purity. What was the cause of its spotlessness? There was nothing between it and the heaven above. It lay open to receive the unstained, unsullied snow sent down from heaven. Oh! that your heart and mine might be as pure. And they may be if there is no known sin between God and us and our lives lie open to the moment by moment infilling of the blessed Holy Spirit.

26

The Believer's Part in Becoming Spirit-filled—
Yielding

IN THE TWO WONDROUS GIFTS of His Son and His Spirit, God has made perfect provision for a life of true spirituality. God's twofold gift to us was not a partial gift. When He gave Christ He gave all of Christ; when He gave the Holy Spirit He gave all of the Holy Spirit. *He withheld nothing from us.* Love not only gave its best but its all. When God gave Christ to us He gave Him in all the fullness of His perfect life and His perfected work. When God gave the Holy Spirit He gave Him to indwell, to infill and to empower. God is not a niggardly, grudging giver. In the glorified Christ through the fullness of the Holy Spirit He has given all that He has to give to make us spiritual. This is the perfection of grace, the acme even of divine giving.

God has made the provision but you must make the decision whether you will be Spirit-filled or not. There is a place in God's dealings with men beyond which He cannot go. He Himself set this boundary line in man's right to will. He sets the feast before you but He cannot compel you to eat. He opens the door into the abundant life but He cannot coerce you to enter. He places in the bank of God a deposit that makes you a spiritual multimillionaire but He cannot write your checks. God has done His part, now you must do yours.

The responsibility for fullness or lack of fullness is now in your hands. He will be limited in the giving of the fullness of His Spirit by one thing only—the room given to Him to fill. "You may have all the fulness you will make room for." To be Spirit-filled requires your active, hearty cooperation with God. You have a very clearly defined part in becoming spiritual.

YIELDING—THE BELIEVER'S PART IN BECOMING SPIRIT-FILLED

The basic principle in a spiritual life lies in its control. The life of the natural man is wholly in the control of "the old man"; the life of the carnal Christian is partially in the control of self. If one determines to become a Spirit-filled Christian the right to reign must be taken altogether from "the old man" and given into the hands of the Lord Jesus. What the Holy

Spirit wishes the believer to do and what He works to bring him to do is to cooperate with Him in this matter by refusing deliberately the further reign of self and by choosing voluntarily the sovereignty of Christ over his life, yielding to Him as Lord and Master.

> Romans 6:16, "Know ye not, that *to whom ye yield yourselves servants to obey,* his servants ye are to whom ye obey; whether of sin unto death, or of obedience unto righteousness?"

> Romans 6:19, "I speak after the manner of men because of the infirmity of your flesh: *for as ye have yielded your members servants to uncleanness* and to iniquity unto iniquity; even *so now yield your members servants to righteousness* unto holiness."

To yield the life unto God is the first step in a continuous walk in the Spirit. This step takes us by our own choice out of the realm of self-will into the realm of God's will. It takes us back to our God-intended, God-provided center. It gives us a base for all future growth in spiritual things. It furnishes us with new headquarters from which all our future life will be directed. In yielding to Christ we definitely align ourselves with the perfect will of God and choose it to be the rule of our lives in all things forever afterward. We adopt the language of Christ which, whether in the great crises of life such as those in the wilderness, in Gethsemane or on Calvary, or in the ordinary walk and work of daily life in the carpenter shop and the home, was invariably "Thy will be done." In yielding to the sovereignty of the Lord Jesus Christ we deliberately choose from that time on to do His will instead of our own in all things and for all time.

THE LIFE YIELDED—WHY?

There are two quite diverse motives that lead people to yield themselves wholly to the Lord. Some make the approach to a yielded life along the avenue of their own need. They hunger and thirst for more of Christ. They long to realize more perfectly their inheritance in Him.

> Ephesians 1:11, "*In whom also we have obtained an inheritance,* being predestinated according to the purpose of him who worketh all things after the counsel of his own will."

Others come into a yielded life over the pathway of Christ's claim. They recognize the loneliness and yearning of Christ's heart for more of them. They desire to have Him possess to the full His inheritance in them.

> Ephesians 1:18, "The eyes of your understanding being enlightened; *that ye may know* what is the hope of his calling, and *what is the riches of the glory of his inheritance in the saints.*"

Both our need of Him and His of us call for the yielding of our lives to Him. Every relationship which Christ bears to us is made ineffectual in an unyielded life. It is impossible for Christ to become all that He designs and desires to become apart from a wholly yielded life. He is handicapped and hindered in all He would do in and through us by our unwillingness to have it done; as Saviour He cannot save us from sin we insist upon retaining; as Head of the Body He cannot direct a stubborn member; as Lord He cannot reveal His will to one who does not want to know it or to obey it; as Life He cannot fill what is already filled with a totally different substance; as Sanctifier He cannot separate us wholly unto Himself when we prefer to live unto self and the world; as Captain He cannot use us to defeat the enemy when we ourselves already have allowed him to defeat us. Christ is checked at every turn in an unyielded life and rendered practically impotent. The realization and enjoyment of our precious inheritance in Him and of His purchased inheritance in us depend upon our unconditional yielding to Him.

There is a basic motive in the yielding of the life to Christ which when discovered is both convincing and compelling. To His glory may I share with you the way in which God graciously led me to this discovery and the revolutionary change it wrought in my relationship to the Lord Jesus.

Becoming a Christian when a girl I experienced deep and real joy in the consciousness of the forgiveness of sins and in the fellowship of Christ. I truly loved my Lord and longed to live so that others, especially members of my family, would see that He was indeed my Saviour. Though born again I knew nothing of a yielded life and consequently some of the old sins continued to manifest themselves in the same old way. One of the most outstanding was temper. Over and over again it was lost and hasty, unkind words said even to those nearest and dearest. Having what often accompanies a quick temper, a sensitive, affectionate heart, I would go apart after an outburst and cry as though my heart would break. Times without number the resolve was made never to lose my temper again and the attempt was made to conquer it by willpower, but all to no avail, and I continued in a life of constant defeat and miserable failure. Conscious of the evident hypocrisy in such a life, all the joy experienced in conversion left me. Truly loving the Lord I hated myself for the caricature of Him I was giving to others.

One day, thoroughly discouraged and disheartened by an overwhelming sense of defeat, I sought the quiet of my own room and shut myself in with the Lord, determined to stay until something happened. I told the Lord that either He must show me *what* a truly Christian life was and *how* to live it or I would renounce my profession of Christ and ask to have my name taken from the church roll. I was desperately in earnest and God always meets one who truly seeks Him. He graciously met me that day and answered both my questions.

Two verses from His Word He used to flood my soul with light. My prayer is that again He may use them to bring similar joy and peace to others discouraged and defeated.

> 1 Corinthians 6:19-20, "What? know ye not that your body is the temple of the Holy Ghost which is in you, which ye have of God, and *ye are not your own? For ye are bought with a price:* therefore glorify God in your body and in your spirit, which are God's."

Through three unforgetable invincible statements of truth God unveiled the essence of a yielded life and revealed its basic motive.

"What? *Know ye not that your body is the temple of the Holy Ghost?*" No, until that day I did not know that my body had any relationship whatsoever to my conversion neither did I know that the Holy Spirit had taken it to be His temple. That God laid claim to my body for His habitation and that the Holy Spirit *had already* made it His home was to me a startling revelation. Think for a moment what that means—God, the Holy One actually dwelling in your human body! Suppose some earthly king would send word that he wanted to spend just one day in your home. What a housecleaning would take place! How all the best and loveliest things would be taken out to use! What preparation would be made that everything would be exactly fitting and worthy of such an honored guest! But oh! what an unclean, unfit, unworthy place we often ask the King of kings and Lord of lords to live in, not for a day but for a lifetime! What an unholy, desecrated temple we offer to the Holy Spirit!

But I have given the Lord my soul, what need hath He of my body? was the question that came into my mind. I saw faintly that day but with growing clearness every day since why God asks for our bodies. Dare we say it—it is His need of a channel through which He may give to a world that knows Him not a revelation of who He is and of His yearning love for men. "The Word was made flesh and dwelt among us" and men saw and knew who the Father was by the presence of the Son on earth. Christ is now in heaven. But oh! is His presence not needed here on earth? Is He not needed in your city? In your church? In your school? In your office? In your social circle? In your home? And how is the glorified Christ to presence Himself here on earth? In what way will He reveal Himself to men now?

Christ has just two ways of making Himself known; one is through His Word. But countless thousands do not even possess a Bible, and countless millions could not read it if they did. The other way is through us in whom He dwells as the Life of our life. Oh! do you not see how He needs your body to be wholly His? Today He needs eyes, ears, lips, hands, feet, minds, hearts, wills and all that makes up a human personality for the manifestation of Himself on earth as truly as these things were needed when He dwelt as the incarnate Son in a human body. When Christ was upon earth it was not merely His teaching and preaching that won men to Him. It was His life, His personal presence, Himself. So today men need to see Christ; to feel His presence; to be brought face to face with Him. The Lord Jesus showed me that day that He wanted and needed my body with my entire human personality to indwell and to use as a medium of revealing Himself to others.

There was something wondrously beautiful in the thought that the Lord of glory could ever have need of me. I knew only too well how desperately I needed Him. Moment by moment I needed to draw all my life from Him as the branch lives in the life of the vine. But to think that He needed me! that there was fruit to be borne that could only be borne on a branch! that some life somewhere would need to see Christ in me! It was a marvelously convincing appeal, yet I am ashamed to record it even now so many years afterward, I hesitated to yield.

Was my life not my own? Was it not asking a great deal to turn it over to the absolute sovereignty of another? Should I relinquish *all* right to its possession and control? Was it safe to do so? Was it reasonable? Was it needful? Oh! the feasible, plausible arguments that self advanced to retain the kingship over my life!

All this reluctance was anticipated by the Lord and He was prepared to meet it. *"What? Know ye that ye are not your own?"* Like a sharp two-edged sword these words penetrated to my innermost being and lodged there. How they cut into shreds every argument advanced against such a wholesale yielding of myself to God! *"Know ye that ye are not your own?"* How they severed the undergirding beneath all my thinking concerning my rights in myself! *"Know ye that ye are not your own?"* How they brought to light the hitherto disguised hypocrisy of my profession as a Christian in saying that I belonged to Jesus Christ yet all the while retaining in my own hands the reins of government! *"Know ye that ye are not your own?"* How these words went straight to the very heart of the issue like an axe laid at the root of the tree—the enthronement of Jesus Christ as Lord over my life or the continued reign of self!

A flood of light entered my soul through that simple but imperative question of the Lord. I was convinced of the rightfulness of God's claim upon me but I was not yet constrained to yield to it. Oh! the incredible, unthinkable stubbornness to resist and refuse in the light of such clear conviction! Oh! the infinite, unwearying patience of the divine heart to continue to woo and to work in the face of such willfulness!

I was not only stubborn but fearful. If I let go and put myself wholly and unconditionally in His possession and control what might He not take from me? What might He not ask of me? I was in the same state of mind as was the college girl who said she would like to yield herself wholly to God but she was afraid He would take advantage of her. To put the truth very bluntly I would have been glad to have turned over to the Lord for His possession and control all the unpleasant, unmanageable, uncontrollable part of myself if He would have left the rest to me!

But God dealt very gently and tenderly with me, drawing me closer and closer to Himself by the cords of love. To master my will He had to melt my heart. "What? know ye that ye are not your own *for ye are bought with a price?*" Bought! *Not my own because bought!* Here again was something new. I had been thinking that by yielding to Christ I would be conferring the ownership of my life upon Him, that I would be making an outright gift to Him. But God showed me that day that *I already belonged to Christ* by the right of purchase and that Christ's claim to the undivided possession and control of my life was an absolutely legitimate one. Who could deny one the right to that which He had purchased?

Convinced again and still not constrained to yield. "Ye are not your own for ye are bought *with a price.*" Oh! *That price!* "Redeemed not with corruptible things, as silver and gold, but with the precious blood of Christ, as of a lamb without blemish and without spot." The precious blood of Christ the price paid for me! The life of the spotless, stainless, sinless Son of God laid down for my paltry, insignificant, sinful, selfish life! A Life given for a life!

> 2 Corinthians 5:15, "And that *he died* for all, *that they which live should not henceforth live unto themselves, but unto him* which died for them, and rose again."

A LIFE FOR A LIFE

"Oh, hands, outstretched upon the tree,
Nail-pierced by shameless cruelty!
Why, blessed Christ, had this to be?
A voice most loving said to me:
'Dear child, these hands of Mine were bruised
That thine in ministry be used
In loving service such as Mine;
My hands were given to purchase thine.'

"Oh, feet of Christ, so rent and torn!
How could such suffering be borne?
In life, so often spent and worn,
In death, must they be given to scorn?

'On mercy's errands thine may go,
A free, glad helpfulness to show;
It was for thee,' the Saviour said,
'My feet for thine so sadly bled.'

"Oh, head of Christ, with thorn-wrought crown!
In grief and agony bowed down;
Why didst Thy heavenly renown
Exchange for earthly jeer and frown?
'My child, beneath those thorns I bought
Thy intellect and all its thought;
The glory-crown was left for thee,
That thou mightst give thy mind to Me.'

"Oh, heart of Christ! Oh, wounded side!
Oh, Man of Sorrows, crucified!
Who in such anguish, sinless, died,
Hast Thou done aught for me beside?
'Ah, child of mine, my heart was riven
That thou mightst live and love in Heaven;
That all thy heart, thy life, might be
Surrendered joyfully to Me.' "

I had been saying "*Must* I give myself to Him?" But on that day kneeling in spirit at the foot of the cross of Christ I said from the depths of my heart "*May* I yield all that I am and have for time and for eternity to Him who gave all for me?"

And what was the basic motive in the yielding? It was the joyous response of love to love following the spiritual apprehension of the reasonableness and rightfulness of Christ's claim upon my life and the use He desired to make of it.

Then let us define yielding. Yielding is the definite, deliberate, voluntary transference of the undivided possession, control and use of the whole being, spirit, soul and body from self to Christ, to whom it rightfully belongs by creation and by purchase. In yielding to Christ we crown Him Lord of all in our lives. "Consecration does not confer ownership, it presumes it. It is not *in order to be His*, but *because we are His*, that we yield up our lives. It is *purchase* that gives *title; delivery* simply gives *possession*. The question is not, 'Do I belong to God?' but 'Have I yielded to God that which already belongs to Him?' " (J. H. McConkey, *The Surrendered Life*, p. 17).

In a city in north China there was a girls' school. The students grew in numbers which necessitated more buildings. Adjoining the school were just the buildings needed, the property of a Chinese family. After much bargaining a sale was effected. The papers were drawn up and the purchase price paid. In the autumn the school fully expected to open work in the new buildings. But they were unable to do so. Why not? *The Chinese family had not moved out.* Purchase gives title but only delivery gives possession.

Christ has the title deed to your life. The price was paid nearly two thousand years ago. It is His by the right of purchase. Have you moved out that He may move in and occupy what He already possesses?

Christ has the right to exempt you from His property; He *is* Lord and He has the right to command you to yield. But Christ's way is to constrain by love rather than to conquer by force. So He beseeches us by the innumerable mercies of God of which we are daily the recipients to yield ourselves to Him.

> Romans 12:1, "*I beseech you* therefore, brethren, *by the mercies of God, that ye present your bodies* a living sacrifice, holy, acceptable unto God, *which is your reasonable service.*"

Yielding is the glad, joyous, willing response of love to love. "We love him because he first loved us." Bought with a price, "therefore" we gladly glorify Him in our body and spirit, which are His. "I beseech you"—I have given My life in death for you, will you not give yours in life for Me? True yielding is the utter abandonment of love. It is the call of the Bridegroom "Rise up, my love, my fair one, and come away," to which the Bride joyfully responds, "I am my beloved's and his desire is toward me."

Oh! my friend, does this not take the "must" out of surrender for you? Does it not answer the question "Is it safe?" Have you only thought of yielding in the light of what you would have to give up? To yield does involve a giving up but it means giving up what really is not yours; it means giving up something only to get something of infinitely greater worth; yes, it means giving up something that He needs for His use to the One we love best; more than all it means giving up something to the One who loves us with a love so great that He died for us and now waits to bestow upon us all the exhaustless treasures that are ours in Him. Can we not trust "the Man who died for us"?

> Romans 8:32, "He that spared not his own Son, but delivered him up for us all, *how shall he not with him also freely give us all things?*"

> 1 Corinthians 3:21-23, "Therefore let no man glory in men. *For all things are yours;* whether Paul or Apollos, or Cephas, or the world, or life, or death, or things present, or things to come; *all are yours; and ye are Christ's;* and Christ is God's."

"Surrender taken alone is a plunge into a cold void. When it is a surrender to the Son of God who loved me and gave Himself for me it is the bright home coming of the soul to the seat and sphere of life and power."

THE LIFE YIELDED—WHAT?

We have seen what yielding is—the transference of the ownership and control of the life from self to Christ. But self will relinquish nothing except under compulsion. So it is necessary to understand at the outset just what the full measurement of a yielded life is.

May we clear the atmosphere by saying what yielding is not? It is not mere subscription to a creed; nor is it a giving of oneself to a certain kind or field of service; nor is it merely stripping the life of certain evil or questionable practices. How many a person has said, "I am afraid to yield myself wholly to the Lord for I know He will make me believe something I can't believe, or will ask me to go somewhere that I do not want to go, or will rob me of something that I want to keep." To such, yielding is altogether a negative thing while in reality it is essentially positive. God wants *us*. It is the whole of ourselves that He asks us to yield to Him that our whole life may be lived unto the will of God.

> Romans 6:13, "Neither yield ye your members as instruments of unrighteousness unto sin: *but yield yourselves unto God,* as those that are alive from the dead, and your members as instruments of righteousness unto God."
>
> 2 Corinthians 8:5, "And this they did, not as we hoped, but *first gave their own selves to the Lord,* and unto us by the will of God."
>
> 1 Peter 4:2, "That he no longer should live the rest of his time in the flesh to the lusts of men, but *to the will of God.*"

Then God specifies the measurement a bit more explicitly lest we be satisfied merely with "the saving of our soul" or "the giving of our heart to the Lord." It is the easiest thing in the world to use the phraseology of consecration while missing the reality of it. It is possible to deceive ourselves by surrendering the invisible and intangible thing while holding on to the visible and tangible. So God asks for the body as well as for the spirit and soul. Read again Romans 12:1.

God leaves no loophole in this matter of yielding. He knows full well how the beauty of a life may be marred and its testimony nullified by the unyieldedness of even one member of the body. Who can read the epistle of James and not know that many a life fails of complete surrender through an unyielded tongue? What possibilities for covetousness through an unyielded eye? What paths of wickedness and worldliness are open before unyielded feet? What a catchall for gossip, slander and idle talk, is an unyielded ear! What a loss to God in His service is an unyielded voice! God specifies the measurement of surrender and it reaches out to include every member of your body. *"Yield your members* as instruments of righteousness unto God."

"Yourselves"
"Your bodies"
"Your members"

It is all-inclusive. Nothing is omitted and nothing is exempt. God has sanctified our whole personality. He has set it all apart as His own personal possession and for His own use. Our consecration is the counterpart of God's sanctification. God has taken us to be His own: He has said, "Thou art mine." We yield ourselves as those belonging unto Him and sanctify Christ, as Lord, in our hearts and say, "Lord, I am Thine, what wilt Thou have me to do?"

> 1 Thessalonians 5:23, "And *the very God of peace sanctify you wholly; and I pray God your whole spirit and soul and body be preserved blameless* unto the coming of our Lord Jesus Christ."
>
> 1 Peter 3:15, R. V., "But *sanctify in your hearts Christ as Lord.*"

The measure of our yielding is the measure of our human life. It includes everything *inside*, spirit, mind, heart, will, affections. It includes everything *outside*, home, children, possessions, occupation. It includes everything *allied*, friendships, time, money, pleasures, life plans.

It includes our past, present and future. No matter what the past has held of sin, sorrow or self it is all handed over to Christ in a once-and-for-all committal. But some can surrender the past who find it difficult to yield the present to Christ's control. There is the desire to reserve a bit of ground. Others can surrender the past and present because driven to it by disheartenment or desperation but they are fearful to put the future wholly into His keeping. How do they know that God can be trusted to be faithful or that they desire to live under His absolute sway for all time?

When giving a message on the yielded life at a conference I noticed the anxious, troubled face of a woman on the front seat. I said, "You are able to trust July to God but fearful to put September into His keeping." Her face lighted up with a smile which was in truth an acknowledgment of being caught in the very act of worry. After the meeting she said, "That remark about committing September to the Lord hit me. I could be very happy here now but I must have an operation in September and I have only half enjoyed this beautiful place because I am worrying over September!"

Yielding includes our worst and our best. Some find it very difficult to believe that God can accept or want them because there is so much of "the worst" that persists in their lives. But "Him that cometh to me I will in no wise cast out" is an invitation extended to the sinning saint as truly as to the sinner. Grace abounds from the beginning clear through to the end of our lives. So no matter how often we have repeated the same sin if we come yielding ourselves unconditionally to Him He waits to receive us, and the blood of Jesus Christ is equal to any demand made upon it for cleansing.

Others find no difficulty in bringing to God the dregs of sin in their unyielded lives but find it extremely hard to yield their best to Him. In fact they see no necessity to do so. Here is someone with very excellent judgment. The superior quality of it is recognized by the possessor who almost believes in his infallibility on all matters. The result is a domineering, overbearing person with whom it is exceedingly difficult for others to work. This point was mentioned once before a group of Christian workers. Afterward a missionary said, "You talked about me this morning! I am that person with the good judgment and I am sure I have made things difficult for my fellow missionaries. I see now that even my good judgment must be yielded to the Lord."

Here is another who is very efficient and she holds the same opinion of herself that a young businesswoman held who said, "Why do I need to ask the Lord how to do something when, if I use my own good sense, I know as well as He how to do it?" That is putting it very crudely but is not our failure often due to a similar self-trust?

Perhaps here is one with a charming personality who is extremely popular and easily draws a crowd about her. She can see the need of some homely, unattractive person yielding herself to the Lord to be made inwardly beautiful. But why should she do so? Does she not attract people already? Oh! but to whom? To herself or to her Lord? Our best can hinder the revelation of Christ through us as truly as our worst.

In taking the measure of our surrender to the Lord Jesus it should be a settled matter that there can be no reservations. We cannot set aside any part of our lives and earmark it "reserved." If Christ is to be Lord, He must be Lord of all. We must let Christ begin at the center and go to the circumference of our lives, laying hold of all in His path and bringing it under His dominion.

It should also be understood that there can be no substitutes offered to the Lord. We cannot buy God off with money or bribe Him to accept our time, talents or service in lieu of ourselves. Having once offered ourselves in a glad, willing yielding to the Lord, all that we have in the way of natural endowment, acquired skill or bestowed wealth will accompany such surrender but can never be accepted by God as a substitute for it. God wants first of all "not yours" but "you."

Let it be understood also that we cannot bring just the troublesome, unmanageable parts of our lives to God, asking Him for spiritual repairs while we withhold the will, the heart, the mind. How much we are like the man who took the hands of his clock to the jeweler and asked him to regulate them as they did not keep time. "Bring me the whole clock," said the jeweler, "the cause of the inaccuracy is not in the hands." "No!" said the owner, "you will take it all to pieces and it will cost me a lot! It is the hands that go wrong!" The measure of our yielding is the measure of our life; the refusal to yield any part of it, however small or insignificant it may seem to us, is an act of rebellion and will make impossible the fullness of the Holy Spirit in our lives. These lines we would do well to repeat frequently:

"Have Thine own way, Lord,
    Have Thine own way;
Thou art the Potter,
    I am the clay.

Make me and mould me
    After Thy will,
While I am waiting
    Silent and still."

THE LIFE YIELDED—HOW?

Perhaps some reader has been brought to say, Lord, I will yield to Thee. I see *why* I should yield, and *what* but now tell me *how.* Because salvation from beginning to end is through God's pure grace, He always takes the initiative in bringing us into a fuller experience of our inheritance in Christ. So the Lord Jesus stands outside every unyielded part of your life and knocks and waits for your response. He wishes to come in and fellowship with you in every part of your spiritual life but in between the knocking and the entering something must take place, for Christ never forces entrance. If He enters, the door must be opened.

> Revelation 3:20, "Behold, I stand at the door, and knock: *if any man hear my voice, and open the door,* I will come in to him, and will sup with him, and he with me."

Yielding to Christ is a *definite* act. It is not a mere expression of a pious desire but it is the declaration of a purposeful determination. It is not an often-repeated wish but it is a decisive act of the will. To yield is to acknowledge Christ's claim to the perfect possession, complete control and unhindered use of one's whole being and then to act upon such an acknowledgment by a definite surrender of it to Him. Desire becomes decision and decision crystallizes into action.

In *A Memorial of a True Life* by Dr. R. E. Speer is recorded such a definite act of surrender by Hugh Beaver, a young man of rare spirituality whose life was very marvelously used among college students in a few brief years of service before God called him Home.

"Kutztown, Pa., Nov. 16, 1895.

" 'Just as I am,—Thy love unknown
Has broken every barrier down;
Now to be Thine, yea, Thine alone
O Lamb of God, I come, I come.'

This 16th day of November 1895, I, Hugh Beaver, do of my own free
will give myself, all that I am and have, entirely, unreservedly, unquali-
fiedly to Him, whom having not seen I love, on whom, though now I see
Him not, I believe. Bought with a price, I give myself to Him who at the
cost of His own blood purchased me. Now committing myself to Him
who is able to guard me from stumbling and to set me before the presence
of His glory without blemish in exceeding joy, I trust myself to Him for
all things, to be used as He shall see fit where He shall see fit. Sealed by
the Holy Spirit, filled with the peace of God that passeth understanding,
to Him be all glory, world without end. Amen.
    Phil. 4:19.

HUGH BEAVER."

Have you by such a definite decisive act of the will yielded yourself, all
that you are, and all that you have, to the Lord Jesus? If not, will you not
close this book for a moment and do it now?

Yielding to Christ is a *voluntary* act. We do not yield because we have
to but because we want to. It is not a matter of coercion but of consecration. The Lord Jesus stands outside the door of that unyielded portion
of your life and knocks but He will not force an entrance. It would mean
very little indeed to be allowed to enter if He did not find fellowship and
comradeship with the one within. It is love that desires to enter but unless love is met by love the entrance would bring heartache rather than
joy. "What fragrance is to the rose, colour to the sunset sky, spotlessness to
the falling snow, voluntariness is to the surrender of the life." Of His own
free will he joyously, gladly laid down His life for us. With a smile and a
song He wants us to open the door to Him.

Yielding to Christ is a *final* act. Such a yielding of the life as we have
been considering is irreversible; it need not be repeated. If it has been
done honestly it is for time and eternity. Great perplexity of heart has
come to countless souls over this matter of repeated surrender so let us be
clear as to what has been done and then we shall see how irrevocable the
act has been.

Through yielding to Christ we have acknowledged that we are not our
own and we have transferred the ownership of our life from self to Christ.
Henceforth the life is no longer ours. A resurrender implies that the trans-
fer had not been honestly made.

Of course one does not know all that is involved in this initial act of surrender or all that it will require of one. When you begin to live only and wholly for God there will be constant revelations of portions of the life still virtually held by self as its own possession. The heart will be made conscious of unwillingness to relinquish certain rights and privileges so long enjoyed. What, then, must one do as these revelations come? Does one need to make a surrender of the life over again? No, that was done once and for all. Simply say, "Lord, this thing which I am still claiming and holding as my own was *part* of that *whole* which I yielded to Thee. It, too, belonged in that initial surrender. I thank Thee for Thy faithfulness in showing me that it is unyielded and just now I give it into Thy possession and place it under Thy control."

There is an *initial act* of yielding that is to be followed by a *continuous attitude* so that as we come to know God and His will better through daily communion we yield instantly to Him any unyielded place or thing. Some-,one has tersely said, "Surrender is a crisis that develops into a process."

May I use a very homely illustration? A man and woman through mutual faith and love yield themselves to each other in marriage. Neither of them knows then all that is involved in this surrender to each other. The wife knew that her time must be given to making the home but she had not realized how little opportunity would be left for the things she had formerly done. She rebels and uses time for things which necessitates neglect of home duties. Misunderstanding and estrangement follow. Or the husband knew that money would be required to care for his wife and supply the needs of the home but he did not know what extravagant tastes she had or what a poor manager she was. So he has to use money he wished to spend on his business or his own pleasure. He rebels and trouble ensues. What do this husband and wife do? Do they remarry each time such a misunderstanding or disagreement comes? Even the idea is absurd. If they are sensible and truly love each other they will acknowledge that there was more in the marriage vows than they realized at the time; each will recognize that all, not a part, was given in the mutual surrender and each will be willing to yield unselfishly and gladly to whatever makes for mutual interest and welfare. Happy and harmonious married life demands not only an initial act of yielding but a continuous attitude of yielding.

We who have loved the Lord and believed in Him are united to Him. "Ye also are become dead to the law, by the body of Christ, *that ye should be married to another,* even to him who is raised from the dead." But no one of us ever knew when he entered into oneness with Christ all that would be involved in such a union. But as we live with Him we learn more of His desires, His will, His purposes, His plans, and we see many things in our lives contrary to these. This does not, however, necessitate another surrender but only as instantaneous yielding of the thing to Him.

From the human standpoint the first condition for a life lived on the highest plane is the definite, voluntary, final yielding of the life to Christ as Lord. The primary requirement for the fullness of the Holy Spirit has been met. "When we surrender our *sins* and believe *we receive* the Holy Spirit; when we surrender our *lives* and believe, we are *filled* with the Holy Spirit. The *receiving* of the Spirit is God's answer to *repentance* and faith; the *fulness* of the Spirit is God's answer to *surrender* and faith. At *conversion* the Spirit enters; at *surrender* the Spirit, *already entered,* takes *full possession.* The supreme human condition of the fulness of the Spirit is a life wholly surrendered to God to do His will" (J. H. McConkey, *The Threefold Secret of the Holy Spirit,* p. 43).

I once visited a college to conduct evangelistic meetings. I was entertained in a home in which the guest room was over the kitchen and was approached by an outside stairway. Very soon my trunk arrived. I was alone in the house. As it was raining very hard, I decided to have the trunk put into the downstairs. I started to open one door but could not— it was locked. I went to another door as there were three in a row, and put my hand on the knob to open it but could not—it too was locked. I tried the third door but with no better success—it also was locked.

Suddenly seized with a strange sense of aloneness I rushed upstairs to the little back-room guest chamber—the only place in the house I was expected to use. To be a bit more conscious of the warm, living, loving presence of my Christ I knelt by the bedside to pray. Instantly He spoke to me, saying, "Do you not know that is the way thousands of people treat Me? They invite Me into their lives and then they put Me away in a little back guest chamber and there they expect Me to stay. But I long to enter into every room of their lives and share all their experiences."

Oh! my friends, where have *you* put the Lord Jesus Christ in your life? Have *you* any locked doors? Have you put Him away in some little hidden corner and given Him no freedom in your life?   Has He longed to get into the social hall of your life where all your pleasures are? Has He put His nail-pierced hand on the door, longing to enter, but could not—for it is locked from the inside? Has He wanted to enter into the room where your business was carried on and share in both its projects and profits? Has He been denied entrance because shady, crooked practices went on there which His all-seeing eye would detect? Has He longed to enter into the room where life plans were being shaped and to help in the fashioning of them? And He tried the door but entrance was denied—locked from the inside? And has He who longs to fill and to bless you gone back to His little upstairs back room with a grieved and sorrowful heart?

I went from that college town to another. My hostess there was a dear widow. Her home was very humble. We ate in the kitchen but oh! such hospitality I have seldom enjoyed. Every good thing which her frugal means would permit her to provide she had for me. The first day she said to me, "Miss Paxson, my home is very humble but while you are here it is all yours. Go where you want to and do just what you want to—just make yourself at home." And I, who traveled constantly, oh! how I spread out over that whole house and made it mine the few days I was there!

Oh! friends, is the Lord Jesus living within you? Have you ever said to Him, "Lord Jesus, I have only a very simple life to offer you as a dwelling place but while you are here *it is all yours.* Go where you want to, do what you want to—*just make yourself at home!*" He waits for just such an invitation. How quickly He will accept it when once honestly offered and how He will spread out over the whole life—truly making Himself at home. If you have not unlocked all the doors from the inside and given Him a gracious and glad invitation to enter, will you do so today? (See Diagram 12.)

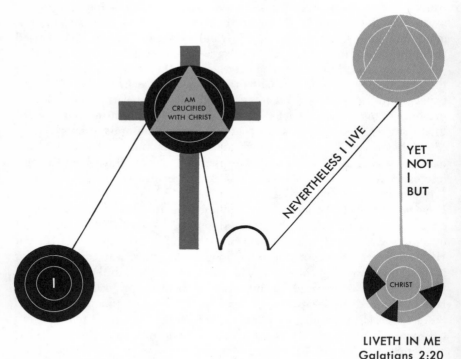

Diagram 12: The Unyielded Life

"I believe on the name of the
    Son of God,
Therefore I am in Him:
Having redemption through His blood
And life through His Spirit.
And He is in me, and all fulness is in Him.
    To Him I belong
    By purchase: conquest and self-surrender.
    To me He belongs for all my hourly need.
    There is no cloud between my Lord and me.
There is no difficulty inward or outward, that
    He is not ready to meet in me to-day.
    The Lord is my keeper."

27

The Believer's Part in Becoming Spirit-filled—
Faith

IT MAY BE SOME READER is saying "As far as I know I have yielded my life unconditionally to Christ yet I have not the life more abundant which He came to bring. There are still the evident marks of the carnal Christian. Is it possible for one to be yielded and still not be filled with the Holy Spirit?" The emptied life must be filled and waits for faith to claim the fullness.

S. D. Gordon tells of a little girl who was praying and who said, "Jesus, I hear you knocking at the door of my heart. Come in Jesus!" Then rising from her knees she said, "He's in!" Surrender, kneeling at the foot of the cross, says, "Lord, I am not my own; I yield myself unto Thee; I present my body a living sacrifice." Faith, looking up to the ascended Lord at the Father's right hand, says, "Christ liveth in me; to me to live is Christ." Surrender says, "Lord, what wilt Thou have me to do? Faith says, "I can do all things through Christ which strengtheneth me." Surrender opens the door; faith believes that Christ enters, fills, abides. You may have crowned Him Lord and yet not have appropriated Him as Life. "And they chose Stephen, a man full of faith and of the Holy Ghost." The spiritual man is one full of faith.

FAITH IS THE COMPLEMENT OF GRACE

Did you ever see a perfect rainbow? Looking out over the ocean I once saw distinctly both ends of a rainbow coming up out of the water, as it were, and forming an unbroken arch. Through this beautiful symbol the Holy Spirit interpreted to me a passage of Scripture which revealed the place of faith in the Christian's life in a new and telling way.

Ye are saved
Ephesians 2:8.

By grace   Through faith
"And that not of yourselves: it is the gift of God."

342

God's arch of salvation is all of grace and it is all of faith. From the God-ward side it is all of grace; from the manward side it is all of faith. God's grace is always perfect and its work is clear and distinct. But oh! how im-perfect is man's faith. Grace has provided in Christ Jesus all that is needed for man's salvation even unto a life of habitual spirituality. But such a life cannot become experiential until faith appropriates in full the provision of God's grace in Christ. Faith is the complement of grace.

Romans 4:16, *"Therefore it is of faith, that it might be by grace."*

With no exception everything in the Christian's life is a gift. Grace gives and faith takes. "Faith is man's one activity." Faith must reach up and lay hold upon all that grace has sent down and bestowed in Christ. Grace provides: faith possesses.

This truth stands out crystal clear in the history of the children of Israel. As an outright gift the land of Canaan with its manifold accom-panying blessings had been bestowed upon them. It *was* theirs through promise years before they ever saw it. God constantly spoke of it as theirs. Yet it was not to be actually in their possession until the soles of their feet trod upon it. Faith must enter in and possess the gift already bestowed in promise.

Joshua 1:2-3, "Moses my servant is dead; now therefore *arise, go over this Jordan,* thou, and all this people, *unto the land which I do give to them,* even to the children of Israel.

Every place that the sole of *your foot shall tread upon,* that *have I given unto you, as I said* unto Moses."

Joshua 1:11, "Pass through the host, and command the people, saying, Prepare you victuals; for within three days ye shall pass over this Jordan, *to go in to possess the land,* which the LORD your *God giveth you to possess it."*

Furthermore the children of Israel might have entered this land of prom-ise forty years earlier. God led them up to the very borderline of this rich, fertile, beautiful country flowing with milk and honey and laden with fruits. But they turned away *through unbelief,* suffered forty years of weary wanderings, and died in the wilderness. Only the two men of faith, Caleb and Joshua, possessed their inheritance.

Hebrews 3:17-19, "But with whom was he grieved forty years? was it not with them that had sinned, whose carcases fell in the wilderness? And to whom sware he that they should not enter into his rest, but *to them that believed not? So we see that they could not enter in because of unbelief."*

My Christian friend, everything you need for life on the highest plane has been given you in Christ. God has bestowed upon you also the Holy Spirit who already indwells you and whose chief task is to make you spiritual. Life on the highest plane is already yours. God hath given you every spiritual blessing in Christ. But this life with all its accompanying blessings can only be actualized through faith. Your faith must make experiential what grace has made possible.

> Ephesians 1:3, R. V., "Blessed be the God and Father of our Lord Jesus Christ, *who hath blessed us with every spiritual blessing* in the heavenly places in Christ."

> Matthew 9:28-30, "And when he was come into the house, the blind men came to him: and Jesus saith unto them, *Believe ye that I am able to do this?* They said unto him, *Yea, Lord.*
> Then touched he their eyes, saying, *According to your faith be it unto you.* And their eyes were opened."

Perhaps through hunger and thirst or through the remembrance of God's gracious promises or through sheer desperation because of your wilderness wanderings you have come up to the borderline of the promised land again and again. It may even be that you have essayed to go to a Keswick or to a Victorious Life Conference to spy out the land, to see if the life was all it promised to be, above all to see "if it works." In the lives of some you met or to whom you listened who are yielded, full-of-faith ones you have seen marvelous clusters of the fruit of the Spirit, "love, joy, peace, longsuffering, gentleness, goodness, faith, meekness, self-control." Yes, you are convinced the life is all that the Bible purports it to be and you have seen it "work" but—but—but *there are giants in the land.* The world, the flesh and the devil loomed large before you and you said, "Greater is he that is in the world than He that is in me." Through unbelief you turned back again into the weariness, the restlessness and the powerlessness of a carnal life.

Dear friend, does this message find you there today, grieving God, rejoicing Satan and robbing yourself? Then it comes as God's own command to you, "Arise, go over this Jordan; go in to possess the land, which the Lord your God giveth you to possess it." Cease grieving your God: possess your possessions in Christ through faith.

Whether one is young or old in the Christian life there is but one way in which our spiritual possessions are actualized—by faith. Faith opens the Christian life to us: faith accompanies us the entire length of life's journey, and faith at last leads us into the land where we see Him as He is and there faith gives place to sight.

> Colossians 2:5-6, "For though I be absent in the flesh, yet am I with you in the spirit, joying and beholding your order, and the stedfastness of

your faith in Christ. As ye have therefore received Christ Jesus the Lord, *so walk ye in him.*"

Colossians 1:23, "*If ye continue in the faith grounded and settled,* and be not moved away from the hope of the gospel, which ye have heard, and which was preached to every creature which is under heaven; whereof I Paul am made a minister."

Faith opens the door to every blessing that is ours in Christ.

2 Timothy 3:15, "And that from a child thou hast known the holy scriptures, which are able to make thee wise unto *salvation through faith which is in Christ Jesus.*"

We have *access* by faith.

Romans 5:2, "By whom also we have *access by faith* into this grace wherein we stand, and rejoice in hope of the glory of God."

We have *sonship* by faith.

Galatians 3:26, "For ye are all *the children of God by faith in Christ Jesus.*"

We have *righteousness* by faith.

Philippians 3:9, "And be found in him, not having mine own righteousness, which is of the law, *but that which is through faith of Christ, the righteousness which is of God by faith.*"

We have *forgiveness of sins* and *sanctification* by faith.

Acts 26:18, "To open their eyes, and to turn them from darkness to light, and from the power of Satan unto God, *that they may receive forgiveness of sins,* and *inheritance among them which are sanctified by faith that is in me.*"

We have *cleansing* by faith.

Acts 15:9, "And put no difference between us and them, *purifying their hearts by faith.*"

We have *Christ's indwelling* by faith.

Ephesians 3:17, "That *Christ may dwell in your heart by faith.*"

We *receive the Holy Spirit* by faith.

Galatians 3:2, "This only would I learn of you, *Received ye the Spirit* by the works of the law, or *by the hearing of faith?*"

We *inherit the promises* by faith.

Hebrews 6:12, "That ye be not slothful, but followers of *them who through faith* and patience *inherit the promises.*"

We have *victory over the world* by faith.

1 John 5:4, "For whatsoever is born of God overcometh the world: and *this is the victory that overcometh the world, even our faith.*"

We have *victory over the evil one* by faith.

Ephesians 6:16, R. V., "Withal *taking up the shield of faith,* wherewith ye shall be able *to quench all the fiery darts of the evil one.*"

We have *victory over circumstances and difficulties* by faith.

Hebrews 11:33-34, "Who *through faith* subdued kingdoms, wrought righteousness, *obtained promises, stopped the mouths of lions.*
Quenched the violence of fire, escaped the edge of the sword, out of weakness were made strong, waxed valiant in fight, turned to flight the armies of the aliens."

We are *kept* through faith.

1 Peter 1:5, "*Who are kept by the power of God through faith* unto salvation ready to be revealed in the last time."

Matthew 21:21-22, "Jesus answered and said unto them, Verily I say unto you, *If ye have faith,* and doubt not, ye shall not only do this which is done to the fig tree, but also if ye shall say unto this mountain, Be thou removed, and be thou cast into the sea; it shall be done. And all things, *whatsoever ye shall ask in prayer, believing,* ye shall receive."

We have *power* through faith.

Matthew 17:19-20, "Then came the disciples to Jesus apart, and said, Why could not we cast him out? And Jesus said unto them, *Because of your unbelief:* for verily I say unto you, *If ye have faith as a grain of mustard seed, ye* shall say unto this mountain, Remove hence to yonder place; and it shall remove; and *nothing shall be impossible unto you.*"

Two things are absolutely essential to a harmonious relationship with God, we must believe that *God is* and that *God does.* Apart from these two fundamental convictions there is no salvation and no blessing.

Hebrews 11:6, "But *without faith it is impossible to please him:* for he that cometh to God must believe that he is, and that he is the rewarder of them that diligently seek him."

Some of Christ's severest rebukes were to unbelief in His disciples. To have His presence, His words, His works fail to inspire faith grieved the Lord Jesus exceedingly. Even though the tempest raged and the waves dashed high and He were asleep—yet *He* was there and why should they fear? Fear and faith are incompatible.

> Matthew 8:26, "And he saith unto them, *Why are ye fearful, O ye of little faith?* Then he arose, and rebuked the winds and the sea; and there was a great calm."

Again even though the wind were boisterous and though Peter did begin to sink yet the Lord of the sea had *said* "Come." The power of His protection accompanied the command, then why should Peter doubt? Doubt and faith are irreconcilable.

> Matthew 14:31, "And immediately Jesus stretched forth his hand, and caught him, and said unto him, *O thou of little faith, wherefore didst thou doubt?*"

The disciples misunderstood the Master's warning concerning the leaven of the Pharisees and of the Sadducees. But there was a far deeper misapprehension of the Lord Jesus Himself in their hearts. They had forgotten to take bread when they went to the other side of the lake and they were very evidently worrying over where and how they would get their next meal. So when He spoke to them of the leaven of the Pharisees they said, "He sees our predicament that we have no bread." Oh! what if they had forgotten their bread? Did they not have with them the One who had satisfied the hunger of five thousand men, besides women and children, with five loaves and two fishes, and had twelve baskets to spare? And had they not just come from seeing Him feed more than four thousand people with seven loaves and a few fishes with seven baskets left over? Would He not be equal to furnishing an evening meal for the twelve of them if need be? Worry and faith cannot dwell together.

> Matthew 16:8-9, "Which when Jesus perceived, he said unto them, *O ye of little faith, why reason ye among yourselves, because ye have brought no bread?* Do ye not yet understand, neither remember the five loaves of the five thousand, and how many baskets ye took up? Neither the seven loaves of the four thousand, and how many baskets ye took up?"

Oh! how we crowd Him out of our lives by that triumvirate of evil—fear, doubt and worry! Failing health, financial losses, waywardness of children, overwhelming burdens, tempests of affliction and adversity, storms of passion from within or of persecution from without—and we become insensible to His presence, we doubt His Word and we forget His works.

A young woman came to me one day to unburden her heart. Spirit and body were both wearied to the point of utter exhaustion. Her face was inexpressibly worn and haggard; furrows of care had left their tracks in her

forehead. Life was hard almost beyond the point of endurance because
of burdens, cares, worries and work. A tempest was raging in her own soul,
her ship was covered with waves and Christ seemed asleep. But He heard
her cry of distress and responded. He commanded the waves of worry to
cease saying, "In nothing be anxious," and besought the calm of peace to
enter her soul through praise, "In everything give thanks."

> Habakkuk 3:17-18, "Although the fig tree shall not blossom, neither shall
> fruit be in the vines; the labour of the olive shall fail, and the fields shall
> yield no meat; the flock shall be cut off from the fold, and there shall be
> no herd in the stalls; *yet I will rejoice in the Lord, I will joy in the God
> of my salvation.*"

Some of Christ's sweetest words of commendation were called forth by
faith in Him and strange to say they were usually spoken to those who
had had the opportunity to know Him the least. A centurion came in person to appeal to the Lord to heal his servant. Christ quickly responded
with a promise to go to him. But faith answered, "Lord, *speak the word
only* and my servant shall be healed." Oh! the joy such faith brought to
Jesus' heart, and the commendation came from His lips, "Verily I say unto
you, I have not found so great faith, no, not in Israel."

There is no record in God's Word and no instance in human experience
where grace and love have failed to respond to faith and trust. God would
be untrue to the very essence of His nature which is love and to the very
heart of His work which is grace if He failed even once to respond to real
faith. Whoever will come to Jesus Christ saying, "If Thou wilt, Thou
canst," will surely hear Him say, "I will."

In the new sphere in Christ into which the believer enters the very atmosphere is grace. To carry the life-giving and life-sustaining qualities of
that atmosphere into the inner life the Christian need only use the lungs
of faith. As a newborn babe begins life in its new sphere by breathing
the air that is all about it as a free gift and as it lives and grows by continued respirations, so the newborn child of God begins life in Christ by
taking Him as God's gift of grace by faith and he "grows up into Christ in
all things" by the continued appropriation of Him through faith. Faith and
nothing but faith avails for us to receive the gifts and graces of our ascended Lord.

> Galatians 5:6, "For *in Jesus Christ neither circumcision availeth any thing,
> nor uncircumcision; but faith* which worketh by love."

In Christ we stand by faith; we walk by faith; we live by faith.

> 2 Corinthians 1:24, "Not for that we have dominion over your faith, but
> are helpers of your joy: for *by faith ye stand.*"

2 Corinthians 5:7, "For *we walk by faith,* not by sight."

Hebrews 10:38, "Now *the just shall live by faith:* but if any man draw back, my soul shall have no pleasure in him."

Perhaps the thought of a life of such complete and continuous faith appalls us and we doubt its possibility. Yet such faith is the simplest thing in the world. Its very simplicity is its chief difficulty to most people. Faith is looking unto Jesus Christ and taking Him at His Word. Faith in itself has no power whatsoever to save or to keep us: it merely links us to the Christ who has that power. Just as grace had a definite method in giving so faith has a definite method in receiving. Let us study some of the operations of faith.

FAITH RESTS ON GOD'S FOUNDATION

The whole superstructure of spiritual experience is built upon a solid and unmovable foundation because it is built upon Jesus Christ Himself.

1 Corinthians 3:11, "For other *foundation* can no man lay than that is laid, *which is Jesus Christ.*"

1 Peter 2:6, "Wherefore also it is contained in the scripture, Behold, I lay in Sion a chief corner stone, elect, precious: and *he that believeth on him shall not be confounded.*"

Christ Jesus Himself is "the way, the truth, and the life." Christ crucified, risen, ascended and exalted is God's foundation. Faith is the cable that connects and transmits the life of the ascended Lord in heaven to the believer on earth.

Can we not rest our faith on such a foundation? Is there any danger of its disintegrating? In His earthly life were all the forces of Satan ever able to overcome Him? From the cross did He not assure us that full salvation had been wrought out for us and that the work was finished? Did not His resurrection prove His victory over every foe? Is He not living today in countless lives as Conqueror, as Life? Upon the triumphant, omnipotent, living, present Christ our faith rests.

Some have made shipwreck of faith because they have built upon the sand of human opinion and speculation rather than upon the rock foundation of God's revealed truth. They have believed certain things *about* Christ but they have not believed *on* Christ Himself. Christ does not act as a guidepost to point out a way of salvation. He Himself is the Way. Christ does not teach principles of truth by which an unregenerate life may be guided and governed from without but Himself is the Truth to be lived out from within. Christ does not show us "a way of life" but He Himself enters to become the Life of our life. God's foundation for a spiritual life is the glorious Person and the gracious work of His crucified, risen, ascended, exalted Son and whosoever rests full-length upon Him for salvation and sanctification will surely become spiritual.

> "On Christ the solid rock I stand;
> All other ground is sinking sand."

Again we may fall into unbelief, doubt and disappointment because we have pinned our faith to a blessing and the blessing is lost; or to an experience and the experience vanishes; or to a person and the person fails. But true faith rests not upon a blessing, however great; or upon an experience, however deep; but upon Him through whom they came; nor does it rest upon any human exponent of victory, however sincere, but upon the Victor. "He that believeth on him shall not be confounded."

FAITH IS ROOTED IN GOD'S GREAT FACTS

Walking along a wooded path in the mountains of Switzerland I saw an interesting tree. On a steep slope was a tall, stately pine tree with a huge boulder lodged right underneath it lifting the main trunk five or six feet from the ground. The tree was fairly sitting on top of this rock yet it shot straight upwards fifty feet or more. Even the winter blasts had not deflected it an iota. How could such a position be maintained with such a handicap? The secret was not hidden from our view. The roots of the tree had spread themselves over that rock and had gone down, deep, deep into the rich earth around so that even the boulder lodged at its very heart could not overturn or overwhelm it.

What a lesson it spoke! What a symbol it was! Afflictions, adversities, sufferings, sorrows, temptations, trials, doubts, disappointments roll in upon us during our pilgrim journey and lodge at the very heart of us. How then can we go on in peace, patience, power, joy and victory? Are such things not enough to overwhelm one? No, not if faith spreads itself out over them and roots itself in the great facts of God. What are some of these eternal facts which furnish faith rich soil in which to root itself? First of all:

God is love.

1 John 4:8, "He that loveth not knoweth not God; for *God is love.*"

It may seem as though God had utterly forsaken and forgotten you or as though His hand of chastening were too heavy upon you. It may seem as though He had closed His eyes and deafened His ear. It may even seem as though He were indifferent altogether to the burden you carry and the heartache you endure. But it is not so for God is love and the love of God shines as the brightness of the sun whether you are warmed and refreshed by its rays or not.

God's grace is sufficient.

> 2 Corinthians 12:9, "And he said unto me, *My grace is sufficient for thee:* for my strength is made perfect in weakness. Most gladly therefore will I glory in my infirmities, that the power of Christ may rest upon me."

There will be temptations but none for which God has not provided a way of escape. Trials will assail; God nowhere promises freedom from them but He does promise endurance to bear them. When our weakness is most pressing His strength is most perfect.

Christ is able to save to the uttermost.

> Hebrews 7:25, "*Wherefore he is able also to save them to the uttermost* that come unto God by him, seeing he ever liveth to make intercession for them."

Has the boulder of doubt rolled in upon you? Look upon the rich soil into which your faith may root itself. If you have come to God through Christ it is a fact that Christ has borne your sins and has forgiven and forgotten them; He has put away your sin and has not only removed its penalty but has freed you from its power; He has overcome the world; He has defeated the devil; He lives in heaven as your great High Priest, your Conqueror, your Advocate, your Intercessor to cleanse you from sin and to keep you from sinning. Then spread the roots of faith over every doubt and let them go deep into these great facts of salvation.

Christ Jesus is in you, and you and Christ are one.

> Colossians 1:27, "To whom God would make known what is the riches of the glory of this mystery among the Gentiles; which is *Christ in you,* the hope of glory."

> John 15:5, "I am the vine, ye are the branches."

Whether you are conscious of His presence or not He is there not as a temporary guest or as One who comes and goes according to our spiritual moods but He is there as an abiding One. We may neglect Him, we may forget Him still He is there. He may be cabined in some back room but if we have ever truly opened the door to Him He is there and into this precious fact He would have faith root itself.

You are God's child and heir.

> Romans 8:16-17, R. V., "The Spirit himself beareth witness with our spirit, that *we are the children of God:* and if children, then heirs; *heirs of God, and joint-heirs with Christ;* if so be that we suffer with him, that we may be also glorified with him."

You may feel far more like a prodigal and a pauper than like a child and

an heir. But if you have put your faith in Christ as your Saviour, you are in God's family and the wealth of the King is yours. God would have your faith spread its roots over all depression caused by failure and go deep down into the soil of the riches of grace in Christ Jesus.

You are complete in Christ.

Your life may be immature in experience but God sees you complete in Christ. Your "old man" has been crucified, you have been baptized into Christ's death and identified with Him in His burial and resurrection. You are now hid with Christ in God and so you are complete in Him. Has the boulder of discouragement over your lack of growth into Christ-likeness settled down upon you? Over your coldness of heart and times of apathy? Then spread the roots of faith over it and let them go down into this great and glorious fact that you are complete in Him.

> Colossians 2:10, "And *ye are complete in him,* which is the head of all principality and power."

You are seated with Christ in the heavenlies.

You may never once have availed yourself of the privileges, possessions and powers of your heavenly position yet it is a fact, nevertheless, that, if you have trusted Christ as your Saviour, you thereby are seated with Him in the heavenlies. The powers of evil may be attacking your spirit, soul and body but they will be unable to overturn or overwhelm you if you spread the roots of faith over them and let them go down into the soil of this peerless truth.

> Ephesians 2:6, And *hath* raised us up together, and *made us sit together in heavenly places in Christ Jesus."*

The Holy Spirit dwells within you.

You may feel that you are left to live the Christian life alone and the weight of this responsibility may rest like a great boulder upon your heart. But you are not left alone. "Another Comforter" who is just like the ascended Lord in heaven lives within you. Spread the roots of faith over all fear and unbelief and let them sink deep down into the fact of the indwelling of the Holy Spirit.

> 1 Corinthians 3:16, "*Know ye not* that ye are the temple of God, and *that the Spirit of God dwelleth in you?*

When the Christian's faith roots itself in these great, eternal facts of God and abides there he becomes spiritual. Faith quietly *accepts* these facts as true and acts as though they were, then no matter what rolls in upon the life to overturn it, it remains steadfast and true and shoots heavenward in its growth into the likeness of Christ.

Look upon the boulders that rolled one after another against the life of the apostle Paul which it would seem might have crushed out his very life.

> 2 Corinthians 11:24-28, "Of the Jews five times received I forty stripes save one. Thrice was I beaten with rods, once was I stoned, thrice I suffered shipwreck, a night and a day I have been in the deep; in journeyings often, in perils of waters, in perils of robbers, in perils of mine own countrymen, in perils by the heathen, in perils in the city, in perils in the wilderness, in perils in the sea, in perils among false brethren; in weariness and painfulness, in watchings often, in hunger and thirst, in fastings often in cold and nakedness.
>
> Beside those things that are without, that which cometh upon me daily, the care of all the churches."

Yet his faith spread itself over all these perils and persecutions, testings and trials and rooted itself in the great, eternal facts of God's grace and love, thus enabling him to grow up to magnificent spiritual stature.

But Paul's life was exceptional you say. He was the giant tree in the forest. There are few who ever have a faith such as his. In the far interior of China was a young missionary who was betrothed. The wedding day drew near; all preparations for it were made. Then word came that her lover was ill. A long three days' journey stretched between her and her loved one living alone. Down upon that woman's heart rolled a terrific boulder of sorrow. Absolutely alone she watched the life of the one dearest to her on earth flicker out, with her own hands she prepared the body for burial, made the coffin, and laid him away to rest, herself conducting the funeral service. Then she turned to the road that led her back to live and toil alone for the rest of her life in the Master's vineyard. Rebellious? Embittered? No, sweetened, enriched with greater tenderness, love and devotion. But how could it be? The roots of faith had spread out over that terrible sorrow and had gone down, down, deep, deep into the facts of God's unchanging love, imperishable goodness and exhaustless grace.

Faith Reckons on God's Faithfulness

Our faith may falter but His faithfulness never. Peter failed Christ oh! so miserably that three times over he could deny his Lord. But the faithfulness of Jesus Christ to Peter remained unshaken. The heavenly Father cannot forget His promises nor can He deny Himself by failing to keep them.

> Psalm 89:33, "Nevertheless my lovingkindness will I not utterly take from him, *nor suffer my faithfulness to fail."*
>
> 2 Timothy 2:13, R. V., *"If we are faithless, he abideth faithful;* for he cannot deny himself."

We may even be ready to give up in defeat to the enemy or to lay down our task in sheer discouragement. We may be on the point of taking our hand from the plow and turning back. But Christ is not discouraged; He will not give up; He acknowledges no victory on the devil's part. He has called us into fellowship with Himself; He has owned us as His possession and has assumed the responsibility for our control and He will not lay it aside. What He has begun in us He will continue. His work in us does not depend upon our love for Him but on His love for us: not faith in our faith but faith in His faithfulness is what He wants from us.

> Philippians 1:6, "*Being confident* of this very thing, *that he which hath begun a good work in you will perform it* until the day of Jesus Christ."

> 1 Thessalonians 5:24, "*Faithful is he that calleth you, who also will do it.*"

I watched two young girls cross a glacier. The path was not clearly marked out; there were great gaping holes in the ice, often the next step had to be fairly cut out. They were not even properly shod with spiked shoes. Yet they tripped along apparently unafraid and in safety because they were roped to one who knew how to avoid the dangers and surmount the difficulties of that icy path and they reckoned on the faithfulness of their guide.

How much more can we reckon upon the faithfulness of our Guide who knows the way before us and whose business it is to lead us safely through all its dangers and difficulties. Our Guide delights to have us throw away all props and helps; to let go of everything outside of Himself and then cast ourselves full-length upon His unfailing faithfulness. "Sarah . . . received power . . . since she counted him faithful who had promised" (Hebrews 11:11, R.V.).

FAITH RECEIVES GOD'S FULLNESS

Are you a child of God? Then by virtue of your sonship you may be filled with the Holy Spirit. Such fullness has been promised to you and it has been provided for you. Then why is it that you do not possess your birthright?

There are several ways for an honest man to gain possession of a thing; he may buy it, he may barter for it, or he may receive it as a gift.

Can one buy the fullness of the Holy Spirit? Simon the sorcerer thought in his heart to purchase Him and the power to confer Him upon others for which he was severely rebuked. Can His fullness be secured through barter? Have you perchance tried to strike a bargain with God offering Him some odd moments of time, some remnants of strength, some segment of talent, in exchange for the fullness of the Holy Spirit? The rich young ruler would no doubt have exchanged *half* his possessions for the life more abundant, but he went away sorrowful. One way remains by which you may possess the Holy Spirit's fullness. It is the gift of God.

1 John 3:24, "And hereby we know that he abideth in us, *by the Spirit which he hath given us.*"

What does one usually do with a gift? He receives it and thanks the giver. This is precisely what God wants you to do with this wondrous gift of the Holy Spirit's fullness. Let me illustrate by a simple incident which brought this message to my own heart with fresh meaning and power.

A dear young Chinese girl came one evening to seek the way of salvation. That night she not only received Christ as Saviour but yielded to Him as Lord. Immediately she was filled with a passion to win to Christ the young man to whom she was betrothed. He was utterly godless. After months of intercession, personal work and, above all, exemplifying Christ in daily life before him she won him to Christ. A marvelous miracle of renewal and transformation was wrought in him. He became a new creation in Christ.

Nearly two years later Mr. and Mrs. Wang were passing through Shanghai and they came to call. Their time was limited and Mr. Wang did not want to waste one moment of it. So as soon as the introduction was over he began conversation upon the theme nearest to his heart—the Lord Jesus Christ.

Oh! how precious Christ was to that young man! What a reality prayer was. Out of every hour of the day he spent at least five minutes in prayer. What a passion he had for souls! He could not sleep at night if he had not made at least an effort to win someone to Christ during the day. What a love for the Word of God he had! It was his meat and drink.

Seeing his love for God's Word I was reminded of a Scofield Bible which had been sent me to give to a Chinese friend. I presented to to Mr. Wang saying, "I see you love the Bible. Here is a Scofield Bible which I should like to give you." At the mention of a Scofield Bible his face grew radiant and the tears of joy filled his eyes. "Oh," said he, "the other day I saw a Scofield Bible in Nanking and how I have wanted to possess one ever since! I began to pray for one. I went to a store to buy one. It cost too much, I couldn't afford it. I had decided I couldn't possess one."

Remember the three ways of gaining possession. Mr. Wang had tried to buy the Bible and it cost too much; no one had offered to exchange one for anything he had. Just one way of possession was open to him—to receive it as a gift. And now the Scofield Bible which he so much desired was being offered to him as a gift. What did he do?

Did he say, "Oh! I want that Bible more than I want any other thing but *I haven't prayed long enough for it*—just wait until I pray a few months more for it!" Or did he say, "*I am really not worthy* to receive that Bible! I must wait until I have made myself a better Christian and am worthy to possess such a Bible!" Or did he reply, "*This Bible is coming too easily*—just receiving it as a gift! I think I should strive harder to get one for myself for I haven't done a thing to merit such a gift." Or did he say, "Oh, that Scofield Bible is what I want and need more than anything else but *it is not for me!* God might give my wife such a gift but not me!" Or did he say, "You say that Bible is for me but *I do not feel that it is mine* so I think I should not take it until I *feel* I possess it!"

If Mr. Wang had made any one of those foolish, absurd remarks I should have been forced to one of two conclusions; either that he was not honest and really did not want a Scofield Bible or else he thought I was not honest and did not really offer that one to him. One of these two conclusions is inescapable.

What did Mr. Wang do? Well, I wish you could have seen the quickness with which he held out his two hands and *took* that Scofield Bible and with a face all aglow with joy and gratitude he immediately kneeled down and thanked God. As he rose to his feet he began to talk of how he would use that gift in winning men to the Lord Jesus.

Have you wanted the fullness of the Holy Spirit? God offers Him in His fullness to you as a gift. What have you done with the offer? Are you still praying for the Holy Spirit's fullness? If so, what do you expect to accomplish through your prayers? The deposit is already placed to your account in the bank. You are still pleading with God to put it there while He pleads with you to cash your checks. "You keep telegraphing to God for supplies, and every year your appeals get more plaintive and piteous; you do not realize that the freight train is already in the station, waiting for you to discharge it; that the heavily burdened ship is in the dock, ready for you to unload."

Or you say, "I am not worthy to be filled with the Holy Spirit" and "I dare not expect Him to fill me until I am a better Christian." Of course you are not worthy to have the Holy Spirit dwell in you much less fill you. Neither was Paul, nor Peter, nor Spurgeon, nor Moody, worthy in himself to be filled with the Holy Spirit. The Holy Spirit is God's gift of grace and grace is pure, unmerited favor. Grace is not something God does because of anything that He finds worthy in us but because of the infinite worth of His Son. The only thing you can do to make yourself worthy of the Holy Spirit's fullness is to take Him as God's proffered gift and let Him make your life a fit and worthy place for His abiding.

Or do you say, "Just receiving the gifts of God's grace is too easy and lazy a way to live the Christian life. I think I ought to work a bit myself and strive to attain to a holy life. I do not like the idea of sitting passive and having spiritual blessings bestowed upon me." This sounds commendable but it runs counter to one of the greatest truths revealed in God's Word concerning faith. "But to him that worketh not, but believeth on him that justifieth the ungodly, his faith is counted for righteousness." There is not a ray of encouragement held out in God's Word to the man who strives to attain spirituality through his own self-effort. There are those who know that salvation cannot be secured by works but who think that spirituality may be so obtained. They know they cannot be *saved* by works but they strive to *grow* by works. We do grow *in* spirituality by faith but we can never grow *into* spirituality by self-effort. Growth is "not of works, lest any man should boast." "Ye can not by taking thought add one cubit to your stature." Making good resolutions, signing pledges, practicing self-denial during certain seasons, and all such self-manufactured methods of obtaining spirituality, will prove futile. If we could grow into holiness through any effort of our own how proud we should become and how independent of God.

Or you say, "Such a standard of spiritual life is too high for the ordinary everyday Christian. It may be possible for the minister or the missionary but it is beyond my reach." Yes, it is beyond the reach of everything in you except your faith. But so long as God says, "All things are possible to him that believeth," the fullness of the Holy Spirit is possible to faith. God has no favorites and, what He offers to one believer, He offers to every believer irrespective of his calling or vocation.

Or you say, "I have been a Christian for years and I have never *felt* the presence of the Holy Spirit in me. Then how can I believe He will fill me? If I just felt He was dwelling within me, I would have faith to believe in His infilling." Your order then is feeling, faith, fact, which is the exact reverse of God's order. God says, "Fact, faith, feeling." We are ever prone to trust our feelings rather than God's facts and it is like having the roots of faith going down into quicksand. The state of the weather, the state of our health, the state of our pocketbook, these and countless other variable conditions may affect our feelings. To place any confidence whatever in them is exceedingly disastrous. God would have you say, "It is a fact that the Holy Spirit dwells within me for God's Word says so. It is a fact that God wants me filled with the Spirit because He commands me to be filled and He has provided for that fullness. Therefore by faith I claim the fullness of the Holy Spirit." Whatever feeling God wishes to accompany or follow this act of faith will come in His own time and way.

So, my friend, if you are coming to God telling Him that you long to be filled with the Holy Spirit and yet saying any of these foolish things, either you are not honest and really do not want to be filled with the Holy Spirit or else you do not believe He is honest when He offers you the gift of the Spirit's fullness.

Are you honest? Do you truly want to be filled with the Holy Spirit? Then acknowledge the presence of the Holy Spirit within you; thank God that He is there; and claim His fullness as your birthright. Take the gift, thank the Giver, and use the gift immediately in winning souls to Christ.

By an act of faith I receive the Spirit's fullness. By a constant succession of acts of faith, the Spirit's fullness becomes habitual. "Let me ask you to remember that there is no such thing as a once-for-all fulness; it is a continuous appropriation of a continuous supply from Jesus Christ Himself:—a moment-by-moment faith in a moment-by-moment Saviour for a moment-by-moment cleansing, and a moment-by-moment filling. As I trust Him, He fills me; so long as I trust Him He fills me, the moment I begin to believe, that moment I begin to receive; and so long as I keep believing, praise the Lord! so long I keep receiving."

28

The Believer's Part in Remaining Spirit-filled— Obedience

IN RESPONSE to surrender and faith the believer is filled with the Holy Spirit. As he is emptied of self, God fills; as he takes of Christ, God gives. Becoming rightly related to the Holy Spirit he becomes spiritual. In him the Spirit dwells in fullness because over him He has unhindered control. But the matter cannot be left there, for many a person has been filled with the Holy Spirit who has not remained filled; and life on the highest plane presumes habitual fullness of the Holy Spirit.

A STEP LENGTHENS INTO A WALK

Surrender and faith as antecedents in becoming Spirit-filled were both acts. By an act of yielding one takes the step out of a life ruled by self into one governed by Christ. By an act of faith one claims his birthright in the fullness of the Holy Spirit and steps out of a life of stagnancy into one of satisfaction and sufficiency.

To many this step marks such a definite and marvelous advance in spiritual living that it is as noteworthy an event in their spiritual history as was their new birth through faith in Christ as Saviour. The blessing of a life in which Christ is really all and in all is so transcendent that many stop short with the enjoyment of the blessing and do not seek to know how it is to be maintained. To their disappointment they wake some day to the realization that their peace and power have gone.

The twofold act of surrender and faith to be of any permanent value must become an attitude. The decisive act must be crystallized into continuous action. Surrender and faith must be merged into obedience. Obedience is just surrender and faith stretched over a lifetime; the step is lengthened into a walk.

Scripture speaks often of the believer's walk and means by the word his whole manner of living from Sunday to Sunday, from morning till morning. Our walk is what we are translated into what we do; it is character expressed in conduct. It is our calling in Christ in the heavenlies actualized in conduct before men in the world.

> 1 Thessalonians 2:12, "That *ye would walk worthy of God,* who hath called you unto his kingdom and glory."

> Ephesians 4:1, "I therefore, the prisoner of the Lord, beseech you that *ye walk worthy of the vocation wherewtih ye are called.*"

To remain spiritual it is of paramount importance that the believer should pay attention to his walk. Let us then study the nature of the walk of a Spirit-filled Christian.

A Walk in Obedience to God's Will

Obedience is the basic principle in the family life of God. The Son's incarnate life opened the door into the home life of heaven and let us see that obedience to the will of the Father is the secret of its happiness and harmony. Indeed Christ said that obedience constitutes the family tie.

> Matthew 12:50, "For *whosoever shall do the will of my Father* which is in heaven, *the same* is my brother, and sister, and mother."

Obedience is likewise the basic principle in the heavenly holy order of which Christ is the Head. To become the Head of the Body He was "obedient even unto death" and each member of the Body partakes of the fullness of the life He bestows only through obedience to the obedient One. The preciousness and permanence of our abiding in the fellowship of His love is determined by our obedience to His will as He was obedient to His Father's.

> Hebrews 5:8-9, "Though he were a Son, yet *learned he obedience by the things* which he suffered; and being made perfect, *he became the author of eternal salvation unto all them that obey him.*"

> John 15:10, "If *ye keep my commandments,* ye shall abide in my love; even as *I have kept my Father's commandments,* and abide in his love."

Obedience is the basic principle in the Kingdom of God. There God's will is everything. The peace, joy, content of heaven are due to the fact that there God's will is done perfectly. So life in the Kingdom of God is conditioned upon willingness to do His will.

> Matthew 6:10, "Thy kingdom come. *Thy will be done in earth, as it is in heaven.*"

> Matthew 7:21, "Not every one that saith unto me, Lord, Lord, shall enter into the kingdom of heaven; but *he that doeth the will of my Father* which is in heaven."

Nothing short of loving obedience can keep us in harmony with God because in His family, His society and His Kingdom, His will is sovereign and supreme.

In yielding his life to God the believer acknowledges that God has a right to expect obedience from him and he accepts God's will as the invariable standard for literally everything in his life. By voluntarily choosing the rule of Christ instead of that of self he places himself in the center of God's will.

Then begins the practice of the will of God in a daily, hourly, moment-by-moment walk. Oh! what a difference there is soon found to be between accepting the will of God in principle and submitting to it in practice. It is one thing by one decisive act to put the hand into God's and say, "Father, I have come to do Thy will," and quite another thing to keep it there in the daily walk of life saying, "Father, I delight to do Thy will; it is my meat and drink." Through the pressure of some particular need or under the power of some special inspiration the step out of self-will into God's will may be taken without the realization that the step must lengthen into a continued, sustained, habitual walk.

We often make the mistake of thinking that life lived in the will of God means all sunshine and no storms; that to be filled with the Spirit means exemption from temptation and suffering. But it is not so. A few days ago I started for a walk down a mountain road. The sun was shining brightly and I anticipated the pure delight of a beautiful sunset over the lake and an unclouded view of the mountains. But before long I walked straight into a rainstorm and for half an hour rain and hail came down upon me. There was nothing to do but walk right on which I did and came out later into the sunshine again. Both the sunshine and the storm were allowed by the Father in heaven. So we find it in our walk with Him in daily life. Two things are bound to be encountered in a walk in obedience to the will of God; one is the temptations of Satan, and the other the testings of God.

Every step of the walk in the will of God will be contested by the evil one whose own greatest sin is self-will. He seduced God's first man into disobedience and self-will and the persistent attack that he made upon the second Man throughout His earthly life had but one motive back of it—to deflect Him from a walk of implicit obedience to His Father. The Spirit-filled man is now his chief target and the temptation of disobedience is the one fiery dart above all others that he constantly aims at him.

The devil tempts the Spirit-filled man along the line of presumption. He tempts him to go beyond the will of God in the matter of the Spirit's manifestation. He says to him, "If thou be Spirit-filled, then speak in tongues." Many earnest people today are being led astray by thinking to prove their reception of the Spirit's fullness by some outer, visible, spectacular manifestation rather than by His inner supernatural presence in power. In this they go beyond the will of God because they go beyond the Word of God.

Satan tempts also through another form of presumption, to lag behind the will of God. He tempts the Spirit-filled man to rely upon his spiritual attainment and to neglect the study of God's Word for personal growth. Resting in his supposed permanent fullness he begins to live on stale manna; to rely for strength upon his own often-repeated testimony; to trust in an unconsciously receding experience. More than one Spirit-filled person has lost his fullness by attempting to live off of it without a constant replenishing.

The devil tempts the Spirit-filled man along the line of pride. The Holy Spirit's motto is "Christ everything"; Satan's motto is "Anything but Christ." So he tempts the Spirit-filled man to look away from Christ and to look in unto self. He has achieved a real victory when he gets the Spirit-filled man to rejoice in his fullness and to testify regarding his blessing rather than to rejoice in the Giver of the fullness and to sing praises unto the Blesser. The grave danger of fixing one's eyes upon an experience, however exalted and blessed, instead of upon Him who bestowed it was expressed very tellingly by Spurgeon when he said,

"I looked at Christ
And the dove of peace flew into my heart;
I looked at the dove of peace—
And it flew away."

The one who places such emphasis upon the blessing is very apt to look reproachfully upon those who have not a similar one. He becomes self-righteous and indulges in criticism and Phariseeism. He looks down upon others with a "holier than thou" attitude which is evidence enough of the diminishing fullness of the Holy Spirit.

Satan tempts the Spirit-filled man along the line of persecution. Satan's one purpose is to deflect him from obedience and if he cannot do it by pressure from within he will attempt it by persecution from without. The Spirit-filled men of the early Church were stoned, beaten, imprisoned and killed. The form of persecution endured today by the Spirit-filled Christian may take a different form but it is nonetheless real. He who stands foursquare for "the whole Gospel in the whole Bible for the whole world" in these days of apostasy is bound to endure persecution. Many a person has given place to the devil in the matter of his faith because he could not endure the taunt of being "unscholarly" or "unintellectual" or because he did not have the courage of his conviction in the atmosphere of opposition and denial. But such persecution is certain to come to every godly believer.

2 Timothy 3:11-12, "Persecutions, afflictions, which came unto me at

Antioch, at Iconium, at Lystra; *what persecutions I endured:* but out of them all the Lord delivered me.

Yea, and all that will live godly in Christ Jesus shall suffer persecution."

In this walk of obedience to God's will we shall be met also by the testings of God. Sometimes it has happened that one who has refused to yield to the temptations of Satan has succumbed to defeat through the testings of God. There is the subtle danger that one who has lived a consistent, yielded, devoted Christian life may think that he has gained thereby a place of special favor in God's family circle and that he merits exoneration from the sufferings of adversity or affliction. A very earnest, active Christian man recently uttered a doubt as to the goodness of God because He had permitted an affliction to come into his home. But let us beware of ever thinking that God's love and goodness mean favoritism, and above all let us not lose the blessing out of even the keenest suffering God permits us to endure by failing to trust Him.

It is good for us to know at the very beginning of our walk in obedience to God that it will mean testing through suffering. We have the pattern for such a walk in the earthly life of our Lord. "Though he were a Son yet learned he obedience by the things which he suffered." Think of it—*He* learned obedience! With a sinless nature that rejoiced above everything else to do His Father's will we would think there would have been no necessity for Him to learn obedience. But the Word tells us that He needed to learn obedience and that this was accomplished through the things that He *suffered*. Is there one of us who does not need to begin in the primary and go clear through the university in the school of obedience? And if our divine Teacher learned what He would teach us on this great theme through suffering can we expect to learn it in any other way? God does not deceive us in this matter and tells us plainly that we shall be partakers of Christ's sufferings, and this in full accord with His will.

1 Peter 4:12-13, "Beloved, *think it not strange concerning the fiery trial which is to try you,* as though some strange thing happened unto you: *but rejoice, inasmuch as ye are partakers of Christ's sufferings;* that, when his glory shall be revealed, ye may be glad also with exceeding joy."

1 Peter 4:19, "*Wherefore let them that suffer according to the will of God* commit the keeping of their souls to him in well doing, as unto a faithful Creator."

We shall suffer through the misunderstanding, reproach and rejection of those who refuse the Lord Jesus the rule over their lives. It may even be that those of our own household will inflict upon us the keenest suffering we will ever endure. "And a man's foes shall be they of his own household." Even our well-doing may be evil spoken of and our work and prayer for the salvation of those we love be wholly misinterpreted. But remember Him who "came unto his own, and his own received him not"; who was accused of "casting out devils through Beelzebub the chief of the devils," and who wept over Jerusalem saying, "How often would I . . . and ye would not."

> 1 Peter 3:16-17, R. V., "Having a good conscience; that, wherein ye are spoken against, they may be put to shame who revile your good manner of life in Christ. *For it is better, if the will of God should so will, that ye suffer for well-doing than for evil-doing.*"

> 1 Peter 4:14, "*If ye be reproached for the name of Christ, happy are ye;* for the spirit of glory and of God resteth upon you: on their part he is evil spoken of, but on your part he is glorified."

We shall suffer through the chastening which in His infinite love God sees is necessary for our spiritual growth. We need to keep constantly in mind the goal which God has set for us—conformity to the image of His Son. "For this is the will of God, even your sanctification." "Be ye holy *even as* I am holy." It is a wondrous thing God wills to work out *in* us and He has His own method of doing it. To polish the vessel into greater perfection God often uses the method of chastening. No words are so clear and comforting on this theme as those of Scripture itself.

> Hebrews 12:6-11, "*For whom the Lord loveth he chasteneth,* and scourgeth every son whom he receiveth. *If ye endure chastening, God dealeth with you as with sons;* for what son is he whom the father chasteneth not? *But if ye be without chastisement,* whereof all are partakers, *then are ye bastards,* and not sons.
>
> Furthermore we have had fathers of our flesh which corrected us, and we gave them reverence: *shall we not much rather be in subjection unto the Father of spirits, and live?* For they verily for a few days chastened us after their own pleasure; but *he for our profit, that we might be partakers of his holiness.* Now no chastening for the present seemeth to be joyous, but grievous: *nevertheless afterward it yieldeth the peaceable fruit of righteousness unto them which are exercised thereby.*"

I think of a dear friend whose life is daily being refined as by fire through a terrible affliction which has come upon her only daughter. While talking with her I have seen her face radiant with the light that can come only from a heart at rest in the will of God at the same time her eyes have been blinded with tears. Through her affliction she has become a partaker of the holiness of God.

A Chinese Christian came to talk with me about her old mother for whom she was greatly burdened. She was an ardent idolater and for more than thirty years had been a devoted vegetarian. The daughter had preached the Gospel to her mother, had prayed for her, and had pled with her to become a Christian, but to no avail. The mother's heart hardened rather than softened. "Why does God not hear my prayer for my mother?" she asked almost as though chiding God. I had watched the daughter's face as she talked; there were hard lines in it that were the outward token of inward rebellion. A bit of gentle probing and soon with a flood of tears came the confession of awful rebellion toward God because He had taken her five boys one after another home to Himself—the baby having gone only a month before. "God is unfair and unloving, yes, even cruel!" such was the language of her soul. The will of God was not good and perfect but unjust and unkind. Hardness of heart followed upon rebellion. But God wrought a miracle of grace that day by enabling her joyously to accept and submit to the gracious will of God. Oh! the riches of His grace! The next day in a way wholly inexplicable except by God's supernatural working the old mother came a long distance in from the country to see her daughter. Startled by something in the daughter's face which she had never seen there before she asked what had happened. Then followed the confession of her rebellion toward God because of her affliction and of the hardness of her heart. The old mother's heart was strangely moved and softened and very shortly it opened to admit the Saviour. "No chastening *for the present* seemeth to be joyous—*nevertheless afterward. . . .*"

We shall suffer through trials and tribulations permitted to test the sincerity of our surrender and the reality of our faith. Abraham was permitted to build the altar, to lay on the wood, to bind Isaac, to lay him on the altar, to stretch forth his hand, even to take the knife to slay his own son, before the angel of the Lord called to him from heaven, "Lay not thine hand upon the lad, neither do thou any thing unto him: for now I know that thou fearest God, *seeing thou hast not withheld thy son, thine only son from me.*" Some such test may be used by God to bring into the light the quality of our surrender and faith.

> 1 Peter 1:6-7, R. V., "Wherein ye greatly rejoice, though now for a little while, if need be, *ye have been put to grief in manifold trials, that the proof of your faith,* being more precious than gold that perisheth *though it is proved by fire, may be found unto praise and glory and honour at the revelation of Jesus Christ.*"

In conversation with a godly man who verily walked with his Lord the fact was disclosed that the life of joy and peace in the Lord which he then enjoyed had come only after he had walked through a hailstorm of trial which had stripped him of several hundreds of thousands of dollars. But you could not have bought him back to his former life had you laid that amount in cash upon his table.

In the recent trouble in Nanking, China, many of the Chinese Christians lost all their earthly possessions. But their hearts were filled with praise that God had counted them worthy to suffer thus for Christ.

Some pamphlets and books which have reached a circulation of hundreds of thousands and have brought untold blessing to countless persons were written by a man whose body is so frail that he can write for only a few moments at a time. But everything that comes from his pen breathes forth the joy and peace of a heart sunk deep into submissiveness to the will of God.

Again some have faltered by the way and failed to walk obediently because they have murmured at God's choice of a path. They rejoiced in the thought of being "made perfect in every good work to do his will" but they mistook a *good* work for a *great* work. Instead God asked for a quiet walk with Him in the obscurity of the home, perchance ministering to the needs of an aged parent or a sick sister. God's will was to live joyously before Him and patiently before others, following the example of Him who as truly did His Father's will when making tables in the carpenter shop and assisting in the support of a widowed mother as when He fed five thousand people or taught the multitude. Only a very few of those who were filled with the Holy Spirit on the day of Pentecost were made apostles; most of the one hundred and twenty were sent back into the ordinary life of business and home.

God wishes us at the very beginning of our walk with Him to accept His will as "good and perfect and acceptable" and then to enter into each day sinking our will into His and submitting with joy and gladness to whatever comes during its hours knowing that every testing and trial is being used by Him to mature our growth into the likeness of our Lord.

> Hebrews 13:21, "*Make you perfect in every good work to do his will,* working in you that which is wellpleasing in his sight, through Jesus Christ; to whom be glory for ever and ever. Amen."

> James 1:2-4, R. V., "*Count it all joy,* my brethren, *when ye fall into manifold temptations [trials]:* knowing that the proving of your faith worketh patience. And let patience have its perfect work, *that ye may be perfect and entire, lacking in nothing.*"

A Walk in Conformity to God's Ways

God's will is not an intangible, indefinite thing. Indeed so practical is it that it stretches itself over our entire manner of living, claiming the authority to fashion our daily walk.

Deuteronomy 5:33, *"Ye shall walk in all the ways which the Lord your God hath commanded you,* that ye may live, and that it may be well with you, and that ye may prolong your days in the land which ye shall possess."

1 Kings 3:14, *"And if thou wilt walk in my ways,* to keep my statutes and my commandments, as thy father David did walk, then I will lengthen thy days."

Over the family life of His children the heavenly Father presides and He fully expects to counsel with them regarding the kind of clothes they wear; the books they read; the studies they pursue; the companions they seek; the business they enter; the money they spend; the possessions they have; the life plans they form; their habits of recreation and play as well as of work; and their food and drink. Radiating from the will of God as the center there are ways of thinking, talking, resting, working, playing, eating, dressing, living which are consistent with our home life in the heavenlies and are worthy of the training which we have received of our Father.

Philippians 1:27, R. V., "Only let *your manner of life* be worthy of the gospel of Christ."

Philippians 2:15, R. V., "That ye may become blameless and harmless, children of God without blemish in the midst of a crooked and perverse generation, *among whom ye are seen as lights in the world."*

Yet there are prodigals in the Father's family who despising the restraints in the Father's home go their own way into the far country. There are others who remain at home but reserve the right in certain matters to conform their ways to those of the world. There are Christian men who contend that in business one must use the methods of the world to succeed even if they are somewhat shady and dishonoring. There are earnest Christian women who in matters of dress follow the extreme fashions of the world. There are both men and women who in most of their ways of life have sought and followed the Lord's guidance, yet in the one supreme choice—that of a partner for life—have disobeyed God's direct command to marry "in the Lord," and a life of suffering and sorrow has often been the result. There are leaders of the Church even who have departed so far from God's ways of financing His work that they have filled the house of prayer with the tables of money changers. Many a Christian has ceased to walk in the will of God because at some definite point he has departed from the ways of God. To be filled again with God's Spirit will mean to return to the place of disobedience in confession of sin and then start aright in God's way.

1 Peter 1:14, R. V., "*As children of obedience, not fashioning yourselves according to your former lusts* in the time of your ignorance."

Romans 12:2, R. V., "And *be not fashioned according to this world:* but be ye transformed by the renewing of your mind, that ye may prove what is the good and acceptable and perfect will of God."

But it is not only in what we do but in what we do not do that we fail to follow the ways of the Lord. In so many homes God seems to figure so little in the ordinary life of weekdays. The family attends church together on Sunday and perhaps the children are sent to Sunday school but there is no family altar, no blessing at the table, no mention of God in conversation.

A WALK IN OBEDIENCE TO THE WORD OF GOD

Some may plead ignorance of the will of God as an excuse for disobedience. But God does not ask us to walk in the dark. God has spoken to us and His will is clearly revealed in His Word. Over and over again in the Old Testament, God commanded the children of Israel to hearken unto His voice and then to do what they heard. And He commanded parents to teach their children that the children also might walk in the will and way of God. "The word 'obey' comes from a Latin compound, it means that you *do* in consequence of what you *hear*." In the New Testament, God makes the same appeal to His children.

Deuteronomy 28:1, "And it shall come to pass, *if thou shalt hearken diligently unto the voice of the Lord thy God, to observe* and *to do* all his commandments which I command this day, that the LORD thy God will set thee on high above all nations of the earth."

James 1:22-24, "But *be ye doers of the word,* and *not hearers only,* deceiving your own selves. For if any be *a hearer of the word, and not a doer,* he is like unto a man beholding his natural face in a glass: for he beholdeth himself, and goeth his way, and straightway forgetteth what manner of man he was."

To walk in the whole will of God requires that we walk in the whole truth of God. Some err and depart from walking in God's ways because they reserve to themselves the right to become critics of God's Word and to accept or reject it according to the dictates of reason. But how can one do the will of God when he has rejected some portion of the Word of God which possibly he most needs? Will one who has rejected the personality of the Holy Spirit pay much attention to the command "Be filled with the Spirit"? Another may have refused to accept the truth of a life of victory over the power of sin, even thinking it an unscriptural doctrine. Then he is not likely to obey the command to reckon himself dead to sin and to let it not reign over him. Walking in the will of God demands a walking in the truth of God.

> 2 John 4, "I rejoiced greatly that I found of thy children *walking in truth,* as we have received a commandment from the Father."

> 3 John 4, "I have no greater joy than to hear that my children *walk in truth.*"

When one has accepted the whole truth of God's inspired Word, he has opened his whole being to the light that streams from the throne of God and he has come into such an adjustment to the Spirit of truth that he can be led into a walk in the pure light of God's Word.

> John 16:13, "Howbeit *when he, the Spirit of truth, is come, he will guide you into all truth:* for he shall not speak of himself; but whatsoever he shall hear, that shall he speak: and he will shew you things to come."

> 1 John 1:7, "But *if we walk in the light, as he is in the light,* we have fellowship one with another, and the blood of Jesus Christ his Son cleanseth us from all sin."

The one who submits himself to the teaching of the Holy Spirit and who takes the Word of God to be the standard by which his life is to be fashioned and directed will be filled with an intense desire to know the will of God. He will make it the most fervent prayer of his life that he may be filled with a knowledge of God's will so that he may walk worthy of his Lord.

> Colossians 1:9-10, "For this cause we also, since the day we heard it, do not cease to pray for you, and to desire that *ye might be filled with the knowledge of his will in all wisdom and spiritual understanding;* that ye might walk worthy of the Lord unto all pleasing."

To such a man the Word of God becomes a new Book and the discovery of God's will therein will not be a duty to be shunned but a delight to be enjoyed. His spiritual life may be marvelously enriched or even quite revolutionized by the discovery of and obedience to some command. The "Unknown Christian" in *How to Live the Victorious Life* gives this personal testimony, "As the writer looks back on his past life nothing so surprises him as the fact that he failed to see, or grasp, or apprehend this Victorious Life teaching, although it is not new, although it is so plainly taught in Scripture."

Think of the change that would be wrought in some life given up to worry, anxiety and fretfulness if the commands "In nothing be anxious" (Philippians 4:6, R.V.) and "Let the peace of God rule in your hearts" (Colossians 3:15) were really obeyed. See the sunshine of joy and praise flood some murmuring, discontented, grumbling heart that begins to live by "Be ye thankful" (Colossians 3:15), "In every thing give thanks: for this is the will of God in Christ Jesus concerning you" (1 Thessalonians 5:18), and "Rejoice in the Lord alway" (Philippians 4:4). What times of defeat and depression we might avoid if we just did as God commanded, "Neither give place to the devil" (Ephesians 4:27), "Resist the devil, and he will flee from you" (James 4:7). What a preventive to yielding to temptation and what a defense against Satan's attacks is for us in this command, "Put on the whole armour of God" (Ephesians 6:11). What a wealth of blessing we might carry even in our casual contacts with people if we were zealous to follow His direction regarding our conversation. "Let no corrupt communication proceed out of your mouth, but that which is good to the use of edifying, that it may minister grace unto the hearers" (Ephesians 4:29). What division among Christians would be displaced by the unity for which our Lord prayed if we obeyed some of His simple, direct commands. "Let nothing be done through strife or vainglory; but in lowliness of mind let each esteem other better than themselves. Look not every man on his own things, but every man also on the things of others" (Philippians 2:3-4), "Be subject one to another . . . be clothed with humility" (1 Peter 5:5). What relief even from physical suffering might result from habitual obedience to His command, "Whether therefore ye eat, or drink, or whatsoever ye do, do all to the glory of God" (1 Corinthians 10:31). What possibilities of testimony to others of the beauty, glory and attractiveness of the life in Christ by simple obedience to His Word, "And whatsoever ye do in word or in deed, do all in the name of the Lord Jesus, giving thanks to God and the Father by him" (Colossians 3:17).

But perhaps to some a walk of such complete obedience seems unattractive; while to others it seems impossible. Whether or not it is attractive and desirable to us will depend upon two things, our confidence in the Lord and our love for Him. Do we truly believe that God is love? Then we must believe that His will is "good and perfect" and that every command is given not only for the sake of His glory but for our welfare. God is not a tyrannical despot who rejoices in lording it over His subjects. He does not command simply to show His authority. God is a Father and every command He gives looks toward both the immediate and the ultimate good of His child. Our unshakeable belief in the infinite goodness and kindness of God is essential to the joyous obedience to His commands. But we cannot force ourselves to love His will. Our love for God must dovetail into His love for us before we joyously obey His commands. When once we truly love Him more than we love ourselves, more than we love any other person, or thing, then God's commands are not grievous but gracious to us; they cease to be a duty and become a delight.

John 14:21, 23, *"He that hath my commandments, and keepeth them, he it is that loveth me:* and he that loveth me shall be loved of my Father, and I will love him, and will manifest myself to him. Jesus answered and said unto him, *If a man love me, he will keep my words:* and my Father will love him, and we will come unto him, and make our abode with him."

But to some it seems an utter impossibility to keep the commandments of God. This leads us to our last thought.

A WALK IN THE SPIRIT

Let us admit without hesitation that a life of obedience to God in our own strength is absolutely impossible. We have not the power in ourselves to obey even one command habitually, to say nothing of the power for a continuous walk in obedience.

But for that reason let us not conclude that God asks something unreasonable or impracticable and therefore impossible and thus excuse ourselves for settling down into habitual disobedience. Frances Ridley Havergal says truly, "We may be quite sure of three things. First, that whatever our Lord commands us, He really means us to do. Secondly, that whatever He commands is 'for our good always.' And thirdly, that whatever He commands He is able and willing to enable us to do, "for all God's biddings are enablings.' "

If "God's bidding is His enabling," then our part is to discover His provision for a walk in obedience to His will, His ways and His Word.

Galatians 5:25, "If we live in the Spirit, let *us also walk in the Spirit.*"

Galatians 5:16, "This I say then, *Walk in the Spirit,* and ye shall not fulfil the lust of the flesh."

By accepting Jesus Christ as Saviour the believer is translated into the sphere of the Spirit. The Holy Spirit, then, stands ready to take all responsibility for a "walk" that is in full accord with such a "life." He comes into the believer to indwell and to infill for that very purpose. He knows the mind and the will of God and He will unfold it to us through the Word of God and give to us the desire and the strength to obey.

1 Peter 1:22, "Seeing ye have purified your souls *in obeying the truth through the Spirit* unto unfeigned love of the brethren, see that ye love one another with a pure heart fervently."

The Holy Spirit knows the ways of God and He will reveal them to us through the Word and guide our footsteps into the right paths so that we may walk step by step in obedience to the will of God. He will restrain us from one course and constrain us toward another. He will rebuke and reprove us whenever we step out into any bypath of the flesh.

If in some particular issue self is allowed to regain supremacy and some part of our walk is dishonoring to God, the Holy Spirit will work within us to guide us back. He not only guides but He guards. He knows every motion and activity of the flesh, every subtle trick and evil design to trip and ensnare the one who walks with God. And He is able even to keep us from stumbling. If we have yielded to Him the control of our lives and have put all authority into His hands, He accepts the responsibility for our walk before God and men.

> Romans 8:14, "For as many as are *led by the Spirit of God,* they are the sons of God."
>
> Jude 24, R. V., "Now *unto him that is able to guard you from stumbling,* and to set you before the presence of his glory without blemish in exceeding joy."

Chafer in his book *He That Is Spiritual* has stated so helpfully the meaning of a walk in the Spirit that I shall quote at length from it. "The passage [referring to Galatians 5:16] is better rendered 'This I say then, By means of the Spirit be walking, and ye shall not fulfil the lust of the flesh!' The child of God has no power within himself whereby he can enter, promote, or maintain a 'walk in the Spirit.' This Scripture when rightly rendered, does not make the impossible demand upon a Christian that he in his own strength is to accomplish a 'walk in the Spirit.' It is rather revealed that the Spirit will do the walking in the Christian. The human responsibility is that of a whole dependence upon the Spirit. Walking by means of the Spirit is simply walking by a definite reliance upon the ability and power of the One who indwells. . . . The third condition of true spirituality is, then, an unbroken reliance upon the Spirit to do what He has come to do and what He alone can do. Such is the Father's provision that sin may be *prevented* in the life of His child. . . . The child of God has an all-engaging responsibility of continuing in an attitude of reliance upon the Spirit. This is his divinely appointed task and place of cooperation in the mighty undertakings of God. The locomotive engineer will accomplish little when pushing at his ponderous train. He is not appointed to such a service. His real usefulness will begin when he takes his place at the throttle. The important conflict in the believer's life is to *maintain* the unbroken attitude of reliance upon the Spirit. Thus, and only thus, can the Spirit possess and vitalize every human faculty, emotion and choice."

If to some a walk in habitual obedience to the will, the ways and the Word of God even in the power of the indwelling Spirit still seems impossible, let us remember that a walk is taken *step by step.* It is a step at a time. And each step taken in obedience makes the next step easier. As we walk in the Spirit our confidence in His power to guide and to guard us deepens and our reliance upon Him grows.

29

The Believer's Part in Remaining Spirit-filled— Bible Study

THE GREATEST PROBLEM of the spiritual man is how to live *habitually* on the highest plane. The question of continuance is the one that perplexes him most. What the Holy Spirit begins in salvation He continues in sanctification. He works for permanence and progress in the spiritual experience of the Christian.

AN ABIDING AND AN ABOUNDING LIFE

Salvation which commences in accepting Christ as Saviour continues in abiding in Him as Life. The last word Christ spoke to His disciples was on the kind of life they were to live after He went away from them. It was not to be a variable up-and-down experience but their life was to be characterized by steadiness and sturdiness. Permanence would be one of its outstanding marks. It was to be an *abiding* life. Abiding is a steady continuance in an already established relationship with the Lord Jesus Christ.

It was to be a life abounding in the exhaustless resources of the Lord of heaven and earth. Life on the highest plane demands growth. There is to be nothing static in experience, stagnant in condition or slothful in action in the spiritual man's life. The language of the spiritual man is always, "Brethren, I count not myself to have apprehended: . . . forgetting those things which are behind, and *reaching forth unto those things which are before,* I press toward the mark for the prize of the high calling of God in Christ Jesus." The passion of the spiritual man is progress in things spiritual. He is not content with bearing "fruit," no not even with bearing "more fruit"; his heart is fixed upon the bearing of the "much fruit" which alone glorifies the Father. Abounding means continually rising to higher ground in the already established relationship in Christ.

Abiding implies reciprocity or mutual giving and taking. It connotes such intimacy of relationship as demands interchange of thought, love, devotion. Abiding means fellowship, the walking and talking together of two who love each other devotedly; the friendship of truly sympathetic persons capable of mutual love and mutual response.

1 John 1:3, "That which we have seen and heard declare we unto you, that ye also may have fellowship with us: and *truly our fellowship is with the Father, and with his Son Jesus Christ.*"

Genesis 5:22, "And *Enoch walked with God.*"

Revelation 3:20, "Behold, I stand at the door, and knock: if any man hear my voice, and open the door, I will come in to him, *and will sup with him, and he with me.*"

But how can such fellowship exist between One in heaven and another on earth? Through what means, by what medium, can such communion be maintained? The answer to this question is to be found in the life of God's second Man. As the Son of Man He maintained unbroken fellowship with His Father in heaven, and as the representative Man He did it through the same means and by the same medium as our fellowship with Him is to be maintained. In this as in all other things He is our Example.

The Holy Spirit was the divine means of communion and the Holy Scriptures were the divine medium of communication between the eternal Father and the incarnate Son. In other words, the Spirit used the Word as the link between heaven and earth.

The incarnate Son lived by the Word of God. He was both obedient to it and dependent upon it. His spiritual growth as a child and His guidance as a Man had their spring in the Word of God.

Luke 2:40, "And *the child grew,* and waxed strong in spirit, filled with wisdom: and the grace of God was upon him."

Strength and stature were His in ever increasing measure. "He was filled with wisdom" that is from above, the wisdom of God. At twelve He astounded the doctors in the Temple by His understanding of the Scriptures.

Luke 4:4, "And Jesus answered him, saying, *It is written,* That man shall not live by bread alone, but by every word of God."

Luke 24:44, "And he said unto them, These are the words which I spake unto you, while I was yet with you, *that all things must be fulfilled, which were written* in the law of Moses, and in the prophets, and in the psalms, concerning me."

The "it is written" of the Scriptures molded His conduct and the "that all things must be fulfilled which were written" marked out His course from the beginning to the end of His ministry. In Scripture He found His Father's plan and path clearly outlined for Him. The loving fellowship which existed between Father and Son was rooted in the Son's habitual obedience to and dependence upon the Word of God.

Is it any wonder, then, that He commended to His disciples a similar life of obedience to and dependence upon the living Word of God if they would abide in Him as He had abided in the Father?

> John 15:10, "*If ye keep my commandments*, ye shall abide in my love; *even as I have kept my Father's commandments*, and abide in his love."

> John 8:31, "Then said Jesus to those Jews which believed on him, *If ye continue in my word*, then are ye my disciples indeed."

> John 15:7, "If ye abide in me, *and my words abide in you*, ye shall ask what ye will, and it shall be done unto you."

We only abide in Him as His Word abides in us and accomplishes its own divinely appointed work. Upon our relationship to the Word of God the permanence and progress of our spiritual life depends. This claim may be easily verified through a study of the Spirit's use of the Word.

THE WORD OF GOD IS THE MEDIUM IN REGENERATION

The instrument used to implant in the human spirit the divine seed of the uncreated life of God is the Word of God. Through the Word we are brought out of death into life.

> 1 Peter 1:23, "*Being born again,* not of corruptible seed, but of incorruptible, *by the word of God,* which liveth and abideth for ever."

THE WORD OF GOD IS THE MEDIUM IN REVELATION

Life requires light. Regeneration presumes revelation. The newborn soul has been "called . . . out of darkness into his marvellous light" (1 Peter 2:9) and the light of God cannot be concealed from the one to whom the life of God has been communicated.

Illumination is absolutely essential to the new life in Christ. To maintain the life, light is imperative.

> John 1:4, "In him was life; and *the life was the light of men.*"

> John 8:12, "Then spake Jesus again unto them, saying, I am the light of the world: he that followeth me shall not walk in darkness, *but shall have the light of life.*"

Illumination is absolutely essential to the new walk in Christ.

> Ephesians 5:8, "For ye were sometimes darkness, but *now are ye light in the Lord: walk as children of light.*"

> 1 John 1:5-7, "God is light, and in him is no darkness at all. If we say that we have fellowship with him, and walk in darkness, we lie, and do not the truth: but *if we walk in the light, as he is in the light,* we have fellowship one with another, and the blood of Jesus Christ his Son cleanseth us from all sin."

When the Holy Spirit enters the human spirit He bestows a spiritual nature which has the capacity to perceive and an appetite to know. An insatiable hunger and an unquenchable thirst for the knowledge of God possesses a Spirit-filled, Spirit-controlled man. He cries with the psalmist, "As the hart panteth after the water brooks, so panteth my soul after thee, O God. My soul thirsteth for the living God."

One of the sure marks of a spiritual man is his ever increasing knowledge of God. Spiritual perception and spiritual enlightenment stamp a man as a growing Christian. God puts no premium on ignorance. Paul prayed that his converts might have spiritual understanding, heaven-born wisdom, divine enlightenment.

> Ephesians 1:17-18, "That the God of our Lord Jesus Christ, the Father of glory, *may give unto you the spirit of wisdom and revelation in the knowledge of him: the eyes of your understanding being enlightened; that ye may know* what is the hope of his calling, and what the riches of the glory of his inheritance in the saints."

> Colossians 1:9, "For this cause we also, since the day we heard it, do not cease to pray for you, and to desire *that ye might be filled with the knowledge of his will in all wisdom and spiritual understanding.*"

God expects every child of His to be growing in the knowledge of Him. Paul did not pray that the Colossian Christians might be filled with the knowledge of God's will in all wisdom and spiritual understanding that they might be equipped to fill a chair in a theological seminary or to go as a missionary to some foreign field, but that wherever they were and whatever their task they might "walk worthily of the Lord unto all pleasing," "be fruitful in every good work," and "be strengthened with might, unto all patience and long-suffering with joyfulness."

The apostle Paul constantly said "Know ye not?" Again and again in the letters to the Ephesians, Philippians and Colossians he speaks of the things we should know. The words "we know" are almost the key words of the first epistle of John. Count for yourself the number of times they are used and write out the things the Christian should "Know." In the realm of the spiritual it is the man who knows who does.

> Daniel 11:32, "And such as do wickedly against the covenant shall be corrupt by flatteries: *but the people that do know their God shall be strong, and do exploits.*"

In Romans 6 God's divine order is "Know" (v. 6); "Reckon" (v. 11); "Yield" (v. 13); "Obey" (v. 17). It is the man who really knows God who believingly reckons on the great facts of salvation, who voluntarily yields himself to the Saviour, and who gladly obeys Christ, the Lord. Growth in grace and growth in the knowledge of God are simultaneous.

> 2 Peter 3:18, "Grow in grace, and *in the knowledge of our Lord and Saviour Jesus Christ.*"

But spiritual knowledge comes through just one channel. The Word of God is the divinely appointed medium of revelation. The entrance of God's Word giveth light. Life and light come from the same source.

> Psalm 36:9, "For with thee is the fountain of life: *in thy light shall we see light.*"

> Psalm 119:130, "*The entrance of thy words giveth light;* it giveth understanding unto the simple."

> Romans 10:17, "So then faith cometh by hearing, and *hearing by the word of God.*"

In the Word of God the Christian finds the revelation of everything needful for salvation, sanctification and service. All that the Father intends His child to know regarding his spiritual possessions, privileges and responsibilities He has revealed in the Bible. The clear revelation of Himself, His will, His way and His purpose is all in the Word.

> John 15:15, "Henceforth I call you not servants; for the servant knoweth not what his lord doeth: but I have called you friends; *for all things that I have heard of my Father I have made known unto you.*"

> Ephesians 1:9, "*Having made known unto us the mystery of his will,* according to his good pleasure which he hath purposed in himself."

The man who gives himself to daily thought and prayerful meditation on God's Word possesses a degree of spiritual perception out of all proportion to his intellectual capacity or attainment, judged from the standpoint of things natural.

The Word of God Is the Medium of Renewal

Even the spiritual man has no resources in himself. He is in daily need of replenishing. "The spiritual blessings, which are given to him according to the everlasting covenant, are all treasured up in heavenly places in Christ Jesus. Once we have begun to draw nigh to God, we must continue to draw nigh. It is both a necessity and a delight. A necessity because we are still as dependent on the creative, supernatural influence of grace. . . . Such pensioners are we of the divine bounty, daily and hourly we must be recipients of His gifts and of His power. Peter imagines he has a stock of courage and loving loyalty in himself; but sad experience teaches him that his nature is feeble and selfish; that not he, but Christ in him, is rock. . . . We have nothing in ourselves; our sufficiency is of God" (Adolph Saphir, *The Hidden Life*, pp. 19-20). The spiritual man never ceases to feel his utter dependence upon God.

God provides for his renewal. The man who is saved by the truth of God's Word is also sanctified by it. The stature and strength of the spiritual man will be in exact proportion to his faithful continuance in the Word of the Lord. The study of God's Word is the divinely appointed means of spiritual culture; the divinely ordained method of spiritual growth.

> John 17:17, "*Sanctify them through thy truth: thy word is turth.*"

> John 8:31, "Then said Jesus to those Jews which believed on him, *If ye continue in my word,* then are ye my disciples indeed."

A careful study of the scriptural names of the Word of God will reveal God's intended use of it in the renewal of the Christian's life.

THE WORD IS A MIRROR TO REVEAL

> James 1:23-25, "For if any [man] be a hearer of the word, and not a doer, *he is like unto a man beholding his natural face in a glass: for he beholdeth himself,* and goeth his way, and straightway forgetteth what manner of man he was. *But whoso looketh into the perfect law of liberty,* and continueth therein, he being not a forgetful hearer, but a doer of the work, this man shall be blessed in his deed."

A mirror reveals the personal appearance of the one who looks into it. The Bible is just such a revelation of man. In it we see the human heart mirrored exactly as it is in the sight of God. We have in the Word full-length portraits of the natural, the carnal and the spiritual man. As one studies the Bible he finds himself; mirrored in the lives of men and women who lived centuries ago he sees himself. In the covetousness of Achan, the backsliding of David, the despondency of Elijah, the avarice of Jacob, the falsehood of Ananias and Sapphira, the denial of Peter, the self-righteousness of Saul of Tarsus and the jealousy, unbelief and self-seeking of the disciples, he looks into his own sinful heart and his own wayward life. The Bible takes the covering off the inmost spirit and unveils its secret thoughts and motives. It shows us to ourselves as we are. But it does not stop there. It unfolds to man's vision the perfect Man. He "beholds as in a glass the glory of the Lord" for in the Word, God gives "the light of the knowledge of the glory of God in the face of Jesus Christ." Then the Bible challenges him, who has seen himself as he is and as he may become, to act upon the vision, to become a doer of the Word in order that he may be conformed to the image of Christ.

THE WORD IS WATER TO CLEANSE AND REFRESH

> Ephesians 5:25-26, "Christ also loved the church, and gave himself for it;

> *that he might sanctify and cleanse it with the washing of water by the word."*
>
> John 15:3, "Now *ye are clean through the word which I have spoken unto you."*
>
> Psalm 119:9, "Wherewithal shall a young man *cleanse his way? by taking heed thereto according to thy word."*

Walking as pilgrims through a world reeking in sin we are in constant contact with its defilement and in constant need of cleansing. In olden times the priests, who were cleansed by the blood at the brazen altar, still needed the washing of water at the laver to make them fit for the worship and the work of the tabernacle. So we, though cleansed from the guilt of sin through the blood of the living Word, yet need daily the washing by the water of the written Word. The Christian's life is kept pure and clean only in the proportion to which the Word of God is hid in the heart and applied to the life.

Water also refreshes. Countless Christians could testify to the removal of weariness of spirit, discouragement of soul and even exhaustion of body through a quiet hour of meditation upon the Word.

THE WORD OF GOD IS FOOD TO NOURISH AND DELIGHT

The Word is milk for the newborn babe; it is strong meat for the spiritual adult; and it is honey for the spiritually minded.

> 1 Peter 2:2, *"As newborn babes, desire the sincere milk of the word,* that ye may grow thereby."
>
> Hebrews 5:14, *"But strong meat belongeth to them that are of full age,* even those who by reason of use have their senses exercised to discern both good and evil."
>
> Psalm 19:10, "More to be desired are they than gold, yea, than much fine gold: *sweeter also than honey and the honeycomb."*

The man who feeds upon God's Word will become strong; the one who neglects it will be dwarfed. Both stature and strength are gauged by the quality of spiritual food eaten and assimilated. Wherever you find a spiritual anemic the reason is improper food.

The Christian who is improperly or insufficiently fed is the prey to all kinds of spiritual disease. He is powerless to resist temptation, blind to discern error, helpless to overcome sin. He is open to all the deceiving devices and subtle strategies of the evil one. He not only makes no progress but he cannot even hold his own and lives a flabby, inconsistent, dishonoring life before the world.

The Christian who is not entering into new possessions of God's grace, love and power through new conquests of the Word is living on the stale manna of some moldy experience or musty testimony. The new nature is starved because forced to exist on denatured emotions and devitalized vocabulary, "he feedeth on ashes" instead of "the bread of life." Christ knew that the only food upon which the new nature could thrive was the Word of God. In His high priestly prayer He said to His Father, "I have given them thy word" (John 17:14).

Sometimes a Christian worker has lost his power for no other reason than neglect of the Bible. Because of this his message is devoid of freshness and fruitfulness. The inevitable result is the giving of his own word in the wisdom, eloquence and energy of the flesh. This God never promises to bless.

> 1 Corinthians 2:4, "And *my speech and my preaching was not with enticing words of man's wisdom,* but in demonstration of the Spirit and of power."
>
> 1 Thessalonians 2:13, "For this cause also thank we God without ceasing, because, *when ye received the word of God* which ye heard of us, *ye received it not as the word of men,* but as it is in truth, the word of God, which effectually worketh also in you that believe."

"Man shall not live by bread alone, but by every word of God" (Luke 4:4). "The words that I speak unto you, they are spirit, and they are life" (John 6:63). Can we think it possible that the food on our tables should be so transmuted in nature's laboratory that it should reappear, now in stalwart muscle of the blacksmith's arm, and now in the fine texture of the poet's brain, and let it seem incredible that the Word of God can reappear in every kind of spiritual power and holy efficiency?

THE WORD OF GOD IS A LAMP TO GUIDE

> Psalm 119:105, "Thy word is *a lamp unto my feet,* and *a light unto my path.*"

Pitfalls are all around the Christian; the devil has well-laid snares to entrap.

> 2 Timothy 2:26, "And *that they may recover themselves out of the snare of the devil,* who are taken captive by him at his will."
>
> Psalm 119:110, "*The wicked have laid a snare for me:* yet I erred not from thy precepts."

The straight and narrow way is not always easily discerned and still less easily followed. In these perilous times when there is so much of the world in the Church and when even the shepherd of the flock may walk in ways quite contrary to the Word of God, many an earnest Christian is perplexed and at a loss to know what is a consistent walk. He surely needs a light upon his path.

But he needs even more than that; he needs to be shown each step of the way. The Word of God is just such a guide and, when it is hid in the heart and heeded in the life, the Christian need not wander nor stumble. His every step may be ordered in full conformity to God's will and ways because in full obedience to God's Word.

> Psalm 119:133, *"Order my steps in thy word:* and let not any iniquity have dominion over me."
>
> Psalm 37:31, "The law of his God is in his heart; *none of his steps shall slide."*

Many mistakes are made by Christians through seeking and following the counsel of men rather than that of God. Some have lost the way altogether and are living outside the will of God because they have listened to man's voice. I know a life that is shipwrecked upon the rock of human counsel, devoid of both peace and power. We cannot be reminded too often of the solemn fact that Adam's sin came through heeding Eve's voice, and Eve sinned by believing and obeying the devil's word instead of God's. There is but one absolutely safe counselor for the Christian, the Word of God.

> Psalm 119:24, *"Thy testimonies also are* my delight and *my counsellors."*
>
> 2 Timothy 3:15, "And that from a child thou hast known *the holy scriptures, which are able to make thee wise unto salvation* through faith which is in Christ Jesus."

The teaching, instruction, warning, correction and guidance which every Christian needs to make him complete and to equip him for service are all to be found in the Bible.

> 2 Timothy 3:16-17, R. V., "Every scripture inspired of God is also *profitable for teaching, for reproof, for correction, for instruction* which is in righteousness: that the man of God may be complete, furnished completely unto every good work."

THE WORD OF GOD IS WEALTH TO ENRICH

> Psalm 119:14, "I have rejoiced in the way of thy testimonies, *as much as in all riches."*
>
> Psalm 119:72, "The law of thy mouth is better unto me *than thousands of gold and silver."*
>
> Psalm 119:127, "Therefore I love thy commandments *above gold; yea, above fine gold."*
>
> Psalm 119:162, "I rejoice at thy word, *as one that findeth great spoil."*

There is constant drain upon the Christian. Everything in his environment tends to impoverishment of spirit. There is unceasing need of renewal through enrichment. But in the Lord Jesus are "hid all the treasures of wisdom and knowledge" (Colossians 2:3); in Him are embodied all the unsearchable riches of grace and glory (Philippians 4:19; Ephesians 1:7). The Spirit opens these to us by opening the Scriptures and enabling us through the Word to know and to claim all the things which He hath given us richly to enjoy.

THE WORD OF GOD IS A CRITIC TO JUDGE

> Hebrews 4:12, "*For the word of God* is quick, and powerful, and sharper than any twoedged sword, piercing even to the dividing asunder of soul and spirit, and of the joints and marrow, and *is a discerner of the thoughts and intents of the heart.*"

The Greek word *Krítikos* means able to judge. The tendency today is that men choose to be critics of the Word rather than to accept the Word as their critic. But one very salutary function of the Bible is its judgment upon the Christian's thoughts and actions. The psalmist who offered that sincere prayer, "Search me, O God, and know my heart: try me, and know my thoughts: and see if there be any wicked way in me, and lead me in the way everlasting," knew the helpfulness of God's righteous judgments.

> Psalm 119:164, "Seven times a day do I praise thee *because of thy righteous judgments.*"

> Psalm 119:175, "Let my soul live, and it shall praise thee; and *let thy judgments help me.*"

What a quickening of spiritual life would take place today if every child of God would put his life under the righteous judgment of the Word of God. The long-prayed-for revival undoubtedly would burst forth like fire if the Bible were permitted to become the critic of men's thoughts, feelings and actions, and if they were willing to act upon its kindly, beneficent criticism.

THE WORD OF GOD IS A MANUAL OF HOLY LIVING

> Psalm 119:1-3, "Blessed are the undefiled in the way, *who walk in the law of the Lord.* Blessed are they that keep his testimonies, and that seek him with the whole heart. They also do no iniquity: *they walk in his ways.*"

God has provision for every step of the way in the life of godliness, which He expects His child to live. In His Word He has given the principles that govern such a life, and the precepts which teach us how to practice them. The Christian who practices the presence of God and who lives the Christ-life most transparently is the one who is most thoroughly saturated with God's Word and who deliberately has given himself to live out that Word in deed.

THE WORD OF GOD IS A WEAPON

> Ephesians 6:17, "And take the helmet of salvation, and *the sword of the Spirit, which is the word of God."*

The Spirit-filled man has enemies; he is engaged in a warfare. The powers of hell are all against him. He is always open to attack and momentarily liable to defeat. He needs both defensive and offensive weapons. He must be able both to stand and to withstand in every assault of Satan.

There is but one way this can be done and it is the way the God-man used. His only weapon in the wilderness was the Sword of the Spirit. "It is written," repeated three times in the threefold attack, repulsed the enemy.

Let us note that the God-man had His sword burnished and ready. He did not wait to draw out the scroll of Scripture and read from it to get an answer for the devil. In the years of seclusion in the Nazareth home He had stored away the words of God in His heart, and in the hours of quiet work in the carpenter's shop He had meditated upon them. It may be that the Son of Man had gone into the wilderness fresh from the study of Deuteronomy. His mind was so saturated with its truth that when Satan attacked, the Spirit instantly brought to remembrance the very words that utterly routed him. The Son of Man was kept in the moment of temptation by the Word hid in His heart.

> Deuteronomy 11:18, *"Therefore shall ye lay up these my words in your heart and in your soul,* and bind them for a sign upon your hand, that they may be as frontlets between your eyes."

> Psalm 119:11, *"Thy word have I hid in mine heart,* that I might not sin against thee."

> Colossians 3:16, *"Let the word of Christ dwell in you richly in all wisdom;* teaching and admonishing one another in psalms and hymns and spiritual songs, singing with grace in your hearts to the Lord."

Often the reason we yield so quickly to temptation is that our sword is rusty. This gives Satan the advantage over us. Temptation comes to us on the street, in the office, when we may not have a Bible with us. It comes unexpectedly. There is no time to stop and search for an effectual portion of Scripture. It is only that part of the Word that is hid in the heart that will become a Sword in action at the moment most needed. It is the portion of the Word of God which we have learned and lived that will be effectual in the fight with Satan.

Another essential to success is confidence in the weapon we use. I feel sure there was the certitude of victory in the very tone of the voice when the Lord Jesus said, "It is written!" To Him the Word was authoritative and final. His confidence in the absolute authority of Deuteronomy had not been weakened by a doubtful attitude toward its authorship. To Him it was the Word of God forever settled in heaven. He had no question concerning its potency because He had no doubt concerning its purity or its permanence.

> Psalm 12:6, "*The words of the Lord are pure words:* as silver tried in a furnace of earth, purified seven times."
>
> Proverbs 30:5, "*Every word of God is pure:* he is a shield unto them that put their trust in him."
>
> Luke 21:33, "Heaven and earth shall pass away: *but my words shall not pass away.*"

Many Christians are defeated today in the warfare against sin and Satan because of doubt regarding their weapon, the Word of God. To them the Word is not the Sword of the Spirit but it is merely a staff of man's making to assist him on the pathway of life which he feels at liberty to whittle down to the measure of his own intellect and experience. Belief in the absolute trustworthiness and final authority of the Word is an essential to the potent use of it as the Sword.

The Word of God is a Fire that Both Burns and Warms

> Jeremiah 20:9, "Then I said, I will not make mention of him, nor speak any more in his name. *But his word was in mine heart as a burning fire* shut up in my bones, and I was weary with forbearing, and I could not stay."

The Bible is like a fire that burns out the dross, purifying and purging. It is a devouring flame before which nothing that is contrary to God's will and ways can stand.

> Jeremiah 5:14, "Wherefore thus saith the Lord God of hosts, Because ye speak this word, behold, *I will make my words in thy mouth fire, and this people wood, and it shall devour them.*"
>
> 1 Peter 1:22, "*Seeing ye have purified your souls in obeying the truth* through the Spirit unto unfeigned love of the brethren, see that ye love one another with a pure heart fervently."

It is at the same time a fire that warms with comfort and cheer the heart desolated by sorrow and distressed through suffering.

1 Thessalonians 4:18, "Wherefore *comfort* one another *with these words.*"

Psalm 119:50, "This is my comfort in my affliction: *for thy word hath quickened me.*"

Psalm 119:165, "*Great peace have they which love thy law:* and nothing shall offend them."

THE WORD OF GOD IS A HAMMER TO BREAK

Jeremiah 23:29, "Is not my word like as a fire? saith the LORD; *and like a hammer that breaketh the rock in pieces?*"

There is such a residue of stubbornness, resistance and rebellion in every life! The man who has been accustomed to go his own way, seek his own pleasure to do his own will is not easily made submissive and humble. There is much in every one of us that is hard which needs to be broken; much that is resisting which needs to be melted.

As the Christian studies the Word and comes under the softening rays of God's loving-kindness, tender mercy, unfailing faithfulness, unquenchable love and exhaustless grace, his heart is melted, his will is broken and his life is turned into joyous, humble submission to the loving will of God.

THE WORD OF GOD IS A SEED THAT MATURES AND MULTIPLIES

Luke 8:11, "Now the parable is this: *The seed is the word of God.*"

James 1:18, "Of his own will *begat he us with the word of truth*, that we should be a kind of firstfruits of his creatures."

Psalm 126:6, "He that goeth forth and weepeth, *bearing precious seed*, shall doubtless come again with rejoicing, *bringing his sheaves with him.*"

A seed in itself is but a small hard substance which, if laid away in a drawer will remain only a seed. But put into suitable soil, given needed nurture, it will become a plant or a tree. The Word of God is seed. Left on the drawing-room table to give semblance of religion to the home or carried when traveling to fulfill a promise to a praying mother at home, or as a sacred charm to ward off disaster, it will never influence or change the life in any way whatsoever. But let that incorruptible seed which has the very germ of life in it—"My words are life"—be sown in the soil of the human heart by the Holy Ghost and it fructifies in a new creation.

Nor is it enough to accept the Bible as historically true. Before it can manifest its power to save and to sanctify it must be engrafted upon the inner life.

James 1:21, "Wherefore lay apart all filthiness and superfluity of naughtiness, and *receive with meekness the engrafted word*, which is able to save your souls."

The seed needs to be fostered and nurtured by earnest study and eager searching. Seed needs time to grow. The Word must be pondered and meditated upon. It must lie fallow in the mind, heart, conscience and will to bring forth its full fruitage. The seed must be kept abiding in the soil of faith. The Christian must continue in the Word. The Word must abide in him by day and by night.

> Psalm 119:97, "O how love I thy law! *it is my meditation all the day.*"
>
> Psalm 119:148, "Mine eyes prevent the night watches, *that I might meditate in thy word.*"
>
> John 15:7, "If ye abide in me, *and my words abide in you,* ye shall ask what ye will, and it shall be done unto you."

Countless times have I seen the maturing, multiplying power of the Word of God when engrafted upon a human life but in none more beautifully illustrated than in the life of a Chinese teacher who came to a summer conference as an interpreter. Although he had been a Christian for many years and was active in Christian work yet he was lamentably ignorant of the Word of God. This fact was so borne in upon him as he interpreted the missionary's message that he determined to leave his position as teacher immediately and devote himself to the study of the Bible. He went to a seminary for a short time, then spent several months alone with only the Holy Spirit as Teacher and Revealer of the deep things of the Book. At the end of a year of such intensive Bible study he returned to the community where he had lived formerly.

Shortly afterward I received a letter from a missionary in that city, in which she said:

> "It would delight your very soul could you see and know all the wonderful way in which the Lord has led and used W—— in the last six or eight months. His Bible classes last fall and winter numbering about two hundred, were very fine indeed. He had them for all classes, from college boys down to the cooks and other servants on our compounds. *His year away made a new man of him.* That year's study did worlds for him in the Scriptures. *His familiarity with the Bible now is as marked as his lack of it was before this year of close application, and of course he is going on too, gaining ground all the time.* He is probably going to be ordained in a few weeks now and become assistant pastor of the —— church. The strongest thing about W—— is his life of prayer. Partly through the instrumentality of him and his sister, if not *mostly*, there are now being held three meetings a day just for prayer. And praise His Name, there have been some extraordinary answers to the prayers of this little circle which has for many months met every Sunday morning very early, really before the dawn. Now they have it every day."

Coldness of heart, callousness of conscience, weakness of will, feebleness of testimony, joylessness in worship, fruitlessness in service, powerlessness in prayer all are traceable to just one thing—ignorance of and indifference to God's Word. "Ye seek to kill me, *because my word hath no place in you*" (John 8:37). But, when the Word is given its rightful place in any life, it has power to convict, to convert, to cleanse, to control, to criticize, to correct and to consecrate. It becomes a mold that fashions the life into ever growing likeness to the image of Christ Jesus. "The Word is an expulsive power to turn out the tyranny of sin; an enlightening power to dispel the darkness of ignorance; an ennobling power to elevate the mind; an eradicating power to cleanse the heart; an endowing power to enrich the being, and an effectual power to bless in every way to the glory of God" (F. E. Marsh, *The Spiritual Life*, p. 49).

Bible Study for Personal Spiritual Growth

I was once asked by a group of high school pupils to lead their Christian Endeavour meeting. The invitation read as follows, "We would like for you to tell us how *to read it so as to get the most out of it*. Most of us read a chapter a day but then I am afraid that we do not do very much else." Doubtless this is the experience of many Christians.

To know how to study the Bible for personal spiritual growth is the need of every Christian, old and young. It is not possible in the confines of this chapter to make suggestions regarding methods of Bible study. Nor is it necessary to do so, for the person who truly desires to know the Word will discover for himself the best method.

But I would mention three things which to me seem essential for the kind of Bible study which will lift a Christian to life on the highest plane. They are *an adequate objective, a right attitude,* and *an obedient response.*

The reason the Bible "has no taste" and why it is so unproductive of spiritual harvest in our lives is partly due to the lack of an adequate objective. To read the Bible aimlessly, to read it because one has signed a pledge promising to read a chapter a day or because of the desire to please a parent, teacher or friend, but without the purpose to remember what is read and to reproduce it in character and conduct, while it may bring blessing, will not lift one to life on the highest plane. To read it spasmodically, to desire comfort in sorrow, to obtain strength in trial, to find wisdom in perplexity and to receive guidance in uncertainty, while all are legitimate motives, yet they are not the highest nor those most productive of spiritual gain.

There is, in fact, but one objective that is altogether adequate and it is that through the Word of God, we may know the Son of God. The Lord Jesus Christ is the central fact, and the commanding Figure of the Bible.

From Genesis to Revelation He is to be found. No book of the Bible will be fully understood until Christ be seen in it. He is the pivot upon which everything in the divine revelation turns and He is the fountain from which everything in spiritual experience springs. *To know Him* is eternal life, to know Him better and better is life abiding and abounding.

> Philippians 3:8, 10, "Yea, doubtless, and I count all things but loss *for the excellency of the knowledge of Christ Jesus* my Lord: for whom I have suffered the loss of all things, and do count them but dung, *that I may win Christ.*
> *That I may know him,* and the power of his resurrection, and the fellowship of his sufferings, being made conformable unto his death."

"That I may know him"—that I may win Christ—this is the objective that will challenge one to earnestly, eagerly search the Scriptures.

The papers of a continent recorded the story of the nonstop flight of Colonel Lindbergh from Washington, D. C., to Mexico City. Alone he flew for twenty-seven hours through an untraversed track of air, enduring loss of sleep and lack of food, surmounting great difficulties and encountering great dangers from the beginning to the end of the trip. He faced all these conditions before he started, but he had an objective that was big enough and worthy enough and challenging enough—to win Mexico City in a nonstop flight. And he reached his goal while the people of a whole continent looked on his achievement with admiration and praise.

Colonel Lindbergh had an adequate objective but how was it attained? Through skill you say. But was there any other contributing cause to the success of his flight? Judging by an article written by the commandant of Bolling Field from which he took off on his flight, half of the success of the trip was won before he ever stepped into his plane at Washington. He says, "The flier *studied everything.* He pored over weather maps; figured time and fuel needed; and examined the field minutely. On three different occasions he walked over the entire airdrome carefully, noting the soft or boggy places, the rough spots, the sound, high, firm or grassy places, the ditches, depressions and obstacles bordering the airdrome, the height of trees, buildings, smoke-stacks, radio towers, etc., within a mile from the field; also the fact that the river level was ten to fifteen feet below the airdrome level at one particular end of the field where no hurdle presented itself." Colonel Lindbergh had an adequate objective which constrained him to make this minute and masterful study of everything pertaining to that flight.

One day on the road to Damascus the young Hebrew, Saul of Tarsus, saw the Lord Jesus Christ. Then and there he was not only converted but captivated. "One figure enraptured him, captivated his being, bound him as with chains, and that figure is Christ Jesus, the Lord. One passion reigns, one motive dominates, that the Lord, in love, devotion and service should be his all-in-all. Everything else is subservient, everything else is counted as refuse that this one object may be altogether his. Nothing of earth is comparable to Him, nothing of earth is desired beside Him. All that once was counted gain is discarded as loss for the priceless possession of the eternal treasure—Jesus Christ the Lord."

Paul, having caught a vision of his risen, exalted Lord, having been captivated by His grace and glory, was consumed with the passion to make "a nonstop flight" to the perfect possession of all his glorious inheritance in Christ Jesus. His objective—"that I may win Christ"—so big, so worthy, so challenging that it made the things of time, sense and earth sink into utter insignificance. His objective—"that I may know him"—so constraining that it carried him away into Arabia for three years where he received the God-inspired revelation which has come down to you and me through his epistles.

What is your objective in Bible study? Is it merely to satisfy intellectual curiosity? Is it only to know the contents of the Bible and to appreciate its literary value as one of the great books in the world's library? Is it even for a purely selfish enrichment of your own life? Or do you come every day to the written Word of God that you may better know the eternal, incarnate, risen, living Word of God as He is revealed in its pages? Your goal will very largely determine your gain. Will you today enter the company of those who, emulating the apostle Paul's example, approach God's Word daily saying "I count all things but loss for the excellency of the knowledge of Christ Jesus my Lord . . . that I may win Christ and be found in him." There will surely be a divine response to such seeking and God will give "the light of the knowledge of the glory of God in the face of Jesus Christ."

> 2 Corinthians 4:6, "For God, who commanded the light to shine out of darkness, hath shined in our hearts, *to give the light of the knowledge of the glory of God in the face of Jesus Christ.*"

The second essential in Bible study for personal spiritual growth is a right attitude. What we get from the Bible is determined very largely by what we bring to it. If we approach the Bible in an attitude of doubt we shall probably leave it in doubt.

A Christian worker whose faith in the Word of God had been so undermined and poisoned that she said she disbelieved and doubted everything in the Book before she even opened it, came one day to me in great distress. She had been asked to give an Easter message and she had none to give. She came to ask that we might read together the accounts of the resurrection in the four gospels. As we read Matthew 28:17, "And when they saw him: they worshipped him: but some doubted," she just dropped her Bible and said, "Oh! it is no wonder they doubted!" I said, "Oh! is *that* the way you read it? As I read it, it is no wonder that they *worshiped!*" "I see," she replied, "it all depends on the attitude you bring to the Bible; if you bring doubt, you will doubt; if you bring worship, you will worship."

The first secret of Bible study is faith born of humility. He that comes to God must believe that He *is* and that He *does*. He must come believing that through the Word, God speaks and therefore he must come humbly and reverently.

> Hebrews 11:6, "But without faith it is impossible to please him: for he that cometh to God must believe *that he is,* and *that he is a rewarder of them* that diligently seek him."
>
> Psalm 119:161, "Princes have persecuted me without a cause: *but my heart standeth in awe of thy word.*"

But we must approach the study of God's Word not only in faith but in love. It will not yield a very abundant harvest to the one who comes to it merely from a sense of duty. To enrich the life Bible study must be regarded as a delight. How well the psalmist knew his Lord. The secret is not hard to discover.

> Psalm 1:2, "*But his delight is in the law of the Lord;* and in his law doth he meditate day and night."
>
> Psalm 119:47, "*And I will delight myself in thy commandments,* which I have loved."

But how contrary is such an attitude to that of most Christians. In what a purely perfunctory, desultory manner many Christians study or read the Bible. It is like a bit of distasteful medicine that is needed for the sake of health but the quicker taken the better. The Bible is opened in a haphazard fashion to any place; the reading is done with no relish; the Book is gladly closed and what was read makes little impression.

The Word of God is a living thing and accordingly responds to the treatment given to it. What a difference it makes when one truly hungers for the bread of life; when one thirsts for the living water; when one comes to the Word of God with a keen appetite for a full meal. The Word of God becomes food to such a one and honey to his taste.

> Jeremiah 15:16, "Thy words were found, and I did eat them; *and thy word was unto me the joy and rejoicing of mine heart:* for I am called by thy name, O LORD of hosts."
>
> Job 23:12, R. V., "I have not gone back from the commandment of his lips; *I have treasured up the words of his mouth more than my necessary food.*"

Psalm 119:103, "*How sweet are thy words unto my taste! Yea, sweeter than honey to my mouth!*"

What a difference it makes when one approaches the Bible as on a quest, when one is really hunting for something as the gold digger hunts for the gold. Then he is content with no superficial reading but he systematically searches; he seeks for great spoil; he diligently digs for the deepest truths. Such a one is saved from intellectual laziness and stands ready for the concentration and meditation required of one who deeply knows God. The Bible becomes a gold mine to such a searcher after truth.

Psalm 119:127, "Therefore *I love thy commandments above gold; yea,* above fine gold."

Psalm 119:162, "*I rejoice at thy word, as one that findeth great spoil.*"

What a difference it makes when one truly loves the Book and longs to know Christ! Then he does not study with an eye on the clock but rather rejoices to find an extra hour or two that he may spend upon the Word. Such a man knows the thrill of "a nonstop flight" even through Genesis, Isaiah or Revelation. He loves the Book of God because he loves the God of the Book.

Psalm 119:140, "Thy word is very pure: therefore *thy servant loveth it.*"

John 14:21, "*He that hath my commandments, and keepeth them, he it is that loveth me: and he that loveth me shall be loved of my Father, and I will love him, and will manifest myself to him.*"

We must approach the Word of God not only in faith and in love but in a willingness to obey. To learn and then not to live is deadly and disastrous. Disobedience to what God said through doubt kept the children of Israel out of Canaan and later took their posterity into captivity and exile. One must become a doer of the Word.

Deuteronomy 6:1, "Now these are the commandments, the statutes, and the judgments, which the LORD your God commanded to teach you, *that ye might do them* in the land whither ye go to possess it."

John 14:23, "Jesus answered and said unto him, *If a man love me, he will keep my words:* and my Father will love him, and we will come unto him, and make our abode with him."

The Bible will never really become ours until we have the consistent and persistent purpose to live what we learn. We might make a very careful study of the constituent elements of foods and know just how much of each we need in our system to ensure health but that knowledge will not give strength of body. Only as we eat, digest and assimilate the food itself does it minister to our bodily needs. So we need to beware of mere head knowledge of the Bible. Apart from the Holy Spirit's inworking of the Word of life into the very fabric of our being it has no saving or sanctifying power. This He cannot do unless there is an obedient response on our part. The Word is not given to us to make our intellects treasure-houses of heavenly wisdom but to make our hearts the sanctuaries of the heavenly One. God's warnings have no value for one unless they are heeded: His precepts profit nothing unless they are followed and His commandments can only bless as they are obeyed. *"If ye keep my commandments."* The whole force of what follows draws its meaning from that little word "if." If we take food into the body, it becomes blood and muscle, so if we incorporate the Word of God into our life, it becomes character and conduct. When studying God's Word we should say to ourselves constantly, "How can this be worked into the very woof and warp of my life?" The Bible to yield its full fruitage demands not only consideration and meditation but application.

Someone had told of a Korean Christian who was examined on the Sermon on the Mount and was able to repeat it without mistake. When the missionary asked, "How did you manage to learn it so perfectly?" the reply came, "I learned it a verse or a few verses at a time. I would learn a verse and then go out and find someone to *practice it on.*"

A native of India read the gospels for the first time and while filled with admiration for the God-man, yet such a life in such a world seemed wholly incredible to him. Then he read on into the epistles and learned that the Christian was one who was like his Lord and whose life was lived in obedience to the Word. So he started out on a quest—*to find a man whose life matched* the Book—determining that if his quest were successful, he would believe. If he had seen you or me would he have found one whose life matched the Book?

Dr. Alex. Smellie wrote of Evan H. Hopkins, "He was a *sermon incarnate.* The sunshine of the Better Country where his days and nights were spent, played on his soul and articulated itself in his speech; it was sunshine not merely visible but audible."

It is the man who obeys the truth as he knows it whose capacity is enlarged to receive larger and fuller revelations of truth. The man who steadfastly lives out what he learns is ever learning more.

> Genesis 13:14, "And the Lord said unto Abram, *after that Lot was separated from him,* Lift up now thine eyes, and look from the place where thou art northward, and southward, and eastward, and westward."

"The Lord said—after that." Here is a most significant sequence. Obedience to God's command brought the fuller revelation of God's purpose to Abram. So will it be with you and me. Disobedience to the known will of God as revealed in His Word is the cause of much of the stagnancy and slothfulness in the churches of today. What a revival would take place in the corporate Body of Christ, the Church, and what a revolution there would be in the individual members if every Christian began to live what he has learned of the Word of God.

Sir Arthur Blackwell has summed up the Christian's relationship to the Bible in four great words.

"admit"— Open your whole being to let it be flooded with light. Let the truth in. Study the Bible sympathetically and lovingly. Let it be God's voice to you direct.

"submit"— Let the truth grip you that it may govern you. "Let the plain declarations of God's Word be the end of all controversy. Whenever we raise an issue with God all growth and all blessing must stop until that issue is settled."

"commit"— Grip the truth by hiding it in your heart. Let today's message be articulated to yesterday's so that a chain is forged that is a veritable anchor to your soul in times of temptation, trouble and trial.

"transmit"—"Don't be a pool; be a stream." Don't hoard your riches; share the bounties of the Lord's table with another. Make every truth tenfold your own by passing it on.

Missionary A—— possessed some strawberry plants which he shared with Missionary B—— who came to live beside him. That year Missionary A's plants were all destroyed by insects and Missionary B—— gave back to Missionary A—— half his plants. So all the plants which Missionary A—— possessed were what he gave away.

The Holy Spirit—The Divine Teacher, Guide and Revealer

There is no reason for ignorance of divine things on the part of any Christian who can read, for God has not only furnished us with a Textbook but with a Teacher: He has given us not only a Guidebook but a Guide: He has unfolded to us not only a Revelation but has bestowed upon us the Revealer.

John 14:26, "But the Comforter, which is *the Holy Ghost,* whom the Father will send in my name, *he shall teach you all things,* and bring all things to your remembrance, whatsoever I have said unto you."

John 16:13, "Howbeit when he, *the Spirit of truth,* is come, *he will guide you into all truth:* for he shall not speak of himself; but whatsoever he shall hear, that shall he speak: and he will shew you things to come."

> 1 Corinthians 2:9-10, "But as it is written, Eye hath not seen, nor ear heard, neither have entered into the heart of man, the things which God hath prepared for them that love him. *But God hath revealed them unto us by his Spirit:* for the Spirit searcheth all things, yea, the deep things of God."

Millions of Christians never have the opportunity to study the Bible in a theological seminary, Bible school or college. Comparatively few even have the privilege of being in a Bible class. But that does not exclude them from knowing all things which God has given in Christ to them that love Him. God not only desires but expects His children to know the way of life, how to enter upon it and how to walk in it. There are some things which God has not revealed to us but all that He has revealed belongs to us and a full knowledge of this revelation is our birthright as His children.

> Deuteronomy 29:29, "The secret things belong unto the LORD our God: *but those things which are revealed belong unto us and to our children for ever,* that we may do all the words of this law."

God has taken our ignorance and inability into account and has made provision for our supernatural illumination and enlightenment. Read 1 Corinthians 1:18–3:4, with this in mind.

The spiritual man then has One who will teach him "all things that pertain to life and godliness" and who will apply them to his life so that the knowledge will not be only intellectual or academic but spiritual and experiential. The Holy Spirit will not only teach us the truth but will guide us *into it,* enabling us to incorporate it into our lives that we may become holy and righteous even as He.

One reason the Bible has no meaning to us but rather seems incredible and unintelligible is because we try to understand it with our unaided and unanointed intellect. God only promises spiritual apprehension to the one who has received the Holy Spirit's anointing. Only a spiritual mind can receive spiritual truth.

> 1 John 2:20, R. V., "And *ye have an anointing* from the Holy One, *and ye know* all things."

> 1 John 2:27, R. V., "And as for you, *the anointing which ye received of him abideth in you,* and ye need not that any one teach you; but as *his anointing teacheth you concerning all things,* and is true, and is no lie, and even as it taught you, ye abide in him."

"Ye have an anointing—ye know," "His anointing—teacheth you." God has a divine order which is irreversible.

I know a Chinese man who has a spiritual apprehension and appreciation of Scripture beyond that of the majority of Christian workers, yet he never attended a Bible school a day in his life or studied in a mission school. But his eyes have been anointed to see, his heart to receive and his mind to understand the deep, eternal verities of the Word of God.

Fellow Christian, have you had that anointing? Have your eyes been anointed to see the beauties and excellencies of the adorable Lord of glory as revealed in the Word? Or are you groping your way through the Bible depending upon your unaided human intellect to fathom the unsearchable riches of God's grace? Have you come from your study of the Bible disappointed and discouraged?

I once visited a wonderful cave in Colorado. Impatient of the delay caused by the slowness of the party gathering together I rushed alone into the cave. All was dark, I could not even see which way to go. Seeing a lantern near the entrance I took that and tried to lift it high enough to see some of the loudly proclaimed beauties of that cave. But I saw nothing and turned back in disappointment. After a while the party came with a guide. He commanded us to follow him very closely. In a few minutes he lifted a big torch, which he carried in his hand, high up to the ceiling of the cave and oh! what exclamations of surprise and delight came from every member of the party as the beauty and wonder of the stalagmites and stalactites burst upon our vision. Every step we took our guide unfolded to us some fresh glory of God's handiwork in the heart of that cave.

And we have such a Guide whose mission is to unveil before us the beauty and glory of our risen, exalted Lord and Saviour. If you would live your life habitually on the highest plane, you must seek His anointing; you must wait upon Him to reveal to you in the Word "the things which God hath prepared for them that love him"; you must through your obedient response allow Him to apply the Word wherever and however He sees it is needed for your conformity to the image of the Lord Jesus Christ.

30

The Believer's Part in Remaining Spirit-filled— Prayer

THE CHRISTIAN LIFE centers in a relationship. It is a divine-human fellowship which has its inward spring in the oneness of life between Christ and the Christian. There are two essential expressions to this heaven-born, earth-bent relationship: communion and cooperation.

AN INNER ROOM—RECIPROCAL COMMUNION

Matthew 6:6, "But thou, *when thou prayest, enter into thy closet,* and *when thou hast shut thy door,* pray to thy Father which is *in secret;* and thy Father which seeth in secret shall reward thee openly."

Matthew 14:23, R. V., "He went up into the mountain *apart to pray:* and when even was come, he was there *alone."*

Mark 6:46-47, R. V., "And after he had taken leave of them, *he departed into the mountain to pray.* And when even was come, the boat was in the midst of the sea, and *he was alone* on the land."

The man who lives habitually on the highest plane will have an inner room and he who remains Spirit-filled will spend some time each day behind a shut door. He who truly follows the example of the God-man will often be alone with his heavenly Father. The spiritual man will be a man of prayer. Communion with the Lord Jesus will be the atmosphere in which he lives, the very air he breathes.

"He went up into the mountain apart to pray." His inner room was a mountainside. There He sought His Father's presence away from every person, out of sight and sound of the things of this world. What took the incarnate Son apart to pray? Two things constrained Him to the solitary place of communion: His love and His need of the Father.

Can we begin to comprehend the longing of the Son on earth for the Father in heaven? He and the Father were one and it was a unity, first of all, in love. Throughout all eternity He had been in the bosom of the Father. He had lived in His ultimate, immediate presence. Oh! it was the hunger and thirst of love that drew the God-man apart even from the friends whose companionship He so prized, apart from the work that He so loved, apart to that inner room in God's out of doors.

Alone with His Father on the mountain slope He could pour out His soul, He could lay bare His heart, He could unburden His spirit. There His desires, His longings, His heartaches, His disappointments, could be expressed! And in that inner room on the mountainside the Father always met Him. He was sure of a listening ear and a sympathetic heart. He always left the place of prayer refreshed. The inner room is the place of reciprocal communion.

Do you have an inner room? A shut door? A place to be alone with your Lord? It may be a real "closet" in your own home or it may be only a place in a streetcar or at a desk or on a mountainside or in a sickroom but it will be a place where the world is shut out and in spirit you are shut in alone with your Lord. It will be a place where heaven and earth meet and the intimate, immediate presence of the Lord of glory will be realized.

Our desire to be alone with the Lover-Christ and our delight in the companionship of our Beloved will reveal the place He really holds in our affections. To have chosen Him as the Lover of one's soul; to have been joined to Him as one spirit; to share His life in its fullness, and then not to hunger and thirst for the privacy of the inner room where His presence may be realized and enjoyed apart from all intrusion of the outer world, is unthinkable. Communion with Christ is the imperative sequence of union with Him because alone with the Lord Jesus behind the closed door one may be both the man that he really is and the man that he longs to be. There he is in the presence of the One who knows what is in him and unto whose eyes "all things are naked and open," yet He is the faithful and merciful High Priest who is touched with the feeling of our infirmities, and who is able to succor us who are tempted because He Himself suffered being tempted. So there alone with the God-man he may frankly and fully confess his sin, his failure, his defeat; and there in the intimate companionship of the victorious, triumphant Lord he may become more than conqueror. In the inner room, the sufferings and sorrows, the trials and tribulations, may be shared with the One who will understand and sympathize. There in the inner room in fellowship with his Lord, new aspirations for higher and holier things will be begotten; there the ambition to "press on toward the mark for the prize of the high calling of God in Christ Jesus" will be quickened; there the determination to live habitually on the highest plane will be strengthened. And from that inner room one will emerge with a shining face even as Moses came from the mount of God. The Christian will always find the inner room the place of reciprocal communion.

Another thing drew the incarnate Son apart to pray. It was His need. Yes, we dare say it—the Son of Man had no other way of replenishing His spiritual supplies save in prayer. In His earthly life He was utterly dependent upon His Father for wisdom, strength, power and guidance. Of Himself He said nothing, He did nothing, He went nowhere. The source of divine supplies for Him was in heaven and the method of their transmission from heaven to earth was prayer. The Son of Man in His representative capacity was limited to this medium of receiving supplies for His day's life and work. His own need drew Him into communion with His Father in heaven.

"Because as he is, so are we in this world." So the Christian has no way of replenishing his ever diminishing spiritual supplies save in prayer. God gives His manna by the day. He would keep us utterly distrustful of self and wholly dependent upon Him—beneficiaries of His exhaustless bounty which can be obtained only as it is sought and claimed in prayer. The source of supplies is in heaven, the realm of need is on earth, the line of communication is prayer. Communion with Christ because of need is a necessary sequence of union with Christ.

Reciprocal communion between Christ and the Christian is an absolute necessity of a Spirit-filled life. Through prayer the Christian is enabled to breathe the exhilarating air of the heavenlies while surrounded by the enervating atmosphere of the world. Through prayer he is able to live in the uplifting, purifying presence of his Saviour while in constant contact with the deteriorating, defiling power of sin. Through prayer the new creation breathes in the very life of God which sustains the new life and maintains it upon the highest plane.

> "Lord, what a change within us one short hour
> Spent in Thy presence will prevail to make—
> What heavy burdens from our bosom take,
> What parched grounds revive, as with a shower!
> We kneel, and all around us seems to lower:
> We rise, and all, the distant and the near,
> Stands forth in sunny outline, brave and clear.
> We kneel how weak; we rise how full of power!
> Why, therefore, should we do ourselves this wrong
> Or others—that we are not always strong,
> That we are ever overborne with care,
> That we should ever weak or heartless be,
> Anxious or troubled, when with us is prayer,
> And joy and strength and courage are with Thee?"
>
> R. C. TRENCH

An Upper Room—Responsive Cooperation

Luke 6:12-13, "And it came to pass in those days, that he went out into a mountain to pray, and *continued all night in prayer to God.*

And when it was day, he called unto him his disciples: and of them *he chose twelve, whom also he named apostles."*

Oh! what a momentous night that was in the world's history! What a stupendous decision confronted the Lord Jesus! A choice was to be made on the following day of those who would become linked with the God-man in the carrying out of that eternal purpose which God purposed in Christ for the salvation of mankind. Humanly speaking everything in the earthward side of God's wondrous plan of redemption hung upon that choice.

"He went out into a mountain to pray and continued all night in prayer to God." For Himself? No, this time that mountaintop was not an inner room where He looked in upon Himself and His needs and then up to God for their satisfaction and supply, but it was an upper room where He looked out upon the world and its need and then up to God for the fulfillment of His purpose.

That night prayer was intercession. Throughout its hours the Son waited to receive the revelation of His Father's will and then responded through intercession to bring that will to pass in the lives of men. That night through intercession Jesus Christ linked heaven with earth; He brought God in touch with man. Through intercession the choice of those twelve men, who were to become the very seed of the Church, was made and they were set apart individually as apostles. Oh! what a night's work was that! Perhaps you and I are thousands of miles in space from that "upper room" on that Palestinian slope, and we are separated nineteen centuries in time from that night of intercession, yet the blessing that flowed from those hours will enrich our lives through time and through eternity.

To the God-man prayer was work; in fact, intercession was the most important work that He did. Greater in power than His preaching, His teaching or His healing was His praying. He commenced, continued and consummated everything in prayer. In the upper room He laid hold upon the supernatural forces of the unseen and brought them to bear upon the world in which men lived. Intercession was the most potential means of responsive cooperation with His Father in accomplishing the task He was sent to do.

Acts 1:13-14, "And when they were come in, *they went up into an upper room,* where abode both Peter, and James, and John, and Andrew, Philip, and Thomas, Bartholomew, and Matthew, James the son of Alpheus, and Simon Zelotes, and Judas the brother of James. *These all continued with one accord in prayer and supplication,* with the women, and Mary the mother of Jesus, and with his brethren."

Acts 2:1, 4, "And when the day of Pentecost was fully come, they were all *with one accord in one place. And they were all filled with the Holy Ghost.*"

Acts 2:41, "Then they that gladly received his word were baptized: and *the same day there were added unto them about three thousand souls.*"

"An upper room," "these all in prayer and supplication," "filled with the Holy Spirit," "added unto them about three thousand souls." A place of prayer, corporate intercession, the outpouring of the Holy Spirit, and three thousand souls saved through one sermon. Is there any reason why such a miracle of grace should not be wrought in the twentieth century as well as in the first?

I would speak a word to pastors. Has your church "an upper room" where men and women gather not to talk or to be talked to but to pray? Where, with all quarrels, divisions, jealousies put away, they with one accord wait upon God for the outpouring of the Holy Spirit not only upon themselves but upon the Body of Christ the world over? Is the power of your preaching on Sunday generated in the prayer meeting on Wednesday? Does every activity of the church reap fruitage that will abide through time and stand the test by fire in eternity (1 Corinthians 3:13) because it is begotten in prayer?

I know the prayer meeting is considered old-fashioned and that it is now either obsolete or so decrepit through lack of virility as to be almost valueless in many churches. Just this week I heard a pastor in a large city full of churches say that he thought that church was perhaps the only one in the city which would observe the "World's Week of Prayer." But I know too, that the Church is losing its power; it is finding it difficult to even hold its own and in some places is resorting to all sorts of entertainments in an attempt to compete with the attractions of the world. Do you desire to see a manifestation of first-century power in your church? If so, are you willing to return to first-century methods which will mean the revival of corporate intercession in your church?

I would speak a word to fellow missionaries. "Has your mission station 'an upper room' where doctors come from the hospital, teachers from the school, evangelists from the field, wives from the home, administrators from the desk to lay before the Lord of heaven and earth the difficulties, problems and needs of the whole parish committed to you?

"What is the outstanding purpose of your life as a missionary? Is it to heal the sick? To teach school? To keep accounts or to keep a home? To preach the Gospel merely? No one of these things is an end in itself but each one a means to an end. What then is the purpose of your life and mine as missionaries? Jesus Christ tells us, 'Ye did not choose me, but I chose you, and appointed you that ye should go and *bear fruit* and that your fruit should abide: that whatsoever ye should ask of the Father in my name, he may give it you.' Jesus Christ said very little to His disciples about work but He said much about fruit-bearing. Upon that He put tremendous emphasis, even to making true discipleship depend upon it. In fact He said that only through much fruit-bearing can we glorify the Father. But work and fruit-bearing are by no means synonymous. Some of our work is the energy of the flesh, the working off of a surplus nervous energy or the dissipation of a limited supply of it. But what is fruit-bearing? We shall know very clearly when someday we stand alone before Him with whom we have to do and render our account. Will it be the number of patients treated or pupils taught or meetings led or hours spent in interviews? No, God keeps but one kind of statistics. He only writes *names* in the book of life. It is not the output of our work but the fruitage of that output that counts with Him. A short time ago a missionary said to me, 'I have never worked so hard as I have this year and have never seen so few results. It is because I have prayed so little!' Oh! if we could but come to believe today that it is the bearing of eternal fruit and not the burning of nervous energy that God wants, we should see that intercession may, no must, have its God-appointed place in our lives" (*Intercession and Evangelism,* a pamphlet by the author).

I would speak a word to parents. Has your home "an upper room"? Will your boy or girl carry out into life as his most priceless possession the prayers offered at the family altar? I know it is out of date. But I know too that juvenile crime is on the increase; that immorality is stalking through the land, robbing thousands upon thousands of boys and girls of the bloom of purity and leaving its black stain upon their souls; that there exists today a junior society for the aggressive promotion of atheism. Everywhere I see and hear that parents have lost both the confidence of and control over their children. I wonder what "an upper room" with a family altar might do in your home! A few days ago a friend whose life is deeply spiritual said that of all the formative influences in her Christian life the family prayers held daily in her home were the greatest. Four times in the book of Acts it is recorded that a whole household was converted and baptized at one time. Will your family circle be unbroken in heaven? "Ye have not because ye ask not."

I would speak a word to each individual Christian. Have you "an upper room" in your life? Oh! I know you have "an inner room" where you pray for yourself and your family and your interests. But do you have "an upper room" where you intercede for others? Where you bear upon your heart the need of the whole world and remember in prayer all the Kingdom interests? A few weeks ago I met a radiant Christian. She had leisure from herself. She enjoyed living. She had not much money and had never gone far from her home city yet she was a citizen of the world through prayer. Her face fairly beamed as she said, "No one will ever know how much she can get out of a dollar until she has used it to buy twenty five-cent stamps!" For what use? On her heart were forty-four missionaries in different countries to whom she wrote and for whom she prayed. Her own life was immeasurably enlarged and enriched through intercession for these friends, most of whom she had never seen.

If you work in an office, a store or a factory, or teach in a school, could you not tithe your noon hour and give ten minutes to God for intercession? If you live at home and are able to control better your own time could you not set aside a longer time as a freewill offering for prayer? If you have a kindred spirit among your friends could you not meet together once a week for intercession? "What, could ye not watch with me one hour?"

If you need help in the establishment of your "upper room" you would find it in such books as Andrew Murray's *Helps to Intercession* or Hugh McKay's *Prayer Cycle for World-wide Missionary Work*. But perhaps you would gain the greatest help from just following the instructions of the Bible on intercessory prayer and then make out your own list of objects for intercession.

> James 5:16, "Confess your faults one to another, *and pray one for another, that ye may be healed.* The effectual fervent prayer of a righteous man availeth much."

This is a command and a call to pray for our friends and for fellow members of the Body of Christ. Our knowledge of another's need is a call to prayer. I cannot tell you what tremendous encouragement and strength came to me this last year to learn from three Christian workers, all ex-tremely busy men with many others on their prayer list whom they knew far better than they knew me, that they prayed *daily* for me.

> "The weary ones had rest, the sad had joy,
>   That day, and wondered 'how,'
> A ploughman singing at his work had prayed,
>   'Lord, help them now.'
>
> "Away in foreign lands they wondered how
>   Their simple word had power.
> At home, the Christians two or three had met
>   To pray an hour.
>
> "Yes, we are always wond'ring, wond'ring 'how';
>   Because we do not see
> Some one, unknown perhaps, and far away,
>   On bended knee."

2 Thessalonians 3:1, "Finally, *brethren, pray for us, that the word of the Lord may have free course, and be glorified,* even as it is with you."

Romans 15:30, "Now I beseech you, brethren, for the Lord Jesus Christ's sake, and for the love of the Spirit, *that ye strive together with me in your prayers to God for me.*"

Here is a call to prayer for the minister and for his preaching of the Word of God. Paul conceived the work of a church to be a sacred partnership between pastor and people through preaching and prayer. Is it possible that the paucity of results from the preaching of God's Word is largely due to the prayerlessness that accompanies it? Do you criticize your preacher? I wonder what would happen if that criticism were converted into prayer? When Mr. Spurgeon was asked for the secret of the power manifested in his ministry, he replied, "My people pray for me." "For the Lord Jesus Christ's sake and for the love of the Spirit," will you strive together with your pastor in your prayers to God for him?

Ephesians 6:18, "Praying always with all prayer and supplication in the Spirit, and watching thereunto with all perseverance and *supplication for all saints.*"

The life of many Christians is confined within its own denominational borders; often even narrowed down to the activities and interests of "my church." We repeat the creed "I believe in the communion of saints" but we practice it but little. Nothing would be so conducive to the dissipation of denominational jealousy, rivalry and overlapping of work and to the real unity of God's people of all tongues and tribes as "prayer and supplication in the Spirit for all saints." Will you begin today to pray for one of God's saints of another nationality in some distant country, in another state or province of your own country, in some city or town of your own state, in another church within your own city, in some family within your own church?

1 Timothy 2:1-2, "I exhort therefore, that, first of all, supplications, prayers, intercessions, and giving of thanks, be made *for all men;*
For kings, and for all that are in authority; that we may lead a quiet and peaceable life in all godliness and honesty."

What a program for worldwide prayer God lays out for His Church in these words! What a call to His people to exercise their Christian priesthood! What a challenge to cooperate with Him in strengthening and sustaining those who are in authority in their endeavors to bring nations out of their existing confusion! Oh! what a change in condition might be wrought in China today if the prayers of all God's people everywhere were focused in believing intercession upon that nation! Andrew Murray says of 1 Timothy 2:2, "What a faith in the power of prayer! A few feeble and despised Christians are to influence the mighty Roman emperors, and help in securing peace and quietness. Let us believe that prayer is a power that is taken up by God in His rule of the world. When God's people unite in this they may count upon their prayer effecting in the unseen world more than they know."

> Matthew 9:37-38, "Then saith he unto his disciples, The harvest truly is plenteous, but the labourers are few; *pray ye therefore the Lord of the harvest, that he will send forth labourers into his harvest."*

If in Christ's time the harvest was plenteous, the laborers few and the need for prayer imperative, it is even more true today. More than nineteen centuries since He gave the commission to preach the Gospel *to every creature,* and there are still hundreds of millions who have never heard the Gospel! Still unoccupied fields, untouched classes, unreached tribes! How can we account for this except that God's people have failed to pray for laborers to enter into these harvest fields?

There are certain mission agencies that are making a serious attempt to secure and send missionaries to the unoccupied fields. There are national home missionary societies in various mission fields which are attempting the evangelization of their own people. Will you not endeavor to acquaint yourselves with the work of such movements and then give yourselves in intercession for their needs? Will you not inquire into the need for laborers in the foreign and home missionary societies of your own denomination and then pray Spirit-taught, Spirit-filled, Spirit-anointed men and women out into these various fields?

Have we not clearly seen that union with Christ necessitates a life of prayer in this twofold aspect: reciprocal communion and responsive cooperation? In the "inner room" we meet Him, there He becomes our satisfaction and our sufficiency. And we go from it to our "upper room" to exercise our mediatorial, priestly ministry in bringing Him to be the Saviour and Satisfier of other men.

THE PREREQUISITES FOR PREVAILING PRAYER

All prayer is not prevailing prayer. It is not enough to pray, we need to pray in power. First let us consider the prerequisites for prevailing prayer on the manward side.

The first prerequisite is *purity of heart.* Only the Christian with a clean heart can pray the effectual prayer. Spurgeon has said, "The goal of prayer is the ear of God." If one cannot even get a hearing, he certainly cannot hope for an answer. Iniquity puts a closed door between the man who prays and the God who listens. Sin in the saint stops the ear of God so that He cannot hear.

> Isaiah 59:1-2, "Behold, the LORD's hand is not shortened, that it cannot save; neither his ear heavy, that it cannot hear: *but your iniquities have separated between you and your God, and your sins have hid his face from you, that he will not hear.*"

If a man is to pray right he must be right. God judges the prayer not by the petition upon the lips but by the purity of the life. Only the pure in heart can offer prayer to God with the assurance of its acceptability and answer.

> 2 Timothy 2:22, R. V., "But flee youthful lusts, and follow after righteousness, faith, love, peace, *with them that call on the Lord out of a pure heart.*"
>
> Hebrews 10:22, "Let us draw near with a true heart in full assurance of faith, *having our hearts sprinkled from an evil conscience,* and our bodies washed with pure water."

The man who prays the effectual prayer must be right in his relationship both to God and to man. He must approach the throne with a conscience void of offense toward God and man (Acts 24:16). If in this life there are sympathy for sin and apathy toward God, if there are indulgence of self and indifference toward God, if there are allegiance to Satan and disloyalty to God, then his prayer is not heard.

> Psalm 66:18, "*If I regard iniquity in my heart,* the Lord will not hear me."

If one would pray the effectual prayer he must be righteous in his relationship with his fellowmen. No pretense of piety will suffice to conceal the presence of dishonesty, greed, jealousy, resentment, unforgiveness or hatred toward others. It has sometimes happened that a truly Spirit-filled man or woman has been shorn of all power in prayer and in preaching because of dishonesty in the handling of funds or because of some unrighteous action in relation to his co-workers.

> James 5:16, "Confess your faults one to another, and pray one for another, that ye may be healed. The effectual fervent prayer of *a righteous man* availeth much."
>
> Mark 11:25, "*And when ye stand praying, forgive,* if ye have ought against any: that your Father also which is in heaven may forgive you your trespasses."

A second prerequisite for prevailing prayer is *detachment of spirit.* True prayer is a spiritual exercise and its field of action is the heavenlies. It deals with the supernatural forces of the unseen world. To pray effectually one must be detached in spirit from the things of time and sense.

But such a thing seems well-nigh impossible in a world where the material, the tangible and the fleshly protrude themselves before one's eyes, press themselves into one's ears, and project themselves into one's life in such a way as almost to submerge and smother the aspiration for higher and holier things. Besides, almost everything in modern life tends to rob one of the solitude which is so essential at times if one is to keep a keen realization of the presence of God. The apartment house instead of the old-fashioned home puts a whole community into one's front yard; the automobile makes the man in a distant city one's next-door neighbor; and the telephone and the radio enable the whole world to enter one's home day and night at will. To be alone is almost a unique experience; to be wholly detached in spirit, even when alone, is far from an easy matter.

But the man who has power with God in prayer must be alone sometimes. Attachment to God and to things eternal and spiritual demands deliberate detachment from the things of earth and sense. The Son of Man deliberately withdrew from the sights and sounds of the life that surged about Him that He might find the solitude of spirit that prepared Him for prayer.

> Luke 5:15-16, "But so much the more went there a fame abroad of him: and great multitudes came together to hear, and to be healed by him of their infirmities. And *he withdrew himself into the wilderness, and prayed.*"

Scripture in its teaching on fasting offers the spiritual man a suggestion regarding a method by which he may secure the detachment of spirit needful for effectual prayer. Fasting connotes two things both of which are essential to vital spirituality: self-denial and discipline.

There are things in the life of every Christian which are perfectly legitimate but which may have a dulling, deadening influence upon the spirit. There are other things which are right in themselves but which often are used in excess and so crowd out more important things. To keep the spirit alert, untrammeled, usable, it must be disciplined through denial. Is not this the essence of fasting? Food is a legitimate thing, even a necessity, yet may not the spirit often have been hindered in the performance of its tasks through the sluggishness of the body caused by overeating? Friends are a legitimate part of one's life. They are a necessity in a normal, balanced life, yet may not many of us have been robbed of power because we have spent more time with them than with the divine Friend? Our recreation and our reading are essential to the health of body and mind yet may we not have become impoverished spiritually because of ill-proportioned time given them?

Did not Jesus Christ intimate that the disciples were impotent to cast the foul spirit out of the epileptic because they were unwilling to forego a meal or to deny themselves the companionship of family and friends?

> Mark 9:29, "And he said unto them, *This kind can come forth by nothing, but by prayer and fasting.*"

The football player, the mountain climber and the soldier in action know the meaning of self-denial and self-discipline. But very few Christians take seriously enough the race into which they have entered or the warfare in which they are engaged. Too few are willing for the sacrificial living which victory over the enemy demands. "It is love of our lives that weakens our spirits, and makes us unfit for the fight." God needs prayer-warriors today who have within them the spirit of the apostle Paul who cared more for the victorious completion of his life's ministry than for life itself.

> Acts 20:24, "But none of these things move me, *neither count I my life dear unto myself,* so that I might finish my course with joy, and the ministry, which I have received of the Lord Jesus, to testify the gospel of the grace of God."

A third prerequisite for prevailing prayer is *definiteness of aim.* Much prayer is very desultory, often forgotten as soon as offered and calls forth no watchful waiting for an answer. We aim at nothing and get what we aim at. There has been no definite petition and so there is no definite answer.

But God invites us to come to Him with clear-cut petitions and teaches us to focus our prayer on particular needs. "What wilt thou that I should do unto thee?" was Christ's word to blind Bartimaeus by the roadside as again and again he cried out his prayer, "Thou Son of David, have mercy on me." "*What* wilt thou that I should do unto thee?" Definitely came the answer, "Lord, that I might receive my sight. And immediately he received his sight, and followed Jesus in the way." God honors a definite prayer with a definite answer. "Every prayer should be with the mind, *a definite desire;* with the heart, *a longed-for need;* with the will, *a claimed petition;* with faith, *an accepted gift;* and with thanksgiving, that praises for *the answer that is assured.* This cleanses the petition list from all generalizing in prayer and gives reality to praying and to receiving."

> John 14:13-14, "And *whatsoever* ye shall ask in my name, *that* will I do, that the Father may be glorified in the Son. If ye shall ask *any thing* in my name, *I will do it.*"

The book of the Acts gives repeated instances of definite answers to definite petitions. But one will be cited. Peter and John had been called into question by the Sanhedrin for the miracle performed on the man born lame and had been threatened and charged to speak no more nor teach in the name of Jesus. They immediately engaged with their fellow Christians in prayer. The prayer was not long nor was it full of generalities. It focused on their one outstanding need.

> Acts 4:29, 31, "And now, Lord, behold their threatenings: and grant unto thy servants, *that with all boldness they may speak thy word.* And when they had prayed, the place was shaken where they were assembled together; and they were all filled with the Holy Ghost, and *they spake the word of God with boldness.*"

A fourth prerequisite of prevailing prayer is *intensity of desire.* God has given us a very gracious promise in Psalm 37:4, "Delight thyself also in the LORD; and he shall give thee *the desires of* thine heart." Do we take in fully the magnitude of the responsibility of this promise? How much and what do we desire? "Ye have not because ye ask not," for "If ye ask—I will do." God frankly says that His doing is limited by our asking: it is dependent upon our desire.

But even when we do ask we often do not want the thing asked for sufficiently to persevere until it comes. Prevailing prayer calls us to persistent perseverance and patient waiting in intense desire until the answer comes.

> Romans 12:12, "Rejoicing in hope; patient in tribulation; *continuing instant in prayer.*"
>
> Colossians 4:2, "*Continue in prayer, and watch in the same* with thanksgiving."

Scripture gives us some very wonderful instances of this intensity of desire in prayer. The children of Israel had fallen into gross idolatry while Moses was upon the mountain with God. Their sin weighed heavily upon his heart. He alone stood as mediator between them and the righteous judgment of God. Witness the sacrificial vicariousness of his intercessory prayer.

> Exodus 32:31-32, "And Moses returned unto the LORD, and said, Oh, this people have sinned a great sin, and have made themselves gods of gold. Yet now, if thou wilt forgive their sin—; and *if not, blot me, I pray thee, out of thy book which thou hast written.*"

The same intensity of desire is in the prayer of the apostle Paul for his kinsmen according to the flesh. His heart's desire was their salvation and he wanted it so much that he could even wish himself outside the fold of Christ if they could be within.

Romans 10:1, "Brethren, *my heart's desire and prayer to God for Israel is, that they might be saved.*"

Romans 9:2-3, "That I have great heaviness and continual sorrow in my heart. *For I could wish that myself were accursed from Christ for my brethren,* my kinsmen according to the flesh."

Such intense desire did David Brainerd have for the salvation of the ignorant, savage Indian tribes to whom he carried the Gospel. He said, "I wrestled for the ingathering of souls, for multitudes of poor souls, personally, in many places. I was in such an agony from sun half an hour high until dark that I was wet all over with sweat." Dr. Jowett rightly said, "True intercession is a sacrifice, a bleeding sacrifice, a perpetuation of Calvary, a filling up of the suffering of Christ. Unquestionably if our intercession blesses it must bleed." How much do we really care for the salvation of the unsaved members of our family? for the unsaved friends in our social circle? for the unsaved millions in the mission fields? How intensely do we desire to see a genuine revival in the Church? Is our desire keen enough to call us to sacrificial, mediatorial intercession and to keep us continuing in it until the answer comes?

A fifth prerequisite in prevailing prayer is *the daring of faith.* God makes staggering promises to the man of prayer. He says "*Whatsoever we ask,* we receive of him" (1 John 3:22). "*If ye shall ask any thing* in my name, I will do it" (John 14:14). "Ye shall *ask what ye will,* and it shall be done unto you" (John 15:7).

As we face such stupendous statements as these we are compelled to ask, "Does God really mean what He says? If He does, is He really able to fulfill such promises? If He is, what does it require of us?"

God really means that if you and I fulfill the conditions He so clearly states in connection with the promises which He has made that He will fulfill the promise. The God of truth cannot lie.

Titus 1:2, "In hope of eternal life, which *God, that cannot lie,* promised before the world began."

God is most assuredly able to fulfill every promise which He has made. Listen to the testimony of those who had put God's faithfulness to the test and had proved both His faithfulness and His power. "God is faithful" (1 Corinthians 10:13) and "God is able" (2 Corinthians 9:8).

Joshua 23:14, "And, behold, this day I am going the way of all the earth: and ye know in all your hearts and in all your souls, *that not one thing hath failed of all the good things which the Lord your God spake concerning you; all are come to pass unto you, and not one thing hath* failed thereof."

1 Kings 8:56, "Blessed be the LORD, that hath given rest unto his people Israel, according to all that he promised: *there hath not failed one word of all his good promise, which he promised* by the hand of Moses his servant."

Then what do such promises require of us? They require the daring of faith. God calls us to take every promise at its face value. He asks us not to drag His promises down to the plane of our unbelief but to lift our faith up to the plane of His promises.

Romans 4:20-21, "*He staggered not at the promise of God through unbelief; but was strong in faith,* giving glory to God; *and being fully persuaded that, what he had promised, he was able also to perform.*"

God challenges us to put Him to the test. He dares us to command the Himalaya, that rears up between Himself and us or between Himself and the one for whom we pray, to be removed and to be cast into the sea and He makes the daring of faith the only condition for the achievement of such a miracle.

Mark 11:23, R.V., "Verily I say unto you, *Whosoever shall say unto this mountain, Be thou taken up and cast into the sea;* and *shall not doubt in his heart, but shall believe that what he saith cometh to pass; he shall have it.*"

Will you enter today, my friend, into a new prayer-partnership with your Lord? The power is His: the faith is yours. Through the daring of faith will you link yourself with the omnipotence of power and bring down from heaven above not only into your own life but into the life of the whole Body of Christ "exceeding abundantly above all that we ask or think"?

Ephesians 3:20, "Now *unto him that is able to do exceeding abundantly above all that we ask or think,* according to the power that worketh in us."

We have considered the prerequisites for prevailing prayer on the manward side. We have been at the foot of the ladder, which connects earth with heaven, looking up. May we now go to the top of the ladder and look down. From the viewpoint of the throne of grace what are the conditions of prevailing prayer? Scripture reveals three qualifying phrases accompanying God's gracious promises.

To be heard and answered prayer must be *according to God's will.* Does this statement need be argued or expounded? Is it not a self-evident fact that God could not grant any petition that is not in accordance with His will? We have learned in the earlier chapters of this book that it is God's purpose that man should think, love and will within the circle of God's will. This, assuredly, means that he must pray within that sphere if his prayer reaches the ear of God. There is a limit then to what we may ask of God and the God-man stated the condition very clearly in the thrice-repeated prayer in Gethsemane, "Not my will but thine be done." Only he who has willed to do the will of God will be able to pray aright.

But there is another side to this. St. Augustine has stated it in these words, "O Lord, grant that I may do Thy will as if it were my will, so that Thou mayest do my will as if it were Thy will." It is possible for Christ and the Christian to live in such abiding oneness that God does the will of His child which is expressed in his prayer.

> John 15:7, "If ye abide in me, and my words abide in you, ye shall ask *what ye will*, and it shall be done unto you."

And we may be so assured of the answer that we can praise Him before we may have received in actual experience the thing prayed for.

> 1 John 5:14-15, "And *this is the confidence that we have in him*, that, *if we ask any thing according to his will*, he heareth us; and if we know that he hear us, *whatsoever we ask, we know that we have the petitions that we desired of him.*"

"When we do what He bids, He does what we ask! Listen to God and God will listen to you. Thus our Lord gives us *'power of attorney'* over His Kingdom, the Kingdom of Heaven, if only we fulfill the condition of abiding in Him" (An Unknown Christian, *The Kneeling Christian, p.* 79).

To be heard and answered prayer must be *in the name of Christ.* No sinner, not even a saved one, has ever made any deposit in the bank of heaven consequently he has no right to open an account in his own name. The spiritual riches which are there for him were placed there through the death, resurrection, ascension and exaltation of the Lord Jesus Christ. The account was opened for him when he put his faith in this Saviour and at that moment Christ placed in his hands blank checks signed with His own name and not one of them has ever been refused at the bank of heaven. Six times in that last conversation with His disciples on earth the Lord Jesus told them that when He went back to the Father He would open an account for each one of them and urged them to make liberal use of His credit in their Father's bank. He taught them that the Father hears but one voice, that only the man in Christ can reach the Father's ear with his petitions.

> John 14:13-14, "And whatsoever ye shall ask *in my name*, that will I do, that the Father may be glorified in the Son. If ye shall ask any thing *in my name*, I will do it."

> John 15:16, "Whatsoever ye shall ask of the Father *in my name*, he may give it you."

> John 16:23-24, 26, "And in that day ye shall ask me nothing. Verily, verily, I say unto you, Whatsoever ye shall ask the Father *in my name,* he will give it you. Hitherto have ye asked nothing *in my name:* ask, and ye shall receive, that your joy may be full. At that day ye shall ask *in my name:* and I say not unto you, that I will pray the Father for you:"

But do not let anyone be deceived into thinking that those are magic words which can be added, as an appendage, to any kind of a prayer. It is only the prayer that will bring honor and glory to His name that can be truly asked in His name. A wrong prayer cannot be made right by the addition of some mystic phrase. It is possible for one to pray in the name of Christ for the salvation of some member of the family in order only that there may be greater harmony in the home. Or a preacher may pray for large additions to his church not for the glory of Christ's name but for his own. There must be identification with Christ in His interests and purposes if there is to be a rightful use of His name in prayer. Only the prayer that is wholly according to God's will can be legitimately asked in the name of Christ.

To be heard and answered, prayer must be *in the Holy Ghost.* The Holy Spirit alone knows what are the mind and will of God; He only understands what prayer will be to the honor and glory of Christ. So only the man who is in the Spirit's sphere and under the Spirit's control will pray aright.

> Jude 20, "But ye, beloved, building up yourselves on your most holy faith, *praying in the Holy Ghost.*"

> Romans 8:26-27, R. V., "And in like manner the Spirit also helpeth our infirmity: *for we know not how to pray as we ought; but the Spirit himself maketh intercession for us* with groanings which cannot be uttered; and he that searcheth the hearts knoweth what is the mind of the Spirit, *because he maketh intercession for the saints according to the will of God.*"

In these two passages of Scripture we see that the divine condition of prevailing prayer becomes at the same time the divine provision for it. We do not know how to pray as we ought but the Holy Spirit does know. Indwelling and infilling us He reveals to us our need, suggests the objects of prayer, sifts and tests our motives, purifies our desires, stiffens our faith and stimulates our hope and expectation of an answer.

Do you honestly wish to live your life habitually on the highest plane? Then you must become a man or woman of prayer, an intercessor after God's heart. Are you willing to let the Holy Spirit deal with you in regard to the actual condition of your prayer life *as it now is?* Will you through the power of His divine enabling determine *what it shall be?*

Has my prayer life been *powerless* because of some besetting sin?

Has my prayer life been *hindered* by haste, irregularity, indefiniteness, insufficient preparation, unbelief, neglect of Bible study?

Has my prayer life been *fruitless?* Have I had such power with God that I have had power with people? Have I had definite answers to prayer week by week?

Has my prayer life been *restricted* merely to short, stated seasons of prayer or have I come to know what it is to "pray without ceasing"?

Has my prayer life been *limited* to prayer for myself? My family? My work? My church? My mission? Or have I taken the world into my heart and into my prayers?

Has my prayer life been *starved?* Or have I devoted time to the study of God's Word about prayer? Do I know His precepts and promises?

Has my prayer life been *joyless?* Do I love to pray? Or is prayer more of a duty than a delight?

Has my prayer life been *growing?* Do I daily know more of the meaning and power of prayer?

Has my prayer life been *sacrificial?* Has it cost me anything in time, strength, vitality, love?

"Lord, teach us to pray."

31

The Works of the Spiritual Man

SALVATION, sanctification, service is the divine order in spiritual experience. The man who is saved from sin and set apart unto God must serve God and his fellowmen in working to bring them into the same spiritual oneness which he enjoys. The Christian's individual relationship to God merges into a corporate relationship with the other members of God's family and the other citizens of God's Kingdom and then stretches on out toward "the other sheep" whom the loving Shepherd longs to bring into His fold.

> Titus 2:14, "Who gave himself for us, that he might redeem us from all iniquity, and purify unto himself a peculiar people, *zealous of good works.*"
>
> 2 Timothy 3:17, "That the man of God may be perfect, *throughly furnished unto all good works.*"
>
> Titus 3:8, "This is a faithful saying, and these things I will that thou affirm constantly, *that they which have believed in God might be careful to maintain good works.* These things are good and profitable unto men."

Works are the natural outcome of faith. Belief in Jesus Christ is not a hollow profession nor a selfish possession. Faith that is real must propagate itself and share its blessing. The apostles Paul and James are not at loggerheads with each other; they are not stating contradictory but complementary truth as they emphasize in turn the necessity of faith and of works. The virility of any true faith is shown in its works.

> James 2:17-18, R. V., "Even so *faith, if it have not works, is dead in itself.* Yea, a man will say, Thou hast faith, and I have works: show me thy faith apart from thy works, and *I by my works will show thee my faith.*"

Works are the natural outcome of love. Love for the Lord Jesus is not shallow sentiment that dissipates itself in words but it is vicarious sacrifice that expresses itself in works. The vitality of true love is shown in service. "Lovest thou me?" "Yea, Lord, thou knowest that I love thee." Then, "Feed my lambs."

1 John 3:16, 18, "Hereby perceive we the love of God, because he laid down his life for us: and we *ought to lay down our lives for the brethren.* My little children, *let us not love in word, neither in tongue; but in deed and in truth."*

Works are the natural outcome of life. The tree is known by its fruits. Life in the tree presumes fruit on the branches. Life in Christ Jesus must reproduce itself in life.

John 15:2, *"Every branch in me that beareth not fruit he taketh away:* and every branch that beareth fruit, he purgeth it, that it may bring forth more fruit."

Acts 4:20, "For *we cannot but speak* the things which we have seen and heard."

Faith, love and life are not passive but active forces and the proportion in which they exist in the believer will determine the part he takes in the work of Christ's Body, the Church. The spiritual man recognizes that the very possessions and privileges which are his in Christ entail responsibilities and duties in the work which Christ desires done in the world.

But no man of himself should determine the nature of his service any more than he can determine the nature of his salvation or of his sanctification. His works are also foreordained of God. It is only the man who does a divinely determined and directed work who is promised the power of God in its accomplishment.

Ephesians 2:10, "For we are his workmanship, *created in Christ Jesus unto good works, which God hath before ordained* that we should walk in them."

God works according to a definite plan which is rooted in an eternal purpose. In the eternity of the past He foresaw the tragedy of sin and all of its evil consequences and formed the purpose which determined the plan by which sin and its accompanying evil would be removed. That plan took into account the conditions to be met in every age, in every century and in every generation of mankind's history, and stretched itself over them all. There is nothing new to God in this twentieth century "modern mind" that either surprises or appalls Him for He has known it all before the foundation of the world.

Ephesians 3:11, *"According to the eternal purpose which he purposed in Christ Jesus our Lord."*

Acts 15:18, *"Known unto God are all his works from the beginning of the world."*

God's purpose centers in Christ and concerns itself with two things only:

the redemption of man and the reconciliation of all things in the universe unto Himself. The salvation of man and the sovereignty of God are the two vital issues at stake and upon their accomplishment God's purpose focuses.

Salvation through a Saviour is God's only plan for the redemption of man. God sent His Son into the world to be a propitiation for its sins.

> 2 Timothy 1:9-10, "*Who hath saved us,* and called us with an holy calling, not according to our own works, but *according to his own purpose and grace, which was given us in Christ Jesus before the world began. But is now made manifest by the appearing of our Saviour Jesus Christ,* who hath abolished death and hath brought life and immortality to light through the gospel."

> 1 John 4:14, "And we have seen and do testify that the *Father sent the Son to be the Saviour of the world.*"

> 1 John 4:10, "Herein is love, not that we loved God, but that he loved us, and *sent his Son to be the propitiation for our sins.*"

God's remedy for the world's revolt against Him and its reconstruction through His restoration to sovereignty over it centers in Christ also; not however in Christ the Saviour but in Christ the King. Through the incarnation He became a Saviour who in the ultimate fulfillment of God's eternal purpose was to become a King of whose Kingdom there would be no end (Luke 1:30-33).

In the fulfillment of His purpose God has a divine order. He accomplishes His task and achieves His goal by stages. The history of God's dealings with man is divided into clearly defined "ages" or periods of time. The scope of this book confines us to the consideration of God's work in this age and the one to come. These two stages are set forth in one passage in the Acts.

> Acts 15:14-17, "Simeon hath declared how God at the first did visit the Gentiles, *to take out of them a people for his name.* And to this agree the words of the prophets; as it is written, *After this I will return, and will build again the tabernacle of David,* which is fallen down; and I will build again the ruins thereof, and I will set it up: *that the residue of men might seek after the Lord,* and all the Gentiles, upon whom my name is called, saith the Lord, who doeth all these things."

In God's plan there are two advents of Christ into this world for two distinct purposes and marking off two distinct ages. In each advent God works through His Son to carry out His purpose for the whole world. In this study we are considering God's purpose in Christ for this age, the period between Christ's first and second advent.

In this age God is not working for the reformation of the world or to put the world right, much as that is needed, but to bring man into a right relationship to His Son. The improvement of conditions in human society has no share in the plan of God for this age. In fact this would run absolutely counter to His purpose in the Saviourhood of His Son, for such a scheme would make this world so comfortable a place in which to live that the natural man in his ease and contentment would feel no need whatever for God and would have no thought for the life to come. God is not working to right the wrongs of a world that still hates and rejects His Son.

Besides, the only possible road to the real reformation of society is through the regeneration of the individual. Sin is the cause of every bit of the suffering and sorrow in the world and the only place where sin is removed is at the cross of Calvary. "The uplift of humanity" depends upon the uplifting of the Christ of the cross. The reformations that have been wrought in the world are the by-product of the work of the Church. Scripture does not tell us that the mission of the Church in this age is the reformation of the world.

Neither is God working in this age for the conversion of the world. God frankly says "that the whole world lieth in the evil one," that Satan is "the god of this age" (2 Corinthians 4:4, R. V.) and that it is in the control of "the prince of this world" (John 14:30). Many passages of Scripture show that "the course of this world" is to grow worse and worse in the last days. One needs only to keep in mind what we have learned in previous studies about the world to see how its very nature precludes the thought of its conversion in this age of grace.

The world is "the flesh" in its corporate capacity. The only place God can meet it is at the foot of the cross and the only way in which the world could be converted would be by the cleansing of its sin in the atoning blood of Christ the Saviour.

But nowhere in the Word of God is there intimation that the whole world ever will come to the cross for that purpose. The whole mass of unbelieving mankind is one vast federation under Satan's leadership and will continue so unto the very end of this age.

> 1 John 5:19, R. V., "We know that we are of God, and *the whole world lieth in the evil one.*"

> Ephesians 2:2, "Wherein in time past ye walked *according to the course of this world, according to the prince of the power of the air,* the spirit that now worketh in the children of disobedience."

> 2 Timothy 3:1, 13, "This know also, that *in the last days perilous times shall come.*
> But *evil men and seducers shall wax worse and worse,* deceiving, and being deceived."

Up to the very end of this age there will be both believers and un-believers, those who will receive and those who will reject Christ the Saviour. At the end of the age the harvest will reveal both wheat and tares in the field; both good and bad fish in the net. The parable of the wicked husbandmen, as given by Christ Himself, shows that the attitude of the world throughout this age continues to be one of hatred and hostility.

> Acts 28:24, "And *some believed* the things which were spoken, and *some believed not."*

> Matthew 13:30, *"Let both grow together until the harvest:* and in the time of harvest I will say to the reapers, *Gather* ye together *first the tares, and bind them in bundles to burn them: but gather the wheat into my barn."*

> Matthew 13:48-49, R. V., margin, "Which, when it was filled, they drew up on the beach; and they sat down, and *gathered the good into vessels,* but *the bad they cast away. So shall it be in the consummation of the age:* the angels shall come forth, and sever the wicked from among the righteous."

God in this age is calling out from the world the Bride of Christ that she may be prepared to meet Him at His coming and to reign with Him in the Kingdom age which is to follow. God is calling individuals out of this present evil world, emancipating them from it and crucifying them to it.

> John 15:19, "If ye were of the world, the world would love his own: but because ye are not of the world, but *I have chosen you out of the world,* therefore the world hateth you."

> Galatians 1:4, "Who gave himself for our sins, *that he might deliver us from this present evil world,* according to the will of God and our Father."

God's plan is in line with His purpose. This plan is the evangelization of the world. Through the proclamation of the Gospel throughout the whole world as a witness God wishes to give every creature the opportunity to accept Jesus Christ as his Saviour. This is the primary meaning of His last commission.

> Luke 24:46-47, "And said unto them, Thus it is written, and thus it be-hooved Christ to suffer, and to rise from the dead the third day: and *that repentance and remission of sins should be preached in his name among all nations,* beginning at Jerusalem."

> Mark 16:15, "And he said unto them, Go ye into all the world, and *preach the gospel to every creature."*

> John 6:40, "And this is the will of him that sent me, *that every one which*

> *seeth the Son, and believeth on him,* may have everlasting life: and I
> will raise him up at the last day."

Having formed this purpose and having fashioned this plan God now has
no other way of working. In giving His Son to die God has done all that
He can do for this world.

> 1 Corinthians 3:11, "For *other foundation can no man lay than that is
> laid, which is Jesus Christ.*"

> Acts 4:12, "*Neither is there salvation in any other:* for there is none other
> name under heaven given among men, whereby we must be saved."

God's plan of working throughout the entire course of this age is perfectly outlined in the Acts. Here we see the invisible Head of the Church
in the heavenlies determining and directing the work of His visible Body
on earth through His Executor and Administrator, the Holy Spirit. Every
type of work in which He would have us engage as Christians today is revealed to us there. Let us now consider the nature of the spiritual man's
work.

GOD'S WORK IN THIS AGE IS EXECUTED THROUGH A DIVINE-HUMAN PARTNERSHIP

Life in Christ necessarily involves identification with Him in His mission
to this world. Real membership in Christ's Body means sharing with Him
His compassionate love for the world and going out into it to seek and to
save the lost. As Christ was sent into the world by the Father for a definitely specified task even so are we sent by Him.

> John 17:18, "As thou hast sent me into the world, *even so have I also sent
> them into the world.*"

> John 20:21, "Then said Jesus to them again, Peace be unto you: *as my
> Father hath sent me, even so send I you.*"

What Christ Jesus began as the incarnate Son, He continues as the
exalted Lord, through the divine-human partnership which exists between
Him and His Body, the Church.

> 1 Corinthians 3:9, "*For we are labourers together with God:* ye are God's
> husbandry, ye are God's building."

> 2 Corinthians 6:1, "*We then, as workers together with him,* beseech you
> also that ye receive not the grace of God in vain."

> Mark 16:20, "And they went forth, and preached every where, *the Lord
> working with them.*"

The Christian, then, is not at liberty to choose what his work will be. He is under the direction of the Head of the Body of which he is but one member. As the Father determined the work of the Son and as Christ executed everything according to His Father's will so the Lord Jesus now chooses and calls the workers and then determines and directs the work. From this viewpoint let us study together the work of the first-century Church, that we may discern our part in this divine-human partnership.

The workers were *chosen of God*. Paul and Peter each had the conviction that they had been chosen by the Lord Himself for their particular task even before receiving His call. Hence the courage of that conviction which was evinced in all their work.

> Acts 9:15, "But the Lord said unto him, Go thy way: *for he is a chosen vessel unto me*, to bear my name before the Gentiles, and kings, and the children of Israel."

> Galatians 1:1, "Paul, an apostle, (*not of men, neither by man, but by Jesus Christ, and God the Father*, who raised him from the dead)."

> Acts 15:7, "Peter rose up, and said unto them, Men and brethren, ye know how that a good while ago *God made choice among us, that the Gentiles by my mouth should hear the word of the gospel, and believe*."

The workers were *called of God*. It is considered somewhat out of date today to speak of a divine call. The term is well-nigh obsolete. Not a divine call, but a sociological appeal takes many a man into the ministry or to the mission field. But the lack of it quite as often takes him out of the ministry into business or out of the mission field when the romance of an ocean trip and of meeting a new people has given place to the daily routine of hard work in an uncongenial environment. But the ministers and missionaries of that early Church were so sure of their call that they would lay down their lives willingly, if need be, in the pursuit of it (Acts 20:24).

> Acts 13:2, "As they ministered to the Lord, and fasted, the Holy Ghost said, Separate me Barnabas and Saul for the work *whereunto I have called them*."

> Acts 13:47, "For so hath the Lord commanded us, saying, *I have set thee to be a light of the Gentiles, that thou shouldest be for salvation unto the ends of the earth*."

The workers were *appointed by the Lord*. The men of the early Church had a direct appointment to a specific task by the Lord Jesus. To them it was a life task—to be laid down only when called into a higher ministry in the immediate presence of their Lord. Is not the reason why so many young men abandon their theological studies before completing their course due to the fact that they were not "put into the ministry" by the Lord Himself? The Church suffers today from man-made ministers.

Acts 26:16, "But rise, and stand upon thy feet: for *I have appeared unto thee for this purpose, to make thee a minister and a witness* both of these things which thou hast seen, and of those things in the which I will appear unto thee."

Acts 20:24, "But none of these things move me, neither count I my life dear unto myself, so *that I might finish* my course with joy, and *the ministry, which I have received of the Lord Jesus,* to testify the gospel of the grace of God."

1 Timothy 1:12, "And I thank Christ Jesus our Lord, who hath enabled me, for that he counted me faithful, *putting me into the ministry.*"

The workers were *sent by the Lord.* Having been chosen and called they were also commissioned by the Lord. With the assurance and authority of a sent one these first-century ministers and missionaries went forth. Laymen, also, like Ananias were divinely commissioned for service.

Acts 22:21, "And he said unto me, Depart: for *I will send thee* far hence unto the Gentiles."

Acts 9:17, "And Ananias went his way, and entered into the house; and putting his hands on him said, Brother Saul, *the Lord, even Jesus,* that appeared unto thee in the way as thou camest, *hath sent me,* that thou mightest receive thy sight, and be filled with the Holy Ghost."

Every Christian is needed somewhere in some kind of work in God's vineyard. Every Christian has been ordained to some task by God. Every member of Christ's Body has been set in his position as an eye, an ear, a hand or a foot so that the Head may work through him for the accomplishment of some particular task. Only as every member of the Body is functioning properly can the work of the Head be perfected.

1 Corinthians 12:14, 18-19, "For *the body is not one member,* but many. But now *hath God set the members every one of them in the body,* as it hath pleased him. *If they were all one member, where were the body?*"

Ephesians 4:11-12, "And *he gave some,* apostles; and some, prophets; and some, evangelists; and some, pastors and teachers; *for the perfecting of the saints, and the work of the ministry, for the edifying of the body of Christ.*"

Not even the weakest, the youngest, or the apparently most ignorant and incapable is left without his share in God's work. In fact, God delights to choose those who in themselves are impotent and inadequate in order that the glory of achievement may be altogether His.

1 Corinthians 12:22, "Nay, much more *those members of the body, which seem to be more feeble, are necessary.*"

> 2 Corinthians 4:7, "But we have this treasure in earthen vessels, *that the excellency of the power may be of God, and not of us.*"

The Lord Jesus determines and directs the work of those whom He has chosen and called. As we study the various phases of the work of the early Church we shall see that the whole field of Christian activity was adequately covered. In the accomplishment of the evangelization of the world the Holy Spirit gave every believer something to do and He set some apart for tasks which required special gifts.

There were witnesses in the first-century Church. In fact, this was the primary work of each. The Holy Spirit came not upon a select group on the day of Pentecost but upon each one of the one hundred and twenty that each might be a witness.

> Acts 2:32, "This Jesus hath God raised up, whereof *we all are witnesses.*"

> Acts 13:31, "And he was seen many days of them which came up with him from Galilee to Jerusalem, *who are his witnesses unto the people.*"

Who is a witness, and of whom, and of what, does he witness? It is very essential to understand this if one would grasp the importance and the power of this form of Christian work. A witness is one who tells what he has *seen* and *knows.*

> Acts 22:15, "For thou shalt be *his witness* unto all men *of what thou hast seen and heard.*"

Of whom did those in the early Church witness? The power of the Holy Spirit was given to those who witnessed of Christ Jesus. From the beginning to the end of Acts we see them witnessing in all places and unto all classes of people of the Lord Jesus Christ.

> Acts 1:8, "But ye shall receive power, after that the Holy Ghost is come upon you: and *ye shall be witnesses unto me* both in Jerusalem, and in all Judea, and in Samaria, and unto the uttermost part of the earth."

> Acts 23:11, "And the night following the Lord stood by him, and said, Be of good cheer, Paul: for *as thou hast testified of me* in Jerusalem, so must thou bear witness also at Rome."

Of what concerning Christ did they witness? Invariably they witnessed not to His work in the flesh but to His work on the cross and from the throne. They told others not of "the Jesus of history" but of the Christ of Calvary.

> Acts 3:15, "And killed the Prince of life, whom God hath raised from the dead; *whereof we are witnesses.*"

> Acts 5:30-32, "The God of our fathers raised up Jesus, whom ye slew and

hanged on a tree. Him hath God exalted with his right hand to be a Prince and a Saviour, for to give repentance to Israel and forgiveness of sins. *And we are his witnesses of these things;* and so is also the Holy Ghost, whom God hath given to them that obey him."

There were preacher-pastors in the first-century Church.

Acts 20:28, "Take heed therefore unto yourselves, and to all the flock, *over the which the Holy Ghost hath made you overseers,* to feed the church of God, which he hath purchased with his own blood."

Definite instructions given them regarding what they were to preach were followed implicitly. They preached *the Word of God.* Will you glance through the book of Acts and note the number of times it is said that they preached the Word? Will you note also its marvelous power both of attraction and conviction? Multitudes, even whole cities, came to the place of worship, not to see a pageant or to hear a concert or a discussion of some notable book or a moralization of current topics or a rhetorical discourse, but to hear the Word of God. And wherever the Word was preached sinners were convicted, converted and baptized by ones and twos, by hundreds and thousands.

Acts 8:4, "Therefore they that were scattered abroad went every where *preaching the word.*"

Acts 13:44, "And the next sabbath day came almost the whole city together *to hear the word of God.*"

They preached *the Gospel.* The Gospel is the heart of the Word of God. Take away the Gospel, which is "that Christ died for our sins, was buried and rose again the third day according to the Scriptures," from the Word of God and you have nothing left but the walls of a gutted building. The core of every sermon, the heart of every message delivered by those first-century preachers, was the death and the resurrection of Jesus Christ. It was this Gospel that pricked the hearts and consciences of men and made them cry out, "What must I do to be saved?"

Acts 8:25, "And they, when they had testified and preached the word of the Lord, returned to Jerusalem, and *preached the gospel* in many villages of the Samaritans."

The preachers of the early Church were not ashamed of the Gospel. They had proved its power in their own lives and knew the miracle it had wrought. They had the compelling conviction that the preaching of the full Gospel of Christ was the only means of changing either the sinful life of an individual or the corporate life of human society.

Romans 1:16, "*For I am not ashamed of the gospel of Christ: for it is the* power of God unto salvation to every one that believeth; to the Jew first, and also to the Greek."

They preached *Christ*. If the Gospel is the heart of the Word, Christ is the heart of the Gospel. The men of that day knew the Jesus of Nazareth, Cana and Capernaum far, far better than any theological historian of the twentieth century, and how they could have entranced their audiences with stories out of His earthly life! How sweet and precious must have been their memories of the years of fellowship with Him! What countless sermons Peter and James and John could have preached about the Jesus who healed the daughter of Jairus, who was transfigured on the mount and who prayed in the Garden of Gethsemane! But "the Jesus of history" was not the theme of their sermons. What pain and anguish of heart must have been mingled with every remembrance of Him as they recalled their faithlessness in the hour of His deepest need; of the cowardly denial in the presence of His enemies; of the traitorous desertion at the cross; and of the doubt and disbelief at the tomb. It was not to the incarnate Son but to the crucified, risen, ascended, exalted Son to whom they owed their deliverance from sin, self and Satan. It was this Christ and Him only whom they preached.

Acts 5:42, "And daily in the temple, and in every house, they ceased not to teach and *preach Jesus Christ*.

Acts 9:20, "And straightway *he preached Christ* in the synagogues, *that he is the Son of God*."

Glance again rapidly through the book of Acts to note the result of the preaching of the Christ of the Gospel of the Word of God. The divine record tells of conversions, baptisms, additions to church membership of individuals, of households, of multitudes of men and women from all classes of society.

Let us take but a few illustrations of the marvelous power of such preaching. The Ethiopian eunuch believed and was baptized when Philip preached Christ to him from Isaiah 53:7-8 (Acts 8). The Roman proconsul Sergius Paulus believed when he heard the doctrine from the mouths of Barnabas and Paul (Acts 13). The households of Cornelius, the Gentile centurion (Acts 10); of Lydia, the businesswoman (Acts 16); of the unnamed Philippian jailor (Acts 16) and of Crispus, the chief ruler of the synagogue (Acts 18), all were convicted of sin, converted and baptized through the preaching of the Christ of the Gospel of the Word.

Acts 6:7, "And the word of God increased; and *the number of disciples multiplied in Jerusalem greatly;* and a great company of the priests were obedient to the faith."

Acts 4:4, "Howbeit many of them which heard the word believed; and *the number of the men was about five thousand.*"

There were evangelists in the first-century Church. Philip was an evangelist and went from place to place preaching the Gospel. Much of the preaching in the early Church was without doubt apologetic, yet there is equal evidence that much of it was evangelistic both in content and in method. The appeal was to the heart and to the will as truly as to the mind and to the conscience, and the audiences were warned and exhorted as well as instructed and edified.

Acts 21:8, "And the next day . . . we entered into the house of *Philip the evangelist,* which was one of the seven."

Acts 2:40, "And *with many other words did he testify and exhort,* saying, Save yourselves from this untoward generation."

There were teachers in the first-century Church. The early Church was thoroughly indoctrinated. New converts were taught the Word of God. Not only were the fundamental truths preached but they were taught to the whole Church. Need we any further proof of this than the epistles which were written to these churches?

Paul's conception of the ministry was that it should be a teaching as well as a preaching ministry. He returned to the places where he had won converts in his missionary tours and sometimes stayed one or two years teaching the things concerning the Lord Jesus. The last word spoken of him in the Acts tells us he was in his own hired house teaching about Jesus Christ.

Acts 18:11, "And he continued there a year and six months, *teaching the word of God among them.*"

Acts 19:10, "And this continued by the space of two years; so that *all which dwelt in Asia heard the word of the Lord Jesus,* both Jews and Greeks."

The apostles of the early Church considered it a definite and essential part of their ministry to establish and confirm the Christians in their faith, to encourage and strengthen them in their work, and to feed and foster their spiritual life.

Acts 16:5, "And *so were the churches established in the faith,* and increased in number daily."

Acts 15:41, "And he went through Syria and Cilicia, *confirming the churches.*"

Acts 18:23, "And after he had spent some time there, he departed, and went over all the country of Galatia and Phrygia in order, *strengthening all the disciples.*"

Not the statistics of church membership but the spiritual status of church members was Paul's concern. He desired passionately that those whom he had begotten in the Gospel might be presented perfect in Christ Jesus. To that end he not only taught them but he warned, reproved and rebuked the Christians under his care.

> Colossians 1:28, "Whom we preach, *warning every man*, and *teaching every man* in all wisdom; *that we may present every man* perfect in Christ Jesus."

There were personal workers in the first-century Church. The passion of the early Church was to win men to Christ. "I am made all things to all men, that I might by all means save some" was its slogan (1 Corinthians 9:22). Tremendous emphasis is laid upon the importance of personal soul-winning by the fact that in three consecutive chapters in the Acts wonderful examples of this type of work are given.

The evangelist Philip was taken from a very successful evangelistic campaign in Samaria to the desert of Gaza to win one man. The Ethiopian eunuch was returning from Jerusalem to his home with a scroll of the prophet Isaiah which he was reading eagerly but without understanding. Philip entered his chariot, explained to him the passage and from it preached Christ. And the eunich believed and was baptized (Acts 8:36-38).

> Acts 8:35, "Then *Philip* opened his mouth, and began at the same scripture, and *preached unto him Jesus.*"

Paul had seen the Lord of glory on the road to Damascus and had fallen before Him believing but blinded; emptied but unfilled. In Damascus was Ananias, the layman. His name appears but once in the annals of Scripture but it is in connection with a bit of personal work that shines upon the page of Scripture as the north star shines in the heavens, for through him as God's own sent messenger Paul received his sight and was filled with the Holy Spirit. The work of salvation begun by the Lord of glory was consummated by his call to sanctification and to service through Ananias.

> Acts 9:17, "And Ananias went his way, and entered into the house; and putting his hands on him said, Brother Saul, *the Lord*, even Jesus, that appeared unto thee in the way as thou camest, *hath sent me, that thou mightest receive thy sight, and be filled with the Holy Ghost.*"

In Caesarea was Cornelius, the centurion, a man with a devout heart and a deep hunger for God. In Joppa was Peter, a man with a passion for souls and a life surrendered to his Lord for service. And in heaven was God who works at both ends of the line sending a prepared messenger to prepared souls. The result was a whole household won to the Lord (Acts 10).

Personal testimony was another form of work in the first-century Church. Who can estimate the fruitage of Paul's testimony of his conversion before the multitude and before Agrippa (Acts 22, 26).

The ministry of intercession was practiced by the first-century Church. To the first Christians intercession was a working force. When Peter and John were threatened because of the healing of the lame man they gave themselves to prayer. When Peter was imprisoned "prayer was made without ceasing." Through praise and prayer Paul and Silas opened not only prison doors but the fast closed hearts of the Philippian jailor and his household. Through prevailing intercession those feeble men and women defeated and routed Satan and his hosts and again and again gained for the triumphant Lord of glory a visible manifestation of His victory on Calvary. They worked through prayer.

> Acts 12:5, "Peter therefore was kept in prison: *but prayer was made without ceasing of the church unto God for him.*"

> Acts 16:25, "And *at midnight Paul and Silas prayed,* and sang praises unto God: and the prisoners heard them."

The grace of giving was manifest in the first-century Church. Filled with the Holy Spirit the first disciples' love for God and their fellowmen led them to lay all they possessed at His feet for His use. The coffers of the early Church were not filled by a finance campaign but by the free-hearted consecration of his material possessions to the Lord on the part of every Christian.

> Acts 4:32, "And the multitude of them that believed were of one heart and of one soul: *neither said any of them that ought of the things which he possessed was his own;* but they had all things common."

Administrators of the business affairs of the Church were to be found in the first-century Church. But these men were not chosen because of their social prestige, their financial income, or their executive ability, but they chose men full of honesty, of wisdom, of faith and of the Holy Spirit. It was a spiritual task to which they were called which required spirituality in those who undertook it.

> Acts 6:3, "Wherefore, brethren, *look ye out among you seven men of honest report, full of the Holy Ghost and wisdom,* whom we may appoint over this business."

Good works were part of the activities of the first-century Church. The practical expression of the love of Christ in kindly deeds for the relief of physical and material needs and for the amelioration of suffering is the natural product of vital spirituality. The genuinely spiritual man is the first to feel the touch upon the hem of his garment and to give most liberally of his sympathy and his support to those in need. The early Church had its "Dorcas" and more than once is it recorded that it sent relief to God's children.

> Acts 9:36, "Now there was at Joppa a certain disciple named Tabitha, which by interpretation is called *Dorcas: this woman was full of good works and almsdeed which she did."*

> Acts 11:29, "Then *the disciples,* every man according to his ability, *determined to send relief unto the brethren which dwelt in Judea."*

The life of the spiritual man is one full of beneficence because "the fruit of the Spirit is kindness." He delights in playing the part of the good Samaritan, he revels in carrying cups of refreshing water.

> Galatians 6:10, "As we have therefore opportunity, *let us do good unto all men, especially unto them who are of the household of faith."*

> Mark 9:41, "For *whosoever shall give you a cup of water to drink in my name,* because ye belong to Christ, verily I say unto you, he shall not lose his reward."

> Titus 2:7, *"In all things shewing thyself a pattern of good works:* in doctrine shewing uncorruptness, gravity, sincerity."

There were missionaries in the first-century Church. No church can lay claim to true, apostolic succession which is not missionary in purpose, passion and program. The early Church was essentially a missionary Church. The power of God was upon it in an exceptional way because it gave itself in obedience to the fulfillment of Christ's last commission to carry the Gospel to the uttermost part of the earth. Persecution sent those first Christians everywhere preaching the Word of life.

> Acts 8:1, 4, "And Saul was consenting unto his death. *And at that time there was a great persecution against the church which was at Jerusalem;* and they were all scattered abroad throughout the regions of Judea and Samaria, except the apostles. Therefore *they that were scattered abroad went every where preaching the word."*

> Acts 11:19-20, "Now *they which were scattered abroad upon the persecution* that arose about Stephen *travelled as far as Phenice, and Cyprus, and Antioch,* preaching the word to none but unto the Jews only. And some of them were men of Cyprus and Cyrene, which, *when they were come to Antioch, spake unto the Grecians,* preaching the Lord Jesus."

There were martyrs in the first-century church. The testimony of Stephen was sealed with martyrdom. How true it was that "the blood of martyrs is the seed of the Church." By the laying down of this faithful life in triumphant death Stephen no doubt did more toward winning Saul of Tarsus to Jesus Christ than he ever could have done in a lifetime of preaching. Paul's conscience was seared by the haunting vision of that victorious death and by the remembrance of his part in it—Stephen, though dead, continued to speak to Saul.

> Acts 7:58, 8:1, "And cast him out of the city, and stoned him: and *the witnesses laid down their clothes at the young man's feet, whose name was Saul.* And Saul was consenting unto his death."

> Acts 22:20, "And *when the blood of thy martyr Stephen was shed, I also was standing by, and consenting unto his death,* and kept the raiment of them that slew him."

The work of the first-century Church bears upon it the seal of God and the scars of Satan. The seal was power and the scars were persecution. Loyalty in preaching the Christ of the Gospel of the Word drew down from heaven the supernatural power of God and it raised up from hell satanic persecution. Study the book of Acts and you will see these two invariably in inevitable succession; power in preaching Christ produced persecution of the Christian and persecution of the Christian precipitated power from Christ.

> Acts 5:14, 16-18, "And *believers were the more added to the Lord, multitudes both of men and women. There came also a multitude out of the cities round about* unto Jerusalem, bringing sick folks, and them which were vexed with unclean spirits: *and they were healed every one. Then the high priest rose up,* and all they that were with him, (which is the sect of the Sadducees,) *and were filled with indignation, and laid their hands on the apostles, and put them in the common prison."*

> Acts 14:1-2, "And it came to pass in Iconium, that they went back together into the synagogue of the Jews, and so spake, that *a great multitude both of the Jews and also of the Greeks believed. But the unbelieving Jews stirred up the Gentiles, and made their minds evil affected against the brethren."*

The work of the early Church was all-comprehensive. The God-man who inaugurated it knew every need of human life and planned adequately to meet and to satisfy it. Though conditions have changed, the fundamental need of human life does not vary from one century to another. The task of the Church at the very beginning was cast into an agelong mold by Christ Jesus and He has given no indication on down through the centuries of any deviation from His purpose and plan so clearly revealed in Scripture.

But no one can look upon the Church today without seeing that it has departed very far from both the purpose and the plan of God. The leaders of Christendom frankly state that the work of the Church is not to save souls but to salvage society, so they have given themselves deliberately to "the purification of Sodom" rather than to "the proclamation of the Saviour." From pulpit and press they declare that "the mission of the Church is to make the world better," and "to interpret to the world the principles of Christ," so that it may win the world into living by His teachings and into following His principles. The supreme question before present-day Christendom is not man's relationship to God's Son but man's relationship to human society; the paramount issue is not God's sovereign reign in righteousness and peace over a world brought into reconciliation with Him through His Son, but it is the equalizing and solidifying of nations, races and classes through foisting upon them for their acceptance the dogma of the Fatherhood of God, whom they do not acknowledge as Father, and the brotherhood of men, whom they do not accept as brothers.

The leaders of Christendom frankly state that they preach such a "social gospel." And anyone who scans the sermon themes for Sunday in the newspaper or who studies the subjects announced on the church calendar has no reason to doubt their word on this point. The marvel is that with such special emphasis on social betterment themes "the world" is not more rapidly approaching the desired millennium of righteousness and peace. "The world" at heart really does not want to be "made better" so it is not going to the place where it will be coaxed or coerced into a reformation of its conduct. It will greatly appreciate anything which the Church does to make its life in sin more full of comfort and will even assist in the matter by making liberal contributions to financial drives or "community chests." But "the world" is not overtaxing the seating capacity of the churches which preach the "social gospel." When "the world" seeks entertainment it usually prefers to have it in its native haunts and its natural setting rather than to have it adulterated and spoiled by an admixture of religion. The "social gospel" is not filling but rather emptying the churches and many are concerned as to what new attractions can be offered to drag "the world" to church.

Let us honestly face the actual condition of the present day pulpit and pew. God still has His "seven thousand" who have not bowed to the worship of "twentieth-century scholarship," who are not devotees at the shrine of "the modern mind" and who will not deify man and humanize God. Praise God that throughout the whole world there are thousands of preachers, evangelists, teachers and missionaries who still preach the Christ of the Gospel of the Word of God and there are millions of laymen who believe that Gospel and who hold inviolate the whole Word of God.

But on the other hand there is a growing number of preachers, teachers and missionaries who today do not preach or teach the Christ of the Gospel of the Word of God. The Christ they preach is "another" Christ, the gospel is "another" gospel and the Bible is "another" Bible.

The reformation of the whole world which the "social gospel" purposes does not need the Saviour of the cross, for man is to be his own savior. To preach the Christ of the cross and of the throne is to leave the realm of the practical and descend to the plane of the doctrinal, the modern teacher reasons. He declares that the world has outgrown this. But to win the world from its naughty ways and to teach it the right "way of life" he does feel the need of an example to hold up before it and of ethical precepts and principles which it can follow. The preacher of the "social gospel" can find no greater example and no better teacher than "the Jesus of history" so he does make use of Him in this capacity.

The reformation of the world which the modern preacher advocates has no place in it for the Gospel of the Word of God which is a Gospel of salvation from sin through a crucified, risen, ascended, exalted Lord. In fact the "social gospel" decries having any creed. It declares that its emphasis is on love rather than on faith and the important thing is not what a man believes but what he is. It does not concern itself with the building of a solid foundation but only with the ornamentation of the roof. If the structure has a lovely, attractive roof garden with sweet music, fragrant flowers, captivating eloquence and happy companionship why have any anxiety over the fact that the foundation is made of sand? The "social gospel" ignores the fact so plainly revealed in Scripture that the divine order is invariably faith and then love, and that it is an absolute impossibility to build the superstructure of a spiritual life on anything but the solid foundation of a crucified, risen Saviour. So the "social gospel" is plainly not "the Gospel of Christ."

The reformation of the world which the modern pulpit so earnestly advocates has no place in it for the Scriptures as the Word of God. "The modern mind" finds it impossible to accept the Bible as such. The Bible cannot be rejected altogether for then the modern preacher would on the very face of it have to leave the evangelical pulpit immediately. But "the modern mind" finds a middle ground of compromise which it hopes the evangelical church will be tolerant and loving enough to accept. It admits that the Bible "contains the Word of God" and modestly claims that it has been ordained by twentieth-century scholarship to tell the pew what parts of it are the Word of God and what parts are not.

Such an arrogant assumption makes the true believer who loves the Bible and who believes that from Genesis to Revelation it is "the Word of God," as God Himself says it is, seek to know what this "modern mind" really is and where it obtained the authority to handle the Book of books in any such fashion.

So one goes to the Bible itself to see if he can run down this "modern mind" that he may know where and how to classify it. He finds only two types of "mind" mentioned: "the mind of Christ" and "the carnal mind." In Philippians 2:5-11 he finds that "the mind of Christ" believes and accepts Christ as the eternal Son, the One who was equal with God because He was God; the incarnate Son who emptied Himself of His divine glory and humbled Himself by entering into this world through the virgin's womb, thus becoming Man; the crucified Son who in obedience to His Father's will went to the death of the cross; the ascended Son who has been exalted to the Father's right hand and given a name above every name; the kingly Son before whom every knee shall bow someday and every tongue shall confess that He is Jesus Christ the Lord. "The mind of Christ" cannot be "the modern mind" which denies and rejects in whole or in part these glorious truths concerning the Lord Jesus.

Then it must be "the carnal mind." But "the carnal mind" is as old as Eden. The only way we can discover whether the self-styled "modern mind" is really the antiquated "carnal mind" dressed in the disguise of twentieth-century scholarship is to take its fingerprints. That will be adequate proof. "Hath God said?" "Ye shall not surely die." "Ye shall be as gods." Doubt and disbelief of God's Word; denial of God's Word; and deification of man and man's intellect! No further evidence is needed. This threefold fingerprint marks "the modern mind" as "the carnal mind" which is enmity toward God, and His arch-antagonist. The Bible of the modern preacher is "another" Bible and not "the Word of God."

Such an appalling condition in the pulpit inevitably creates an equally appalling condition in the pew. The people in many churches today are starved; they are like the famine sufferers, having to live on shrubs, bark, husks and fodder. Probably the Church was never so perfectly organized as it is today, yet it is pitifully ineffective before its tremendous task. The apostasy in the pulpit has created dwindling congregations, doubting Christians and drifting churches. The Church has drifted so far back toward the world that ofttimes the boundaryline between the two spheres is almost indiscernible. Worldly policies are resorted to in the conduct of the affairs of the Church; worldly methods are employed to attract people to attend its services; worldly entertainments are given them after they come. Whatsoever a church soweth, that shall it also reap. There is a tragic harvest of thoroughly worldly churches in Christendom today.

Let us come back to the individual Christian's responsibility for the kind of work he does as a member of the Body of Christ. The works of every believer in Christ will be judged and he will receive or lose his reward according to the kind of work which he has done. If he has built a super-structure upon the foundation of the pure Gospel that is gold, silver and precious stones, then his work will abide. But, if he has fashioned the superstructure out of the wood, hay and stubble of "another gospel which is not the gospel" (Galatians 1:6-7) then his work will be burned. It will not stand the test of the fire of God's judgment.

> 1 Corinthians 3:8, "Now he that planteth and he that watereth are one: and *every man shall receive his own reward according to his own labour.*"

> 2 Corinthians 5:10, "For *we must all appear before the judgment seat of Christ;* that every one may receive the things done in his body, *according to that he hath done, whether it be good or bad.*"

> 1 Corinthians 3:11-15, "For other foundation can no man lay than that is laid, which is Jesus Christ. Now if any man build upon this foundation gold, silver, precious stones, wood, hay, stubble; *every man's work shall be made manifest:* for the day shall declare it, because it shall be revealed by fire; and the fire shall try every man's work of what sort it is. *If any man's work abide which he hath built thereupon, he shall receive a reward. If any man's work shall be burned, he shall suffer loss:* but he himself shall be saved; yet so as by fire."

It is a terrifically solemn thought that in the work which we do we are either the tool of Christ or of Satan and that in the message we give we are either the mouthpiece of Christ or of the devil.

> Romans 6:13, "*Neither yield ye your members as instruments of unrighteousness unto sin:* but yield yourselves unto God, as those alive from the dead, and *your members as instruments of righteousness unto God.*"

> Matthew 16:23, "But he turned, and *said unto Peter, Get thee behind me, Satan:* thou art an offence unto me: for thou savourest not the things that be of God, but those that be of men."

But there is no need for any Christian to be ignorant of the kind of work that abides nor will he have any excuse to present to Christ at the judgment seat if he does the kind that must be burned. God has given us the pattern in His Book and has bestowed upon us the power in His Spirit to accomplish our part in this blessed partnership. If we fail to do it, it will be because we have failed to discern.

GOD'S WORK IN THIS AGE IS ACCOMPLISHED THROUGH SUPERNATURAL POWER

The works of the incarnate Son were supernatural and beyond the power of any man to accomplish in himself. Those who tried to copy or to counterfeit them failed miserably. Yet He told His disciples that they were to do the same works and even greater. It is truly a supernatural task which Christ gives the Christian to do. Bringing spiritually dead men to life and making them into the image of the Son of God is in deed and truth a task beyond human power.

> John 14:12, "Verily, verily, I say unto you, He that believeth on me, *the works that I do shall he do also; and even greater works than these shall he do;* because I go unto my Father."

In the last clause of this wonderful promise He gives a clue as to how they were to be empowered for such a work. "Because I go unto my Father." By His return to heaven supernatural power to do supernatural tasks was to be transmitted to them. Let us follow this clue until we find the secret.

After His crucifixion and resurrection and immediately preceding His ascension He gives to His disciples the commission in which He makes mention of this power. He tells them three things: first, that all power in heaven and upon earth resides in Him; second, that they will be endued with this power; third, that they will receive this power through the anointing of the Holy Spirit.

> Matthew 28:18, "And Jesus came and spake unto them, saying, *All power is given unto me in heaven and in earth.*"

> Luke 24:49, "And, behold, I send the promise of my Father upon you: but tarry ye in the city of Jerusalem, until ye be *endued with power from on high.*"

> Acts 1:8, "*Ye shall receive power, after that the Holy Ghost is come upon you.*"

The crucified, risen, ascended, exalted Lord in whom dwells all power in heaven and upon earth Himself lives in all the fullness of His supernatural power in the believer through the infilling and anointing of the Holy Spirit. Someone has tersely said, "Calvary creates the worker; Pentecost empowers him."

The disciples and apostles of the first-century Church were equipped and energized to do "the greater works" by the limitless power of God through the fullness of the Holy Spirit.

> Acts 4:8, "Then *Peter, filled with the Holy Ghost,* said unto them, Ye rulers of the people, and elders of Israel."

> Acts 13:9, "Then Saul, (who also is called Paul,) *filled with the Holy Ghost,* set his eyes on him."

> Romans 15:18-19, "For I will not dare to speak of any of *those things*

which Christ hath not wrought by me, to make the Gentiles obedient, by word and deed, through mighty signs and wonders, *by the power of the Spirit of God;* so that from Jerusalem, and round about unto Illyricum, I have freely preached the gospel of Christ."

1 Thessalonians 1:5, "For our gospel came not unto you in word only, *but also in power, and in the Holy Ghost,* and in much assurance; as ye know what manner of men we were among you for your sake."

The same power bestowed by the same Person is open to every disciple of the twentieth-century Church for the accomplishment of the same God-given task. Is that power yours today? Have you been anointed by the Holy Spirit? Are you doing "the greater works"?

32

The Relationships of the Spiritual Man

NO MAN CAN LIVE UNTO HIMSELF. Every man has a corporate as well as an individual life. God has ordained that we live in families, neighborhoods, nations and races, nevertheless the whole human race is a unit and each person is a unit within a unit.

God intended that between the units in this vast organism there should be perfect adjustment. Godliness, holiness and righteousness were the fundamentals upon which God meant human society to be built.

But sin entered and as we have seen, cosmos became chaos. Maladjustment distorted every relationship; first, between God and man; second, within man's own being; third, between man and man. In God's original creation the divine order was God, others, oneself. Sin completely reversed this. Selfishness supplanted love. Today the whole fabric of human society is threatened. Family life is being rent in twain by divorce of parents and disobedience of children; communities are agog with frightful crimes and civic corruptions; nations and races are at war at heart, if not in fact. Family, civic, national and international life is shot through and through with division.

The only hope for readjustment within human society rests in a return to God's original order. In Christ and in Him alone can man come into a right relationship with God, with himself and with his fellow men. In Christ all dislocations in relationships may be set right and there may be a reproduction of moral order in which the processes of disintegration and degeneration may cease. Life on the highest plane both demands and provides for such readjustment.

The Christian life is a fellowship which is rooted in faith and nurtured by love. The soil out of which it springs is faith in God. The atmosphere in which it thrives is love for God, out of which is begotten love toward man. This divine order is irreversible. It is impossible for one to have a love for his fellow man with sufficient power to conquer the innate selfishness of his own heart apart from faith in God. It is utter folly to preach "the brotherhood of man" to those who do not know "the Fatherhood of

God" through a new birth based on faith in the cleansing blood of a Saviour.

Primacy is always given in Scripture to man's relationship to God; his relationship to man is secondary and dependent. Godliness is an essential precedent to righteousness. When men have become children of God through faith in Jesus Christ then they become brothers in the Lord. This is the only "fatherhood of God" and "brotherhood of man" which Scripture sanctions and which works out in practical experience. After Paul calls himself Christ's apostle then he calls himself Timothy's brother.

> Colossians 1:4, "Since we heard of *your faith in Christ Jesus, and of the love which ye have to all the saints.*"

> Philemon 5, "Hearing of thy love and faith, which thou hast *toward the Lord Jesus, and toward all saints.*"

> Colossians 1:1, "Paul, an *apostle of Jesus Christ* by the will of God, and Timotheus *our brother.*"

Let us then consider the Christian's corporate relationships in their divinely appointed order.

The Spiritual Man's Relationship to God

Life on the highest plane demands a radical reversal in man's affections. The natural man lives unto himself because he loves self supremely; the spiritual man lives unto God because he loves God supremely.

> 2 Timothy 3:2-4, "For *men shall be lovers of their own selves, ...* traitors, heady, highminded, *lovers of pleasures more than lovers of God.*"

> 2 Corinthians 5:15, "And he died for all, *that they which live should not henceforth live unto themselves, but unto him* which died for them, and rose again."

God's love bridged the gulf between the natural and the spiritual man. "God *so loved* that he gave his only begotten Son." His gift was the measure of His love. He gave His best, His all. He gave the costliest gift in His treasure-house, the crown jewel of heaven. Such love comprehended by faith conquers the rebellion of the will and constrains the heart to love Him who first so loved us. Our love for Him is rooted in His love for us.

> 1 John 4:9-10, "*In this was manifested the love of God toward us,* because that God sent his only begotten Son into the world, that we might live through him. *Herein is love, not that we loved God, but that he loved us, and sent his Son* to be the propitiation for our sins."

> 1 John 4:19, "*We love him, because he first loved us.*"

The spiritual man not only loves God more than he loves himself but also more than he loves any other one. His love for God is paramount. It is so far above the love he has even for his own kith and kin that it is in a class by itself.

> Matthew 22:37-38, "Thou shalt love the Lord thy God *with all thy heart,* and *with all thy soul,* and *with all thy mind.* This is *the first* and great *commandment."*

> Matthew 10:37, "He that *loveth father or mother more than me* is not worthy of me: and he that *loveth son or daughter more than me* is not worthy of me."

When the Christian becomes a son in God's family thereafter his first filial obedience and love is to be given to his heavenly Father. This does not mean for one moment that God discounts the human love of parent for child or child for parent or friend for friend. On the contrary God commands both parental and filial love, and experience proves that when one loves God supremely all human love is both enhanced and enriched. To the heavenly Father His child not only owes the gift of physical life through creation but he owes the still more priceless gift of spiritual life through re-creation. This makes him far more of a debtor to God than he is even to his earthly parents, and parents and children alike should acknowledge with joy the primacy of their relationship to God.

But this is not always so and oftentimes the hardest place to live one's Christian life is in the home and one's greatest enemies are those of his own household. One knows many instances of heartbreaking experiences and well-nigh intolerable situations caused by the ridicule, opposition and persecution of Christians by members of their own family. Many a boy or girl has been disowned by parents for no other reason than that he became a Christian! Many a young person has had to go to the mission field over the wishes of parents or friends. To have chosen to do the will of God when it went counter to the will of loved ones has been the severest test in Christian experience. But God has never failed to honor love that expresses itself in sacrificial obedience to Himself. And Christ knows how to sympathize with and to succor all who are so tested. He met opposition in His own family and His mother and brothers tried to dissuade Him from the path that led to Calvary. This action called out from Him that remarkable statement that those children of God who were united in doing the will of their heavenly Father were more closely bound together than those who are put together by family ties. The blood of Christ unites His own by a tie that supersedes that made through human blood.

> Matthew 10:36, "And a man's foes shall be they of his own household."

> Matthew 12:50, "For whosoever shall do the will of my Father which is in heaven, *the same is my brother, and sister, and mother."*

Strength to suffer and to endure, to bear and to forbear will be given to the one who gives Christ the supreme place in his affections. God will cause him to triumph and to be a sweet savor of Christ unto Him in every place. Love to God, preeminent and paramount, is rewarded by victory and fruitage. His love in us manifested even in silence will be like a light shining in a dark place.

> 2 Corinthians 2:14-16, R. V., "But thanks be unto God, *who always lead-eth us in triumph in Christ, and maketh manifest through us the savour of his knowledge in every place.* For we are a sweet savour of Christ unto God, in them that are saved and in them that perish; to the one a savour from death unto death; to the other a savour from life unto life."

The relationship of the spiritual man to God is marked also by loyalty. By virtue of sonship in God's family he has citizenship in God's Kingdom. Loyalty to his heavenly country and to the interests of his Father's Kingdom takes precedence over citizenship in his earthly domain and supersedes the nationalism which is earthborn.

While acknowledging that "the powers that be are ordained of God," while submitting obediently to the laws of the country in which he lives, while taking his full responsibility for support of that government during his sojourn on earth, yet the man who lives his life on the highest plane discerns clearly that his real home center is in the heavenlies and that his first allegiance must be to the Kingdom of God.

> Titus 3:1, "*Put them in mind to be subject to principalities and powers, to obey magistrates,* to be ready to every good work."
>
> Romans 13:1, "*Let every soul be subject unto the higher powers.* For there is no power but of God: *the powers that be are ordained of God.*"
>
> Philippians 3:20, R. V., "*For our citizenship is in heaven.*"

The spiritual man must acknowledge the sovereignty of his Lord over all other rulers. To him Christ Jesus is already the King of kings and the Lord of lords and his prayer to the Father invariably breathes forth the intense desire to see God's sovereignty extend from sea to sea until His will is done on earth as it is in heaven.

> 1 Timothy 1:17, "Now *unto the King eternal, immortal, invisible, the only wise* God, be honour and glory for ever and ever. Amen."
>
> Matthew 6:9-10, "After this manner therefore pray ye: *Our Father which art in heaven, Hallowed be thy name. Thy kingdom come. Thy will be done in earth, as it is in heaven.*"

The Christian serves his Master in an official capacity. Disloyalty is treason. He is a servant of the Lord of heaven and God requires uncompromising faithfulness in a servant. He is a soldier in the army of Christ and a soldier dare not be enmeshed in entangling alliances. He is an ambassador of the King at the court of a foreign country and an ambassador must maintain absolute loyalty to the statutes of his own country.

> Romans 1:1, "Paul, *a servant of Jesus Christ,* called to be an apostle, separated unto the gospel of God."

> 2 Timothy 2:3-4, "Thou therefore endure hardship, *as a good soldier of Jesus Christ. No man that warreth entangleth himself with the affairs of this life;* that he may please him who hath chosen him to be a soldier."

> 2 Corinthians 5:20, "Now then *we are ambassadors for Christ,* as though God did beseech you by us: we pray you in Christ's stead, be ye reconciled to God."

An ambassador of Christ has definite instructions from his Sovereign and he cannot act independently of them. He has had committed unto him the Gospel of Christ as a sacred trust and loyalty to Christ requires loyalty to this Gospel.

> 1 Timothy 1:11, "According to *the glorious gospel of the blessed God,* which was committed to my trust."

> Romans 15:16, "That I should be the minister of Jesus Christ to the Gentiles, *ministering the gospel of God.*"

Some of the religious leaders in Paul's day had departed from the faith. They would not endure sound doctrine and resisted the truth to such an extent that Paul openly called them blasphemers. They had made shipwreck of their faith and were busily engaged in trying to steer the ship of other men's lives onto the same rocks.

> 2 Timothy 3:8, "Now as Jannes and Jambres withstood Moses, *so do these also resist the truth:* men of corrupt minds, *reprobate concerning the faith.*"

> 1 Timothy 1:19-20, "Holding faith, and a good conscience; *which some having put away concerning faith have made shipwreck;* of whom is Hymenaeus and Alexander; whom I have delivered unto Satan, *that they may learn not to blaspheme.*"

Paul wrote to the young minister who was his son in the faith urging him to loyalty to his Lord. He pointed out to Timothy the fallacy of the scholarship of that day, which was the cause of this departure from the true faith, and warned him to have nothing to do with it but to give himself afresh to a study of the Word.

> 1 Timothy 6:20-21, R. V., "O Timothy, guard that which is committed

unto thee, *turning away from the profane babblings and oppositions of the knowledge which is falsely so called; which some professing have erred concerning the faith."*

2 Timothy 2:16-18, R. V., "But *shun profane babblings:* for they will proceed further in ungodliness, *and their word will eat as doth a gangrene;* of whom is Hymenaeus and Philetus; *men who concerning the truth have erred,* saying that the resurrection is past already, and *overthrow the faith of some."*

2 Timothy 2:15, *"Study to shew thyself approved unto God,* a workman that needeth not to be ashamed, *rightly dividing the word of truth."*

Paul also warned the little flock at Ephesus and the whole Church under his care of the grievous wolves and the false hirelings who would enter in among them to draw the flock away from the Shepherd. He faithfully exposed these men and their seductive methods in his epistles to the churches.

Acts 20:29-30, "For I know this, that after my departure shall *grievous wolves enter in among you, not sparing the flock. Also of your own selves shall men arise, speaking perverse things, to draw away disciples after them."*

2 Corinthians 11:13-15, *"For such are false apostles, deceitful workers, transforming themselves into the apostles of Christ.* And no marvel; for Satan himself is transformed into an angel of light. *Therefore it is no great thing if his ministers also be transformed as the ministers of righteousness; whose end shall be according to their works."*

Paul declared that these men were guilty of bringing division into the Church. When they departed from the faith of the Gospel instead of separating also from the Church that had preached and taught this Gospel from its inception, and establishing an organization upon their new tenets, they did the very unethical thing of remaining within the Church and of attempting to gain control over it. Though teaching a doctrine contrary to that which the Christians had been taught yet they apparently used such a vocabulary that it would be difficult for their simple-hearted hearers to detect its falseness. They ensnared many through genial manners and fair words. Such was the beginning of apostasy.

Romans 16:17-18, R. V., "Now I beseech you, brethren, *mark them that are causing the divisions* and occasions of stumbling, *contrary to the doctrine which ye learned:* and turn away from them, *For they that are such serve not our Lord Christ, but their own belly; and by their smooth and fair speech they beguile the hearts of the innocent."*

Colossians 2:4, 8, "And this I say, *lest any man beguile you with enticing words. Beware lest any man spoil you through philosophy and vain deceit,* after the tradition of men, after the rudiments of the world, and not after Christ."

Under the inspiration of the divine Spirit Paul foretold the apostasy that would sweep the entire professing Church and would eat at its very vitals. Into a veritable whirlpool of doubt, disbelief and disloyalty multitudes would be drawn.

> 1 Timothy 4:1-2, R. V., "But *the Spirit saith expressly, that in the later times some shall fall away from the faith,* giving heed to seducing spirits and doctrines of demons, *through the hypocrisy of men that speak lies,* branded in their own conscience as with a hot iron."

> 2 Timothy 4:3-4, R. V., "*For the time will come when they will not endure the sound doctrine;* but having itching ears, *will heap to themselves teachers after their own lusts; and will turn away their ears from the truth, and turn aside unto fables.*"

No Spirit-taught student of the Word of God and of the universal condition of Christendom doubts that the day of this prophesied apostasy is already upon us. In the churches of the mission field as well as in those of the homelands this declension from the true faith and this disloyalty to Him who is the Truth is in everyday evidence (In China about twenty-five hundred missionaries, representing all denominations and nationalities, united in a Bible Union as a testimony before the native Christians of their loyalty to Jesus Christ and to His Word, and as a protest to the inroads of Modernism, into a field where for more than one hundred years the pure Gospel seed had been sown and nurtured by thousands of missionaries loyal to Christ and to His truth.)

Today many religious leaders in all parts of Christendom have departed from the faith and are openly in revolt against the truth. They will not endure sound doctrine but are actively declaring war upon the foundational truths of Christianity. Just last week a minister, still occupying an evangelical pulpit, was assisting in the ordination of a Unitarian minister. On that occasion he made this pronouncement, "The Church is in revolt against Fundamentalism and Puritanism," which means that he is openly in favor of liberalism and license. Such men are at heart unitarian because they deny every truth of the Word which makes the Lord Jesus Christ the unique Son of God. Their place is entirely outside the evangelical Church and, if they practiced even the most elementary principles of the ethical gospel which they preach, they would pack up their ecclesiastical belongings, depart from the evangelical pulpit, and establish themselves either with their unitarian brethren or seek virgin soil in which to plant their tares.

But they have no intention whatever of leaving the evangelical pulpit, rather they purpose deliberately to stretch forth their hands and stealthily lay hold upon the entire machinery of the Church both at home and upon the mission field and secure its control. They usually are such adepts in the manipulation of language that through the use of "good words and fair speeches" (Romans 16:18) they deceive even the true people of God. They preach sermons filled with the rankest poison but sugarcoated with sweet words and eloquent phrases, patronizing the Jesus of history. Only those who have the discernment which the Holy Spirit alone gives detect the deception. And, when the men and women who love their Lord better than they love their own lives cry out in protest against such high-handed dishonesty, they have the blatant effrontery to charge them with bringing division into the Church and to accuse them with lack of love.

The conflict between Fundamentalism and Modernism is dividing organized Christianity in twain. There are some who live near the border line of both camps who earnestly desire neutrality between these opposing forces. They plead for unity; they plan for union; they pray for unanimity. But those who live at the headquarters of both camps know that this can never be. The only unity which the Bible enjoins is "the unity of the Spirit" which is based on "one body, one Spirit, one hope, one Lord, one faith, one baptism and one God."

Such unity is not something which we attempt to "make" but rather is something already created by the Holy Spirit which we "keep." Such unity does not "become" for it "is" wherever there is oneness in Christ Jesus. This and only this is the unity for which our Lord prayed and which He expects of His children.

> Ephesians 4:3-6, "*Endeavouring to keep the unity of the Spirit* in the bond of peace. There is *one body*, and *one Spirit*, even as ye are called in *one hope* of your calling; *one Lord, one faith, one baptism, one God* and Father of all, who is above all, and through all, and in you all."

Such unity can never exist between Fundamentalism and Modernism for they are as far apart as darkness and light, as death and life. Let me quote from an editorial of *The Christian Century:* "The God of the Fundamentalist is one God; the God of the Modernist is another. The Christ of the Fundamentalist is one Christ; the Christ of the Modernist is another. The Bible of Fundamentalism is one Bible; the Bible of Modernism is another. The Church, the kingdom, the salvation, the consummation of all things— these are one thing to the Fundamentalist and another thing to the Modernist. Which God is the Christian God, which Christ is the Christian Christ, which Bible is the Christian Bible, which church, which kingdom, which salvation, which consummation are the Christian Church, the Christian kingdom, the Christian salvation, the Christian consummation? The future will tell. You may sing 'Blest be the tie' till doomsday, but it cannot bind these worlds together."

Thus according to the testimony of Modernism itself we see that between Fundamentalism and Modernism a great gulf is fixed which nothing or no one can bridge. The issue admits of no neutrality. Loyalty to the Lord Jesus Christ demands that every Christian study to know and declare himself either for or against the Christ of the Fundamentalist or the Christ of the Modernist. In such a conflict as this silence is cowardice—it may even be construed to be desertion and treachery. Loyalty to God in these difficult days of deepening apostasy calls every Christian to three things; discernment, devotion and division.

Christians should be able to discern between false and true teaching even when the former is given in its most subtle form, so that there shall not be the slightest deviation from the truth of God's Word. It is not enough to believe God's truth, we are to "walk" in it.

> 2 John 1-4, "The elder unto the elect lady and her children, *whom I love in the truth;* and not I only, but also *all they that have known the truth; for the truth's sake,* which *dwelleth in us,* and shall be with us for ever. . . . I rejoiced greatly that I found of *thy children walking in truth,* as we have received a commandment from the Father."

> 3 John 3-4, "For I rejoiced greatly, when the brethren came and testified of *the truth that is in thee, even as thou walkest in the truth.* I have no greater joy than to hear that *my children walk in truth.*"

Discernment requires watchfulness; it required a continuous prayerful study under the tutelage of the Holy Spirit of God's Word and a careful comparison of what one hears and reads with what one studies. Paul told the Ephesian elders that from among themselves men would arise speaking perverse things to draw men away after them and cautioned them to watch and to remember his warnings.

> Acts 20:31-32, *"Therefore watch,* and *remember,* that by the space of three years *I ceased not to warn every one* night and day with tears. And now, brethren, *I commend you to God and to the word of his grace,* which is able to build you up, and to give you an inheritance among all them which are sanctified."

He warned Timothy to be on his guard continuously against false teaching and unsound doctrine.

> 2 Timothy 4:3, 5, "For the time will come when they will not endure sound doctrine; but after their own lusts shall they heap to themselves teachers, having itching ears; and they shall turn away their ears from the truth, and shall be turned unto fables. *But watch thou in all things,*

endure afflictions, do the work of an evangelist, make full proof of thy ministry."

He warned the Christians against deception and urged them to become adults in the faith that they might always be able to discern the false and the true.

> Ephesians 5:6, *"Let no man deceive you with vain words:* for because of these things cometh the wrath of God upon the children of disobedience."

> Ephesians 4:14, *"That we henceforth be no more children,* tossed to and fro, *and carried about with every wind of doctrine,* by the sleight of men, and cunning craftiness, *whereby they lie in wait to deceive."*

Loyalty to the Lord Jesus demands devotion to the truth at any cost as the Holy Spirit has taught us. When men and women everywhere are departing from the faith, possibly even members of our own family and our friends, God asks of us a faithfulness to the faith of our fathers that beats no retreat.

> 2 Timothy 3:14, *"But continue thou in the things which thou hast learned and hast been assured of,* knowing of whom thou hast learned them."

> 2 Timothy 4:7, "I have fought a good fight, I have finished my course, *I have kept the faith."*

> 1 Corinthians 16:13, "Watch ye, *stand fast in the faith,* quit you like men, be strong."

> 2 Timothy 1:13, *"Hold fast the form of sound words, which thou hast heard of me,* in faith and love which is in Christ Jesus."

Devotion to Jesus Christ calls us to a loyalty to truth that brooks no neutrality. It even challenges us to take our place in the front ranks and "to fight the good fight of faith."

> 1 Timothy 6:12, *"Fight the good fight of faith,* lay hold on eternal life, whereunto thou art called, and *hast professed a good profession before many witnesses."*

> Jude 3-4, "Beloved, when I gave all diligence to write unto you of the common salvation, it was needful for me to write unto you, and *exhort you that ye should earnestly contend for the faith* which was once delivered unto the saints. *For there are certain men crept in unawares,* who were before of old ordained to this condemnation, *ungodly men, turning the grace of our God into lasciviousness, and denying the only Lord God, and our Lord Jesus Christ."*

There is pseudounion in Christendom today that is tantamount to dishonoring disloyalty. Its slogan is "For the sake of peace we must have union even at the cost of truth." It bids the Fundamentalist sit silently while the Modernist seeks and secures control of the machinery of the Church both at home and abroad. If he protests he is accused of being divisive.

As one studies the gospel of Matthew he will find a place where the Lord Jesus Christ made a definite, deliberate break with the men who had willfully rejected Him. There was a clean-cut cleavage between Him and the religious leaders of that day and He withdrew from them and from that time on devoted Himself exclusively to those who were His own.

We have not only His example but we have the clear teaching of Scripture to guide us in this very delicate and difficult matter. God calls His children into complete separation from all those who are traitors to the truth. He commands His loyal ones to have no fellowship with them and not to be partakers of their sins.

> 1 Timothy 6:3-5, "If any man teach otherwise, and consent not to wholesome words, even the words of our Lord Jesus Christ, and to the doctrine which is according to godliness; . . . He is proud, knowing nothing, but doting about questions and strifes of words, whereof cometh envy, strife, railings, evil surmisings, . . . Perverse disputings of men of corrupt minds, and destitute of the truth, supposing that gain is godliness, *from such withdraw thyself.*"

> 2 John 9-11, "Whosoever transgresseth, *and abideth not in the doctrine of Christ,* hath not God. He that abideth in the doctrine of Christ, he hath both the Father and the Son. . . . *If there come any unto you, and bring not this doctrine, receive him not into your house, neither bid him God speed:* For he that biddeth him God speed is *partaker of his evil deeds.*"

Such loyalty to the Lord Jesus is bound to mean suffering to the man or woman of sensitive spirit. It will incur a persecution as real as anything endured by the Christians of the first century, even though of a different nature. The intellectuals of the twentieth century consign the conservative to the slums of scholarship and the worldlings regard him as an antique. But for the joy that is set before him the Fundamentalist endures the ignominy and reproach of the cross.

> 2 Timothy 3:12, "Yea, and *all that will live godly in Christ Jesus shall suffer persecution.*"

> 2 Timothy 1:8, "Be not thou therefore ashamed of the testimony of our Lord, nor of me, his prisoner: *but be thou partaker of the afflictions of the gospel according to the power of God.*"

THE SPIRITUAL MAN'S RELATIONSHIP TO FELLOW CHRISTIANS

A right adjustment to God necessitates a right adjustment with all to whom God is related. Coming into God's family brings one into relationship with other members of that family as brothers and sisters. God is love so love is the atmosphere of the home in the heavenlies.

> 1 John 4:8, 12, *"God is love. . . . If we love one another, God dwelleth in us, and his love is perfected in us."*

The love of the children for one another is rooted in the love of God. His heart of love is reflected in the heart of each because His very nature, which is love, is imparted to each one at the new birth. The proof of God's indwelling in the believer is his love for the brethren. Unlove or hatred toward a brother or sister in the family of God is incontrovertible proof that the love of God does not dwell in one. The love-nature is shown in a love-life.

> 1 John 4:7, "Beloved, *let us love one another* for love is of God; and *every one that loveth is born of God* and knoweth God."
>
> 1 John 3:14, "We know that we have passed from death unto life *because we love the brethren. He that loveth not his brother abideth in death.*"
>
> 1 John 4:20, *"If a man say, I love God, and hateth his brother he is a liar:* for he that loveth not his brother whom he hath seen, how can he love God whom he hath not seen?"

Obedience in the family life of God requires love for one another. The law of Christ is love upon the very highest plane—the plane of the cross. There on Calvary in laying down His life in death for those who were not only sinners but rebels the Lord Jesus manifested love at its highest and purest. It is love of this same nature and extent that Christ commands Christians to have. The cross of Christ is to be both the birthplace and the pattern of the love which brethren are to bear one to another. Rooted in a love that has its lifeblood flowing from the cross the spiritual man's life becomes adjusted to that of every other member of God's family.

> John 13:34, *"A new commandment,* I give unto you, *That ye love one another; as I have loved you,* that ye also love one another."
>
> John 15:12, "This is my commandment, *That ye love one another, as I have loved you."*

Then love for one another in the family of God is not optional but obligatory. To love one another as Christ hath loved us rests upon a divine "ought." There is no escape and no excuse.

> 1 John 4:11, "Beloved, if God so loved us, *we ought also to love one another."*
>
> 1 John 3:16, "Hereby perceive we the love of God, because he laid down his life for us: And *we ought to lay down our lives for the brethren."*

This spiritual adjustment between fellow Christians is revealed in the inner circle of fellowship by unity and in touch with the outer world by solidarity.

Unity in the inner circle of the Father's family life is the very heart of the Son's high-priestly prayer. In church circles today there is much emphasis laid upon union. All kinds of associations and federations are being formed. There is an attempt on a vast scale to bring about a universal consolidation of denominations, and even a federation of the two bodies into which the visible church is divided—Protestant and Roman Catholic.

But there is a vast and crucial difference between union and unity. According to Webster's dictionary union means "junction; coalition; combination," while unity means "a state of being one, oneness, agreement, harmony." Union is junction; unity is conjunction. Union is coalition; unity is concord.

The unity for which our Lord prayed was not a forced union, worked up and organized by man, based on common ideas and ideals, but it was a spontaneous oneness which grew inevitably out of the sharing of a common life—the life of Christ Himself. Christ prayed that the disciples might be one *even as* He and the Father were one. The significance of that *"even as"* is tremendous; it is descriptive and explanatory. It describes a unity that is based not on organization but on organism; it is not a union of denominations or of communions but it is a welding into essential oneness of those who are drawn together magnetically as it were, by the power of the supernatural life indwelling each. "Father, thou in me and I in them that they may be made perfect in one." It is the unity of spirit with spirit through oneness in Christ Jesus.

> John 17:21, 23, *"That they all may be one: as thou, Father, art in me, and I in thee, that they also may be one in us:* that the world may believe that thou hast sent me. . . . I in them, and thou in me, *that they may be made perfect in one."*

> Galatians 3:28, "There is neither Jew nor Greek, there is neither bond nor free, there is neither male nor female: *for ye are all one in Christ Jesus."*

Such unity is based on a common, clearly defined relationship to God the Father, God the Son, and God the Holy Spirit, and it is "kept" through a mutual, right adjustment to the Spirit.

> Ephesians 4:4-6, *"Endeavoring to keep the unity of the Spirit* in the bond of peace. There is *one body,* and *one Spirit,* even as ye are called in *one hope* of your calling; *one Lord, one faith, one baptism, one God* and Father of all, who is above all, and through all, and in you all."

Such unity comprehends a universal brotherhood of men on the ground of a blood tie. They who are separated as far as the east is from the west by racial antagonisms and prejudices, by national division and friction, by personal suspicion and hatred, are made one by the blood of Christ. Enmities are put away at the cross and those who were far apart are made nigh by the blood of a common Redeemer.

The synchronizing into one of people from the two great divisions of the human race—Jew and Gentile—through faith in Jesus Christ, as recorded in the book of Acts, is one of the great supernatural achievements of the ascended Lord. Through the shed blood of their common Saviour, Jew and Gentile were made fellow heirs and fellow members of the Body of Christ. Typifying the racial divisions and international antipathies of the present day they show us the only possible way to world peace.

> Ephesians 2:14-16, *"For he is our peace, who hath made both one,* and hath broken down the middle wall of partition between us; *having abolished in his flesh the enmity,* even the law of commandments contained in ordinances; *for to make in himself of twain one new man, so making peace;* and that he might reconcile both unto God *in one body by the cross, having slain the enmity thereby."*

Such unity comprehends far more than just "the Fatherhood of God" and "the brotherhood of man." It goes infinitely deeper. Trusting in the blood of Christ for salvation Christians are baptized into the Body of Christ, and each member is united to every other member in an organic bond as real and as close as that which exists between the members of the physical body. Brought into oneness through the death of Christ Christians are welded together into unity through the life of Christ. The life of the Head flows through the whole Body uniting it in an inevitable oneness of faith, love and service. Every Christian is not only a member of Christ but Christians are members one of another.

> 1 Corinthians 12:12, 14, 27, "For as *the body is one, and hath many members,* and all the members of that one body, being many, are one body: so also is Christ. *For the body is not one member, but many. Now ye are the body of Christ, and members in particular."*

> Romans 12:5, "So *we,* being many, *are one body in Christ, and every one members one of another."*

> Ephesians 4:25, *"For we are members one of another."*

The members of Christ's Body are fitly framed together and compacted into one. Each member is complementary and supplementary to every other member of the Body.

> Ephesians 4:16, "From whom *the whole body fitly joined together and compacted by that which every joint supplieth,* according to the effectual

working in the measure of every part, maketh increase of the body unto
the edifying of itself in love."

Colossians 2:19, "And not holding the Head, *from which all the body by
joints and bands having nourishment ministered, and knit together*, in-
creaseth with the increase of God."

Unity between members of the Body of Christ was very marvelously
manifested in several ways in the first-century Church. It was first of all
a unity *in faith*. The apostles and disciples believed alike concerning their
Lord. Their oneness centered in their crucified, risen, ascended Lord.
Around Him they gathered as one heart and one soul because of one mind.
They loved each other in the truth and so were one.

Acts 2:42, "And *they continued stedfastly in the apostles' doctrine and
fellowship*, and in breaking of bread and in prayers."

3 John 1, "The elder unto the well beloved Gaius, *whom I love in the
truth*."

It was a unity *in love*. They shared mutually with one another as fellow
members of one Body their material possessions and spiritual blessings in
Christ. The need of one was the need of all and each one considered that
what he had was for the benefit of all.

Acts 2:44-46, "*And all that believed were together, and had all things common;* and sold their possessions and goods, and parted them to all men,
as every man had need. And they, *continuing daily with one accord
in the temple, and breaking bread from house to house*, did eat their
meat with gladness and singleness of heart."

It was a unity *in purpose*. Repeatedly it says in the Acts that they were
'of one accord." They were single-eyed and so were single-hearted. It was
a society of kindred spirits with a consuming passion to know Jesus Christ
and the consuming purpose to make Him known.

Acts 2:1, "And when the day of Pentecost was fully come, they were all
with one accord in one place."

Acts 5:12, "And by the hands of the apostles were many signs and wonders wrought among the people; (and they were all *with one accord* in
Solomon's porch)."

It was a unity *in fellowship*. Difficulties and problems were shared mutually as well as joys and blessings. What affected one member of the Body
affected all the members. That first-century Church knew in experience
the meaning of "the communion of saints."

Acts 4:23, "And being let go, *they went to their own company, and re-
ported all* that the chief priests and elders had said unto them."

Acts 20:36, "And when he had thus spoken, he kneeled down, and *prayed with them all.*"

Members of the Body of Christ were united also in solidarity in service. Believers who were "added unto the Lord" were also "added unto the church."

Acts 5:14, "And *believers were the more added to the Lord,* multitudes both of men and of women."

Acts 2:47, "Praising God, and having favour with all the people. *And the Lord added to the church* daily such as should be saved."

Confession of cleansing from sin and separation from life in the old sphere and of entrance into new life through a new birth was made through the act of baptism. Induction into the new order of which Christ is the Head was made public, through this divinely appointed rite.

Acts 2:41, "Then *they that gladly received his word were baptized:* and the same day there were added unto them about three thousand souls."

Through the unity and solidarity of the Body of Christ in its corporate life God revealed Himself to the world and worked to accomplish its evangelization. Christ, the Head, worked through the members of His Body with mighty power to carry the Gospel out into the enemy's territory and to deliver thousands upon thousands of men and women from his power.

Against this unity and solidarity in passion and purpose the archenemy of Christ aimed his deadliest darts. The most harmful thing Satan could do to that Spirit-filled, Spirit-empowered Church was to work to diminish its power through disunion. This he succeeded to a certain extent in doing. There are recorded divisions between individuals because of a difference in personal viewpoint (Acts 15:37-40); between groups because of a difference in doctrinal conviction (Acts 15:1, 5, 24). Then there arose factions within certain churches and each faction sought to gain control of affairs (1 Corinthians 1:11-13). Again one man in the Church who loved preeminence and power was the cause of great dissension (3 John 9-10).

All down through the centuries the devil has continued to use this method of opposing Christ. A most serious condition exists within the Church today which calls for very deep heart searching. In view of the need of the unsaved millions and of the growing apostasy in Christendom the dissensions that exist between individuals, and between groups within the Body of Christ, are deplorable. It calls for a careful diagnosis of causes and for a scriptural prescription of a cure.

The first cause is temperamental differences. Perhaps the majority of dislocations within the Body of Christ could be traced ultimately to this source. Earnest Christians are often diametrically opposite in temperament and even the grace of God has not made them congenial companions. They grate on each other. One is mystical and the other is practical; one is militant and the other is gentle; one is refined and the other is rough; one is social and the other is seclusive; one is scholarly and the other is scatter-brained; one is intense and the other is sluggish; one is Mary and the other is Martha. These people have to live under the same roof and work at the same tasks. By nature and possibly by training their way of looking at things is antipodal and their methods are as different as day and night. Such temperamental differences with their resultant dissensions are the cause of quarrels in the churches at home and of physical breakdowns and enforced furloughs in the Christian ranks upon the mission field.

A second cause is doctrinal differences. Reference is not made here to the disagreement upon fundamentals mentioned above, which is inevitable, but to that which could and should be avoided. I refer especially to the overemphasis upon some particular truth which separates a section of the Body of Christ and segregates it to an exclusive corner of the fold. Many sects have been started in this way and today even some of the larger denominations are divided into several different branches, differing possibly in but one or two matters of belief. The difficulty arises in studying the Bible from the limited angle of one segment of truth rather than studying that segment of truth from the lofty viewpoint of the whole Bible. Thus this particular truth is dislocated from its proper setting and given a preeminence which the Bible never gives it. To those whose lives have been enriched and blessed by it, it becomes all-important. Sometimes deeply spiritual Christians are excluded from fellowship with such groups simply because they do not put the same interpretation or the same emphasis upon this one particular truth.

Another phase of this same thing is onesidedness in viewpoint caused by some particular experience passed through which makes one critical of others who have not walked in precisely the same footprints. It is such a natural thing to interpret and to judge others' spiritual experiences by one's own yet it is a very dangerous thing to do. One man may feel just as deeply as another yet it may be impossible for him to shout "Hallelujah." He may love his Lord devotedly and yet not be able to use the vocabulary of highly emotional souls. The language with which he testifies of his life of victory and sanctification may not be cast into the mold of any particular school of thought along these deeper lines yet the experience of it may be none the less real. As God has made no two persons alike so He has no stereotyped mold into which He casts the spiritual experience of His children. The truth of His Word is the same for all but the manner of its appropriation and assimilation varies according to the Spirit's dealing with each separate personality. The divine One knows each life through and through and He takes into account the temperament and training, the opportunities and advantages, as He works with infinite patience to bring each one into full maturity of life in Christ. But unsympathetic judgment and censorious criticism of others who have not yet attained to the same degree of experience or who have not come to it by the same road is one of the commonest sins of earnest Christians and the cause of no little trouble within the Body of Christ.

Still another phase is that of a legal attitude that makes for intolerance in matters not clearly revealed in Scripture. An earnest Christian may have convictions not only on essentials but on secondary matters as well. One's belief in the truth should affect one's conduct. God has a clearly defined standard of conduct for those living on the highest plane. There are some things which by the precepts of Scripture God shows us to be wholly outside His will for the new man in Christ; but in other things He guides by principles. Within this realm there will inevitably be a wide difference in interpretation and in understanding. The conduct of every Christian should be undergirded with deep conviction by which he himself abides unswervingly but he should be very careful to give to his equally devout and spiritual fellow Christian the same right to follow his conviction. At least he should not indulge in backbiting and evil speaking and self-righteous judgment of his brother, but if he feels his fellow Christian is dishonoring God through something he permits in his life, he should give himself to prayer that fuller light and greater apprehension in this particular matter may be given.

A third cause of division is jealousy and envy owing partly to the diversity of gifts. We are distinctly told that this diversity of gifts is intentional on God's part and that He has "divided to every man severally as He will" making one an apostle, another a prophet, another a pastor, another an evangelist and still another a teacher for the express purpose of "perfecting of the saints, for the work of the ministry, for the edifying of the body of Christ" (Ephesians 4:11-12). In order to bring the whole Body of Christ "unto a perfect man, unto the measure of the stature of the fulness of Christ" the gifts of all these varied types of workers are needed.

And yet behold what takes place! The teacher looks with something akin to contempt upon the evangelist or the preacher. The development and enrichment of the mind seem to him to be all-inclusive of a person's need. He argues that if one is educated he is fully equipped to become what he ought to be. Any work that deals more directly with the heart and the will he dubs "emotionalism" which is to be studiously avoided. The teacher is in great danger of having that obnoxious thing, "a superiority complex." On the other hand the evangelist and preacher may look with suspicion and doubt upon the teacher; they may misjudge him and, because of his apparent absorption in educational pursuits, charge him with no interest in spiritual matters. Such an attitude often produces a censorious spirit that results in bitter backbiting.

Oftentimes church quarrels start among the laymen. Petty jealousies, trivial enmities between individuals produce factions; people take sides; the trouble is broadcasted by gossiping tongues, and God's name is disgraced before unbelievers by a full-fledged church quarrel.

> 1 Corinthians 1:11-13, "For it hath been declared unto me of you, my brethren, by them which are of the house of Chloe, *that there are contentions among you.* Now this I say, that every one of you saith, *I am of Paul;* and *I of Apollos;* and *I of Cephas;* and *I of Christ.* Is Christ divided? Was Paul crucified for you? or were ye baptized in the name of Paul?"

We have given at least a partial diagnosis of the serious malady from which the Body of Christ suffers today and its resultant weakness. But is there no cure? Is Christ the Head nonplussed before these awful maladjustments within His own Body? Does He stand impotent before these hindering dislocations? A thousand times no!

Let us remind ourselves again and again that the true Church, the Body of Christ, is of divine construction. God is the Architect; the Church is His wondrous workmanship; God Himself "fitly framed together" the parts that make up His holy temple; He "knits together" the living members of the Body of Christ. Then He is amply able to readjust any dislocated part of this wondrous organism.

May we suggest what seems to be the scriptural cure for these manifold dissensions within the Body of Christ? It reaches to the very seat of the trouble and effects a double cure, one both of mind and of heart. If Christians were thinking rightly and loving purely every dislocation would be corrected. The whole Church needs a fresh immersion into the very mind of Christ and a new baptism of His love. This double cure was the apostle Paul's unfailing prescription for the disease of division.

Over and over again he beseeches the Christians under his care to be of one mind. It is possible for differences in opinion, judgment and conviction to be adjusted without compromise if Christians truly seek to be of one mind. If there is an honest, selfless yielding to know the mind of the Lord, there will surely be like-mindedness as a result.

> Philippians 2:5, "*Let this mind be in you, which was also in Christ Jesus.*"

> 1 Corinthians 1:10, "Now I beseech you, brethren, by the name of our Lord Jesus Christ, that ye all speak the same thing, and that there be no divisions among you; *but that ye be perfectly joined together in the same mind and in the same judgment.*"

2 Corinthians 13:11, "Finally, brethren, farewell. Be perfect, be of good comfort, *be of one mind, live in peace;* and the God of love and peace shall be with you."

The second part of the cure for division is a baptism of love. The whole Body of Christ needs to eat, digest, and assimilate 1 Corinthians 13 as its daily food. It needs to be filled and to be refilled with the Holy Spirit whose first fruit is love. It needs a deluging and a saturating with the purifying, perfecting love of God until love increases and abounds in the hearts of God's children.

1 Thessalonians 3:12, "And *the Lord make you to increase and abound in love one toward another,* and toward all men, even as we do toward you."

Philippians 1:9, "And this I pray, *that your love may abound yet more and more* in knowledge and in all judgment."

1 Peter 1:22, "Seeing ye have purified your souls in obeying the truth through the Spirit *unto unfeigned love of the brethren, see that ye love one another with a pure heart fervently.*"

Twice in Colossians Paul speaks of the members of the Body being "knit together." The Greek means "compacted," implying firm consolidation. What can so unite members of the Body differing so greatly in temperament, taste, thought and training? Only one thing, a divinely imparted, supernaturally sustained love, can do it. Such unity comes when all things are done in love.

Colossians 2:2, "That their hearts might be comforted, *being knit together in love.*"

Ephesians 4:15, "But speaking the truth *in love.*"

Ephesians 4:2, "With all lowliness and meekness, with longsuffering, *forbearing one another in love.*

Ephesians 4:16, R. V., "From whom all the body fitly framed and knit together through that which every joint supplieth, according to the working in due measure of each several part, maketh the increase of the body *unto the building up of itself in love.*"

Ephesians 3:17-19, "That Christ may dwell in your hearts by faith; *that ye, being rooted and grounded in love,* may be able to comprehend with all saints what is the breadth, and length, and depth, and height; *and to know the love of Christ, which passeth knowledge,* that ye might be filled with all the fulness of God."

The spiritual man is big enough to recognize that it takes all the millions upon millions of believers in the past, present and future, until the coming of Christ completes it, to make up that wondrous Body. He grasps the truth of that incomparable passage, Ephesians 3:17-19, where words fail even the apostle Paul as he tries to show that it will take all the saints of all the ages to know the love of God that passeth knowledge. In the apprehension of this transcendent truth the spiritual man sees the terrible sin of jealousy, envy, unlove, strife, enmity, hatred, intolerance, selfishness, quarreling between members of the Body of Christ. He gladly acknowledges that in the Church of God there are both room and need for the mystical, the practical, the philosophical, the scientific, the meditative, the active temperament. He acknowledges the greatness of truth and the absolute inability of any one person or sect to comprehend all truth or to embody its teachings perfectly. He joyfully acquiesces in God's plan of sharing His ministry gifts with all His children, dividing to each according to His divine will that His purpose for the world may be accomplished.

There is a clearly defined attitude which every Christian must take toward his fellow Christians if he means to live his life on the highest plane. It is an attitude of forbearance, humility, unselfishness, sympathy, frankness, helpfulness, peace and cooperation.

> Colossians 3:13, *"Forbearing one another,* and forgiving one another, if any man have a quarrel against any: even as Christ forgave you, so also do ye."

> Philippians 2:3-4, "Let nothing be done through strife or vainglory; *but in lowliness of mind let each esteem other better than themselves. Look not every man on his own things,* but every man also on the things of others."

> 1 Corinthians 12:25-26, "That there should be no schism in the body; *but that the members should have the same care one for another.* And whether one member suffer, *all the members suffer with it;* or one member be honoured, *all the members rejoice with it."*

> Romans 12:9, R. V., "Let love be *without hypocrisy."*

> Galatians 6:2, *"Bear ye one another's burdens,* and so fulfil the law of Christ."

> Romans 14:19, *"Let us therefore follow after the things which make for peace,* and things wherewith one may edify another."

> Galatians 5:13, *"By love serve one another."*

Such unity in the Body of Christ is the most convincing of all arguments to an unbelieving, maladjusted world of the power of the living Christ. Christ prayed that this oneness of mind and heart manifested in His disciples would bring many to believe in Him as the God-sent One. God would glorify Himself through solidarity in the Body of Christ Jesus.

> John 13:35, "By this shall all men know that ye are my disciples, *if ye have love one to another.*"

> John 17:21, "That they all may be one; as thou, Father, art in me, and I in thee, that they also may be one in us: *that the world may believe that thou hast sent me.*"

Dear fellow member of the Body of Christ, are you living in harmonious and peaceful adjustment to every other member of that Body? Is there something between you and a fellow Christian for which you are responsible? If so, are you satisfied to have such a condition continue or are you ready to let the great Physician heal the breach? He is able to do it if you will cooperate with Him. Your part is threefold.

First, will you lay aside by confession all sin of your heart toward another?

> 1 Peter 2:1, "Wherefore *laying aside all malice,* and all guile, and hypocrisies, and envies, and all evil speakings."

Second, will you live by 1 Corinthians 13 every day of your life? Will you let the love-truth of that chapter become your code of conduct? Will you take your spiritual pulse by this infallible thermometer? Will you judge yourself, rather than your fellows, by this divine standard of love? Will you let the Holy Spirit clothe you with love?

> Colossians 3:14, R. V., "And above all these things *put on love,* which is the bond of perfectness."

Third, will you unite your prayer with that of your Lord that you may be "made perfect in one" with every other member of His Body? And will you allow nothing to remain in your mind or in your heart that separates you even a hair's breadth from any other child of God?

> John 17:23, "I in them, and thou in me, *that they may be made perfect in one.*"

THE SPIRITUAL MAN'S RELATIONSHIP TO THE WORLD

A right adjustment with God necessitates a readjustment of relationship to the world. The boundary line between the spiritual man and the worldling is clearly marked and a wall of separation is built by God. The spiritual man is a nonconformist in his relationship to the world.

> Romans 12:2, "*And be not conformed to this world:* but be ye transformed by the renewing of your mind, that ye may prove what is that good, and acceptable, and perfect, will of God."

> 2 Corinthians 6:14-15, 17, "*Be ye not unequally yoked together with unbelievers:* for what fellowship hath righteousness with unrighteousness?

and what communion hath light with darkness? And what concord hath Christ with Belial? or what part hath he that believeth with an infidel? *Wherefore come out from among them, and be ye separate,* saith the Lord."

The Christian is taken out of the world yet he is sent back into it. For what purpose?

John 17:18, "As thou hast sent me into the world, *even so have I also sent them into the world.*"

John 20:21, "Then said Jesus unto them again, Peace be unto you: as my Father hath sent me, *even so send I you.*"

Christ came into the world as the Father's Ambassador. Into a world alienated from God He brought "the good tidings of great joy" that a way was opened through Himself back to the Father's heart and home.

The Christian now goes forth as an ambassador of the Kingdom of heaven into the enemy's territory to carry the message of reconciliation to those who are alienated from God. Having experienced the joy of restoration to God through faith in Christ he cannot rest satisfied until he has brought others into the same joy. So he gladly accepts the responsibilities and obligations resting upon him through this ministry of reconciliation and gives himself to the winning of souls.

2 Corinthians 5:18-20, "And all things are of God, who hath reconciled us to himself by Jesus Christ, and *hath given to us the ministry of reconciliation;* to wit, that God was in Christ, reconciling the world unto himself, not imputing their trespasses unto them; and *hath committed unto us the word of reconciliation. Now then we are ambassadors for Christ,* as though God did beseech you by us: *we pray you in Christ's stead, be ye reconciled to God.*"

Christ came into a world enveloped in densest darkness to be its light. Into that same world every Christian is sent to be a light. In the beauty of the Christian's character and in the blessing of the Christian's service Christ would radiate the sweetness and strength of His own life and draw sinners unto Himself.

Matthew 5:14, *"Ye are the light of the world."*

Philippians 2:15, "That ye may be blameless and harmless, the sons of God, without rebuke, in the midst of a crooked and perverse nation, *among whom ye shine as lights in the world."*

THE HOLY SPIRIT—THE DIVINE AGENT IN THIS THREEFOLD ADJUSTMENT

The adjustment which brings the Christian into a right relationship with God, with his fellow Christians and with the world, is made by the Holy

Spirit who indwells and infills the spiritual man. It is He who takes of the love of the crucified, risen and ascended Christ and sheds it abroad in the heart of the Christian until each one loves the Father as the Son loves Him, and loves the fellow members of the Body of Christ as the Head loves them, and loves the unsaved in the world as the Saviour loves them.

> Romans 5:5, "And hope maketh not ashamed; *because the love of God is shed abroad in our hearts by the Holy Ghost which is given unto us.*"

> 1 Thessalonians 2:8, "So being affectionately desirous of you, *we were willing to have imparted unto you, not the gospel of God only, but also our own souls,* because ye were dear unto us."

Are you rightly related to God? To your fellow Christians? To the world? If not,

"Be filled with the Spirit."

33

The Hope of the Spiritual Man

THE CHRISTIAN IS UNITED to Christ by a golden cord of three strands, faith, love and hope (1 Corinthians 13:13; 1 Thessalonians 1:3). Faith and love look back to the cross and up to the throne and, claiming the fruits of salvation for the past and the present, use them to the glory of the Lord. But hope looks up into the heavens and waits for that future day when faith shall be merged into sight, when the labor of love shall be rewarded, when the salvation begun in grace shall be consummated in glory.

As the object of the believer's faith and love is the Lord Jesus Himself so is He the object of his hope. The glorious appearing of Christ Jesus, the Saviour, is the Christian's blessed hope.

> Titus 2:13, "*Looking for that blessed hope, and the glorious appearing of the great God and our Saviour Jesus Christ.*"

> Hebrews 9:28, "So Christ was once offered to bear the sins of many; and *unto them that look for him shall he appear the second time* without sin unto salvation."

OUR LORD'S RETURN—ANNOUNCED

Through prophecies added to those already given through the Old Testament, Jesus Christ gave birth to this hope in the hearts of those first believers. According to His prophecy His second advent was to be of a totally different nature and for a totally different purpose than His first advent had been. In the first He had come in weakness and humiliation; in the second He would come in regal power and glorious splendor. In the first He had come as a Saviour, to be despised of men and to be crucified upon a cross set up by wicked men for Him, but in the second He would come as a Sovereign to set up a Kingdom for Himself in which all nations and all men would bow down and serve Him.

> Mark 13:26, (see also Luke 21:27), "And then shall they see *the Son of man coming in the clouds with great power and glory.*"

> Matthew 25:31, "*When the Son of man shall come in his glory,* and all the holy angels with him, *then shall he sit upon the throne of his glory.*"

460

Upon the eve of His exodus He comforted the hearts of His disciples with two promises. One was the promise of another Comforter, the Holy Spirit, during His absence. This promise was fulfilled literally as we have seen. The other was that one day He Himself would return in person to receive them unto Himself to be with Him forever.

> John 14:2-3, "In my Father's house are many mansions: if it were not so, I would have told you. *I go to prepare a place for you.* And if I go and prepare a place for you, *I will come again, and receive you unto myself;* that where I am, there ye may be also."

As the disciples watched Him ascending into heaven this promise was reiterated by two men who stood by in white apparel.

> Acts 1:11, "Which also said, Ye men of Galilee, why stand ye gazing up into heaven? *this same Jesus, which is taken up from you into heaven, shall so come in like manner as ye have seen him go into heaven.*"

In the words "this *same* Jesus," "shall *so* come," in *like* manner," wonderful light was thrown upon the manner of Christ's return to earth. It was to be a personal, visible, bodily coming. Thus the Lord Jesus Himself instilled into the hearts of His first disciples the blessed hope of His literal return to earth.

OUR LORD'S RETURN—ANTICIPATED

This promise of His personal return was ever before them. That little group lived and worked in confident assurance and eager anticipation of the speedy return of the Lord they loved. On the day of Pentecost only ten days after His ascension He fulfilled the promise to send another Comforter; why should they not expect just as truly and even as speedily that His other promises would likewise be fulfilled?

When fifteen and finally twenty years passed by and some of those who had this hope had died, the hearts of others were very disquieted. What would it mean to these loved ones that this blessed hope had not yet been realized? To still this fear Paul writes to them at Thessalonica counseling patient waiting and comforting them with fuller teaching on this precious truth.

> 1 Thessalonians 4:13-18, "But I would not have you to be ignorant, brethren, concerning them which are asleep, that ye sorrow not, even as others which have no hope. *For if we believe that Jesus died and rose again, even so them also which sleep in Jesus will God bring with him.* For this we say unto you by the word of the Lord, that *we which are alive and remain unto the coming of the Lord shall not prevent them which are asleep. For the Lord himself shall descend from heaven* with a shout, with the voice of the archangel, and with the

trump of God: and *the dead in Christ shall rise first: then we which are alive and remain shall be caught up together with them in the clouds, to meet the Lord in the air:* and so shall we ever be with the Lord. Wherefore comfort one another with these words."

So the steadfast confidence of their faith and the intense longing of their love crystallized into an undimmed patience of hope which dominated the everyday life. How fully this blessed hope permeated and possessed the thought and the testimony of the apostles is revealed in a study of the New Testament. In the closing chapters of the gospels, throughout the book of the Acts and in every epistle except three Christ's second advent is taught and it is the major theme of Revelation. Three hundred and eighteen times it is mentioned; one verse out of every twenty-five is devoted to it. It was the hope of Paul, Peter, John, James, Jude and the writer of Hebrews.

> 1 Timothy 6:14, "That thou keep this commandment without spot, un-rebukeable *until the appearing of our Lord Jesus Christ.*"

> 1 Peter 1:13, "Wherefore gird up the loins of your mind, be sober, and hope to the end for the grace that is to be brought unto you *at the revelation of Jesus Christ.*"

> 1 John 2:28, "And now, little children, abide in him; that, *when he shall appear,* we may have confidence, and *not be ashamed before him at his coming.*"

> James 5:8, "Be ye also patient; stablish your hearts: *for the coming of the Lord draweth nigh.*"

> Jude 14, "And Enoch also, the seventh from Adam, prophesied of these, saying, *Behold, the Lord cometh with ten thousands of his saints.*"

> Hebrews 10:37, "For yet a little while, *and he that shall come will come, and will not tarry.*"

Our Lord's Return—Actualized

Nineteen centuries have passed since Christ Jesus said that He would return and the prophecies and promises regarding His second advent are still unfulfilled. The greater part of the professing Church has ceased to expect Him. In fact Christendom has set itself to the task of establishing the Kingdom without the King and scoffs at those who, believing that the Lord's promise will be fulfilled literally, still look for His return. Indeed this very scoffing is in itself a part of the fulfillment of prophecy regarding the last days.

> 2 Peter 3:2-4, "That ye may be mindful of the words which were spoken before by the holy prophets, and of the commandment of us the apostles of the Lord and Saviour: knowing this first, that *there shall come in*

the last days scoffers, walking after their own lusts, and saying, Where is the promise of his coming? for since the fathers fell asleep, all things continue as they were from the beginning of the creation."

Many preachers and teachers have applied "the blessed hope" of our Lord's return to the death of the believer, to the destruction of Jerusalem, to the descent of the Holy Spirit at Pentecost and to the gradual dissemination of the Gospel and the diffusion of Christianity over the whole earth. But the spiritually minded Christian believes that every prophecy regarding His second advent will be fulfilled as literally as were those of His first and waits for the coming of the Lord Himself from heaven.

The return of the Lord Jesus Christ has a special relationship to three groups of people, to Israel, to the Church and to the Gentile nations. A comprehensive study of this subject in all its bearings will deeply repay every Christian. But in these studies we must confine ourselves to the bearing of Christ's return upon the redemption of the individual believer from sin and all its consequences, upon the reconciliation of all things unto God and upon the restoration to God of sovereignty over the universe.

The return of the Lord Jesus Christ will mean the consummation of the believer's identification with Christ. The believer will be identified with his Lord as regards place, personality and power. Where Christ is he will be; what Christ is he will become; what Christ does he will share.

Where Christ is the Christian will be. Christ promised this to His disciples. "Where I am, there ye may be also" (John 14:3). He prayed that they might be with Him in glory. "Father, I will that they also, whom thou hast given me, be with me where I am; that they may behold my glory" (John 17:24). Then He went back into the glory. The disciples remained on earth and He came to be with them through the indwelling Holy Spirit. But one day He is coming to take His own to be with Him.

> Colossians 3:4, "When Christ, who is our life, shall appear, *then shall ye also appear with him in glory."*

What Christ is the Christian will become for he shall become a partaker of Christ's glory. He shall be glorified together with Him in spirit and in body.

> Romans 8:17, "And if children, then heirs; heirs of God, and joint-heirs with Christ; if so be that we suffer with him, *that we may be also glorified together."*

> 1 Peter 5:1, 10, "The elders which are among you I exhort, who am also an elder, and a witness of the sufferings of Christ, *and also a partaker of the glory that shall be revealed.* But the God of all grace, *who hath called us unto his eternal glory by Christ Jesus,* after that ye have suffered a while, make you perfect, stablish, strengthen, settle you."

The glorification of the Christian will involve the full redemption of his body which for the dead in Christ means resurrection and for the living means translation.

"The wages of sin is death" and there can be no final victory over sin that does not include victory over death. Death has laid claim all these ages to the bodies of God's saints, and still holds them captive in the grave. "But the sky not the grave is the goal of the Christian" and this will be proven when at the sound of the trump of God the graves of those asleep in Christ shall be opened and they shall be raised from the dead.

A few days ago I visited the cemetery on the hillside and saw there one tombstone in the form of a broken pillar. What a symbol it is of what every grave there means—a broken family circle! A broken thread of life that spelled manifold severed relationships! Will there ever be a reunion? Praise God there will be for those in Christ Jesus! The resurrection of Jesus Christ is the sure pledge of the resurrection of every believer. "Because I live, ye shall live also," He has said and He will do. Through His resurrection He became "the firstfruits of them that sleep" and thus made not only certain but essential the resurrection of every member of His Body.

> 1 Thessalonians 4:16, "For the Lord himself shall descend from heaven with a shout, with the voice of the archangel, and with the trump of God: *and the dead in Christ shall rise first.*"
>
> 1 Corinthians 15:20-23, "But now is Christ risen from the dead, and *become the firstfruits of them that slept. For since by man came death, by man came also the resurrection of the dead.* For as in Adam all die, *even so in Christ shall all be made alive.* But every man in his own order: Christ the firstfruits; *afterward they that are Christ's at his coming.*"

Oh! what comfort this can bring to those called upon to watch at the bedside of one whose life is slowly ebbing away; to endure the suffering of laying that loved one in the grave and to return to the loneliness of the home bereft of that presence. The blessed hope of our Lord's return calls the Christian to turn his gaze toward that resurrection morning when that loved one in Christ will come forth from the darkness of the grave to live in the power of an endless life. "O death, where is thy sting? O grave, where is thy victory?"

> 1 Corinthians 15:54, "So when this corruptible shall have put on incorruption, and this mortal shall have put on immortality, then shall be brought to pass the saying that is written, *Death is swallowed up in victory.*"

For those who are alive at Christ's coming it will mean a marvelous victory over death also, the conquering of death through not dying! It will not be the victory of resurrection but of translation.

Through the new birth the human body is dignified by being made the habitation of God, the temple of the Holy Spirit. Through the Holy Spirit's indwelling it is fitted to be the channel for the revelation of the Lord Jesus and to be an instrument for His use. Grace has done much to purify and magnify the human body.

Yet it often grows so tired, weak and sick. It is so full of limitations and oftentimes a hindrance and a drag. And it is such a target for Satan and such an instrument of sin. It is liable at any moment to fall a victim to death's precursor, disease. So Scripture pictures the body as groaning under its burden of weariness and weakness and as crying out for the day of its release.

> Romans 8:23, R. V., "And not only so, but ourselves also, who have the firstfruits of the Spirit, *even we ourselves groan within ourselves, waiting for our adoption, to wit, the redemption of our body.*"

> 2 Corinthians 5:2-4, "*For in this we groan, earnestly desiring to be clothed upon with our house which is from heaven: if so be that being clothed we shall not be found naked. For we that are in this tabernacle do groan, being burdened:* not for that we would be unclothed, but clothed upon, that mortality might be swallowed up of life."

But one day in a moment, in the twinkling of an eye, those who are alive will be changed. "The twinkling of an eye takes two motions, the downward and the upward one." Just recently a friend has suffered anguish of spirit in watching a dearly loved sister slowly starve to death through the cruel ravages of disease until death seemed a happy release. But oh! when He comes, in the twinkling of the eye—apart from disease, death and decay—our mortal body shall have put on immortality. One moment here in bodies weak and worn; the next moment there in bodies powerful and glorious!

> "O joy, O delight, should we go without dying,
> No sickness, no sadness, no sorrow, and no crying,
> Caught up in the clouds to meet Him in glory,
>   When Jesus receives His own."

> 1 Thessalonians 4:17, "*Then we which are alive and remain shall be caught up together with them in the clouds, to meet the Lord in the air:* and so shall we ever be with the Lord."

> 1 Corinthians 15:51-53, "Behold, I shew you a mystery; We shall not all sleep, but we shall all be changed, *in a moment, in the twinkling of an eye,* at the last trump: for the trumpet shall sound, and the dead shall

be raised incorruptible, *and we shall be changed.* For this corruptible must put on incorruption, and this mortal must put on immortality."

Sin robbed the human body of the garment of light which the Creator gave it. But grace will give to it a robe of glory beautiful beyond anything we can conceive, for we are someday to be wholly conformed to the body of His glory. On the mount of transfiguration the curtain was drawn aside momentarily to give just a little idea of what our glorified body will be like. "His face did shine as the sun, and his raiment was white as the light." And of us Christ Himself said, "Then shall the righteous shine forth as the sun in the Kingdom of their Father."

> 1 Corinthians 15:49, "As we have borne the image of the earthly, *we shall also bear the image of the heavenly.*"

> Philippians 3:20-21, R. V., "For our citizenship is in heaven; *whence also we wait for a Saviour,* the Lord Jesus Christ: *who shall fashion anew the body of our humiliation, that it may be conformed to the body of his glory,* according to the working whereby he is able even to subject all things unto himself."

The Weymouth translation is "The Lord Jesus will transform this body . . . until it resembles the body of His glory." And this is just what identification with Christ in glory will mean to the body of the believer.

The glorification of the Christian will mean the consummating of his sanctification. Through identification with the Lord Jesus Christ in His death, resurrection and ascension the believer's sanctification is begun, through the Holy Spirit's indwelling and infilling it is continued but it will not be completed until we are identified with Him in His glory.

> 1 Thessalonians 5:23, "And the very God of peace sanctify you wholly; and I pray God your whole spirit soul and body be preserved blameless *unto the coming of our Lord Jesus Christ.*"

> Philippians 1:6, "Being confident of this very thing, that he which hath begun a good work in you *will perform it until the day of Jesus Christ.*"

Will our deep-rooted desire for real likeness to Him ever be fulfilled? Praise God that that also belongs to our blessed hope. Our spirit often eager and earnest, yet as often dulled and deadened by sin, will then be like His in all the fullness of His glorified, divine being. The purpose of our sonship will have been consummated in our perfected likeness to the Son. When we shall see Him face to face we shall be like Him; we shall ever bear His name, which stands for His nature, in our foreheads as His own personal seal to our full conformity to Himself.

> 1 John 3:2, "Beloved, now are we the sons of God, and it doth not yet

appear what we shall be: but *we know that, when he shall appear, we shall be like him;* for we shall see him as he is."

Revelation 22:4, "And they shall see his face; *and his name shall be in their foreheads.*"

The completion of sanctification is perfection; it is the deliverance not only from the penalty and power of sin but from its very presence. So long as we are in the body of flesh and in the world, within is a sinful nature and without is a sinful environment. But at the coming of the Lord the believer in Christ will be removed from the presence of sin both within and without. He will then breathe the pure air of the Glory-land and be himself purified. Then he will be:

"Without spot"—absolutely free from the stain of sin;

"Without wrinkle"—beyond the reach of suffering or sorrow, anxiety or anguish or aught that causes the furrows of care;

"Holy"—even as He is holy—"as the bush was luminous with the divine fire, so shall the luminosity of the divine nature make us aflame with the holiness of Jehovah";

"Without blemish"—delivered from inner corruption and outer contamination we shall be perfected with His perfection. Our Saviour will then see the travail of His soul and be satisfied, for He shall present us "faultless before the presence of his glory with exceeding joy."

Ephesians 5:27, "That he might present it to himself a glorious church, *not having spot, or wrinkle,* or any such thing; but *that it should be holy and without blemish.*"

Jude 24, "Now unto him who is able to keep you from falling, and *to present you faultless before the presence of his glory with exceeding joy.*"

When Christ returns, the Christian will be identified with Him in dominion. What Christ does he will share in doing. He will be a partner of His power. The God-man shall have recovered His rightful dominion over His universe and the saints, as "heirs of God and joint-heirs with Jesus Christ," shall be given their share in this inheritance and together with Him shall reign upon the earth.

Daniel 7:18, "*But the saints of the most High shall take the kingdom, and possess the kingdom for ever,* even for ever and ever."

Revelation 5:10, "And hast made us unto our God kings and priests: and *we shall reign on the earth.*"

Revelation 20:6, "Blessed and holy is he that hath part in the first resurrection: on such the second death hath no power, but they shall be priests of God and of Christ, and *shall reign with him a thousand years.*"

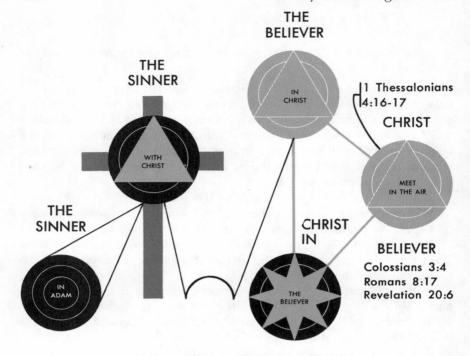

Diagram 13: Hope of the Spiritual Man

The God-man is now in heaven. The Father is on the throne and the Son is at His Father's right hand. But some day when He shall have conquered every enemy the Son is to have His own throne. This throne He promises to share with everyone who, while here on earth, has lived the life of an overcomer.

> Matthew 22:44, "The LORD said unto my Lord, *Sit thou on my right hand, till I make thine enemies thy footstool."*

> Revelation 3:21, *"To him that overcometh will I grant to sit with me in my throne,* even as I also overcame, and am set down with my Father in his throne." (See Diagram 13.)

The return of the Lord Jesus Christ will effect the consummation of the reconciliation of all things unto Himself. A time is coming when Jesus Christ will be the center of everything in heaven and upon earth; when everything will be directly related to Him and will head up in Him.

> Ephesians 1:10, *"That in the dispensation of the fulness of times he might gather together in one all things in Christ,* both which are in heaven and which are on earth; even in him."

That time will usher in the last of the divinely ordered ages which condition human life upon the earth; it will register the answer to the prayer "Thy kingdom come," and it will mark the fulfillment of the prophecy that Jesus Christ, as the seed of David, should be King over His own Kingdom upon this earth.

2 Samuel 7:12-13 [spoken to David], "And when thy days be fulfilled, and thou shalt sleep with thy fathers, *I will set up thy seed after thee, which shall proceed out of thy bowels, and I will establish his kingdom.* He shall build an house for my name, and *I will stablish the throne of his kingdom for ever.*"

Isaiah 9:6-7, "For unto us a child is born, unto us a son is given: *and the government shall be upon his shoulder. . . . Of the increase of his government and peace there shall be no end, upon the throne of David,* and upon his kingdom, to order it, and to establish it with judgment and with justice from henceforth even for ever. The zeal of the LORD of hosts will perform this."

Luke 1:32-33, "He shall be great, and shall be called the Son of the Highest: and *the Lord God shall give unto him the throne of his father David: and he shall reign over the house of Jacob for ever; and of his kingdom there shall be no end.*"

Scripture constantly speaks of a day that is coming when the Heir of all things will claim His possessions and exercise His power. It is called "the day of the Lord." In that day all that is proud and haughty and lifted up against Him in rebellion and resistance shall be brought low and the Lord alone shall be exalted and magnified as King of kings and Lord of lords.

Isaiah 2:12, 17, "*For the day of the Lord of hosts shall be upon every one that is proud and lofty,* and upon every one that is lifted up; and he shall be brought low. And the loftiness of man shall be bowed down, and the haughtiness of men shall be made low: *and the Lord alone shall be exalted in that day.*"

Revelation 19:11, 15-16, "And I saw heaven opened, and behold a white horse; and he that sat upon him was called Faithful and True, and in righteousness he doth judge and make war. And out of his mouth goeth a sharp sword, that with it he should smite the nations: and he shall rule them with a rod of iron: and he treadeth the winepress of the fierceness and wrath of Almighty God. And he hath on his vesture and on his thigh a name written, KING OF KINGS, AND LORD OF LORDS."

Men everywhere are acknowledging the awful confusion and chaos which exist in the moral world. Some are working to effect reconciliation within Satan's world-system through world courts, peace conferences, leagues of nations and international community houses. Others, believing such things are inadequate, hope that the millennial state will be ultimately produced by the progressive betterment of the world through the Holy Spirit's work and the preaching of the Gospel. Through the gradual diffusion of the Kingdom of God throughout the world they expect the kingdom of evil to be conquered and, as it were, absorbed into it. But the spiritually minded man who knows and accepts the prophetical teaching of God's Word believes there is no hope of universal peace until the Prince of Peace sits on His throne and Himself rules in justice and righteousness. He believes there can be no Millennium such as Scripture portrays until the satanic world-system based on self-love, self-interest, self-exaltation and self-will is overthrown.

A careful study of the word "until" as used repeatedly in the Bible in connection with our Lord's return amply justifies such a belief. The Christ who came once *in grace* must come a second time *in government* before He recovers all that was lost to Him through the Fall and before there can be a reconciliation of all things unto Himself.

> Ezekiel 21:27, "I will overturn, overturn, overturn it: and it shall be no more, *until he come whose right it is; and I will give it him.*"

> Acts 3:20-21, "And he shall send Jesus Christ, which before was preached unto you: whom the heaven must receive *until the times of restitution of all things,* which God hath spoken by the mouth of all his holy prophets since the world began."

> 1 Timothy 6:14-15, "That thou keep this commandment without spot, unrebukeable, *until the appearing of our Lord Jesus Christ: which in his times he shall shew,* who is the blessed and only Potentate, the King of kings, and Lord of lords."

Seiss says on this point, "My Bible tells of no millennium which existing processes are to bring about. Neither does it tell me of a millennium which is to precede the Saviour's second advent. The only millennium I read of in the Holy Book is that which is to be introduced by the glory and power of Christ's coming and the chief excellence of which is His personal presence and reign with His saints upon the earth. It is not the reign of art, science, human culture or free governments, for which the Bible teaches me to look; nor yet for the universal triumph of Christianity or the Church as we now have it; nor yet for the reign of justice, holiness or any mere abstract principles; *but the personal reign of Jesus my Lord.*"

But when the Man comes whom God has appointed to rule the world, the righteous King, He will rule in righteousness and the result will be peace. Then all problems will be solved; all wrongs righted; all breaches healed; all wars ended, because all things in God's moral universe shall be readjusted and reestablished according to the perfect will of God. "All the universe will feel the beneficence of His rule and the benediction of His peace."

> Isaiah 32:1, *"Behold, a king shall reign in righteousness,* and princes shall rule in judgment."
>
> Isaiah 11:4-5, *"But with righteousness shall he judge the poor, and reprove with equity for the meek of the earth:* and he shall smite the earth with the rod of his mouth, and with the breath of his lips shall he slay the wicked. *And righteousness shall be the girdle of his loins,* and faithfulness the girdle of his reins."
>
> Jeremiah 23:5-6, "Behold, the days come, saith the LORD, that I will raise unto David a righteous Branch, and *a King shall reign and prosper, and shall execute judgment and justice in the earth.* In his days Judah shall be saved, and Israel shall dwell safely: and this is his name whereby he shall be called, THE LORD OUR RIGHTEOUSNESS."
>
> Psalm 67:4, "O let the nations be glad and sing for joy: *for thou shalt judge the people righteously, and govern the nations upon earth.*"

When Christ, the King, reigns there will be *national peace.* Now the whole world is in a state of incipient war. "All Europe is armed to the teeth and the nations all watching each other with acute suspicion, and trembling with fear over the volcano of a suppressed Armageddon." The newspapers almost daily chronicle "rumours of war." But the coming of the Prince of Peace will end war.

> Isaiah 2:4, "And he shall judge among the nations, and shall rebuke many people: *and they shall beat their swords into plowshares, and their spears into pruninghooks: nation shall not lift up sword against nation, neither shall they learn war any more.*"
>
> Micah 4:2, "And *many nations shall come, and say,* Come, and let us go up to the mountain of the LORD, and to the house of the God of Jacob; and *he will teach us of his ways, and we will walk in his paths:* for the law shall go forth from Zion, and the word of the LORD from Jerusalem."

When Christ, the King, reigns there will be *social reconstruction.* The day of oppression, greed, selfishness, injustice will be ended because sin will be instantly detected, judged and punished. "When the Prince of Peace comes He will allay every disturbing element; hush the din caused by sin; put down every wrong; still every clamouring tongue; calm every raging sea of unrest; touch and heal every inflamed sore of society; unite into the harmony of accord every quarrelsome crowd; pilot every perplexed barque of humanity tossed on the sea of life, into the harbour of rest; heal every epileptical tourture of suffering; adjust every turmoil of difference by His rule of equity, and harmonize all conflicting claims in the melting fire of His love" (F. E. Marsh, *What Will Take Place When Christ Returns?*, p. 122).

> Isaiah 26:9, "When thy judgments are in the earth, *the inhabitants of the world will learn righteousness.*"

> Psalm 72:3-4, 12-14, "The mountains shall bring peace to the people, and the little hills, by righteousness. *He shall judge the poor of the people, he shall save the children of the needy, and shall break in pieces the oppressor. For he shall deliver the needy when he crieth, the poor also, and him that hath no helper. He shall spare the poor and needy, and shall save the souls of the needy. He shall redeem their soul from deceit and violence: and precious shall their blood be in his sight.*"

> Zechariah 14:20, "In that day shall there be upon the bells of the horses, HOLINESS UNTO THE LORD; and the pots in the LORD's house shall be like the bowls before the altar."

When Christ the King reigns there will be *material prosperity*. Vast fortunes will not be massed in the hands of a few but each man shall have sufficient and shall live in contentment.

> Micah 4:4, "*But they shall sit every man under his vine and under his fig tree;* and none shall make them afraid: for the mouth of the LORD of hosts hath spoken it."

> Isaiah 65:21-23, "*And they shall build houses, and inhabit them; and they shall plant vineyards, and eat the fruit of them.* They shall not build, and another inhabit; they shall not plant, and another eat: for as the days of a tree are the days of my people, and mine elect shall long enjoy the work of their hands. They shall not labour in vain, nor bring forth for trouble; for they are the seed of the blessed of the LORD, and their offspring with them."

When Christ the King reigns there will universal health and longevity.

> Isaiah 33:24, "*And the inhabitant shall not say, I am sick.*"

> Isaiah 35:5-6, "*Then the eyes of the blind shall be opened, and the ears of the deaf shall be unstopped. Then shall the lame man leap as an hart, and the tongue of the dumb sing:* for in the wilderness shall waters break out, and streams in the desert."

> Isaiah 65:20, "*There shall be no more thence an infant of days, nor an old man that hath not filled his days: for the child shall die an hundred years old;* but the sinner being an hundred years old shall be accursed."

In the coming age under the kingship of the Lord Jesus Christ mankind will be given a chance to attain to a perfection of personality, spiritual, intellectual and physical which is impossible for us to conceive of and the human race will enter upon a life of harmony and concord that the most optimistic cannot picture today.

When our Lord comes again it will mean redemption and renovation within His whole creation. Sin brought a curse upon the earth and upon the animal creation. Its destructive power and extensive reach are seen in the terrible disturbance caused within the divine harmony of creation. Everything in God's inanimate world is touched by death and decay and is robbed of its greatest utility and beauty by the blasting curse which sin brought.

So there is a minor key even in nature. The whole creation is weighted by a burden that constrains it to groan; it is subjected to a slavery that compels it to cry out for emancipation. It waits with impatience for the manifestation of the sons of God which will usher in that glad day when it too will be delivered from the bondage of corruption into the glorious liberty of the sons of God.

> Romans 8:19-22, R. V., "For the earnest expectation *of the creation waiteth for the revealing of the sons of God. For the creation was subjected to vanity,* not of its own will, but by reason of him who subjected it, in hope *that the creation itself also shall be delivered from the bondage of corruption into the liberty of the glory of the children of God. For we know that the whole creation groaneth and travaileth in pain together until now.*"

But "in the day of the Lord" all these conditions will be changed. "The miserere of Nature will become a jubilate." Even the life of the jungle will be lived in harmony. The earth will then yield her increase and the whole creation will sing its praises unto God, its Maker and Redeemer.

> Isaiah 55:12-13, "For ye shall go out with joy, and be led forth with peace: *the mountains and the hills shall break forth before you into singing, and all the trees of the field shall clap their hands. Instead of the thorn shall come up the fir tree, and instead of the brier shall come up the myrtle tree:* and it shall be to the LORD for a name, for an everlasting sign that shall not be cut off."

> Isaiah 11:6-9, "*The wolf also shall dwell with the lamb, and the leopard shall lie down with the kid; and the calf and the young lion and the fatling together; and a little child shall lead them.* And the cow and the bear shall feed; their young ones shall lie down together: *and the lion shall eat straw like the ox.* And the sucking child shall play on the hole of the asp, and the weaned child shall put his hand on the cockatrice' den. *They shall not hurt nor destroy in all my holy mountain:* for the earth shall be full of the knowledge of the LORD, as the waters cover the sea."

Finally, the return of the Lord Jesus Christ will effect the consummation of the restoration to God of sovereignty over His universe. Can such a victory ever be won until the usurping "prince of this world" is dispossessed and destroyed? There can be no Millennium while Satan remains in the heavenlies or on earth for it is impossible to be rid of his world-system until the world is rid of him. Through His regenerating power the Holy Spirit can and does deliver the believer from the power of Satan but He cannot deliver him from his presence. Satan is still here and will be until the Lord returns.

Genesis records Satan's victory and the rejection of God; Revelation records the dethronement of Satan and the enthronement of Christ. "The seed of the woman" born in the manger-cradle of Bethlehem and crucified on the cross of Calvary must stand upon the Mount of Olivet before the bruising of the serpent's head is finally consummated and the perpetual curse pronounced upon Satan is executed. When the Lord Jesus Christ returns Satan will be bound and cast into the bottomless pit for one thousand years.

> Zechariah 14:4, "*And his feet shall stand in that day upon the mount of Olives,* which is before Jerusalem on the east, and the mount of Olives shall cleave in the midst thereof toward the east and toward the west, and there shall be a very great valley; and half of the mountain shall remove toward the north, and half of it toward the south."

> Revelation 20:1-3, "And I saw an angel come down from heaven, having the key of the bottomless pit and a great chain in his hand. *And he laid hold on the dragon, that old serpent, which is the Devil, and Satan, and bound him a thousand years, and cast him into the bottomless pit, and shut him up, and set a seal upon him,* that he should deceive the nations no more, till the thousand years should be fulfilled: and after that he must be loosed a little season."

With the head of the world-system dethroned the triumphant Lord is restored to His rightful rule over the earth.

> Zechariah 14:9, "*And the Lord shall be king over all the earth: in that day there shall be one Lord, and his name one.*"

> Revelation 11:15, "And the seventh angel sounded; and there were great voices in heaven, saying, *The kingdoms of this world are become the kingdoms of our Lord, and of his Christ; and he shall reign for ever and ever.*"

> Revelation 19:6, "And I heard as it were the voice of a great multitude, and as the voice of many waters, and as the voice of mighty thunderings, saying, *Allelulia: for the Lord God omnipotent reigneth.*"

At the end of the thousand years Satan will be loosed for a season. He will reveal his unchanging and unchangeable disposition to self-will and his implacable hatred toward God by going forth to deceive the nations and by making a futile effort to regain his lost dominion.

> Revelation 20:7-9, "And *when the thousand years are expired, Satan shall be loosed out of his prison.* And shall go out to deceive the nations which are in the four quarters of the earth, Gog and Magog, to gather them together to battle: the number of whom is as the sand of the sea. And they went up on the breadth of the earth, and compassed the camp of the saints about, and the beloved city: and fire came down from God out of heaven, and devoured them."

This rebellion ends in his utter undoing and destruction. God's full and final judgment is now meted out upon him. He is cast into the lake of fire and brimstone to be tormented forever.

> Revelation 20:10, "*And the devil that deceived them was cast into the lake of fire and brimstone,* where the beast and the false prophet are, *and shall be tormented day and night for ever and ever.*"

Then God's victory is consummated. Every enemy is at last under His feet and the sovereignty of the triune God is absolute.

> 1 Corinthians 15:24-25, 28, R. V., "Then cometh the end, when he shall deliver up the kingdom to God, even the Father; *when he shall have abolished all rule and all authority and power. For he must reign, till he hath put all his enemies under his feet.* And when all things have been subjected unto him, then shall the Son also himself be subjected to him that did subject all things unto him, *that God may be all in all.*"

Is it any wonder that Satan hates the truth of the Lord's return and that he does all within his power to discredit, discourage and destroy those who hold and preach this blessed hope? He has no place for the second coming of the Lord in his "gospel" and his "ministers" either rail at or ridicule those who have it in theirs. One reason why we may well believe that we are in the last days is the fact of the violent and venomous attacks of Satan's instruments upon this glorious truth on the one hand and the growing preciousness and deepening influence of this hope upon those who love His appearing on the other.

Our Lord's Return—Attitude

With such a glorious prospect before the believer, one would expect him to have just one possible attitude toward our Lord's return—that of eager expectancy and ardent desire. Yet strange to say there are four very evident attitudes manifested in the professing Church toward this blessed hope; aggressive hostility, listless apathy, fearful apprehension and loving expectancy. Some hate it; some are totally ignorant of it; some are afraid of it and some love it. In which group do you find yourself?

God shows very clearly in Scripture what is the attitude of the spiritual man toward our Lord's return. May He now speak to the heart of every reader through His own Word.

> 2 Peter 1:19, "We have also a more sure word of prophecy: *whereunto ye do well that ye take heed,* as unto a light that shineth in a dark place, until the day dawn, and the day star arise in your hearts."

"Take heed." Think of how much both of the Old and the New Testament is devoted to prophecy—the foretelling of things to come. God tells us here that these prophetic words are reliable, they will most assuredly come to pass. Should we not then give heed to that which God thinks to be of such tremendous importance? Surely to be apathetic to that to which God commands us "to give attention with heart intentness" would be sin. In these dark days what can so truly keep us from depression over conditions in the world and in the Church and from discouragement over ourselves and our work as to concentrate our attention upon and become absorbed with this sure word of prophecy that shines like a light in the darkness?

> 2 Timothy 4:8, "Henceforth there is laid up for me a crown of righteousness, which the Lord, the righteous judge, shall give to me at that day: and not to me only, *but unto all them also that love his appearing.*"

"Love." The aged apostle knew that his lifework was nearly ended. Perhaps his body still bore the marks of the stripes and was weakened from the periods of hunger and thirst; his heart still felt the wounds caused by the persecutions of his own countrymen and the desertions of false brethren; his spirit was still burdened by the spiritual need of all the churches under his care; yet his whole being was aglow with joy. He had fought a good fight, he had finished his course, he had kept the faith through all the hardships and heartaches. And what had been the incentive for such a life? Paul had loved his Lord's appearing. Even in the darkest experiences of his life he had ever before him the anticipation of "that day" when the Lord, the righteous Judge, would give him a crown of righteousness, and within the heart of Paul there burned like a fire a love for his Lord's appearing that eclipsed every other love. Do you ever waken in the morning or fall asleep at night with the thought, "O, today, tonight, my Beloved may come?" Do you "love His appearing" to such a degree that you are longing for His return with eagerness and expectancy?

> 2 Peter 3:12, R. V., "*Looking for and earnestly desiring the coming of the*

day of God, by reason of which the heavens being on fire shall be dissolved, and the elements shall melt with fervent heat?"

"Look." Who could ever be apprehensive of our Lord's return who understands what that coming will mean to this dark, sin-cursed world? In times of exceptional calamity the hearts of ignorant ones are terrified by the thought that it is "the end of the world." Others, equally ignorant of the great prophetic truths, charge those who hold this blessed hope with being pessimistic and with looking upon world conditions in too somber and gloomy a way. Such men shudder at the very thought of what they call the "catastrophic cataclysm" of the premillennial view.

But the Christian who looks expectantly for our Lord's return is the only true optimist because he alone sees things both as they are and as they will be. To shut one's eyes to actual conditions and to deny the self-evident trend of affairs and their logical, inevitable outcome as revealed in the Word of God is not optimism but folly. The man who believes the sure word of prophecy and takes it as his compass knows that perilous times are ahead; he sees the way the world's ship of life is taking; he sights the rocks ahead and he knows that a frightful disaster is unavoidable.

Recently I read in the newspaper this account of a wrecked steamer, "The steamer *Robert E. Lee,* crack passenger liner bound from Boston to New York with 150 passengers and an equal number in the crew, went ashore in a blinding storm on the Mary Ann Rocks four miles off shore about eight o'clock in the evening. The ship struck one of the three jagged rocks that project about five feet above the low water mark." The next day the paper gave the reason for this catastrophe as stated by the ship's commander. "The wreck of the steamer *Robert E. Lee* on the rocks off Manonut *was due to a faulty compass.* Because of the consequent inaccuracy of the vessel's course, the ship would have piled up on the shore at Indian Head, three miles farther on, even if she had escaped the treacherous Mary Ann Rocks on which she grounded." The captain of the vessel attributed the changing of the compass largely "to the penetration into the pilot house of large quantities of snow, driven in through the windows by the severe gale."

The existing world-system has a faulty compass. The wintry drifts of enmity toward God have settled in upon it and made it wholly inaccurate. The world is steering straight for the rocks upon which it will sooner or later be wrecked.

But back of the "catastrophic cataclysm" that ends the rule of "the prince of this world" and overthrows this world-system the spiritual man sees the glorious appearing of the great God and Saviour Jesus Christ to rule the world, and beyond "the dissolving of the heavens" and "the melting of the elements" he sees "the new heavens and the new earth wherein dwelleth righteousness." So with almost impatient longing he "looks" for the coming of the Lord.

> 1 Thessalonians 1:10, *"And to wait for his Son from heaven,* whom he raised from the dead, even Jesus, which delivered us from the wrath to come."

> 1 Corinthians 1:7, "So that ye come behind in no gift; *waiting for the coming of our Lord Jesus Christ."*

"*Wait.*" Let us not miss the sweetness of this precious truth by failing to apprehend the inwardness of its meaning. We have told some of the blessings that will come to the Christian through our Lord's return, his resurrection from the dead or his translation without dying; his removal from the very presence of sin; his release from all bondage to self and to Satan; his reign with the Lord as coheir of the Kingdom. Yes, all these and other blessings await us upon the coming of the Lord.

Yet the chiefest of all blessings will be missed if we stop here. What we wait for is not a blessing but a Person. We wait for God's Son, our Saviour; it is the Bridegroom, our Beloved, for whom we wait. He has promised to come for His own to receive them unto Himself. When He comes, we shall meet *Him* in the air; we shall see *Him* face to face; we shall be like *Him*; and we shall forever be with *the Lord*.

I was travelling once in China from Shanghai to Foochow. A missionary who had been separated from his family for a year was returning home. At Shanghai he had received a large number of letters from his wife which he read and reread apparently devouring every word with a hungry heart. But long before we were near enough to Foochow to discern even the outline of the city he had cast aside his letters and was standing with eyes fixed in the direction of that city. As we drew still nearer he shaded his eyes with his hand; he waited, he watched with steady, fixed intentness. Why did the letters which had so engrossed him when he left Shanghai not satisfy him now? For whom was he looking so intently? Soon in the distance we saw a little boat coming and in it was a woman—his wife and Oh! what joy was theirs when hope was rewarded by sight and those two so long separated were together once again.

Our Lord has gone away to prepare a place that we may be with Him forever. During His absence our hearts are comforted and cheered through His Word and we find precious companionship with Him in its study. But He promised to come back and, as we draw nearer and nearer to "the day of Christ" with hearts fixed intently upon this blessed hope, we wait for the *Son Himself* from heaven.

> Matthew 24:36-42, R. V., "But of that day and hour knoweth no one, not even the angels of heaven, neither the Son, but the Father only. And

as were the days of Noah, so shall be the coming of the Son of man. For as in those days which were before the flood they were eating and drinking, marrying and giving in marriage, until the day that Noah entered into the ark, and they knew not until the flood came, and took them all away; so shall be the coming of the Son of man. Then shall two men be in the field; one is taken, and one is left: two women shall be grinding at the mill: one is taken, and one is left. *Watch therefore:* for ye know not on what day your Lord cometh."

Mark 13:33-37, R. V., "Take ye heed, *watch* and pray: for ye know not when the time is. It is as when a man, sojourning in another country, having left his house, and given authority to his servants, to each one his work, *commanded also the porter to watch. Watch* therefore: for ye know not when the Lord of the house cometh, whether at even, or at midnight, or at cockcrowing, or in the morning; *lest coming on you suddenly he find you sleeping. And what I say unto all, Watch.*"

"*Watch.*" Life will be flowing on in its ordinary channels when "the day of Christ" finally comes. We will rise to the ordinary tasks; we will be in our accustomed haunts; we will be eating, drinking, working and sleeping as usual.

No warning will be given us that we may hastily prepare ourselves to meet the Lord. No time will be given to change our occupation or our garments. So there is but one attitude for the Christian to have toward the coming of the Lord and that is the attitude of watchfulness. He may come *any* moment, therefore I should be watching *every* moment.

Revelation 2:25, "But that which ye have already *hold fast till I come.*"

"*Hold fast.*" In these days of growing apostasy the Christian is meeting with very severe tests to his faith, love, zeal and fidelity. The man who rejects the foundation truths of God's Word considers the man who holds them fast an intellectual outcast and consigns him to the slums of scholarship. This is a day in which men are suffering persecution for their faith. As the shadows deepen and the darkness of the apostasy falls more heavily over Christendom every man who is loyal to his Lord will have to "go forth . . . without the camp, bearing his reproach" (Hebrews 13:13). But with a tenacity of faith that nothing can shake; with an ardency of love that nothing can quench; with a warmth of zeal that nothing can dampen; and with a constancy of fidelity that nothing can weaken, the spiritual man will "hold fast" to all that is his in Christ till He comes.

Luke 19:12-13, "He said therefore, A certain nobleman went into a far country to receive for himself a kingdom, and to return. And he called his ten servants, and delivered them ten pounds, and said unto them, *Occupy till I come.*"

"Occupy." The Christian who looks and longs for the Lord's return is sometimes accused by those who reject this truth of being a visionary, impracticable stargazer, waiting idly for something to happen to release him from a doomed world. They even claim that such a hope "cuts the nerve of service." Nothing could be further from the truth. In fact, the exact opposite of this is true. From the early Church on down to the present time it is the men and women who have held this truth who have been the most zealous, ardent, active soul-winners. Their one passion was to trade with the pound which their Lord had given them until it had brought Him ten pounds. Their chief concern was not that they themselves might be released from a doomed world but that they might be the channels which the Lord would use to deliver others from it. With unwearied devotion and unflagging zeal they have obeyed the Lord's commission to preach the Gospel to every creature. The paramount purpose of their lives was to "occupy" faithfully till He comes.

Our Lord's Return—Approach

Is the time for the fulfillment of the Christian's hope drawing near? Is the Lord's return near at hand? We are told explicitly in Scripture that we know neither the day nor the hour that our Lord will come. Then of course, it is impossible to fix a date for this glorious event. Yet some, attempting to do this, have brought great discredit upon this precious truth.

> Matthew 25:13, "Watch therefore, for *ye know neither the day nor the hour wherein the Son of man cometh.*"

Yet our Lord Himself in His great prophetic address in the last week of His earthly life stated that there would be signs that would indicate the approach of His return in power and glory and He exhorted His disciples to watch for such signs.

> Luke 21:25-28, "And *there shall be signs* in the sun, and in the moon, and in the stars; and upon the earth distress of nations, with perplexity; the sea and the waves roaring; men's hearts failing them for fear, and for looking after those things which are coming on the earth: for the powers of heaven shall be shaken. And then shall they see the Son of man coming in a cloud with power and great glory. *And when these things begin to come to pass,* then look up, and lift up your heads; *for your redemption draweth nigh.*"

The Bible unfolds the divine program in the carrying out of God's eternal purpose in Christ. It is divided into definite cycles. There are certain signs which will precede the consummation of the cycle or "age" we are now in and the Spirit-taught Christian will be able to discern these "signs of the times." Today "the children of light" see in the conditions prevailing both in the world and in the Church a marvelous fulfillment of prophetic truth regarding "the last days" of this age and they believe it indicates the approach of the Lord from glory.

> 1 Thessalonians 5:4-6, *"But ye, brethren, are not in darkness,* that that day should overtake you as a thief. *Ye are all the children of light, and the children of the day:* we are not of the night, nor of darkness. Therefore let us not sleep, as do others; but let us watch and be sober."

> Hebrews 10:25, "Not forsaking the assembling of ourselves together, as the manner of some is; but exhorting one another: and so much the more, *as ye see the day approaching."*

> Luke 21:31, "So likewise ye, *when ye see these things come to pass,* know ye that the kingdom of God is nigh at hand."

In the limited scope of this study we can mention only four signs which Scripture says will immediately precede "the day of the Lord" and indicate its approach.

> Matthew 24:31-33, "And he shall send his angels with a great sound of a trumpet, and *they shall gather together his elect from the four winds,* from one end of heaven to the other. Now learn a parable of the fig tree; *When his branch is yet tender, and putteth forth leaves, ye know the summer is nigh: so likewise ye, when ye shall see all these things, know that it is near, even at the doors."*

The prophecies of God if they relate to the fulfillment of His divine purposes on earth center in the Jewish race and in the land of Palestine. Repeatedly He says that this people, who have been scattered among all peoples and have lived as exiles for two thousand years, are to be gathered out from all the nations and restored to their own land. As the prophecy that God would take them from their land was fulfilled literally so will the prophecies that He will return them to their land and give it to them as an everlasting possession be as literally fulfilled.

Israel is typified by the fig tree. For centuries she has been withered, dead, fruitless nationally. Yet the Jewish race has been divinely preserved as a distinct people and has never been absorbed by the nations among whom it has been scattered.

But in the last few years there has been marked evidence of new national life in Israel. Through the Zionist Movement which has as its purpose the restoration of Israel to Palestine, through the action of the Allies since World War I in committing themselves to the return of Palestine to the Jews, the fig tree is again putting forth leaves.

"Since General Allenby entered Jerusalem on that never-to-be-forgotten day December 9th, 1918, the fig tree has been putting 'forth leaves' with amazing rapidity. Over 55,000 Jews have returned to Palestine since the Balfour Declaration. The population has more than doubled during the five years of Sir Herbert Samuel's Commissionership. A Hebrew University on Mount Scopus was opened on April 1st, 1925. Trade has flourished and the revenue shows a surplus of one and a quarter millions. The sacred custom of going up to the Passover was observed in the spring of 1922 for the first time in nearly 2,000 years. The Sanhedrin has been revived. Schools have been established. A shipping company has been formed by wealthy American Jews for the purpose of carrying Jews back to Palestine" (E. E. Hotchell, *Signs of Christ's Coming*, p. 914).

> Matthew 24:33, "When ye shall see all these things, know that it is near, even at the doors."

> Luke 21:24, "And they shall fall by the edge of the sword, and shall be led away captive into all nations: *and Jerusalem shall be trodden down of the Gentiles, until the times of the Gentiles be fulfilled.*"

Perhaps no sign is more significant than this one. In World War I a prophetic prediction became an historical fact. Christ had said that the liberation of Jerusalem from Gentile overlordship would not take place "*until*" a certain time and then stated what that time would be. "The times of the Gentiles" refers to the period from the captivity of Judah under Nebuchadnezzar and the dispersion of Israel from her land until the setting up of the Kingdom by the return of the King and His reestablishment of His chosen people in the land He gave them. Jerusalem has been emancipated and is today virtually in the control of the Jews. Then may we not confidently believe that "the times of the Gentiles" are at least nearing fulfillment and the coming of the Lord draweth nigh?

> Luke 21:25-26, "Upon the earth *distress of nations*, with perplexity; . . . *men's hearts failing them for fear*, and for looking after those things which are coming on the earth."

One needs only to observe conditions and to read the daily newspaper to be convinced that this prophecy is being fulfilled at the present time. Everywhere one looks there is tumult and turmoil. World leaders are distressed knowing not what to do to put the world right. Universal anarchy threatens the world and they do not know how to cope with it. To the man with this blessed hope the very hopelessness in present world conditions demands the coming of the only One who can set the world right and indicates that His coming must be near.

> 2 Thessalonians 2:3-4, "Let no man deceive you by any means: *for that day shall not come, except there come a falling away first, and that man*

> *of sin be revealed,* the son of perdition; who opposeth and exalteth himself above all that is called God, or that is worshipped; so that he as God sitteth in the temple of God, shewing himself that he is God."

2 Timothy 3:1-5, "This know also, that *in the last days perilous times shall come.* For men shall be lovers of their own selves, covetous, boasters, proud, blasphemers, disobedient to parents, unthankful, unholy, without natural affection, trucebreakers, false accusers, incontinent, fierce, despisers of those that are good, traitors, heady, highminded, lovers of pleasures more than lovers of God; having a form of godliness, but denying the power thereof: from such turn away."

These passages reveal the truth that in the apostasy of the last days there will be two outstanding marks, religious decadence and moral deterioration. These signs are appallingly evident today. Every distinctive foundational truth of the Christian faith, the virgin birth, the deity of Christ, the substitutionary atonement, the literal resurrection and the Lord's return, are openly and avowedly denied in the pulpit and in the religious press and, as a result, in the pew. With almost incredible arrogance men are tearing the Bible to pieces and retaining only what suits their desire.

Following inevitably upon this rejection of God's Word and refusal of His authority is the breaking loose from all other bonds, parental and magisterial. A wave of lawlessness is sweeping irresistibly over the world and is bound to engulf it ultimately.

Liberalism in belief produces license in conduct. The laws of human society are disregarded and every man becomes a law unto himself. This is the day of divorce, free love, companionate marriage. It is the day of the discarding of parental authority and advice. It is the day of shameless immodesty and indecency in dress. It is the day of bold corruption and dishonesty in high places in governmental affairs. It is the day of traitors and truce breakers, when friends may become enemies over night, and when treaties, solemnly made, may be lightly broken. It is the day of moral deterioration.

God says that "evil men and seducers shall wax worse and worse" so that there would be nothing for this world to look forward to but moral suicide unless the Lord Jesus Christ were to return to save it from itself. But these things are to happen in *"the last days"* so the hope of the spiritual man burns brightly for they are to him a sign that the approach of the Lord is sure.

These signs constitute both a call and a challenge to the Christian. A call to reaffirm his hope, to lift up his head and to rejoice that his redemption draweth nigh. And a challenge to fill his lamps with oil and to prepare his bridal robes that he may be prepared for the coming of the Lord.

OUR LORD'S RETURN—APPEAL

The coming of the Lord will be with suddenness and without warning. The constraining appeal that this blessed truth makes to every man is for readiness. The Lord Jesus warns us of the terrible peril of unpreparedness for His return and appeals to all men to be ready and watching so that whether He comes in the second or in the third watch they will not be caught unawares but will be ready to welcome Him.

> Luke 12:35-36, 40, *"Let your loins be girded about, and your lights burning; and ye yourselves like unto men that wait for their lord,* when he will return from the wedding; that when he cometh and knocketh, they may open unto him immediately. *Be ye therefore ready also: for the Son of man cometh at an hour when ye think not."*

What appeal does the truth of our Lord's return make to the unsaved person? It appeals to him to accept without delay the Lord Jesus as his personal Saviour. Christ warns us that in the day when He shall be revealed unsaved men will be as indifferent as in the days of Noah. They will be engrossed in business and in pleasure, utterly forgetful of their Lord. Suddenly He will come—a wife will be taken and the husband left; a child will be snatched from the mother's arms; a business associate will be caught away to meet his Lord in the air and his partner will be left to carry on alone.

> Matthew 24:40-41, "Then shall two be in the field; *the one shall be taken, and the other left.* Two women shall be grinding at the mill; *the one shall be taken, and the other left."*

And what will it mean to the one who is left? It will mean the ending of the day of grace and the beginning of the day of judgment. The rejected Saviour will then be the righteous Judge before whom the ungodly must stand and receive his punishment for He has come to execute judgment.

> 2 Thessalonians 1:7-9, "And to you who are troubled rest with us, when the Lord Jesus shall be revealed from heaven with his mighty angels, *in flaming fire taking vengeance on them that know not God, and that obey not the gospel of our Lord Jesus Christ: who shall be punished with everlasting destruction from the presence of the Lord, and from the glory of his power."*

All down through the ages there have been those who have mockingly said "Where is the promise of his coming?" (2 Peter 3:4). Ten days after His return to glory He fulfilled the promise to send another Comforter. More than nineteen centuries have passed and He has not yet fulfilled the promise that He would come again. Oh! why does He not come?

> 2 Peter 3:9, "The Lord is not slack concerning his promise, as some men count slackness; *but is longsuffering to us-ward, not willing that any should perish, but that all should come to repentance.*"

Oh! my friend, perhaps He delays His coming for *your* sake. He may be waiting for *you* to accept Him. *You* may be the last one needed to complete the Body of the Lord Jesus Christ. God may be holding the door of grace open a little longer for *you* to enter. Will *you* do so today?

What appeal does the truth of the Lord's return make to the saved person? It is a threefold appeal, to purity of life, to separation from the world and to zeal in service.

The outstanding appeal of the blessed hope is to purity of life. It challenges us to be both holy and righteous, to be void of offense both to God and to men. It calls us to so live that we would be unashamed to meet Him face to face at any moment.

> 1 John 3:3, "And every man that hath this hope in him *purifieth himself, even as he is pure.*"
>
> 2 Peter 3:14, "Wherefore, beloved, seeing that ye look for such things, *be diligent that ye may be found of him in peace, without spot, and blameless.*"
>
> 1 John 2:28, "And now, little children, abide in him; that when he shall appear, *we may have confidence, and not be ashamed before him at his coming.*"

If Christ should come today would He find you with a clean heart? Or would it be filled with rebellion toward Him? With jealousy, unforgiveness, hatred, anger, malice, bitterness toward another? Would He call you to Himself out of the midst of a church quarrel? If Christ should come today would you leave behind unpaid debts? unfulfilled promises? unconfessed sins? Oh, Christian, He may come at any moment, "be diligent that ye may be found of him *in peace, without spot and blameless.*"

The hope of our Lord's return appeals to us to live a separated life. In the twinkling of an eye we shall have left earth and earthly things and shall be in the pure atmosphere of His holy presence which is to be our abiding place throughout eternity. God would have us prepared to breathe that heavenly air by a separation now unto the things that are unseen and eternal; He would deafen our ears to the jazz noises of earth that we might be prepared to appreciate the melodious symphonies of heaven. He would deepen within us the consciousness that we are already citizens of heaven and only pilgrims on earth that we might be freed from encumbersome luggage, that we might be ready to go at a moment's notice.

Philippians 3:20, R. V., *"For our citizenship is in heaven; whence also we wait for a Saviour."*

1 Peter 1:13-14, R. V., "Wherefore girding up the loins of your mind, *be sober and set your hope perfectly on the grace that is to be brought unto you at the revelation of Jesus Christ;* as children of obedience, *not fashioning yourselves according to your former lusts in the time of your ignorance."*

The hope of our Lord's return appeals to us to live a fruitful life. When the Lord Jesus Christ returns He will bring rewards and will bestow crowns for faithful service. A special crown is waiting for those who have zealously won souls to Christ. Will you be in line for coronation? Are you doing your part to hasten the day of His coming by winning souls to Him?

Revelation 22:12, "And, behold, I come quickly; *and my reward is with me,* to give every man according as his work shall be."

1 Thessalonians 2:19, "For *what is our* hope, or joy, or *crown of rejoicing? Are not even ye* in the presence of our Lord Jesus Christ at his coming?"

"Just a few days—and our tears will have ended;
Just a few hours—and our task will be done;
    Yet still hear them calling,
    From darkness appalling,
While we rest in the light of the fast-setting sun.

"Just a few days—and the gifts we've withholden,
Just a few hours—and the call we refuse—
    Will rush on forever,
    Or return to us never,
And Eternity's crown we no longer may choose.

"Just a few days—and then nought will avail us,
The thought of the crown that we might yet have won;
    And ah! what the sorrow
    If we miss on the morrow
Our share in that joy, when He whispers, 'Well done!'

"Just a few days—Oh Lord, strengthen our courage;
Just a few moments—to publish Thy Name.
    In our weakness enfold us,
    Through darkness uphold us,
'Till He Come,' make us faithful Thy love to proclaim."

"Surely, I come quickly.
Even so, come, Lord Jesus."

34

The Story of Salvation Told in Five Chapters

(See Diagram 14.)

CHAPTER 1

THE SINNER IN ADAM—WITHOUT CHRIST.

The penalty of sin is upon him.
The power of sin is over him.
The presence of sin is in him.
    Without Christ.
The sinner. Without hope.

CHAPTER 2

THE SINNER AT THE CROSS—WITH CHRIST.

The penalty of sin is removed by Christ, the Saviour.
Pardon is granted.
Righteousness is imputed.
    Justification.
The sinner's past. Covered.

CHAPTER 3

THE BELIEVER IN THE HEAVENLIES—IN CHRIST

The power of sin is broken by Christ, the Lord.
A new sphere is entered.
A new life is implanted.
A new nature is imparted.
    Regeneration.
The believer's present. Assured.

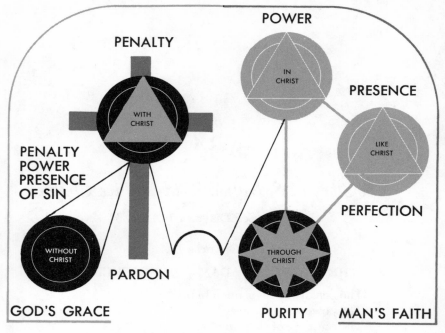

POWER

PENALTY

IN CHRIST

PRESENCE

WITH CHRIST

LIKE CHRIST

PENALTY
POWER
PRESENCE
OF SIN

PERFECTION

WITHOUT CHRIST

THROUGH CHRIST

PARDON

GOD'S GRACE   PURITY   MAN'S FAITH

Diagram 14: The Story of Salvation

CHAPTER 4

THE BELIEVER ON THE EARTH—THROUGH CHRIST.

The place of sin is taken by Christ, the Life.

Dead to $\left\{ \begin{array}{l} \text{Sin.} \\ \text{Self.} \end{array} \right.$

Alive to God.

   Sanctification.
The believer's present. Secured.

CHAPTER 5

THE BELIEVER IN THE AIR. LIKE CHRIST.

The presence of sin is effaced by Christ, the King.
He is perfected into His likeness.
He is conformed to His image.
   Glorification.
The believer's future. Transfigured.

Ephesians 2:8-9

"For by grace are ye saved through faith,
And that not of yourselves:
It is the gift of God:
Not of works, lest any man should boast."

"It is finished."

Bibliography

CHAPTER 1

Chafer, L. S. *He That Is Spiritual*. Grand Rapids: Zondervan, 1918.

CHAPTER 2

McDonough, Mrs. Mary. *God's Plan of Redemption*. 2d ed. Boston: Mansfield, n.d.
Murray, Andrew. *The Spirit of Christ*. Fort Washington, Pa.: CLC, 1970.
Penn-Lewis, Mrs. Jessie. *Soul and Spirit*. Fort Washington, Pa.: CLC, 1962.
Pierson, A. T. *The Bible and Spiritual Life*. New York: Gospel Publishing, 1908.

CHAPTER 3

Bartoli, Giorgio. *The Biblical Story of Creation*. New York: Harper, 1926.
Keyser, L. S. *Man's First Disobedience*. New York: Macmillan, 1924.
Pember, G. H. *Earth's Earliest Ages*. Old Tappan, N.J.: Revell, 1976.
Pink, Arthur. *Gleanings in Genesis*. Chicago: Moody, 1922.

CHAPTER 4

Newell, W. R. *Romans*. Chicago: Moody, 1947.
Tucker, W. Leon. *Studies in Romans*. New York: Charles C. Cook, 1915.

CHAPTER 5

Blackstone, W. E. *Satan: His Kingdom and Its Overthrow*. New York: Revell, 1900.
Chafer, L. S. *Satan*. Grand Rapids: Zondervan, 1919.
Penn-Lewis, Mrs. Jessie. *The Warfare with Satan and the Way of Victory*. 3d rev. ed. London: Marshall, 1908.
Pink, Arthur. *Satan and His Gospel*. Swengel, Pa.: Reiner, n.d.

CHAPTER 6

Haldeman, I. M. *Can Morality Save Us?* 2d ed. New York: Book Stall, n.d.
Machen, Gresham. *Christianity and Liberalism*. Grand Rapids: Eerdmans, 1923.
Trumbull, C. G. *What is the Gospel?* Philadelphia: S.S. Times, 1918.

CHAPTER 7

Armour, J. M. *Atonement and Law.* Chicago: B. I. C. A., 1885.
Mabie, H. C. *The Divine Reason of the Cross.* New York: Revell, 1911.
Morgan, G. Campbell. *The Bible and the Cross.* Grand Rapids: Baker, 1975.

CHAPTER 8

De Vries, Henri. *The Incarnate Son of God.* New York: Christian Alliance, 1921.
Pierson, A. T. *Many Infallible Proofs.* New York: Revell, 1886.

CHAPTER 9

Morgan, G. Campbell. *The Crises of the Christ.* Old Tappan, N.J.: Revell, 1903.
Orr, James. *The Christian View of God and the World.* Grand Rapids: Eerdmans, 1954.
Torrey, R. A. *The Christ of the Bible.* New York: Doran, 1924.
———. *The Real Christ.* Grand Rapids: Zondervan, 1966.
Wood, N. E. *The Person and Work of Jesus Christ.* Philadelphia: American Baptist, 1909.

CHAPTER 10

Anderson, Sir Robert. *The Gospel and Its Ministry.* Grand Rapids: Kregel, 1955.
Boyd, Eleanor. *The Meaning of the Cross.* Cleveland: Union Gospel, n.d.
Denney, James. *The Death of Christ.* Chicago: Inter-Varsity, 1952.
Dixon, A. C. *The Glories of the Cross.* London: Partridge, n.d.
Marsh, F. E. *The Greatest Theme in the World.* New York: Alliance, 1908.
Watt, Gordon. *The Meaning of the Cross.* New York: Harper, 1923.

CHAPTER 11

Gaebelein, A. C. *The Work of Christ.* N.Y.: Our Hope, 1913.
Moule, H. C. G. *Outlines of Christian Doctrine.* London: Hodder, 1910.

CHAPTER 12

Patterson, A. *The Greater Life and Work of Christ.* New York: Christian Alliance, 1928.

CHAPTER 13

Gordon, A. J. *The Ministry of the Spirit.* Minneapolis: Bethany Fellowship, 1964.
Soltau, George. *Person and Mission of the Holy Spirit.* 2d ed. New York: Charles C. Cook, 1908.
Torrey, R. A. *The Holy Spirit: Who He Is and What He Does.* Old Tappan, N.J.: Revell, 1927.

CHAPTER 14

Chafer, L. S. *Salvation*. Grand Rapids: Zondervan, 1972.
Dean, I. R. *In Christ or in Adam*. 2d ed. Philadelphia: Philadelphia School of the Bible, 1925.
Saphir, Adolph. *The Sinner and the Saviour*. New York: Gospel Publishing, n.d.
Thomas, W. H. Griffith. *"What Is 'Justification'?"* In *The Victorious Life*. Philadelphia: Board of Managers, Victorious Life Conference, 1918.

CHAPTER 16

Brookes, J. H. *From Death unto Life*. New York: Revell, 1896.
Mackintosh, C. H. *Ruined, Redeemed, Regenerated*. Chicago: B.I.C.A., 1922.
Torrey, R. A. *Real Salvation*. 5th ed. New York: Revell, 1905.

CHAPTER 17

Gordon, A. J. *In Christ*. New York: Revell, 1880.
Pierson, A. T. *In Christ Jesus*. Chicago: Moody, 1974.
Trotter, I. Lilias. *Parables of the Christ-life*. N.p., n.d.
———. *Parables of the Cross*. London: Marshall, Morgan & Scott, n.d.

CHAPTER 18

Murray, Andrew. *Like Christ*. Minneapolis: Bethany Fellowship, 1974.
Nicholson, W. R. *Oneness with Christ*. Grand Rapids: Kregel, 1951.

CHAPTER 19

Mauro, Philip. *Sanctification*. New York: Gospel Publishing, n.d.
Murray, Andrew. *Holy in Christ*. Minneapolis: Bethany Fellowship, 1969.
Thomas, W. H. Griffith. *Grace and Power*. New York: Revell, 1916.

CHAPTER 20

Gaebelein, A. C. *Types in Joshua*. New York: Our Hope, n.d.
Penn-Lewis, Mrs. Jessie. *The Conquest of Canaan*. Fort Washington, Pa.: CLC, 1956.

CHAPTER 21

Harrison, J. East. *Reigning in Life*. Grand Rapids: Zondervan, 1922.
Richardson, A. E. *The Happy Christian*. Chicago: Moody, n.d.

CHAPTER 22

Mackay, W. P. *Grace and Truth*. New York: Revell, 1876.
Murray, Andrew. *The Spiritual Life*. New ed. New York: Revell, 1895.
Victory in Christ. *Sunday School Times* conference report.

CHAPTER 23

Haldeman, I. M. *The Two Natures*. N.p., n.d.
Mantle, J. Gregory. *Beyond Humiliation: The Way of the Cross*. 7th ed., rev. Chicago: Moody, n.d.
Mauro, Philip. *The Christian's Choice*. New York: Gospel Publishing, n.d.

CHAPTER 24

Holden, Stuart. *The Price of Power*. New York: Revell, 1908.
McConkey, James. *The Threefold Secret of the Holy Spirit*. Lincoln, Nebr.: Back to the Bible, 1958.
MacNeil, John. *The Spirit-Filled Life*. New York: Revell, 1896.

CHAPTER 25

Marsh, F. E. *Emblems of the Holy Spirit*. Grand Rapids: Kregel, 1963.

CHAPTER 26

McConkey, James. *The Surrendered Life*. Pittsburgh: Silver, 1930.
Speer, R. E. *Memorial of a True Life*. New York: Revell, 1898.

CHAPTER 27

Pierson, A. T. *George Muller of Bristol*. Old Tappan, N.J.: Revell, 1971.
Smith, H. W. *The Christian's Secret of a Happy Life*. Old Tappan, N.J.: Spire, 1968.
Taylor, F. Howard, and Taylor, M. Geraldine. *Hudson Taylor and the China Inland Mission: The Growth of a Work of God*. London: Morgan, 1920.

CHAPTER 28

Murray, Andrew. *The School of Obedience*. Chicago: Moody, n.d.

CHAPTER 29

Pierson, A. T. *Knowing the Scriptures*. New York: Gospel Publishing, 1910.
Saphir, Adolph. *Christ and the Scriptures*. New York: Revell, n.d.
Thomas, W. H. Griffith. *Life Abiding and Abounding*. Chicago: B.I.C.A., 1915.
Torrey, R. A. *How to Study the Bible*. New York: Revell, 1896.

CHAPTER 30

Murray, Andrew. *The Ministry of Intercession*. Old Tappan, N.J.: Revell, 1952.
———. *With Christ in the School of Prayer*. Old Tappan, N.J.: Revell, 1895.
Torrey, R. A. *The Power of Prayer and the Prayer of Power*. Grand Rapids: Zondervan, 1971.

CHAPTER 31

Cook, C. C. *The Christian's Present Duty.* New York: Charles C. Cook, n.d.
Wilkes, A. Paget. *The Dynamic of Service.* Kansas City, Mo.: Beacon Hill,
    1944.

CHAPTER 32

Andrews, S. J. *Christianity and Anti-Christianity.* 2d ed. New York: Putnam,
    1899.
Gordon, Ernest. *The Leaven of the Sadducees.* Chicago: B.I.C.A., 1926.

CHAPTER 33

Chafer, L. S. *Seven Biblical Signs of the Times.* Philadelphia: S.S. Times, 1919.
Marsh, F. E. *What Will Take Place When Christ Returns?* 2d ed. London:
    Thynne, n.d.
Pankhurst, Christabel. *The World's Unrest: Visions of the Dawn.* London:
    Morgan & Scott, 1926.

CHAPTER 34

Frost, Henry. *Outline Bible Studies.* Philadelphia: S.S. Times, 1924.
Miller, Herbert S. *Christian Worker's Manual.* New York: Doran, 1922.